Fodor's 2015

HAWAII

WELCOME TO HAWAII

Hawaii overflows with natural beauty. Piercing the surface of the Pacific from the ocean floor, the Hawaiian Islands are garlanded with soft sand beaches and dramatic volcanic cliffs. Long days of sunshine and fairly mild year-round temperatures make this an all-season destination, and the islands' offerings—from urban Honolulu on Oahu to the luxury resorts of Maui to the natural wonders of Kauai and the Big Island—appeal to all kinds of visitors. Less-developed Lanai and Molokai are quieter, but all the islands are rich in Hawaiian culture.

TOP REASONS TO GO

★ **Beaches:** Every island claims its share of postcard-perfect strands.

★ **Resorts:** Spas, pools, lavish gardens, and golf courses make relaxing easy.

★ **Pearl Harbor:** This historic memorial site on Oahu is not to be missed.

★ **Napali Coast:** Kauai's jagged emerald-green coast makes an unforgettable excursion.

★ **Whale-Watching:** In winter humpback whales swim right off Maui's shores.

★ **Volcanoes National Park:** On the Big Island you can explore the world's most active volcano.

Fodor's HAWAII 2015

Publisher: Amanda D'Acierno, *Senior Vice President*

Editorial: Arabella Bowen, *Editor in Chief;* Linda Cabasin, *Editorial Director*

Design: Fabrizio La Rocca, *Vice President, Creative Director;* Tina Malaney, *Associate Art Director;* Chie Ushio, *Senior Designer;* Ann McBride, *Production Designer*

Photography: Melanie Marin, *Associate Director of Photography;* Jessica Parkhill and Jennifer Romains, *Researchers*

Maps: Rebecca Baer, *Senior Map Editor;* David Lindroth and Mark Stroud; *Cartographers*

Production: Linda Schmidt, *Managing Editor;* Evangelos Vasilakis, *Associate Managing Editor;* Angela L. McLean, *Senior Production Manager*

Sales: Jacqueline Lebow, *Sales Director*

Marketing & Publicity: Heather Dalton, *Marketing Director;* Katherine Punia, *Senior Publicist*

Business & Operations: Susan Livingston, *Vice President, Strategic Business Planning;* Sue Daulton, *Vice President, Operations*

Fodors.com: Megan Bell, *Executive Director, Revenue & Business Development;* Yasmin Marinaro, *Senior Director, Marketing & Partnerships*

Copyright © 2015 by Fodor's Travel, a division of Random House LLC

Writers: Karen Anderson, Kristina Anderson, Eliza Escaño-Vasquez, Bonnie Friedman, Trina Kudlacek, Heidi Pool, Charles E. Roessler, Michele Bigley, Joan Conrow, James Cave, Lesa Griffith, Chris Oliver, Catherine E. Toth, Anna Weaver

Editors: Perrie Hartz, Luke Epplin, Doug Stallings, Eric Wechter

Production Editor: Evangelos Vasilakis

ISBN 978-0-8041-4252-6

ISSN 0071-6421

All details in this book are based on information supplied to us at press time. Always confirm information when it matters, especially if you're making a detour to visit a specific place. Fodor's expressly disclaims any liability, loss, or risk, personal or otherwise, that is incurred as a consequence of the use of any of the contents of this book.

SPECIAL SALES

This book is available at special discounts for bulk purchases for sales promotions or premiums. For more information, e-mail specialmarkets@randomhouse.com

PRINTED IN THE UNITED STATES OF AMERICA

10 9 8 7 6 5 4 3 2 1

CONTENTS

Fodor's Features

MAPS

ABOUT
THIS GUIDE

Fodor's Recommendations
Everything in this guide is worth doing—
we don't cover what isn't—but exceptional sights, hotels, and restaurants are
recognized with additional accolades.
Fodor's Choice★ indicates our top recommendations; and **Best Bets** call attention to
notable hotels and restaurants in various
categories. Care to nominate a new place?
Visit Fodors.com/contact-us.

Trip Costs
We list prices wherever possible to help
you budget well. Hotel and restaurant
price categories from $ to $$$$ are noted
alongside each recommendation. For
hotels, we include the lowest cost of a
standard double room in high season.
For restaurants, we cite the average price
of a main course at dinner or, if dinner
isn't served, at lunch. For attractions,
we always list adult admission fees; dis-
counts are usually available for children,
students, and senior citizens.

Hotels
Our local writers vet every hotel to recom-
mend the best overnights in each price cat-
egory, from budget to expensive. Unless
otherwise specified, you can expect pri-
vate bath, phone, and TV in your room.
For expanded hotel reviews, visit Fodors.
com.

Restaurants
Unless we state otherwise, restaurants are
open for lunch and dinner daily. We men-
tion dress code only when there's a specific
requirement and reservations only when
they're essential or not accepted. To make
restaurant reservations, visit Fodors.com.

Credit Cards
The hotels and restaurants in this guide
typically accept credit cards. If not, we'll
say so.

Top Picks
★ Fodor's Choice

Listings
✉ Address
✉ Branch address
☎ Telephone
🖷 Fax
⊕ Website
✉ E-mail
🎫 Admission fee
🕐 Open/closed times
Ⓜ Subway
✛ Directions or Map coordinates

Hotels & Restaurants
🖬 Hotel
↗ Number of rooms
🍽 Meal plans
✕ Restaurant
🥂 Reservations
👔 Dress code
🚫 No credit cards
$ Price

Other
⇨ See also
☞ Take note
⛳ Golf facilities

EXPERIENCE HAWAII

WHAT'S WHERE

Hanalei

Mt. Waialeale
5,148 ft. ▲

5

Waimea   Lihue

Poipu   KAUAI

NIIHAU

Kaulakahi Channel

Kapaa

Kauai Channel

Kahuku Pt.

OAHU

Haleiwa   Laie

Kaena Pt.   2

Pearl Harbor   Kaneohe

HONOLULU   Waikiki

P A C I F I C

Kaiwi Channel

O C E A N

*Numbers correspond to
chapters in this book.*

2 Oahu. Honolulu and
Waikiki are here—and it's a
great big luau. It's got hot
restaurants and lively nightlife
as well as gorgeous white-
sand beaches, knife-edged
mountain ranges, and cultural
sites including Pearl Harbor.

3 Maui. The phrase *Maui no
ka oi* means Maui is the best,
the most, the tops. There's
good reason for the superlatives. It's got a little of everything, perfect for families with
divergent interests.

4 Big Island of Hawaii. It
has two faces, watched over
by snowcapped Mauna Kea
and steaming Mauna Loa. The
Kona side has parched, lava-
strewn lowlands, and eastern
Hilo is characterized by lush
flower farms and waterfalls.

5 Kauai. This is the
"Garden Isle," and it's where
you'll find the lush, green
folding sea cliffs of Napali
Coast, the colorful and
awesome Waimea Canyon,
and more beaches per mile
of coastline than any other
Hawaiian island.

6 Molokai. It's the least
changed, most laid-back of
the Islands. Come here to
ride a mule down a cliff to
Kalaupapa Peninsula; experience the Kamakou Preserve,
a 2,774-acre wildlife refuge;
and for plenty of peace and
quiet.

7 Lanai. For years there
was nothing here except
for pineapples and red-dirt
roads. Today it attracts the
well-heeled in search of
privacy, with two upscale
resorts, archery and shooting, four-wheel-drive excursions, and superb scuba
diving.

0   30 mi

0   30 km

Kalaupapa   MOLOKAI

6   Halawa

Kaunakakai

Kahului Bay

Lahaina   Kahului   MAUI

Lanai City   7   Hana

LANAI   Kihei   3

Wailea   *Puu Ulaula*   Kipahulu
10,023 ft.

KAHOOLAWE

Alenuihaha Channeel

Hawi

Honokaa

Kohala Coast   Waimea

Mauna Kea
▲ *13,796 ft*

Hilo

Kailua-Kona   4

Captain Cook   Pahoa

Kona Coast   ▲ *Mauna Loa*
BIG ISLAND   *13,677 ft.*   Volcano
OF HAWAII

Hoopuloa   Pahala

Naalehu

HAWAII PLANNER

When You Arrive

Honolulu's International Airport is the main stopover for most domestic and international flights, but all of Hawaii's major islands have their own airports. Flights to the Neighbor Islands leave from Honolulu almost every half hour daily.

Visitor Information

Oahu Visitors Bureau ☎ 877/525–6248 ⊕ www.gohawaii.com/oahu.

Maui Visitors & Convention Bureau ☎ 800/525–6284 ⊕ www.gohawaii.com/maui.

Big Island Visitors Bureau ☎ 808/961–5797, 800/648–2441 ⊕ www.gohawaii.com/big-island.

Kauai Visitors Bureau ☎ 808/245–3971, 800/262–1400 ⊕ www.gohawaii.com/kauai.

Hawaii Island Chamber of Commerce ☎ 808/935–7178 ⊕ www.hicc.biz.

Hawaii Beach Safety ⊕ oceansafety.ancl.hawaii.edu.

Hawaii Department of Land and Natural Resources ☎ 808/587–0400 ⊕ www.hawaii.gov/dlnr.

Hawaii Visitors and Convention Bureau ☎ 808/923–1811, 800/464–2924 ⊕ www.gohawaii.com.

Getting Here

Oahu: Honolulu International Airport is 20 minutes (40 during rush hour) from Waikiki. Car rental is across the street from baggage claim. An inefficient airport taxi system requires you to line up to a taxi wrangler who radios for cars (about $36 to Waikiki). Other options: TheBus ($2.50, one lap-size bag allowed), SpeediShuttle ($12.95), and the Roberts Hawaii Express Shuttle ($13).

Maui: Most visitors arrive at Kahului Airport in Central Maui. For trips to Molokai or Lanai, ferries are available to both islands and have room for your golf clubs and mountain bike. If you prefer to travel to Molokai or Lanai by air, and you're not averse to flying on 4- to 12-seaters, your best bet is a small air taxi.

Big Island: The Big Island's two airports are directly across the island from each other. Kona International Airport on the west side is about a 10-minute drive from Kailua-Kona and 30 to 45 minutes from the Kohala Coast. On the east side, Hilo International Airport, 2 miles from downtown Hilo, is about 40 minutes from Volcanoes National Park.

Kauai: All commercial flights use the Lihue Airport, 2 miles east of the town of the same name. It has just two baggage-claim areas, each with a visitor information center.

Dining and Lodging

Hawaii is a melting pot of cultures, and nowhere is this more apparent than in its cuisine. From luau and "plate lunch" to sushi and steak, there's no shortage of interesting flavors and presentations. As for lodging, there are many top-notch resorts in Hawaii, as well as a wide variety of condos and vacation rentals to choose from.

1

Getting Around

Oahu: If you want to travel around the island on your own schedule, renting a car is a must. Heavy traffic toward downtown Honolulu begins as early as 6:30 am and lasts until 9 am. In the afternoon, expect traffic departing downtown to back up beginning around 3 pm until approximately 7 pm.

Maui: Driving from one point on Maui to another can take longer than the mileage indicates. It's 52 miles from Kahului Airport to Hana, but the drive can take three hours. As for driving to Haleakala, the 38-mile drive from the mountain's base to its summit will take you about two hours. Traffic on Maui's roads can be heavy, especially during the rush hours of 6 am to 8:30 am and 3:30 pm to 6:30 pm.

Big Island: It's a good idea to rent a car with four-wheel drive, such as a Jeep, on the Big Island. Some of the island's best sights (and most beautiful beaches) are at the end of rough or unpaved roads. Most agencies make you sign an agreement that you won't drive on the path to Mauna Kea and its observatories. Keep in mind that, while a good portion of the Saddle Road is smoothly paved, it is also remote, winding, and bumpy in certain areas, unlighted, and bereft of gas stations.

Kauai: A rental car is the best way to get to your hotel, though taxis and some hotel shuttles are available. From the airport it will take you about 15 to 25 minutes to drive to Wailua or Kapaa, 30 to 40 minutes to reach Poipu, and 45 minutes to an hour to get to Princeville or Hanalei. Kauai roads are subject to some pretty heavy traffic, especially going through Kapaa and Lihue.

ISLAND DRIVING TIMES

Oahu: Waikiki to Downtown Honolulu	4 miles/10 mins
Oahu: Waikiki to Honolulu Int'l Airport	12 miles/25 mins
Oahu: Waikiki to Haleiwa	34 miles /45 mins
Maui: Kahului to Wailea	17 miles /30 mins
Maui: Kahului to Kaanapali	25 miles /45 mins
Maui: Kahului to Kapalua	36 miles /1 hr 15 mins
Big Island: Kailua-Kona to Kohala Coast	32 miles /50 mins
Big Island: Kailua-Kona to Hilo	86 miles /2.5 hrs
Kauai: Hanalei to Lihue	32 miles /1 hr 5 mins
Kauai: Lihue to Poipu	13 miles /25 mins

Hawaii's Best Festivals and Events

February: Chinese New Year: Lahaina, Maui, and in Chinatown on Oahu. Waimea Town Celebration: Waimea, Kauai.

March: Prince Kuhio Day Celebration: Lihue, Kauai.

April: Maui County Agricultural Festival: Maui. Merrie Monarch Hula Festival: Hilo, Big Island. East Maui Taro Festival: Hana, Maui. Kona Chocolate Festival: Big Island.

May: World Fire-Knife Dance Championships & Samoa Festival: Polynesian Cultural Center, Laie, Oahu. Maui Onion Festival: Kaanapali, Maui.

June: Hawaiian Slack-Key Guitar Festival: Kahului, Maui. King Kamehameha Hula Competition: Honolulu, Oahu. Flavors of Honolulu: Oahu. Maui Film Festival: Maui.

July: Fourth of July celebrations: Magic Island, Kailua Beach, and at Pearl Harbor's Schofield Barracks, Oahu. In Honolulu, displays light up the skies.

October: Ironman Triathalon World Championship: Kailua-Kona, Big Island. Halloween festivities: Lahaina, Maui, and Chinatown and Waikiki on Oahu. Plantation Days: Lahaina, Maui.

November: Kona Coffee Cultural Festival: Kona, Big Island. Triple Crown of Surfing: North Shore, Oahu.

HAWAII TODAY

Hawaiian culture and tradition here have experienced a renaissance over the last few decades. There's a real effort to revive traditions and to respect history as the Islands go through major changes. New developments often have a Hawaiian cultural expert on staff to ensure cultural sensitivity and to educate newcomers.

Nonetheless, development remains a huge issue for all Islanders—land prices are skyrocketing, putting many areas out of reach for the native population. Traffic is becoming a problem on roads that were not designed to accommodate all the new drivers, and the Islands' limited natural resources are being seriously tapped. The government, though sluggish to respond at first, is trying to make development in Hawaii as sustainable as possible.

Sustainability

Although sustainability is an effective buzzword and authentic direction for the Islands' dining establishments, 90% of Hawaii's food and energy is imported.

Most of the land was used for monocropping of pineapple or sugarcane, both of which have all but vanished. Sugarcane is now produced in only two plants on Kauai and Maui, while pineapple production has dropped precipitously. Dole, once the largest pineapple company in Hawaii, closed its plants in 1991, and after 90 years, Del Monte stopped pineapple production in 2008. The next year, Maui Land and Pineapple Company also ceased its Maui Gold pineapple operation, although in early 2010 a group of executives took over one third of the land and created a new company. Low cost of labor and transportation from Latin American and Southeast Asian pineapple producers are factors contributing to the industry's demise in Hawaii. Although this proves daunting, it also sets the stage for great agricultural change to be explored.

Back-to-Basics Agriculture

Emulating how the Hawaiian ancestors lived and returning to their simple ways of growing and sharing a variety of foods has become a statewide initiative. Hawaii has the natural conditions and talent to produce far more diversity in agriculture than it currently does.

The seed of this movement thrives through various farmers' markets and partnerships between restaurants and local farmers. Localized efforts such as the Hawaii Farm Bureau Federation are collectively leading the organic and sustainable agricultural renaissance. From home-cooked meals to casual plate lunches to fine-dining cuisine, these sustainable trailblazers enrich the culinary tapestry of Hawaii and uplift the Islands' overall quality of life.

Tourism and the Economy

The $10-plus billion tourism industry represents a third of Hawaii's state income. Naturally, this dependency causes economic hardship as the financial meltdown of recent years affects tourists' ability to visit and spend.

One way the industry has changed has been to adopt more eco-conscious practices, as many Hawaiians feel that development shouldn't happen without regard for impact to local communities and their natural environment.

Belief that an industry based on the Hawaiians' *aloha* should protect, promote, and empower local culture and provide more entrepreneurial opportunities for local people has become more important to tourism businesses. More companies are incorporating authentic Hawaiiana in their programs and aim not only to provide a commercially viable

tour but also to ensure that the visitor leaves feeling connected to his or her host.

The concept of *kuleana*, a word for both privilege and responsibility, is upheld. Having the privilege to live in such a sublime place comes with the responsibility to protect it.

Sovereignty

Political issues of sovereignty continue to divide Native Hawaiians, who have formed myriad organizations, each operating with a separate agenda and lacking one collectively defined goal. Ranging from achieving complete independence to solidifying a nation within a nation, existing sovereignty models remain fractured and their future unresolved.

The introduction of the Native Hawaiian Government Reorganization Act of 2009 attempts to set up a legal framework in which Native Hawaiians can attain federal recognition and coexist as a self-governed entity. Also known as the Akaka Bill after former Senator Daniel Akaka of Hawaii, this bill has been presented before Congress and is still pending.

Rise of Hawaiian Pride

After the overthrow of the monarchy in 1893, a process of Americanization began. Traditions were duly silenced in the name of citizenship. Teaching Hawaiian language was banned from schools and children were distanced from their local customs.

But Hawaiians are resilient people, and with the rise of the civil rights movement they began to reflect on their own national identity, bringing an astonishing renaissance of the Hawaiian culture to fruition.

The people rediscovered language, hula, chanting, and even the traditional Polynesian arts of canoe building and wayfinding (navigation by the stars without use of instruments). This cultural resurrection is now firmly established in today's Hawaiian culture, with a palpable pride that exudes from Hawaiians young and old.

The election of President Barack Obama increased Hawaiian pride. The president's strong connection and commitment to Hawaiian values of diversity, spirituality, family, and conservation have restored confidence that Hawaii can inspire a more peaceful, tolerant, and environmentally conscious world.

The Arts

The Hawaiian Islands have inspired artistic expression from the time they were first inhabited. From ancient hula to digital filmmaking, the arts are alive and well. Honolulu is the artistic hub of the state. The Honolulu Museum of Art has an impressive permanent collection and hosts major exhibitions throughout the year. It comprises four locations including the spectacular Shangri La, the former home of heiress Doris Duke, filled with Islamic treasures. The Hawaii Theater in Honolulu—a restored art deco palace—stages theatrical productions, concerts, and films. The Maui Arts & Cultural Center (MACC) has a 1,200-seat theater for concerts, theatrical productions, and film, as well as an amphitheater and art gallery. Numerous art galleries thrive on the Islands.

HAWAII
TOP ATTRACTIONS

Hike Maui's Haleakala

(A) Trek down into Maui's Haleakala National Park's massive bowl and see proof, at this dormant volcano, of how very powerful the earth's exhalations can be. You won't see landscape like this anywhere, outside of visiting the moon. The barren terrain is deceptive, however— many of the world's rarest plants, birds, and insects live here.

Surf at Waikiki Beach on Oahu

(B) Waikiki, with its well-shaped but diminutive waves, remains the perfect spot for grommets (surfing newbies), though surf schools operate at beaches (and many hotels) around the island. Most companies guarantee at least one standing ride in the course of a lesson. And catching your first wave? We guarantee you'll never forget it.

Visit Oahu's Pearl Harbor

(C) This top Honolulu site is not to be missed. Spend the better part of a day touring the *Missouri*, the *Arizona* Memorial, and, if you have time, the *Bowfin*.

Hit the Road to Hana on Maui

(D) Spectacular views of waterfalls, lush forests, and the sparkling ocean are part of the pleasure of the twisting drive along the North Shore to tiny, timeless Hana in East Maui. The journey is the destination, but once you arrive, kick back and relax.

Enjoy Oahu After Hours

(E) Yes, you can have an umbrella drink at sunset. But in the multicultural metropolis of Honolulu, there's so much more to it than that. Sip a glass of wine and listen to jazz at the Dragon Upstairs in Chinatown, or join the beach-and-beer gang at Duke's Waikiki.

Whale-Watch on Maui
(F) Maui is the cradle for hundreds of humpback whales that return every year to frolic in the warm waters and give birth. Watch a mama whale teach her 1-ton calf how to tail wave. You can eavesdrop on them, too: book a tour boat with a hydrophone or just plunk your head underwater to hear the strange squeaks, groans, and chortles of the cetaceans.

See a Lava Show on the Big Island
(G) At Hawaii Volcanoes National Park, watch as fiery red lava pours, steaming, into the ocean; stare in awe at nighttime lava fireworks; and hike across the floor of a crater.

Attend a Luau
(H) There are luau that are spectacles and those that lean toward the more authentic. Both have their merits, depending on the experience you're after. Two that are worthy of mention are the Old Lahaina Luau on Maui and the thrilling performances at the Polynesian Cultural Center on Oahu.

Catch the Views at Kauai's Waimea Canyon
(I) From its start in the west Kauai town of Waimea to the road's end some 20 uphill miles later at Puu O Kila Lookout, you'll pass through several microclimates—from hot, desertlike conditions at sea level to the cool, deciduous forest of Kokee—and navigate through the traditional Hawaiian system of land division called *ahupuaa*.

Explore Kauai's Napali Coast
(J) Experiencing Kauai's emerald green Napali Coast is a must-do. You can see these awesome cliffs on the northwest side of the island by boat, helicopter, or by hiking the Kalalau Trail. Whichever you pick, you won't be disappointed.

Drive Big Island's Hamakua Coast
The views of the Pacific are absolutely breathtaking along this stretch of road between Kohala and Hilo. Make sure to take the Old Mamalahoa Highway's scenic 4-mile detour off Hawaii Belt Road.

THE HAWAIIAN ISLANDS

Oahu. The state's capital, Honolulu, is on Oahu; this is the center of Hawaii's economy and by far the most populated island in the chain—976,000 residents add up to 71% of the state's population. At 597 square miles Oahu is the third-largest island in the chain; the majority of residents live in or around Honolulu, so the rest of the island still fits neatly into the tropical, untouched vision of Hawaii. Situated southeast of Kauai and northwest of Maui, Oahu is a central location for island-hopping. Pearl Harbor, iconic Waikiki Beach, and surfing contests on the legendary North Shore are all here.

Maui. The second-largest island in the chain, Maui is northwest of the Big Island and close enough to be visible from its beaches on a clear day. The island's 729 square miles are home to only 150,000 people but host more than 2 million tourists every year. With its restaurants and lively nightlife, Maui is the only island that competes with Oahu in terms of entertainment; its charm lies in the fact that although entertainment is available, Maui's towns still feel like island villages compared to the heaving modern city of Honolulu.

Hawaii (The Big Island). The Big Island has the second-largest population of the Islands (almost 190,000) but feels sparsely settled due to its size. It's 4,038 square miles and growing—all the other Islands could fit onto the Big Island and there would still be room left over. The southernmost island in the chain (slightly southeast of Maui), the Big Island is home to Kilauea, the most active volcano on the planet. It percolates within Volcanoes National Park, which draws nearly 3 million visitors every year.

Kauai. The northernmost island in the chain (northwest of Oahu), Kauai is, at approximately 622 square miles, the fourth-largest of all the Islands and the least populated of the larger Islands, with 68,000 residents. Known as the Garden Isle, this island is home to lush botanical gardens as well as the stunning Napali Coast and Waimea Canyon. The island is a favorite with honeymooners and others wanting to get away from it all—lush and peaceful, it's the perfect escape from the modern world.

Molokai. North of Lanai and Maui, and east of Oahu, Molokai is Hawaii's fifth-largest island, encompassing 260 square miles. On a clear night, the lights of Honolulu are visible from Molokai's western shore. Molokai is sparsely populated, with about 7,300 residents, the majority of whom are Native Hawaiians. Most of the island's 79,000 annual visitors travel from Maui or Oahu to spend the day exploring its beaches, cliffs, and former leper colony on Kalaupapa Peninsula.

Lanai. Lying just off Maui's western coast, Lanai looks nothing like its sister Islands, with pine trees and deserts in place of palm trees and beaches. Still, the tiny 140-square-mile island is home to about 3,200 residents and draws an average of 75,000 visitors each year to two resorts (one in the mountains and one at the shore), both operated by Four Seasons, and the small, 11-room Hotel Lanai.

Hawaii's Geology

The Hawaiian Islands comprise more than just the islands inhabited and visited by humans. A total of 19 islands and atolls constitute the State of Hawaii, with a total landmass of 6,423.4 square miles.

The Islands are actually exposed peaks of a submersed mountain range called

the Hawaiian Ridge-Emperor Seamounts chain. The range was formed as the Pacific plate moves very slowly (around 32 miles every million years—or about as much as your fingernails grow in one year) over a hot spot in the Earth's mantle. Because the plate moves northwestwardly, the Islands in the northwest portion of the archipelago (chain) are older, which is also why they're smaller—they have been eroding longer and have actually sunk back into the sea floor.

The Big Island is the youngest, and thus the largest, island in the chain. It is built from five different volcanoes, including Mauna Loa, which is the largest mountain on the planet (when measured from the bottom of the sea floor). Mauna Loa and Kilauea are the only Hawaiian volcanoes still erupting with any sort of frequency. Mauna Loa last erupted in 1984. Kilauea has been continuously erupting since 1983.

Mauna Kea (Big Island), Hualalai (Big Island), and Haleakala (Maui) are all in what's called the post-shield-building stage of volcanic development—eruptions decrease steadily for up to a million years before ceasing entirely. Kohala (Big Island), Lanai (Lanai), and Waianae (Oahu) are considered extinct volcanoes, in the erosional stage of development; Koolau (Oahu) and West Maui (Maui) volcanoes are extinct volcanoes in the rejuvenation stage—after lying dormant for hundreds of thousands of years, they began erupting again, but only once every several thousand years.

There is currently an active undersea volcano to the south and east of the Big Island called Kamaehu that has been erupting regularly. If it continues its current pattern, it should breach the ocean's surface in tens of thousands of years.

Hawaii's Flora and Fauna

More than 90% of native Hawaiian flora and fauna are endemic (they evolved into unique species here), like the koa tree and the yellow hibiscus. Long-dormant volcanic craters are perfect hiding places for rare native plants. The silversword, a rare cousin of the sunflower, grows on Hawaii's three tallest peaks: Haleakala, Mauna Kea, and Mauna Loa, and nowhere else on Earth. Ohia trees—thought to be the favorite of Pele, the volcano goddess—bury their roots in fields of once-molten lava, and one variety sprouts ruby pom-pom–like lehua blossoms. The deep yellow petals of ilima (once reserved for royalty) are tiny discs, which make elegant lei.

But most of the plants you see while walking around aren't Hawaiian at all and came from Tahitian, Samoan, or European visitors. Plumeria is ubiquitous; alien orchids run rampant on the Big Island; bright orange relatives of the ilima light up the mountains of Oahu. Though these flowers are not native, they give the Hawaiian lei their color and fragrance.

Hawaii's state bird, the nene goose, is making a comeback from its former endangered status. It roams freely in parts of Maui, Kauai, and the Big Island. Rare Hawaiian monk seals breed in the northwestern Islands. With only 1,500 left in the wild, you probably won't catch many lounging on the beaches, though they have been spotted on the shores of Kauai in recent years. Spinner dolphins and sea turtles can be found off the coast of all the Islands; and every year from November to April, the humpback whales migrate past Hawaii in droves.

CHOOSING YOUR ISLANDS

You've decided to go to Hawaii, but should you stay put and relax on one island or try sampling more than one? If all you have is a week, it is probably best to stick to just one island. You traveled all this way, why spend your precious vacation time at car-rental counters, hotel check-in desks, and airports? But, with seven or more nights, a little island-hopping is a great way to experience the diversity of sights and experiences that are packed into this small state. Here are some of our favorite island-pairing itineraries for every type of trip.

Family Travel: Oahu and Maui

If you're traveling with children, Oahu and Maui have the most options.

Why Oahu: Oahu is by far the most kid-friendly island. For sea life, visit the Waikiki Aquarium and Sea Life Park or let the little ones get up close and personal with fish at Hanauma Bay. At Pearl Harbor you can visit an aircraft carrier or, if the kids are at least four, a World War II submarine. Then there's the Honolulu Zoo and a slippery slide–filled water park, not to mention some very family-friendly and safe beaches. *Plan to spend 4 nights.*

Why Maui: Whales! Though you can see whales from any island between November and April, there's no better place than Maui. If your visit doesn't fall during peak whale-watching season, visit the Whalers Village Museum, the Hawaiian Islands Humpback Whale National Marine Sanctuary, or the Maui Ocean Center (to get an up close look at some of Hawaii's smaller sea creatures). Away from the water, there's the Sugar Cane Train. *Plan to spend at least 3 nights.*

Romance: Maui and Kauai

If you're getting away for seclusion, romantic walks along the beach, and the pampering at world-class spas, consider Maui and Kauai.

Why Maui: You'll find waterfalls, salt-and-pepper sand beaches, and incredible views as you follow the twisting turning Road to Hana. The luxury resorts in Wailea or Kaanapali provide lots of fine dining and spa treatment options. And for those who want to start their day early, there's the drive up to Haleakala to see the sun rise—or for couples who prefer to sleep in, there's the arguably even more spectacular sunset from the summit. *Plan to spend 4 nights.*

Why Kauai: The North Shore communities of Hanalei and Princeville provide the opportunity to get away from crowds and indulge in some spectacular beaches, hiking, and helicopter rides. At Princeville you can experience views straight out of *South Pacific* as well as excellent dining and spas at the St. Regis Hotel, while a drive to Kee Beach at the end of the road provides innumerable options for pulling over and grabbing a beach, all for just the two of you. *Plan to spend at least 3 nights.*

Golf, Shopping, and Luxury: Maui and the Big Island

For luxurious travel, great shopping, restaurants, and accommodations you can't beat Maui and the Big Island.

Why Maui: The resorts at Wailea and Kaanapali have endless options for dining, shopping, and spa treatments. And, the golf on Maui can't be beat with Kapalua, the Dunes at Maui Lani, and Makena Resort topping the list of spectacular courses. *Plan to spend 4 nights.*

Why the Big Island: In addition to having incredible natural scenery, the Big Island

offers world-class resorts and golfing along the Kohala Coast. The Mauna Kea and Hapuna golf courses rank among the top in state while the courses at Mauna Lani Resort and Waikoloa Village allow the unusual experience of playing in and around lava flows. Gourmet dining and spa treatments are readily available at the top resorts and you'll find shopping opportunities at King's Shops at Waikoloa Village as well as within many of the resorts themselves. Or, travel to Hawi or Waimea (Kamuela) for original island boutiques. *Plan to spend at least 3 nights.*

Natural Beauty and Pristine Beaches: The Big Island and Kauai

Really want to get away and experience nature at its most primal? The Big Island is the place to start, followed by a trip to Kauai.

Why the Big Island: Home to 11 different climate zones, the Big Island is large enough to contain all the other Hawaiian Islands. There are countless options for those who want to get off the beaten track and get their hands (and feet) dirty—or sandy as the case may be. See lava flowing or steam rising from Kilauea. Visit beaches in your choice of gold, white, green, or black sand. Snorkel or dive just offshore from an ancient Hawaiian settlement. Or, hike through rain forests to hidden waterfalls. The choices are endless on this island. *Plan to spend at least 4 nights.*

Why Kauai: The Napali Coast is the main draw for those seeking secluded beaches and incredible scenery. If you're interested in hiking to otherwise inaccessible beaches along sheer sea cliffs, this is as good as it gets. Or, head up to Waimea Canyon to see the "Grand Canyon of the Pacific." Want waterfalls? Opaekaa Falls outside Lihue is one of the state's most

breathtaking. And there's no better place for bird-watching than Kilauea Point National Wildlife Refuge. *Plan to spend at least 3 nights.*

Volcanic Views: The Big Island and Maui

For those coming to Hawaii for the volcanoes, there are really only two options: the Big Island and Maui.

Why the Big Island: Start by flying into Hilo and head straight to Hawaii Volcanoes National Park and Kilauea Volcano. Plan to spend at least two days at Kilauea—you'll need time to really explore the caldera, drive to the end of Chain of Craters Road, and have some time for hiking in and around this active volcano. While eruptions are unpredictable, helicopter companies can get you views of otherwise inaccessible lava flows. You can also make a visit up to the summit of Mauna Kea with a tour company. From here you'll see views not only of the observatories (Mauna Kea is one of the best places in the world for astronomy), but also Kilauea and Haleakala volcanoes, which loom in the distance. *Plan to spend at least 4 nights.*

Why Maui: Though all the islands in Hawaii were built from the same hot spot in Earth's crust, the only other island to have had volcanic activity in recorded history was Maui, at Haleakala. The House of the Sun (as Haleakala is known) has great hiking and camping opportunities. *Plan to spend 3 nights.*

ISLAND-FINDER CHART

Not sure which Hawaiian island is your kind of paradise? Any island would make a memorable vacation, but not every one has that particular mix of attributes that makes it perfect for you. Use this chart to compare how each island measures up to your vacation dreams. Looking for great nightlife and world-class surfing? Oahu would fit the bill. Hate crowds but love scuba? Lanai is your place. You can also consult What's Where to learn more about the specific attractions of each island.

	OAHU	MAUI	BIG ISLAND	KAUAI	MOLOKAI	LĀNAI
Beaches						
Activities & Sports	●	●	●	◑	◑	◑
Deserted	◑	◑	◑	●	●	◑
Party Scene	●	◑	◑	○	○	○
City Life						
Crowds	●	◑	◑	◑	○	○
Urban Development	●	◑	◑	◑	○	○
Entertainment						
Hawaiian Cultural Events	●	●	●	◑	◑	○
Museums	●	◑	◑	◑	○	○
Nightlife	●	◑	○	○	○	○
Performing Arts	●	◑	○	○	○	○
Shopping	●	●	◑	◑	○	○
Lodging						
B&Bs	◑	◑	●	●	○	○
Condos	●	●	●	●	◑	○
Hotels & Resorts	●	●	●	●	○	●
Vacation Rentals	◑	●	◑	●	◑	○
Nature						
Rainforest Sights	◑	◑	◑	●	◑	○
Volcanic Sights	○	◑	●	○	○	○
Wildlife	○	◑	●	●	◑	◑
Sports						
Golf	●	●	●	◑	○	●
Hiking	◑	●	●	●	◑	◑
Scuba	◑	●	●	◑	○	●
Snorkeling	◑	●	●	◑	◑	◑
Surfing	●	●	◑	◑	◑	○
Windsurfing	◑	●	◑	◑	◑	○

KEY: ● Noteworthy ◑ Some ○ Little or None

WHEN TO GO

Long days of sunshine and fairly mild year-round temperatures make Hawaii an all-season destination. Most resort areas are at sea level, with average afternoon temperatures of 75°F to 80°F during the coldest months of December and January; during the hottest months of August and September the temperature often reaches 90°F. Only at high elevations does the temperature drop into the colder realms, and only at mountain summits does it reach freezing.

Most travelers head to the Islands in winter. From mid-December through mid-April, visitors find Hawaii's sun-splashed beaches and balmy trade winds appealing. This high season means that fewer travel bargains are available; room rates average 10% to 15% higher during this season than the rest of the year. The highest rates you're likely to pay are between Christmas and New Year's. Spring break (the month of March) and even summer can be pricey. A general rule of thumb: when kids are on recess from school, it's high season in Hawaii.

Rainfall can be high in winter, particularly on the north and east shores of each island. Generally speaking, you're guaranteed sun and warm temperatures on the west and south shores no matter what time of year.

Only-in-Hawaii Holidays

If you happen to be in the Islands on March 26 or June 11, you'll notice light traffic and busy beaches—these are state holidays not celebrated anywhere else. March 26 recognizes the birthday of Prince Jonah Kuhio Kalanianaole, a member of the royal line who served as a delegate to Congress and spearheaded the effort to set aside homelands for Hawaiian people. June 11 honors the first island-wide monarch, Kamehameha the Great; locals drape his statues with lei and stage elaborate parades.

May 1 isn't an official holiday, but it's the day when schools and civic groups celebrate the quintessential Islands gift, the flower lei, with lei-making contests and pageants.

Statehood Day is celebrated on the third Friday in August (Admission Day was August 21, 1959).

Another holiday much celebrated is Chinese New Year, in part because many Hawaiians married Chinese immigrants. Homes and businesses sprout bright red good-luck mottoes, lions dance in the streets, and everybody eats *gau* (steamed pudding) and *jai* (vegetarian stew).

The state also celebrates Good Friday as a spring holiday.

Climate

Moist trade winds drop their precipitation on the north and east sides of the Islands, creating tropical climates, while the south and west sides remain hot and dry with desertlike conditions. Higher "Upcountry" elevations typically have cooler, and often misty conditions.

Average maximum and minimum temperatures for Honolulu are listed here; temperatures throughout the Hawaiian Islands are similar.

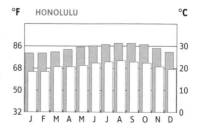

HAWAIIAN PEOPLE AND THEIR CULTURE

By 2013, Hawaii's population was more than 1.3 million with the majority of residents living on Oahu. Ten percent are Hawaiian or other Pacific Islander, almost 40% are Asian American, 9% are Latino, and about 26% Caucasian. Nearly a fifth of the population list two or more races, making Hawaii the most diverse state in the United States.

Among individuals 18 and older, about 89% finished high school, half attained some college, and 29% completed a bachelor's degree or higher.

The Role of Tradition

The kingdom of Hawaii was ruled by a spiritual class system. Although the *alii*, or chief, was believed to be the direct descendent of a deity or god, high priests, known as *kahuna*, presided over every imaginable aspect of life and *kapu* (taboos) that strictly governed the commoners.

Each part of nature and ritual was connected to a deity—Kane was the highest of all deities, symbolizing sunlight and creation; Ku was the god of war; Lono represented fertility, rainfall, music, and peace; Kanaloa was the god of the underworld or darker spirits. Probably the most well known by outsiders is Pele, the goddess of fire.

The kapu not only provided social order, they also swayed the people to act with reverence for the environment. Any abuse was met with extreme punishment, often death, as it put the land and people's *mana*, or spiritual power, in peril.

Ancient deities play a huge role in Hawaiian life today—not just in daily rituals, but in the Hawaiians' reverence for their land. Gods and goddesses tend to be associated with particular parts of the land, and most of them are connected with many places, thanks to the body of stories built up around each.

One of the most important ways the ancient Hawaiians showed respect for their gods and goddesses was through the hula. Various forms of the hula were performed as prayers to the gods and as praise to the chiefs. Performances were taken very seriously, as a mistake was thought to invalidate the prayer, or even to offend the god or chief in question. Hula is still performed both as entertainment and as prayer; it is not uncommon for a hula performance to be included in an official government ceremony.

Who Are the Hawaiians Today?

To define the Hawaiians in a page, let alone a paragraph, is nearly impossible. Those considered to be indigenous Hawaiians are descendants of the ancient Polynesians who crossed the vast ocean and settled Hawaii. According to the government, there are Native Hawaiians or native Hawaiians (note the change in capitalization), depending on a person's background.

Federal and state agencies apply different methods to determine Hawaiian lineage, from measuring blood percentage to mapping genealogy. This has caused turmoil within the community because it excludes many who claim Hawaiian heritage. It almost guarantees that, as races intermingle, even those considered Native Hawaiian now will eventually disappear on paper, displacing generations to come.

Modern Hawaiian Culture

Perfect weather aside, Hawaii might be the warmest place anyone can visit. The Hawaii experience begins and ends with *aloha*, a word that envelops love, affection, and mercy, and has become a salutation for hello and good-bye. Broken

down, *alo* means "presence" and *ha* means "breath"—the presence of breath. It's to live with love and respect for self and others with every breath. Past the manicured resorts and tour buses, aloha is a moral compass that binds all of Hawaii's people.

Hawaii is blessed with some of the most unspoiled natural wonders, and aloha extends to the land, or *aina*. Hawaiians are raised outdoors and have strong ties to nature. They realize as children that the ocean and land are the delicate sources of all life. Even ancient gods were embodied by nature, and this reverence has been passed down to present generations who believe in *kuleana,* their privilege and responsibility.

Hawaii's diverse cultures unfold in a beautiful montage of customs and arts—from music, to dance, to food. Musical genres range from slack key to *Jawaiian* (Hawaiian reggae) to *hapa-haole* (Hawaiian music with English words). From George Kahumoku's Grammy-worthy laid-back strumming to the late Iz Kamakawiwoole's "Somewhere over the Rainbow" to Jack Johnson's more mainstream tunes, contemporary Hawaiian music has definitely carved its ever-evolving niche.

The Merrie Monarch Festival is celebrating more than 50 years of worldwide hula competition and education. The fine-dining culinary scene, especially in Honolulu, has a rich tapestry of ethnic influences and talent. But the real gems are the humble hole-in-the-wall eateries that serve authentic cuisines of many ethnic origins in one plate, a deliciously mixed plate indeed.

And perhaps, the most striking quality in today's Hawaiian culture is the sense of family, or *ohana*. Sooner or later, almost everyone you meet becomes an uncle or auntie, and it is not uncommon for near strangers to be welcomed into a home as a member of the family.

Until the last century, the practice of *hanai*, in which a family essentially adopts a child, usually a grandchild, without formalities, was still prevalent. While still practiced to a somewhat lesser degree, the *hanai*, which means to feed or nourish, still resonates within most families and communities.

How to Act Like a Local

Adopting local customs is a firsthand introduction to the Islands' unique culture. So live in T-shirts and shorts. Wear cheap rubber flip-flops, but call them slippers. Wave people into your lane on the highway, and, when someone lets you in, give them a wave of thanks in return. Never, ever blow your horn, even when the pickup truck in front of you is stopped for a long session of "talk story" right in the middle of the road.

Holoholo means to go out for the fun of it—an aimless stroll, ride, or drive. "Wheah you goin', braddah?" "Oh, holoholo." It's local speak for Sunday drive, no plan, it's not the destination but the journey. Try setting out without an itinerary. Learn to *shaka*: pinky and thumb extended, middle fingers curled in, waggle sideways. Eat white rice with everything. When someone says, "Aloha!" answer, "Aloha no!" ("And a real big aloha back to you"). And, as the locals say, "No make big body" ("Try not to act like you own the place").

THE HISTORY OF HAWAII

Hawaiian history is long and complex; a brief survey can put into context the ongoing renaissance of native arts and culture.

The Polynesians

Long before both Christopher Columbus and the Vikings, Polynesian seafarers set out to explore the vast stretches of the open ocean in double-hulled canoes. From western Polynesia, they traveled back and forth between Samoa, Fiji, Tahiti, the Marquesas, and the Society Isles, settling on the outer reaches of the Pacific, Hawaii, and Easter Island, as early as AD 300. The golden era of Polynesian voyaging peaked around AD 1200, after which the distant Hawaiian Islands were left to develop their own unique cultural practices and subsistence in relative isolation.

The Islands' symbiotic society was deeply intertwined with religion, mythology, science, and artistry. Ruled by an *alii*, or chief, each settlement was nestled in an *ahupuaa*, a pie-shaped land division from the uplands where the *alii* lived, through the valleys and down to the shores where the commoners resided. Everyone contributed, whether it was by building canoes, catching fish, making tools, or farming land.

A United Kingdom

When the British explorer Captain James Cook arrived in 1778, he was revered as a god. With guns and ammunition purchased from Cook, the Big Island chief, Kamehameha the Great, gained a significant advantage over the other *alii*. He united Hawaii into one kingdom in 1810, bringing an end to the frequent interisland battles that dominated Hawaiian life.

Tragically, the new kingdom was beset with troubles. Native religion was abandoned, and *kapu* (laws and regulations) were eventually abolished. The European explorers brought foreign diseases with them, and within a few short decades the Native Hawaiian population was decimated.

New laws regarding land ownership and religious practices eroded the underpinnings of pre-contact Hawaii. Each successor to the Hawaiian throne sacrificed more control over the island kingdom. As Westerners permeated Hawaiian culture, Hawaii became more riddled with layers of racial issues, injustice, and social unrest.

Modern Hawaii

In 1893, the last Hawaiian monarch, Queen Liliuokalani, was overthrown by a group of Americans and European businessmen and government officials, aided by an armed militia. This led to the creation of the Republic of Hawaii, and it became a U.S. territory for the next 60 years. The loss of Hawaiian sovereignty and the conditions of annexation have haunted the Hawaiian people since the monarchy was deposed.

Pearl Harbor was attacked in 1941, which engaged the United States immediately into World War II. Tourism, from its beginnings in the early 1900s, flourished after the war and naturally inspired rapid real estate development in Waikiki. In 1959, Hawaii officially became the 50th state. Statehood paved the way for Hawaiians to participate in the American democratic process, which was not universally embraced by all Hawaiians. With the rise of the civil rights movement in the 1960s, Hawaiians began to reclaim their own identity, from language to hula.

HAWAII AND THE ENVIRONMENT

Sustainability—it's a word rolling off everyone's tongues these days. In a place known as the most remote island chain in the world (check your globe), Hawaii relies heavily on the outside world for food and material goods—estimates put the percentage of food arriving on container ships as high as 90. Like many places, though, efforts are afoot to change that. And you can help.

Shop Local Farms and Markets

From Kauai to the Big Island, farmers' markets are cropping up, providing a place for growers to sell fresh fruits and vegetables. There is no reason to buy imported mangoes, papayas, avocadoes, and bananas at grocery stores, when the ones you'll find at farmers' markets are not only fresher but tastier, too. Some markets allow the sale of fresh-packaged foods—salsa, say, or smoothies—and the on-site preparation of food—like pork *laulau* (pork, beef, and fish or chicken with taro, or luau, leaves wrapped and steamed in *ti* leaves) or roasted corn on the cob— so you can make your run to the market a dining experience.

Not only is the locavore movement vibrantly alive at farmers' markets, but Hawaii's top chefs are sourcing more of their produce—and fish, beef, chicken, and cheese—from local providers as well. You'll notice this movement on restaurant menus, featuring Kilauea greens or Hamakua tomatoes or locally caught mahimahi.

And while most people are familiar with Kona coffee farm tours on Big Island, if you're interested in the growing slow-food movement in Hawaii, you'll be heartened to know many farmers are opening up their operations for tours— as well as sumptuous meals.

Support Hawaii's Merchants

Food isn't the only sustainable effort in Hawaii. Buying local goods like art and jewelry, Hawaiian heritage products, crafts, music, and apparel is another way to "green up" the local economy. The County of Kauai helps make it easy with a program called **Kauai Made** (⊕ *www. kauaimade.net*), which showcases products made on Kauai, by Kauai people, using Kauai materials. The Maui Chamber of Commerce does something similar with **Made in Maui** (⊕ *www.madeinmaui. com*). Think of both as the Good Housekeeping Seal of Approval for locally made goods.

Then there are the crafty entrepreneurs who are diverting items from the trash heap by repurposing garbage. Take Oahu's **Muumuu Heaven** (⊕ *www.muumuuheaven. com*). They got their start by reincarnating vintage aloha apparel into hip new fashions.

Choose Green Tour Operators

Conscious decisions when it comes to island activities go a long way to protecting Hawaii's natural world. The **Hawaii Ecotourism Association** (⊕ *www.hawaiiecotourism. org*) recognizes tour operators for, among other things, their environmental stewardship. The **Hawaii Tourism Authority** (⊕ *www.hawaiitourismauthority.org*) recognizes outfitters for their cultural sensitivity. Winners of these awards are good choices when it comes to guided tours and activities.

TOP 10 HAWAIIAN FOODS TO TRY

Food in Hawaii is a reflection of the state's diverse cultural makeup and tropical location. Fresh seafood, organic fruits and vegetables, free-range beef, and locally grown products are the hallmarks of Hawaii regional cuisine. Its preparations are drawn from across the Pacific Rim, including Japan, the Philippines, Korea, and ThailanVd—and "local food" is a cuisine in its own right. Don't miss Hawaiian-grown coffee, either, whether it's smooth Kona from the Big Island or coffee grown on other Islands.

Saimin

The ultimate hangover cure and the perfect comfort food during Hawaii's mild winters, saimin ranks at the top of the list of local favorites. In fact, it's one of the few dishes deemed truly local, having been highlighted in cookbooks since the 1930s. Saimin is an Asian-style noodle soup so ubiquitous, it's even on McDonald's menus statewide. In mom-and-pop shops, a large melamine bowl is filled with homemade dashi, or broth, and wheat-flour noodles and then topped off with strips of omelet, green onions, bright pink fish cake and char siu (Chinese roast pork) or canned luncheon meat, such as SPAM. Add shoyu (the "local" name for soy sauce) and chili pepper water, lift your chopsticks, and slurp away.

SPAM

Speaking of SPAM, Hawaii's most prevalent grab-and-go snack is SPAM musubi. Often displayed next to cash registers at groceries and convenience stores, the glorified rice ball is rectangular, topped with a slice of fried SPAM and wrapped in nori (seaweed). Musubi is a bite-sized meal in itself. But just like sushi, the rice part hardens when refrigerated. So it's best to gobble it up right after purchase.

Hormel Company's SPAM actually deserves its own recognition—way beyond as a mere musubi topping. About 5 million cans are sold per year in Hawaii, and the Aloha State even hosts a festival in its honor. It's inexpensive protein and goes a long way when mixed with rice, scrambled eggs, noodles or, well, anything. The spiced luncheon meat gained popularity in World War II days, when fish was rationed. Gourmets and those with aversions to salt, high cholesterol, or high blood pressure may cringe at the thought of eating it, but SPAM in Hawaii is here to stay.

Manapua

Another savory snack is manapua, fist-sized dough balls fashioned after Chinese bao (a traditional Chinese bun) and stuffed with fillings such as char siu (Chinese roast pork) and then steamed. Many mom-and-pop stores sell them in commercial steamer display cases along with pork hash and other dim sum. Modern-day fillings include curry chicken.

Fresh Ahi or Tako Poke

There's nothing like fresh ahi or tako (octopus) poke to break the ice at a backyard party, except, of course, the cold beer handed to you from the cooler. The perfect pupu, poke (pronounced poh-kay) is basically raw seafood cut into bite-sized chunks and mixed with everything from green onions to roasted and ground kukui nuts. Other variations include mixing the fish with chopped round onion, sesame oil, seaweed, and chili pepper water. Shoyu is the constant. These days, grocery stores sell a rainbow of varieties such as kimchi crab and anything goes, from adding mayonnaise to tobiko (caviar). Fish lovers who want to take it to the next level order sashimi, the best cuts of ahi sliced and dipped in a mixture of shoyu and wasabi.

Tropical Fruits

Tropical fruits such as apple banana and strawberry papaya are plucked from trees in island neighborhoods and eaten for breakfast—plain or with a squeeze of fresh lime. Give them a try; the banana tastes like an apple and the papaya's rosy flesh explains its name. Locals also love to add their own creative touches to exotic fruits. Green mangoes are pickled with Chinese five spice, and Maui Gold pineapples are topped with *li hing mui* powder (heck, even margarita glasses are rimmed with it). Green papaya is tossed in a Vietnamese salad with fish paste and fresh prawns.

Plate Lunch

It would be remiss not to mention the plate lunch as one of the most beloved dishes in Hawaii. It generally includes two scoops of sticky white rice, a scoop of macaroni or macaroni-potato salad, heavy on the mayo, and perhaps kimchi or *koko* (salted cabbage). There are countless choices of main protein such as chicken *katsu* (fried cutlet), fried mahimahi, and beef tomato. The king of all plate lunches is the Hawaiian plate. The main item is *laulau* (pork or fish wrapped in taro leaf) or *kalua* pig (cooked in an underground oven or *imu*) and cabbage along with poi, *lomilomi* salmon (salmon-and-tomato salad), chicken long rice, and sticky white rice.

Bento Box

The bento box gained popularity back in the plantation days, when workers toiled in the sugarcane fields. No one brought sandwiches to work then. Instead it was a lunch box with the ever-present steamed white rice, pickled *ume* (plum) to preserve the rice, and main meats such as fried chicken or fish. Today, many stores sell prepackaged bentos or you may go to an *okazuya* (Japanese deli) with a hot buffet counter and create your own.

Malasadas

The Portuguese have contributed much to Hawaii cuisine in the form of sausage, soup, and sweetbread. But their most revered food is *malasadas*, hot, deep-fried doughnuts rolled in sugar. *Malasadas* are crowd-pleasers. Buy them by the dozen, hot from the fryer, placed in brown paper bags to absorb the grease. Or bite into gourmet *malasadas* at restaurants, filled with vanilla or chocolate cream.

Shave Ice

Much more than just a snow cone, shave ice is what locals crave after a blazing day at the beach or a hot-as-Hades game of soccer. If you're lucky, you'll find a neighborhood store that hand-shaves the ice, but it's rare. Either way, the counter person will ask you first if you'd like ice cream and/or adzuki beans scooped into the bottom of the cone or cup. Then they shape the ice into a giant mound and add colorful fruit syrups. First-timers should order the Rainbow, of course.

Crack Seed

There are dozens of varieties of crack seed in dwindling specialty shops and at the drugstores. Chinese call the preserved fruits and nuts *see mui* but somehow the Pidgin English version is what Hawaiians prefer. Those who like hard candy and salty foods will love *li hing* mangoes and rock salt plums, and those with an itchy throat will feel relief from the lemon strips. Peruse large glass jars of crack seed sold in bulk or smaller hanging bags—the latter make good gifts to give to friends back home.

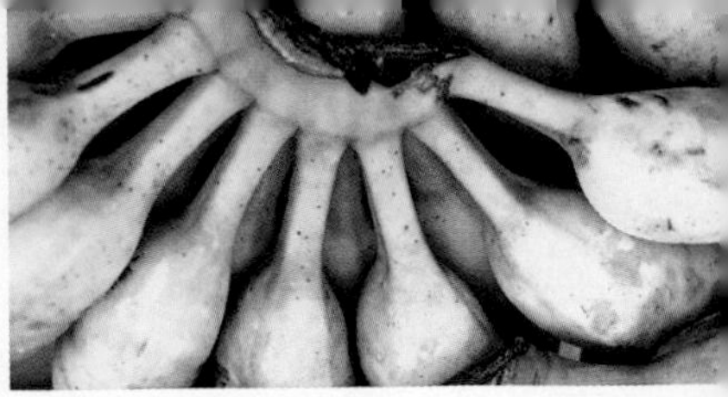

BEST FARMERS' MARKETS IN HAWAII

Oahu

Although there are exceptions, the **People's Open Market** dominates farmers' markets on Oahu. Others include the **Saturday Farmers' Market** at Kapiolani Community College on Diamond Head Road in Honolulu, **Kailua Town Farmers' Market** on Thursday morning in the parking lot of the Kailua District Park at 21 South Kainalu Drive and another on Thursday evening at the Kailua Town Center Parking Garage at 609 Kailua Rd, **Kakaako Farmers' Market,** held at Ward Warehouse, and the **North Shore Country Market** in Haleiwa. The Hawaii Farm Bureau (🌐 *hfbf.org/markets*) has information and weekly tip sheets about farmers' markets on Oahu. The Oahu Visitors Bureau site (🌐 *www.gohawaii.com/oahu*) also has good information.

Maui

Exotic oddities and fresh organic produce delight attendees of the **Ono Organic Farms** farmers' market on Monday and Thursday near Hasegawa General Store in Hana, where you can taste such items as durian, star apple, and egg fruit. **Maui Swap Meet** at the University of Hawaii Maui College is a great place to spend your Saturday. Peruse coconuts sliced open for you by a machete-wielding Tongan, banana bread just out of the oven, and more. There are plenty of crafts as well. **The Upcountry Farmers' Market,** near the Longs Drug Center in Pukalani, sells wonderful local produce every Saturday morning. **Kula Country Farms** (on Kula Highway across from Rice Park) boasts 100% local produce from as many as 50 local farmers. Those heading back to the condo from the beach on Saturday morning should make a pit stop at the farmers' markets in **Kihei** (on Lipoa Street). On the west side, the **Farmers' Market of Maui-Honokowai** is open on Monday, Wednesday, and Friday morning in the Hawaiian Motors parking lot.

Big Island

Because of its vast size, Big Island boasts specialties from its various regions in its farmers' markets. For instance, those who shop at **Kau Farmers' Market,** in front of Ace Hardware at South Point, will find the best local Kau oranges.

Head to **Hilo's Farmers' Market** on the corner of Kamehemeha Avenue and Mamo Street along with Keaau Village Market on Old Volcano Road and you'll discover the ripest and most colorful papaya at the state's lowest prices, along with jams, salsas, and an incredible variety of Asian street-food treats and gorgeous local flowers.

Kona Farmers' Market, at the corner of Alii Drive and Hualalai Road, has produce, macadamia nuts, and, of course, Kona coffee. For a taste of all things "hippie" and "New Age," **Pahoa Village Farmers' Market** in eccentric Pahoa can't be beat. On Saturday morning the **Waimea Homestead Farmers' Market** is a lively stop if you're in Waimea.

Kauai

Sunshine Markets has a near-monopoly on Kauai with weekly displays all over the island. Luckily, the selection is good and the produce is quality. **Kekaha Neighborhood Center** on Elepaio Road in Kekaha is just one of six produced by Sunshine Markets. Others include **Kalaheo Neighborhood Center** on Papalina Road in Kalaheo, **Kapaa New Town Park** on Kahau Road in Kapaa, **Kilauea Neighborhood Center** off Lighthouse Road in Kilauea, **Koloa Ball Park** on Maluhia Road in Koloa, and **Vidinha Stadium** in Lihue.

KIDS AND FAMILIES

With dozens of adventures, discoveries, and fun-filled beach days, Hawaii is a blast with kids. Even better, the things to do here do not appeal only to small fry. The entire family, parents included, will enjoy surfing, discovering a waterfall in the rain forest, and snorkeling with sea turtles. And there are plenty of organized activities for kids that will free parents' time for a few romantic beach strolls.

Choosing a Place to Stay

Resorts: All the big resorts make kids' programs a priority, and it shows. When you are booking your room, ask about "kids eat free" deals and the number of kids' pools at the resort. Also check out the size of the groups in the children's programs, and find out whether the cost of the programs includes lunch, equipment, and activities.

Condos: Condo and vacation rentals are a fantastic value for families vacationing in Hawaii. You can cook your own food, which is cheaper than eating out and sometimes easier (especially if you have a finicky eater in your group), and you'll get twice the space of a hotel room for about a quarter of the price. If you decide to go the condo route, be sure to ask about the size of the complex's pool (some try to pawn a tiny soaking tub off as a pool) and whether barbecues are available.

Ocean Activities

Hawaii is all about getting your kids outside—away from TV and video games. And who could resist the turquoise water, the promise of spotting dolphins or whales, and the fun of bodyboarding or surfing?

On the Beach: Most people like being in the water, but toddlers and school-age kids are often completely captivated by Hawaii's beaches. The swimming pool at your condo or hotel is always an option, but don't be afraid to hit the beach with a little one in tow. There are several in Hawaii that are nearly as safe as a pool—completely protected bays with pleasant white-sand beaches. As always, use your judgment, and heed all posted signs and lifeguard warnings.

On the Waves: Surf lessons are a great idea for older kids, especially if Mom and Dad want a little quiet time. Beginner lessons are always on safe and easy waves and last anywhere from two to four hours.

The Underwater World: If your kids are ready to try snorkeling, Hawaii is a great place to introduce them to the underwater world. Even without the mask and snorkel, they'll be able to see colorful fish darting this way and that, and they may also spot turtles and dolphins at many of the island beaches.

Land Activities

In addition to beach experiences, Hawaii has rain forests, botanical gardens, aquariums (Oahu and Maui), and even petting zoos and hands-on children's museums that will keep your kids entertained and out of the sun for a day.

After Dark

At night, younger kids get a kick out of luau, and many of the shows incorporate young audience members, adding to the fun. The older kids might find it all a bit lame, but there are a handful of new shows in the Islands that are more modern, incorporating acrobatics, lively music, and fire dancers. If you're planning on hitting a luau with a teen in tow, we highly recommend going the modern route.

ONLY IN HAWAII

Traveling to Hawaii is as close as an American can get to visiting another country while staying within the United States. There's much to learn and understand about the state's indigenous culture, the hundred years of immigration that resulted in today's blended society, and the tradition of aloha that has welcomed millions of visitors over the years.

Aloha Shirt

To go to Hawaii without taking an aloha shirt home is almost sacrilege. The first aloha shirts from the 1920s and 1930s—called "silkies"—were classic canvases of art and tailored for the tourists. Popular culture caught on in the 1950s, and they became a fashion craze. With the 1960s more subdued designs, Aloha Friday was born, and the shirt became appropriate clothing for work, play, and formal occasions. Because of its soaring popularity, cheaper and mass-produced versions became available.

Hawaiian Quilt

Although ancient Hawaiians were already known to produce fine *kapa* (bark) cloth, the actual art of quilting originated from the missionaries. Hawaiians have created designs to reflect their own aesthetic, and bold patterns evolved over time. They can be pricey because the quilts are intricately made by hand and can take years to finish. These masterpieces are considered precious heirlooms that reflect the history and beauty of Hawaii.

Popular Souvenirs

Souvenir shopping can be intimidating. There's a sea of Islands-inspired and often kitschy merchandise, so we'd like to give you a breakdown of popular and fun gifts that you might encounter and consider bringing home. If authenticity is important to you, be sure to check labels and ask shopkeepers. Museum shops are good places for authentic, Hawaiian-made souvenirs.

Fabrics. Purchased by the yard or already made into everything from napkins to bedspreads, modern Hawaiian fabrics make wonderful keepsakes.

Home accessories. Deck out your kitchen or dining room in festive luau style with bottle openers, pineapple mugs, tiki glasses, shot glasses, slipper and surfboard magnets, and salt-and-pepper shakers.

Lei and shell necklaces. From silk or polyester flower lei to kukui or puka shell necklaces, lei have been traditionally used as a welcome offering to guests (although the artificial ones are more for fun, as real flowers are always preferable).

Lauhala products. *Lauhala* weaving is a traditional Hawaiian art. The leaves come from the *hala*, or *pandanus*, tree and are hand-woven to create lovely gift boxes, baskets, bags, and picture frames.

Spa products. Relive your spa treatment at home with Hawaiian bath and body products, many of them manufactured with ingredients found only on the Islands.

Vintage Hawaii. You can find vintage photos, reproductions of vintage postcards or paintings, heirloom jewelry, and vintage aloha wear in many specialty stores.

Traditional Canoe

Hawaii's ancestors voyaged across 2,500 miles from Polynesia on board a double-hulled canoe with the help of the stars, the ocean swells, and the flight pattern of birds. The creation of a canoe spanned months and involved many religious ceremonies by the *kahuna kalai waa*, or high priest canoe builder. In 1973, the Polynesian Voyaging Society was founded to rediscover and preserve this ancestral

tradition. Since 1975, the group has built and launched the majestic *Hokulea* and *Hawaiiloa*, which regularly travel throughout the South Pacific. In 2014, Hokulea began an historic, three-year, around-the-world voyage.

Luau

The luau's origin, which was a celebratory feast, can be traced back to the earliest Hawaiian civilizations. In the traditional luau, the taboo or *kapu* laws were very strict, requiring men and women to eat separately. Nevertheless, in 1819 King Kamehameha II broke the great taboo and shared a feast with women and commoners, ushering in the modern-era luau. Today, traditional luau usually commemorate a child's first birthday, graduation, wedding, or other family occasion. They also are a Hawaiian experience that most visitors enjoy, and resorts and other companies have incorporated the fire-knife dance and other Polynesian dances into their elaborate presentations.

Nose flutes

The nose flute is an instrument used in ancient times to serenade a lover. For the Hawaiians, the nose is romantic, sacred, and pure. The Hawaiian word for kiss is *honi*. Similar to an Eskimo's kiss, the noses touch on each side sharing one's spiritual energy or breath. The Hawaiian term, *ohe hano ihu*, simply translated to "bamboo," with which the instrument is made; "breathe," because one has to gently breathe through it to make soothing music; and "nose," as it is made for the nose and not the mouth.

Slack-Key Guitar and the Paniolo

Kihoalu, or slack-key music, evolved in the early 1800s when King Kamehameha III brought in Mexican and Spanish vaqueros to manage the overpopulated cattle that had run wild on the Islands. The vaqueros brought their guitars and would play music around the campfire after work. When they left, supposedly leaving their guitars to their new friends, the Hawaiian *paniolo*, or cowboys, began to infuse what they learned from the vaqueros with their native music and chants, and so the art of slack-key music was born.

Today, the paniolo culture thrives where ranchers have settled.

Ukulele

The word *ukulele* literally translates to the "the jumping flea" and came to Hawaii in the 1880s by way of the Portuguese and Spanish. Once a fading art form, today it brings international kudos as a solo instrument, thanks to tireless musicians and teachers who have worked hard to keep it by our fingertips.

One such teacher is Roy Sakuma. Founder of four ukulele schools and a legend in his own right, Sakuma and his wife, Kathy, produced Oahu's first Ukulele Festival in 1971. Since then, they've brought the tradition to the Big Island, Kauai, and Maui. The free event annually draws thousands of artists and fans from all over the globe.

Hula

"Hula is the language of the heart, therefore the heartbeat of the Hawaiian people." —Kalakaua, the Merrie Monarch.

Thousands—from tots to seniors—devote hours each week to hula classes. All these dancers need some place to show off their stuff. The result is a network of hula competitions (generally free or very inexpensive) and free performances in malls and other public spaces. Many resorts offer hula instruction.

BEST BEACHES

No one ever gets as much beach time in Hawaii as they planned to, it seems, but it's a problem of time, not beaches. Beaches of every size, color (even green), and description line the state's many shorelines.

They have different strengths: some are great for sitting, but not so great for swimming. Some offer beach-park amenities like lifeguards and showers, whereas others are more private and isolated. Read up before you head out.

Oahu

Makapuu Beach. Quite possibly Oahu's most breathtaking scenic view—with a hiking trail to a historic lighthouse, offshore views of two rocky islets, home to thousands of nesting seabirds, and hang gliders launching off nearby cliffs.

While the white-sand beach and surroundings adorn many postcards, the treacherous ocean's currents invite experienced bodyboarders only.

Kailua Beach Park. This is a true family beach, offering something for everyone: A long stretch of sand for walking, turquoise seas set against cobalt skies for impressive photographs, a sandy-bottom shoreline for ocean swimming, and grassy expanses underneath shade trees for picnics.

You can even rent a kayak and make the short paddle to Popia (Flat) Island. This is Windward Oahu, so expect wind—all the better if you're an avid windsurfer or kiteboarder.

Waimea Bay. This is the beach that makes Hawaii famous every winter when monster waves and the world's best surfers roll in.

Show up to watch, not partake. If the rest of us want to get in the water here, we have to wait until summer when the safe, onshore break is great for novice bodysurfers.

White Plains. This beach is equal parts Kailua Beach Park with its facilities and tree-covered barbecue areas and Waikiki with its numerous surf breaks—minus the crowds and high-rises.

Pack for the day—cooler with food and drink, snorkel gear, inflatables, and bodyboard—as this destination is 35 minutes from downtown Honolulu.

Maui

Napili Beach. There is much to love about this intimate, crescent-shaped beach. Sunbathing, snorkeling, swimming, bodysurfing, and—after a full day of beach fun—startling sunsets. Bring the kids; they'll love the turtles that nosh on the *limu* (seaweed) growing on the lava rocks.

Makena (Big Beach). Don't forget the camera for this one. A bit remote and tricky to find, the effort is worth it—a long, wide stretch of golden sand and translucent offshore water. It's beautiful, yes, but the icing on the cake is this beach is never crowded. Use caution for swimming because the steep, onshore break can get big.

Waianapanapa State Park. The rustic beauty will capture your heart here—a black-sand beach framed by lava cliffs and backed by bright green *naupaka* bushes. Ocean currents can be strong, so cool off in one of two freshwater pools.

Get an early start, because your day's destination is just shy of Hana and requires a short, quarter-mile walk.

Big Island

Hapuna Beach State Recreation Area. It's hard to know where to start with this beach—the long, perfect crescent of sand,

the calm, turquoise waters, rocky points for snorkeling, even surf in winter. Just about everyone can find something to love here. With its west-facing views, this is a good spot for sunsets.

Kaunaoa Beach (Mauna Kea Beach). This is like the big brother, more advanced version of Hapuna Beach with snorkeling, bodysurfing, and board surfing but trickier currents, so be careful. Still, it's worth it. Try them both and let us know which you prefer. For most, it's a toss-up.

Papakolea Beach (Green Sand Beach). Papakolea makes our list, because, really, how often do you run across a green-sand beach? That's right, green. The greenish tint here is caused by an accumulation of olivine crystals that formed in volcanic eruptions.

This isn't the most swimmable of beaches, but the sand, sculpted cliffs, and dry, barren landscape make it quite memorable. A steep, 2-mile hike is required to access the beach.

Punaluu Beach Park (Black Sand Beach). This might as well be called Turtle Beach. Both the endangered Hawaiian green sea turtle and hawksbill turtle bask on the rocky, black-sand beach here.

We prefer to stay dry at this beach—due to strong rip currents—and snap pictures of the turtles and picnic under one of the many pavilions.

Kauai

Haena Beach Park (Tunnels Beach). Even if all you do is sit on the beach, you'll leave here happy. The scenic beauty is unsurpassed, with verdant mountains serving as a backdrop to the turquoise ocean.

Snorkeling is the best on the island during the calm, summer months. When the winter's waves arrive, surfers line up on the outside break.

Hanalei Bay Beach Park. When you dream of Hawaii, this is what comes to mind: a vast bay rimmed by a wide beach and waterfalls draping distant mountains. Everyone finds something to do here—surf, kayak, swim, sail, sunbathe, walk, and celebrity-watch.

Like most north shore beaches in Hawaii, Hanalei switches from calm in summer to big waves in winter.

Poipu Beach Park. The *keiki* (child's) swimming hole makes Poipu a great family beach, but it's also popular with snorkelers and moderate-to-experienced surfers. And while Poipu is considered a tourist destination, the Kauai residents come out on the weekends, adding a local flavor.

Be mindful of the endangered Hawaiian monk seals; they like it here, too.

Polihale State Park. If you're looking for remote, if you're looking for guaranteed sun, or if you're thinking of camping on the beach, drive the 5-mile-long cane-haul road to the westernmost point of Kauai. Be sure to stay for the sunset.

Unless you're an experienced water person, we advise staying out of the water due to a steep, onshore break. You can walk for miles along this beach, the longest in Hawaii.

BEST OUTDOOR ADVENTURES

In a place surrounded by the ocean, water sports like surfing, snorkeling, and scuba diving abound. Hawaii has it all—and more. But that's just the sea. Interior mountains and valleys offer a never-ending stream of other outdoor adventures. Here are our picks for the best water and land adventures around the state.

Oahu

Dive and snorkel at Shark's Cove. Some of the best things in life require a wait. That's the case with Shark's Cove—you have to wait for summer until it's safe to enter the water and swim with an amazing array of marine life thanks to the large boulders and coral heads dotting the sea floor and forming small caves and ledges. This is both a spectacular shore dive and snorkeling destination in one—perfect for the diver-snorkeler couple.

Bike the Aiea Loop Trail. This 4.5-mile, single-track, loop trail offers some of the most fun mountain biking in central Oahu. Although it's listed as an intermediate trail, some sections are a bit more difficult, with steep drop-offs. We recommend it for the weekend warrior who has a bit more experience. Caution: Do not attempt in wet weather.

Golf at the Royal Hawaiian Golf Club. Carved out of the middle of a tropical rain forest, this peaceful setting offers an antidote to the hustle and bustle of Waikiki. Bring your "A" game and a full bag, because club selection is key here. You'll want to hit each and every fairway.

Learn to surf at Waikiki Beach. You've heard the age-old saying that goes, "When in Rome, do as the Romans do." Well, when in Hawaii, surf. The sport that was once reserved for *alii*, or royalty, knows no class barrier these days. And there is no better place to learn than Waikiki, with its long and gentle rolling swells.

Hike to Kaena Point. For a raw and rugged look at Oahu's coastline, head to hot, dry Kaena Point. Head out early in the morning as Kaena Point is situated at the northwestern tip of the island (about 45 minutes from Waikiki). The 5-mile round-trip hike—rather, walk—ends at the westernmost tip of the island.

Maui

Explore Molokini Crater. Snorkeling here is like swimming in a tropical-fish aquarium. Molokini is a crescent-shaped crater that barely peeks its ridged spine above the ocean's surface, and the reef fish love it. If you're not comfortable leaping off the side of a boat into the open ocean, you may not go for this. Go early before the winds pick up.

Golf at Kapalua Resort. The Plantation Course at Kapalua is the site of the PGA Tour's first event each January, in which only champions from the previous PGA season can play. You can take them on—sort of—by playing in their footsteps. The wind will challenge the best of golfers here.

Hike in Haleakala Crater. How about hiking on black sand on the top of a mountain? There aren't many places you can do that. Thirty miles of trails await here—everything from day hikes to multiday pack trips. At 10,000 feet and summit temperatures ranging from 40 to 60 degrees, you might forget you're in Hawaii.

Snorkel at Kekaa. We like Kekaa Point for its big marine life: a turtle the size of a small car, eagle rays with three-foot wingspans, and all kinds of Hawaii's colorful endemic fish. But keep an eye out above, too, because this is a popular cliff-diving spot.

Big Island

Bike Kulani Trails. Stands of 80-foot eucalyptus. Giant tree ferns. The sweet song of honeycreepers overhead. Add single-track of rock and root—no dirt here—and we're talking a technically difficult ride. Did we mention this is a rain forest? That explains the perennial slick coat of slime on every possible surface. Advanced cyclists only.

Snorkel at Kealakekua Bay. Yes, the snorkeling here is tops for Big Island but, to be real, the draw here is the Hawaiian spinner dolphins that rest in the bay during the daytime. While it's enticing to swim with wild dolphins, doing so can disrupt their sleep patterns and make them susceptible to predators—aka sharks—so stick to an early morning or late afternoon schedule and give the dolphins their space between 9 and 3.

Watch the lava flow at Volcanoes National Park. It isn't too often that you can witness the creation of land in action. That's just what happens at Volcanoes National Park. The most dramatic example occurs where lava enters the sea. While Mother Nature rarely gives her itinerary in advance, if you're lucky, a hike, helicopter flight, or boat ride may pay off with spectacular views of nature's wonder. Sunrise and sunset make for the best viewing opportunities.

Go horseback riding in Waipio Valley. The Valley of the Kings owes its relative isolation and off-the-grid status to the 2,000-foot cliffs book-ending the valley. Really, the only way to explore this sacred place is on two legs—or four. We're partial to the horseback rides that wend deep into the rain forest to a series of waterfalls and pools—the setting for a perfect romantic getaway.

Kauai

Tour the Napali Coast by boat. Every one of the Hawaiian Islands possesses something spectacularly unique to it, and this stretch of folding cliffs is it for Kauai. To see it, though, you'll want to hop aboard a boat. You may opt for the leisurely ride aboard a catamaran or the more adventurous inflatable raft. You can even stop for snorkeling or a walk through an ancient fishing village. Whatever you do, don't forget your camera.

Kayak the Wailua River. The largest river in all Hawaii, the Wailua River's source is the center of the island—a place known as Mt. Waialeale—the wettest spot on Earth. And yet it's no Mighty Mississippi. There are no rapids to run. And that makes it a great waterway for learning to kayak. Guided tours will take you to a remote waterfall. Bring the whole family on this one.

Hike the Kalalau Trail. The Sierra Club allegedly rates this famous cliffside trail a difficulty level of 9 out of 10. But don't let that stop you. You don't have to hike the entire 11 miles. A mile hike will reward you with scenic ocean views—where in winter you might see breaching whales—sights of soaring seabirds and tropical plant life dotting the trail sides. Wear sturdy shoes, pack your camera, and be prepared to ooh and aah.

Enjoy a Helicopter Ride. If you drive from Kee Beach to Polihale, you may think you've seen all of Kauai, but we're here to tell you there's more scenic beauty awaiting you. Lots more. Save up for this one. It's not cheap, but a helicopter ride over the Garden Island will make you think you're watching a movie with 3-D glasses.

TOP SCENIC SPOTS

Every Hawaiian island has spectacular scenery; from any angle, panoramic Pacific vistas span the sky, the sea, and the land. Yet each island has its own special charm—from sparkling waterfalls and lush rain forests, to glistening beaches and stark lavascapes. Here are some spots for enjoying Hawaii's breathtaking scenery.

Oahu

Nuuanu Pali Lookout. With sweeping views of the verdant Koolau Mountains and Kaneohe Bay, the point where Kamehameha I forced enemy warriors over the cliff is a must-stop on any tour around the island.

Waikiki Beach at sunset. This is quintessential Oahu: sailboats and catamarans cruise offshore, Diamond Head glows magenta in the last rays of sunlight while the turquoise Pacific washes gently up to pristine beaches.

Bellows Beach Park. With sugary coral sand and jade green waters, this giant arc of a beach is why people come to Hawaii. While the colors of the sea and sand and few crowds are its best features, the jagged Koolau Mountains provide a backdrop for this idyllic tropical spot.

Maui

The Road to Hana. Calling the Road to Hana a "scenic spot" may be playing it down. With innumerable waterfalls, black-sand beaches, views over taro patches, and the sheer engineering involved in the narrow bridges and switchback curves, this stretch of highway in a tropical paradise provides scenic views around every corner.

Haleakala. Most known for its views at sunrise, the summit of Haleakala volcano is equally spectacular at sunset. On clear days the Big Island, Molokai, Lanai, Kahoolawe, and Molokini Crater are visible.

Makena Beach. Rolling waves, views of Kahoolawe, and golden sand make this wide beach a weekend favorite for locals.

The Big Island

Top of Mauna Kea at sunset. At almost 14,000 feet, a view from this cinder-covered summit at sunset provides an opportunity not only to see the sun slip into the Pacific through the pristine alpine atmosphere but also fabulous views of Maui's Haleakala.

Waipio Valley Overlook. The road along the Hamakua Coast ends with a view into one of the Big Island's most remote areas. From this point, view sheer black cliffs and the wide green valley that was once home to between 4,000 and 20,000 Hawaiians.

Hawaii Tropical Botanical Garden. Drive past waterfalls, ponds, orchids, and lush green vegetation on one of the Big Island's most scenic roads.

Kauai

Waimea Canyon. The oft-used term *breathtaking* does not do justice to your first view of Waimea Canyon (otherwise known as the "Grand Canyon of the Pacific"). Narrow waterfalls tumble thousands of feet to streams that cut through the rust-colored volcanic soil. Continue on to the end of the road for a view through the clouds of otherworldly Kalalau Valley.

Hanalei Valley Lookout. On the way to Hanalei (just past the Princeville shops), this pullout provides views of the Hanalei River winding its way through wet *loi kalo* (taro patches) framed by jagged green mountains.

Kee Beach. At the end of the road on the North Shore, Kee Beach is as far as you can drive and as close as you can get to the fabled cliffs of Bali Hai.

ULTIMATE HAWAIIAN INDULGENCES

Many indulgences in Hawaii don't require reservations, appointments, or making a serious dent in your credit card. They can be as simple as lingering a bit longer in a botanical garden, smelling the plumeria or ginger flowers, or stealing a bit of time away for yourself and a book under an umbrella at one of countless secluded beaches. However, because of Hawaii's world-class spas, chefs, and scenery, extravagant indulgences for the hedonist or gastronome abound.

Oahu

SpaHalekulani at the Halekulani Hotel in Waikiki offers a truly indulgent experience for two. Its Romance Remembered package is a five-and-a-half-hour experience, which features a *furo* (Japanese tub) soak, massage, and a champagne lunch in a terrace setting, and concludes with a manicure and pedicure in the salon. For individuals, choose from an extensive menu of massages, body treatments, facials, hair care, and nail care.

Looking for a gastronomic experience? **La Mer** in Waikiki offers a gourmet menu degustation that includes abalone "meuniere," filet of prime beef with foie gras and truffle mousseline, and hazelnut cake.

Maui

The traditional *lomilomi* massage at **The Spa at the Four Seasons Resort Maui** is given in their *hale* (a small replica of an ancient Hawaiian home) overlooking Wailea Bay. The pair of therapists works in unison as they chant and dance while providing a restorative treatment that seeks to unite both mind and body.

The treatments at the **Waihua Spa, Ritz-Carlton, Kapalua,** are based on Native Hawaiian healing and utilize plants, flowers, fruits, and herbs found in Hawaii. In addition to a full menu of spa treatments and a fitness center, this luxurious retreat has private outdoor gardens and spacious, private couples' cabanas.

Big Island

Mauna Lani Spa has a unique Lava Watsu treatment that features pressure point techniques and stretching, but the treatment itself is only the beginning. Built inside a natural lava tube, this saltwater Watsu pool is heated to body temperature. Clients float weightlessly throughout a treatment experience that is enhanced by a waterfall and underwater music.

Kauai

Kauai's natural wonders are a perfect opportunity to indulge in a helicopter ride. **Jack Harter Helicopters** offers an aerial tour of dramatic waterfalls and the spectacular Napali coastline—to avoid reflections in your photos, opt for a doors-off trip.

Those who prefer a more soothing experience can relax in a private cabana in a tropical garden setting of orchids, ti, and other tropical greenery, as you experience the Kauai Clay Escape at The Grand Hyatt Kauai's **ANARA Spa.** This spa package features a kava root scrub, mask made from local volcanic clays of Kauai, and a soothing massage with botanical lotions.

WEDDINGS AND HONEYMOONS

There's no question that Hawaii is one of the country's foremost honeymoon destinations. Romance is in the air here, and the white, sandy beaches, turquoise water, swaying palm trees, balmy tropical breezes, and perpetual sunshine put people in the mood for love. It's easy to understand why Hawaii is fast becoming a popular wedding destination as well, especially as the cost of airfare is often discounted, new resorts and hotels entice visitors, and same-sex marriage is now legal in the state. A destination wedding is no longer exclusive to celebrities and the superrich. You can plan a traditional ceremony in a place of worship followed by a reception at an elegant resort, or you can go barefoot on the beach and celebrate at a luau. There are almost as many wedding planners in the Islands as real estate agents, which makes it oh-so-easy to wed in paradise, and then, once the knot is tied, stay and honeymoon as well.

The Big Day

Choosing the Perfect Place. When choosing a location, remember that you really have two choices to make: the ceremony location and where to have the reception, if you're having one. For the former, there are beaches, bluffs overlooking beaches, gardens, private residences, resort lawns, and, of course, places of worship. As for the reception, there are these same choices, as well as restaurants and even luau. If you decide to go outdoors, remember the seasons—yes, Hawaii has seasons. If you're planning a winter wedding outdoors, be sure you have a backup plan (such as a tent), in case it rains. Also, if you're planning an outdoor wedding at sunset—which is very popular—be sure you match the time of your ceremony to the time the sun sets at that time of year. If you choose an indoor spot, be sure to ask

for pictures of the location when you're planning. You don't want to plan a pink wedding, say, and wind up in a room that's predominantly red. Or maybe you do. The point is, it should be your choice.

Finding a Wedding Planner. If you're planning to invite more than an officiant and your loved one to your wedding ceremony, seriously consider an on-island wedding planner who can help select a location, help design the floral scheme and recommend a florist as well as a photographer, help plan the menu and choose a restaurant, caterer, or resort, and suggest any Hawaiian traditions to incorporate into your ceremony. And more: Will you need tents, a cake, music? Maybe transportation and lodging? Many planners have relationships with vendors, providing packages—which mean savings.

If you're planning a resort wedding, most have on-site wedding coordinators; however, there are many independents around the Islands and even those who specialize in certain types of ceremonies—by locale, size, religious affiliation, and so on. A simple "Hawaii weddings" Google search will reveal dozens. What's important is that you feel comfortable with your coordinator. Ask for references and call them. Share your budget. Get a proposal—in writing. Ask how long they've been in business, how much they charge, how often you'll meet with them, and how they select vendors. Request a detailed list of the exact services they'll provide. If your idea of your wedding doesn't match their services, try someone else. If you can afford it, you might want to meet the planner in person.

Getting Your License. The good news about marrying in Hawaii is that there is no waiting period, no residency or citizenship

requirement, and no blood test or shots are required. You can apply and pay the fee online; however, both the bride and groom must appear together in person before a marriage-license agent to receive the marriage license (the permit to get married). You'll need proof of age—the legal age to marry is 18. (If you're 19 or older, a valid driver's license will suffice; if you're 18, a certified birth certificate is required.) Upon approval, a marriage license is immediately issued and costs $60 (credit cards accepted online and in person; cash only accepted in-person). After the ceremony, your officiant will mail the marriage certificate (proof of marriage) to the state. Approximately four months later, you will receive a copy in the mail. (For $10 extra, you can expedite this process. Ask your marriage-license agent when you apply.) For more detailed information, visit ⊕ *marriage. ehawaii.gov.*

Also—this is important—the person performing your wedding must be licensed by the Hawaii Department of Health, even if he or she is a licensed officiant. Be sure to ask.

Wedding Attire. In Hawaii, basically anything goes, from long, formal dresses with trains to white bikinis. Floral sundresses are fine, too. For men, tuxedos are not the norm; a pair of solid-colored slacks with a nice aloha shirt is. In fact, tradition in Hawaii for the groom is a beautiful white aloha shirt (they do exist) with slacks or long shorts and a colored sash around the waist. If you're planning a wedding on the beach, barefoot is the way to go.

If you decide to marry in a formal dress and tuxedo, you're better off making your selections on the mainland and hand-carrying them aboard the plane. Yes, it can be a pain, but ask your wedding-gown retailer to provide a special carrying bag. After all, you don't want to chance losing your wedding dress in a wayward piece of luggage.

Local Customs. The most obvious traditional Hawaiian wedding custom is the lei exchange in which the bride and groom take turns placing a lei around the neck of the other—with a kiss. Bridal lei are usually floral, whereas the groom's is typically made of *maile*, a green leafy garland that drapes around the neck and is open at the ends. Brides often also wear a *lei poo*—a circular floral headpiece. Other Hawaiian customs include the blowing of the conch shell, hula, chanting, and Hawaiian music.

The Honeymoon

Do you want champagne and strawberries delivered to your room each morning? A breathtaking swimming pool in which to float? A five-star restaurant in which to dine? Then a resort is the way to go. If, however, you prefer the comforts of a home, try a bed-and-breakfast. A small inn is also good if you're on a tight budget or don't plan to spend much time in your room. On the other hand, maybe you want your own private home in which to romp naked—or just laze around recovering from the wedding planning. Maybe you want your own kitchen so you can whip up a gourmet meal for your loved one. In that case, a private vacation-rental home is the answer. Or maybe a condominium resort. That's another beautiful thing about Hawaii: the lodging accommodations are almost as plentiful as the beaches, and there's one that will perfectly match your tastes and your budget.

CRUISING THE HAWAIIAN ISLANDS

Cruising has become popular in Hawaii. Cruises are a comparatively inexpensive way to see all of Hawaii, and you'll save travel time by not having to check in at hotels and airports on each island. The limited amount of time in each port can be an argument against cruising, but you can make reservations for tours, activities, rental cars, and more aboard the cruise ship. This will also give you more time for sightseeing and shopping at ports.

The larger cruise lines such as Carnival, Princess, and Holland America offer itineraries of 10–16 days departing from the West Coast of the United States, most with stops at all the major Hawaiian Islands. Some cruise lines, such as Crystal, Cunard, and Disney, include ports in Hawaii on around-the-world cruises. All have plenty on board to keep you busy during the 4–5 days that you are at sea between the U.S. mainland and Hawaii.

Cruise ships plying the Pacific from the continental United States to Hawaii are floating resorts complete with pools, spas, rock-climbing walls, restaurants, nightclubs, shops, casinos, children's programs, and much more. Most hold thousands of passengers with an average staff-to-passenger ratio of three to one.

Prices for cruises are based on accommodation type: interior (no window, in an inside corridor); outside (includes a window or porthole); balcony (allows you to go outside without using a public deck); and suite (larger cabin, more amenities and perks). Passages start at about $1,000 per person for the lowest class accommodation (interior) and include room, on-board entertainment, and food. Ocean-view, balcony, and suite accommodations can run up to $6,500 and beyond per person.

Cruising to Hawaii

Carnival Cruises is great for families, with plenty of kid-friendly activities. Departing from Los Angeles or Vancouver, Carnival's "fun ships" show your family a good time, both on board and on shore (☎ 888/227–6482 ⊕ www.carnival.com). The grand dame of cruise lines, Holland America has a reputation for service and elegance. Their 14-day Hawaii cruises leave from and return to San Diego, with a brief stop at Ensenada (☎ 877/932–4259 ⊕ www.hollandamerica.com). More affordable luxury is what Princess Cruises offers. While their prices seem a little higher, you get more bells and whistles on your trip (more affordable balcony rooms, more restaurants to chose from, personalized service) (☎ 800/774–6237 ⊕ www.princess.com).

Cruising within Hawaii

Norwegian Cruise Lines is the only major operator to begin and end cruises in Hawaii. Pride of Hawaii (vintage America theme, family focus with lots of connecting staterooms and suites) offers a seven-day itinerary that includes stops on Maui, Oahu, the Big Island, and Kauai. This is the only ship to cruise Hawaii that does not spend days at sea visiting a foreign port, allowing you more time to explore destinations (☎ 800/327–7030 ⊕ www.ncl.com). Ocean conditions in the channels between Islands can be a consideration when booking an interisland cruise on a smaller vessel such as Un-Cruise Adventures—a stately yacht accommodating only 36 passengers. This yacht's small size allows it to dock at less frequented islands such as Molokai and Lanai. The cruise is billed as "all inclusive"—your passage includes shore excursions, water activities, and a massage (☎ 888/862–8881 ⊕ www.un-cruise.com).

OAHU

WELCOME TO OAHU

TOP REASONS TO GO

★ **Waves:** Bodyboard or surf some of the best breaks on the planet.

★ **Pearl Harbor:** Remember Pearl Harbor with a visit to the *Arizona* Memorial.

★ **Diamond Head:** Scale the crater whose iconic profile looms over Waikiki.

★ **Nightlife:** Raise your glass to the best party scene in Hawaii.

★ **The North Shore:** See Oahu's countryside—check out the famous beaches from Sunset to Waimea Bay and hike to the remote tip of the island.

1 Honolulu. The vibrant capital city holds the nation's only royal palace, free concerts under the tamarind trees in the financial district, and the art galleries, hipster bars, and open markets of Nuuanu and China-town. It also encompasses

Waikiki—dressed in lights at the base of Diamond Head, famous for its world-class shopping, restaurants, and surf—and Pearl Harbor, Hawaii's largest natural harbor and the resting place of the USS *Arizona*, sunk on December 7, 1941.

Waialee

Waimea Bay

NORTH SHORE 4

83

Haleiwa

Dillingham Airfield
930

Waialua Bay

KAENA POINT

Yokohama Bay

WAIANAE MOUNTAINS

803

Kaala

CENTRAL OAHU 5

80

Wahiawa

Wheeler Air Force Base

Makaha
93

WEST (LEEWARD) OAHU 6

Waianae

Mililani Town
99

H2

Maili

Palikea

Puu Manawahua

750

Nanakuli

93

H1

Ewa

76

Kapolei

76

2 Southeast Oahu. Honolulu's main bedroom communities crawl up the steep-sided valleys that flow into Maunalua Bay. Also here are snorkelers' favorite Hanauma Bay and a string of wild and often hidden beaches.

3 Windward Oahu. The sleepy neighborhoods at the base of the majestic Koolau Mountains offer a respite from the bustling city with long stretches of sandy beaches, charming eateries, ancient Hawaiian fishponds, and offshore islands to explore.

4 The North Shore. Best known for its miles of world-class surf breaks and green sea-turtle sightings, this plantation town also boasts farms, restaurants, and hiking trails.

5 Central Oahu. Though the interstate cuts through much of this fertile region, it's an integral part of Hawaii's rich cultural history. This valley, between the Waianae and Koolau mountains, is an eclectic mix of farms, planned communities, and strip malls.

6 West (Leeward) Oahu. This rugged part of the island is finding a new identity as a "second city" of suburban homes, golf courses, and tech firms.

GETTING ORIENTED

Oahu, the third-largest of the Hawaiian Islands, is not just Honolulu and Waikiki. It's looping mountain trails on the western Waianae and eastern Koolau ranges. It's monster waves breaking on the golden beaches of the North Shore. It's country stores and beaches where turtles are your only swimming companions.

GREAT ITINERARIES

To experience even a fraction of Oahu's charms, you need a minimum of four days and a bus pass. Five days and a car is better: Waikiki is at least a day, Honolulu and Chinatown another, Pearl Harbor the better part of another. Each of the rural sections can swallow a day each, just for driving, sightseeing, and stopping to eat. And that's before you've taken a surf lesson, hung from a parasail, hiked a loop trail, or visited a botanical garden. The following itineraries will take you to our favorite spots on the island.

First Day in Waikiki

You'll be up at dawn due to the time change and dead on your feet by afternoon due to jet lag. Have a dawn swim, change into walking gear, and head east along Kalakaua Avenue to Monsarrat Avenue toward Diamond Head. Either climb to the summit (about 1½ hours round-trip) or enjoy the view from the lookout. After lunch—there are plenty of options along Monsarrat—take a nap in the shade, do some shopping, or visit the nearby East Honolulu neighborhoods of Moiliili and Kaimuki, rife with small shops and quaint restaurants. End the day with an early and inexpensive dinner at one of these neighborhood spots.

Southeast and Windward Exploring

For sand, sun, and surf, follow H1 east to the keyhole-shaped Hanauma Bay for picture-perfect snorkeling, then round the southeast tip of the island with its windswept cliffs and the famous Halona Blowhole. Watch bodysurfers at Sandy Beach or walk up the trail leading to the Makapuu Point Lighthouse. If you like, stop in at Sea Life Park. In Waimanalo, stop for local-style plate lunch or punch on through to Kailua, where there's intriguing shopping and good eating.

Lounge at Lanikai Beach until sunset, then grab dinner at one of the area's many restaurants.

The North Shore

Hit H1 westbound and then H2 to get to the North Shore. You'll pass through pineapple fields before dropping down a scenic winding road to Waialua and Haleiwa. Stop in Haleiwa town to shop, enjoy shave ice, and pick up a guided dive or snorkel trip. On winding Kamehameha Highway, stop at famous big-wave beaches, take a dip in a cove with a turtle, and buy fresh island fruit from roadside stands.

Pearl Harbor

Pearl Harbor is almost an all-day investment. Be on the grounds by 7:30 am to line up for USS *Arizona* Memorial tickets. Clamber all over the USS *Bowfin* submarine. Finally, take the free trolley to see the "Mighty Mo" battleship. If it's Wednesday, Saturday, or Sunday, make the five-minute drive *mauka* (toward the mountains) for bargain-basement shopping at the sprawling Aloha Stadium Swap Meet.

Town Time

If you are interested in history, devote a day to Honolulu's historic sites. Downtown, see Iolani Palace, the Kamehameha Statue, and Kawaiahao Church. A few blocks east, explore Chinatown, gilded Kuan Yin Temple, and artsy Nuuanu with its galleries. On the water is the informative Hawaii Maritime Center. Hop west on H1 to the Bishop Museum, the state's anthropological and archaeological center. And 1 mile up Pali Highway is Queen Emma Summer Palace, whose shady grounds were a royal retreat. The Foster Botanical Garden is worth a visit for plant lovers.

2

Updated by James Cave, Lesa Griffith, Trina Kudlacek, Chris Oliver, Catherine E. Toth, Anna Weaver

Oahu is one-stop Hawaii—all the allure of the Islands in a chop-suey mix that has you kayaking around offshore islets by day and sitting in a jazz club 'round midnight, all without ever having to take another flight or repack your suitcase. It offers both the buzz of modern living in jam-packed Honolulu (the state's capital) and the allure of slow-paced island life on its northern and eastern shores. Sometimes called "The Gathering Place," it is, in many ways, the center of the Hawaiian universe.

There are more museums, staffed historic sites, and walking tours here than you'll find on any other island. And only here do a wealth of renovated buildings and well-preserved neighborhoods so clearly spin the story of Hawaii's history. It's the only place to experience island-style urbanity, since there are no other true cities in the state. And yet you can get as lost in the rural landscape and be as laid-back as you wish.

Oahu is home to Waikiki, the most famous—though not the most beautiful—Hawaiian beach, as well as some of the world's most famous surf on the North Shore and the Islands' best known historical site—Pearl Harbor. If it's isolation, peace, and quiet you want, Oahu shouldn't be your only stop, but if you'd like a bit of spice with your piece of paradise, this island provides it.

GEOLOGY

Encompassing 597 square miles, Oahu is the third-largest island in the Hawaiian chain. Scientists believe the island was formed about 4 million years ago by two volcanoes: Waianae and Koolau. Waianae, the older of the two, created the mountain range on the western side of the island, whereas Koolau shaped the eastern side. Central Oahu is an elevated plateau bordered by the two mountain ranges, with Pearl Harbor to the south. Several of Oahu's most famous natural landmarks, including Diamond Head and Hanauma Bay, are tuff rings and cinder cones formed during a renewed volcanic stage (roughly 1 million years ago).

Koko Head in Hawaii Kai is a volcanic cinder cone near Hanauma Bay.

FLORA AND FAUNA

The eastern (Koolau) side of Oahu is much cooler and wetter than the western side of the island, which tends to be dry and arid. The island's official flower, the little orange *ilima,* grows predominantly in the east, but lei throughout the island incorporate *ilima.* Numerous tropical fish call the reef at Hanauma Bay home, migrating humpback whales can be spotted off the coast past Waikiki and Diamond Head from December through April, spinner dolphins pop in and out of the island's bays, and dozens of islets off Oahu's eastern coast provide refuge for endangered seabirds.

HISTORY

Oahu is the most populated island because early tourism to Hawaii started here. Although Kilauea volcano on Hawaii was a tourist attraction in the late 1800s, it was the building of the Moana Hotel on Waikiki Beach in 1901 and subsequent advertising of Hawaii to wealthy San Franciscans that really fueled tourism in the Islands. Oahu was drawing tens of thousands of guests yearly when, on December 7, 1941, Japanese Zeros appeared at dawn to bomb Pearl Harbor. Though tourism understandably dipped during the war (Waikiki Beach was fenced with barbed wire), the subsequent memorial only seemed to attract more visitors, and Oahu remains hugely popular with tourists—especially the Japanese—to this day.

CLOSE UP

Seeing Pearl Harbor

Pearl Harbor is a must-see for many, but there are things to know before you go. The collection of historic sights and ships is now called Valor in the Pacific National Monument.

Consider whether you want to see only the USS *Arizona* Memorial, or the USS *Bowfin* and USS *Missouri* as well. Allow approximately an hour and 15 minutes for the USS *Arizona* tour, which includes a 23-minute documentary of the Pearl Harbor attack and a ferry ride to the memorial itself.

Plan to arrive early—tickets for the USS *Arizona* Memorial are free and given out on a first-come, first-served basis. They can disappear within an hour. Take some time to enjoy the newly upgraded visitor center, which houses two exhibits using state-of-the-art technology to tell the story of the attack on December 7, 1941.

Strict security measures prohibit purses, backpacks, diaper bags, and camera cases (although cameras are allowed). Strollers are allowed in the visitor center but not in the theaters or on the shuttle boats. Baggage lockers are available for a small fee. Also, don't forget your ID.

Children under four years of age are not allowed on the USS *Bowfin* for safety reasons, and may not enjoy the crowds or waiting in line at other sights.

Older kids are likely to find the more experiential, hands-on history of the USS *Bowfin* and USS *Missouri* memorable.

For more information, visit ⊕ *www.nps.gov/valr.*

OAHU PLANNER

GETTING HERE AND AROUND
AIR TRAVEL

Honolulu International Airport is 20 minutes (40 during rush hour) from Waikiki. Car-rental companies have booths at baggage claim; shuttle buses then take you to the car pickup areas.

An inefficient airport taxi system requires you to line up to a taxi wrangler who radios for cars (about $25 to Waikiki). Other options include the city's reliable bus system ($2.50) with stops throughout Honolulu and Waikiki, or the Airport Waikiki Express shuttle ($9), which transports you to any hotel in Waikiki. Ask the driver to take Interstate H1, not Nimitz Highway, or your introduction to paradise will be via Honolulu's industrial backside.

CAR TRAVEL

You can get away without renting a car if you plan on staying in Waikiki. But if you want to explore the rest of the island (a wise choice), there's no substitute for having your own wheels. Avoid the obvious tourist cars—candy-colored convertibles, for example—and never leave anything valuable inside, even if you've locked the car. Get a portable GPS navigator, as some of Oahu's streets can be confusing.

Reserve your vehicle in advance, especially when traveling during the Christmas holidays and summer breaks. This will not only ensure that you get a car but also that you get the best rates. *See Travel Smart Hawaii for more information on renting a car and driving.*

Don't let maps fool you. Although the distance between Waikiki and, say, the North Shore is roughly 40 miles, it may take more than an hour to get there, thanks to heavy traffic, construction, and other factors. Many of Oahu's main roads are single lanes in each direction, with no alternate routes. So if you're stuck behind a slow-moving vehicle, you may have no other choice than to hope it turns soon. If you are the slow-moving vehicle, consider turning off and letting locals pass. Heavy traffic moving toward downtown can begin as early as 6 am, with after-work traffic starting at 3 pm.

Here are average driving times—without traffic—that will help you plan your excursions accordingly.

DRIVING TIMES	
Waikiki to airport	25 mins
Waikiki to downtown Honolulu	10 mins
Waikiki to Hawaii Kai	25 mins
Waikiki to Kailua	30 mins
Hawaii Kai to Kailua	25 mins
Waikiki to Haleiwa	45 mins
Haleiwa to Turtle Bay	20 mins
Kaneohe to Turtle Bay	1 hr
Waikiki to Ko Olina	1 hr

HOTELS

Most of Oahu's lodging options are located in Waikiki. While the Royal Hawaiians and Hilton Hawaiian Villages get a lot of the airtime when TV shows try to capture this resort area, most of us stay at places that are a bit less flashy but still have their charms. Aqua Hotels have recently taken over several properties that create that boutique feel without the price tag, while the Outrigger chain carries broad appeal for those traveling with kids.

Prices in the reviews are the lowest cost of a standard double room in high season. For expanded hotel reviews, visit www.Fodors.com

RESTAURANTS

Honolulu is home to some of the world's most famous chefs, from Sam Choy and his down-home cooking to the artistic Roy Yamaguchi. While there are plenty of glitzy and recognizable names, some of the best cuisine is off Waikiki's beaten path. Look to Kapahulu and Waialae Avenues for fantastic hole-in-the-wall sushi joints and local favorites. Chinatown is the spot for not just dim sum but the best of Italian, French, and Cuban dishes.

Prices in the reviews are the average cost of a main course at dinner or, if dinner is not served, at lunch.

GUIDED TOURS

Guided tours are convenient; you don't have to worry about finding a parking spot or getting admission tickets. Most of the tour guides have taken special classes in Hawaiian history and lore, and many are certified by the state of Hawaii. On the other hand, you won't have the freedom to proceed at your own pace, nor will you have the ability to take a detour trip if something else catches your attention.

BUS AND VAN TOURS

Polynesian Adventure. This company leads tours of Pearl Harbor and other historic Honolulu sights and also offers a circle-island tour by motor coach, van, and minicoach. ☎ *808/833–3000* ⊕ *www. polyadhawaiitours.com/.*

Roberts Hawaii. Choose from a large selection of tours, including downtown Honolulu ghost tours, underwater submarine tours, and the more traditional Pearl Harbor excursions. Tours are conducted via everything from vans to president-worthy limousines. ☎ *808/539–9400* ⊕ *www. robertshawaii.com.*

THEME TOURS

Discover Hawaii Tours. In addition to circle-island and other Oahu-based itineraries on motor and minicoaches, this company can also get you from Waikiki to the lava flows of the Big Island or to Maui's Hana Highway and back in one day. ☎ *808/690–9050* ⊕ *www. discoverhawaiitours.com.*

E Noa Tours. This outfitter's certified tour guides conduct circle-island, Pearl Harbor, nature, and shopping tours. ☎ *808/591–2561* ⊕ *www. enoa.com.*

Home of the Brave Victory Tours. Perfect for military history buffs, these narrated tours visit Oahu's military bases and the National Memorial Cemetery of the Pacific. Tours also include a visit to the company's private "brewseum," which displays artifacts and memorabilia from World War II. Evening "Night at the Brewseum" tours also include stops in Honolulu and craft beer tastings. ☎ *808/396–8112* ⊕ *www. pearlharborhq.com.*

VISITOR INFORMATION

Before you go, contact the Oahu Visitors Bureau (OVB). For general information on all the Islands, contact the Hawaii Visitors & Convention Bureau (HVCB). The HVCB website has a calendar section that shows what local events will be taking place during your stay.

Contacts Hawaii Visitors & Convention Bureau ☎ *800/464–2924 for brochures* ⊕ *www.gohawaii.com.* **Oahu Visitors Bureau** ☎ *877/525–6248* ⊕ *www.gohawaii.com/oahu.*

EXPLORING

HONOLULU

Updated by
Anna Weaver

Here is Hawaii's only true metropolis, its seat of government, center of commerce and shipping, entertainment and recreation mecca, a historic site, and an evolving urban area—conflicting roles that engender endless debate and controversy. For the visitor, Honolulu is every person's delight: hipsters and scholars, sightseers and foodies, nature lovers, and culture vultures all can find their bliss.

Once there was the broad bay of Mamala and the narrow inlet of Kou, fronting a dusty plain occupied by a few thatched houses and the great Pakaka *heiau* (shrine). Nosing into the narrow passage in the early 1790s, British sea captain William Brown named the port Fair Haven. Later, Hawaiians would call it Honolulu, or "sheltered bay." As shipping traffic increased, the settlement grew into a Western-style town of streets and buildings, tightly clustered around the single freshwater source, Nuuanu Stream. Not until piped water became available in the early 1900s did Honolulu spread across the greening plain. Long before that, however, Honolulu gained importance when King Kamehameha I reluctantly abandoned his home on the Big Island to build a chiefly compound near the harbor in 1804 to better protect Hawaiian interests from the Western incursion.

Two hundred years later, the entire island is, in a sense, Honolulu—the City and County of Honolulu. The city has no official political boundaries, extending across the flatlands from Pearl Harbor to Waikiki and high into the hills behind.

WAIKIKI
3 miles east of downtown Honolulu.

A short drive from downtown Honolulu, Waikiki is Oahu's primary resort area. A mix of historic and modern hotels and condos front the sunny 2-mile stretch of beach, and many have clear views of Diamond Head to the east. The area is home to much of the island's upscale dining, nightlife, and shopping scene—from posh boutiques to hole-in-the-wall eateries to craft booths at the International Marketplace.

Waikiki was once a favorite retreat for Hawaiian royalty. In 1901 the Moana Hotel debuted, introducing Waikiki as an international travel destination. The region's fame continued to grow when Duke Kahanamoku helped popularize the sport of surfing, offering lessons to visitors at Waikiki. You can see Duke immortalized in a bronze statue, with a surfboard, on Kuhio Beach. Today, there is a decidedly "urban resort" vibe here; streets are clean, gardens are manicured, and the sand feels softer than at beaches farther down the coast. There isn't much of a local culture—it's almost exclusively tourist crowds—but you'll still find the relaxed surf-y vibe that has drawn people here for more than a century.

Diamond Head Crater (*see Greater Honolulu and Diamond Head*) is perhaps Hawaii's most recognizable natural landmark and creates

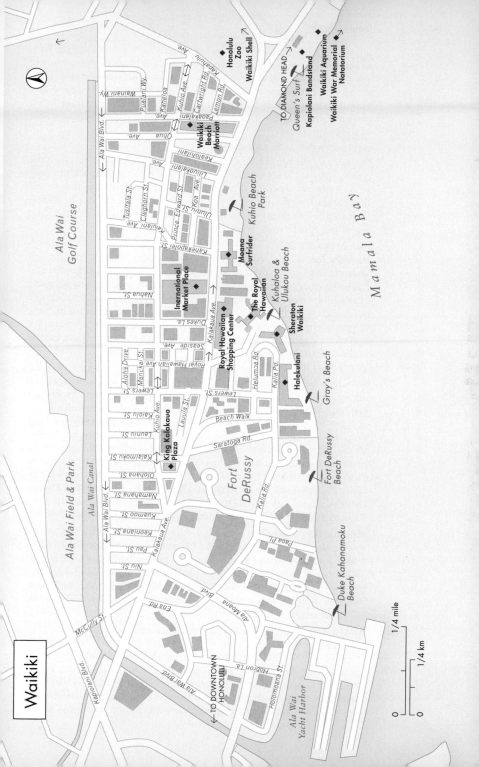

Waikiki

Ala Wai Golf Course

Ala Wai Field & Park

Ala Wai Canal

Mamala Bay

Honolulu Zoo
Waikiki Shell

TO DIAMOND HEAD
Queen's Surf
Kapiolani Bandstand
Waikiki Aquarium
Waikiki War Memorial Natatorium

Kapahulu Ave.
Walina Wy.
Pualani Wy.
Kanekoa
Kuhio Ave.
Cartwright Rd.
Paoakalani Ave.
Lemon Rd.
Kealohilani Ave.
Ala Wai Blvd.
Ohua Ave.
Ave.
Liliuokalani Ave.
Koa Ave.
Kaiulani Ave.
Kanekapolei St.
Prince Edward St.
Uluniu St.
Nohonani St.
Cleghorn St.
Tusitala St.
Nahua St.
Dukes La.
Royal Hawaiian Ave.
Seaside Ave.
Aloha Drive
Lewers St.
Kaiolu St.
Launiu St.
Kalaimoku St.
Namahana St.
Olohana St.
Nahua St.
Kalakaua Ave.
Kalakaua Ave.
Ala Wai Blvd.
Kuamoo St.
Keoniana St.
Pau St.
Niu St.
McCully St.

Waikiki Beach Marriott

International Market Place

Moana Surfrider

Kuhio Beach Park

The Royal Hawaiian

Royal Hawaiian Shopping Center

Kuhaloa & Uluikou Beach

Sheraton Waikiki

Halekulani

Helumoa Rd.
Kalia Rd.
Kalia Pd.

Gray's Beach

Beach Walk

Lewers St.

Saratoga Rd.

King Kalakaua Plaza

Fort DeRussy

Fort DeRussy Beach

Kalia Rd.

Paoa Pl.

Ala Moana Blvd.

Ena Rd.

Duke Kahanamoku Beach

Hobron La.

Holomoana St.

Ala Wai Yacht Harbor

TO DOWNTOWN HONOLULU

Kalakaua Blvd.

0   1/4 mile
0   1/4 km

a postcard-perfect backdrop against Waikiki's beach. Kapiolani Park lies in the shadow of the crater, providing a 500-acre expanse where you can play all sorts of field sports, enjoy a picnic, see wild animals at the Honolulu Zoo, or hear live music at the Waikiki Shell or the Kapiolani Bandstand. King David Kalakaua established the park in 1887, named it after his queen, and dedicated it "to the use and enjoyment of the people."

GETTING HERE AND AROUND

Bounded by the Ala Wai Canal on the north and west, the beach on the south, and the Honolulu Zoo to the east, Waikiki is compact and easy to walk around. TheBus runs multiple routes here from the airport and downtown Honolulu. By car, finding Waikiki from H1 can be tricky; look for the Punahou exit for the western end of Waikiki, and the King Street exit for the eastern end.

TOP ATTRACTIONS

FAMILY **Honolulu Zoo.** There are bigger and better zoos, but this one, though showing signs of neglect due to budget constraints, is a lush garden and has some great programs. To get a glimpse of the endangered nene, the Hawaii state bird, check out the zoo's Kipuka Nene Sanctuary. Though many animals prefer to remain invisible, particularly the elusive big cats, the monkeys appear to enjoy being seen and are a hoot to watch. It's best to get to the zoo right when it opens, since the animals are livelier in the cool of the morning.

The Wildest Show in Town is a 10-week summer concert series ($3 participation fee), and you can have a family sleepover inside the zoo during Snooze in the Zoo on Saturday nights between May and October. Or just head for the petting zoo, where kids can make friends with a llama or stand in the middle of a koi pond. There's an exceptionally good gift shop. On weekends, the Art on the Zoo Fence, on Monsarrat Avenue on the Diamond Head side outside the zoo, has affordable artwork by contemporary artists. Metered parking is available all along the *makai* (ocean) side of the park and in the lot next to the zoo—but it can fill up early. TheBus makes stops here along the way to and from Ala Moana Center and Sea Life Park (routes 8 and 22). ⊠ *151 Kapahulu Ave., Waikiki* ☎ *808/971-7171* ⊕ *honoluluzoo.org* ⌖ *$14* ☉ *Daily 9–4:30.*

Kapiolani Bandstand. The Victorian-style Kapiolani Bandstand, which was originally built in the late 1890s and was recently renovated, is Kapiolani Park's stage for community entertainment and concerts. The nation's only city-sponsored band, the Royal Hawaiian Band, performs free concerts at the bandstand as well as at Iolani Palace and the Moana Surfrider. Local newspapers list event information. ⊠ *2805 Monsarrat Ave., Waikiki* ☎ *808/922-5331.*

FAMILY **Waikiki Aquarium.** This amazing little attraction harbors more than 3,500 organisms and 500 species of Hawaiian and South Pacific marine life, endangered Hawaiian monk seals, sharks, and the only chambered nautilus living in captivity. The Edge of the Reef exhibit showcases five different types of reef environments found along Hawaii's shorelines. Check out the new endangered green sea turtle exhibit, the Northwestern Hawaiian Islands display that explains the formation of the

2

island chain, the Ocean Drifters jellyfish exhibit, the outdoor touch pool, and the self-guided audio tour, which is included with admission. The aquarium offers activities of interest to adults and children alike, including the Aquarium After Dark program when visitors grab a flashlight and view fish going about their rarely observable nocturnal activities. ✉ *2777 Kalakaua Ave., Waikiki* ☏ *808/923–9741* ⊕ *www. waquarium.org* 🖅 *$12* ⊙ *Daily 9–5; last entrance 4:30.*

WORTH NOTING

Waikiki Shell. Grab one of the 6,000 "grass seats" (i.e., lawn seating) for music under the stars (there are actual seats, as well). An eclectic array of musical acts put on concerts at this landmark venue throughout the summer and occasionally during the winter, weather permitting. Check newspaper entertainment sections to see who is performing. ✉ *2805 Monsarrat Ave., Waikiki* ☏ *808/768–5400* ⊕ *blaisdellcenter.com/venues/waikiki-shell.*

Waikiki War Memorial Natatorium. This Beaux-Arts style, 1927 World War I monument, dedicated to the 102 Hawaiian servicemen who lost their lives in battle, stands proudly in Waikiki. The 100-meter saltwater swimming pool, the training spot for Olympians Johnny Weissmuller and Buster Crabbe and the U.S. Army during World War II, has been closed for decades, as the pool needs repair. Plans are under study to tear down the natatorium, though a nonprofit group continues fighting to save the facility. The site is closed to visitors, but you can stop by and look at it from the outside. ✉ *2777 Kalakaua Ave., Waikiki* ⊕ *www.natatorium.org.*

DIAMOND HEAD

Besides hiking Diamond Head, visitors will enjoy the eclectic shops and restaurants along Monsarrat Avenue like Diamond Head Market & Grill. Don't forget the amazing *poke* (seasoned raw fish) and other local goodies at Fort Ruger Market, and the Saturday farmers' market at Kapiolani Community College is arguably the best on the island.

TOP ATTRACTIONS

Diamond Head State Monument and Park. Panoramas from this 760-foot extinct volcanic peak, once used as a military fortification, extend from Waikiki and Honolulu in one direction and out to Koko Head in the other, with surfers and windsurfers scattered like confetti on the cresting waves below. This 360-degree perspective is a great orientation for first-time visitors. On a clear day, look east past Koko Head to glimpse the outlines of the islands of Maui and Molokai.

To enter the park from Waikiki, take Kalakaua Avenue east, turn left at Monsarrat Avenue, head a mile up the hill, and look for a sign on the

---

WAIKIKI'S BEST FREE ENTERTAINMENT

Waikiki's entertainment scene isn't just dinner shows and lounge acts. There are plenty of free or nearly free offerings right on the beach and at Kapiolani Park. Queen's Surf Beach hosts the popular Sunset on the Beach, which brings big-screen showings of recent Hollywood blockbusters to the great outdoors. Also, during the summer months, the Honolulu Zoo has weekly concerts, and admission is just $1.

right. Drive through the tunnel to the inside of the crater. The ¾-mile trail to the top begins at the parking lot. Be aware that the hike to the crater is an upward ascent with numerous stairs to climb; if you aren't in the habit of getting occasional exercise, this might not be for you. At the top, you'll find a somewhat awkward scramble through a tunnel and bunker out into the open air, but the view is worth it.

Take bottled water with you to stay hydrated under the tropical sun. ■TIP➜ **To beat the heat and the crowds, rise early and make the hike before 8 am.** As you walk, note the color of the vegetation; if the mountain is brown, Honolulu has been without significant rain for a while; but if the trees and undergrowth glow green, you'll know it's the wet season (winter) without looking at a calendar. This is when rare Hawaiian marsh plants revive on the floor of the crater. Keep an eye on your watch if you're here at day's end: the gates close promptly at 6. ⊠ *Diamond Head Rd. at 18th Ave., Diamond Head* ☎ *808/587–0300* ⊕ *www. hawaiistateparks.org/parks/oahu/?park_id=15* ⊠ *$1 per person, $5 per vehicle* ⊗ *Daily 6–6; last trail entry at 4:30.*

PEARL HARBOR

Approximately 9 miles west of downtown Honolulu, beyond Honolulu International Airport.

December 7, 1941. Every American then alive recalls exactly what he or she was doing when the news broke that the Japanese had bombed Pearl Harbor, the catalyst that brought the United States into World War II. More than 2,000 people died that day, and a dozen ships were sunk.

Here, in what is still a key Pacific naval base, the attack is remembered every day by thousands of visitors. In recent years, the memorial has been the site of reconciliation ceremonies involving Pearl Harbor veterans from both sides.

TOP ATTRACTIONS

Fodor's Choice ★ **Pearl Harbor Visitor Center.** The Pearl Harbor Visitor Center, reopened after a $58 million renovation and is now the gateway to the World War II Valor in the Pacific National Monument and the starting point for visitors to this historic site. Pearl Harbor is a must-see for many, but there are things to know before you go. Consider whether you want to see only the *Arizona* Memorial, or the USS *Bowfin* and USS *Missouri* as well (the latter two charge separate admission fees). Allow approximately an hour and 15 minutes for the USS *Arizona* tour. The majority of *Arizona* tickets are now given out at ⊕ *recreation.gov* where you book a specific time slot. But if you didn't get a ticket online, arrive early for a limited number of same-day tickets and prepare to wait for your time slot. There are restrictions on what you can bring with you, including purses, backpacks, and camera cases (although cameras are allowed). Baggage lockers are available for a small fee. Also, don't forget ID. *For much more detailed information, see the highlighted feature in this chapter.* ⊠ *World War II Valor in the Pacific National Monument, 1 Arizona Memorial Pl., Pearl Harbor* ☎ *808/422–3300* ⊕ *www.nps.gov/valr/* ⊠ *Arizona admission is free with a $1.50 online reservation charge; separate fees for Bowfin, Missouri, Arizona audio*

Continued on page 63

USS *West Virginia* (BB48), 7 December 1941

PEARL HARBOR

December 7, 1941. Every American then alive recalls exactly what he or she was doing when the news broke that the Japanese had bombed Pearl Harbor, the catalyst that brought the United States into World War II.

Although it was clear by late 1941 that war with Japan was inevitable, no one in authority seems to have expected the attack to come in just this way, at just this time. So when the Japanese bombers swept through a gap in Oahu's Koolau Mountains in the hazy light of morning, they found the bulk of America's Pacific fleet right where they hoped it would be: docked like giant stepping stones across the calm waters of the bay named for the pearl oysters that once prospered there. More than 2,000 people died that day, including 49 civilians. A dozen ships were sunk. And on the nearby air bases, virtually every American military aircraft was destroyed or damaged. The attack was a stunning success, but it lit a fire under America, which went to war with "Remember Pearl Harbor" as its battle cry. Here, in what is still a key Pacific naval base, the attack is remembered every day by thousands of visitors, including many curious Japanese, who for years heard little World War II history in their own country. In recent years, the memorial has been the site of reconciliation ceremonies involving Pearl Harbor veterans from both sides.

GETTING AROUND

Pearl Harbor is both a working military base and the most-visited Oahu attraction. Four distinct destinations share a parking lot and are linked by footpath, shuttle, and ferry.

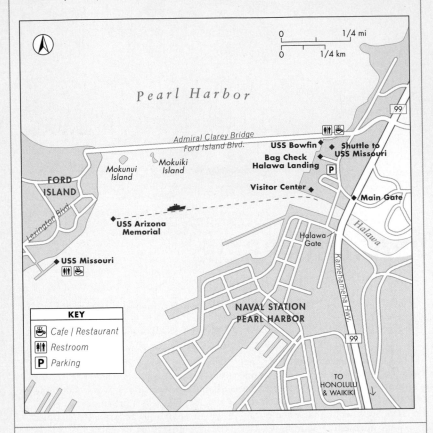

The visitor center is accessible from the parking lot. The USS *Arizona* Memorial itself is in the middle of the harbor; get tickets for the ferry ride at the visitor center. The USS *Bowfin* is also reachable from the parking lot.

The USS *Missouri* is docked at Ford Island, a restricted area of the naval base. Vehicular access is prohibited. To get there, take a shuttle bus from the station near the *Bowfin*.

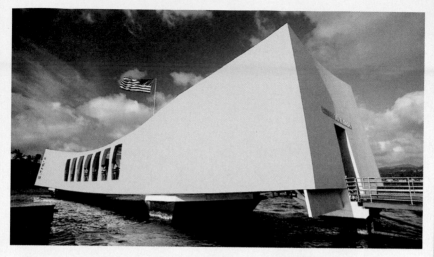

ARIZONA MEMORIAL

Snugged up tight in a row of seven battleships off Ford Island, the USS *Arizona* took a direct hit that December morning, exploded, and rests still on the shallow bottom where she settled.

The swooping, stark-white memorial, which straddles the wreck of the USS *Arizona*, was designed to represent both the depths of the low-spririted, early days of the war, and the uplift of victory.

A visit here begins at the Pearl Harbor Visitor Center, which recently underwent a $58 million renovation. High definition projectors and interactive exhibits were installed, and the building was modernized. From the visitor center, a ferry takes you to the memorial itself, and a new shuttle hub now gives access to sites that were previously inaccessible, like the USS *Utah* and USS *Oklahoma*.

A somber, contemplative mood descends upon visitors during the ferry ride to the *Arizona*; this is a place where 1,177 crewmen lost their lives. Gaze at the names of the dead carved into the wall of white marble. Scatter flowers (but no lei—the string is bad for the fish). Salute the flag. Remember Pearl Harbor.

☎ *808/422–0561*
⊕ *www.nps.gov/valr*

USS *MISSOURI* (BB63)

Together with the *Arizona* Memorial, the *Missouri's* presence in Pearl Harbor perfectly bookends America's WWII experience that began December 7, 1941, and ended on the "Mighty Mo's" starboard deck with the signing of the Terms of Surrender.

Surrender of Japan, USS *Missouri*, 2 September 1945

In the parking area behind the USS *Bowfin* Museum, board a shuttle for a breezy, eight-minute ride to Ford Island and the teak decks and towering superstructure of the *Missouri*, docked for good in the very harbor from which she first went to war on January 2, 1945. The last battleship ever built, the *Missouri* famously hosted the final act of WWII, the signing of the Terms of Surrender. The commission that governs this floating museum has surrounded her with buildings tricked out in WWII style—a canteen that serves as an orientation space for tours, a WACs and WAVEs lounge with a flight simulator the kids will love ($10 per person), Truman's Line restaurant serving Navy-style meals, and a Victory Store housing a souvenir shop and covered with period mottos ("Don't be a blabateur").
■ **TIP→** Definitely hook up with a tour guide (additional charge) or audio tour— these add a great deal to the experience.

The *Missouri* is all about numbers: 209 feet tall, six 239,000-pound guns, capable of firing up to 23 mi away. Absorb these during the tour, then stop to take advantage of the view from the decks. The Mo is a work in progress, with only a handful of her hundreds of spaces open to view.

☎ *808/423–2263* or ☎ *888/877–6477*
⊕ *www.ussmissouri.com*

USS *BOWFIN* (SS287)

SUBMARINE MUSEUM & PARK

Launched one year to the day after the Pearl Harbor attack, the USS *Bowfin* sank 44 enemy ships during WWII and now serves as the centerpiece of a museum honoring all submariners.

Although the *Bowfin* no less than the *Arizona* Memorial commemorates the lost, the mood here is lighter. Perhaps it's the childlike scale of the boat, a metal tube just 16 feet in diameter, packed with ladders, hatches, and other obstacles, like the naval version of a jungle gym. Perhaps it's the World War II-era music that plays in the covered patio. Or it might be the museum's touching displays—the penciled sailor's journal, the Vargas girlie posters. Aboard the boat nicknamed "Pearl Harbor Avenger," compartments are fitted out as though "Sparky" was away from the radio room just for a moment, and "Cooky" might be right back to his pots and pans. The museum includes many artifacts to spark family conversations, among them a vintage dive suit that looks too big for Shaquille

O'Neal. A caution: The *Bowfin* could be hazardous for very young children; no one under four allowed.

☎ *808/423–1341*
⊕ *www.bowfin.org*

THE PACIFIC AVIATION MUSEUM

This museum opened on December 7, 2006, as phase one of a four-phase tribute to the air wars of the Pacific. Located on Ford Island in Hangar 37, an actual seaplane hangar that survived the Pearl Harbor attack, the museum is made up of a theater where a short film on Pearl Harbor kicks off the tour, an education center, a shop, and a restaurant. Exhibits—many of which are interactive and involve sound effects—include an authentic Japanese Zero in a diorama setting a chance to don a flight suit and play the role of a World War II pilot using one of six flight simulators. Various aircrafts are employed to narrate the great battles: the Doolittle Raid on Japan, the Battle of Midway, Guadalcanal, and so on. The actual Stearman N2S-3 in which President George H. W. Bush soloed is another exhibit. ☎ *808/441-1000* ⊕ *www.pacificaviationmuseum.org* ✉ $25.

PLAN YOUR PEARL HARBOR DAY LIKE A MILITARY CAMPAIGN

DIRECTIONS

Take H–1 west from Waikiki to Exit 15A and follow signs. Or take The-Bus route 20 or 47 from Waikiki. Beware high-priced private shuttles. It's a 30-minute drive from Waikiki.

WHAT TO BRING

Picture ID is required during periods of high alert; bring it just in case.

You'll be standing, walking, and climbing all day. Wear something with lots of pockets and a pair of good walking shoes. Carry a light jacket, sunglasses, hat, and sunscreen.

No purses, packs, or bags are allowed. Take only what fits in your pockets. Cameras are okay but without the bags. A private bag storage booth is located in the parking lot near the visitors' center. Leave nothing in your car; theft is a problem despite bicycle security patrols.

HOURS

Hours are 7 AM to 5 PM for the visitor center, though the attractions open at 8 AM. The *Arizona* Memorial starts giving out tickets on a first-come, first-served basis at 7:30 AM; the last tickets are given out at 3 PM. Spring break, summer, and holidays are busiest, and tickets sometimes run out by noon or earlier.

TICKETS

Arizona: Free. Add $7.50 for museum audio tours.

Aviation: $25 adults, $15 children. Add $10 for aviator's guided tour.

Missouri: $25 adults, $13 children. Add $25 for in-depth, behind-the-scenes tours.

Bowfin: $12 adults, $5 children. Children under 4 may go into the museum but not aboard the *Bowfin*.

KIDS

This might be the day to enroll younger kids in the hotel children's program. Preschoolers chafe at long waits, and attractions involve some hazards for toddlers. Older kids enjoy the *Bowfin* and *Missouri*, especially.

MAKING THE MOST OF YOUR TIME

Expect to spend at least half a day; a whole day is better if you're a military history buff.

At the *Arizona* Memorial, you'll get a ticket, be given a tour time, and then have to wait anywhere from 15 minutes to 3 hours. You must pick up your own ticket so you can't hold places. If the wait is long, skip over to the *Bowfin* to fill the time.

SUGGESTED READING

Pearl Harbor and the USS Arizona Memorial, by Richard Wisniewski. $5.95. 64-page magazine-size quick history.

Bowfin, by Edwin P. Hoyt. $14.95. Dramatic story of undersea adventure.

The Last Battleship, by Scott C. S. Stone. $11.95. Story of the Mighty Mo.

tour, package deals ⊗ *Daily 7–5; Arizona Memorial tours daily 8–3* ☞ *Call 877/444–6777 or go to recreation.gov for timed reservations.*

DOWNTOWN

Honolulu's past and present play a delightful counterpoint throughout the downtown sector, which is approximately 6 miles east of Honolulu International Airport. Postmodern glass-and-steel office buildings look down on the Aloha Tower, built in 1926 and, until the early 1960s, the tallest structure in Honolulu. Hawaii's history is told in the architecture of these few blocks: the cut-stone turn-of-the-20th-century storefronts of Merchant Street, the gracious white-columned American-Georgian manor that was the home of the Islands' last queen, the jewel-box palace occupied by the monarchy before it was overthrown, the Spanish-inspired stucco and tile-roofed Territorial Era government buildings, and the 21st-century glass pyramid of the First Hawaiian Bank Building.

GETTING HERE AND AROUND

To reach downtown Honolulu from Waikiki by car, take Ala Moana Boulevard to Alakea Street and turn right; three blocks up on the right, between South King and Hotel, there's a municipal parking lot in Alii Place on the right. There are also public parking lots (75¢ per half hour for the first two hours) in buildings along Alakea, Smith, Beretania, and Bethel streets (Gateway Plaza on Bethel Street is a good choice). The best parking downtown, however, is metered street parking along Punchbowl and King Streets—when you can find it.

Another option is to take Route 19 or 20 of highly popular and convenient TheBus to the Aloha Tower Marketplace, or take a trolley from Waikiki.

WALKING TOURS

American Institute of Architects (AIA) Honolulu Walking Tour. Join an AIA tour to see downtown Honolulu from an architectural perspective, including the restored Hawaii Theatre, city seat Honolulu Hale, and the open-air state capitol. Advance reservations are required. Tours are offered only on Saturday mornings. ☎ 808/628–7243 ⊕ www.aiahonolulu.org 🎫 $10.

Hawaii Geographic Society. The society offers three historic downtown Honolulu walking tours focusing on the monarchy era, architecture, and temples. Email the organization for more information. ☎ 808/538–3952 ✉ hawaiigeographicsociety@gmail.com 🎫 $15.

TIMING

Plan a couple of hours for exploring downtown's historic buildings, more if you're taking a guided tour or walk. The best time to visit is in the cool and relative quiet of morning or on the weekends when downtown is all but deserted except for the historic sites.

TOP ATTRACTIONS

Fodor'sChoice **Iolani Palace.** America's only royal residence was built in 1882 on the site
★ of an earlier palace. It contains the thrones of King Kalakaua and his successor (and sister) Queen Liliuokalani, who was imprisoned in her home after the 1893 overthrow. Bucking the stereotype of simple island life, the palace had electricity and telephone lines installed even before

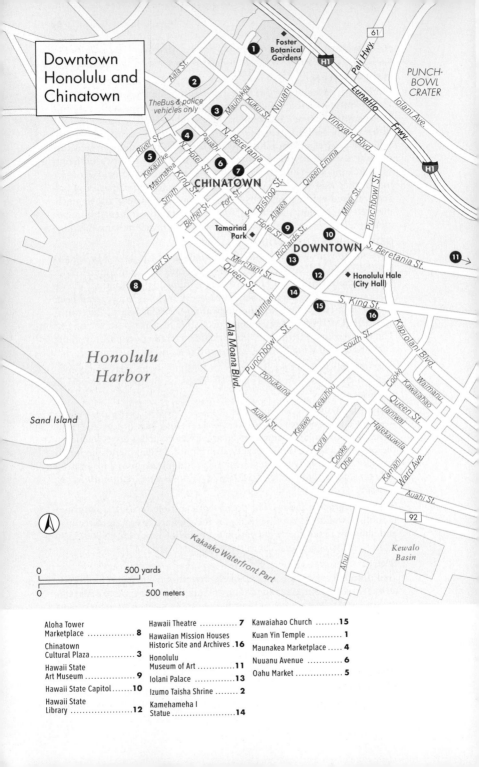

Downtown Honolulu and Chinatown

PUNCH-BOWL CRATER

Foster Botanical Gardens

TheBus & police vehicles only

CHINATOWN

Tamarind Park

DOWNTOWN

Honolulu Hale (City Hall)

Honolulu Harbor

Sand Island

Kakaako Waterfront Park

Kewalo Basin

0   500 yards
0   500 meters

the White House. Downstairs galleries showcase the royal jewelry and a kitchen and offices restored to the glory of the monarchy. The palace is open for guided tours or self-guided audio tours, and reservations are recommended. ■TIP➜ If you're set on taking a guided tour, call for reservations a few days in advance. The main gift shop was formerly the Iolani Barracks, built to house the Royal Guard. ✉ *King and Richards Sts., Downtown Honolulu* ☎ *808/522–0832* ⊕ *www.iolanipalace.org* ✉ *$21.75 guided tour, $14.75 audio tour, $7 downstairs galleries only* ⊙ *Mon.– Sat. 9–4; guided tours every 15 min. Tues.–Sat. mornings.*

Kamehameha I Statue. Paying tribute to the Big Island chieftain who united all the warring Hawaiian Islands into one kingdom at the turn of the 18th century, this statue, which stands with one arm outstretched in welcome, is one of three originally cast in Paris, France, by American sculptor T. R. Gould. The original statue, lost at sea and replaced by this one, was eventually salvaged and is now in Kapaau, on the Big Island, near the king's birthplace. Each year on the king's birthday, June 11, the more famous copy is draped in fresh lei that reach lengths of 18 feet and longer. A parade proceeds past the statue, and Hawaiian civic clubs, women in hats and impressive long *holoku* dresses, and men in sashes and cummerbunds, pay honor to the leader whose name means "The One Set Apart." ✉ *417 S. King St., outside Aliiolani Hale, Downtown Honolulu.*

Kawaiahao Church. Fancifully called Hawaii's Westminster Abbey, this historic house of worship witnessed the coronations, weddings, and funerals of generations of Hawaiian royalty. Each of the building's 14,000 coral blocks was quarried from reefs offshore at depths of more than 20 feet and transported to this site. Interior woodwork was created from the forests of the Koolau Mountains. The upper gallery has an exhibit of paintings of the royal families. The graves of missionaries and of King Lunalilo are adjacent. Services in English and Hawaiian are held each Sunday, and the church members are exceptionally welcoming, greeting newcomers with lei; their affiliation is United Church of Christ. Although there are no guided tours, you can look around the church at no cost. ✉ *957 Punchbowl St., at King St., Downtown Honolulu* ☎ *808/469–3000* ⊕ *www.kawaiahao.org* ✉ *Free* ⊙ *Services Sun. at 9 am.*

MONEY-SAVING TIPS

■ Take advantage of coupons in the free publications stacked at the airport and in racks all over Waikiki.

■ Access to beaches and most hiking trails is free to the public.

■ For inexpensive fresh fruit and produce, check out farmers' markets and farm stands along the road—they'll often let you try before you buy.

■ For cheap and quick lunches, consider a food truck. Part of the culinary landscape of Oahu for generations, these lunch wagons charge substantially less than restaurants.

WORTH NOTING

FAMILY **Aloha Tower Marketplace.** In two stories of shops and kiosks, you can find island-inspired clothing, jewelry, art, and home furnishings. The Marketplace also has indoor and outdoor restaurants and live entertainment. For a bird's-eye view of this working harbor, take a free ride up to the observation deck of

WORD OF MOUTH

"Everyone should at least see the view of Diamond Head curving around from the beach. To me, that IS Hawaii, and I've been more than once to the four major Islands."   —carolyn

Aloha Tower. Cruise ships usually dock at piers 10 and 11 alongside the Marketplace, making it a prime visitor spot. ⊠ *1 Aloha Tower Dr., at Piers 10 and 11, Downtown Honolulu* ☎ *808/566–2337 entertainment info* ⊕ *www.alohatower.com* ☉ *Mon.–Sat. 9–9, Sun. 9–6; restaurants open later.*

Hawaii State Art Museum. Hawaii was one of the first states in the nation to legislate that a portion of the taxes paid on commercial building projects be set aside for the purchase of artwork. The state purchased an ornate period-style building (that once was the Armed Services YMCA Building) and in 2002 opened a 12,000-square-foot museum on the second floor dedicated to the art of Hawaii in all its ethnic diversity. HiSAM, as it's nicknamed, has a **Diamond Head Gallery** featuring new acquisitions and thematic shows from the State Art Collection and the Hawaii State Foundation on Culture and the Arts. The **Ewa Gallery** houses more than 150 works documenting Hawaii's visual-arts history since becoming a state in 1959. Also included are a sculpture gallery, a gift shop, a café, and educational meeting rooms. Check for occasional evening events as on First Fridays in Chinatown. ⊠ *250 S. Hotel St., 2nd fl., Downtown Honolulu* ☎ *808/586–0300* ⊕ *www.hawaii.gov/sfca* ☜ *Free* ☉ *Tues.–Sat. 10–4.*

Hawaii State Capitol. The capitol's architecture is richly symbolic: the columns resemble palm trees, the legislative chambers are shaped like volcanic cinder cones, and the central court is open to the sky, representing Hawaii's open society. Replicas of the Hawaii state seal, each weighing 7,500 pounds, hang above both its entrances. The building, which in 1969 replaced Iolani Palace as the seat of government, is surrounded by reflecting pools, just as the Islands are embraced by water. A pair of statues, often draped in lei, flank the building: one of the beloved Queen Liliuokalani and the other of the sainted Father Damien de Veuster, famous for helping Molokai leprosy patients. Free guided and self-guided tours are available. ⊠ *415 S. Beretania St., Downtown Honolulu* ☎ *808/586–0178, 808/586–0221* ⊕ *governor.hawaii.gov/ about/capitol-tour-information* ☜ *Free* ☉ *Guided tours Tues.–Fri. at 1 pm; self-guided tours Mon.–Fri. 9–3.*

Hawaii State Library. This beautifully renovated main library was built in 1913. Its Samuel M. Kamakau Reading Room, on the first floor in the Mauka (Hawaiian for "mountain") Courtyard, houses an extensive Hawaii and Pacific book collection and pays tribute to Kamakau, a missionary student whose 19th-century writings in English offer rare and vital insight into traditional Hawaiian culture. ⊠ *478 S. King St.,*

2

Downtown Honolulu ☎ *808/586–3617* 📠 *Free* ☉ *Mon. and Wed. 10–5; Tues., Fri., and Sat. 9–5; Thurs. 9–8.*

Honolulu Museum of Art. Originally built around the collection of a Honolulu matron who donated much of her estate to the museum, the academy is housed in a maze of courtyards, cloistered walkways, and quiet, low-ceilinged spaces. There's an impressive permanent collection that includes Hiroshige's *ukiyo-e* Japanese prints, donated by James Michener; Italian Renaissance paintings; and American and European art. The newer Luce Pavilion complex, nicely incorporated into the more traditional architecture of the place, has a traveling-exhibit gallery, a Hawaiian gallery, an excellent café, and a gift shop. The Doris Duke Theatre screens art films. This is also the jumping-off point for tours of Doris Duke's estate, Shangri-La. Admission here includes same-day entry to Spalding House, formerly the Contemporary Museum. Call or check the website for special exhibits, concerts, and films. ✉ *900 S. Beretania St., Downtown Honolulu* ☎ *808/532–8700* ⊕ *www.honolulumuseum.org* 📠 *$10; free 1st Wed. and 3rd Sun. of month* ☉ *Tues.–Sat. 10–4:30, Sun. 1–5.*

Hawaiian Mission Houses. The determined Hawaii missionaries arrived in 1820, gaining royal favor and influencing a wide array of island life. Their descendants became leaders in government and business. At Hawaiian Mission Houses Historic Site and Archives (previously Mission Houses Museum), you can learn about their influence and walk through their original dwellings, including Hawaii's oldest wooden structure, a white-frame house that was prefabricated in New England and shipped around the Horn. Certain areas of the museum may be seen only on a one-hour guided tour given every hour. Docents paint an excellent picture of what mission life was like. Rotating displays showcase such arts as Hawaiian quilting, portraits, even toys, and a rich archival library is also open to the public. ✉ *553 S. King St., Downtown Honolulu* ☎ *808/447–3910* ⊕ *www.missionhouses.org* 📠 *$10* ☉ *Tues.–Sat. 10–4; guided tours hourly 11–3.*

CHINATOWN

Chinatown's original business district was made up of dry-goods and produce merchants, tailors and dressmakers, barbers, herbalists, and dozens of restaurants. The meat, fish, and produce stalls remain, but the mix is heavier now on gift and curio stores, art galleries, lei stands, jewelry shops, and bakeries, with a smattering of noodle makers, travel agents, Asian-language video stores, and dozens of restaurants.

The name *Chinatown* here has always been a misnomer. Though three-quarters of Oahu's Chinese lived closely packed in these 25 acres in the late 1800s, even then the neighborhood was half Japanese. Today, you hear Vietnamese and Tagalog as often as Mandarin and Cantonese, and there are voices of Japan, Singapore, Malaysia, Korea, Thailand, Samoa, and the Marshall Islands, as well.

Perhaps a more accurate name is the one used by early Chinese: *Wah Fau* ("Chinese port"), signifying a landing and jumping-off place. Chinese laborers, as soon as they completed their plantation contracts, hurried into the city to start businesses here. It's a launching point for today's immigrants, too: Southeast Asian shops almost outnumber Chinese; stalls carry Filipino specialties like winged beans and goat meat; and in one tiny space, knife-wielding Samoans skin coconuts to order.

In the half century after the first Chinese laborers arrived in Hawaii in 1851, Chinatown was a link to home for the all-male cadre of workers who planned to return to China rich and respected. Merchants not only sold supplies, they held mail, loaned money, wrote letters, translated documents, sent remittances to families, served meals, offered rough bunkhouse accommodations, and were the center for news, gossip, and socializing.

Though much happened to Chinatown in the 20th century—beginning in January 1900, when almost the entire neighborhood was burned to the ground to halt the spread of bubonic plague—it remains a bustling, crowded, noisy, and odiferous place bent primarily on buying and selling, and sublimely oblivious to its status as a National Historic District or the encroaching gentrification on nearby Nuuanu Avenue.

GETTING HERE AND AROUND

Chinatown occupies 15 blocks immediately north and west of downtown Honolulu—it's flat, compact, and very walkable.

TIMING

This area is easily explored in half a day. The best time to visit is morning, when the *popos* (grandmas) shop—it's cool out, and you can enjoy a cheap dim-sum breakfast. Chinatown is a seven-days-a-week operation. Sundays are especially busy with families sharing dim sum in raucous dining hall–size restaurants.

If you're here between January 20 and February 20, check local newspapers for Chinese New Year activities. Bakeries stock special sweets, stores and homes sprout bright-red scrolls, and lion dancers cavort through the streets feeding on *li-see* (money envelopes). The Narcissus Queen is chosen, and an evening street fair draws crowds.

GUIDED TOURS

Hawaii Food Tours. Come hungry for food writer Matthew Gray's culinary "Hole-in-the-Wall Tour" through Honolulu, which includes discussion of Hawaiian culinary history and the diversity of the island's food culture, along with 15- to 20-plus samples of local favorites as you walk to a variety of ethnic restaurants, markets, and bakeries, including two hours in Chinatown. It's a great way to get a delicious taste of Hawaii's culture. The tour costs $99 per person. Gray also has a progressive dinner tour through Honolulu and a new North Shore Food Tour. ☎ 808/926–3663 ⊕ *www.hawaiifoodtours.com* ✉ *$99 for Hole in the Wall Tour.*

TOP ATTRACTIONS

Chinatown Cultural Plaza. This sprawling multistory shopping square surrounds a courtyard with an incense-wreathed shrine and Moongate stage for holiday performances. The Chee Kung Tong Society has a beautifully decorated meeting hall here; a number of such *tongs* (meeting places) are hidden on upper floors in Chinatown. Outside, near the canal, local members of the community play cards and mah-jongg. ✉ *100 N. Beretania St., Chinatown.*

Izumo Taisha Shrine. From Chinatown Cultural Plaza, cross a stone bridge to the Izumo Taishakyo Mission of Hawaii to visit this shrine established in 1906. It honors Okuninushi-no-Mikoto, a *kami* (god) who is believed in Shinto tradition to bring good fortune if properly courted (and thanked afterward). ⊠ *215 N. Kukui St., at the canal, Chinatown* ☎ *808/538–7778.*

Kuan Yin Temple. A couple of blocks *mauka* (toward the mountains) from Chinatown is the oldest Buddhist temple in the Islands. Mistakenly called a goddess by some, Kuan Yin, also known as Kannon, is a *bodhisattva*—one who chose to remain on earth doing good even after achieving enlightenment. Transformed from a male into a female figure centuries ago, she is credited with a particular sympathy for women. You will see representations of her all over the Islands: holding a lotus flower (beauty from the mud of human frailty), as at the temple; pouring out a pitcher of oil (like mercy flowing); or as a sort of Madonna with a child. Visitors are permitted but be aware this is a practicing place of worship. ⊠ *170 N. Vineyard Blvd., Chinatown.*

Maunakea Marketplace. On the corner of Maunakea and Hotel streets is this busy plaza surrounded by shops, an indoor market, and a food court. It gets packed every year for the annual Chinese Lunar New Year. ■TIP➜ **If you appreciate fine tea, visit the unpretentious tea counter in the Tea Hut, a curio shop filled with Chinese gifts and good luck charms.** ⊠ *1120 Maunakea St., Chinatown* ☎ *808/524–3409.*

Hawaiian Chinese Multicultural Museum & Archives. Within the Maunakea Marketplace, the small Hawaiian Chinese Multicultural Museum and Archives displays historic photographs and artifacts and is where you can learn about events like the Great Chinatown Fire of 1900 that burned down most of the neighborhood. ⊠ *Maunakea Marketplace, 1120 Maunakea St., 2nd Floor, Chinatown* ☎ *808/524–3409* ▣ *$2* ⊙ *Mon.–Sat. 10–2.*

Oahu Market. In this market founded in 1904, you'll find a taste of old-style Chinatown, where you might be hustled aside as a whole pig (dead, of course) is wrestled through the crowd and where glassy-eyed fish of every size and hue lie stacked forlornly on ice. Try the bubble tea (juices and flavored teas with tapioca bubbles inside) or pick up a bizarre magenta dragonfruit for breakfast. ⊠ *N. King St. at Kekaulike St., Chinatown.*

WORTH NOTING

Hawaii Theatre. Opened in 1922, this theater earned rave reviews for its neoclassical design, with Corinthian columns, marble statues, and plush carpeting and drapery. Nicknamed the "Pride of the Pacific," the facility was rescued from demolition in the early 1980s and underwent a $30 million renovation. Listed on both the State and National Register of Historic Places, it has become the centerpiece of revitalization efforts of Honolulu's downtown area. The 1,400-seat venue hosts concerts, theatrical productions, dance performances, and film screenings. Guided tours of the theater (reservations required) end with a mini-concert on the historic orchestral pipe organ and can be booked through the box office. ⊠ *1130 Bethel St., Chinatown* ☎ *808/528–0506*

⊕ *www.hawaiitheatre.com* ✉ *$10* ⊙ *Tours Tues. at 11 am, subject to performances.*

Nuuanu Avenue. Here on Chinatown's main mauka-makai drag and on Bethel Street, which runs parallel, are clustered art galleries, restaurants, a wine shop, an antiques auctioneer, a dress shop or two, one small theater/exhibition space (the Arts at Mark's Garage), and one historic stage (the Hawaii Theatre). **First Friday** art nights, when galleries stay open until 9 pm, draw crowds. Many stay later and crowd Chinatown's bars. If you like art and people-watching and are fortunate enough to be on Oahu the first Friday of the month, this event shouldn't be missed. ✉ *Nuuanu Ave., Chinatown.*

GREATER HONOLULU

One reason to venture beyond the areas of Honolulu that have a wider range of tourist sights (primarily Waikiki, Pearl Harbor, downtown, and Chinatown) is the chance to glimpse Honolulu's residential neighborhoods. Species of classic Hawaii homes include the tiny green-and-white plantation-era house with its corrugated tin roof, two windows flanking a central door and small porch; or the breezy bungalow with its swooping Thai-style roofline and two wings flanking screened French doors through which breezes blow into the living room. Note the tangled "Grandma-style" gardens and many *ohana* houses—small homes in the backyard of a larger home or built as apartments perched over the garage, allowing extended families to live together. Carports, which rarely house cars, are the island's version of rec rooms, where parties are held and neighbors sit to "talk story." Sometimes you see gallon jars on the flat roofs of garages or carports: these are pickled lemons fermenting in the sun. Also in the neighborhoods, you find the folksy restaurants and takeout spots favored by the islanders.

GETTING HERE AND AROUND

For those with a Costco card, the cheapest gas on the island is at the Costco station on Arakawa Street between Dillingham Boulevard and Nimitz Highway, though the line can sometimes wind into the street.

TOP ATTRACTIONS

Fodor's Choice
★

Bishop Museum. Founded in 1889 by Charles R. Bishop as a memorial to his wife, Princess Bernice Pauahi Bishop, the museum began as a repository for the royal possessions of this last direct descendant of King Kamehameha the Great. Today it's the state's designated hstory and cultural museum. Its five exhibit halls house almost 25 million items that tell the history of the Hawaiian Islands and their Pacific neighbors. The latest addition to the complex is a 16,500 square-foot natural-science wing with a three-story simulated volcano at its center, where twice-daily "lava melt" shows take place much to the enjoyment of younger museum patrons. Newly renovated Pacific Hall (formerly Polynesian Hall) now focuses on the history of the entire Pacific region.

The Hawaiian Hall, with state-of-the art and often interactive displays, teaches about the Hawaiian culture. Spectacular Hawaiian artifacts—lustrous feather capes, bone fish hooks, the skeleton of a giant sperm whale, photography and crafts displays, and an authentic, well-preserved grass house—are displayed inside a three-story 19th-century

2

SHOPPING IN CHINATOWN

Chinatown is rife with ridiculously inexpensive gifts: folding fans for $1 and coconut purses for $5 at **Maunakea Marketplace,** for example.

Curio shops sell everything from porcelain statues to woks, ginseng to Mao shoes. If you're in the mood for a snack, visit the Hong Kong Supermarket in the Wo Fat Chop Sui building (at the corner of N. Hotel and Maunakea) for fresh fruit, crack seed (Chinese dried fruit popular for snacking), and row upon row of boxed, tinned delicacies with indecipherable names.

Chinatown Cultural Plaza offers fine-quality jade. Chinatown is Honolulu's lei center, with shops strung along Beretania and Maunakea; the locals have favorite shops where they're greeted by name. In spring, look for gardenia nosegays wrapped in ti leaves.

Victorian-style gallery. The building alone, with its huge Victorian turrets and immense stone walls, is worth seeing. Also check out the planetarium, daily tours, hula and science demonstrations, special exhibits, and the Shop Pacifica. ⊠ *1525 Bernice St., Kalihi* ☎ *808/847–3511* ⊕ *www.bishopmuseum.org* 🖾 *$19.95* ۞ *Wed.–Mon. 9–5.*

Queen Emma Summer Palace. Queen Emma, King Kamehameha IV's wife, used this stately white home, built in 1848, as a retreat from the rigors of court life in hot and dusty Honolulu during the mid-1800s. It has an eclectic mix of European, Victorian, and Hawaiian furnishings and has excellent examples of Hawaiian quilts and koawood furniture. ⊠ *2913 Pali Hwy., Nuuanu* ☎ *808/595–3167* ⊕ *www. queenemmasummerpalace.org* 🖾 *$10 guided tours, $8 self-guided tours* ۞ *Daily 9–4 (last tour at 3).*

WORTH NOTING

National Memorial Cemetery of the Pacific. Nestled in the bowl of Puowaina, or Punchbowl Crater, this 112-acre cemetery is the final resting place for more than 50,000 U.S. war veterans and family members and is a solemn reminder of their sacrifice. Among those buried here is Ernie Pyle, the famed World War II correspondent who was killed by a Japanese sniper on Ie Shima, an island off the northwest coast of Okinawa. There are intricate stone maps providing a visual military history lesson. Puowaina, formed 75,000–100,000 years ago during a period of secondary volcanic activity, translates as "Hill of Sacrifice." Historians believe this site once served as an altar where ancient Hawaiians offered sacrifices to their gods. ■TIP➜ **The entrance to the cemetery has unfettered views of Waikiki and Honolulu—perhaps the finest on Oahu.** ⊠ *2177 Puowaina Dr., Nuuanu* ☎ *808/532–3720* ⊕ *www.cem. va.gov/cem/cems/nchp/nmcp.asp* 🖾 *Free* ۞ *Mar.–Sept., daily 8–6:30; Oct.–Feb., daily 8–5:30.*

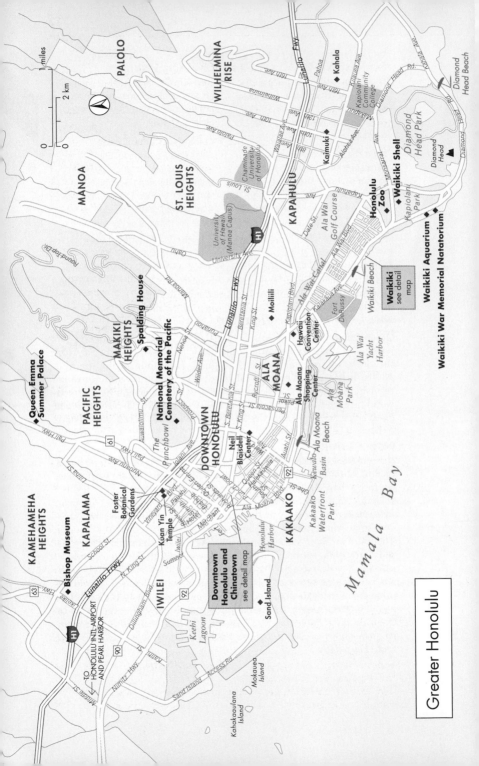

Greater Honolulu

PALOLO

WILHELMINA RISE

Kahala

Kaimuki

KAPAHULU

Diamond Head Park

Diamond Head

Diamond Head Beach

Kapiolani Community College

Waikiki Shell

Honolulu Zoo

Kapiolani Park

Waikiki Aquarium

Waikiki War Memorial Natatorium

MANOA

ST. LOUIS HEIGHTS

Chaminade University of Honolulu

University of Hawaii (Manoa Capus)

University Ave.

Moilili

Ala Wai Golf Course

Ala Wai Canal

Hawaii Convention Center

Ala Wai Yacht Harbor

Waikiki Beach

Fort DeRussy

Waikiki
see detail map

MAKIKI HEIGHTS

Spalding House

National Memorial Cemetery of the Pacific

The Punchbowl

DOWNTOWN HONOLULU

Ala Moana Shopping Center

Ala Moana Park

ALA MOANA

Ala Moana Beach

Queen Emma Summer Palace

PACIFIC HEIGHTS

Neil Blaisdell Center

Kewalo Basin

KAKAAKO

Kakaako Waterfront Park

Mamala Bay

KAMEHAMEHA HEIGHTS

KAPALAMA

Foster Botanical Gardens

Kuan Yin Temple

Honolulu Harbor

Downtown Honolulu and Chinatown
see detail map

Bishop Museum

IWILEI

Sand Island

TO HONOLULU INTL AIRPORT AND PEARL HARBOR

Keehi Lagoon

Mokauea Island

Sand Island Access Rd.

Kahakaulana Island

1 mile

2 km

0

0

SOUTHEAST OAHU

Approximately 10 miles southeast of Waikiki.

Driving southeast from Waikiki on busy four-lane Kalanianaole Highway, you'll pass a dozen bedroom communities tucked into the valleys at the foot of the Koolau Range, with fleeting glimpses of the ocean from a couple of pocket parks. Suddenly, civilization falls away, the road narrows to two lanes, and you enter the rugged coastline of Koko Head and Ka Iwi.

This is a cruel coastline: dry, windswept, and rocky shores, with untamed waves that are notoriously treacherous. The first rule of beach safety is to never turn your back on the ocean. Don't venture close to wet areas where high waves occasionally reach, and be sure to heed warning signs.

At this point, you're passing through Koko Head Regional Park. On your right is the bulging remnant of a pair of volcanic craters that the Hawaiians called Kawaihoa, known today as Koko Head. To the left is Koko Crater and an area of the park that includes a short but extraordinarily steep hiking trail, a dryland botanical garden, a firing range, and a riding stable. Ahead is a sinuous shoreline with scenic pullouts and beaches to explore. Named the Ka Iwi Coast (*iwi,* "ee-vee," are bones—sacred to Hawaiians and full of symbolism) for the channel just offshore, this area was once home to a ranch and small fishing enclave that were destroyed by a tidal wave in the 1940s.

GETTING HERE AND AROUND

Driving straight from Waikiki to Makapuu Point takes from a half to a full hour, depending on traffic. There aren't a huge number of sights per se in this corner of Oahu, so a couple of hours should be plenty of exploring time, unless you make a lengthy stop at a particular point.

TOP ATTRACTIONS

Halona Blowhole. Below a scenic turnout along the Koko Head shoreline, this oft-photographed lava tube sucks the ocean in and spits it out. Don't get too close, as conditions can get dangerous. ■ TIP➔ Look to your right to see the tiny beach below that was used to film the wavewashed love scene in From Here to Eternity. In winter this is a good spot to watch whales at play. Offshore, the islands of Molokai and Lanai call like distant sirens, and every once in a while Maui is visible in blue silhouette. Take your valuables with you and lock your car, because this scenic location is overrun with tourists and therefore a hot spot for petty thieves. ⊠ *Kalanianaole Hwy., 1 mile east of Hanauma Bay, Hawaii Kai.*

Makapuu Point. This spot has breathtaking views of the ocean, mountains, and the windward Islands. The point of land jutting out in the distance is **Mokapu Peninsula,** site of a U.S. Marine base. The spired mountain peak is **Mt. Olomana.** On the long pier is part of the **Makai Undersea Test Range,** a research facility that's closed to the public. Offshore is **Manana Island (Rabbit Island),** a picturesque cay said to resemble a swimming bunny with its ears pulled back. Ironically enough, Manana Island was once overrun with rabbits, thanks to a rancher who let a few hares run wild on the land. They were eradicated in 1994

Exploring
Oahu

Turtle Bay Resort
Waialee
83

Sunset Beach
Ehukai Beach
The Bonzai Pipeline
◆ Puuomahuka Heiau
Waimea Bay
◆ Waimea
Valley Park

TO
KAUAI

Haleiwa Alii Beach Park
Mokuleia Beach
Waialua Bay
83

**Kaena Point
State Recreation Area**
Haleiwa

KAENA
POINT
930
Kamehameha Hwy

Dillingham
Airfield
803

W A I A N A E

Yokohama Bay
Keawaula Beach
(Yokohama Bay)

Dole Plantation

M O U N T A I N S

Kaala
Schofield
Barracks
80
Wahiawa
Wheeler
Air Force Base

Makaha Beach Park
Makaha
Pokai Bay Beach Park
93
Waianae

Mililani
Town
99
H2

Maili

Palikea

Puu
Manawahua

750

Nanakuli

Farrington Hwy

**Hawaii's
Plantation
Village**
H1

76

Ko Olina
Ewa
764

Kapolei

Blue Plains

76

White Plains

Elevation

feet	meters
4,019	1,225
2,952	900
2,624	800
2,296	700
1,968	600
1,640	500
1,312	400
984	300
656	200
328	100
feet	meters

0   5 mi

0   5 km

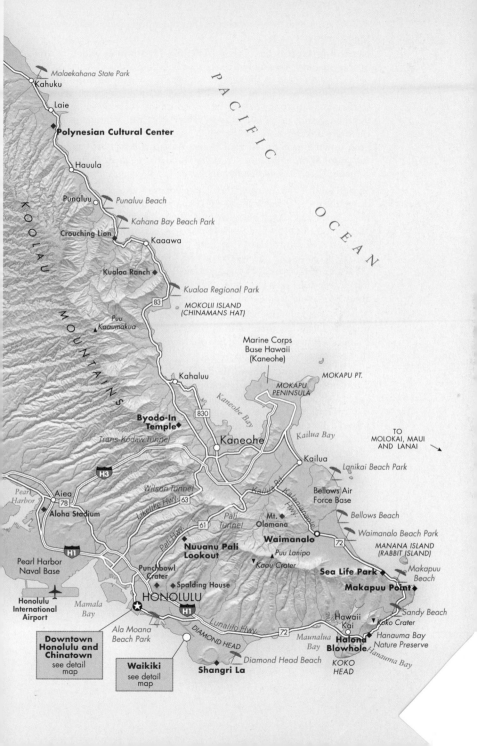

PACIFIC OCEAN

Malaekahana State Park
Kahuku
Laie
Polynesian Cultural Center
Hauula
Punaluu
Punaluu Beach
Kahana Bay Beach Park
Crouching Lion
Kaaawa
Kualoa Ranch
Kualoa Regional Park
MOKOLII ISLAND
(CHINAMANS HAT)
Puu
Kaaumakua
Marine Corps
Base Hawaii
(Kaneohe)
MOKAPU PT.
Kahaluu
MOKAPU
PENINSULA
KOOLAU MOUNTAINS
Byodo-In
Temple
Kaneohe Bay
Trans-Koolau Tunnel
Kailua Bay
Kaneohe
TO
MOLOKAI, MAUI
AND LANAI
Kailua
H3
Lanikai Beach Park
Pearl
Harbor
Aiea
Wilson Tunnel
78
Aloha Stadium
Likelike Hwy.
63
Kailua Rd.
Bellows Air
Force Base
Bellows Beach
Pali
Tunnel
Mt.
Olomana
61
Waimanalo Beach Park
Pali Hwy.
Waimanalo
72
MANANA ISLAND
(RABBIT ISLAND)
Pearl Harbor
Naval Base
H1
Nuuanu Pali
Lookout
Puu Lanipo
Kaau Crater
Sea Life Park
Makapuu
Beach
Punchbowl
Crater
Spalding House
HONOLULU
Makapuu Point
Honolulu
International
Airport
Mamala
Bay
H1
Hawaii
Kai
Sandy Beach
Koko Crater
Ala Moana
Beach Park
Lunalilo Hwy.
72
Hanauma Bay
Nature Preserve
Downtown
Honolulu and
Chinatown
see detail
map
DIAMOND HEAD
Maunalua
Bay
Halona
Blowhole
Hanauma Bay
Waikiki
see detail
map
Diamond Head Beach
Shangri La
KOKO
HEAD

by biologists who grew concerned that the rabbits were destroying the island's native plants.

Nestled in the cliff face is the **Makapuu Lighthouse,** which became operational in 1909 and has the largest lighthouse lens in America. The lighthouse is closed to the public, but near the Makapuu Point turnout you can find the start of a mile-long paved road (closed to vehicular traffic). Hike up to the top of the 647-foot bluff for a closer view of the lighthouse and, in winter, a great whale-watching vantage point. For the more adventurous, at the whale-watching sign on the main path, head down a switchback trail to the **Makapuu tidepools** below. ✉ *Ka Iwi State Scenic Shoreline, Kalanianaole Hwy., at Makapuu Beach, Kaneohe ⊕ www.hawaiistateparks.org.*

Shangri La. In 1936, heiress Doris Duke bought five acres at Black Point, down the coast from Waikiki, and began to build and furnish the first home that would be all her own. She called it Shangri La. For more than 50 years, the home was a work in progress as Duke traveled the world, buying art and furnishings, picking up ideas for her Mughul garden, for the playhouse in the style of a 17th-century Irani pavilion, and for the water terraces and tropical gardens. When she died in 1993, Duke left instructions that her home was to become a public center for the study of Islamic art.

To walk through the house and its gardens—which have remained much as Duke left them with only some minor conservation-oriented changes—is to experience the personal style of someone who saw everything as raw material for her art.

With her trusted houseman, Jin de Silva, she helped build the elaborate Turkish Room, trimming tiles and painted panels to retrofit the existing space (including raising the ceiling and lowering the floor) and building a fountain of her own design. Among many aspects of the home inspired by the Muslim tradition is the entry: an anonymous gate, a blank white wall, and a wooden door that bids you "Enter herein in peace and security" in Arabic characters. Inside, tiles glow, fountains tinkle, and shafts of light illuminate artworks through arches and high windows. This was her private world, entered only by trusted friends.

The house is open by guided tour only and reservations are highly recommended. Tours take 2½ hours including transportation from the Academy of Arts. Children under 12 are not admitted. All tours begin at the Honolulu Academy of Arts (✉ *900 S. Beretania*) in downtown Honolulu. ✉ *Hawaii Kai* ☎ *808/532–3853 Honolulu Academy of Arts ⊕ www.shangrilahawaii.org or honolulumuseum.org/385-about_shangri_la* ☛ *Tour $25; $1.50 for online reservations; $2 for phone reservations ⊙ Wed.–Sat. at 9, 10:30, and 1:30 by reservation only.*

WINDWARD OAHU

2

Approximately 15 miles northeast of downtown Honolulu (20–25 minutes by car), approximately 25 miles southeast of downtown Honolulu via Ka Iwi and Waimanalo (35–45 minutes by car).

Looking at Honolulu's topsy-turvy urban sprawl, you would never suspect the windward side existed. It's a secret Oahuans like to keep, so they can watch the awe on the faces of their guests when the car emerges from the tunnels through the mountains and they gaze for the first time on the panorama of turquoise bays and emerald valleys watched over by the knife-edged Koolau ridges. Jaws literally drop. Every time. And this just a 20-minute drive from downtown.

It's on this side of the island where many native Hawaiians live. Evidence of traditional lifestyles is abundant in crumbling fishponds, rock platforms that once were altars, taro patches still being worked, and throw-net fishermen posed stock-still above the water (though today, they're invariably wearing polarized sunglasses, the better to spot the fish).

Here, the pace is slower, more oriented toward nature. Beach-going, hiking, diving, surfing, and boating are the draws, along with a visit to the Polynesian Cultural Center, and poking through little shops and wayside stores.

GETTING HERE AND AROUND

For a driving experience you won't soon forget, take the H3 freeway over to the windward side. As you pass through the tunnels, be prepared for one of the most breathtaking stretches of road anywhere. Flip a coin before you leave to see who will drive and who will gape.

TIMING

You can easily spend an entire day exploring Windward Oahu, or you can just breeze on through, nodding at the sights on your way to the North Shore. Waikiki to Windward is a drive of less than half an hour; to the North Shore via Kamehameha Highway along the Windward Coast is one hour, minimum.

TOP ATTRACTIONS

Byodo-In Temple. Tucked away in the back of the Valley of the Temples cemetery is a replica of the 11th-century Temple at Uji in Japan. A 2-ton carved wooden statue of the Buddha presides inside the main temple building. Next to the temple building are a meditation pavilion and gardens set dramatically against the sheer, green cliffs of the Koolau Mountains. You can ring the 5-foot, 3-ton brass bell for good luck and feed some of the hundreds of carp, ducks, and swans that inhabit the garden's 2-acre pond. Or, you can enjoy the peaceful surroundings and just relax. ✉ *47-200 Kahekili Hwy., Kaneohe* ☎ *808/239–8811* ⊕ *www. byodo-in.com* 🎟 *$3* ☉ *Daily 9–5.*

NEED A BREAK?

Kalapawai Market. Generations of children have purchased their beach snacks and sodas at Kalapawai Market, near Kailua Beach. A Windward Oahu landmark since 1932, the green-and-white market has distinctive charm. You'll see slipper-clad locals sitting in front sharing a cup of coffe

The Byodo-In Temple on the windward side of Oahu is a replica of an 11th-century temple in Japan.

and talking story at picnic tables or in front of the market. It's a good source for your carryout lunch, since there's no concession stand at the beach. With one of the better selections of wine on the island, the market is also a great place to pick up a bottle. There's a sister Kalapawai Cafe with a sit-down menu closer to the entrance to Kailua. ⊠ *306 S. Kalaheo Ave., Kailua* ☎ *808/262–4359* ⊕ *www.kalapawaimarket.com* ⊙ *Daily 6 am– 9 pm; deli 6:30 am–7 pm.*

Nuuanu Pali Lookout. This panoramic perch looks out to expansive views of Windward Oahu. It was in this region that King Kamehameha I drove defending forces over the edges of the 1,000-foot-high cliffs, thus winning the decisive battle for control of Oahu. ■ TIP→ From here you can see views that stretch from Kaneohe Bay to Mokolii (little lizard), a small island off the coast, and beyond. Temperatures at the summit are several degrees cooler than in warm Waikiki, so bring a jacket along. Hang on tight to any loose possessions and consider wearing pants; it gets extremely windy at the lookout, which is part of the fun. Lock your car in the pay-to-park lot; break-ins have occurred here (this wayside is in the most trafficked state park in Hawaii). ⊠ *Top of Pali Hwy., Kaneohe* ⊕ *www.hawaiistateparks.org/parks/oahu/nuuanu.cfm* ⊙ *Daily during daylight hours.*

NEED A BREAK?

Island Snow. Long a favorite of Windward Oahu residents for its shave ice counter within the clothing store, Island Snow has more recently become known as the place where President Obama and his daughters have gone to for the sweet treat when they vacation in Hawaii. Extra fluffy shave ice topped off with local syrup flavors and a milky "snow cap" make this one of the best shave ice stops on the island. ⊠ *130 Kailua Rd., separate entrance from clothing shop, Kailua* ☏ *808/263–6339* ⊕ *www.islandsnow.com* ⊙ *Mon.–Thurs. 10–6, Fri.–Sun. 10–7.*

EN
ROUTE

Mokolii. As you drive the Windward and North shores along Kamehameha Highway, you'll note a number of interesting geological features. At Kualoa look to the ocean and gaze at the uniquely shaped little island of Mokolii (little lizard), a 206-foot-high sea stack also known as Chinaman's Hat. According to Hawaiian legend, the goddess Hiiaka, sister of Pele, slew the dragon Mokolii and flung its tail into the sea, forming the distinct islet. Other dragon body parts—in the form of rocks, of course—were scattered along the base of nearby Kualoa Ridge. ■TIP➔ In Laie, if you turn right on Anemoku Street, and right again on Naupaka, you come to a scenic lookout where you can see a group of islets, dramatically washed by the waves. ⊠ *49-479 Kamehameha Hwy., Kaneohe* ⊕ *www1.honolulu.gov/parks/programs/beach/kualoa.htm.*

FAMILY **Polynesian Cultural Center.** Recreated individual villages showcase the lifestyles and traditions of Hawaii, Tahiti, Samoa, Fiji, the Marquesas Islands, New Zealand, and Tonga. Focusing on individual islands within its 42-acre center, 35 miles from Waikiki, the Polynesian Cultural Center was founded in 1963 by the Church of Jesus Christ of Latter-day Saints. It houses restaurants, hosts luaus, and demonstrates cultural traditions such as tribal tattooing, fire dancing, and ancient customs and ceremonies. The expansive open-air shopping village carries Polynesian handicrafts. ■TIP➔ If you're staying in Honolulu, see the center as part of a van tour so you won't have to drive home late at night after the two-hour evening show. There are multiple packages available, from basic admission to an all-inclusive deal. Every May, the PCC hosts the World Fireknife Dance Competition, an event that draws the top fire-knife dance performers from around the world. Get tickets for that event in advance. ⊠ *55-370 Kamehameha Hwy., Laie* ☏ *808/293–3333, 800/367–7060* ⊕ *www.polynesia.com* ⊠ *From $50; $8 parking fee* ⊙ *Mon.–Sat. noon–9:15 (Village noon–6).*

WORTH NOTING

FAMILY **Sea Life Park.** Dolphins leap and spin and penguins frolic at this marine-life attraction 15 miles from Waikiki at scenic Makapuu Point. The park has a 300,000-gallon Hawaiian reef aquarium, a breeding sanctuary for Hawaii's endangered *honu* sea turtle, a penguin habitat, and many more marine attractions. Sign up for a dolphin, seal, stingray or shark encounter and get up close and personal in the water with these sea creatures (don't worry, the rays' stingers have been removed, and you'll be behind a wire mesh with the sharks). ⊠ *41-202 Kalanianaole Hwy., Waimanalo* ☏ *808/259–2500* ⊕ *www.sealifeparkhawaii.com* ⊠ *$30* ⊙ *Daily 10:30–5.*

Waimanalo. This modest little seaside town flanked by chiseled cliffs is worth a visit. Home to more native Hawaiian families than Kailua to the north or Hawaii Kai to the south, Waimanalo's biggest draws are its beautiful beaches, offering glorious views to the windward side.

CLOSE UP

Windward Oahu Villlages

Tiny villages—generally consisting of a sign, store, a beach park, possibly a post office, and not much more—are strung along Kamehameha Highway on the windward side. Each has something to offer. In **Waiahole**, look for fruit stands and an ancient grocery store. In **Kaaawa**, there's a lunch spot and convenience store–gas station. In **Punaluu**, stop at the gallery of fanciful landscape artist Lance Fairly and the woodworking shop, Kahaunani Woods & Crafts, plus venerable Ching General Store or the Shrimp Shack. Kim Taylor Reece's photo studio, featuring haunting portraits of hula dancers, is between Punaluu and Hauula. **Hauula** has Hauula Gift Shop and Art Gallery, formerly yet another Ching Store, now a clothing shop where sarongs wave like banners, and, at Hauula Kai Shopping Center, Tamura Market, with excellent seafood and the last liquor before Mormon-dominated Laie.

Bellows Beach is great for swimming, bodysurfing, and camping, and **Waimanalo Beach Park** is also safe for swimming. Down the side roads, as you head *mauka* (toward the mountains), are little farms that grow a variety of fruits and flowers. Toward the back of the valley are small ranches with grazing horses. ■TIP➔ If you see any trucks selling corn and you're staying at a place where you can cook it, be sure to get some in Waimanalo. It may be the sweetest you'll ever eat, and the price is the lowest on Oahu. ⊠ *Kalanianaole Hwy., Waimanalo.*

THE NORTH SHORE

Approximately 35 miles (one hour) north of downtown Honolulu; approximately 25 miles (one hour) from Kualoa Regional Park (Chinaman's Hat) in Windward Oahu.

An hour from town and a world away in atmosphere, Oahu's North Shore, roughly from Kahuku Point to Kaena Point, is about small farms and big waves, tourist traps and otherworldly landscapes. Parks and beaches, roadside fruit stands and shrimp shacks, a bird sanctuary, and a valley preserve offer a dozen reasons to stop between the onetime plantation town of Kahuku and the surf mecca of Haleiwa.

Haleiwa has had many lives, from resort getaway in the 1900s to plantation town through the 20th century to its life today as a surf and tourist magnet. Beyond Haleiwa is the tiny village of Waialua, a string of beach parks, an airfield where gliders, hang gliders, and parachutists play, and, at the end of the road, Kaena Point State Recreation Area, which offers a brisk hike, striking views, and whale-watching in season.

Pack wisely for a day's North Shore excursion: swim and snorkel gear, light jacket and hat (the weather is mercurial, especially in winter), sunscreen and sunglasses, bottled water and snacks, towels and a picnic blanket, and both sandals and close-toed shoes for hiking. A small cooler is nice; you may want to pick up some fruit or fresh corn. As always, leave valuables in the hotel safe and lock the car whenever you park.

GETTING HERE AND AROUND

From Waikiki, the quickest route to the North Shore is H1 east to H2 north, and then the Kamehameha Highway past Wahiawa; you'll hit Haleiwa in less than an hour. The windward route (H1 east, H3, Like Like or Pali Highway, through the mountains, or Kamehameha Highway north) takes at least 90 minutes to Haleiwa, but the drive is far prettier.

TIMING

It's best to dedicate an entire day for an excursion to the North Shore, as it's about an hour from downtown Honolulu, depending on traffic.

TOP ATTRACTIONS

Haleiwa. Today Haleiwa is a fun mix of old and new, with charming general stores and contemporary boutiques, galleries, and eateries. During the 1920s this seaside hamlet boasted a posh hotel at the end of a railroad line (both long gone), while the 1960s saw hippies gathered here, followed by surfers from around the world. Be sure to stop in at **Liliuokalani Protestant Church,** founded by missionaries in the 1830s. It's fronted by a large, stone archway built in 1910 and covered with night-blooming cereus. ⊠ *Haleiwa ✛ Follow H1 west from Honolulu to H2 north, exit at Wahiawa, follow Kamehameha Hwy. 6 miles, turn left at signaled intersection, then right into Haleiwa.*

NEED A BREAK?

Matsumoto's. For a real slice of Haleiwa life, stop at Matsumoto's, a family-run business in a building dating from 1910, for shave ice in every flavor imaginable. For something different, order a shave ice with adzuki beans—the red beans are boiled until soft, mixed with sugar, and then placed in the cone with the ice on top. ⊠ *66-087 Kamehameha Hwy., Haleiwa* ☎ *808/637-4827* ⊕ *www.matsumotoshaveice.com* ⊙ *Daily 9–6.*

Kaena Point State Recreation Area. The name means "the heat" and, indeed, this windy barren coast lacks both shade and freshwater (or any man-made amenities). Pack water, wear sturdy closed-toed shoes, don sunscreen and a hat, and lock the car. The hike is along a rutted dirt road, mostly flat and 3 miles long, ending in a rocky, sandy headland. It is here that Hawaiians believed the souls of the dead met with their family gods, and, if judged worthy to enter the afterlife, leapt off into eternal darkness at Leinaakauane, just south of the point. In summer and at low tide, the small coves offer bountiful shelling; in winter, don't venture near the water. Rare native plants dot the landscape. If you're lucky, you might spot seals sunbathing on the rocks. From November through March, watch for humpbacks, spouting and breaching. Binoculars and a camera are highly recommended. ⊠ *69-385 Farrington Hwy., Makua* ⊕ *www.hawaiistateparks.org/parks/oahu.*

See colorful wildlife at the Waimea Valley Audubon Center on Oahu's North Shore.

Waimea Valley Park. Waimea may get lots of press for the giant winter waves in the bay, but the valley itself is a newsmaker and an ecological treasure in its own right. The Office of Hawaiian Affairs is working to conserve and restore the natural habitat. Follow the Kamananui Stream up the valley through the 1,800 acres of gardens. The botanical collections here include more than 5,000 species of tropical flora, including a superb gathering of Polynesian plants. It's the best place on the island to see native species, such as the endangered Hawaiian moorhen. You can also see the remains of the Hale O Lono *heiau* (temple) along with other ancient archaeological sites; evidence suggests that the area was an important spiritual center. Daily activities include hula lessons, native plant walks, and traditional Hawaiian games, depending on how many staff members are working on a given day. At the back of the valley, **Waihi Falls** plunges 45 feet into a swimming pond. ■TIP➔ Bring your board shorts—a swim is the perfect way to end your hike. Be sure to bring mosquito repellent, too; it can get buggy. ⊠ *59-864 Kamehameha Hwy., Haleiwa* ☎ *808/638-7766* ⊕ *www.waimeavalley.net* ⊑ *$15* ⊙ *Daily 9–5.*

QUICK
BITES
Ted's Bakery. The chocolate *haupia* (coconut pudding) pie at Ted's Bakery is legendary. Stop in for a take-out pie or for a quick plate lunch or sandwich. ⊠ *59-024 Kamehameha Hwy., near Sunset Beach, Haleiwa* ☎ *808/638–8207* ⊕ *www.tedsbakery.com* ⊙ *Open daily 7 am–8 pm.*

WORTH NOTING

Puuomahuka Heiau. Worth a stop for its spectacular views from a bluff high above the ocean overlooking Waimea Bay, this sacred spot was once the site of human sacrifices. It's now on the National Register of Historic Places. Turn up the road at the Haleiwa Foodland, and follow the road up to the heiau. ⊠ *Pupukea Rd., ½ mile north of Waimea Bay, Haleiwa* ⊹ *From Rte. 83, turn right on Pupukea Rd. and drive 1 mile uphill.*

CENTRAL OAHU

Wahiawa is approximately 20 miles (30–35 minutes by car) north of downtown Honolulu; 15 miles (20–30 minutes by car) south of the North Shore.

Oahu's central plain is a patchwork of old towns and new residential developments, military bases, farms, ranches, and shopping malls, with a few visit-worthy attractions and historic sites scattered about. Central Oahu encompasses the Moanalua Valley, residential Pearl City and Mililani, and the old plantation town of Wahiawa, on the uplands halfway to the North Shore.

GETTING HERE AND AROUND

All sights in Central Oahu are most easily reached by either the H1 or H2 freeway.

TIMING

In Central Oahu, check out the Dole Plantation for all things pineapple. This area is about 35 minutes' drive from downtown Honolulu and might make a good stop on the drive to the North Shore or after a morning at Pearl Harbor, but the area is probably not worth a separate visit, particularly if you're short on time.

TOP ATTRACTIONS

Dole Plantation. Pineapple plantation days are nearly defunct in Hawaii, but you can still celebrate Hawaii's famous golden fruit at this promotional center with exhibits, a huge gift shop, a snack concession, educational displays, and the world's largest maze. Take the self-guided Garden Tour, plant your own pineapple, or hop aboard the *Pineapple Express* for a 20-minute train tour to learn a bit about life on a pineapple plantation. Kids love the more than 3-acre Pineapple Garden Maze, made up of 14,000 tropical plants and trees. If you do nothing else, stop by the cafeteria in the back for a delicious pineapple soft-serve Dole Whip. This is about a 40-minute drive from Waikiki, a suitable stop on the way to or from the North Shore. ⊠ *64-1550 Kamehameha Hwy., Wahiawa* ☎ *808/621–8408* ⊕ *www.dole-plantation.com* ⊠ *Pavilion free, maze $6, train $8.50, garden tour $5* ☉ *Daily 9:30–5:30; train, maze, and garden 9:30–5.*

WEST (LEEWARD) OAHU

Approximately 20 miles (30 minutes by car) west of downtown Honolulu; 12 miles (20 minutes by car) from Mililani; traffic can add significantly to driving time.

West (or Leeward) Oahu has the island's fledgling "second city"—the planned community of Kapolei, where the government hopes to attract enough jobs to lighten inbound traffic to downtown Honolulu—then continues on past the far-flung Ko Olina resort to the Hawaiian communities of Nanakuli and Waianae, to the beach and the end of the road at Keaweula, aka Yokohama Bay.

A couple of cautions as you head to the leeward side: Highway 93 is a narrow, winding, two-lane road notorious for accidents. There's an abrupt transition from freeway to highway at Kapolei, and by the time you reach Nanakuli, it's a country road, so *slow down.* ⚠ Car break-ins and beach thefts are common here.

GETTING HERE AND AROUND

West Oahu begins at folksy Waipahu and continues past Makakilo and Kapolei on H1 and Highway 93, Farrington Highway.

TIMING

If you've got to leave one part of this island for the next trip, this is the part to skip. It's a longish drive to West Oahu by island standards—30 minutes to Kapolei from Waikiki and 90 minutes to Waianae. The Waianae Coast is naturally beautiful, but the area doesn't have the tourist amenities you'll find elsewhere on the island. The attraction most worth the trek to West Oahu is Hawaii's Plantation Village in Waipahu, about a half hour out of town; it's a living-history museum built from actual homes of turn-of-the-20th-century plantation workers.

Hawaii's Plantation Village. Starting in the 1800s, immigrants seeking work on the sugar plantations came to these islands like so many waves against the shore. At this living museum 30 minutes from downtown Honolulu, visit authentically furnished buildings, original and replicated, that re-create and pay tribute to the plantation era. See a Chinese social hall; a Japanese shrine, sumo ring, and saimin stand; a dental office; and historic homes. The village is open for guided tours only. ✉ *Waipahu Cultural Gardens Park, 94-695 Waipahu St., Waipahu* ☎ *808/677–0110* ⊕ *www.hawaiiplantationvillage.org* 💲 *$13* ⊗ *Tours on the hr, Mon.–Sat. 10–2.*

BEACHES

Updated by
Trina Kudlacek

Tropical sun mixed with cooling trade winds and pristine waters make Oahu's shores a literal heaven on earth. But contrary to many assumptions, the island is not one big beach. There are miles and miles of coastline without a grain of sand, so you need to know where you're going to fully enjoy the Hawaiian experience.

Much of the island's southern and eastern coast is protected by inner reefs. The reefs provide still coastline water but not much as far as sand is concerned. However, where there are beaches on the south and east shores, they are mind-blowing. In West Oahu and on the North Shore you can find the wide expanses of sand you would expect for enjoying the sunset. Sandy bottoms and protective reefs make the water an adventure in the winter months. Most visitors assume the seasons don't change a bit in the Islands, and they would be mostly right—except for the waves, which are big on the South Shore in summer and placid in winter. It's exactly the opposite on the north side, where winter storms bring in huge waves, but the ocean becomes glasslike come May and June.

HONOLULU

WAIKIKI

The 2-mile strand called Waikiki Beach extends from Hilton Hawaiian Village on one end to Kapiolani Park and Diamond Head on the other. Although it's one contiguous piece of beach, it's as varied as the people that inhabit the Islands. Whether you're an old-timer looking to enjoy the action from the shade or a sports nut wanting to do it all, you can find every beach activity here without ever jumping in the rental car.

FAMILY **Duke Kahanamoku Beach.** Named for Hawaii's famous Olympic swimming champion, Duke Kahanamoku, this is a hard-packed beach with the only shade trees on the sand in Waikiki. It's great for families with young children because it has both shade and the calmest waters in Waikiki, thanks to a rock wall that creates a semiprotected cove. The ocean clarity here is not as brilliant as most of Waikiki because of the stillness of the surf, but it's a small price to pay for peace of mind about youngsters. The beach fronts the Hilton Hawaiian Village Beach Resort and Spa. **Amenities:** food and drink; showers; toilets. **Best for:** sunset; walking. ⊠ *2005 Kalia Rd.*

FAMILY **Fort DeRussy Beach Park.** This is one of the finest beaches on the south side of Oahu. A wide, soft, ultrawhite beachfront with gently lapping waves makes it a family favorite for running-jumping-frolicking fun (this also happens to be where the NFL holds its rookie sand football game when Hawaii hosts the Pro Bowl). The new, heavily shaded grass grilling area, sand volleyball courts, and aquatic rentals make this a must for the active visitor. The beach fronts Hale Koa Hotel as well as Fort DeRussy. **Amenities:** food and drink; lifeguards; showers; toilets; water sports. **Best for:** swimming; walking. ⊠ *2161 Kalia Rd.*

Kahaloa and Ulukou Beaches. The beach widens back out here, creating the "it" spot for the bikini crowd. Beautiful bodies abound. This is where you find most of the catamaran charters for a spectacular sail out to Diamond Head, or surfboard and outrigger canoe rentals for a ride on the rolling waves of the Canoe surf break. Great music and outdoor dancing beckon the sand-bound visitor to Duke's Canoe Club, where shirt and shoes not only aren't required, they're discouraged. The Royal Hawaiian Hotel and the Moana Surfrider are both on this beach. **Amenities:** food and drink; lifeguards; parking (fee); showers; toilets; water sports. **Best for:** partiers; surfing. ⊠ *2259 Kalakaua Ave.*

FAMILY **Kuhio Beach Park.** This beach has experienced a renaissance after a recent face-lift. Now bordered by a landscaped boardwalk, it's great

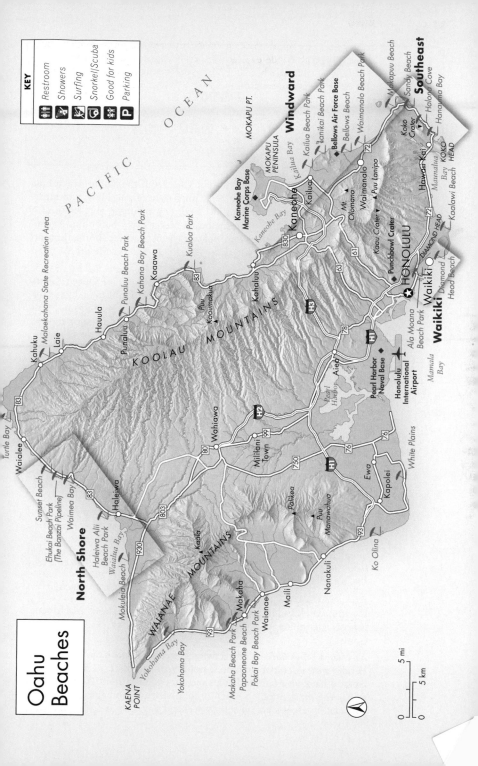

Oahu Beaches

KEY
- Restroom
- Showers
- Surfing
- Snorkel/Scuba
- Good for kids
- Parking

PACIFIC OCEAN

North Shore

Windward

Southeast

Waikiki

KOOLAU MOUNTAINS

WAIANAE MOUNTAINS

KAENA POINT

Turtle Bay
Waialee
Kahuku
Laie
Hauula
Malaekahana State Recreation Area
Punaluu Beach Park
Kahana Bay Beach Park
Kaaawa
Kualoa Park
Punaluu
Kahaluu
Puu Kaaumakua
Puu
Kaoumaku
Mokapu Beach
MOKAPU PT.
MOKAPU PENINSULA
Kaneohe Bay Marine Corps Base
Kaneohe Bay
Kaneohe
Kailua Bay
Kailua Beach Park
Kailua
Lanikai Beach Park
Bellows Air Force Base
Bellows Beach
Waimanalo Beach Park
Waimanalo
Puu Lanipo
Mt. Olomana
Kaau Crater
Punchbowl Crater
Makapuu Beach
Sandy Beach
Koko Crater
Halona Cove
KOKO HEAD
Hanauma Bay
Kaalawi Beach
Maunalua Bay
Hawaii Kai
HONOLULU
Waikiki
Ala Moana Beach Park
DIAMOND HEAD
Diamond Head Beach
Mamala Bay
Honolulu International Airport
Pearl Harbor Naval Base
Pearl Harbor
Aiea
Wahiawa
Wahiawa
Mililani Town
Ewa
White Plains
Kapolei
Ko Olina
Nanakuli
Maili
Waianae
Pokai Bay Beach Park
Papaoneone Beach
Makaha Beach Park
Makaha
Puu Manawahua
Palikea
Puu Kaala
Yokohama Bay
Yokohama Bay
Mokuleia Bay
Waialua Bay
Waialua Beach
Haleiwa
Haleiwa Alii Beach Park
Ehukai Beach Park (The Banzai Pipeline)
Sunset Beach
Waimea Bay

5 mi

5 km

for romantic walks any time of day. Check out the Kuhio Beach hula mound Tuesday to Sunday at 6:30 for free hula and Hawaiian-music performances and a torch-lighting ceremony at sunset. Surf lessons for beginners are available from the beach center every half hour. **Amenities:** food and drink; lifeguards; showers; toilets; water sports. **Best for:** surfing; walking. ⊠ *2461 Kalakaua Ave.* ✢ *Go past the Moana Surfrider Hotel to the Kapahulu Ave. pier.*

FAMILY **Queen's Surf Beach.** So named as it was once the site of Queen Liliuokalani's beach house, this beach draws a mix of families and gay couples—and it seems as if someone is always playing a steel drum. Many weekends, movie screens are set up on the sand, and major motion pictures are shown after the sun sets (⊕ *www.sunsetonthebeach.net*). In the daytime, there are banyan trees for shade and volleyball nets for pros and amateurs alike. The water fronting Queen's Surf is an aquatic preserve, providing the best snorkeling in Waikiki. **Amenities:** lifeguards; showers; toilets. **Best for:** snorkeling; swimming; walking. ⊠ *2598 Kalakaua Ave., across from the entrance to Honolulu Zoo.*

FAMILY **Sans Souci State Recreational Park.** Nicknamed Dig-Me Beach because of its outlandish display of skimpy bathing suits, this small rectangle of sand is nonetheless a good sunning spot for all ages. Children enjoy its shallow, safe waters, which are protected (for now) by the walls of the historic natatorium, an Olympic-size saltwater swimming arena that's been closed for decades. Serious swimmers and triathletes also swim in the channel here, beyond the reef. Sans Souci is favored by locals wanting to avoid the crowds while still enjoying the convenience of Waikiki. The New Otani Kaimana Beach Hotel is next door. **Amenities:** lifeguards; parking (fee and no fee); showers; toilets. **Best for:** swimming; walking. ⊠ *2776 Kalakaua Ave., across from Kapiolani Park, between the New Otani Kaimana Beach Hotel and the Waikiki War Memorial Natatorium.*

ALA MOANA

Downtown Honolulu has only one beach, the monstrous Ala Moana. It hosts everything from Dragon Boat competitions to the Aloha State Games.

FAMILY **Ala Moana Beach Park.** A protective reef makes Ala Moana essentially a ½-mile-wide saltwater swimming pool. Very smooth sand and no waves create a haven for families and stand-up paddle surfers. After Waikiki, this is the most popular beach among visitors, and the free parking area can fill up quickly on sunny weekend days. On the Waikiki side is

BEACH SAFETY

Hawaii's world-renowned, beautiful beaches can be dangerous at times due to large waves and strong currents—so much so that the state rates wave hazards using three signs: a yellow square (caution), a red stop sign (high hazard), and a black diamond (extreme hazard). Signs are posted and updated three times daily or as conditions change.

Visiting beaches with lifeguards is strongly recommended, and you should swim only when there's a normal caution rating. Never swim alone or dive into unknown water or shallow breaking waves. If you're unable to swim out of a rip current, don't fight the pull but instead tread water and wave your arms in the air to signal for help.

Even in calm conditions, there are other dangerous things in the water to be aware of, including razor-sharp coral, jellyfish, eels, and sharks.

Jellyfish cause the most ocean injuries, and signs are posted along beaches when they're present. Reactions to a sting are usually mild (burning sensation, redness, welts); however, in some cases they can be severe (breathing difficulties). If you're stung, pick off the tentacles, rinse the affected area with water, and apply ice.

The chances of getting bitten by a shark in Hawaiian waters are very low; sharks attack swimmers or surfers fewer than three or four times per year. Of the 40 species of sharks found near Hawaii, tiger sharks are considered the most dangerous because of their size and indiscriminate feeding behavior. They're easily recognized by their blunt snouts and vertical bars on their sides.

The website ⊕ *oceansafety.soest. hawaii.edu* provides statewide beach-hazard maps as well as weather and surf advisories, listings of closed beaches, and safety tips.

a peninsula called Magic Island, with shady trees and paved sidewalks ideal for jogging. Ala Moana also has playing fields, tennis courts, and a couple of small ponds for sailing toy boats. This beach is for everyone, but only in the daytime. It's a high-crime area, with lots of homeless people, after dark. **Amenities:** food and drink; lifeguards; parking (no fee); showers; toilets. **Best for:** swimming; walking. ⊠ *1201 Ala Moana Blvd., Ala Moana ⊕ From Waikiki take Bus 8 to Ala Moana Shopping Center and cross Ala Moana Blvd.*

SOUTHEAST OAHU

Much of Southeast Oahu is surrounded by reef, making most of the coast uninviting to swimmers, but the spots where the reef opens up are true gems. The drive along this side of the island is amazing, with its sheer lava-rock walls on one side and deep blue ocean on the other. There are plenty of restaurants in the suburb of Hawaii Kai, so you can make a day of it, knowing that food isn't far away.

FAMILY **Hanauma Bay Nature Preserve.** Picture this as the world's biggest open-air aquarium. You go here to see fish, and fish you'll see. Due to their

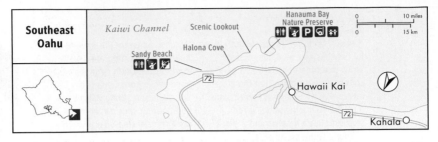

exposure to thousands of visitors every week, these fish are more like family pets than the skittish marine life you might expect. An old volcanic crater has created a haven from the waves where the coral has thrived. There's an educational center where you must watch a nine-minute video about the nature preserve before being allowed down to the bay. ■ TIP→ **The bay is best early in the morning (around 7), before the crowds arrive; it can be difficult to park later in the day.**

Snorkel equipment and lockers are available for rent, and there's an entry fee for nonresidents. Smoking is not allowed, and the beach is closed on Tuesday. Wednesday to Monday, the beach is open from 6 am to 6 pm. There's a tram from the parking lot to the beach, or you can walk the short distance on foot. Need transportation? Hanauma Bay Dive Tours runs snorkeling, snuba, and scuba tours to Hanauma Bay with transportation from Waikiki hotels on Monday, Wednesday, Thursday, and Friday only. *See Scuba Diving in Water Sports and Tours.* **Amenities:** food and drink; lifeguards; parking (fee); showers; toilets. **Best for:** snorkeling; swimming. ⊠ *7455 Kalanianaole Hwy., Hawaii Kai* 🕾 *808/396–4229* 🗹 *Nonresident fee $7.50; parking $1; mask, snorkel, and fins rental $12; tram from parking lot to beach $1.75 round-trip* ⊗ *Wed.–Mon. 6–6.*

Fodor'sChoice
★
Sandy Beach. Probably the most popular beach with locals on this side of Oahu, the broad, sloping beach is covered with sunbathers there to watch the "Show" and soak up rays. The Show is a shore break that's like no other in the Islands. Monster ocean swells rolling into the beach combined with the sudden rise in the ocean floor causes waves to jack up and crash magnificently on the shore. Expert surfers and bodyboarders young and old brave this danger to get some of the biggest barrels you can find for bodysurfing. ⚠ **But keep in mind that the beach is nicknamed "Break-Neck Beach" for a reason: many neck and back injuries are sustained here each year.** Use extreme caution when swimming here, or just kick back and watch the drama unfold from the comfort of your beach chair. **Amenities:** lifeguards; parking (no fee); showers; toilets. **Best for:** surfing; walking. ⊠ *7850 Kalanianaole Hwy., makai (toward the ocean) of Kalanianaole Hwy., 2 miles east of Hanauma Bay., Hawaii Kai.*

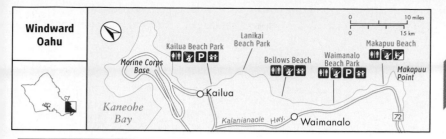

WINDWARD OAHU

The windward side of the island lives up to its name, with ideal spots for windsurfing and kiteboarding, or for the more intrepid, hang gliding. For the most part the waves are mellow, and the bottoms are all sand—making for nice spots to visit with younger kids. The only drawback is that this side does tend to get more rain. But the vistas are so beautiful that a little sprinkling shouldn't dampen your experience; plus, it benefits the waterfalls that cascade down the Koolaus.

Bellows Beach. Bellows is the same beach as Waimanalo, but it's under the auspices of the military, making it more friendly for visitors—though that also limits public beach access to weekends. The park area is excellent for camping, and ironwood trees provide plenty of shade. ■TIP→ The beach is best before 2 pm. After 2, the trade winds bring clouds that get hung up on steep mountains nearby, causing overcast skies until midafternoon. There are no food concessions, but McDonald's and other takeout fare, including *huli huli* (rotisserie) chicken on weekends, are right outside the entrance gate. **Amenities:** lifeguards; parking (no fee); showers; toilets. **Best for:** solitude; swimming. ⊠ *520 Tinker Rd., Waimanalo* ⊕ *Entrance on Kalanianaole Hwy. near Waimanalo town center.*

FAMILY **Kahana Bay Beach Park.** Local parents often bring their children here to wade in safety in the very shallow, protected waters. This pretty beach cove, surrounded by mountains, has a long arc of sand that is great for walking and a cool, shady grove of tall ironwood and pandanus trees that is ideal for a picnic. An ancient Hawaiian fishpond, which was in use until the 1920s, is visible nearby. The water here is not generally a clear blue due to the runoff from heavy rains in the valley. **Amenities:** lifeguards; parking (no fee); showers; toilets. **Best for:** swimming; walking. ⊠ *52-201 Kamehameha Hwy., north of Kualoa Park, Kaneohe.*

FAMILY **Kailua Beach Park.** A cobalt-blue sea and a wide continuous arc of powdery sand make Kailua Beach Park one of the island's best beaches, illustrated by the crowds of local families who spend their weekend days here. This is like a big Lanikai Beach, but a little windier and a little wider, and a better spot for spending a full day. Kailua Beach has calm water, a line of palms and ironwoods that provide shade on the sand, and a huge park with picnic pavilions where you can escape the heat. This is the "it" spot if you're looking to try your hand at windsurfing or kiteboarding. You can rent kayaks nearby at Kailua Sailboards and Kayaks (*130 Kailua Rd.*) and take them to the Mokulua Islands

Fodor's Choice
★

For a hopping scene with everything from surfing to volleyball, head to Waikiki Beach.

for the day. Two-seaters cost $69 for four hours or $79 for a full day. *See Windsurfing and Kiteboarding in Water Sports and Tours.* **Amenities:** lifeguards; parking (no fee); showers; toilets; water sports. **Best for:** walking; windsurfing. ✉ *437 Kawailoa Rd., Kailua* ✛ *Near Kailua town, turn right on Kailua Rd. At market, cross bridge, then turn left into beach parking lot.*

Kualoa Park. Grassy expanses border a long, narrow stretch of beach with spectacular views of Kaneohe Bay and the Koolau Mountains, making Kualoa one of the island's most beautiful picnic, camping, and beach areas. Dominating the view is an islet called Mokolii, better known as Chinaman's Hat, which rises 206 feet above the water. You can swim in the shallow areas year-round. The one drawback is that it's usually windy here, but the wide-open spaces are ideal for kite flying. **Amenities:** lifeguards; showers; toilets. **Best for:** solitude; swimming. ✉ *49-479 Kamehameha Hwy., north of Waiahole, Kaaawa.*

Fodor's Choice **Lanikai Beach Park.** Think of the beaches you see in commercials: peaceful
★ jade-green waters, powder-soft white sand, families and dogs frolicking mindlessly, offshore islands in the distance. It's an ideal spot for camping out with a book. Though the beach hides behind multimillion-dollar houses, by state law there is public access every 400 yards. You'll find street parking on Mokulua Drive for the various public-access points to the beach. ■TIP→ **Look for walled or fenced pathways every 400 yards, leading to the beach. Be sure not to park in the marked bike/ jogging lane.** There are no shower or bathroom facilities here—they are a two-minute drive away at Kailua Beach Park. **Amenities:** None.

Best for: swimming; walking. ✉ *974 Mokulua Dr., past Kailua Beach Park, Kailua.*

Fodor's Choice
★
Makapuu Beach. A magnificent beach protected by Makapuu Point welcomes you to the windward side. Hang gliders circle above the beach, and the water is filled with bodyboarders. Just off the coast you can see Bird Island, a sanctuary for aquatic fowl, jutting out of the blue. The currents can be heavy, so check with a lifeguard if you're unsure of safety. Before you leave, take the prettiest (and coldest) outdoor shower available on the island. Being surrounded by tropical flowers and foliage while you rinse off that sand will be a memory you will cherish from this side of the rock. **Amenities:** lifeguards; parking (no fee); showers; toilets. **Best for:** swimming; walking. ✉ *41-095 Kalanianaole Hwy, across from Sea Life Park, 2 miles south of Waimanalo, Waimanalo.*

FAMILY
Waimanalo Beach Park. One of the most beautiful beaches on the island, Waimanalo is a local pick, busy with picnicking families and active sports fields. Expect a wide stretch of sand; turquoise, emerald, and deep blue seas; and gentle shore-breaking waves that are fun for all ages. Theft is an occasional problem, so lock your car. **Amenities:** lifeguards; parking (no fee); showers; toilets. **Best for:** sunrise; swimming; walking. ✉ *41-849 Kalanianaole Hwy., south of Waimanalo town center, Waimanalo.*

THE NORTH SHORE

"North Shore, where the waves are mean, just like a washing machine," sing the Kaau Crater Boys about this legendary side of the island. And in winter they are absolutely right. At times the waves overtake the road, stranding tourists and locals alike. When the surf is up, there are signs on the beach telling you how far to stay back so that you aren't swept out to sea. The most prestigious big-wave contest in the world, the Eddie Aikau, is held at Waimea Bay only when waves reach the size of a five- or six-story building. The Triple Crown of Surfing roams across three North Shore beaches in the winter months each year.

All this changes come summer when this tiger turns into a kitten, with water smooth enough to water-ski on and ideal for snorkeling. The fierce Banzai Pipeline surf break becomes a great dive area, allowing you to explore the coral heads that, in winter, have claimed so many lives on the ultrashallow but big, hollow tubes created here. Even with the monster surf subsided, this is still a time for caution: lifeguards are scarce, and currents don't subside just because the waves do.

That said, it's a place like no other on earth, and must be explored. From the turtles at Mokuleia to the tunnels at Shark's Cove, you could spend your whole trip on this side of the island and not be disappointed.

Ehukai Beach Park. What sets Ehukai apart is the view of the famous Banzai Pipeline. Here the winter waves curl into magnificent tubes, making it an experienced wave-rider's dream. It's also an inexperienced swimmer's nightmare, though spring and summer waves are more accommodating to the average person, and there's good snorkeling. Except when the surf contests are going on, there's no reason to stay on the

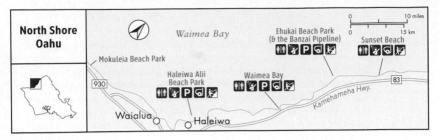

central strip. Travel in either direction from the center, and the conditions remain the same but the population thins out, leaving you with a magnificent stretch of sand all to yourself. **Amenities:** lifeguards; parking (no fee); showers; toilets. **Best for:** snorkeling; surfing. ✉ *59-406 Kamehameha Hwy., 1 mile north of Foodland at Pupukea, Haleiwa.*

FAMILY **Haleiwa Alii Beach Park.** The winter waves are impressive here, but in summer the ocean is like a lake, ideal for family swimming. The beach itself is big and often full of locals. Its broad lawn off the highway invites volleyball and Frisbee games and groups of barbecuers. This is also the opening break for the Triple Crown of Surfing, and the grass is often filled with art festivals or carnivals. **Amenities:** lifeguards; parking (no fee); showers; toilets. **Best for:** surfing; swimming. ✉ *66-162 Haleiwa Rd., north of Haleiwa town center and past harbor, Haleiwa.*

Mokuleia Beach Park. There is a reason why the producers of the TV show *Lost* chose this beach for their set. On the remote northwest point of the island, it is about 10 miles from the closest store or public restroom; you could spend a day here and not see another living soul. And that is precisely its beauty—all the joy of being stranded on a deserted island without the trauma of the plane crash. The beach is wide and white, the waters bright blue (but a little choppy) and full of sea turtles and other marine life. Mokuleia is a great secret find; just remember to pack supplies and use caution, as there are no lifeguards. **Amenities:** parking (no fee). **Best for:** solitude. ✉ *68-67 Farrington Hwy., west of Haleiwa town center, across from Dillingham Airfield, Haleiwa.*

Sunset Beach. The beach is broad, the sand is soft, the summer waves are gentle, making for good snorkeling, and the winter surf is crashing. Many love searching this shore for the puka shells that adorn the necklaces you see everywhere. Food trucks selling shave ice, plate lunches, and sodas usually line the adjacent highway. **Amenities:** food and drink; lifeguards; parking (no fee); showers; toilets. **Best for:** snorkeling; sunset; surfing. ✉ *59 Kamehameha Hwy., 1 mile north of Ehukai Beach Park, Haleiwa.*

Turtle Bay. Now known more for its resort (the Turtle Bay Resort) than its magnificent beach, Turtle Bay is mostly passed over on the way to the better-known beaches of Sunset and Waimea. But for the average visitor with average swimming capabilities, this is a good place to be on the North Shore. The crescent-shaped beach is protected by a huge sea wall. You can see and hear the fury of the northern swell while blissfully floating in cool, calm waters. The convenience of this spot is also hard to

pass up—there is a concession selling sandwiches and sunblock right on the beach. The resort has free parking for beach guests. **Amenities:** food and drink; parking (no fee); showers; toilets. **Best for:** sunset; swimming. ⊠ *57-20 Kuilima Dr., 4 miles north of Kahuku, Kahuku ⊹ Turn into Turtle Bay Resort, and let guard know where you are going.*

Fodor's Choice ★ **Waimea Bay.** Made popular in that old Beach Boys song "Surfin' U.S.A.," Waimea Bay is a slice of big-wave heaven, home to king-size 25- to 30-foot winter waves. Summer is the time to swim and snorkel in the calm waters. The shore break is great for novice bodysurfers. Due to its popularity, the postage-stamp parking lot is quickly filled, but it's also possible to park along the side of the road and walk in. **Amenities:** lifeguards; parking (no fee); showers; toilets. **Best for:** snorkeling (in summer); surfing (in winter); swimming (in summer). ⊠ *61-31 Kamehameha Hwy., across from Waimea Valley, 3 miles north of Haleiwa, Haleiwa.*

WEST (LEEWARD) OAHU

The North Shore may be known as "Country," but the west side is truly the rural area on Oahu. There are commuters from this side to Honolulu, but many are born, live, and die on this side with scarcely a trip to town. For the most part, there's little hostility toward outsiders, but occasional problems have flared up, mostly due to drug abuse that has ravaged the fringes of the island. The problems have generally been car break-ins, not violence. So, in short, lock your car, don't bring valuables, and enjoy the amazing beaches.

The beaches on the west side are expansive and empty. Most Oahu residents and tourists don't make it to this side simply because of the drive; in traffic it can take almost 90 minutes to make it all the way to Kaena Point from downtown Honolulu. But you'll be hard-pressed to find a better sunset anywhere.

FAMILY **Ko Olina.** This is the best spot on the island if you have small kids. The resort area commissioned a series of four man-made lagoons, but, as it has to provide public beach access, you are the winner. Huge rock walls protect the lagoons, making them into perfect spots for the kids to get their first taste of the ocean without getting bowled over. The large expanses of seashore grass and hala trees that surround the semicircle beaches are made-to-order for naptime. A 1½-mile jogging track connects the lagoons. Due to its appeal for *keiki* (children), Ko Olina is popular, and the parking lot fills up quickly when school is out and on weekends, so try to get here before 10 am. The biggest parking lot is at the farthest lagoon from the entrance. There are actually three resorts here: Aulani (the Disney resort), the J.W. Marriott Ihilani Resort & Spa, and the Ko Olina Beach Villas Resort (which has a time-share section as well). **Amenities:** food and drink; parking (no fee); showers; toilet. **Best for:** sunset; swimming; walking. ⊠ *92 Aliinui Dr., 23 miles west of Honolulu, Kapolei ⊹ Take Ko Olina exit off H1 West and proceed to guard shack.*

Makaha Beach Park. This beach provides a slice of local life most visitors don't see. Families string up tarps for the day, fire up hibachis, set up

Continued on page 102

Imagine picking your seat for free at the Super Bowl or wandering the grounds of Augusta National at no cost during The Masters, and you glimpse the opportunity you have when attending the Vans Triple Crown of Surfing on the North Shore.

NORTH SHORE SURFING & THE TRIPLE CROWN

10-FOOT WAVES.
10,000 FANS.
TOP 50 SURFERS.

Long considered the best stretch of surf breaks on Earth, the North Shore surf area encompasses 6 miles of coastline on the northwestern tip of Oahu from Haleiwa to Sunset Beach. There are over 20 major breaks within these 6 miles. Winter storms in the North Pacific send huge swells southward which don't break for thousands of miles until they hit the shallow reef of Oahu's remote North Shore. This creates optimum surfing all winter long and was the inspiration for having surf competitions here each holiday season.

Every November and December the top 50 surfers in world rankings descend on "The Country" to decide who is the best all-around surfer in the world. Each of the three invitation-only contests that make up the Triple Crown has its own winner; competitors also win points based on the final standings. The surfer who excels in all three contests, racking up the most points overall, wins the Vans Triple Crown title. The first contest is held at **Haleiwa Beach,** the second at **Sunset Beach.** The season reaches its crescendo at the most famous surf break in the world, the **Banzai Pipeline.**

The best part is the cost to attend the events—nothing; your seat for the show—wherever you set down your beach towel. Just park your car, grab your stuff, and watch the best surfers in the world tame the best waves in the world.

The only surfing I understand involves the TV.

The contests were created not only to name an overall champion, but to attract the casual fan to the sport. Announcers explain each ride over the loudspeakers, discussing the nuances and values being weighed by the judges. A scoreboard displays points and standings during the four days of each event.

If this still seems incomprehensible to you, the action on the beach can also be exciting as some of the most beautiful people in the world are attracted to these contests.

For more information, see www.triplecrownofsurfing.com.

What should I bring?

Pack for a day at the Triple Crown the way you would for any day at the beach—sun block, beach towel, bottled water, and if you want something other than snacks, food.

These contests are held in rural neighborhoods (read: few stores), so pack anything you might need during the day. Also, binoculars are suggested, especially for the contest at Sunset. The pros will be riding huge outside ocean swells, and it can be hard to follow from the beach without binoculars. Haleiwa's breaks and Pipeline are considerably closer to shore, but binoculars will let you see the intensity on the contestants' faces.

Haleiwa Alii Beach Park
Vans Triple Crown Contest #1: Reef Pro Hawaii

The Triple Crown gets underway with high-performance waves (and the know-how to ride them) at Haleiwa. Though lesser known than the other two breaks of the Triple Crown, it is the perfect wave for showing off: the contest here is full of sharp cutbacks (twisting the board dramatically off the top or bottom of the wave), occasional barrel rides, and a crescendo of floaters (balancing the board on the top of the cresting wave) before the wave is destroyed on the shallow tabletop reef called the Toilet Bowl. The rider who can pull off the most tricks will win this leg, evening the playing field for the other two contests, where knowledge of the break is the key. Also, the beach park is walking distance from historic Haleiwa town, a mecca to surfers worldwide who make their pilgrimage here every winter to ride the waves. Even if you are not a fan, immersing yourself in their culture will make you one by nightfall.

Sunset Beach
Vans Triple Crown Contest #2: Vans World Cup of Surfing

At Sunset, the most guts and bravado win the day. The competition is held when the swell is at 8 to 12 feet and from the northwest. Sunset gets the heaviest surf because it is the exposed point on the northern tip of Oahu. Surfers describe the waves here as "moving mountains." The choice of waves is the key to this contest as only the perfect one will give the competitor a ride through the jigsaw-puzzle outer reef, which can kill a perfect wave instantly, all the way into the inner reef. Big bottom turns (riding all the way down the face of the wave before turning dramatically back onto the wave) and slipping into a super thick tube (slowing down to let the wave catch you and riding inside its vortex) are considered necessary to carry the day.

Banzai Pipeline

Vans Triple Crown Contest #3: Billabong Pipeline Masters

Surfing competitions are generally judged on the top three waves ridden by the competitors. In the Pipeline Masters, however, instead of accruing points through tricks and jumps, the surfers score high by dropping in the deepest and staying inside the tube the longest. The best trick at Pipeline is surviving this incredibly hollow and heavy wave, no other artistry is necessary.

How does the wave become hollow in the first place? When the deep ocean floor ascends steeply to the shore, the waves that meet it will pitch over themselves sharply, rather than rolling. This pitching causes a tube to form, and in most places in the world that tube is a mere couple of feet in diameter. In the case of Pipeline, however, its unique, extremely shallow reef causes the swells to open into 10-foot-high moving hallways that surfers can pass through. Only problem: a single slip puts them right into the raggedly sharp coral heads that caused the wave to pitch in the first place. Broken arms and boards are the rule rather than the exception for those who dare to ride and fail.

■ TIP➔ The Banzai Pipeline is a surf break, not a beach. The best place to catch a glimpse of the break is from Ehukai Beach.

When Are the Contests?

The first contests at Haleiwa begin the second week of November, and the Triple Crown finishes up right before Christmas.

Surfing, more so than any other sport, relies on Mother Nature to allow competition. Each contest in the Triple Crown requires only four days of competition, but each is given a window of twelve days. Contest officials decide by 7 AM of each day whether the contest will be held or not, and they release the information to radio stations and via a hotline (the number changes each year, unfortunately). By 7:15, you will know if it is on or not. Consult the local paper's sports section for the hotline number or listen to the radio announcement. The contests run from 8:30 to 4:30, featuring half-hour heats with four to six surfers each.

If big crowds bother you, go early on in the contests, within the first two days of each one. While the finale of the Pipeline Masters may draw about 10,000 fans, the earlier days have the same world-class surfers with fewer than a thousand fans.

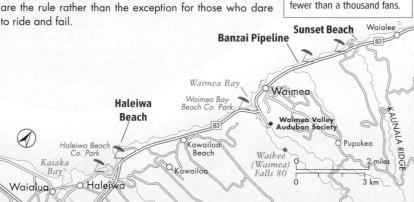

How Do I Get There?

If you hate dealing with parking and traffic, take TheBus. It will transport you from Waikiki to the contest sites in an hour for two bucks and no hassle.

If you must drive, watch the news the night before. If they are expecting big waves that night, there is a very good chance the contest will be on in the morning. Leave by 6 AM to beat the crowd. When everybody else gets the news at 7:15 AM that the show is on, you will be parking your car and taking a snooze on the beach waiting for the surfing to commence.

Parking is limited so be prepared to park alongside Kamehameha Highway and trek it in.

But I'm not coming until Valentine's Day.

There doesn't need to be a contest underway for you to enjoy these spots from a spectator's perspective. The North Shore surf season begins in October and concludes at the end of March. Only the best can survive the wave at Pipeline. You may not be watching 11-time world champ Kelly Slater ripping, but, if the waves are up, you will still see surfing that will blow your mind. Also, there are surf contests year-round on all shores of Oahu, so check the papers to see what is going on during your stay. A few other events to be on the lookout for:

Buffalo's Annual Big Board Surfing Classic

Generally held in March at legendary waterman "Buffalo" Keaulana's home beach of Makaha, this is the Harlem Globetrotters of surfing contests. You'll see tandem riding, headstands, and outrigger canoe surfing. The contest is more about making the crowds cheer than beating your competitors, which makes it very accessible for the casual fan.

Converse Hawaiian Open

During the summer months, the waves switch to the south shore, where there are surf contests of one type or another each week. The Open is one of the biggest and is a part of the US Professional Longboard Surfing Championships. The best shoot it out every August on the waves Duke Kahanamoku made famous at Queen's Beach in Waikiki.

Quiksilver in Memory of Eddie Aikau Big Wave Invitational

The granddaddy of them all is a one-day, winner-take-all contest in 25-foot surf at Waimea Bay. Because of the need for huge waves, it can be held only when there's a perfect storm. That could be at any time in the winter months, and there have been many years when it didn't happen at all. When Mother Nature does comply, however, it is not to be missed. You can hear the waves from the road, even before you can see the beach or the break.

BOARD SHAPES

Longboard: Lengthier (about 2.5–3 m/9–10.5 feet), wider, thicker, and more buoyant than the often-miniscule shortboards. Offers more flotation and speedier paddling, which makes it easier to get into waves. Great for beginners and those with relaxed surf styles. Skill level: Beginner to Intermediate.

Funboard: A little shorter than the longboard with a slightly more acute nose and blunt tail, the Funboard combines the best attributes of the longboards with some similar characteristics of the shorter boards. Good for beginners or surfers looking for a board more maneuverable and faster than a longboard. Skill level: Beginner to Intermediate.

Fishboard: A stumpy, blunt-nosed, twin-finned board that features a "V" tail (giving it a "fish" like look, hence the name) and is fast and maneuverable. Good for catching small, steep, slow waves and pulling tricks. At one point this was the world's best-selling surfboard. Skill level: Intermediate to Expert.

Shortboard: Shortboards came on the scene in 1967-70 when the average board length dropped from 9'6" to 6'6" (2.9m to 2m) and changed the wave riding styles in the surf world forever. This board is a short, light, high-performance stick that is designed for carving the wave with a high amount of maneuverability. These boards need a fast steep wave, completely different than a longboard break, which tends to be slower with shallower wave faces. Skill level: Expert.

Beginner **Expert**

Funboards
Fishboards
Longboards
Shortboards

Shallow wave faces, easiest surfing — Steeper wave faces, difficult surfing

lawn chairs, get out the fishing gear, and strum ukulele while they "talk story" (chat). Legendary waterman Buffalo Keaulana can be found in the shade of the palms playing with his grandkids and spinning yarns of yesteryear. In these waters Buffalo not only invented some of the most outrageous methods of surfing, but also raised his world-champion son Rusty. He also made Makaha the home of the world's first international surf meet in 1954 and still hosts his Big Board Surfing Classic. With its long, slow-building waves, it's a great spot to try out longboarding. The swimming is generally decent in summer, but avoid the big winter waves. The only parking is along the highway, but it's free. **Amenities:** lifeguards; showers; toilets. **Best for:** surfing; swimming. ⊠ *84-450 Farrington Hwy., Waianae ✛ Go 32 miles west of Honolulu on the H1, then exit onto Farrington Hwy. The beach will be on your left.*

FAMILY **White Plains.** Concealed from the public eye for many years as part of
Fodor's Choice the former Barbers Point Naval Air Station, this beach is reminiscent
★ of Waikiki but without the condos and the crowds. It is a long, sloping beach with numerous surf breaks, but it is also mild enough at shore for older children to play freely. It has views of Pearl Harbor and, over that, Diamond Head. Although the sand lives up to its name, the real joy of this beach comes from its history as part of a military property for the better part of a century. Expansive parking, great restroom facilities, and numerous tree-covered barbecue areas make it a great day-trip spot. As a bonus, a Hawaiian monk seal takes up residence here several months out of the year (seals are rare in the Islands). **Amenities:** lifeguards; parking (no fee); showers; toilets. **Best for:** surfing; swimming. ⊠ *Essex Rd. and Tripoli Rd., off H1 W., Kapolei ✛ Take the Makakilo exit off H1 West, then turn left. Follow it into base gates; make a left. Blue signs lead to beach.*

WATER SPORTS AND TOURS

Updated by
Trina Kudlacek

From snorkeling on the North Shore to kayaking to small islands off Kailua Beach to stand-up paddleboarding in Waikiki—when you're on Oahu, there's always a reason to get wet. You can swim with native fish in a protected bay, surf waves in an outrigger canoe, take to the skies in a parasail above Diamond Head, or enjoy panoramic views of Waikiki aboard a 45-foot catamaran. Diving into the ocean—whether in a boat, on a board, or with your own finned feet—is a great way to experience Oahu.

But as with any physical activity, heed the warnings. The ocean is unpredictable and unforgiving, and it can be as dangerous as it can be awe-inspiring. But if you respect it, it can offer you the kind of memories that last well after your vacation.

BOAT TOURS AND CHARTERS

Being on the water can be the best way to enjoy the Islands. Whether you want to see the fish in action or experience how they taste, there is a tour for you.

For a sailing experience in Oahu, you need go no farther than the beach in front of your hotel in Waikiki. Strung along the sand are seven beach catamarans that will provide you with one-hour rides during the day and 90-minute sunset sails. Expect to spend around $23 to $25 for day sails and $30 to $34 for sunset rides. ■TIP➔ Feel free to haggle, especially with the smaller boats. Some provide drinks for free, some charge for them, and some let you pack your own, so keep that in mind when pricing the ride.

Hawaii Nautical. With one location in Waikiki and one on the Waianae Coast, this outfit offers a wide variety of cruise options including guaranteed dolphin sightings, gourmet dinners, lunches, snorkeling, scuba diving, or sunset viewing. Three-hour cruises, including lunch and two drinks, depart from the Hilton in Waikiki.

For those interested in leaving from the Waianae Coast, three-hour morning and two-hour afternoon snorkel tours are available from the Waianae Boat Harbor on Farrington Hwy. (✉ *91-607 Malakole St.* ☎ *808/234–7245*). Prices include all gear, food, and two alcoholic beverages. The dock in the Waianae Boat Harbor is a little more out of the way, but this is a much more luxurious option than what is offered in Waikiki. Three-hour morning and two-hour afternoon tours of the west side of Oahu include stops for observing dolphins from the boat and a snorkel spot well populated with fish. All gear, snacks, sandwiches, and two alcoholic beverages make for a more complete experience. Pickup in Ko Olina is free, but the company will also pick you up and take you back to Waikiki for an additional fee. ✉ *Hilton Pier at Hilton Hawaiian Village, 2005 Kalia Rd., Waikiki, Honolulu* ☎ *808/234–7245* ⊕ *www. hawaiinautical.com* ✑ *From $109.*

Maitai Catamaran. Taking off from the stretch of sand between the Sheraton Waikiki and the Halekulani Hotel, this 44-foot cat is the fastest and sleekest on the beach. There are a variety of tours to choose from, including a sunset sail and a snorkel excursion. If you have a need for speed and enjoy a little more upscale experience, this is the boat for you. ✉ *Waikiki Beach, between the Sheraton Waikiki and the Halekulani Hotel, Waikiki, Honolulu* ☎ *808/922–5665, 800/462–7975* ⊕ *www. maitaicatamaran.net* ✑ *From $28.*

Na Hoku II Catamaran. The tour features a variety of music and free booze in its $30 price tag. The 45-foot catamaran is tied up near the Westin Moana Surfrider hotel and sails four times daily. ■TIP➔ Make reservations in advance for the sunset sail as the boat fills up quickly. ✉ *Waikiki Beach, between the Moana Surfrider Hotel and Duke's Barefoot Bar, Waikiki, Honolulu* ☎ *808/554–5990* ⊕ *www.waikikicat.com* ✑ *From $30.*

Star of Honolulu Cruises. Founded in 1957, this company recently expanded its fleet to include the 65-foot *Dolfin Star,* docked on Oahu's west coast. It offers everything from snorkeling cruises in the pristine waters off the Waianae coast to gourmet-dinner cruises with live entertainment to seasonal whale-watching sails on one of two vessels. Popular cruises teach you how to string lei and dance hula. Two-hour whale-watching-excursion rates begin at $33 per person, while dinner

The windward side has many good spots for bodyboarding.

cruises start at $84 and go up to $184. The company has a second location at 85-491 Farrington Highway in Waianae. ✉ *Aloha Tower Marketplace, 1 Aloha Tower Dr., Downtown Honolulu, Honolulu* ☏ *808/983–7827* 🖨 *808/983–7780* ⊕ *www.starofhonolulu.com.*

Tradewind Charters. This company's half-day private excursions can include sailing, snorkeling, reef fishing, and whale-watching. Traveling on these luxury yachts not only gets you away from the crowds, but also gives you the opportunity to "take the helm" if you wish. The cruises may include snorkeling at an exclusive anchorage, as well as hands-on snorkeling and sailing instruction. Base charter prices cover up to six passengers. ✉ *Kewalo Basin Harbor, 1125 Ala Moana Blvd., Ala Moana, Honolulu* ☏ *808/227–4956* ⊕ *tradewindvacationshawaii. com* ◨ *From $495.*

BODYBOARDING AND BODYSURFING

Bodyboarding (or sponging) has long been a popular alternative to surfing for a couple of reasons. First, the start-up cost is much less—a usable board can be purchased for $30 to $40 or can be rented on the beach for $5 an hour. Second, it's a whole lot easier to ride a bodyboard than to tame a surfboard. All you have to do is paddle out to the waves, then turn toward the beach as the wave approaches and kick like crazy.

Most grocery and convenience stores sell bodyboards. Though these boards don't compare to what the experts use, beginners won't notice a difference in their handling on smaller waves. ■**TIP→ Another small investment you'll want to make is surf fins.** These smaller, sturdier versions of dive fins sell for $25 to $60 at surf and dive stores, and sporting-goods stores. Most beach stands don't rent fins with the boards. Though they are not necessary for bodyboarding, fins do give you a tremendous advantage when you're paddling. If you plan to go out into bigger surf, we would also suggest getting a leash, which reduces the chance you'll lose your board.

Bodysurfing requires far less equipment—just a pair of swim fins with heel straps—but it can be a lot more challenging to master. Typically, surf breaks that are good for bodyboarding are good for bodysurfing.

If the direction of the current or dangers of the break are not readily apparent to you, don't hesitate to ask a lifeguard for advice.

BEST SPOTS

Bodyboarding and bodysurfing can be done anywhere there are waves, but due to the paddling advantage surfers have over spongers, it's usually more fun to go to surf breaks exclusively for bodyboarding.

Bellows Beach. On Oahu's windward side, Bellows Field Beach has shallow waters and a consistent break that makes it an ideal spot for bodyboarders and bodysurfers. (Surfing isn't allowed between the two lifeguard towers.) But take note: the Portuguese man-o-war, a blue jellyfish-like invertebrate that delivers painful and powerful stings, is often seen here. ✉ *41-043 Kalanianaole Hwy., Waimanalo.*

Kuhio Beach Park. This beach is an easy spot for first-timers to check out the action. The Wall, a break near the large pedestrian walkway called Kapahulu Groin, is the quintessential bodyboarding spot. The soft, rolling waves make it perfect for beginners. Even during summer's south swells, it's relatively tame because of the outer reefs. ✉ *Waikiki Beach, between the Sheraton Moana Surfrider Hotel and the Kapahulu Groin, Honolulu.*

Makapuu Beach. With its extended waves, Makapuu Beach is a sponger's dream. If you're a little more timid, go to the far end of the beach to **Keiki's,** where the waves are mellowed by Makapuu Point. Although the main break at Makapuu is much less dangerous than Sandy's, check out the ocean floor—the sands are always shifting, sometimes exposing coral heads and rocks. Always check (or ask lifeguards about) the currents, which can get pretty strong. ✉ *41-095 Kalanianaole Hwy., across from Sea Life Park.*

EQUIPMENT

There are more than 30 rental spots along Waikiki Beach, all offering basically the same prices. But if you plan to bodyboard for more than just an hour, we would suggest buying an inexpensive board for $20 to $40 at an ABC Store—there are more than 30 in the Waikiki area—and giving it to a kid at the end of your vacation. It will be more cost-effective for you, and you'll be passing along some aloha spirit in the process.

DEEP-SEA FISHING

Fishing isn't just a sport in Hawaii, it's a way of life. A number of charter boats with experienced crews can take you on a sportfishing adventure throughout the year. Sure, the bigger yellowfin tuna (ahi) are generally caught in summer, and the coveted spearfish are more frequent in winter, but you can still hook them any day of the year. You can also find dolphinfish (mahimahi), wahoo (ono), skip jacks, and the king—Pacific blue marlin—ripe for the picking on any given day. The largest marlin ever caught, weighing in at 1,805 pounds, was reeled in along Oahu's coast.

When choosing a fishing boat in the Islands, keep in mind the immensity of the surrounding ocean. Look for veteran captains who have decades of experience. Better yet, find those who care about Hawaii's fragile marine environment. Many captains now tag and release their catches to preserve the state's fishing grounds.

The general rule for the catch is an even split with the crew. Unfortunately, there are no "freeze-and-ship" providers in the state, so unless you plan to eat the fish while you're here, you'll probably want to leave it with the boat. Most boats do offer mounting services for trophy fish; ask your captain.

Besides the gift of fish, a gratuity of 10% to 20% is standard, but use your own discretion depending on how you felt about the overall experience.

BOATS AND CHARTERS

Maggie Joe Sport Fishing. The oldest sportfishing company on Oahu boasts landing one of the largest marlins every caught out of Kewalo Basin. With a fleet of three boats including the 53-foot custom *Maggie Joe* (which can hold up to 15 anglers and has air-conditioned cabins, hot showers, and cutting-edge fishing equipment) they can offer a variety of off-shore fishing packages including night shark fishing. A marine taxidermist can mount the monster you reel in. Half-day exclusive on the 41-foot *Sea Hawk* or the 38-foot *Ruckus* can accommodate up to six people and are the cheapest option. Charters on the larger *Maggie Joe* can start at ¾-day or a full day (but not a half-day). ⊠ *Kewalo Basin, 1025 Ala Moana Blvd., Ala Moana, Honolulu* ☎ *808/591–8888, 877/806–3474* ⊕ *www.maggiejoe.com* ⊠ *Half-day charters from $850.*

Magic Sportfishing. This 50-foot Pacifica fishing yacht, aptly named *Magic*, boasts a slew of sportfishing records, including some of largest marlins caught in local tournaments and the most mahimahi hooked during a one-day charter. This yacht is very comfortable, with twin diesel engines that provide a smooth ride, air-conditioning, and a cozy seating area. The boat can accommodate up to six passengers and offers both shared and full charters. ⊠ *Kewalo Basin Harbor, 1025 Ala Moana Blvd., Ala Moana, Honolulu* ☎ *808/596–2998, 808/286–2998* ⊕ *www. magicsportfishing.com* ⊠ *From $200 per person for shared charter; from $975 for a private charter.*

Sashimi Fun Fishing. With a glass-bottomed boat, speed boat, and two 65-foot fishing vessels, Sashimi Fun Fishing offers a variety of water activities. Choose a shark hunt, rock 'n' roll blues cruise, or traditional deep sea fishing. Or, for those who aren't quite ready to troll for big game in the open-ocean swells, you can take a trip that combines a dinner cruise with fishing and music. The boat keeps close enough to shore so that while you're hooking reef fish, you can still see Oahu.

The cruise includes a local barbecue dinner or you can cook what you catch. Rates can include hotel transportation. ✉ *Kewalo Basin Harbor, 1125 Ala Moana Blvd., Ala Moana, Honolulu* ☎ *808/955–3474* ⊕ *www.808955fish.com* ✉ *From $63 per person for shared trips.*

KAYAKING

Kayaking is an easy way to explore the ocean—and Oahu's natural beauty—without much effort or skill. It offers a vantage point not afforded by swimming or surfing, and a workout you won't get lounging on a catamaran. Even novices can get in a kayak and enjoy the island's scenery.

The ability to travel long distances can also get you into trouble. ⚠ **Experts agree that rookies should stay on the windward side.** Their reasoning is simple: if you get tired, break or lose an oar, or just plain pass out, the onshore winds will eventually blow you back to the beach. The same cannot be said for the offshore breezes of the North Shore and West Oahu.

Kayaks are specialized: some are better suited for riding waves while others are designed for traveling long distances. Your outfitter can address your needs depending on your skill level. Sharing your plans with your outfitter can lead to a more enjoyable—and safer—experience.

BEST SPOTS

If you want to try your hand at surfing kayaks, **Bellows Field Beach** (near Waimanalo Town Center, entrance on Kalanianaole Highway) on the windward side and **Mokuleia Beach** (across from Dillingham Airfield) on the North Shore are two great spots. Hard-to-reach breaks, the ones that surfers exhaust themselves trying to reach, are easily accessed by kayak. The buoyancy of the kayak also allows you to catch the wave earlier and get out in front of the white wash. One reminder on these spots: if you're a little green, stick to Bellows Field Beach with those onshore winds. Generally speaking, you don't want to be catching waves where surfers are; in Waikiki, however, pretty much anything goes.

The perennial favorite of kayakers is **Lanikai Beach,** on the island's windward side. Tucked away in an upscale residential area, this award-winning beach has become a popular spot for amateur kayakers because of its calm waters and onshore winds. More adventurous paddlers can head to the Mokulua Islands, two islets less than 1 mile from the beach. You can land on Moku Nui, which has surf breaks and small beaches great for picnicking. Take a dip in Queen's Bath, a small saltwater swimming hole.

For something a little different, try the Kahana River on the island's windward side, which empties into the ocean at **Kahana Bay Beach Park.** The river may not have the blue water of the ocean, but the majestic Koolau Mountains, with waterfalls during rainy months, make for a picturesque backdrop. It's a short jaunt, about 2 miles round-trip from the beach, but it's tranquil and packed with rain-forest foliage. Bring mosquito repellent. *For more information on this and other beaches in Oahu, see Beaches.*

EQUIPMENT, LESSONS, AND TOURS

Go Bananas. Staffers make sure that you rent the appropriate kayak for your abilities, and can also outfit your rental car with soft racks to transport your boat to the beach. (The racks are included in the rental fee.) The store also carries clothing and kayaking accessories and rents stand-up paddleboards. Full-day rates begin at $30 for single kayaks, $45 for doubles, and $30 for stand-up paddleboards. ⊠ *799 Kapahulu Ave., Kapahulu, Honolulu* ☎ *808/737–9514* 🖷 *808/732–7646* ⊕ *www. gobananaskayaks.com.*

Kailua Sailboards and Kayaks. One of the best places for beginners to rent kayaks is Kailua Beach, and Kailua Sailboards and Kayaks has an ideal location just across the street. Guided kayak tours start at $130 for four hours or, for the more adventurous, rent a kayak and venture to the Mokulua Islands off Lanikai. They also rent snorkeling equipment, stand-up paddleboards, kiteboarding gear, and bikes. Kayak rentals start at $69 for a half day in a double kayak, $59 for single. ⊠ *Kailua Beach Shopping Center, 130 Kailua Rd., Kailua* ☎ *808/262–2555* 🖷 *808/261–7341* ⊕ *www.kailuasailboards.com.*

Twogood Kayaks Hawaii. The outfitter offers kayak rentals, lessons, and guided tours. Guides are trained in the history, geology, and birds of the area. Full-day rental rates begin at $45 for single kayaks, $55 for doubles. Fully guided kayak excursions are $125, including lunch, snorkeling gear, and transportation to and from Waikiki. ⊠ *134B Hamakua Dr., Kailua* ☎ *808/262–5656* 🖷 *808/261–3111* ⊕ *www. twogoodkayaks.com.*

SCUBA DIVING

Not all of Hawaii's beauty is above water. What lurks below can be just as magnificent. While snorkeling and snuba (more on that later) provide adequate access to this underwater world, nothing gives you the freedom—or depth, quite literally—as scuba.

The diving on Oahu is comparable with any you might do in the tropics, but its uniqueness comes from the isolated environment of the Islands. There are literally hundreds of species of fish and marine life that you can find only in this chain. In fact, about 25% of Hawaii's marine life can be seen here only—nowhere else in the world. Adding to the singularity of diving off Oahu is the human history of the region. Military activities and tragedies of the 20th century filled the waters surrounding Oahu with wreckage that the ocean creatures have since turned into their homes.

Although instructors certified to license you in scuba are plentiful in the Islands, we suggest that you get your PADI certification before coming, as a week of classes may be a bit of a commitment on a short vacation. ■TIP➔ **You can go on introductory dives without the certification, but the best dives require it.**

2

BEST SPOTS

Hanauma Bay Nature Preserve. On Oahu's southeast shore, Hanauma Bay Nature Preserve is home to more than 250 different species of fish, of which a quarter can be found nowhere else in the world. This has made this volcanic crater bay one of the most popular dive sites in the state. It's a long walk from the parking lot to the beach—even longer lugging equipment—so consider hooking up with a licensed dive-tour operator. Preservation efforts have aided the bay's delicate ecosystem, so expect to see various butterfly fish, surgeonfish, tangs, parrot fish, and endangered Hawaiian sea turtles. ⊠ *7455 Kalanianaole Hwy., Honolulu* ☎ *808/396–4229.*

Mahi Waianae. Hawaii's waters are littered with shipwrecks, but one of the most intact and accessible is the *Mahi Waianae,* a 165-foot minesweeper that was sunk in 1982 off the Waianae Coast. It lays upright in about 90 feet of calm and clear water, encrusted in coral and patrolled by white spotted eagle rays and millet seed butterfly fish. The wreck serves as an artificial reef for such Hawaii aquatic residents as bluestriped snappers, puffer fish, lionfish, moray eels, and octopus. Visibility averages about 100 feet, making this one of the most popular dives on the island. ⊠ *Waianae.*

Fodor's Choice
★

Shark's Cove. Oahu's best shore dive is accessible only during the summer months. Shark's Cove, on Oahu's North Shore, churns with monster surf during the winter, making this popular snorkeling and diving spot extremely dangerous. In summer, the cavernous lava tubes and tunnels are great for both novices and experienced divers. Some dive-tour companies offer round-trip transportation from Waikiki. ⊠ *Haleiwa.*

Three Tables. A short walk from Shark's Cove is Three Tables, named for a trio of flat rocks running perpendicular to shore. There are lava tubes to the right of these rocks that break the surface and then extend out about 50 feet. While this area isn't as active as Shark's Cove, you can still spot octopus, moray eels, parrot fish, green sea turtles, and the occasional shark. ⊠ *Haleiwa.*

EQUIPMENT, LESSONS, AND TOURS

Captain Bruce's Hawaii. Focusing on the island's western shore, this full-service company offers refresher and introductory dives as well as more advanced drift and night dives. Everything is provided, including transportation to and from Waikiki. Most important, the boat has hot showers. The company is based in the Waianae Boat Harbor. ⊠ *Waianae Boat Harbor, 85-491 Farrington Hwy, Waianae* ☎ *808/234–7245* ⊕ *www.captainbruce.com* 🖃 *From $150 for 2-tank dives.*

Hanauma Bay Dive Tours. You can guess the specialty here. This company offers introductory courses in the federally protected reserve for divers ages 12 and above. ⊠ *460 Ena Rd., Honolulu* ☎ *808/256–8956, 800/505–8956* ⊕ *www.hanaumabaydivetours.com* 🖃 *From $120 (1-tank dive).*

Surf 'N Sea. The North Shore headquarters for all things water-elated is also great for diving. An interesting perk—a cameraman can shoot a video of you diving. It's hard to see facial expressions under the water, but it still might be fun for those who want to prove that they took the

Oahu's North Shore has the island's biggest waves as well as some of the best snorkeling—but not at the same time of year.

plunge. Two-tank shore dives are the most economical choice (prices for non-certified divers are higher), but the company also offers boat dives, and in the summer, night dives are available for only slightly more. ✉ 62-595 Kamehameha Hwy., Haleiwa ☎ 800/899–7873 📠 808/637–3008 ⊕ www.surfnsea.com ✉ From $100 (2-tank shore dives).

SNORKELING

If you can swim, you can snorkel. And you don't need any formal training, either.

Snorkeling is a favorite pastime for both visitors and residents, and can be done anywhere there's enough water to stick your face in. Each spot will have its great days depending on the weather and time of year, so consult with the purveyor of your gear for tips on where the best viewing is that day. Keep in mind that the North Shore should be attempted only when the waves are calm, namely in the summertime.

■TIP→ Think of buying a mask and snorkel as a prerequisite for your trip—they make any beach experience better. Just make sure you put plenty of sunscreen on your back because once you start gazing below, your head may not come back up for hours. If you'd prefer to go with a guide, several outfitters offer snorkel tours around the island.

BEST SPOTS

Electric Beach. Directly across from the electricity plant—hence the name—Electric Beach is a haven for tropical fish, making it a great snorkeling spot. The expulsion of hot water from the plant raises the temperature of the ocean, attracting Hawaiian green sea turtles, spotted moray eels, and spinner dolphins. Although the visibility is not always the best, the crowds are small and the fish are guaranteed. ⊠ *Farrington Hwy., 1 mile west of Ko Olina Resort, Kapolei.*

Hanauma Bay Nature Preserve. What Waimea Bay is to surfing, Hanauma Bay in Southeast Oahu is to snorkeling. Easily the most popular snorkeling spot on the island, it's home to more than 250 different species of marine life. Due to the protection of the narrow mouth of the cove and the prodigious reef, you will be hard-pressed to find a place you will feel safer while snorkeling. ⊠ *7455 Kalanianaole Hwy., Honolulu* ☎ *808/396–4229.*

EQUIPMENT AND TOURS

Snorkel Bob's. This place has all the stuff you'll need—and more—to make your water adventures more enjoyable. Bob makes his own gear and is active in protecting reef fish species. Feel free to ask the staff about good snorkeling spots, as the best ones can vary with weather and the seasons. ⊠ *700 Kapahulu Ave., Kapahulu, Honolulu* ☎ *808/735–7944* ⊕ *www.snorkelbob.com.*

SUBMARINE TOURS

Atlantis Submarines. This is the underwater adventure for the unadventurous. Not fond of swimming, but want to see what you've been missing? Board this 64-passenger vessel for a ride past shipwrecks, turtle breeding grounds, and coral reefs. The tours, which depart from the pier at the Hilton Hawaiian Village, are available in several languages. A smaller 48-passenger boat with underwater viewing windows is a bit cheaper than the submarine trip. ⊠ *Hilton Hawaiian Village Beach Resort and Spa, 2005 Kalia Rd., Honolulu* ☎ *808/973–1296, 800/548–6262* ⊕ *www.atlantisadventures.com* ⊠ *From $119.*

STAND-UP PADDLING

From the lakes of Wisconsin to the coast of Lima, Peru, stand-up paddling (or SUP, for short) is taking the sport of surfing to the most unexpected places. Still, the sport remains firmly rooted in the Hawaiian Islands.

Back in the 1960s, Waikiki beach boys would paddle out on their long boards using a modified canoe paddle. It was longer than a traditional paddle, enabling them to stand up and stroke. It was easier this way to survey the ocean and snap photos of tourists learning how to surf. Eventually it became a sport unto itself, with professional contests at world-class surf breaks and long-distance races across treacherous waters.

Stand-up paddling is easy to learn—though riding waves takes some practice—and most outfitters on Oahu offer lessons for all skill levels. It's also a great workout; you can burn off yesterday's dinner buffet, strengthen your core, and experience the natural beauty of the island's coastline all at once.

If you're looking to learn, go where there's already an SUP presence. Avoid popular surf breaks, unless you're an experienced stand-up paddle surfer, and be wary of ocean and wind conditions. You'll want to

Stand-up paddling has become one of Hawaii's most popular water activities.

find a spot with calm waters, easy access in and out of the ocean, and a friendly crowd that doesn't mind the occasional stand-up paddler.

BEST SPOTS

Ala Moana Beach Park. About a mile west of Waikiki, Ala Moana is the most SUP-friendly spot on the island. In fact, the state installed a series of buoys in the flat-water lagoon to separate stand-up paddlers and swimmers. There are no waves here, making it a great spot to learn, but beware of strong trade winds, which can push you into the reef.

Waikiki. There are a number of outfitters on Oahu's south shore that take beginners into the waters off Waikiki. **Canoes,** the surf break fronting the Duke Kahanamoku statue, and the channels between breaks are often suitable for people learning how to maneuver their boards in not-so-flat conditions. But south swells here can be deceptively menacing, and ocean conditions can change quickly. Check with lifeguards before paddling out and be mindful of other surfers in the water.

EQUIPMENT AND LESSONS

Hawaiian Watersports. Paddle in the picturesque Kailua Bay or in the waters off Waikiki with Hawaiian Watersports. Two-hour lessons are offered in groups or in one-on-one sessions. Look for deals on the website. Half-day rentals are also available. There's also a branch in Kailua. ✉ *415 Kapahulu Ave., Waikiki, Honolulu* ☎ *808/262–5483, 808/739–5483* ⊕ *www.hawaiianwatersports.com* 🖥 *Rentals from $49, lessons from $99.*

Paddle Core Fitness. Paddling is a way of life for Reid Inouye, who now shares his passion for the sport with students. (He's also the publisher of *Standup Paddle Magazine.*) His company offers introductory classes as well as fitness programs for serious paddlers. Lesssons are held in the flat waters of Ala Moana Beach, where there's a designated area for paddling, and you can have either group or private lessons. ✉ *Ala Moana Beach Park, Ala Moana Blvd., Ala Moana, Honolulu* ☎ *808/385–0717* ⊕ *www.paddlecorefitness.com* ✉ *Lessons from $50.*

SURFING

Perhaps no word is more associated with Hawaii than surfing. Every year the best of the best gather on Oahu's North Shore to compete in their version of the Super Bowl: the prestigious Vans Triple Crown of Surfing. The pros dominate the waves for a month, but the rest of the year belongs to folks just trying to have fun.

Oahu is unique because it has so many famous spots: Banzai Pipeline, Waimea Bay, Kaiser Bowls, and Sunset Beach. But the island also has miles of coastline with surf spots that are perfect for everyday surfers. But remember this surfer's credo: when in doubt, don't go out. If you're unsure about conditions, stay on the beach.

BEST SPOTS

Makaha Beach Park. If you like to ride waves, try Makaha Beach on Oahu's west side. It has legendary, interminable rights that allow riders to perform all manner of stunts: from six-man canoes with everyone doing headstands to bully boards (oversize bodyboards) with whole families along for the ride. Mainly known as a longboarding spot, it's predominantly local but respectful to outsiders. Use caution in the winter, as the surf can get huge. It's not called Makaha—which means "fierce"—for nothing. ✉ *84-369 Farrington Hwy., Waianae.*

Ulukou Beach. In Waikiki you can paddle out to **Populars,** a break at Ulukou Beach. Nice and easy, Populars—or Pops—never breaks too hard and is friendly to both newbies and veterans. It's one of the best places to surf during pumping south swells, as this thick wave breaks in open ocean, making it more rideable. The only downside is the long paddle out to the break from Kuhio Beach, but that keeps the crowds manageable. ✉ *Waikiki Beach, in front of the Sheraton Waikiki hotel, Honolulu.*

EQUIPMENT AND LESSONS

Aloha Beach Services. It may sound like a cliché, but there's no better way to learn to surf than from a beach boy in Waikiki. And there's no one better than Harry "Didi" Robello, a second-generation beach boy and owner of Aloha Beach Services. Learn to surf in an hour-long group lesson, a semiprivate lesson, or with just you and an instructor. You can also rent a board here. ✉ *2365 Kalakaua Ave., on the beach near the Moana Surfrider, Waikiki, Honolulu* ☎ *808/922–3111* ⊕ *www.alohabeachservices.com* ✉ *Lessons from $40, board rentals from $15.*

Faith Surf School. Professional surfer Tony Moniz started his own surf school in 2000, and since then he and his wife Tammy have helped thousands of people catch their first waves in Waikiki. The 90-minute group lessons include all equipment and are the cheapest option. You can pay more (sometimes a lot more) for semiprivate lessons with up to three people or private lessons. You can also book an all-day surf tour with Moniz, riding waves with him at his favorite breaks. ⊠ *Sheraton Waikiki, 2255 Kalakaua Ave., Waikiki, Honolulu* ☎ *808/931–6262* ⊕ *www.faithsurfschool.com* ✉ *From $50.*

FAMILY **Hawaiian Fire.** Learn how to surf from some of Hawaii's most knowledgeable water-safety experts at this school, owned and operated by Honolulu firefighters. Lessons include 45 minutes of ocean safety instruction and 75 minutes in the water at a secluded beach near Barbers Point. Transportation is available to and from the Ko Olina area only. Both cheaper group lessons and private lessons are offered. A great option for kids ages seven and up. ⊠ *Ko Olina Resorts, 92-1047 Olani St., Suite 1-109, Kapolei* ☎ *808/737–3473* ⊕ *www.hawaiianfire. com* ✉ *From $119.*

Surf 'N Sea. This is a one-stop shop for surfers (and other water-sports enthusiasts) on the North Shore. Rent a shortboard by the hour or for a full day. Three-hour group lessons are offered, as well as surf safaris for experienced surfers, which can last between four to five hours. ⊠ *62-595 Kamehameha Hwy., Haleiwa* ☎ *800/899–7873, 808/637-9887* ⊕ *www.surfnsea.com* ✉ *Lessons from $85; rentals from $5 per hour.*

WHALE-WATCHING

November is marked by the arrival of snow in much of America, but in Hawaii it marks the return of the humpback whale. These migrating behemoths move south from their North Pacific homes during the winter months for courtship and calving, and they put on quite a show. Watching males and females alike throwing themselves out of the ocean and into the sunset awes even the saltiest of sailors. Newborn calves riding gently next to their 2-ton mothers will stir you to your core. These gentle giants can be seen from the shore as they make a splash, but there is nothing like having your boat rocking beneath you in the wake of a whale's breach.

Wild Side Specialty Tours. Boasting a marine-biologist crew, this company takes you to undisturbed snorkeling areas. Along the way you may see dolphins and turtles. The company promises a sighting of migrating whales year-round on some itineraries. Tours may depart as early as 8 am from Waianae, so it's important to plan ahead. The three-hour deluxe wildlife tour is the most popular option. ⊠ *Waianae Boat Harbor, 87-1286 Farrington Hwy., Waianae* ☎ *808/306–7273* ⊕ *www. sailhawaii.com* ✉ *From $175.*

WINDSURFING AND KITEBOARDING

Those who call windsurfing and kiteboarding cheating because they require no paddling have never tried hanging on to a sail or kite. It will turn your arms to spaghetti quicker than paddling ever could, and the speeds you generate earn these sports the label of "extreme."

Windsurfing was born here in the Islands. For amateurs, the windward side is best because the onshore breezes will bring you back to land even if you don't know what you're doing. The newer sport of kiteboarding is tougher but more exhilarating, as the kite will sometimes take you in the air for hundreds of feet. We suggest only those in top shape try the kites, but windsurfing is fun for all ages.

EQUIPMENT

Kailua Sailboards and Kayaks. Within walking distance of Kailua Beach, this outfitter offers everything you'll need for a day on the water including kayak and stand-up paddleboarding lessons, rentals, and guided tours. Kayak rentals start at $59 for a single for a half-day or $69 for 24 hours. Double kayaks run $10 more. Guided kayak tours start at $129. ⊠ *Kailua Beach Center, 130 Kailua Rd., Kailua* ☎ *808/262–2555* ⊕ *www.kailuasailboards.com.*

GOLF, HIKING, AND OUTDOOR ACTIVITIES

Updated by Trina Kudlacek

Although much is written about the water surrounding this little rock known as Oahu, there is as much to be said for the rock itself. It's a wonder of nature, thrust from the ocean floor thousands of millennia ago by a volcanic hot spot that is still spitting out islands today. Hawaii is the most remote island chain on earth, and there are creatures and plants that can be seen here and nowhere else. And there are dozens of ways for you to check them all out.

AERIAL TOURS

Taking an aerial tour of the Islands opens up a world of perspective. Look down from the sky at the outline of the USS *Arizona* where it lies in its final resting place below the waters of Pearl Harbor, or get a glimpse of the vast carved expanse of a volcanic crater—here are views only seen by an "eye in the sky." Don't forget your camera.

Blue Hawaiian Helicopters. This company stakes its claim as Hawaii's largest copter company, with tours on all the major islands and more than two dozen choppers in its fleet. The 45-minute Oahu tour seats up to 12 passengers and includes narration from your friendly pilot along with sweeping views of Waikiki, the beautiful Windward Coast, and the North Shore. If you like to see the world from above or are just pinched for time and want to get a quick overview of the whole island without renting a car, this is the way to go. ⊠ *99 Kaulele Pl., Honolulu* ☎ *808/831–8800* ⊕ *www.bluehawaiian.com* 🖭 *From $233.*

Island Seaplane Service. Harking back to the days of the earliest air visitors to Hawaii, the seaplane has always had a special spot in island lore. The only seaplane service still operating in Hawaii takes off from Keehi Lagoon. Flight options are either a half-hour south and eastern Oahu shoreline tour or an hour-long island circle tour. The *Pan Am Clipper* may be gone, but you can revisit the experience with this company. ⊠ *85 Lagoon Dr., Honolulu* ☎ *808/836–6273* ⊕ *www.islandseaplane. com* 🖭 *From $169.*

Makani Kai Helicopters. This may be the best way to see the beautiful Sacred Falls on the windward side of the island, as the park around the falls was closed to hikers after a deadly 1999 rock slide. Makani Kai

Take a helicopter tour for a unique perspective of the island.

dips the helicopter down to show you one of Hawaii's former favorite trails and the pristine waterfall it leads to. Tours can last either a half-or full hour. Customized private charters are available for up to six passengers. ✉ *130 Iolana Pl., Honolulu* ☎ *808/834–5813* ⊕ *www.makanikai.com* ✉ *From $170.*

The Original Glider Rides. "Mr. Bill" has been offering piloted glider (sailplane) rides over the northwest end of Oahu's North Shore since 1970. Choose from piloted scenic rides for one or two passengers in sleek, bubble-top, motorless aircraft with aerial views of mountains, shoreline, coral pools, windsurfing sails, and, in winter, humpback whales. Seeking more thrills? You can also take a more acrobatic ride or take control yourself in a "mini lesson." Flights range from 15 to 60 minutes long and depart continuously from 10 to 5 daily. ✉ *Dillingham Airfield, 69-132 Farrington Hwy., Waialua* ☎ *808/677–3404* ⊕ *www.honolulusoaring.com* ✉ *From $79.*

GOLF

Unlike on the Neighbor Islands, the majority of Oahu's golf courses are not associated with hotels and resorts. In fact, of the island's three-dozen-plus courses, only five are tied to lodging.

Municipal courses are a good choice for budget-conscious golfers. Your best bet is to call the day you want to play and inquire about walk-on availability. Greens fees are standard at city courses: walking rate, $49 for visitors; riding cart $20 for 18 holes; pull carts $4.

Greens fees listed here are the highest course rates per round on weekdays and weekends for U.S. residents. (Some courses charge non-U.S. residents higher prices.) Discounts are often available for resort guests and for those who book tee times online. Twilight fees are usually offered; call individual courses for information.

WAIKIKI

Ala Wai Municipal Golf Course. Just across the Ala Wai Canal from Waikiki, this municipal golf course is said to host more rounds than any other U.S. course—up to 500 per day. Not that it's a great course, just really convenient. Although residents can obtain a city golf card that allows automated tee-time reservation over the phone, the best bet for a visitor is to show up and expect to wait at least an hour. The course itself is flat. Robin Nelson did some redesign work in the 1990s, adding mounding, trees, and a lake. The Ala Wai Canal comes into play on several holes on the back nine, including the treacherous 18th. There's also an on-site restaurant and bar. ⊠ *404 Kapahulu Ave., Waikiki, Honolulu* ☎ *808/733–7387 starter's office, 808/738–4652 golf shop* ⊕ *www1.honolulu.gov/des/golf/alawai.htm* ⊟ *$55* ⅃ *18 holes, 5861 yards, par 70.*

SOUTHEAST OAHU

Hawaii Kai Golf Course. The Championship Golf Course (William F. Bell, 1973) winds through a Honolulu suburb at the foot of Koko Crater. Homes (and the liability of a broken window) come into play on many holes, but they are offset by views of the nearby Pacific and a crafty routing of holes. With several lakes, lots of trees, and bunkers in all the wrong places, Hawaii Kai really is a "championship" golf course, especially when the trade winds howl. The **Executive Course** (1962), a par-55 track, is the first of only three courses in Hawaii built by Robert Trent Jones Sr. Although a few changes have been made to his original design, you can find the usual Jones attributes, including raised greens and lots of risk-reward options. Greens fees include cart. ⊠ *8902 Kalanianaole Hwy., Hawaii Kai* ☎ *808/395–2358* ⊕ *www. hawaiikaigolf.com* ⊟ *$110 for Championship Course; $39 for Executive Course* ⅃ *Championship Course: 18 holes, 6222 yards, par 72; Executive Course: 18 holes, 2223 yards, par 54.*

WINDWARD OAHU

Koolau Golf Club. Koolau Golf Club is marketed as the toughest golf course in Hawaii and one of the most challenging in the country. Dick Nugent and Jack Tuthill (1992) routed 10 holes over jungle ravines that require at least a 110-yard carry. The par-4 18th may be the most difficult closing hole in golf. The tee shot from the regular tees must carry 200 yards of ravine, 250 from the blue tees. The approach shot is back across the ravine, 200 yards to a well-bunkered green. Set at the windward base of the Koolau Mountains, the course is as much beauty as beast. Kaneohe Bay is visible from most holes, orchids and yellow ginger bloom, the shama thrush (Hawaii's best singer since Don Ho) chirps, and waterfalls flute down the sheer, green mountains above. Greens fee includes cart. ⊠ *45-550 Kionaole Rd., Kaneohe* ☎ *808/236–4653* ⊕ *www.koolaugolfclub.com* ⊟ *$145* ⅃ *18 holes, 6406 yards, par 72.*

Olomana Golf Links. Bob and Robert L. Baldock are the architects of record for this layout, but so much has changed since it opened in 1969 that they would recognize little of it. A turf specialist was brought in to improve fairways and greens, tees were rebuilt, new bunkers added, and mangroves cut back to make better use of natural wetlands. But what really puts Olomana on the map is that this is where wunderkind Michelle Wie learned the game. ✉ *41-1801 Kalanianaole Hwy., Waimanalo* ☎ *808/259–7926* ⊕ *www.olomanagolflinks.com* 💳 *$59 for 9 holes, $95 for 18 holes* ⛳ *18 holes, 5896 yards, par 72.*

Fodor's Choice **Royal Hawaiian Golf Club.** In the cool, lush Maunawili Valley, Pete and
★   Perry Dye created what can only be called target jungle golf. In other words, the rough is usually dense jungle, and you may not hit a driver on three of the four par-5s, or several par-4s, including the perilous 18th that plays off a cliff to a narrow green protected by a creek. Mt. Olomana's twin peaks tower over the course. ■TIP➜ **The back nine wanders deep into the valley, and includes an island green (par-3 11th) and perhaps the loveliest inland hole in Hawaii (par-4 12th).** ✉ *770 Auloa Rd., at Luana Hills Rd., Kailua* ☎ *808/262–2139* ⊕ *www. royalhawaiiangolfclub.com* 💳 *$155* ⛳ *18 holes, 6609 yards, par 72.*

NORTH SHORE

Turtle Bay Resort & Spa. When the Lazarus of golf courses, the **Fazio Course** at Turtle Bay (George Fazio, 1971), rose from the dead in 2002, Turtle Bay on Oahu's rugged North Shore became a premier golf destination. Two holes had been plowed under when the **Palmer Course** at Turtle Bay (Arnold Palmer and Ed Seay, 1992) was built, while the other seven lay fallow, and the front nine remained open. Then new owners came along and re-created holes 13 and 14 using Fazio's original plans, and the Fazio became whole again. It's a terrific track with 90 bunkers. The gem at Turtle Bay, though, is the Palmer Course. The front nine is mostly open as it skirts Punahoolapa Marsh, a nature sanctuary, while the back nine plunges into the wetlands and winds along the coast. The short par-4 17th runs along the rocky shore, with a diabolical string of bunkers cutting diagonally across the fairway from tee to green. ✉ *57-049 Kuilima Dr., Kahuku* ☎ *808/293–8574* ⊕ *www.turtlebaygolf.com* 💳 *Fazio Course, $115 for 18 holes, $75 for 9 holes; Palmer Course, $185* ⛳ *Fazio Course: 18 holes, 6769 yards, par 72; Palmer Course: 18 holes, 6795 yards, par 72.*

CENTRAL OAHU

Royal Kunia Country Club. At one time the PGA Tour considered buying Royal Kunia Country Club and hosting the Sony Open there. It's that good. ■TIP➜ **Every hole offers fabulous views from Diamond Head to Pearl Harbor to the nearby Waianae Mountains.** Robin Nelson's eye for natural sight lines and dexterity with water features adds to the visual pleasure. ✉ *94-1509 Anonui St., Waipahu* ☎ *808/688–9222* ⊕ *www. royalkuniacc.com* 💳 *$150* ⛳ *18 holes, 6507 yards, par 72.*

Waikele Country Club. Outlet stores are not the only bargain at Waikele. The adjacent golf course is a daily-fee course that offers a private clublike atmosphere and a terrific Ted Robinson (1992) layout. The target off the tee is Diamond Head, with Pearl Harbor to the right.

Robinson's water features are less distinctive here but define the short par-4 fourth hole, with a lake running down the left side of the fairway and guarding the green; and the par-3 17th, which plays across a lake. The par-4 18th is a terrific closing hole, with a lake lurking on the right side of the green. ☒ *94-200 Paioa Pl., Waipahu* ☏ *808/676–9000* ⊕ *www.golfwaikele.com* ✉ *$130* ⅄ *18 holes, 6261 yards, par 72.*

WEST (LEEWARD) OAHU

Coral Creek Golf Course. On the Ewa Plain, 4 miles inland, Coral Creek is cut from ancient coral—left from when this area was still underwater. Robin Nelson (1999) does some of his best work in making use of the coral, and of some dynamite, blasting out portions to create dramatic lakes and tee and green sites. They could just as easily call it Coral Cliffs, because of the 30- to 40-foot cliffs Nelson created. They include the par-3 10th green's grotto and waterfall, and the vertical drop-off on the right side of the par-4 18th green. An ancient creek meanders across the course, but there's not much water, just enough to be a babbling nuisance. ☒ *91-1111 Geiger Rd., Ewa Beach* ☏ *808/441–4653* ⊕ *www.coralcreekgolfhawaii.com* ✉ *$140* ⅄ *18 holes, 6810 yds, par 72.*

Ko Olina Golf Club. Hawaii's golden age of golf-course architecture came to Oahu when Ko Olina Golf Club opened in 1989. Ted Robinson, king of the water features, went splash-happy here, creating nine lakes that come into play on eight holes, including the par-3 12th, where you reach the tee by driving behind a Disney-like waterfall. Tactically, though, the most dramatic is the par-4 18th, where the approach is a minimum 120 yards across a lake to a two-tiered green guarded on the left by a cascading waterfall. Today, Ko Olina, affiliated with the adjacent Ihilani Resort and Spa (guests receive discounted rates), has matured into one of Hawaii's top courses. You can niggle about routing issues—the first three holes play into the trade winds (and the morning sun), and two consecutive par-5s on the back nine play into the trades—but Robinson does enough solid design to make those of passing concern. ■ **TIP→ The course provides free transportation from Waikiki hotels.** ☒ *92-1220 Aliinui Dr., Kapolei* ☏ *808/676–5300* ⊕ *www.koolinagolf.com* ✉ *$89 for 9 holes; $189 for 18 holes* ⅄ *18 holes, 6432 yards, par 72.*

HIKING

The trails of Oahu cover a full spectrum of environments: desert walks through cactus, slippery paths through bamboo-filled rain forest, and scrambling rock climbs up ancient volcanic calderas. The only thing you won't find is an overnighter, as even the longest of hikes won't take you more than half a day. In addition to being short in length, many of

the prime hikes are within 10 minutes of downtown Waikiki, meaning that you won't have to spend your whole day getting back to nature.

BEST SPOTS

Diamond Head Crater. Every vacation has requirements that must be fulfilled so that when your neighbors ask, you can say, "Yeah, did it." Climbing Diamond Head is high on that list of things to do on Oahu. It's a moderately easy hike if you're in good physical condition, but be prepared to climb many stairs along the way. Be sure to bring a water bottle because it's hot and dry. Only a mile up, a clearly marked trail with handrails scales the inside of this extinct volcano. At the top, the fabled final 99 steps take you up to the pillbox overlooking the Pacific Ocean and Honolulu. It's a breathtaking view and a lot cheaper than taking a helicopter ride for the same photo op. Last entry for hikers is 4:30 pm. ⊠ *Diamond Head Rd. at 18th Ave., Honolulu ⊹ Enter on the east side of the crater; there's limited parking inside, so most park on street and walk in ⊕ www.hawaiistateparks.org/hiking/oahu* ⊠ *$1 per person; $5 to park* ⊙ *Daily 6–6.*

Fodor's Choice ★ **Kaena Point Trail.** This hike is a little longer (a 5-mile round-trip) and both hotter and more exposed than the Makapuu Lighthouse Trail, but it is right next to the beach, and there are spots where you can get in and cool off. Sea-carved cliffs give way to lava-rock beaches and sea arches. Halfway to the point, there is a double blowhole, which is a good indicator of sea conditions. If it is blowing good, stay out of the water. Though the area is hot and dry, there is still much wildlife here, as it is the only nesting ground for many rare sea birds. ■TIP→ **Keep a lookout for the Laysan albatrosses; these enormous birds have recently returned to the area. Don't be surprised if they come in for a closer look at you, too.** There has been a cave-in of an old lava tube, so be careful when crossing it, but enjoy the view in its enormous mouth. ⊠ *81-780 Farrington Hwy, Waianae ⊹ Take Farrington Hwy. to its end at Yoko-hamas. Hike in on the old 4WD trail.*

Fodor's Choice ★ **Manoa Falls Trail.** Travel up into the valley beyond Honolulu to make the Manoa Falls hike. Though only a mile long, this well-trafficked path—visited by an estimated 100,000 hikers a year—passes through so many different ecosystems that you feel as if you're in an arboretum—and you're not far off. (The beautiful Lyon Arboretum is right near the trail-head, if you want to make another stop.) Walk among the elephant ear ape plants, ruddy fir trees, and a bamboo forest straight out of China. At the top is a 150-foot waterfall, which can be an impressive cascade, or, if rain has been sparse, the falls can be little more than a trickle. This hike is more about the journey than the destination; make sure you bring some mosquito repellent because they grow 'em big up here. ⊠ *3998 Manoa Rd., Manoa, Honolulu ⊹ West Manoa Rd. is behind Manoa Valley in Paradise Park. Take West Manoa Rd. to end, park on side of road or in the parking lot for a small fee, and follow trail signs in.*

Makapuu Lighthouse Trail. For the less adventurous hiker and anyone look-ing for a great view, this paved trail that runs up the side of Makapuu Point in Southeast Oahu fits the bill. Early on, the trail is surrounded by lava rock but, as you ascend, foliage—the tiny white *koa haole* flower and the cream-tinged spikes of the *kiawe*—begins taking over the barren rock. At the easternmost tip of Oahu, where the island divides the sea, this trail gives you a spectacular view of the cobalt ocean meeting the land in a cacophony of white caps. To the south are several tide pools and the lighthouse, while the eastern view looks down upon Rabbit and Kaohikaipu islands, two bird sanctuaries just off the coast. The 2-mile round-trip hike is a great break on a circle-island trip. ■**TIP→ Be sure not to leave valuables in your car as break-ins are common.** ⊠ *Makapuu Lighthouse Rd., Honolulu ⚓ Take Kalanianaole Hwy. to base of Makapuu Point. Look for asphalt strip snaking up mountain.*

GOING WITH A GUIDE

FAMILY **Hawaii Nature Center.** A good choice for families, the center in upper Makiki Valley conducts a number of programs for both adults and children. There are guided hikes into tropical settings that reveal hidden waterfalls and protected forest reserves. They don't run tours every day so it's a good idea to get advance reservations. ⊠ *2131 Makiki Heights Dr., Makiki Heights, Honolulu* ☎ *808/955–0100* ⊕ *www. hawaiinaturecenter.org.*

Oahu Nature Tours. Guides explain the native flora and fauna and history that are your companions on their Manoa Waterfall, Mountain Rainforest, and Diamond Head walking tours. Tours include pick-up at centralized Waikiki locations. ☎ *808/924–2473* ⊕ *www.oahunaturetours. com.*

HORSEBACK RIDING

A great way to see the island is atop a horse, leaving the direction to the pack while you drink in the views of mountains or the ocean. It may seem like a cliché, but there really is nothing like riding a horse down a stretch of beach to put you in a romantic state of mind.

FAMILY **Happy Trails Hawaii.** Take a guided horseback ride above the North Shore's Waimea Bay along trails that offer panoramic views from Kaena Point to the famous surfing spots. Specializing in families, they have groups of no more than 10 and provide instruction. Children 6 and older are welcome. You can take either a 90-minute or 2-hour ride. Reservations are required. ⊠ *59-231 Pupukea Rd., Pupukea ⚓ Go 1 mile mauka (toward the mountain) up Pupakea Rd. The office is on the right* ☎ *808/638–7433* ⊕ *happytrailshawaii.com* 💲 *From $80.*

FAMILY **Kualoa Ranch.** This ranch across from Kualoa Beach Park on the windward side leads trail rides in the Kaaawa Valley. The most basic offering is a one-hour trail ride. Kualoa has other activities such as bus and Jeep tours, all-terrain-vehicle trail rides, and children's activities, which may be combined for half- or full-day package rates. ⊠ *49-560 Kamehameha Hwy., Kaneohe* ☎ *800/231-7321* ⊕ *www.kualoa.com* 💲 *From $69.*

Turtle Bay Stables. Trail rides follow the coast line and even step out onto sandy beaches. The stables here are part of the North Shore resort but can be utilized by nonguests. The sunset ride is a definite must if you are a friend of our four-legged friends. A basic trail ride lasts 45 minutes. ⊠ *Turtle Bay Resort, 57-091 Kamehemeha Hwy., Kahuku*

☎ *808/293–6024* ⊕ *www.turtlebayresort.com/experiences/outdoor_activities/horseback_riding/* 🏷 *From $70.*

SHOPPING

Updated by
Chris Oliver

Eastern and Western traditions meet on Oahu, where savvy shoppers find luxury goods at high-end malls and scout tiny boutiques and galleries filled with pottery, blown glass, woodwork, and Hawaiian-print clothing by local artists.

Exploring downtown Honolulu, Kailua on the windward side, and the North Shore often yields the most original merchandise. Some of the small stores carry imported clothes and gifts from around the world—a reminder that, on this island halfway between Asia and the United States, shopping is a multicultural experience.

HONOLULU

WAIKIKI

SHOPPING CENTERS

DFS Galleria Waikiki. Hermès, Cartier, Michael Kors, and Marc Jacobs are among the shops on the Waikiki Luxury Walk in this enclosed mall, as well as Hawaii's largest beauty and cosmetic store. The third floor caters to duty-free shoppers only and features an exclusive Watch Shop. The Kalia Grill and Starbucks offer a respite for weary shoppers. ✉ *330 Royal Hawaiian Ave., Waikiki* ☎ *808/931–2700* ⊕ *www.dfsgalleria.com.*

Royal Hawaiian Center. An open and inviting facade has made this three-block-long shopping center a garden of Hawaiian shops. There are more than 100 stores and restaurants, including local gems such as Aloha Aina Boutique, Honolulu Home Collection, and Koi Boutique. Check out tropical Panama hats at Hawaiian Island Arts, or offerings at Island Soap & Candleworks while Bob's Ukulele may inspire musicians to learn a new instrument. Nine restaurants round out the dining options, along with the Paina Lanai Food Court, the Five-O Bar & Lounge, plus a theater and nightly outdoor entertainment. ✉ *2201 Kalakaua Ave., Waikiki* ☎ *808/922–0588* ⊕ *www.royalhawaiiancenter.com.*

2100 Kalakaua. Tenants of this elegant, town house–style center known as "Luxury Row" include Chanel, Coach, Tiffany & Co., Yves Saint Laurent, Bottega Veneta, Gucci, Hugo Boss, and Tod's. ✉ *2100 Kalakaua Ave., Waikiki* ⊕ *www.2100kalakaua.com.*

Waikiki Beach Walk. This open-air shopping center greets visitors at the west end of Waikiki's Kalakaua Avenue with 70 locally owned stores and restaurants. Get reasonably priced, fashionable resort wear for yourself at Mahina; find unique pieces by local artists at Under the Koa Tree; or buy local treats from Coco Cove. Or you can browse Koa and sandalwood gifts at Martin & MacArthur in the nearby Outrigger Reef hotel, The mall also features free local entertainment on the outdoor fountain stage at least once a week. ✉ *226 Lewers St., Waikiki* ☎ *808/931–3591* ⊕ *www.waikikibeachwalk.com.*

CLOTHING

Newt at the Royal. Newt is known for high-quality, hand-woven Panama hats and tropical sportswear for men and women. ⊠ *The Royal Hawaiian Hotel, 2259 Kalakaua Ave., Waikiki* ☏ *808/949–4321* ⊕ *www.newtattheroyal.com.*

GIFTS

Sand People. This little shop stocks beach-inspired, easy-to-carry gifts, such as fish-shaped Christmas ornaments, Hawaiian-style notepads, frames, charms in the shape of flip-flops (known locally as "slippahs"), soaps, kitchen accessories, and ceramic clocks. There's another branch in Kailua as well as three each on Kauai and Maui. ⊠ *Moana Surfrider, 2369 Kalakaua, Waikiki* ☏ *808/924–6773* ⊕ *www.sandpeople.com.*

JEWELRY

Philip Rickard. The heirloom design collection of this famed jeweler features custom Hawaiian jewelry, particularly its Wedding Collection often sought by various celebrities. Visitors to the factory and showroom in Ala Moana may watch jewelers and craftsmen designing, engraving, and polishing their work. ⊠ *Ala Moana Shopping Center, 1450 Ala Moana Blvd., Ala Moana* ☏ *808/946-6720* ⊕ *www.philiprickard.com.*

DOWNTOWN

Downtown shopping is an entirely different, constantly changing experience from what you'll find elsewhere in Honolulu. Focus on the small galleries—which are earning the area a strong reputation for its arts and culture renaissance—and the burgeoning array of hip, home-decor stores tucked between ethnic restaurants. ■TIP→ Don't miss the festive atmosphere on the first Friday of every month, when stores, restaurants, and galleries stay open from 5 pm to 9 pm for the "Downtown Gallery Walk."

SHOPPING CENTERS

Aloha Tower Marketplace. Billing itself as a festival marketplace, Aloha Tower cozies up to Honolulu Harbor. Along with restaurants and entertainment venues, it has about two-dozen shops and kiosks selling mostly visitor-oriented merchandise, from sunglasses to apparel to souvenir refrigerator magnets. To get there from Waikiki take the E-Transit Bus, which goes along TheBus routes every 15 minutes. ⊠ *1 Aloha Tower Dr., at Piers 8, 9, and 10, Downtown Honolulu* ☏ *808/566–2337* ⊕ *www.alohatower.com.*

HOME DECOR

Robyn Buntin Galleries. Chinese antiques, Japanese art, Buddhist sculptures, and important works by Hawaiian artists are among the international pieces sold here as well as jewelry and an extensive selection of prints. The gallery has more than 7,000 items available online. ⊠ *Robyn Buntin Gallery, 848 S. Beretania St., Downtown Honolulu* ☏ *808/523–5913* ⊕ *www.robynbuntin.com.*

CHINATOWN
GALLERIES
Louis Pohl Gallery. Stop in this gallery to browse modern works from some of Hawaii's finest artists. In addition to pieces by resident artists, there are monthly exhibitions by local and visiting artists. ⊠ *1142 Bethel St., Chinatown* ☎ *808/521–1812* ⊕ *www.louispohlgallery.com.*

KAKAAKO
CLOTHING
Anne Namba Designs. This designer combines the beauty of classic kimonos with contemporary styles to make unique pieces for career and evening. In addition to women's apparel, she designs a men's line and a wedding couture line. ⊠ *324 Kamani St., Kakaako* ☎ *808/589–1135* ⊕ *www.annenamba.com.*

ALA MOANA
■ TIP→ Getting to the Ala Moana shopping centers from Waikiki is quick and inexpensive thanks to TheBus and the Waikiki Trolley.

SHOPPING CENTERS
Ala Moana Shopping Center. The world's largest open-air shopping mall is five minutes from Waikiki by bus. More than 240 stores and 60 restaurants make up this 50-acre complex, which is a unique mix of national and international chains as well as smaller, locally owned shops and eateries—and everything in between. Thirty-five luxury boutiques in residence include Gucci, Louis Vuitton, Christian Dior, and Emporio Armani. All of Hawaii's major department stores are here, including the state's only Neiman Marcus and Nordstrom, plus Macy's. To get to the mall from Waikiki, catch TheBus line 8, 19, 20, 23, 24 or 42; a one-way ride is $2.50. Or hop aboard the Waikiki Trolley's Pink Line for $2 each way, which comes through the area every 10 minutes. ⊠ *1450 Ala Moana Blvd., Ala Moana* ☎ *808/955–9517* ⊕ *www. alamoanacenter.com.*

Ward Centers. Heading west from Waikiki toward downtown Honolulu, you'll run into a section of town with five distinct shopping-complex areas; there are more than 80 specialty shops and 40 eateries here. The Ward Entertainment Center features 16 movie theaters, including a state-of-the-art, 3-D, big-screen auditorium. For distinctive Hawaiian gifts, such as locally made muumuu, koa wood products, and Niihau shell necklaces, visit Nohea Gallery, Martin & MacArthur, and Native Books/Na Mea Hawaii. Island Soap and Candle Works makes all of its candles and soaps on-site with Hawaiian flower scents. Take TheBus routes 19, 20, and 42; fare is $2.50 one way. Or hop on the Waikiki Trolley Red Line, which comes through the area every 40 minutes. There also is free parking nearby and a valet service. ⊠ *1050–1200 Ala Moana Blvd., Ala Moana* ☎ *808/591–8411* ⊕ *www.wardcenters.com.*

BOOKS
Native Books/Na Mea Hawaii. In addition to island-style clothing for adults and children, Hawaian cultural items, and unusual artwork such as Niihau shell necklaces, this boutique's book selection covers Hawaiian history and language, and offers children's books set in the Islands.

✉ *Ward Warehouse, 1050 Ala Moana Blvd.* ☎ *808/597–8967* ⊕ *www.nativebookshawaii.com.*

CLOTHING

Reyn Spooner. This clothing store is a good place to buy the aloha-print fashions residents wear. Look for the limited-edition Christmas shirt, a collector's item manufactured each holiday season. Reyn Spooner has eight locations statewide and offers styles for both men and children. ✉ *Ala Moana Shopping Center, 1450 Ala Moana Blvd., Ala Moana* ☎ *808/949–5929* ⊕ *www.reynspooner.com.*

FOOD

Honolulu Chocolate Company. To really impress those back home, pick up a box of gourmet chocolates here. Choose from dozens of flavors of Hawaii, from Kona coffee to macadamia nuts, dipped in fine chocolate. ✉ *Ward Centers, 1200 Ala Moana Blvd., Ala Moana* ☎ *808/591–2997* ⊕ *www.honoluluchocolate.com.*

Longs Drugs. For gift items in bulk, try one of the many outposts of Longs, the perfect place to stock up on chocolate-covered macadamia nuts—at reasonable prices—to carry home. ✉ *Ala Moana Shopping Center, 1450 Ala Moana Blvd., 2nd level, Ala Moana* ☎ *808/941–4433* ⊕ *www.alamoana.com/Stores/Longs-Drugs.*

GALLERIES

Nohea Gallery. This shop is really a gallery representing more than 450 artisans who specialize in koa furniture, bowls, and boxes, as well as art glass and ceramics. Original paintings and prints—all with an island theme—add to the selection. They also carry unique handmade Hawaiian jewelry with ti leaf, maile, and coconut-weave designs. ■TIP→ The koa photo albums in these stores are easy to carry home and make wonderful gifts. ✉ *Ward Warehouse, 1050 Ala Moana Blvd., Ala Moana* ☎ *808/596–0074* ⊕ *www.noheagallery.com.*

GIFTS

Blue Hawaii Lifestyle. The Ala Moana store carries a large selection of locally made products, including soaps, honey, tea, salt, chocolates, art, and CDs. Every item, in fact, is carefully selected from various Hawaii companies, artisans, and farms, from the salt fields of Molokai to the lavender farms on Maui to the single-estate chocolate on Oahu's North Shore. ✉ *Ala Moana shopping Center, 1450 Ala Moana Blvd., Ala Moana* ☎ *808/949–0808* ⊕ *www.bluehawaiilifestyle.com.*

HAWAIIAN ARTS AND CRAFTS

Hawaiian Quilt Collection. Traditional island comforters, wall hangings, pillows, bags, and other Hawaiian-print quilt accessories are the specialty here. There are also three locations in Waikiki hotels. ✉ *Ala Moana Shopping Center, 1450 Ala Moana Blvd., Ala Moana* ☎ *808/946–2233* ⊕ *www.hawaiian-quilts.com.*

Na Hoku. If you look at the wrists of *kamaaina* (local) women, you might see Hawaiian heirloom bracelets fashioned in either gold or silver and engraved in a number of island-inspired designs. Na Hoku sells traditional and modern jewelry in designs that capture the heart of the Hawaiian lifestyle in all its elegant diversity. ✉ *Ala Moana Center, 1450 Ala Moana Blvd., Ala Moana* ☎ *808/946–2100* ⊕ *www.nahoku.com.*

MOILIILI
JEWELRY

Maui Divers Design Center. For a look into the harvesting and design of coral and black pearl jewelry, visit this shop and its adjacent factory near the Ala Moana Shopping Center. ⊠ *1520 Liona St., Moiliili* ☎ *808/946–7979* ⊕ *www.mauidivers.com/tour.*

IWILEI
CLOTHING

Hilo Hattie. Busloads of visitors pour in through the front doors of the world's largest manufacturer of Hawaiian and tropical aloha wear. Once shunned by Honolulu residents for its three-shades-too-bright tourist wear, it has become a favorite source for island gifts, jewelry, macadamia nut and chocolate packages, and clothing for elegant island functions. Free shuttle service is available from Waikiki hotels. ⊠ *700 N. Nimitz Hwy., Iwilei* ☎ *808/535–6500* ⊕ *www.hilohattie.com.*

GREATER HONOLULU

Kapahulu, like many older neighborhoods, should not be judged at first glance. It begins at the Diamond Head end of Waikiki and continues up to the H1 freeway and is full of variety; shops and restaurants are located primarily on Kapahulu Avenue. The upscale residential neighborhood of Kahala, near the slopes of Diamond Head, is 10 minutes by car from Waikiki and has a shopping mall and some gift stores.

SHOPPING CENTERS

Kahala Mall. The upscale residential neighborhood of Kahala, near the slopes of Diamond Head, is 10 minutes by car from Waikiki. The only shopping of note in the area is located at the indoor mall, which has more than 100 stores and restaurants, including Macy's, Reyn Spooner, an Apple store, Island Sole footwear, and T&C Surf. Shops include local and national retailers. Don't miss fashionable boutiques such as **Ohelo Road** (☎ *808/735–5525*), where contemporary clothing for all occasions fills the racks. You can also browse local foods and products at Whole Foods. Eight movie theaters provide post-shopping entertainment. ⊠ *4211 Waialae Ave., Kahala* ☎ *808/732–7736* ⊕ *www. kahalamallcenter.com.*

CLOTHING

Bailey's Antiques & Aloha Shirts. Vintage aloha shirts are the specialty at this kitschy store. Prices range from $3.99 to $8,000 for the 15,000 shirts in stock; thousands of them are used while others come from top designers. The tight space and musty smell are part of the thrift-shop atmosphere. ■ **TIP→** Antiques hunters can also buy old-fashioned postcards, authentic military clothing, funky hats, and denim jeans from the 1950s. ⊠ *517 Kapahulu Ave., Kapahulu* ☎ *808/734–7628* ⊕ *alohashirts.com.*

GIFTS

Island Treasures at the Marina. Popular with local residents, who shop here for gifts that are both unique and within reach of almost every budget, this store's range of goods runs the gamut, from cards costing $1 to a koa table costing $18,000. Next to Zippy's and overlooking the ocean, it carries handmade items including koa wood furniture, ceramics, handbags, toys, jewelry, home accessories, soaps and lotions, and locally made original artwork. It's certainly the most interesting shop in Hawaii Kai's suburban-mall atmosphere. ⊠ *Koko Marina Center, 7192 Kalanianaole Hwy., Hawaii Kai* ☎ *808/396–8827.*

WINDWARD OAHU

Fodor's Choice
★
Bookends. The perfect place to shop for gifts, or just take a break with the family, this independent bookstore feels more like a small-town library, welcoming browsers to linger for hours. The large children's section is filled with toys and books to read. ⊠ *600 Kailua Rd., Kailua* ☎ *808/261–1996.*

Fodor's Choice
★
Global Village. Tucked into a tiny strip mall near Maui Tacos, this boutique features jewelry, clothing, and housewares made by local artists, as well as Hawaiian-style children's clothing and unusual gifts from all over the world. Look for wooden beach signs, placemats made from lauhala and other natural fibers, and accessories you won't find anywhere else. ⊠ *Kailua Village Shops, 539 Kailua Rd., No. 104, Kailua* ☎ *808/262–8183* ⊕ *www.globalvillagehawaii.com.*

Fodor's Choice
★
Under a Hula Moon. Exclusive tabletop items and Pacific home decor, such as shell wreaths, shell night-lights, Hawaiian quilts, frames, and unique one-of-a-kind gifts with an island influence define this eclectic shop. ⊠ *Kailua Shopping Center, 600 Kailua Rd., Kailua* ☎ *808/261–4252* ⊕ *www.hulamoonhawaii.com.*

NORTH SHORE

Global Creations Interiors. Look for Hawaiian bath products, pikake perfume, locally made jewelry, island bedding, and a carefully chosen selection of Hawaiian music CDs. Popular picks include Hawaiian sarongs and island-inspired kitchen items. ⊠ *66-079 Kamehameha Hwy., Haleiwa* ☎ *808/637–1780* ⊕ *www.globalcreationsinteriors.com.*

The Growing Keiki. Frequent visitors return to this store year after year for a fresh supply of original, handpicked, Hawaiian-style clothing for youngsters. ⊠ *66-051 Kamehameha Hwy., Haleiwa* ☎ *808/637–4544* ⊕ *www.thegrowingkeiki.com.*

Fodor's Choice
★
Silver Moon Emporium. The small boutique carries everything from Brighton jewelry and designer wear to fashionable T-shirts, shoes, and handbags. Shoppers get attentive yet casual and personalized service. The stock changes frequently, and there's always something wonderful on sale. No matter what your taste, you'll find something for everyday wear or special occasions. ⊠ *North Shore Marketplace, 66-250 Kamehameha Hwy., Haleiwa* ☎ *808/637–7710* ⊕ *www.silvermoonhawaii. blogspot.com.*

WEST (LEEWARD) OAHU

Aloha Stadium Swap Meet. This thrice-weekly outdoor bazaar attracts hundreds of vendors and even more bargain hunters. Every Hawaiian souvenir imaginable can be found here, from coral shell necklaces to bikinis, as well as a variety of ethnic wares, from Chinese brocade dresses to Japanese pottery. There are also ethnic foods, silk flowers, and luggage in aloha floral prints. Shoppers must wade through the typical sprinkling of used and stolen goods to find value. Wear comfortable shoes, use sunscreen, and bring bottled water. The flea market takes place in the Aloha Stadium parking lot Wednesday and Saturday from 8 to 3; Sunday from 6:30 to 3. Admission is $1 per person ages 12 and up.

Several shuttle companies serve Aloha Stadium for the swap meet, including VIP Shuttle (☎ *808/839–0911*); Reliable Shuttle (☎ *808/924–9292*); and Hawaii Supertransit (☎ *808/841–2928*). The average cost is $12 per person, round-trip. For a cheaper but slower ride, take TheBus (⊕ *www.thebus.org*). ✉ *Aloha Stadium, 99-500 Salt Lake Blvd., Aiea* ☎ *808/486–6704* ⊕ *www.alohastadiumswapmeet.net.*

Waikele Premium Outlets. AIX Armani Exchange, Calvin Klein, Coach Luggage, and Saks Fifth Avenue Outlet anchor this discount destination of around 50 stores. You can take a shuttle from Waikiki for the 30-minute ride to the outlets for $15 round-trip, but the companies do change frequently. Reservations are recommended. ✉ *94-790 Lumiaina St., Waipahu, Waikele* ☎ *808/676–5656* ⊕ *www.premiumoutlets.com.*

SPAS

Updated by
Chris Oliver

Many of Oahu's spas draw from the traditions and resources of the Islands to provide the ultimate in luxury and relaxation. If you're getting a massage at a spa, there's a spiritual element to the *lomilomi* that calms the soul while the muscles release tension. During a hot-stone massage, smooth rocks, taken from the earth with permission from Pele, the goddess of volcanoes, are heated and placed at focal points on the body. Others are covered in oil and rubbed over tired limbs, feeling like powerful fingers. For an alternative, refresh skin with mango scrubs so fragrant they seem edible. Savor the unusual sensation of bamboo tapped against the arches of the feet. Indulge in a scalp massage that makes the entire body tingle. Day spas provide additional options to the self-indulgent services offered in almost every major hotel on the island.

HONOLULU

WAIKIKI

Mandara Spa at the Hilton Hawaiian Village Beach Resort & Spa. From its perch in the Kalia Tower, Mandara Spa, an outpost of the chain that originated in Bali, overlooks the mountains, ocean, and downtown Honolulu. Fresh Hawaiian ingredients and traditional techniques headline an array of treatments. Try an exotic upgrade, such as reflexology or a Balinese body polish. Or relieve achy muscles with a traditional Thai poultice massage. The delicately scented, candlelit foyer can fill up quickly with robe-clad conventioneers, so be sure to make a reservation. There are spa suites for couples, a private infinity pool, and a boutique. ✉ *Hilton Hawaiian Village Beach Resort and Spa, 2005 Kalia Rd., Waikiki* ☎ *808/945–7721* ⊕ *www.mandaraspa.com* ✂ *50-min. massages from $135.*

Na Hoola Spa at the Hyatt Regency Waikiki Resort & Spa. Na Hoola is the premier resort spa in Waikiki, with 16 treatment rooms sprawling across 10,000 square feet and two floors of the Hyatt on Kalakaua Avenue. Arrive early for your treatment to enjoy the postcard views of Waikiki Beach. Four packages identified by Hawaii's native healing plants—noni, kukui, awa, and kalo—combine various body, face, and hair treatments; the spa also has luxurious packages that last three to six hours. The Kele Kele body wrap employs a self-heating mud wrap to release tension and stress. The small exercise room is for use by hotel guests only. ⊠ *Hyatt Regency Waikiki Resort and Spa, 2424 Kalakaua Ave., Waikiki* ☎ *808/923–1234, 808/237–6330 Reservations* ⊕ *www.waikiki.hyatt.com/hyatt/pure/spas* ☞ *50-min. massages from $155.*

Fodor's Choice **SpaHalekulani.** SpaHalekulani mines the traditions and cultures of
★ the Pacific Islands with massages, body, and facial therapies. Try the Samoan Nonu, which uses warm stones and healing nonu gel to relieve muscle tension. The exclusive line of bath and body products is scented by maile, lavender orchid, or coconut passion. Facilities specific to treatment but may include Japanese furo bath or steam shower. ⊠ *Halekulani Hotel, 2199 Kalia Rd., Waikiki* ☎ *808/931–5322* ⊕ *www.halekulani.com/living/spahalekulani* ☞ *55-min. massages from $180.*

The Spa at Trump Waikiki. One of the newest in Waikiki, The Spa at Trump offers private changing and showering areas for each room, creating an environment of uninterrupted relaxation. No matter what treatment you choose, it is inspired by "personal intention," such as purify, balance, heal, revitalize, or calm, to elevate the senses throughout your time there. Don't miss the signature gemstone treatments, which feature products by Shiffa; or treat yourself to a Kate Somerville facial to emerge with younger-looking skin. The Hawaiian pineapple lime exfoliation massage is the most popular, as it is exclusive to this spa. ⊠ *Trump International Hotel Waikiki, 223 Saratoga Rd., Waikiki* ☎ *808/683–7466* ✎ *waikikispa@trumphotels.com* ⊕ *www.trumpwaikikihotel.com* ☞ *80-min. massages from $165.*

ALA MOANA

Hoala Salon and Spa. This Aveda concept spa has everything from Vichy showers to hydrotherapy rooms to customized aromatherapy. Ladies, they'll even touch up your makeup for free before you leave. ⊠ *Ala Moana Shopping Center, 3rd fl., 1450 Ala Moana Blvd.* ☎ *808/947–6141* ⊕ *www.hoalasalonspa.com* ☞ *75-min. massages from $155.*

THE NORTH SHORE

Nalu Kinetic Spa at Turtle Bay Resort. Luxuriate at the ocean's edge in this renovated spa on Oahu's North Shore. Try one of the spa's body wraps, including the lilikoi citrus polish using Hawaiian cane sugar and organic lehua honey in its Vichy shower treatment room. Or book an ashiatsu massage, which utilizes foot pressure to release soft tissue constrictions and improve circulation. There are private spa suites, an outdoor treatment cabana that overlooks the surf, an outdoor exercise studio, and a lounge area and juice bar. ⊠ *Turtle Bay Resort, 57-091 Kamehameha*

Hwy., Kahuku ☎ *808/447–6868* ⊕ *www.turtlebayresort.com/oahu–spa* ☞ *50-min. massages from $150.*

WEST (LEEWARD) OAHU

Fodor's Choice ★ **JW Marriott Ihilani Resort & Spa.** Soak in warm seawater among velvety orchid blossoms at this unique Hawaiian hydrotherapy spa. Thalassotherapy treatments combine underwater jet massage with color therapy and essential oils. Specially designed treatment rooms have a hydrotherapy tub, a Vichy-style shower, and a needle shower with 12 heads. The spa's Ohia Ai Mountain Apple line of natural aromatherapy products uses the essence of the mountain apple fruit in lotions, bath salts, shampoos, and conditioners. ⊠ *JW Marriott Ihilani Resort, 92-1001 Olani St., Ko Olina* ☎ *808/679–3321* ⊕ *www.ihilanispa.com* ☞ *50-min. massages from $145.*

Laniwai Spa at Aulani, A Disney Resort & Spa. Every staff member at this spa, or "cast member," as they call themselves, is extensively trained in Hawaiian culture and history to ensure they are projecting the right *mana*, or energy, in their work. To begin each treatment, you select a special *pohaku* (rock) with words of intent, then cast it into a reflective pool. Choose from about 150 spa therapies, and indulge in Kulu Wai, the only outdoor hydrotherapy garden on Oahu—with private vitality pools, co-ed mineral baths, six different "rain" showers, whirlpool jet spas, and more. ⊠ *Aulani, A Disney Resort & Spa, 92-1185 Aliinui Dr., Ko Olina, Kapolei* ☎ *714/520–7001* ⊕ *resorts.disney.go.com/aulani-hawaii-resort* ☞ *50-min. massages from $165.*

ENTERTAINMENT AND NIGHTLIFE

Updated by James Cave

Many people arrive in Oahu expecting to find white-sand beaches, swaying palm trees, and the kind of picturesque scenery you'd see in postcards. If they think about nightlife at all, it's sunsets over Waikiki.

But Oahu does have an after-dark scene, ranging from torch-lit luau shows to hip bars to sleek nightclubs. Posh bars are found in many of the larger hotels, and smaller neighborhoods hide comfortable local watering holes. Every night of the week you can find musicians in venues from Kailua to Ko Olina—and everywhere in between. Or you can simply walk down Kalakaua Avenue to be entertained by Waikiki's street performers.

And if all-night dancing isn't for you, Oahu boasts a thriving arts and culture scene, with community-theater productions, stand-up comedy, outdoor concerts, film festivals, and chamber-music performances. Major Broadway shows, dance companies, rock stars, and comedians come through the Islands, too. Check local newspapers—the *Honolulu Star-Advertiser, Midweek, Honolulu Weekly*—for the latest events. Websites like ⊕ *www.nonstophonolulu.com* and ⊕ *www.honolulupulse.com* also have great information.

Whether you stay out all night or get up early to catch the morning surf, there's something for everyone on Oahu.

ENTERTAINMENT

DINNER CRUISES AND SHOWS

Dinner cruises depart either from the piers adjacent to the Aloha Tower Marketplace in downtown Honolulu or from Kewalo Basin, near Ala Moana Beach Park, and head along the coast toward Diamond Head. There's usually a buffet-style dinner with a local accent, dancing, drinks, and a sensational sunset. Except as noted, dinner cruises cost approximately $40 to $110, cocktail cruises $25 to $40. Most major credit cards are accepted. In all cases, reservations are essential. Check the websites for savings of up to 15%.

Alii Kai **Catamaran.** Patterned after an ancient Polynesian vessel, this 170-foot catamaran casts off from Aloha Tower with 1,000 passengers. The deluxe dinner cruise has two bars, a huge dinner, and an authentic Polynesian show with dancers, drummers, and chanters. The menu is varied, and the after-dinner show is loud and fun. Cost is around $80. Vegetarian meals are available. ⊠ *Aloha Tower Marketplace, 1 Aloha Tower Dr.* ☎ *808/954–8652, 866/898–2519* ⊕ *www.aliikaicatamaran.com.*

Atlantis Cruises. The sleekly high-tech *Navatek,* designed to sail smoothly in rough waters, powers farther along Waikiki's coastline than its competitors, sailing past Diamond Head. Enjoy sunset dinners or moonlight cruises aboard the 300-passenger boat, feasting on tenderloin or whole Maine lobster. Rates begin at $96 for a bountiful buffet; five-course dinners start at $128. ⊠ *Aloha Tower Marketplace, 1 Aloha Tower Rd., Pier 6* ☎ *808/973–1311, 800/548–6262* ⊕ *www.atlantisadventures.com.*

Creation: A Polynesian Journey. A daring Samoan fire-knife dancer is the highlight of this show that traces Hawaii's culture and history from its origins of discovery to statehood. The buffet dinner is priced at $110; a sit-down dinner with steak and lobster is $160. You can also choose to see the show without dinner for $65. ⊠ *Ainahau Showroom, Sheraton Princess Kaiulani Hotel, 120 Kaiulani Ave.* ☎ *808/931–4660* ⊕ *www.creationshow.com* ☉ *Tues. and Thurs.–Sun. at 7:15pm.*

Magic of Polynesia. Hawaii's top illusionist, John Hirokawa, displays mystifying sleight of hand in this highly entertaining show, which incorporates contemporary hula and island music into its acts. It's held in the Holiday Inn Waikiki's $7.5 million showroom. Reservations are required for dinner and the show; a teriyaki short rib dinner starts at $80, while a deluxe steak and lobster dinner is $144. Walk-ups are permitted if you just want the entertainment for $55. ⊠ *Holiday Inn Waikiki Beachcomber Hotel, 2300 Kalakaua Ave., Waikiki* ☎ *808/971–4321, 866/898–2519* ⊕ *www.magicofpolynesia.com* ☉ *Nightly at 8.*

LUAU

The luau is an experience that everyone, both local and tourist, should have. Today's luau still offer traditional foods and entertainment, but there's often a fun, contemporary flair. With many, you can watch the roasted pig being carried out of its *imu,* a hole in the ground used for cooking meat with heated stones.

Luau average around $100 per person—some are cheaper, others twice that amount—and are held around the island, not just in Waikiki. Reservations—and a camera—are a must.

Fia Fia Luau. Just after sunset at the Marriott Ko Olina Beach Club, the charismatic Chief Sielu Avea leads the Samoan-based Fia Fia, an entertaining show that takes guests on the journey through the South Pacific. Every show is different and unscripted, but always a good look at Polynesian culture. It's the only recurring show with eight fire-knife dancers in a blazing finale. Admission costs $95 and includes a buffet. ⊠ 92-161 Waipahe Place, Kapolei ☏ 808/679–4700, 888/236–2427 ⊙ Tuesdays at 4:30.

Germaine's Luau. More than 3 million visitors have come to this luau, held about 45 minutes west of Waikiki in light traffic. Widely considered one of the most folksy and laid-back, Germaine's offers a tasty, multicourse, all-you-can-eat buffet. Admission for adults is $78 and includes a buffet, three drinks, and shuttle transport from Waikiki. ⊠ 91-119 Olai St., Kapolei ☏ 808/949–6626, 800/367–5655 ⊕ www.germainesluau.com ⊙ Tues.–Sun. at 6 pm.

Paradise Cove Luau. One of the largest shows on Oahu, the lively Paradise Cove Luau is held in the Ko Olina resort area, about 45 minutes from Waikiki. Drink in hand, you can stroll through the authentic village, learn traditional arts and crafts, and play local games. The stage show includes a fire-knife dancer, singing emcee, and both traditional and contemporary hula and other Polynesian dances. A finale dance features participation from the audience. Admission includes the buffet, activities, and the show, as well as shuttle transport from Waikiki. You pay extra for table service and box seating. The stunning sunsets are free. ⊠ 92-1089 Alii Nui Dr., Kapolei ☏ 808/842–5911, 800/775–2683 ⊕ www.paradisecove.com ☏ $88–$153 ⊙ Daily at 5.

Fodor's Choice ★ **Polynesian Cultural Center Alii Luau.** While this elaborate luau has the sharpest production values, there is no booze allowed (it's a Mormon-owned facility in the heart of Laie—Mormon country). It's held amid the seven re-created villages at the Polynesian Cultural Center in the North Shore town of Laie, about an hour-and-a-half's drive from Honolulu. The luau—considered one of the most authentic on the island—includes the "Ha: Breath of Life" show that has long been popular with both residents and visitors. Rates start at $95 and go up depending on activities and amenities (personalized tours, reserved seats, or table service, for example). Waikiki transport is available. ⊠ Polynesian Cultural Center, 55-370 Kamehameha Hwy., Laie ☏ 808/293–3333, 800/367–7060 ⊕ www.polynesia.com ⊙ Mon.–Sat. at 5.

FILM

Hawaii International Film Festival. One of the biggest film events in the state, the festival in the middle of October showcases top films from all over the world, as well as some by local filmmakers (many are Hawaii premieres; a few are world premieres) screened day and night to packed crowds. It's a must-see for film adventurers. A majority of films are screened at the Regal Dole Cannery Theaters, but recently festival organizers have branched out to other venues as well. Check the official

HIFF website for updated locations. ⊠ *Regal Dole Cannery Theaters, 680 Iwilei Rd.* ☎ *808/792-1577* 🖷 *877/749-7783* ⊕ *www.hiff.org.*

Sunset on the Beach. It's like watching a movie at the drive-in, minus the car and the speaker box. Bring a blanket and find a spot on the sand to enjoy live entertainment, food from top local restaurants, and a movie on a 30-foot screen. Held six to seven times each year on Queen's Surf Beach across from the Honolulu Zoo, Sunset on the Beach is a favorite event for both locals and visitors. Additionally, season premiers of some current television shows are celebrated at Sunset on the Beach. Get there early if you want a good spot to view the film. If the weather is blustery, beware of flying sand. ⊠ *Queen's Surf Beach, Kalakaua Ave., Waikiki* ☎ *808/923-1094* ⊕ *www.waikikiimprovement.com.*

MUSIC

First Friday. Rain or shine, on the first Friday of every month, the downtown Honolulu and Chinatown districts come alive. The more family-friendly late afternoon art tours evolve into an adults-only club atmosphere with a lively street party. Art galleries and restaurants stay open late, and local musicians and DJs provide the soundtrack for the evening. ⊠ *Downtown Honolulu* ☎ *808/739-9797* ⊕ *www.hcadhawaii. org* 🖾 *Free entrance to galleries, cover for nightclubs.*

Hawaii Opera Theatre. Locals refer to it as "HOT," probably because the Hawaii Opera Theatre has been turning the opera-challenged into opera lovers since 1960. All operas are sung in their original language with a projected English translation. Tickets range from $34 to $125. ⊠ *Neal S. Blaisdell Center Concert Hall, 777 Ward Ave.* ☎ *808/596-7372, 800/836-7372* ⊕ *www.hawaiiopera.org.*

Honolulu Zoo Concerts. Since the early 1980s the Honolulu Zoo Society has sponsored hour-long evening concerts branded the "Wildest Show in Town." They're held at 6 pm on Wednesday from June to August. Listen to local legends play everything from Hawaiian to jazz to Latin music. ■TIP➔ At just $3 admission, this is one of the best deals in town. Take a brisk walk through the zoo, or join in the family activities. This is an alcohol-free event, and there's food for those who haven't brought their own picnic supplies. ⊠ *Honolulu Zoo, 151 Kapahulu Ave., Waikiki* ☎ *808/971-7171* ⊕ *www.honoluluzoo.org* 🖾 *$3* 🕐 *Gates open at 4:30.*

Ke Kani O Ke Kai. Every other Thursday evening in June and July, the Waikiki Aquarium holds an ocean-side concert series called "Ke Kani O Ke Kai." You can listen to top performers while enjoying food from local restaurants. The aquarium stays open throughout the night, so you can see the marine life in a new light. Bring your own beach chairs. Proceeds support the aquarium, the third oldest in the United States. ⊠ *Waikiki Aquarium, 2777 Kalakaua Ave., Waikiki* ☎ *808/923-9741* ⊕ *www.waquarium.org* 🖾 *$30.*

NIGHTLIFE

Oahu is the best of all the Islands for nightlife. The locals call it *pau hana,* but you might call it "off the clock and ready for a cocktail." (The literal translation of the Hawaiian phrase means "done with work.") On weeknights, it's likely that you'll find the working crowd, still in their casual business attire, downing chilled beers even before the sun goes down. Those who don't have to wake up in the early morning should change into a fresh outfit and start the evening closer to 10 pm.

On the weekends, it's typical to have dinner at a restaurant before hitting the clubs around 9:30. Some bar-hoppers start as early as 7, but partygoers typically don't patronize more than two establishments a night. That's because getting from one Oahu nightspot to the next usually requires packing your friends into the car and driving.

You can find a bar in just about any area on Oahu. Most of the clubs, however, are in Waikiki, near Ala Moana, and in and around downtown Honolulu. The drinking age is 21 on Oahu and throughout Hawaii. Many bars will admit younger people but will not serve them alcohol. By law, all establishments that serve alcoholic beverages must close by 2 am. The only exceptions are those with a cabaret license, which can stay open until 4 am. ■TIP→ Most places have a cover charge of $5 to $10, but with some establishments, getting there early means you don't have to pay.

HONOLULU

WAIKIKI

Addiction Nightclub. Traditional banquettes offer intimate seating for VIP tables, and bottle service lends a New York City nightclub feel at The Modern Honolulu. Red-velvet ropes guide you to the entrance; once inside you can dance to house and hip-hop music under a stunning ceiling installation of 40,000 round lights. But Addiction comes with a price—there's a $20 cover (if you're not on the guest list) and drinks aren't cheap. ⊠ *The Modern Honolulu, 1775 Ala Moana Blvd., Waikiki* ☎ *808/943–5800* ⊕ *www.addictionnightclub.com.*

Duke's Waikiki. Making the most of its spot on Waikiki Beach, Duke's presents live music every Friday, Saturday, and Sunday. Contemporary Hawaiian musicians like Henry Kapono and Maunalua have performed here, as have nationally known musicians like Jimmy Buffett. Solo Hawaiian musicians take the stage nightly, and it's not unusual for surfers to leave their boards outside to step in for a casual drink after a long day on the waves. The bar and grill's surf theme pays homage to Duke Kahanamoku, who popularized the sport in the early 1900s. ⊠ *Outrigger Waikiki, 2335 Kalakaua Ave., Suite 116, Waikiki* ☎ *808/922–2268* ⊕ *www.dukeswaikiki.com.*

Hula's Bar and Lei Stand. Hawaii's oldest and best-known gay-friendly nightspot offers panoramic views of Diamond Head by day and high-energy club music by night. Check out the soundproof, glassed-in dance floor. Patrons have included Elton John, Adam Lambert, and Dolly Parton. ⊠ *Waikiki Grand Hotel, 134 Kapahulu Ave., 2nd fl., Waikiki* ☎ *808/923–0669* ⊕ *www.hulas.com.*

Experience one of Hawaii's most spectacular luau at the Polynesian Cultural Center.

Lewers Lounge. A great spot for predinner drinks or post-sunset cocktails, Lewers Lounge offers a relaxed but chic atmosphere in the middle of Waikiki. There are classic and contemporary cocktails; the bar is helmed by Colin Field, known as one of the best bartenders in the industry; he has created several digestifs exclusively for Halekulani. He's also ditched the soda guns and mixes and brought back the craft of cocktails, using fresh and natural ingredients. Some standouts include the ginger lychee caipirissima and the blackberry julep. Enjoy your libation with live jazz and tempting desserts, such as the hotel's famous coconut cake. Or just sit back and relax in the grand setting of the luxurious lounge, which is decked in dramatic drapes and cozy banquettes. ⊠ *Halekulani Hotel, 2199 Kalia Rd., Waikiki* ☎ *808/923–2311* ⊕ *www.halekulani.com.*

Lulu's Waikiki. Even if you're not a surfer, you'll love this place's retro vibe and the unobstructed second-floor view of Waikiki Beach. The open-air setting, casual dining menu, and tropical drinks are all you need to help you settle into your vacation. The venue transforms from a nice spot for lunch or dinner to a bustling, high-energy club with live music lasting into the wee hours. ⊠ *Park Shore Waikiki Hotel, 2586 Kalakaua Ave., Waikiki* ☎ *808/926–5222* ⊕ *www.luluswaikiki.com.*

Mai Tai Bar at the Royal Hawaiian. The bartenders here sure know how to mix up a killer mai tai. This is, after all, the establishment that first concocted the famous drink. The umbrella-shaded tables at the outdoor bar are front-row seating for sunsets and also have an unobstructed view of Diamond Head. Contemporary Hawaiian musicians

If it's nightlife you're after, there's no better place in Hawaii than Waikiki Beach.

hold jam sessions onstage. ⊠ *Royal Hawaiian Hotel, 2259 Kalakaua Ave., Waikiki* ☎ *808/923–7311* ⊕ *www.royal-hawaiian.com.*

Fodor's Choice
★ **Moana Terrace.** Three floors up from Waikiki Beach, this casual, open-air terrace where the Keawe Ohana, a family comprised of some of Hawaii's finest musicians, plays on Thursday evenings. Order a drink served in a fresh pineapple and watch the sun dip into the Pacific Ocean. ⊠ *Waikiki Beach Marriott Resort, 2552 Kalakaua Ave., Waikiki* ☎ *808/922–6611.*

Nashville Waikiki. Country music in the tropics? You bet! Dress up like a *paniolo* (Hawaiian cowboy) and mosey on out to the giant dance floor at Nashville Waikiki. There's line dancing and free dance lessons five nights a week. Look for wall-to-wall crowds on the weekend. Pool tables, dartboards, and Wii consoles keep them occupied. ⊠ *Ohana Waikiki West Hotel, 2330 Kuhio Ave., Waikiki* ☎ *808/926–7911* ⊕ *www.nashvillewaikiki.com.*

RumFire. Locals and visitors head here for the convivial atmosphere, trendy decor, and the million-dollar view of Waikiki Beach and Diamond Head. Come early to get a seat for happy hour, which is from 4 to 6 nightly and 9:30 to 11 pm Sunday through Thursday. If you're feeling peckish, there's a menu of Asian-influenced dishes. RumFire also features original cocktails, signature shots, and live music. ⊠ *Sheraton Waikiki, 2255 Kalakaua Ave., Waikiki* ☎ *808/922–4422* ⊕ *www.rumfirewaikiki.com.*

The Study. It's tricky to find The Study at the Modern Honolulu—it's behind a huge, revolving bookcase in the lobby behind the registration desk. It's an überchic space, with intimate alcoves and oversized sofas that are both hip and inviting. The literary-themed cocktails, like the

"Huckle Berry Finn" and the "War and Peace," are pricey but cool. ⊠ *The Modern Honolulu, 1775 Ala Moana Blvd., Waikiki* ☎ *808/943–5800* ⊕ *www.themodernstudy.com.*

Tiki's Grill & Bar. Tiki torches light the way to this restaurant and bar overlooking Kuhio Beach. A mix of locals and visitors head here on the weekend to get their fill of kitschy cool. There's nightly entertainment featuring contemporary Hawaiian musicians. Don't leave without sipping on the Lava Flow, served in a whole coconut, or noshing on the famous coconut shrimp. ⊠ *Aston Waikiki Beach Hotel, 2570 Kalakaua Ave., Waikiki* ☎ *808/923–8454* ⊕ *www.tikisgrill.com.*

The Veranda. The Veranda at the Moana Surfrider—Waikiki's first hotel—has its own interesting history. From this location, the radio program *Hawaii Calls* first broadcast the sounds of Hawaiian music to a U.S. mainland audience in 1935. Hawaiian entertainers continue to provide the perfect accompaniment to the sounds of the waves. There's a small bar in the dining area—this space turns into the Beachhouse at the Moana for dinner—or mosey to The Beach Bar below and enjoy live Hawaiian music nightly. ⊠ *Moana Surfrider, 2365 Kalakaua Ave., Waikiki* ☎ *808/922–3111* ⊕ *www.moana-surfrider.com.*

DOWNTOWN

Murphy's Bar & Grill. On the edge of Chinatown, this bar has served drinks to such locals and visitors as King Kalakaua and Robert Louis Stevenson since the late 1800s. The kind of Irish pub you'd find in Boston, Murphy's is a break from all the tropical fruit-garnished drinks found in Waikiki, and it's definitely the place to be on St. Patrick's Day. Its block party fundraiser on that day is one of the most popular on the island. On Friday it serves some of the best homemade fruit pies around. They're so good, they sell out during lunch. ⊠ *2 Merchant St., Downtown Honolulu* ☎ *808/531–0422* ⊕ *www.murphyshawaii.com.*

Nocturna Lounge. This is Hawaii's first self-described NextGen lounge, a stylish and sophisticated karaoke and gaming lounge at the Waterfront Plaza. It boasts a full bar, four private suites with state-of-the-art karaoke, and video game consoles around the lounge featuring the latest in social gaming. Play "Street Fighter" in the open lounge, perfect your moves in "Dance Central" on the Xbox Kinect in a side room, or wander through the noisy club while sipping one of Nocturna's creative cocktails with names like "Sonic Boomtini" and "Yuzu is About to Die." The crowd isn't as young as you'd expect at a club outfitted with video game consoles—in fact, you must to be at least 21 to enter. ⊠ *Waterfront Plaza, 500 Ala Moana Blvd., Downtown Honolulu* ☎ *808/521–1555* ⊕ *www.nocturnalounge.com.*

CHINATOWN

The Dragon Upstairs. In the heart of Chinatown, this cool club—formerly a tattoo parlor, hence the dragon mural—serves up classic cocktails along with loungy jazz performances most nights of the week. You'll hear local vocalists, as well as small combos, in this unique venue upstairs from Hank's Cafe Honolulu. ⊠ *1038 Nuuanu Ave., Chinatown* ☎ *808/526–1411* ⊕ *www.thedragonupstairs.com.*

ALA MOANA

Fodor's Choice
★
Mai Tai Bar. After a long day of shopping at Ala Moana Shopping Center, the fourth-floor Mai Tai Bar is a perfect spot to relax. There's live entertainment and happy hour specials for both food and drink. There's never a cover charge and no dress code. To avoid waiting in line, get here before 9 pm. ⊠ *Ala Moana Center, 1450 Ala Moana Blvd., Ala Moana* ☎ *808/947–2900* ⊕ *www.maitaibar.com.*

Fodor's Choice
★
Rumours. It may not be the hippest club in town, but Rumours prides itself on its theme events and its retro vibe, spinning hits from the 1970s and '80s. It's got free pupu to nibble on and cages to dance inside. ⊠ *Ala Moana Hotel, 410 Atkinson St., Ala Moana* ☎ *808/955–4811.*

SOUTHEAST OAHU

The Shack. This sports bar and restaurant is one of the the only late-night spots you can find in Southeast Oahu. After a day of snorkeling at Hanauma Bay, stop by to kick back, have a beer, eat a burger, or play a game of pool. ⊠ *Hawaii Kai Shopping Center, 377 Keahole St., Hawaii Kai* ☎ *808/396–1919.*

WINDWARD OAHU

Boardrider's Bar & Grill. Tucked away in Kailua town, Boardrider's has long been the place for local bands to strut their stuff. Look for live music—reggae to rock and roll—every Friday and Saturday night. The spruced-up space includes a pool table, dartboards, and eight TVs for watching the game. ⊠ *201-A Hamakua Dr., Kailua* ☎ *808/261–4600.*

THE NORTH SHORE

Breaker's Restaurant. Just about every surf competition post-party is celebrated at this family-owned establishment. (The owner's son, Benji Weatherly, is a pro surfer.) Surfing memorabilia, including longboards hanging from the ceiling, fill the space. A tasty late-night menu is available until midnight. There's live music on Saturday. ⊠ *Marketplace Shopping Center, 66-250 Kamehameha Hwy., #G120, Haleiwa* ☎ *808/637–9898* ⊕ *www.breakersnsh.com.*

WHERE TO EAT

Updated by
Lesa Griffith

Oahu, where the majority of the Islands' 2,000-plus restaurants are located, offers the best of all worlds: it has the exoticness and excitement of Asia and Polynesia, but when the kids need McDonald's, or when you just have to have a Starbucks latte, they're here, too.

Budget for a pricey dining experience at the very top of the restaurant food chain, where chefs Alan Wong, Roy Yamaguchi, George Mavrothalassitis, and others you've seen on the Food Network and Travel Channel put a sophisticated and unforgettable spin on local foods and flavors. Savor seared ahi tuna in sea urchin beurre blanc or steak marinated in Korean kimchi sauce.

Spend the rest of your food dollars where budget-conscious locals do: in plate-lunch places and small ethnic eateries, at roadside stands and lunch wagons, or at window-in-the-wall delis. Snack on a *musubi* (a handheld rice ball wrapped with seaweed and often topped with Spam),

BEST BETS FOR OAHU DINING

Fodor's Choice ★

12th Avenue Grill, $$, p. 158

Alan Wong's, $$$$, p. 156

Chef Mavro, $$$$, p. 156

Honolulu Burger Co., $, p. 155

Opal Thai Food, $, p. 161

The Pig and the Lady, $$, p. 151

Salt Bar & Kitchen, $$, p. 158

Town, $$, p. 158

Vintage Cave Honolulu, $$$$, p. 154

By Price

$

Little Village Noodle House, p. 150

Lucky Belly, p. 150

Kakaako Kitchen, p. 152

Ono Hawaiian Foods, p. 157

To Chau, p. 151

Wailana Coffee House, p. 148

$$

Kalpawai Café & Deli, p. 160

Keo's in Waikiki, p. 143

Ola at Turtle Bay Resort, p. 161

Pah Ke's Chinese Restaurant, p. 160

$$$

3660 on the Rise, p. 157

Buzz's Original Steakhouse, p. 159

Nobu, p. 145

Roy's, p. 159

$$$$

Alan Wong's, p. 156

Chef Mavro, p. 156

Hoku's at the Kahala, p. 159

By Cuisine

HAWAIIAN

Alan Wong's, $$$$, p. 156

Hoku's at the Kahala, $$$$, p. 159

Roy's, $$$, p. 159

PLATE LUNCH

Ono Hawaiian Foods, $, p. 157

Ted's Bakery, $, p. 162

SUSHI

Nobu, $$$, p. 145

Sushi Sasabune, $$$$, p. 157

Yanagi Sushi, $$$, p. 150

slurp shave ice with red-bean paste, or order up Filipino pork adobo with two scoops of rice and macaroni salad.

In Waikiki, where most visitors stay, you can find choices from gracious rooms with a view to surprisingly authentic Japanese noodle shops. But hop in the car, or on the trolley or bus, and travel just a few miles in any direction, and you can save your money and get in touch with the real food of Hawaii.

Prices in the reviews are the average cost of a main course at dinner or, if dinner is not served, at lunch.

HONOLULU

WAIKIKI

$$$$
STEAKHOUSE

✕ **dk Steakhouse.** Honolulu has its share of national chain steak houses—but you're in Hawaii, why not go local? D.K. Kodama's second-floor restaurant serves Vintage Natural Beef, sourced from mainland ranchers who use no hormones or antibiotics. Choose from wet- and dry-aged cuts. The 22-ounce "Paniolo" (cowboy) rib-eye steak is dry-aged 30 days on the bone and seasoned with a house-made rub. The potato au gratin, topped with Maui onions and Parmesan, is addictive. The accommodating management even has menus for the gluten-free and vegan (!). The restaurant shares space, but not a menu, with Kodama's Sansei Seafood Restaurant & Sushi Bar; sit at the bar perched between the two and you can order from either menu. [$] *Average main: $55* ✉ *Waikiki Beach Marriott Resort and Spa, 2552 Kalakaua Ave., Waikiki* ☎ *808/931–6280* 🌐 *www.dksteakhouse.com* 🕑 *No lunch.*

$$$ AMERICAN 🍴 **Duke's Canoe Club.** Locals often take visiting friends and family from the mainland to this hotel restaurant for the beachfront setting—it's right in front of the famed Canoes surf break in Waikiki. Named for the father of modern surfing, and filled with Duke Kahanamoku memorabilia, Duke's is a popular open-air bar and steak-and-seafood grill. Two words: salad bar. Duke's has one—a huge one—which gives you an idea of the aim-to-please food. Pick one of the four catches of the day—such as mahimahi and opa (moonfish)—then choose one of four preparations. The prime rib and *huli huli* (rotisserie) chicken are also good options. The atmosphere can be raucous when live music by A-list Hawaiian performers fills the air. Sit back and enjoy your mai tai. ■ **TIP→ You can experience many of the same great flavors and pay half the price by siting in the bar.** [$] *Average main: $28* ✉ *Outrigger Waikiki on the Beach, 2335 Kalakaua Ave., Waikiki* ☎ *808/922–2268* 🌐 *www.dukeswaikiki.com.*

$$$$ AMERICAN 🍴 **Hau Tree Lanai.** The vine-like *hau* tree is ideal for sitting under, and it's said that the one that spreads itself over this beachside courtyard is the very one that shaded Robert Louis Stevenson as he mused and wrote about Hawaii. Today diners are still enjoying the shade and the view at this romantic beachside hotel restaurant. The restaurant is known for its rich, classic eggs Benedict for breakfast, papaya chicken salad at lunch, and workmanlike fresh catch of the day or steak at dinner. Dinner entrée portions are quite large. During the day you get a nice sightline of bodies beautiful prancing on Kaimana Beach. [$] *Average main: $48* ✉ *New Otani Kaimana Beach Hotel, 2863 Kalakaua Ave., Waikiki* ☎ *808/921–7066* 🌐 *www.kaimana.com* ✍ *Reservations essential.*

$$ THAI 🍴 **Keo's in Waikiki.** Many Islanders—and many Hollywood stars—have gotten their first taste of pad thai noodles, lemongrass, and coconut milk curry at one of veteran restaurateur Keo Sananikone's eateries. This one, perched at the entrance to Waikiki, characterizes his formula: a bright, clean space awash in flowers with intriguing menu titles and reasonable prices. Evil Jungle Prince, a stir-fry redolent of Thai basil, flecked with chilis and rich with coconut milk, is a classic; also try the apple bananas (smaller, sweeter variety of banana) in coconut milk. The Eastern and Western breakfasts are popular. [$] *Average main: $23* ✉ *2028 Kuhio Ave., Waikiki* ☎ *808/951–9355* 🌐 *keosthaicuisine.com.*

$$$$ FRENCH 🍴 **La Mer.** Looking out on its namesake, La Mer is the prettiest dining room on Oahu, with carved wooden screens setting an elegant art deco-ish tone. The classic haute-cuisine French food may be a little tired, but the restaurant remains a popular "special occasion" restaurant. Three prix-fixe options are offered (three or four courses, or a seven-course tasting menu)—choose from dishes such as sautéed baby squid with onion marmalade and coriander pesto, and roasted duck breast with

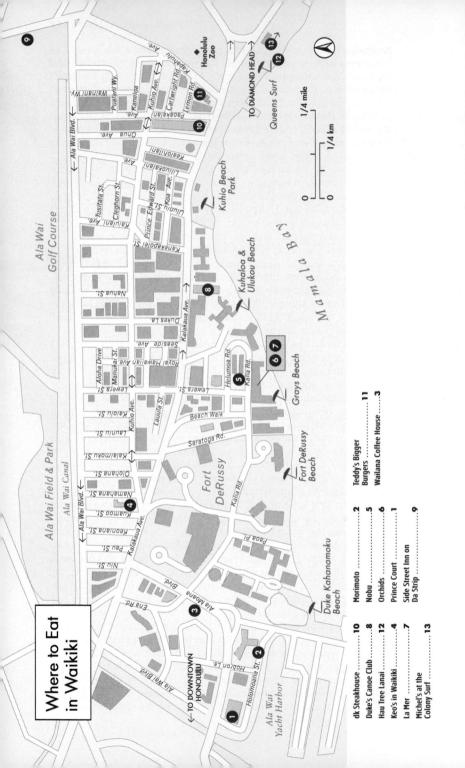

Where to Eat in Waikiki

dk Steakhouse **10**
Duke's Canoe Club **8**
Hau Tree Lanai **12**
Keo's in Waikiki **4**
La Mer **7**
Michel's at the
Colony Surf **13**

Morimoto **2**
Nobu **5**
Orchids **6**
Prince Court **1**
Side Street Inn on
Da Strip **9**

Teddy's Bigger
Burgers **11**
Wailana Coffee House **3**

TO DOWNTOWN HONOLULU

TO DIAMOND HEAD →

Honolulu Zoo

Ala Wai Golf Course

Ala Wai Field & Park

Ala Wai Canal

Ala Wai Yacht Harbor

Fort DeRussy

Mamala Bay

Queens Surf

Kuhio Beach Park

Kuhaloa & Ulukou Beach

Grays Beach

Fort DeRussy Beach

Duke Kahanamoku Beach

0   1/4 mile
0   1/4 km

2

beetroot and red fruit mousseline—as well as several rather expensive supplements. Place yourself in the sommelier's hands for wine choices from the hotel's exceptional cellar. Jacket or long-sleeved shirt required for gentlemen. ■TIP→ **For an elegant cocktail experience in Waikiki, visit L'Aperitif bar located inside the restaurant. Each cocktail comes with a paired gourmet bite.** Ⓢ *Average main: $142* ✉ *Halekulani, 2199 Kalia Rd., Waikiki* ☎ *808/923–2311* ⊕ *www.halekulani.com/living/ dining/la_mer* ⌕ *Reservations essential* ◷ *No lunch.*

$$$$ ✕**Michel's at the Colony Surf.** Consistently voted "most romantic res-
FRENCH taurant" in local publications' reader polls, Michel's is an old-school French favorite on Waikiki's tranquil Gold Coast. You pay for the beachside view, which you watch turn from blue to fireball orange at sunset. (To get a window table you need to reserve at *least* a month in advance.) Opened in 1962, the place retains a *Mad Men* feel, with lots of wood and stone and bow-tied servers preparing things like steak tartare tableside. Among the French classics (garlicky escargots, mustard-crusted rack of lamb) are local twists, such as Kauai-raised prawns with passion-fruit vinaigrette and Chinese-style steamed pink snapper. Brunch is served the first Sunday of every month. Ⓢ *Average main: $55* ✉ *Colony Surf, 2895 Kalakaua Ave., Waikiki* ☎ *808/923–6552* ⊕ *michelshawaii.com* ⌕ *Reservations essential* ◷ *No lunch.*

$$$$ ✕**Morimoto.** Iron Chef Masahara Morimoto of Food Network fame is
JAPANESE a big part of the dining scene in Honolulu. He's always in town for the annual Hawaii Food & Wine Festival, which takes place in September and includes an Asia-Pacific night at The Modern led by Morimoto. In the sleek white-and-chartreuse room you'll find the signature dishes served at his restaurants around the world—like Duck Duck Duck (duck three ways) and *ishi yaki buri bop* (yellowtail and rice cooked at your table in a hot stone pot) along with original creations taking cues from local cuisine, such as the chef's *loco moto* (wagyu beef with a sunny-side up egg and gravy), and, of course, sushi. ■TIP→ **Try the tofu, which is made right at your table.** You can choose to sit at the sushi bar, the regular bar, or at a table, but try to get a seat outside, with a view overlooking the yacht harbor. The place is also a popular spot for breakfast (Japanese style!) and brunch, and the lunch set menus are a bargain. Ⓢ *Average main: $41* ✉ *The Modern, 1775 Ala Moana Blvd., Waikiki* ☎ *808/943–5900* ⊕ *morimotowaikiki.com.*

$$$ ✕**Nobu.** Nobu Waikiki remains a magnet for visiting celebrities and local
JAPANESE bigwigs—and lots of Japanese tourists. Part of an ever-growing global
FUSION chain, this outpost serves Nobu Matsuhisa's decades-old Japanese-Peruvian signatures such as black cod lacquered with sweet den miso, along with original dishes like sous vide kurobuta pork belly with jalapeño, and ahi poke made with a sweet soy-mustard sauce, *ogo* (seaweed) from Molokai, and Big Island hearts of palm. The intense flavors can lead to unabandoned ordering—and the cost quickly adds up. The dramatically lit sushi bar serves some of the finest nigiri on the island. For a quick bite and cocktails, head to the lounge for happy hour, when pretty young things languish on the banquettes. ■TIP→ **Gluten-free diners can choose from a short but delicious special menu that includes an addictive pepperoncini with threads of hearts of palm standing in**

A typical Hawaiian "plate lunch" usually includes meat along with one scoop of rice and another of macaroni salad.

for the spaghetti, and wheat-free soy sauce is always available for the asking. [$] *Average main: $33* ✉ *Waikiki Parc Hotel, 2233 Helumoa Rd., Waikiki* ☎ *808/237–6999* 🌐 *www.noburestaurants.com.*

$$$$ SEAFOOD 🍴 **Orchids.** Perched along the seawall at historic Gray's Beach, Orchids in the luxe Halekulani resort is open all day—it's a locus of power breakfasters, ladies who lunch, celebrating families at the over-the-top Sunday brunch, and the gamut at dinner. The louvered walls are open to the breezes, sprays of orchids add color, the seafood is perfectly prepared, and the wine list is intriguing. The contemporary menu of international flavors reflects the hotel's well-traveled clientele—you can go around the world in one dinner, zigzagging from smoked duck carpaccio to marlin and Asian pear tartare to chicken tagine to steamed sesame pink snapper with shiitake mushrooms. Collard shirts are required for gentlemen. **■ TIP→ Halekulani executive chef Vikram Garg offers Table One, a custom dining experience within Orchids. He asks you your food preferences and makes culinary magic. It's not mentioned on the website—call to book.** [$] *Average main: $42* ✉ *Halekulani, 2199 Kalia Rd., Waikiki* ☎ *808/923–2311* 🌐 *www.halekulani.com* ✍ *Reservations essential.*

$$$$ ECLECTIC 🍴 **Prince Court.** This restaurant overlooking Ala Wai Yacht Harbor is a multifaceted success, with exceptional high-end lunches and dinners, daily breakfast buffets, weekly dinner seafood buffets, and sold-out weekend brunches (Sunday only). With a truly global mix of offerings, the overall style is Eurasian. Their ever-changing prix-fixe buffet includes offerings such as Australian rack of lamb, Kahuku prawns, and medallions of New York Angus beef. You can order à la carte as well.

CLOSE UP

Oahu Food Trucks

Lunch wagons, or food trucks, as they are now known around the country, have been a staple for plate lunches around Hawaii for decades, even before they were trendy. But now, with the taco-truck craze and the emergence of social media, more food trucks are popping up, serving an amazing variety of local flavors.

You can check the trucks' locations and daily menus on Twitter, or try a sampling from more than two-dozen vendors at the monthly Eat the Street food-truck rally or the weekly Tacoako Tuesdays. Visit 🌐 *www.streetgrindz.com* for details.

Here are some of our favorite lunch wagons:

Camille's on Wheels (🌐 *twitter.com/camillesonwheel*) combines Mexican, American, and Asian flavors in tacos and other dishes. Check out the shoyu chicken tacos, homemade salsas, and any of the homemade desserts. Camille's uses local ingredients whenever possible.

Elena's (🌐 *twitter.com/elenasfilipino*) is an extension of the popular, family-run Filipino restaurant in Waipahu. There are three trucks, in Campbell, Mililani, and the airport area. Try the AFRO, an adobo-fried rice omelet, or the famous *lechón* (roast pork with onions and tomatoes) special.

Ono To Go (🌐 *twitter.com/onotogo*) has a regular spot on Sheridan Street off King Street. It's open Monday through Saturday from 11 am until the food sells out—which is often, as the plate lunches are restaurant quality at lower prices. Best sellers are pork chops, teriyaki-citrus salmon, *pulehu* (fire-broiled) short ribs, poke, and roast turkey. Park on the street or at the car-repair shop next door.

Shogunai Tacos (🌐 *twitter.com/shogunai_tacos*) serves up hearty tacos with unique fillings that have Greek, Korean, Italian, Indian, Mexican, Thai, and Japanese flavors. The most popular item is the Osaka Jo taco, which is brimming with pork marinated in ginger, shoyu, garlic, lemon, a special sauce, sprouts, and then sprinkled with *furikake* (shredded dried seaweed). Make it a meal with the Moroccan-inspired french fries.

[$] *Average main: $42* ✉ *Hawaii Prince Hotel Waikiki, 100 Holomoana St., Waikiki* ☎ *808/944–4494* 🌐 *www.princeresortshawaii.com.*

$$ ECLECTIC 🍴 **Side Street Inn on Da Strip.** The original Hopaka Street pub is famous as the place where celebrity chefs gather after hours; this second location, also run by Colin Nishida, is on bustling Kapahulu Avenue, closer to Waikiki. Local-style bar food—salty pan-fried pork chops with a plastic tub of ketchup; fried rice; and passion fruit–glazed ribs—comes in huge, shareable portions. This is a place to dress any way you like, nosh all night, and watch sports on TV. Pupu (in portions so large as to be dinner) are served from 3 pm to 11:30 pm daily. [$] *Average main: $20* ✉ *614 Kapahulu Ave., Waikiki* ☎ *808/739–3939* 🌐 *www.sidestreetinn.com* ⏲ *No lunch.*

$ BURGER 🍴 **Teddy's Bigger Burgers.** Modeled after 1950s diners, this local franchise serves classic moist and messy burgers, along with turkey and veggie burgers, as well as chicken breast and fish sandwiches. The fries are crisply perfect, the shakes rich and sweet. The original location in Waikiki combines burger shack simplicity with surf-boy cool—there's even a place to store your surfboard while you have your burger. This popular location has given birth to several others around the state. $ *Average main: $10* ⊠ *134 Kapahulu Ave., Waikiki* ☎ *808/926–3444* ⊕ *teddysbiggerburgers.com.*

$ ✕ **Wailana Coffee House.** Coffee shops are a dying breed in Honolulu,
AMERICAN but the 24-hour Wailana Coffee House, opened in 1969, is still going strong. Budget-conscious snowbirds, night owls with a yen for karaoke, all-day drinkers of both coffee and the stronger stuff, hearty eaters, and post-clubbing club kids all crowd this venerable, family-run diner and cocktail lounge at the edge of Waikiki. Banana pancakes and corned beef hash at breakfast; French dips, burgers, and Salisbury steak (!) at lunch; and trademark "broasted" chicken at dinner—this place is a trip down food memory lane. Most checks are under $11, and there's a $2.50 children's menu. It's open 24 hours a day, seven days a week, 365 days a year (except Tuesday, when the restaurant closes from 10 pm to 6 am), but the place fills up, and a line forms around the corner at breakfast time, so arrive early or late. $ *Average main: $12* ⊠ *1860 Ala Moana Blvd., atf Ena Rd., Waikiki* ☎ *808/955–1764* ⚄ *Reservations not accepted.*

DOWNTOWN

$ ✕ **Bac Nam.** Tam and Kimmy Huynh's menu is much more extensive
VIETNAMESE than most, ranging far beyond the usual *pho* (beef noodle soup) and *bun* (cold noodle dishes). Lamb curry, tapioca dumplings, tamarind head-on shrimp, an extraordinary crab noodle soup, and other dishes hail from North and South Vietnam. The no-frills atmosphere is welcoming and relaxed at this go-to spot for locals. At lunch it's packed with people who work in the neighborhood. Reservations are not accepted for groups fewer than six. $ *Average main: $12* ⊠ *1117 S. King St., Ala Moana* ☎ *808/597–8201.*

$ ✕ **Honolulu Museum of Art Cafe.** The Honolulu Museum of Art's cool
AMERICAN courtyards and galleries filled with works by masters from Monet to Hokusai are well worth a visit and, afterward, so is this popular lunch restaurant. The open-air café is flanked by a burbling water feature and eight-foot-tall ceramic "dumplings" by artist Jun Kaneko—a tranquil setting in which to eat your salade niçoise (featuring seared ahi) or fork-tender filet mignon sandwich with Dijon-caper relish. You'll rub shoulders with a who's who of the local art and business communities. Reservations are recommended. $ *Average main: $17* ⊠ *Honolulu Museum of Art, 900 S. Beretania St., Downtown Honolulu* ☎ *808/532–8734* ⊕ *www.honolulumuseum.org* ☾ *No dinner.*

$$ ✕ **Vino.** Island oenophiles make a beeline for this wine bar and restau-
WINE BAR rant, which regularly holds special tastings and dinners. Chef Keith Endo creates his take on contemporary Italian cuisine with some local accents. Housemade pastas, jumbo shrimp in a resonant cioppino sauce, and Big Island smoked pork pair well with wines selected by nationally recognized Master Sommelier Chuck Furuya. He makes sure food and service are grade-A quality amid a let-your-hair-down atmosphere. You

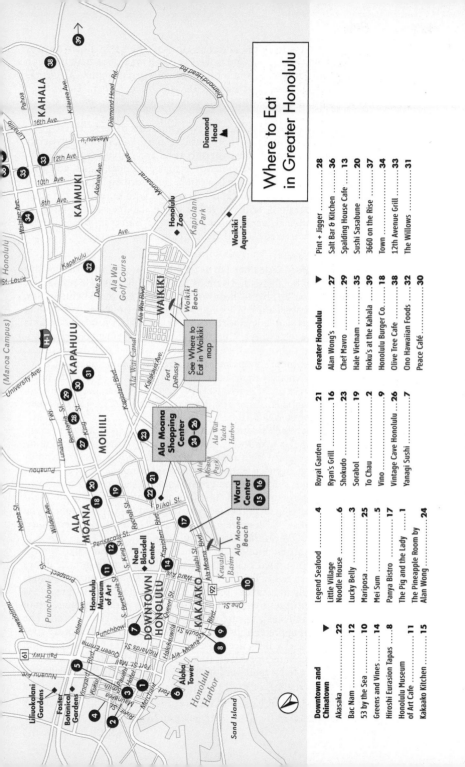

Where to Eat in Greater Honolulu

Downtown and Chinatown

Restaurant	No.
▶	
Akasaka	22
Bac Nam	12
53 by the Sea	10
Greens and Vines	14
Hiroshi Eurasion Tapas	8
Honolulu Museum of Art Cafe	11
Kakaako Kitchen	15
Legend Seafood	4
Little Village Noodle House	6
Lucky Belly	3
Mariposa	25
Mei Sum	5
Panya Bistro	17
The Pig and the Lady	1
The Pineapple Room by Alan Wong	24
Royal Garden	21
Ryan's Grill	16
Shokudo	23
Sorabol	19
To Chau	2
Vino	9
Vintage Cave Honolulu	26
Yanagi Sushi	7

Greater Honolulu

Restaurant	No.
Alan Wong's	27
Chef Mavro	29
Hale Vietnam	35
Hoku's at the Kahala	39
Honolulu Burger Co.	18
Olive Tree Cafe	38
Ono Hawaiian Foods	32
Peace Café	30
Pint + Jigger	28
Salt Bar 8 Kitchen	36
Spalding House Cafe	13
Sushi Sasabune	20
3660 on the Rise	37
Town	34
12th Avenue Grill	33
The Willows	31

can order items from the adjacent Hiroshi's Eurasion Tapas, as they share a kitchen. ■ **TIP→ Vino is well situated for stopping off between downtown sightseeing and a return to your Waikiki hotel.** [$] *Average main: $25* ✉ *Waterfront Plaza, 500 Ala Moana Blvd., Downtown Honolulu* ☎ *808/524–8466* 🌐 *vinohawaii.com* ⏰ *No lunch. Closed Sun.–Tues.*

$$$ JAPANESE 🍴 **Yanagi Sushi.** One of relatively few restaurants to serve the complete menu until 2 am (Sunday only until 10 pm), Yanagi is a full-service Japanese restaurant offering not only sushi and sashimi around a small bar, but also *teishoku* (combination menus), tempura, stews, and grill-it-yourself shabu-shabu. The fish can be depended on for freshness and variety. Try the baked volcano roll stuffed with crabmeat, the spicy shrimp tempura roll, or if you're brave, the abalone sashimi—straight out of the tank. [$] *Average main: $28* ✉ *762 Kapiolani Blvd., Downtown Honolulu* ☎ *808/597–1525* 🌐 *yanagisushi-hawaii.com.*

CHINATOWN

$ CHINESE 🍴 **Legend Seafood Restaurant.** Do as the locals do: start your visit to Chinatown with breakfast dim sum at this Hong Kong–style restaurant. If you want to be able to hear yourself think, get there before 9 am, especially on weekends. And don't be shy: use your best cab-hailing technique and sign language to make the cart ladies stop at your table and show you their wares. The pork-filled steamed buns, spinach dumplings, taro-and-pork *gok* (bite-size fried balls), and still-warm custard tarts are excellent pre-shopping fortification. Dim sum dishes cost $2.75 to $5.75, so knock yourself out. The place also has à la carte lunch and dinner menus. [$] *Average main: $13* ✉ *Chinese Cultural Plaza, 100 N. Beretania St., Suite 108, Chinatown* ☎ *808/532–1868* 🌐 *www.legendseafoodhonolulu.com.*

$ CHINESE 🍴 **Little Village Noodle House.** Unassuming and budget-friendly, Little Village is so popular with locals that it expanded to the space next door. The extensive pan-China menu is filled with crowd pleasers such as shredded beef, spinach with garlic, Shanghai noodles, honey-walnut shrimp, orange chicken, dried green beans. Reservations are accepted for parties of five or more. ■ **TIP→ Two hours of free parking are available in the parking lot immediately to the right of the restaurant (if you can nab a space).** [$] *Average main: $10* ✉ *1113 Smith St., Chinatown* ☎ *808/545–3008* 🌐 *littlevillagehawaii.com.*

$ ASIAN 🍴 **Lucky Belly.** At Honolulu's answer to New York's Momofuku Noodle Bar, a hip local crowd sips cocktails and slurps familiar noodle dishes with a modern twist. Try the Belly Bowl with smoked bacon, sausage, and pork belly in a savory broth loaded with noodles. At dinner, the pupu menu features trendy small plates such as pork belly buns, oxtail dumplings, and steak tartare spiced with Japanese chili powder. The service here is unpretentious and attentive, and you can also order your food to go. Lucky Belly accepts dinner reservations for 5 to 6:30 pm only, so be prepared for a wait if you dine after that. ■ **TIP→ Arrive by 11:30 if you want a table for lunch; this place quickly fills up with the downtown crowd.** [$] *Average main: $12* ✉ *50 N. Hotel St., Chinatown* ☎ *808/531–1888* ⏰ *Closed Sun.*

Authentic Asian food can be found all over Hawaii and some of the best is in Chinatown in downtown Honolulu.

$ ✕ **Mei Sum Chinese Dim Sum Restaurant.** In contrast to the sprawling,
CHINESE noisy halls in which dim sum is generally served, Mei Sum is compact and shiny bright. It's open daily, one of the few places that serves dim sum from 8 am all the way to 9 pm. Be ready to guess and point at the color photos of dim sum favorites as not much English is spoken, but the charades pay off when you get your delicate buns and tasty bites. Other menu items and specials are also served. $ *Average main: $11* ✉ *1170 Nuuanu Ave., Suite 102, Chinatown* ☎ *808/531–3268.*

$$ ✕ **The Pig and the Lady.** After making waves as sous chef at Chef Mavro,
MODERN ASIAN then operating pop-up nights and a noodle stand at farmers' markets
Fodor'sChoice for two years—not to mention a six-month stage at San Francisco's
★ Rich Table—rising star Andrew Le opened his own place in November 2013. The Pig and the Lady is a casual noodle house by day, attracting downtown office workers, but becomes a creative contemporary restaurant by night, when serious chowhounds come out. Drawing on both his Vietnamese heritage and multicultural island flavors, the talented, playful Le is a wizard with spice and acid, turning out dishes of layered flavor such as "coffee can bread" (which is baked in Café du Monde coffee cans) with chicken liver paté, Kyoho grapes, and pink peppercorns. Another innovative dish is porchetta with pomegranate-arugula salsa verde. A young, creative crowd, craft cocktails, and affordable prices keep the DIY-chic space (Le's family and friends did everything!) with exposed brick hopping. $ *Average main: $20* ✉ *83 N. King St., Chinatown* ☎ *808/585–8255* ⊕ *www.thepigandthelady.com.*

$ ✕ **To Chau.** Wonder why people are standing in line on River Street? To
VIETNAMESE get bowls of steaming *pho* (Vietnamese beef noodle soup) at To Chau.

This spot was a pho pioneer. Many Vietnamese restaurants have since opened and surpassed To Chau's quality, but eating habits die hard in this city. The divey storefront is open only until 2:30 pm, but you may be turned away if the food runs out earlier. $ *Average main: $8* ⊠ *1007 River St., Chinatown* ☎ *808/533–4549* ⌖ *Reservations not accepted* ▬ *No credit cards* ⊘ *No dinner.*

KAKAAKO

$$$$
CONTEMPORARY

✕ **53 by the Sea.** Housed in a McVilla aimed at attracting a Japanese wedding clientele, this restaurant serves contemporary Continental food that focuses primarily on well-prepared standards you'd find at a reception (crab cakes in lemon purée, mahimahi with a mango beurre blanc, lamb chops in a red wine reduction)—albeit with a million-dollar view of Honolulu, from Kakaako to Diamond Head. Perched at water's edge, with famed surf break Point Panic offshore, 53 by the Sea uses its setting to great advantage—the crescent-shaped dining room faces the sea, so even if you're not at a table nestled against the floor-to-ceiling windows, you have a fine view. It's the stuff marriage proposals are made of. If you aren't proposing or dining, you can have cocktails and appetizers at the bar's little outdoor balcony and watch the city light up as the sun goes down. Sublime. $ *Average main: $50* ⊠ *53 Ahui St., Kakaako* ☎ *808/536–5353* ⊕ *www.53bythesea.com* ⌖ *Reservations essential.*

$
MODERN
HAWAIIAN
FAMILY

✕ **Kakaako Kitchen.** Russell Siu was the first of the local-boy fine dining chefs to open a place of the sort he enjoys when he's off-duty, serving high-quality plate lunches (he uses house-made sauce instead of from-a-mix brown gravy, for example). Here you can get a crab-and-avocado salad sandwich and honey-soy sauce pork chops with two scoops of either brown or white rice, and green salad instead of the usual macaroni salad. Breakfast is especially good, with combos like corned-beef hash and eggs, as well as exceptional baked goods. You order at the counter (be prepared to stand in line if you go right at noon), stake out a table, and wait for the food to come. $ *Average main: $13* ⊠ *Ward Centres, 1200 Ala Moana Blvd., Kakaako* ☎ *808/596–7488* ⊕ *kakaakokitchen.com* ⌖ *Reservations not accepted.*

$$
ECLECTIC

✕ **Panya Bistro.** The newest location of this local chainlet is an easy-breezy café run by Hong Kong–born sisters Alice and Annie Yeung. The crowd-pleasing menu is a mix of contemporary American (salads, sandwiches, pastas) and Asian (Thai-style steak salad, Japanese-style fried chicken, Singaporean *laksa*), served in a disco-tinged space (there's also a full bar!) in the fast-developing neighborhood of Kakaako. Across the street is the new Ward Village Shops complex housing TJ Maxx and Nordstrom Rack. $ *Average main: $18* ⊠ *Hokua, 1288 Ala Moana Blvd., Kakaako* ☎ *808/597-8880* ⊕ *www.panyagroup.com.*

$$
AMERICAN

✕ **Ryan's Grill at Ward Centre.** An all-purpose food and drink emporium, lively and popular Ryan's has an exceptionally well-stocked bar, with 20 beers on tap, an outdoor deck, and TVs broadcasting sports. Lunch, dinner, and small plates are served until the midnight. The eclectic menu ranges from an addictive hot crab-and-artichoke dip with focaccia to grilled fresh fish, pasta, salads, and sophisticated versions of local favorites, such as the Kobe beef hamburger steak. $ *Average main: $20*

✉ *Ward Centre, 1200 Ala Moana Blvd., Kakaako* ☎ *808/591–9132* 🌐 *ryansgrill.com.*

ALA MOANA

$$ JAPANESE 🍴 **Akasaka.** Step inside this tiny sushi bar tucked behind the Ala Moana Hotel, and you'll swear you're in an out-of-the-way Edo neighborhood in some indeterminate time. Don't be deterred by its location between strip clubs or its reputation for inconsistent service. Greeted with a cheerful "*Iraishaimase!*" (Welcome!), sink down at a diminutive table or perch at the handful of seats at the sushi bar. It's safe to let the sushi chefs here decide (*omakase*-style) or you can go for the grilled specialties, such as scallop *battayaki* (grilled in butter). [$] *Average main: $21* ✉ *1646 B Kona St., Suite B, Ala Moana* ☎ *808/942–4466.*

$ VEGETARIAN 🍴 **Greens and Vines.** Honolulu's only raw-food restaurant was an immediate hit when it opened in 2012, having filled a healthy hole in the city's dining landscape. Dishes such as the Living Lasagna, made with layers of seasoned zucchini, basil pesto, sun-dried tomato "marinara," macadamia nut "ricotta," and spinach have meat eaters convinced that raw and vegan food is delicious. The casual café also has a refrigerated case of entrées, spreads, and crackers to go. ■ **TIP→ Chef-owner Sylvia Thompson and her husband are oenophiles and hold periodic wine-tasting dinners.** [$] *Average main: $15* ✉ *NineONine, 909 Kapiolani Blvd., Ala Moana* ☎ *808/536–9680* 🌐 *greensandvines.com* 🕒 *Closed Sun.*

$$$ ASIAN FUSION 🍴 **Hiroshi Eurasion Tapas.** Founding chef Hiroshi Fukui is no longer with the restaurant, but the new young team continues his signature style of "West & Japan" cuisine. With an emphasis on local ingredients (one of the chefs has served tilapia that he raised himself in his backyard!) mixed with French technique, the menu always intrigues. Order a slew of small plates and share, or go with a more traditional big plate entrée. Signatures include red wine steamed veal cheeks, locally raised *kampachi* fish carpaccio, and *misoyaki* (marinated in a rich miso-soy blend, then grilled) butterfish. For a decadent treat, try the foie gras *sushi*. You can also order off the menu from Vino, next door, as they share a kitchen. ■ **TIP→ During Happy Hour, from 5:30 to 6:30, everything on the menu is half-price when you sit at the bar—and the seats go fast.** [$] *Average main: $27* ✉ *Waterfront Plaza, 500 Ala Moana Blvd., Ala Moana* ☎ *808/533–4476* 🌐 *www.hiroshihawaii.com* 🕒 *No lunch.*

$$$ ASIAN 🍴 **Mariposa.** Yes, the popovers and the wee cups of bouillon are there at lunch, but in every other regard, this Neiman Marcus restaurant menu departs from the classic model, incorporating a clear sense of Pacific place. The breezy open-air veranda, with a view of Ala Moana Park, twirling ceiling fans, and life-size hula-girl murals say Hawaii. The menu at this headquarters for ladies who lunch gives the calorie and gluten info for contemporary American dishes such as braised pork belly and scallops with pickled watercress and passionfruit brown butter, and a pork chop with sun-dried cherry port wine sauce. Make sure to leave room for the warm lilikoi pudding cake for dessert. [$] *Average main: $35* ✉ *Nieman Marcus, Ala Moana Center, 1450 Ala Moana, Ala Moana* ☎ *808/951–8887* 🌐 *www.neimanmarcushawaii.com/restaurant.aspx* ✍ *Reservations essential.*

$$$ MODERN HAWAIIAN 🍴 **The Pineapple Room by Alan Wong.** For some people, this restaurant is the only reason to go to Macy's. At Alan Wong's more casual second spot the chef de cuisine plays intriguing riffs on local food themes. Power lunchers confer over the stack-'em-high burger—made with locally raised grass-fed beef, bacon, cheddar cheese, hoisin-mayonnaise spread, avocado salsa, and huge onion ring—it's one of the best in town. Ladies more often lean toward lighter fare like the Caesar salad with island-style grilled chicken or sesame-crusted *opah* (moonfish) in a yuzu ponzu sauce. Service is professional; reservations are recommended. [$] *Average main: $35* ✉ *Ala Moana Center, 1450 Ala Moana Blvd., Ala Moana* ☎ *808/945–6573* 🌐 *www.alanwongs.com* ⏲ *No dinner Sun.*

$$ CHINESE 🍴 **Royal Garden.** Royal Garden is one of the best dim sum spots in town, and people don't mind paying a little more for the quality they get (about $4 per four-piece dish). From 10 am to 2 pm, when dim sum is offered, just point to the steamed and baked morsels that look good; chances are, they're as good as they look. The regular menu features Hong Kong–style dishes, from the pedestrian shrimp with walnuts to the crazy poetic signature "osmanthus flower" made with dried scallops, crab, bean sprouts, and egg, and, of course, sweet, fragrant osmanthus flowers. [$] *Average main: $21* ✉ *Ala Moana Hotel, 410 Atkinson Dr., Ala Moana* ☎ *808/942–7788.*

$$ JAPANESE 🍴 **Shokudo.** With a soaring ceiling, crazy red mobile sculpture, contemporary Japanese grazing plates, fruity vodka "sodas," and hungry young people, Shokudo is a culinary house of fun. Whether you go for new-wave fusion dishes such as sushi pizza (a flat, baked square of rice topped with salmon, scallop, crab, and pickled jalapeño), or more traditional noodle bowls and sushi, the food is all good. Do get the signature honey toast for dessert—a hollowed-out loaf of Japanese sandwich bread stuffed with cubes of its toasted innards and vanilla ice cream that's drizzled with honey. ■ **TIP→ Shokudo is one of Honolulu's few late-night eateries that is not a fast-food joint. Last orders are taken at 1 am.** [$] *Average main: $21* ✉ *Ala Moana Pacific Center, 1585 Kapiolani Blvd., Ala Moana* ☎ *808/941–3701* 🌐 *www.shokudojapanese.com.*

$$ KOREAN 🍴 **Sorabol.** The largest Korean restaurant in the city, this 24-hour eatery, with its tiny parking lot and maze of booths and private rooms, offers a vast menu encompassing the entirety of day-to-day Korean cuisine, plus sushi. English menu translations are cryptic at best. Still, it's great for wee hour "grinds" (local slang for food): *bi bim bap* (veggies, meats, and eggs on steamed rice), *kal bi* and *bulgogi* (barbecued meats), meat or fish *jun* (thin fillets battered with egg then fried), and kimchi pancakes. [$] *Average main: $24* ✉ *805 Keeaumoku St., Ala Moana* ☎ *808/947–3113* 🌐 *sorabolhawaii.com.*

$$$$ CONTEMPORARY Fodor's Choice ★ 🍴 **Vintage Cave Honolulu.** The opening of Vintage Cave Honolulu in December 2012 was the most exciting culinary thing to happen on the island in almost a decade. Billionaire Japanese developer Takeshi Sekiguchi gave rising star chef Chris Kajioka, an alum of New York's Per Se and San Francisco's Aziza, carte blanche to create his dream kitchen and menu in a dark, brick-lined space that was once the storage basement of the Japanese department store Shiryokiya, which Sekiguchi also owns. (The space is also a private wine club—hence the name.) Today

chefs from across the country and Japan clamor to be a part of Kajioka's "collaboration dinner" program. He turns out the most progressive, enchanting food in the state, each plate in a progressive multicourse dinner a jewel-like composition that dazzles with color, texture, and, most important, flavor. Strong Japanese and French influences converge in his food, which mixes grade-A international ingredients (osetra caviar, foie gras, dry-aged organic beef, Tsukiji Market fish) from around the world with the freshest local produce (such as sea beans plucked from the banks of an ancient Hawaiian fishpond). Signature creations include a "seafood platter" of bite-size raw-fish constructions, a maple-glazed rectangle of brioche topped with caviar, and charred caraflex cabbage (grown specially for Kajioka on the Big Island) stacked in a dainty square and served in a resonant kombu-anchovy broth with a dollop of miso-crème fraîche. It's prix-fixe tasting menu only, and worth every cent of the considerable price. $ *Average main: $295* ⊠ *Ala Moana Center, 1450 Ala Moana Blvd., Suite 2250, Ala Moana* ☎ *808/441–1744* ⊕ *www.vintagecave.com* ⌧ *Reservations essential.*

MAKIKI HEIGHTS

$
BURGER
Fodor'sChoice
★

× **Honolulu Burger Co.** Owner Ken Takahashi retired as a nightclub impresario on the Big Island to become a real-life burger king. This modest storefront is the home of the locavore burger, made with range-fed beef, Manoa lettuce, and tomatoes that are all island-raised—and you can taste the difference. Go classic with a single hand-shaped patty, the meat loosely packed to let the juices run free, or one of Takahashi's creations such as the Miso Kutie burger topped with red miso glaze and Japanese cucumber slices. The Korean Big Bang—braised short ribs with a spicy *ko choo jang* aioli—is as delicious as it is messy. And do get the truffle fries. There's a second location across the street from Kahala Mall (⊠ *4210 Waialae Ave.* ☎ *808/735–5202*). $ *Average main: $11* ⊠ *1295 S. Beretania St., Makiki* ☎ *808/626–5202* ⊕ *www. honoluluburgerco.com* ⌧ *Reservations not accepted.*

$
AMERICAN

× **Spalding House Cafe.** In the exclusive Makiki Heights neighborhood above the city, the Honolulu Museum of Art Spalding House's casual café spills out of the ground floor of the museum onto the lush, expansive lawn with a million-dollar view of the city and Diamond Head. Sit inside when it's hot, grab an outdoor table when the tradewinds are blowing. The short, Mediterranean-accented menu features items such as housemade soups, gourmet sandwiches, a hummus plate with fresh pita, and a roasted vegetable salad with curried quinoa. The cafe offers a $30 "Lauhala and Lunch" picnic for two, which includes a choice of sandwich or salad for each person, dessert bars, and beverage packed in a picnic basket—grab a tatami mat and lay your spread under the huge monkeypod tree on the museum grounds. $ *Average main: $12* ⊠ *2411 Makiki Heights Dr., Makiki* ☎ *808/237–5225* ⊗ *No dinner. Closed Mon.*

MOILIILI

$$$$ ✕ **Alan Wong's Restaurant Honolulu.** Alan Wong is the undisputed king of
MODERN Hawaiian Regional Cuisine, earning love and respect for his humble
HAWAIIAN demeanor and practice as much as for his food. The "Wong Way," as
Fodor'sChoice it's not-so-jokingly called by his staff, includes an ingrained under-
★ standing of the aloha spirit, evident in the skilled but unstarched service, and creative and playful interpretations of island cuisine. Try crab
mousse and lobster medallions in kudzu dashi, his signature ginger-
crusted *onaga* (snapper), or, if you're feeling indulgent, the chef's tasting
menu. With warm tones of koa wood, and *lauhala* grass weaving, you'll
forget you're on the third floor of an office building. There's a reason
the president dines here whenever he's in town. $ *Average main: $38*
✉ *McCully Court, 1857 S. King St., 3rd fl., Moiliili* ☎ *808/949–2526*
⊕ *www.alanwongs.com* ⌂ *Reservations essential* ⊘ *No lunch.*

$$$$ ✕ **Chef Mavro.** George Mavrothalassitis, who took two hotel restaurants
MODERN to the top of the ranks before opening this James Beard Award–win-
EUROPEAN ning restaurant in 1998, admits he's crazy. Crazy because of the care
Fodor'sChoice he takes to draw out the truest and most concentrated flavors, to track
★ down the freshest fish, to create one-of-a-kind wine pairings. But for
this passionate Marseilles transplant, there's no other way. He marries
French technique with global flavors and local ingredients. The menu
changes quarterly, every dish (including dessert) matched with a select
wine. Choose from a four- or six-course menu or the grand degustation
(vegetarian and gluten-free options are available). Etched-glass windows screen the busy street-corner scene, and all within is mellow and
serene with starched white tablecloths, fresh flowers, wood floors, and
contemporary island art. This is a memorable gastronomic experience.
$ *Average main: $130* ✉ *1969 S. King St., Moiliili* ☎ *808/944–4714*
⊕ *www.chefmavro.com* ⌂ *Reservations essential* ⊘ *No lunch.*

$ ✕ **Peace Café.** This tranquil little storefront with a rustic country com-
VEGETARIAN munal table is a nurturing sanctuary on a fast-food-loving island. Place
your order at the counter, serve yourself lemon-infused water from a
large glass beverage jar, and wait for your Yogini plate (a mountain of
brown rice, beans, greens, and seaweed), soy soba salad, Moroccan
chickpea stew, barbecue tempeh sandwich, and other vegan bites. Peace
Café also has a selection of coffees, lattes, and teas—'cause you don't
want to get *too* peaceful. $ *Average main: $10* ✉ *2239 S. King St., Moiliili* ☎ *808/951–7555* ⊕ *www.peacecafehawaii.com* ⊘ *No dinner Sun.*

$ ✕ **Pint + Jigger.** Dining trends are late to arrive in Honolulu, and the
ECLECTIC gastropub phenomenon is no exception. Opened in 2012 by a group
of people that includes a former Nobu Waikiki bar manager, Pint +
Jigger is the best of the genre. Sit at one of the "beer garden" communal benches or perch at a high top in this welcoming wood-and-brick
room for Dave Newman's farm-to-glass cocktails and craft beers. They
pair well with bites such as a Scotch egg made with pork rillettes,
strips of double-cut bacon spiced up with a jalapeño-corn salsa, and
a burger topped with stout cheese. Plates are diverse enough to provide everything from a nibble (house-made barbecue potato chips) to
a full meal (pan-seared salmon in lemon beurre blanc). After work and
on weekends it is packed. $ *Average main: $13* ✉ *1936 S. King St.,*

Moiliili ☎ *808/744–9593* 🌐 *www.pintandjigger.com* ✍ *Reservations not accepted* ⏲ *No lunch.*

$$$$ JAPANESE 🍴 **Sushi Sasabune.** Be sure to get a seat at the counter (tables are for plebes) and prepare for an unforgettable sushi experience—if you behave. Part of a chainlet with locations in Los Angeles, Beverly Hills, and New York, this is the home of Seiji Kumagawa—Honolulu's sushi nazi. The way to go is the *omakase*-style (oh-*mah*-ka-*say*, roughly, "trust me"), letting the chef send out his choices of the highest-grade sea creatures for the night. The dishes are served with instructions: "Please, no shoyu on this one." "One piece, one bite." People who defy Kumagawa and go ahead and dip their nigiri in shoyu anyway have been kicked out of the restaurant mid-meal. The parade of dishes always includes the signature California baby squid stuffed with Louisiana crab. A caution: the courses come rapidly until you cry uncle. You pay by the course, which is generally two pieces of sushi or six to eight slices of sashimi, and they can add up fast. The final price depends on how far you can go. [$] *Average main: $115* ✉ *1419 S. King St., Moiliili* ☎ *808/947–3800* 🌐 *sushisasabune.tumblr.com* ✍ *Reservations essential* ⏲ *Closed Sun and Mon. No lunch Sat.*

$$$$ HAWAIIAN 🍴 **The Willows.** Locals come to this buffet-only spot to celebrate things like graduations and showers, and it has its share of wedding receptions (there's a chapel on site). It's an acre oasis of pavilions overlooking a network of ponds (once natural streams flowing from mountain to sea). The island-style comfort food includes the trademark chicken curry (*Joy of Cooking* style, not Indian) along with Hawaiian dishes such as *laulau* (a steamed bundle of ti leaves containing pork, butterfish, and taro tops) and *kalua* pig. [$] *Average main: $38* ✉ *901 Hausten St., Moiliili* ☎ *808/952–9200* 🌐 *willowshawaii.com* ✍ *Reservations essential.*

KAPAHULU

$ HAWAIIAN Fodor's Choice ★ 🍴 **Ono Hawaiian Foods.** The adventurous in search of traditional Hawaiian food (teriyaki chicken with two scoops of rice is not traditional Hawaiian food) should head to this no-frills hangout, where residents patiently wait in line on the sidewalk. You can sample *poi* (a paste made from pounded taro root), *lomilomi* salmon (salmon massaged until tender and served with minced onions and tomatoes), *laulau* (pork wrapped in taro leaves and steamed), smoky *kalua* pork (roasted in an underground oven), and *haupia* (like coconut Jell-O). The Hawaiian word *ono* means "delicious"—and locals agree with the name. [$] *Average main: $15* ✉ *726 Kapahulu Ave., Kapahulu* ☎ *808/737–2275* ✍ *Reservations not accepted* 💳 *No credit cards* ⏲ *Closed Sun.*

KAIMUKI

$$$$ MODERN HAWAIIAN 🍴 **3660 on the Rise.** This casually stylish eatery is a 10-minute drive from Waikiki in restaurant-packed Kaimuki. Sample Chef Russell Siu's New York Steak Alae (steak grilled with Hawaiian clay salt), the crab cakes, or the signature ahi katsu wrapped in nori and deep-fried with a wasabi-ginger butter sauce. Siu combines a deep understanding of local flavors with a sophisticated palate, making this place especially popular with homegrown gourmands. ■ **TIP→ The dining room can feel a bit snug when it's full (as it usually is); go early or late.** [$] *Average main: $37*

✉ *3660 Waialae Ave., Kaimuki* ☎ *808/737–1177* 🌐 *www.3660.com* ⏲ *No lunch. Closed Mon.*

$$ MODERN HAWAIIAN Fodor's Choice ★

🍴 **12th Avenue Grill.** Until October 2013, it was hard to get a table at this popular contemporary American spot—that's when it moved down the street to larger, airier digs with a big bar serving handcrafted cocktails. Now you have a better chance of trying chef Jason Schoonover's locavore, seasonal food. Bright flavors in sometimes surprising combinations mark dishes like kampachi sashimi dusted with coriander and lime and served with serrano chimichurri, and grilled chicken marinated in ginger, tarragon, honey, and mustard. The specials are always excellent, and the passion-fruit mochi cake with vanilla-ginger syrup is one of the best desserts in town. [$] *Average main: $26* ✉ *1120 12th Ave., Kaimuki* ☎ *808/732–9469* 🌐 *12thavegrill.com* ⏲ *No lunch.*

$ VIETNAMESE

🍴 **Hale Vietnam.** One of Oahu's first Vietnamese restaurants, this neighborhood spot, popular with budget-minded college kids, expresses its friendly character with its name: *hale* (hah-lay) is the Hawaiian word for house or home. You'll find the region's expected staples—green-papaya salad, summer rolls, pho, bun (rice noodles). If you're not sure what to order, just ask. The staff is known for their willingness to help those who don't know much about Vietnamese food. Reservations are taken for larger groups only. [$] *Average main: $12* ✉ *1140 12th Ave., Kaimuki* ☎ *808/735–7581.*

$$ CONTEMPORARY Fodor's Choice ★

🍴 **Salt Bar & Kitchen.** Hipsters and good-food hunters take their time grazing and drinking at this inviting two-level space, where the cocktails are crisp and the charcuterie house-cured. Sit at the bar or one of the tables on the second loft level and order small plates to share. Oxtail empanadas and grilled octopus with chorizo are perennial faves, but the offerings also include beautiful salad compositions (hearts of palm, sea asparagus, Thai basil, and charred tomato water), the charcuterie board accented with housemade pickles, or big plates like a Korean-flavored pastrami sandwich and a flatiron steak with fried egg purée. The food is innovative yet comforting at this sister of 12th Avenue Grill. [$] *Average main: $21* ✉ *3605 Waialae Ave, Kaimuki* ☎ *808/744–7567* 🌐 *www.salthonolulu.com* ⏲ *No lunch.*

$$ INTERNATIONAL Fodor's Choice ★

🍴 **Town.** Opened in 2005, stylish Town remains a hot spot for Honolulu's creative class and farm-to-table diners. Chef-owner Ed Kenney and his partner Dave Caldiero offer a Mediterranean-eclectic menu ranging from hand-cut pastas and refreshing composed salads (pastas and salads) to clean preparations of fish and meat (polenta with egg and asparagus or buttermilk panna cotta). Get a bunch of tasting plates to share—ahi tartare on risotto cakes and mussels in a fennel-Cinzano broth are instant winners—or go big with dishes such as *opah* (moonfish) in a Meyer-lemon-butter sauce and pork belly with salsa verde and polenta. If you're a vegetarian, ask for the bountiful veggie plate, which isn't on the menu. The restaurant serves breakfast and lunch, too. [$] *Average main: $25* ✉ *3435 Waialae Ave., Kaimuki* ☎ *808/735–5900* 🌐 *www.townkaimuki.com* ✍ *Reservations essential* ⏲ *Closed Sun.*

2

KAHALA

$$$$
ASIAN FUSION
✕ **Hoku's at the Kahala.** Everything about this room speaks of quality and sophistication: the wall of windows with their beach views, the avant-garde cutlery and dinnerware, the solicitous staff, and the carefully constructed Euro-Pacific cuisine. The menu constantly changes, but you can count on Chef Wayne Hirabayashi to use fresh, local ingredients when possible in his innovative dishes such as braised short-rub tempura, salt-crusted rack of lamb with tomato confit, and butter-poached lobster with passionfruit jus. It's an excellent and popular choice for special occasions or for Sunday brunch. The dress code is collared shirts, no beachwear. $ *Average main: $55* ⊠ *The Kahala Hotel & Resort, 5000 Kahala Ave., Kahala* ☎ *808/739–8760* ⊕ *www.kahalaresort.com* ⌂ *Reservations essential* ⊙ *Closed Mon. and Tues. No lunch.*

$
GREEK
✕ **Olive Tree Cafe.** An Iranian Hellenophile owns this bustling, self-serve café that serves the best taramasalata, falafel, and souvlaki in town. Stand in line at the counter to order while your companion tries to shanghai one of the outdoor tables. It's BYOB, and you can get good wines next door at Olive Tree's sister gourmet shop, Oliver. There's no corkage fee, and they'll even lend you a corkscrew. Located behind Kahala Mall, this is a great option if you're headed back to town late from a day at the beach on the east side. $ *Average main: $13* ⊠ *4614 Kilauea Ave., Suite 107, Kahala* ☎ *808/737–0303* ⌂ *Reservations not accepted* ▭ *No credit cards* ⊙ *No lunch.*

SOUTHEAST OAHU

$$$
MODERN
HAWAIIAN
✕ **Roy's.** Roy Yamaguchi is one of the 12 founding chefs of Hawaiian Regional Cuisine—a culinary movement that put Hawaii on the food map back in 1991. Opened in 1988, his flagship restaurant across the highway from Maunalua Bay is still packed every night. Food-savvy visitors on a Hawaiian Regional Cuisine pilgrimage mix with well-heeled residents. (If you're sensitive to pressure to turn the table, it's best to visit later in the evening.) The wide-ranging and ever-interesting Hawaiian fusion menu is made up of his longtime classics, like Szechuan-spiced baby back ribs and blackened ahi with soy mustard butter sauce, and contemporary creations such as a pork chop with Hawaiian-chili chimichurri sauce and *andagi* (an Okinawan donut hole) made with poi. There's also an exceptional wine list. The Waikiki location is equally busy and has a four-course menu for vegans and gluten-free eaters. $ *Average main: $34* ⊠ *Hawaii Kai Corporate Plaza, 6600 Kalanianaole Hwy., Hawaii Kai, Honolulu* ☎ *808/396–7697* ⊕ *www.royshawaii.com* ⌂ *Reservations essential* ⊙ *No lunch.*

WINDWARD OAHU

$$$
STEAKHOUSE
✕ **Buzz's Original Steakhouse.** Virtually unchanged since it opened in 1967, this neighborhood institution opposite Kailua Beach Park is filled with the enticing aroma of grilling steaks. It doesn't matter if you're a bit sandy (though bare feet are not allowed). Find a spot in the cozy maze of rooms, stop at the salad bar, and order up a steak, a burger, teriyaki chicken, or the fresh fish special. If you sit at the bar, expect to make

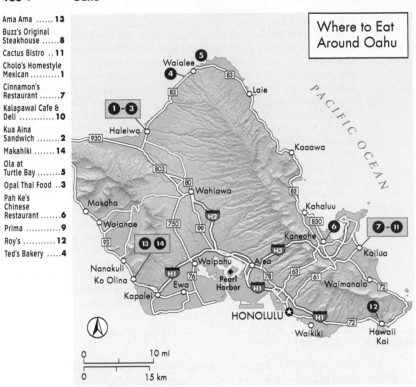

Where to Eat
Around Oahu

friends. ■TIP➔ Be warned: the mai tais here are the strongest you'll find anywhere. $ *Average main: $35* ✉ *413 Kawailoa Rd.* ☎ *808/261–4661* ⊕ *www.buzzssteakhouse.com* ⌂ *Reservations essential.*

$$ ✕ **Kalapawai Cafe & Deli.** Chef Jason Iwane, born and raised in Kailua,
ECLECTIC   always keeps things interesting at this one-stop Mediterranean-leaning café, wine bar, bakery, and gourmet deli. The green-and-white Kailua landmark is a meeting spot for Windward residents. Come in on your way to the beach for a cup of coffee and bagel and stop back for a gourmet pizza or bruschetta (how does eggplant confit, sweet peppers, honey, and goat cheese sound?) at lunchtime. The menu changes frequently, but at dinner you may find tempting choices such as duck ragout with dried cherries and mushrooms, or fresh grilled fish with lemongrass risotto and red curry aioli. ■TIP➔ If you're staying in a Kailua vacation rental, the is the place to pick up prepared foods such as stuffed grape leaves and crab cakes to take home. $ *Average main: $19* ✉ *750 Kailua Rd, Kailua, Honolulu* ☎ *808/262-3354* ⊕ *www. kalapawaimarket.com.*

$$ ✕ **Pah Ke's Chinese Restaurant.** If you happen to be on the windward side
CHINESE   at dinner time, this out-of-the-ordinary Chinese restaurant—named for the local pidgin term for Chinese (literally translated this is Chinese's Chinese Restaurant)—is a good option. Ebullient owner and chef Raymond Siu, a former hotel pastry chef, focuses on healthier cooking

techniques and local ingredients. The menu offers all the usual suspects (like kung pao chicken), but you should hone in on the "house specialties" such as braised short ribs rubbed with Kona coffee and curry, and scallops with flash-fried spinach leaves. Call ahead to find out if he's got any cool specials and to alert them to dietary restrictions—they are very accommodating. [$] *Average main: $22* ✉ *46-018 Kamehameha Hwy., Kaneohe* ☎ *808/235–4505* 🌐 *www.pahke.com.*

$$ PIZZA 🍴 **Prima.** The beautifully blistered pies are cooked in a white-tiled Ferrara wood-burning oven that you can see in the open kitchen of this bright, light pizzeria with robin's egg–blue Eames shell chairs. This is as Neapolitan as it gets on Oahu, and these are the best pizzas on the island, topped with such ingredients as soppressata, prosciutto, and spicy meatballs. At dinner, look for a short menu of chef specials, perhaps a grilled octopus salad or square of roasted pork belly. [$] *Average main: $18* ✉ *Kailua Foodland Marketplace, 108 Hekili St., Kailua, Honolulu* ☎ *808/888–8933* 🌐 *www.primahawaii.com.*

THE NORTH SHORE

$ MEXICAN 🍴 **Cholo's Homestyle Mexican.** There are a few places on the North Shore that are the area's great gathering places. Foodland is one. Another is Cholo's. Festively done up with Mexican tchotchkes, this longtime spot serves up decent rice-and-beans plates of Mexican standards (steak fajitas, burritos, enchiladas) at affordable prices. The fish tacos are made with sashimi-grade ahi—caught just offshore and brought in from Haleiwa Pier—and the margaritas are made with locally sourced fruit. (You won't find a sweeter fresh mango margarita anywhere.) Early birds should check out the morning menu; the restaurant opens at 9 am and serves different variations of the breakfast burrito. [$] *Average main: $13* ✉ *North Shore Marketplace, 66-250 Kamehameha Hwy* ☎ *808/637–3059* 🌐 *www.cholos.mx.*

$ BURGER 🍴 **Kua Aina Sandwich.** This North Shore spot has gone from funky burger shack (it first opened in 1975) to institution, with crowds of tourists and locals standing in line to order the large, hand-formed burgers heaped with bacon, cheese, salsa, and pineapples. The patties are packed tight, so they tend to be on the dry side. Kua Aina also has a Honolulu location in the Ward Centre. [$] *Average main: $10* ✉ *66-160 Kamehameha Hwy.* ☎ *808/637–6067* ✍ *Reservations not accepted.*

$$$ MODERN HAWAIIAN 🍴 **Ola at Turtle Bay Resort.** In a rustic-beam-and-concrete-floor pavilion literally on the sand, Ola's draw is its ocean-view location at the Turtle Bay Resort on the North Shore. In an area where a quasi-Mexican cantina is considered a big night out, this spot with reliable Hawaiian regional cuisine is a favorite standby. Dishes such as five-spiced braised beef short ribs with corn relish or a catch of the day with a macadamia nut pesto cream deliver bold flavors. [$] *Average main: $42* ✉ *Turtle Bay Resort, 57-091 Kamehameha Hwy., Kahuku* ☎ *808/293–0801* 🌐 *olaislife.com.*

$ THAI Fodor's Choice ★ 🍴 **Opal Thai Food.** When you go on your big adventure to the North Shore, you might want to stop at this crowded little room, which serves the best Thai food on the island. Sanith "Opel" Sirichandhra and his wife Aoy are neighborhood celebrities for their down-to-earth ways and pungent, addictive *tom kha* (coconut curry) soup, green curry, and drunken noodles. Opel (yes, the spelling is different from that of the restaurant's name) is a vegetarian, so he's tuned in to accommodating herbivores and people with food sensitivities. [$] *Average main: $10* ✉ *Haleiwa Town Center, 66-197 C Kamehameha Hwy.* ☎ *808/637–7950* ⏲ *Closed Sun. and Mon.*

$ AMERICAN 🍴 **Ted's Bakery.** Sunburned tourists and salty surfers rub shoulders in their quest for Ted's famous chocolate *haupia* pie (layered coconut and chocolate puddings topped with whipped cream) and hearty plate lunches—like gravy-drenched hamburger steak and mahimahi. Parking spots and the umbrella-shaded tables are a premium, be prepared to grab and go. [$] *Average main: $9* ✉ *59-024 Kamehameha Hwy.* ☎ *808/638–8207* 🌐 *www.tedsbakery.com* ✍ *Reservations not accepted.*

WEST (LEEWARD) OAHU

$$$$ MODERN HAWAIIAN 🍴 **Ama Ama.** There's nothing Mickey Mouse about the food at the fine-dining restaurant of this Disney resort. Chef Kevin Chong was chef de cuisine at Chef Mavro for seven years, and his food has a brightness and innovation not always seen in resort retaurants. Add to that the view of the Ko Olina lagoons and Pacific Ocean—and live music by top local performers—and you have an evening worth the pretty penny. From a Thai seafood curry to a pork chop with a mushroom ragout, the ingredients are largely local, but the flavors are international. And the puffed potatoes are a fun side. If you're on a budget, skip dinner—breakfast and lunch entrées are half the price (although menu offerings vary). [$] *Average main: $40* ✉ *Aulani, a Disney Resort & Spa, 92-1185 Aliinui Dr., Ko Olina, Kapolei* ☎ *808/674–6200* 🌐 *disneyparks.disney.go.com* ✍ *Reservations essential.*

$$$$ HAWAIIAN FAMILY 🍴 **Makahiki—The Bounty of the Islands.** The buffet restaurant at Disney's Aulani resort offers a wide variety of locally produced items, as well as familiar dishes from the mainland and the rest of the world. You'll find sustainable Hawaiian seafood, Asian selections, familiar grilled meats and vegetables, and a kids' menu. If you have children, plan months in advance to get a reservation for the Character Breakfast, as it's only offered on select days and is always sold out. An à la carte menu is also available. **■ TIP→ Arrive early for dinner and have a drink at the adjacent Olelo Room, where the staff are fluent in Hawaiian; you can get a language lesson along with your libation.** [$] *Average main: $43* ✉ *Aulani, a Disney Resort & Spa, 92-1185 Aliinui Dr., Ko Olina, Kapolei* ☎ *808/674–6200* 🌐 *resorts.disney.go.com* ✍ *Reservations essential.*

WHERE TO STAY

Updated by Catherine E. Toth

As in real estate, location matters. And though Oahu is just 44 miles long and 30 miles wide—meaning you can circle the entire island before lunch—it boasts neighborhoods and lodgings with very different vibes and personalities. If you like the action and choices of big cities, consider Waikiki, a 24-hour playground with everything from surf to karaoke bars. Those who want an escape from urban life look to the island's

2

leeward or windward sides, or the North Shore, whose surf culture creates a laid-back atmosphere.

Most of the island's major hotels and resorts are in Waikiki, which has a lot to offer within a small area, namely shopping, restaurants, nightlife, and nearly 3 miles of sandy beach. You don't need a car in Waikiki; everything is nearby, from the Honolulu Zoo and Waikiki Aquarium, the 300-acre Kapiolani Park, running and biking paths, grocery stores, and access to public transportation that can take you to museums, shopping centers, and historic landmarks around the island.

You'll find places to stay along the entire stretch of Kalakaua Avenue, with smaller and quieter hotels and condos at the eastern end, and more business-centric accommodations on the western edge of Waikiki, near the Hawaii Convention Center, and Ala Moana Center. Look for better value in hotels off the beach.

The majority of tourists who come to Oahu stay in Waikiki, but choosing accommodations away from the center of Waikiki can afford you the opportunity to be closer to shopping and restaurants at Ala Moana Center, the largest shopping mall in the state. It also provides easier access to the airport.

If you want to get away from the bustle of the city, consider a stay on Oahu's Leeward Coast—namely, at the Ko Olina resort area, about 20 minutes from the Honolulu International Airport and 40 minutes from Waikiki. Here, there are great golf courses and quiet beaches and coves that make for a relaxing getaway. But you'll need a car to get off the property if you want to explore the rest of the island.

Other more low-key options are in elegant Kahala or on the North Shore. Both are charming, with nearby eateries and coffee shops, unique shops, and some of the island's best beaches—plus one of the top resorts, Turtle Bay, on the North Shore.

Prices shown in reviews are the lowest price of a standard double room in high season. For expanded hotel reviews, visit Fodors.com.

HONOLULU

WAIKIKI

$$$ **Aston at the Waikiki Banyan.** Families and active travelers love the convenience and action of this hotel, just a block from Waikiki Beach and bustling Kalakaua Avenue. **Pros:** many rooms have great views; walking distance to shops and restaurants. **Cons:** trekking to the beach (a block away) with all of your gear; no on-site restaurant. $ *Rooms from: $331* ✉ *201 Ohua Ave., Waikiki* ☎ *808/922–0555, 877/997–6667* ⊕ *www. astonwaikikibanyan.com* ⟳ *876 units* ❗ *No meals.*

RENTAL
FAMILY

$$$$ **Aston Waikiki Beach Tower.** You'll find the elegance of a luxury all-suites condominium combined with the intimacy and service of a boutique hotel right on bustling Kalakaua Avenue. **Pros:** *very* large rooms—big enough to move into. **Cons:** no on-site restaurants; you must cross a busy street to the beach. $ *Rooms from: $499* ✉ *2470 Kalakaua Ave., Waikiki* ☎ *877/997–6667* ⊕ *www.astonwaikikibeachtower.com* ⟳ *140 units* ❗ *No meals.*

RENTAL

BEST BETS FOR OAHU LODGING

Fodor's Choice★

Ala Moana Hotel, $$$, p. 171
Halekulani, $$$$, p. 165
The Kahala Hotel & Resort, $$$$, p. 171
The Royal Hawaiian, $$$$, p. 169

By Price

$

The Breakers, p. 164
Royal Grove Hotel, p. 169

$$

The Doubletree Alana, p. 164
The Equus Hotel, p. 165
Hilton Hawaiian Village, p. 165
Hilton Waikiki Beach Hotel, p. 165

$$$

Ala Moana Hotel, p. 171
Hyatt Regency Resort and Spa, p. 167

$$$$

Halekulani, p. 165
JW Marriott Ihilani Resort & Spa, p. 172
The Kahala Hotel & Resort, p. 171
Marriott Ko Olina, p. 172
Moana Surfrider, p. 168
Outrigger Reef on the Beach, p. 168
The Royal Hawaiian, p. 169

By Experience

BEST FOR ROMANCE

Halekulani, $$$$, p. 165
The Kahala Hotel & Resort, $$$$, p. 171
Moana Surfrider, $$$$, p. 168
The Royal Hawaiian, $$$$, p. 169

BEST BEACH

Hilton Hawaiian Village, $$, p. 165
JW Marriott Ihilani Resort and Spa, $$$$, p. 172
The Kahala Hotel & Resort, $$$$, p. 171
Marriott Ko Olina, $$$$, p. 172

$ RENTAL **The Breakers.** Despite an explosion of high-rise construction all around it, the low-rise Breakers continues to offer a taste of 1960s Hawaii in this small complex a mere half-block from Waikiki Beach. **Pros:** intimate atmosphere; great location. **Cons:** a bit worn down; parking space is limited though free. [$] *Rooms from: $140* ✉ *250 Beach Walk, Waikiki* ☎ *808/923–3181, 800/426–0494* 📠 *808/923–7174* ✉ *breakers@aloha.net* 🌐 *www.breakers-hawaii.com* 🛏 *64 units* 🍴 *No meals.*

$$$ RENTAL **Castle Waikiki Shore.** Nestled between Fort DeRussy Beach Park and the Outrigger Reef on the Beach, this is the only condo hotel directly on Waikiki Beach. **Pros:** great security; great views; great management; free high-speed Wi-Fi available in rooms. **Cons:** beach out front is kind of thin; two-night stay minimum; no on-site dining. [$] *Rooms from: $270* ✉ *2161 Kalia Rd., Waikiki* ☎ *808/952–4500, 800/367–5004* 📠 *808/952–4580* 🌐 *www.castleresorts.com/Home/accommodations/waikiki-shore* 🛏 *168 units.*

$$ HOTEL **Doubletree Alana Waikiki.** Its location—a 10-minute walk from the Hawaii Convention Center—and its 24-hour business center and gym meet the requirements of the Doubletree's global business clientele. **Pros:** free Wi-Fi in lobby; professional staff; pleasant public spaces; walk-in glass showers with oversized rain showerheads. **Cons:** it's a 10-minute walk to the beach. [$] *Rooms from: $209* ✉ *1956 Ala Moana*

Blvd., Waikiki ☎ *808/941–7275* 🌐 *doubletree3.hilton.com* 🛏 *317 rooms* 🍴 *No meals.*

$$$ RESORT FAMILY 🏨 **Embassy Suites Waikiki Beach Walk.** In a place where space is at a premium, the only all-suites resort in Hawaii offers families and groups traveling together a bit more room to move about, with two 21-story towers housing one- and two-bedroom suites. **Pros:** great location next to Waikiki Beach Walk and all of its shops and restaurants; great vibe; nice pool deck; complimentary hot breakfast served daily. **Cons:** no direct beach access. [$] *Rooms from: $319* ✉ *201 Beachwalk St., Waikiki* ☎ *800/362–2779, 808/921–2345* 🌐 *www.embassysuiteswaikiki.com* 🛏 *300 1-bedroom suites, 69 2-bedroom suites* 🍴 *Breakfast.*

$$ HOTEL 🏨 **The Equus Hotel.** This small hotel has been completely renovated with a Hawaiian country theme that pays tribute to Hawaii's polo-playing history. **Pros:** casual; fun atmosphere; attentive staff; nicely furnished rooms. **Cons:** on a very busy road you must cross to get to the beach. [$] *Rooms from: $190* ✉ *1696 Ala Moana Blvd., Waikiki* ☎ *808/949–0061, 800/669–7719* 🌐 *www.equushotel.com* 🛏 *66 rooms, 1 suite* 🍴 *No meals.*

$$$$ RESORT Fodor's Choice ★ 🏨 **Halekulani.** The luxurious Halekulani exemplifies the translation of its name—the "house befitting heaven"—and from the moment you step into the lobby, the attention to detail and impeccable service wrap you in privilege at this beachfront location away from Waikiki's bustle. **Pros:** location on small (private-feeling) beach; heavenly interior spaces; wonderful dining opportunities in-house; world-class service; artsy perks. **Cons:** might feel a bit formal for Waikiki; pricey. [$] *Rooms from: $500* ✉ *2199 Kalia Rd., Waikiki* ☎ *808/923–2311, 800/367–2343* 🌐 *www.halekulani.com* 🛏 *411 rooms, 43 suites* 🍴 *No meals.*

$$$$ HOTEL 🏨 **Hawaii Prince Hotel & Golf Club Waikiki.** This slim high-rise with 538 oceanfront rooms including 57 luxury suites fronts Ala Wai Yacht Harbor at the *ewa* (west) edge of Waikiki. **Pros:** fantastic views; all very elegant; easy exit from complicated-to-maneuver Waikiki; smoking and non-smoking rooms available. **Cons:** no free Internet; no beach access. [$] *Rooms from: $415* ✉ *100 Holomoana St., Waikiki* ☎ *888/977–4623, 808/956–1111* 🌐 *www.hawaiiprincehotel.com* 🛏 *481 rooms, 57 suites* 🍴 *No meals.*

$$ RESORT FAMILY 🏨 **Hilton Hawaiian Village Beach Resort and Spa.** Location, location, location: this megaresort and convention destination sprawls over 22 acres on Waikiki's widest stretch of beach, with the green lawns of neighboring Fort DeRussy creating a buffer zone to the high-rise lineup of central Waikiki. **Pros:** activities and amenities can keep you and the kids busy for weeks; stellar spa. **Cons:** ongoing renovations and construction noise might be a problem; oceanfront rooms in the Rainbow Tower may have obstructed views as the hotel is repairing its famous mural; size of property can be overwhelming; the hotel charges a resort fee of $30 (plus tax) per room, per night. [$] *Rooms from: $239* ✉ *2005 Kalia Rd., Waikiki* ☎ *808/949–4321, 800/774–1500* 🌐 *www.hiltonhawaiianvillage.com* 🛏 *3,616 rooms, 244 suites, 639 condominiums* 🍴 *No meals.*

$$ HOTEL 🏨 **Hilton Waikiki Beach Hotel.** Two blocks from Kuhio Beach, this 37-story high-rise, located on the Diamond Head end of Waikiki, is great for

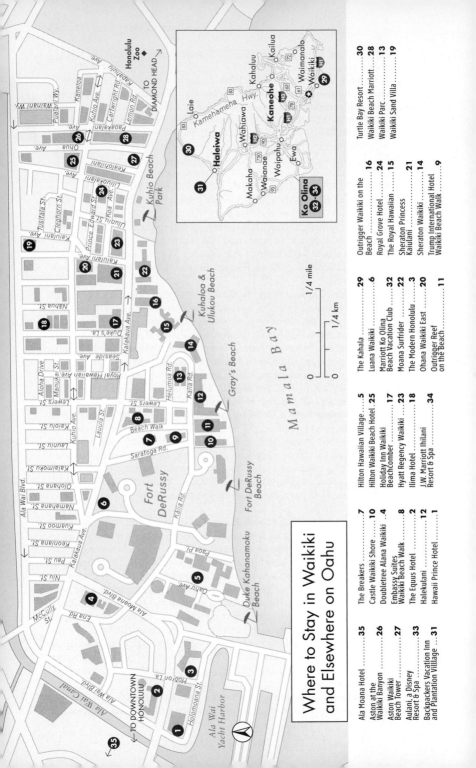

Where to Stay in Waikiki and Elsewhere on Oahu

2

WHERE TO STAY ON OAHU

	Local Vibe	Pros	Cons
Honolulu	Lodging options are limited in downtown Honolulu, but if you want an urban feel look no farther. Farther afield in Kahala you'll find one of the island's top resorts.	Access to a wide selection of art galleries, boutiques, and new restaurants as well as Chinatown.	If you're looking to get away from it all, downtown Honolulu is not the place.
Waikiki	Lodgings abound in Waikiki, from youth hostels to five-star accommodations. The area is always abuzz with activity and anything you desire is within walking distance.	You can surf in front of the hotels, wander miles of beach, and explore hundreds of restaurants and bars.	This is tourist central. Prices are high, and you are not going to get the true Hawaii experience.
North Shore	This is true country living, with one luxurious resort exception. It's bustling in the winter (when the surf is up) but pretty slow-paced in the summer.	Amazing surf and long stretches of sand truly epitomize the beach culture in Hawaii. Historic Haleiwa has enough stores to keep shopaholics busy.	Accommodations are limited, there is zero nightlife, and traffic can get heavy during winter months.
West (Leeward) Oahu	This is the resort side of the rock; there is little outside of these resorts, but plenty on the grounds to keep you occupied for a week.	Ko Olina's lagoons offer the most kid-friendly swimming on the island, and the golf courses on this side are magnificent. Rare is the rainy day out here.	You are isolated from the rest of Oahu, with little in the way of shopping or jungle hikes.

travelers who want to be near the action, but not right in it. **Pros:** good value; central location; very helpful staff; pleasant, comfortable public spaces. **Cons:** a bit of a distance to the beach; very few rooms with views. [$] *Rooms from: $219* ✉ *2500 Kuhio Ave., Waikiki* ☎ *808/922–0811, 888/370–0980* 🌐 *www3.hilton.com* 🛏 *601 rooms, 8 suites* 🍴 *No meals.*

$$$ HOTEL FAMILY 🏨 **Holiday Inn Waikiki Beachcomber Resort.** Located almost directly across from the upgraded Royal Hawaiian Center, next door to the International Marketplace, and 300 steps from the beach, the Holiday Inn is a well-situated family-friendly hotel. **Pros:** lots of freebies; in the thick of Waikiki action. **Cons:** very busy area; no direct beach access; no on-site cultural activities. [$] *Rooms from: $319* ✉ *2300 Kalakaua Ave., Waikiki* ☎ *808/922–4646, 877/317–5756* 🌐 *www.waikikibeachcomberresort.com* 🛏 *491 rooms, 5 suites* 🍴 *No meals.*

$$$ RESORT FAMILY 🏨 **Hyatt Regency Waikiki Resort and Spa.** Though it's across the street from Kuhio Beach, the Hyatt is actually considered oceanfront, as there's no resort between it and the Pacific Ocean. **Pros:** public spaces are open; elegant and very professional spa; kid-friendly; close to the beach. **Cons:** in a very busy and crowded part of Waikiki; on-site pool is quite small; can feel a bit like you're staying in a shopping mall. [$] *Rooms from:*

$300 ⊠ Hyatt Regency Waikiki Resort and Spa, 2424 Kalakaua Ave., Waikiki ☎ 808/923–1234, 800/633–7313 ⊕ www.hyattregencywaikiki. com ⟿ 1,230 rooms, 18 suites ⦿ No meals.

$$
RENTAL
⚏ **Ilima Hotel.** Tucked away on a residential side street near Waikiki's Ala Wai Canal, this locally owned 17-story condominium-style hotel is a gem. **Pros:** big rooms are great for families; free parking in Waikiki is a rarity; on-site coin-operated laundry facilities; smoking rooms available. **Cons:** limited hotel parking, and street parking can be difficult to find; not the most luxurious accomodations; 10-minute walk to the beach. ⓢ *Rooms from: $215 ⊠ Ilima Hotel, 445 Nohonani St., Waikiki ☎ 808/923–1877, 800/801–9366 ⊕ www.ilima.com ⟿ 99 units ⦿ No meals.*

$$$$
RESORT
⚏ **Moana Surfrider, A Westin Resort & Spa.** Outrageous rates of $1.50 per night were the talk of the town when the "First Lady of Waikiki" opened her doors in 1901; today, this historic beauty—the oldest hotel in Waikiki—is still a wedding and honeymoon favorite with a sweeping main staircase and period furnishings in its historic Moana wing. **Pros:** elegant; historic property; best place on Waikiki Beach to watch hula and have a drink; can't beat the location. **Cons:** you'll likely dodge bridal parties in the lobby; the hotel now charges a mindboggling resort fee of $31.41 per room, per day. ⓢ *Rooms from: $570 ⊠ 2365 Kalakaua Ave., Waikiki ☎ 808/922–3111, 866/500–8313 ⊕ www.moana-surfrider.com ⟿ 750 rooms, 46 suites ⦿ No meals.*

$$$$
HOTEL
⚏ **The Modern Honolulu.** Gen Xers will immediately feel at home in this edgy hotel with an eye to slick design. **Pros:** excellent design; unpretentious feel; great bars and restaurants; nice spa. **Cons:** not kid-friendly; on the outer edge of Waikiki; direct beach access a 5-minute walk away. ⓢ *Rooms from: $450 ⊠ 1775 Ala Moana Blvd., Waikiki ☎ 808/943–5800, 866/970–4161 ⊕ www.themodernhonolulu.com ⟿ 353 rooms; 30 suites ⦿ No meals.*

$$$
HOTEL
⚏ **Ohana Waikiki East.** If you want to be in central Waikiki and don't want to pay beachfront lodging prices, consider the Ohana Waikiki East. **Pros:** close to the beach and reasonable rates; decent on-site eateries, including a piano bar. **Cons:** some rooms with no lanai and very basic public spaces. ⓢ *Rooms from: $279 ⊠ 150 Kaiulani Ave., Waikiki ☎ 808/922–5353, 866/956–4262 ⊕ www.ohanahotelsoahu. com/ohana_east/ ⟿ 403 rooms, 38 suites ⦿ No meals.*

$$$
HOTEL
⚏ **Luana Waikiki.** At the entrance to Waikiki near Fort DeRussy is this welcoming hotel offering both rooms and condominium units, and in January 2014 it came under the umbrella of Aqua Hospitality. **Pros:** on-site full service spa; sundeck with barbecue grills (rare for Waikiki); walking distance to shops and restaurants; on-site coin-operated laundry; free Wi-Fi. **Cons:** no direct beach access. ⓢ *Rooms from: $265 ⊠ 2045 Kalakaua Ave., Waikiki ☎ 808/955-6000, 866/940–2782 ⊕ www.aqualuanawaikiki.com ⟿ 225 units ⦿ No meals.*

$$$$
HOTEL
FAMILY
⚏ **Outrigger Reef on the Beach.** Multimillion-dollar renovations have drastically updated this beachfront property, adding a new entrance that incorporates a Hawaiian voyaging design theme; expanded guest rooms; larger and more contemporary bathrooms; and a new signature restaurant—the poolside Kani Ka Pila Grille, with nightly live music by legendary Hawaiian entertainers—though the Shore Bird Restaurant & Beach

2

Bar and Ocean House Restaurant also remain. **Pros:** no resort fees; on beach; direct access to Waikiki Beach Walk. **Cons:** views from non-oceanfront rooms are uninspiring; can be pricey. $ *Rooms from: $489 ☒ 2169 Kalia Rd., Waikiki ☎ 808/923–3111, 866/956–4262 ⊕ www.outriggerreef-onthebeach.com ↗ 631 rooms, 38 suites* ¶©| *No meals.*

ASK FOR A LANAI

Islanders love their porches, balconies, and verandas—all wrapped up in a single Hawaiian word: *lanai.* You may not want to look at a parking lot, so when booking, ask about the lanai and be sure to specify the view (understanding that top views command top dollars). Also, check that the lanai is not merely a step-out or Juliet balcony, with just enough room to lean against a railing—you want a lanai that is big enough for patio seating.

$$$$
RESORT
Outrigger Waikiki on the Beach. Renovated in 2012, this star of Outrigger Hotels & Resorts sits on one of the finest strands of Waikiki Beach. **Pros:** no resort fee; the best bar on the beach is downstairs; free Wi-Fi in lobby; on-site coin-operated laundry. **Cons:** the lobby feels a bit like an airport with so many people using it as a throughway to the beach. $ *Rooms from: $489 ☒ 2335 Kalakaua Ave., Waikiki ☎ 808/923–0711, 808/956–4262 ⊕ www.outriggerwaikikihotel.com ↗ 479 rooms, 30 suites* ¶©| *No meals.*

$
HOTEL
Royal Grove Hotel. Two generations of the Fong family have put their heart and soul into the operation of this tiny (by Waikiki standards), pink six-story hotel that feels like a throwback to the days of boarding houses, where rooms were outfitted for function, not style, and served up with a wealth of home-style hospitality at a price that didn't break the bank. **Pros:** very economical Waikiki option; lots of character. **Cons:** no a/c in some rooms; rooms are dated; no on-site parking. $ *Rooms from: $70 ☒ 151 Uluniu Ave., Waikiki ☎ 808/923–7691 ⊕ www.royalgrovehotel.com ↗ 80 rooms, 7 suites* ¶©| *No meals.*

$$$$
RESORT
Fodor's Choice
★
The Royal Hawaiian, a Luxury Collection Resort. There's nothing like the legendary Pink Palace of the Pacific, and an $85 million face-lift in 2009, the iconic hotel set on 14 acres of prime Waikiki Beach is a unique blend of luxury and tradition. **Pros:** can't be beat for history; mai tais and sunsets are amazing; there's a doctors-on-call service. **Cons:** history is not cheap; you'd better like pink; resort fee of $36.65 per room per day. $ *Rooms from: $765 ☒ 2259 Kalakaua Ave., Waikiki ☎ 808/923–7311, 866/716–8110 ⊕ www.royal-hawaiian.com ↗ 495 rooms, 33 suites* ¶©| *No meals.*

$$$
HOTEL
Sheraton Princess Kaiulani. This hotel sits across the street from its upscale sister property, the Moana Surfrider. **Pros:** in the heart of everything in Waikiki; on-site surfboard storage (for a fee). **Cons:** no direct beach access; kids' activities off-site; pool closes early; no spa; hotel charges a resort fee of $26.18 tax inclusive, per room per day. $ *Rooms from: $310 ☒ 120 Kaiulani Ave., Waikiki ☎ 808/922–5811, 866/716–8109 ⊕ www.princess-kaiulani.com ↗ 1,142 rooms, 14 suites* ¶©| *No meals.*

$$$$
HOTEL
Sheraton Waikiki. If you don't mind crowds, this could be the place for you: towering over its neighbors on the prow of Waikiki's famous

sands, the enormous Sheraton Waikiki is center stage on Waikiki Beach. **Pros:** location in the heart of everything. **Cons:** busy atmosphere clashes with laid-back Hawaiian style. $ *Rooms from: $515* ✉ *2255 Kalakaua Ave., Waikiki* ☎ *808/922–4422, 866/716–8109* ⊕ *www.sheraton-waikiki.com* ⊷ *1,634 rooms and suites* ⦿*No meals.*

$$$$
HOTEL
⌨ **Trump International Hotel Waikiki Beach Walk.** One of the chicest hotels on the Waikiki scene, Trump has been drawing rave reviews since its opening in November 2009. **Pros:** beautifully appointed rooms; on the edge of Waikiki so a bit quieter; great views of Friday fireworks. **Cons:** must cross street to reach the beach; pricey. $ *Rooms from: $509* ✉ *223 Saratoga Rd., Waikiki* ☎ *808/683–7777, 877/683–7401* ⊕ *www.trumphotelcollection.com/waikiki/* ⊷ *305 rooms, 127 suites* ⦿*No meals.*

> ## CONDO COMFORTS
>
> The local **Foodland** (✉ *Market City, 2939 Harding Ave., near intersection with Kapahulu Ave. and highway overpass, Kaimuki* ☎ *808/734-6303* ✉ *Ala Moana Center, 1450 Ala Moana Blvd., ground level, Ala Moana* ☎ *808/949-5044*) grocery-store chain has two locations near Waikiki. A smaller version of larger Foodland, **Food Pantry** (✉ *2370 Kuhio Ave., across from Miramar hotel, Waikiki* ☎ *808/923-9831* ✉ *2370 Kuhio Ave., across from Miramar hotel, Waikiki* ☎ *808/923-9831*) also has apparel, beach stuff, and tourist-oriented items.

$$$$
RESORT
⌨ **Waikiki Beach Marriott Resort & Spa.** On the eastern edge of Waikiki, this flagship Marriott sits on about 5 acres across from Kuhio Beach and close to Kapiolani Park, the Honolulu Zoo, and Waikiki Aquarium. **Pros:** stunning views of Waikiki; professional service; airy tropical public spaces; unbeatable location. **Cons:** large impersonal hotel; Kalakaua Avenue can be noisy. $ *Rooms from: $390* ✉ *2552 Kalakaua Ave., Waikiki* ☎ *808/922–6611, 800/367–5370* ⊕ *www.marriottwaikiki.com* ⊷ *1,175 rooms, 135 suites* ⦿*No meals.*

$$$
HOTEL
⌨ **Waikiki Parc.** In contrast to the stately vintage-Hawaiian elegance of her sister hotel, the Halekulani, the Waikiki Parc makes a contemporary statement, offering the same attention to detail in service and architectural design but lacking the beachfront location and higher prices. **Pros:** modern; great access to Waikiki Beach Walk. **Cons:** no direct beach access. $ *Rooms from: $285* ✉ *2233 Helumoa Rd., Waikiki* ☎ *808/921–7272, 800/422–0450* ⊕ *www.waikikiparc.com* ⊷ *297 rooms* ⦿*No meals.*

$
HOTEL
⌨ **Waikiki Sand Villa.** Families and those looking for an economical rate without sacrificing proximity to Waikiki's beaches, dining, and shopping return to the Waikiki Sand Villa year after year. **Pros:** fun bar; fitness center; economical choice. **Cons:** the noise from the bar might annoy some; 10-minute walk to the beach. $ *Rooms from: $165* ✉ *2375 Ala Wai Blvd., Waikiki* ☎ *808/922–4744, 800/247–1903* ⊕ *www.sandvillahotel.com* ⊷ *214 rooms* ⦿*No meals.*

ALA MOANA

$$$
HOTEL
Fodor'sChoice
★

⊡ Ala Moana Hotel. A great value in a pricey hotel market, this well located and nicely appointed hotel is connected to Oahu's largest mall, the Ala Moana Center, by a pedestrian ramp, and is a 10-minute walk to Waikiki. **Pros:** great value; adjacent to Ala Moana Center and all of its shops and restaurants; rooms nicely appointed; quick walk to the beach. **Cons:** outside the heartbeat of Waikiki; not right on the beach; large, impersonal hotel. $ *Rooms from: $289* ✉ *410 Atkinson Dr., Ala Moana* ☎ *808/955–4811, 866/956–4262* ⊕ *www.alamoanahotelhonolulu. com* 📮 *1,090 studios, 44 suites* ⦿ *No meals.*

KAHALA

$$$$
RESORT
Fodor'sChoice
★

⊡ The Kahala Hotel & Resort. Hidden away in the upscale residential neighborhood of Kahala (on the other side of Diamond Head from Waikiki), this elegant oceanfront hotel has played host to celebrities, princesses, the Dalai Lama, and nearly every president since Lyndon Johnson as one of Hawaii's very first luxury resorts. **Pros:** away from hectic Waikiki; beautiful rooms and public spaces; heavenly spa; pet-friendly. **Cons:** Waikiki is a drive away. $ *Rooms from: $495* ✉ *5000 Kahala Ave., Kahala* ☎ *808/739–8888, 800/367–2525* ⊕ *www. kahalaresort.com* 📮 *306 rooms, 32 suites* ⦿ *No meals.*

HOTELS' CULTURAL PROGRAMS

Hotels, especially in Waikiki, are fueling a resurgence of Hawaiian culture, thanks to repeat visitors who want a more authentic island experience. In addition to lei-making and hula-dancing lessons, you can learn how to strum a ukulele, listen to Grammy Award–winning Hawaiian musicians, watch a revered master *kumu* (teacher) share the art of ancient hula and chant, chat with a marine biologist about Hawaii's endangered species, or get a lesson in the art of canoe making. Check with the concierge for daily Hawaiian activities at the hotel or nearby.

NORTH SHORE

$
B&B/INN

⊡ Backpackers Vacation Inn and Plantation Village. Laid-back Haleiwa surfer chic at its best, Backpackers is spartan in furnishings, rustic in amenities, and definitely very casual in spirit. **Pros:** friendly, laid-back staff who can offer recommendations; prices you won't find anywhere else. **Cons:** many rooms are plainly furnished. $ *Rooms from: $62* ✉ *59-788 Kamehameha Hwy., Haleiwa, Haleiwa* ☎ *808/638-7838* 🖷 *808/638-7515* ⊕ *www.backpackers-hawaii.com* 📮 *25 rooms* ⦿ *No meals.*

$$$
RESORT

⊡ The Turtle Bay Resort. Sprawling over 880 acres of natural landscape on the edge of Kuilima Point in Kahuku, the Turtle Bay Resort boasts spacious guest rooms averaging nearly 500 square feet, with lanai that showcase stunning peninsula views. **Pros:** great open, public spaces in a secluded area of Oahu; beautiful two-level spa. **Cons:** renovation work planned for 2014 may cause disruptions; very far from anything else—even Haleiwa is a 20-minute drive; hotel charges a $25 per night resort fee. $ *Rooms from: $289* ✉ *57-091 Kamehameha Hwy., Box 187, Kahuku* ☎ *808/293–6000, 800/203–3650, 866/827–5321* *reservations* 🌐 *www.turtlebayresort.com* 🛏 *397 rooms, 40 suites, 42 beach cottages, 56 ocean villas* 🍴 *No meals.*

WEST (LEEWARD) OAHU

$$$$ RESORT FAMILY 🏨 **Aulani, A Disney Resort & Spa.** In September 2011, Disney opened its first property in Hawaii, an elaborate, full-service complex in the resort area of Ko Olina about a 40-minute drive from Waikiki on Oahu's leeward side. **Pros:** tons to do on premises; very kid-friendly; a 1,500-square-foot teens-only spa with a private entrance, yogurt bar, and teen-specific treatments. **Cons:** a long way from Waikiki; Character Breakfasts are often sold out. [$] *Rooms from: $480* ✉ *92-1185 Aliinui Dr., Ko Olina, Kapolei* ☎ *714/520–7001, 808/674–6200, 866/443–4763* 🌐 *resorts.disney.go.com/aulani-hawaii-resort* 🛏 *359 rooms, 16 suites, 481 villas* 🍴 *No meals.*

$$$$ RESORT 🏨 **JW Marriott Ihilani Resort & Spa.** Forty-five minutes and a world away from the bustle of Waikiki, this sleek, 17-story resort anchors the Ko Olina Resort and Marina on Oahu's Leeward Coast. **Pros:** beautiful property; impeccable service; pool is stunning at night. **Cons:** a bit of a drive from Honolulu; rental car a must; there's a daily resort fee of $25. [$] *Rooms from: $545* ✉ *92-1001 Olani St., Ko Olina, Kapolei* ☎ *808/679–0079, 800/626–4446* 🌐 *www.ihilani.com* 🛏 *351 rooms, 36 suites* 🍴 *No meals.*

$$$$ RENTAL FAMILY 🏨 **Marriott Ko Olina Beach Vacation Club.** Though primarily a time-share property, Marriott Ko Olina also offers nightly rentals, which range from hotel-style standard guest rooms to expansive and elegantly appointed one- or two-bedroom guest villa apartments. **Pros:** suites are beautifully decorated and have ample space for families; full kitchens; nice views; fairly private lagoon; on-site weekly Polynesian dinner show. **Cons:** at least a half-hour drive to Honolulu [$] *Rooms from: $349* ✉ *92-161 Waipahe Pl., Ko Olina, Kapolei* ☎ *808/679–4700, 800/307–7312* 🌐 *www.marriottvacationclub.com* 🛏 *544 units* 🍴 *No meals.*

MAUI

WELCOME TO MAUI

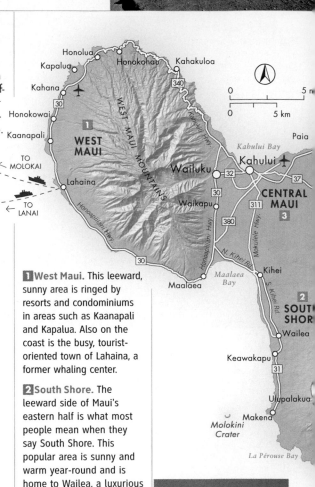

TOP REASONS TO GO

★ **The Road to Hana:** Each curve of this legendary cliff-side road pulls you deeper into the lush green rain forest of Maui's eastern shore.

★ **Haleakala National Park:** Explore the lava bombs, cinder cones, and silverswords at the gasp-inducing, volcanic summit of Haleakala, the House of the Sun.

★ **Hookipa Beach:** On Maui's North Shore, the world's top windsurfers will dazzle you as they maneuver above the waves like butterflies shot from cannons.

★ **Waianapanapa State Park:** Head to East Maui and take a dip at the stunning black-sand beach or in the cave pool where an ancient princess once hid.

★ **Resorts, Resorts, Resorts:** Opulent gardens, pools, restaurants, and golf courses make Maui's resorts some of the best in the Islands.

1 West Maui. This leeward, sunny area is ringed by resorts and condominiums in areas such as Kaanapali and Kapalua. Also on the coast is the busy, tourist-oriented town of Lahaina, a former whaling center.

2 South Shore. The leeward side of Maui's eastern half is what most people mean when they say South Shore. This popular area is sunny and warm year-round and is home to Wailea, a luxurious resort area.

3 Central Maui. Between Maui's two mountain areas is Central Maui, the location of the county seat of Wailuku and the commercial center of Kahului. Kahului Airport is here.

Map labels: Honolua, Kapalua, Honokohau, Kahakuloa, Kahana, 340, Honokowai, 30, Kaanapali, **WEST MAUI** 1, WEST MAUI MOUNTAINS, TO MOLOKAI, Lahaina, TO LANAI, Honoapiilani Hwy., Kahului Bay, Paia, Wailuku, 32, Kahului, **CENTRAL MAUI** 3, 37, Waikapu, 30, 311, 380, N. Kihei Rd., Kihei, Maalaea Bay, Maalaea, **SOUTH SHORE** 2, Wailea, Keawakapu, 31, Ulupalakua, Makena, Molokini Crater, La Pérouse Bay, 0 — 5 mi, 0 — 5 km

4 **Upcountry.** Island residents affectionately call the regions climbing up the slope of Haleakala Crater Upcountry. This is farm and ranch country.

5 **North Shore.** The North Shore has no large resorts, just plenty of picturesque small towns like Paia and Haiku—and great surfing action at Hookipa Beach.

6 **Road to Hana.** The island's northeastern, windward side is largely one great rain forest, traversed by the stunning Road to Hana. The town of Hana preserves the slow pace of the past.

GETTING ORIENTED

Maui consists of two distinct circular landmasses: the western area includes the rain-chiseled West Maui Mountains, and the larger eastern landmass includes Haleakala, with its cloud-wreathed volcanic peak. Maui has very different areas, from the resorts of sunny West Maui and the South Shore to the funky small towns of the North Shore, the ranches and farms of Upcountry, and the remote village of Hana in unspoiled East Maui.

3

Hookipa Beach

NORTH SHORE
5
Hana Hwy. 36
Haiku
Ulumalu
Huelo
Kailua
Road to Hana
Baldwin
Haliimaile Rd.
365
Makawao
4
UPCOUNTRY
Pukalani
377
Kula
378
37
Keokea
HALEAKALA NATIONAL PARK
Haleakala Crater

Wailua
Nahiku
360
Hana Hwy.
6
ROAD TO HANA
Kaeleku
Waianapanapa State Park
Hana

Oheo Gulch

31
Kaupo

GREAT ITINERARIES

Maui's landscape is incredibly diverse, offering everything from underwater encounters with eagle rays to treks across moonlike terrain. Although daydreaming at the pool or on the beach may fulfill your initial island fantasy, Maui has much more to offer. The following one-day itineraries will take you to our favorite spots on the island.

Beach Day in West Maui
West Maui has some of the island's most beautiful beaches, though many of them are hidden by megaresorts. If you get an early start, you can begin your day snorkeling at Slaughterhouse Beach (in winter, D.T. Fleming Beach is a better option as it's less rough). Then spend the day beach hopping through Kapalua, Napili, and Kaanapali as you make your way south. You'll want to get to Lahaina before dark so you can spend some time exploring the historic whaling town before choosing a restaurant for a sunset dinner.

Focus on Marine Life on the South Shore
Start your South Shore trip early in the morning, and head out past Makena into the rough lava fields of rugged La Perouse Bay. At the road's end there are areas of the Ahihi-Kinau Marine Preserve open to the public (others are closed indefinitely) that offer good snorkeling. If that's a bit too far afield for you, there's excellent snorkeling at Polo Beach. Head to the right (your right while facing the ocean) for plenty of fish and beautiful coral. Head back north to Kihei for lunch, and then enjoy the afternoon learning more about Maui's marine life at the outstanding Maui Ocean Center at Maalaea.

Haleakala National Park, Upcountry, and the North Shore
If you don't plan to spend an entire day hiking in the crater at Haleakala National Park, this itinerary will at least allow you to take a peek at it. Get up early and head straight for the summit of Haleakala (if you're jet-lagged and waking up in the middle of the night, you may want to get there in time for sunrise). Bring water, sunscreen, and warm clothing; it's freezing at sunrise. Plan to spend a couple of hours exploring the various lookout points in the park. On your way down the mountain, turn right on Makawao Avenue and head into the little town of Makawao. You can have lunch here, or make a left on Baldwin Avenue and head downhill to the North Shore town of Paia, which has a number of great lunch spots and shops to explore. Spend the rest of your afternoon at Paia's main strip of sand, Hookipa Beach.

The Road to Hana
This cliff-side driving tour through rainforest canopy reveals Maui's lushest and most tropical terrain. It will take a full day to explore this part of the North Shore and East Maui, especially if you plan to make it all the way to Oheo Gulch. You'll pass through communities where old Hawaii still thrives, and where the forest runs unchecked from the sea to the summit. You'll want to make frequent exploratory stops. To really soak in the magic of this place, consider staying overnight in Hana town. That way you can spend a full day winding toward Hana, hiking and exploring along the way, and the next day traveling leisurely back to civilization.

3

Those who know Maui well understand why it's earned all its superlatives. The island's miles of perfect beaches, lush green valleys, historic villages, top-notch water sports and outdoors activities, and amazing marine life have made it an international favorite. But nature isn't all Maui has to offer: it's also home to a wide variety of cultural activities, stunning ethnic diversity, and stellar restaurants and resorts.

At 729 square miles, Maui is the second-largest Hawaiian Island, but offers more miles of swimmable beaches than any of its neighbors. Despite rapid growth over the past few decades, the local population still totals less than 200,000.

GEOLOGY

Maui is made up of two volcanoes, one now extinct and the other dormant but which erupted long ago, joined into one island. The resulting depression between the two is what gives the island its nickname, the Valley Isle. West Maui's 5,788-foot Puu Kukui was the first volcano to form, a distinction that gives that area's mountainous topography a more weathered look. Rainbows seem to grow wild over this terrain as gentle mists fill the deeply eroded canyons. The Valley Isle's second volcano is the 10,023-foot Haleakala, where desertlike terrain abuts tropical forests.

HISTORY

Maui's history is full of firsts—Lahaina was the first capital of Hawaii and the first destination of the whaling industry (early 1800s), which explains why the town still has that seafaring vibe. Lahaina was also the first stop for missionaries on Maui (1823). Although they suppressed aspects of Hawaiian culture, the missionaries did help invent the Hawaiian alphabet and built a printing press—the first west of the Rockies— that rolled out the news in Hawaiian, as well as, not surprisingly, Hawaii's first Bibles. Maui also boasts the first sugar plantation in Hawaii (1849) and the first Hawaiian luxury resort (1946), now called the Travaasa Hana.

ON MAUI TODAY

In the mid-1970s savvy marketers saw a way to improve Maui's economy by promoting the Valley Isle to golfers and luxury travelers. The ploy worked well; Maui's visitor count is about 2.5 million annually. Impatient traffic now threatens to overtake the ubiquitous aloha spirit, development encroaches on agricultural lands, and county planners struggle to meet the needs of a burgeoning population. But Maui is still carpeted with an eyeful of green, and for every tailgater there's a local on "Maui time" who stops for each pedestrian and sunset.

MAUI PLANNER

GETTING HERE AND AROUND

AIR TRAVEL

Most visitors arrive at Kahului Airport in Central Maui. A rental car is the best way to get from the airport to your destination. The major car-rental companies have desks at the airport and can provide a map and directions to your hotel. ■ TIP→ Flights from the mainland tend to arrive around the same time, leading to long lines at car-rental windows. If possible, send one person to pick up the car while the others wait for the baggage.

CAR TRAVEL

If you want to travel around on your own schedule, a rental car is a must on Maui. It's also one of your biggest trip expenses, especially given the price of gasoline—higher on Maui than on Oahu or the mainland. If you need to ask for directions, try your best to pronounce the multivowel road names. Locals don't use (or know) highway route numbers and will respond with looks as blank as yours. Also, they will give you directions by the time it takes to get somewhere rather than by the mileage.

Kahului is the transportation hub—the main airport and largest harbor are here. Traffic on Maui's roads can be heavy, especially during the rush hours of 6 am to 8:30 am and 3:30 pm to 6:30 pm.

See Travel Smart Hawaii for more information on renting a car and driving.

ISLAND DRIVING TIMES Driving from one point on Maui to another can take longer than the mileage indicates. It's 52 miles from Kahului Airport to Hana, but the drive will take you about three hours if you stop to smell the flowers, which you certainly should do. As for driving to Haleakala, the 38-mile drive from sea level to the summit will take about two hours. The roads are narrow and winding; you must travel slowly. Kahului is the transportation hub—the main airport and largest harbor are here. Traffic on Maui's roads can be heavy, especially during the rush hours of 6 am to 8:30 am and 3:30 pm to 6:30 pm. Here are average driving times.

DRIVING TIMES	
Kahului to Wailea	17 miles/30 mins
Kahului to Kaanapali	25 miles/45 mins
Kahului to Kapalua	36 miles/1 hr, 15 mins
Kahului to Makawao	13 miles/25 mins
Kapalua to Haleakala	73 miles/3 hrs
Kaanapali to Haleakala	62 miles/2 hrs, 30 mins
Wailea to Haleakala	54 miles/2 hrs, 30 mins
Kapalua to Hana	88 miles/5 hrs
Kaanapali to Hana	77 miles/5 hrs
Wailea to Hana	69 miles/4 hrs, 30 mins
Wailea to Lahaina	20 miles/45 mins
Kaanapali to Lahaina	4 miles/15 mins
Kapalua to Lahaina	12 miles/25 mins

RESTAURANTS

There's a lot going on for a place the size of Maui, from ethnic holes-in-the-wall to fancy oceanfront fish houses. Much of it is excellent, but some of it is overpriced and touristy. Choose menu items made with products that are abundant on the island, including local fish. Local cuisine is a mix of foods brought by ethnic groups since the late 1700s, blended with the foods Native Hawaiians have enjoyed for centuries. For a food adventure, take a drive into Central Maui and eat at one of the "local" spots recommended here. *Prices in the reviews are the average cost of a main course at dinner or, if dinner is not served, at lunch.*

HOTELS

Maui is well known for its lovely resorts, some of them very luxurious; many cater to families. But there are other options, including abundant and convenient apartment and condo rentals for all budgets. The resorts and rentals cluster largely on Maui's sunny coasts, in West Maui and the South Shore. For a different, more local experience, you might spend part of your time at a small bed-and-breakfast. Check Internet sites and ask about discounts and packages. *Prices in the reviews are the lowest cost of a standard double room in high season or, for rentals, the lowest per-night cost for a one-bedroom unit in high season.*

VISITOR INFORMATION

The Hawaii Visitors and Convention Bureau (HVCB) has plenty of general and vacation-planning information for Maui and all the Islands, and offers a free official vacation planner. The Maui Visitors & Convention Bureau website includes information on accommodations, sights, events, and suggested itineraries.

Information Hawaii Visitors and Convention Bureau ✉ *2270 Kalakaua Ave., Suite 801, Honolulu, Hawaii* ☎ *808/923–1811, 800/464–2924 to order free visitor guide* ⊕ *www.gohawaii.com.* **Maui Visitors Bureau** ✉ *Hawaii* ☎ *808/244–3530, 800/525–6284* ⊕ *www.visitmaui.com.*

EXPLORING

Updated by
Michele Bigley

Maui is more than sandy beaches and palm trees. Puu Kukui, the 5,788-foot interior of the West Maui Mountains, also known as Mauna Kahalawai, is one of Earth's wettest spots—annual rainfall of 400 inches has sculpted the land into impassable gorges and razor-sharp ridges. On the opposite side of the island, the blistering lava fields at Ahihi-Kinau receive scant rain. Just above this desertlike landscape, *paniolo* (Hawaiian cowboys) herd cattle on rolling, fertile ranchlands. On the island's rugged east side is the lush, tropical Hawaii of travel posters.

In small towns like Paia and Hana you can see remnants of the past mingling with modern-day life. Ancient *heiau* (stone platforms once used as places of worship) line busy roadways. Old coral and brick missionary homes now house broadcasting networks. The antique smokestacks of sugar mills tower above communities where the children blend English, Hawaiian, Japanese, Chinese, Portuguese, Filipino, and more into one colorful language. Hawaii is a melting pot like no other. Visiting an eclectic mom-and-pop shop—such as Upcountry Makawao's Komoda Store & Bakery—can feel like stepping into another country, or back in time. The more you look here, the more you find.

WEST MAUI

Separated from the remainder of the island by steep *pali* (cliffs), West Maui has a reputation for attitude and action. Once upon a time this was the haunt of whalers, missionaries, and the kings and queens of Hawaii. Today the main drag, Front Street, is crowded with T-shirt and trinket shops, art galleries, and restaurants. Farther north is Kaanapali, Maui's first planned resort area. Its first hotel, the Sheraton, opened in 1963. Since then, massive resorts, luxury condos, and a shopping center have sprung up along the white-sand beaches, with championship golf courses across the road. A few miles farther up the coast is the ultimate in West Maui luxury, the resort area of Kapalua. In between, dozens of strip malls line both the *makai* (toward the sea) and *mauka* (toward the mountains) sides of the highway. There are gems here, too, like Napili Bay and its jaw-dropping crescent of sand.

LAHAINA

27 miles west of Kahului; 4 miles south of Kaanapali.

Lahaina, a bustling waterfront town packed with visitors from around the globe, is considered the center of Maui. Some may describe Lahaina as tacky, with too many T-shirt vendors and not enough mom-and-pop shops, but this historic village houses some of Hawaii's most excellent restaurants, boutiques, cafés, and galleries. ■TIP→ **If you spend Friday afternoon exploring Front Street, hang around for Art Night, when the galleries stay open late and offer entertainment along with artists demonstrating their work.**

Sunset cruises and other excursions depart from Lahaina Harbor. At the southern end of town an important archaeological site—Mokuula—is currently being researched, excavated, and restored. This was once a spiritual and political center, as well as home to Maui's chiefs.

Old Lahaina Luau: "A beautiful picture while waiting for the best luau in Hawaii." –Tammy Davis, Fodors.com photo contest participant

GETTING HERE AND AROUND

It's about a 45-minute drive from Kahului Airport to Lahaina (take Route 380 to Route 30) depending on the traffic on this heavily traveled route. Traffic can be slow around Lahaina, especially between 4 and 6 pm. Shuttles and taxis are available from Kahului Airport. The Maui Bus Lahaina Islander route runs from Queen Kaahumanu Center in Kahului to the Wharf Cinema Center on Front Street, Lahaina's main thoroughfare.

TOP ATTRACTIONS

Baldwin Home Museum. If you want some insight into 19th-century life in Hawaii, this informative museum is an excellent place to start. Begun in 1834 and completed the following year, the coral-and-stone house was originally home to missionary Dr. Dwight Baldwin and his family. The building has been carefully restored to reflect the period; many of the original furnishings remain. You can view the family's grand piano, carved four-poster bed, and most interestingly, Dr. Baldwin's dispensary. During a brief tour by Lahaina Restoration Foundation volunteers, you'll be shown the "thunderpot" and told how the doctor single-handedly inoculated 10,000 Maui residents against smallpox. Friday at 6 pm are special candlelight tours. ⊠ *696 Front St., Lahaina, Hawaii* ☎ *808/661–3262* ⊕ *www.lahainarestoration.org* ✉ *$7, also includes admission to Wo Hing Museum* ☉ *Sat.–Thurs. 10–4, Fri. 10–8:30.*

Banyan Tree. Planted in 1873, this massive tree is the largest of its kind in the state and provides a welcome retreat and playground for locals and visitors, who rest, play music, and climb under (and atop) its awesome branches. ■ TIP➔ The Banyan Tree is a popular and hard-to-miss

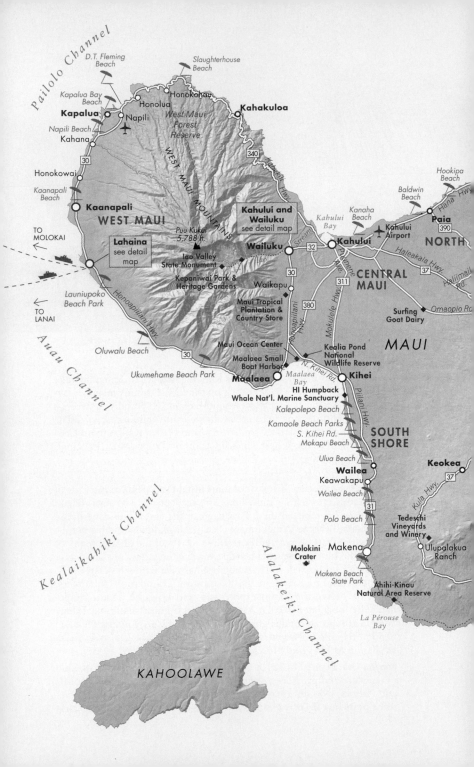

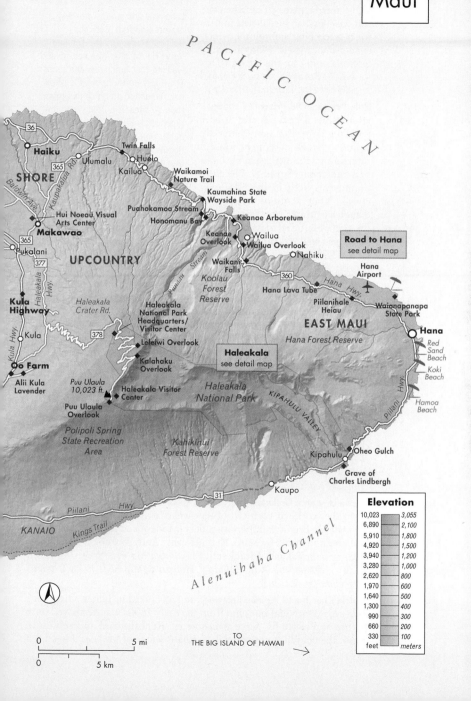

meeting place if your party splits up for independent exploring. It's also a terrific place to be when the sun sets—mynah birds settle in here for a screeching symphony, which is an event in itself. Many Lahaina festivals center on the Banyan Tree as well. ⊠ *Front St., between Hotel and Canal Sts., Lahaina, Hawaii.*

Hale Paahao (Old Prison). Lahaina's jailhouse is a reminder of rowdy whaling days. Its name literally means "stuck-in-irons house," referring to the wall shackles and ball-and-chain restraints. The compound was built in the 1850s by

WALKING TOURS

Lahaina's side streets are best explored on foot. Both the Baldwin Home and the Lahaina Court House offer free self-guided walking-tour brochures and maps. The Court House booklet is often recommended and includes more than 50 sites. The Baldwin Home brochure is less well known but, in our opinion, easier to follow. It details a short but enjoyable loop tour of the town.

convict laborers out of blocks of coral that had been salvaged from the demolished waterfront fort. Most prisoners were sent here for desertion, drunkenness, or reckless horse riding. Today, a wax figure representing an imprisoned old sailor tells his recorded tale of woe. ⊠ *Wainee and Prison Sts., Lahaina, Hawaii* ⊡ *Free* ☉ *Mon.–Sat. 10–4.*

Fodor'sChoice
★ **Lahaina Court House.** The Lahaina Arts Society and the Lahaina Heritage Museum occupy this charming old government building in the center of town that recently opened a massive exhibit about Lahaina's history. Wander among the terrific displays, pump the knowledgeable museum staff for interesting trivia, and ask for the walking-tour brochure covering historic Lahaina sites. There's also a theater with a rotating array of films about everything from whales to canoes. The nonprofit Lahaina Town Action Committee, which oversees Lahaina's attractions, can be found here as well. Erected in 1859 and restored in 1999, the building has served as a customs and court house, governor's office, post office, vault and collector's office, and police court. On August 12, 1898, its postmaster witnessed the lowering of the Hawaiian flag when Hawaii became a U.S. territory. The flag now hangs above the stairway. ■TIP→ There's a public restroom in the building. ⊠ *648 Wharf St., Lahaina, Hawaii* ☎ *808/661–0111 Lahaina Arts Society, 808/667–9175 Lahaina Town Action Committee* ⊕ *www.lahaina-arts. com* ⊡ *Free* ☉ *Daily 9–5.*

Fodor'sChoice
★ **Martin Lawrence Galleries.** In business since 1975, Martin Lawrence displays the works of such world-renowned artists as Picasso, Erté, and Chagall in a bright and friendly gallery. Modern and pop-art enthusiasts will also find pieces by Miró, Keith Haring, Andy Warhol, and Japanese creative icon Takashi Murakami. ⊠ *Lahaina Market Place, 790 Front St., at Lahainaluna Rd., Lahaina, Hawaii* ☎ *808/661–1788* ⊕ *www. martinlawrence.com.*

Fodor'sChoice
★ **Waiola Church and Wainee Cemetery.** Immortalized in James Michener's *Hawaii*, the original building from the early 1800s was destroyed once by fire and twice by fierce windstorms. Repositioned and rebuilt in 1954, the church was renamed Waiola ("water of life") and has been

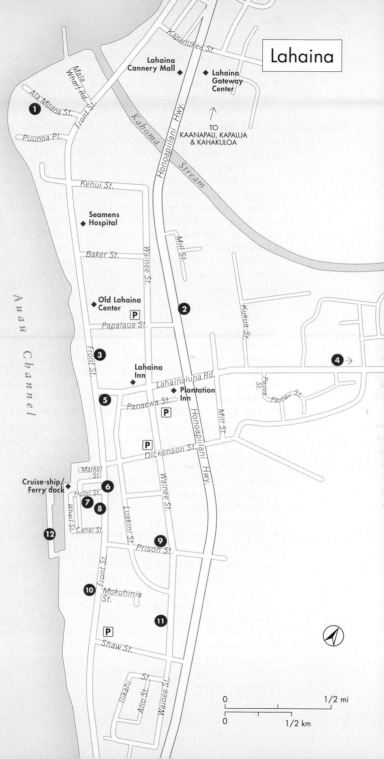

standing proudly ever since. The adjacent cemetery was the region's first Christian cemetery and is the final resting place of many of Hawaii's most important monarchs, including Kamehameha the Great's wife, Queen Keopuolani, who was baptized during her final illness. ⊠ *535 Wainee St., Lahaina, Hawaii* ☏ *808/661–4349* ⊕ *www.waiolachurch. org* ▨ *Free* ☉ *Daily 9–4.*

Fodor's Choice
★

Wo Hing Museum. Smack-dab in the center of Front Street, this eye-catching Chinese temple reflects the importance of early Chinese immigrants to Lahaina. Built by the Wo Hing Society in 1912, the museum contains beautiful artifacts, historic photos of old Lahaina, and a Taoist altar. Don't miss the films playing in the rustic theater next door— some of Thomas Edison's first films, shot in Hawaii circa 1898, show Hawaiian wranglers herding steer onto ships. Ask the docent for some star fruit from the tree outside, for the altar or for yourself. ■TIP→ **If you are in town in late January or early February, this museum hosts a nice Chinese New Year festival.** ⊠ *858 Front St., Lahaina, Hawaii* ☏ *808/661–5553* ▨ *$7, includes admission to Baldwin Home* ☉ *Sat.– Thurs. 10–4, Fri. 1–8 pm.*

WORTH NOTING

Hale Pai. Protestant missionaries established Lahainaluna Seminary as a center of learning and enlightenment in 1831. Six years later, they built this printing shop, where they and their young Hawaiian scholars created a written Hawaiian language and used it to produce a Bible, history texts, and a newspaper. An exhibit displays a replica of the original Rampage press and facsimiles of early printing. The oldest U.S. educational institution west of the Rockies, the seminary now serves as Lahaina's public high school. ⊠ *980 Lahainaluna Rd., Lahaina, Hawaii* ☏ *808/661–3262* ▨ *Donations accepted* ☉ *Mon.–Wed. 10–4.*

Holy Innocents' Episcopal Church. Built in 1927, this beautiful open-air church is decorated with paintings depicting Hawaiian versions of Christian symbols (including a Hawaiian Madonna and child), rare or extinct birds, and native plants. At the afternoon services, the congregation is typically dressed in traditional clothing from Samoa and Tonga. Anyone is welcome to slip into one of the pews, carved from native woods. Queen Liliuokalani, Hawaii's last reigning monarch, lived in a large grass house on this site as a child. ⊠ *561 Front St., near Mokuhina St., Lahaina, Hawaii* ☏ *808/661–4202* ⊕ *www.holyimaui.org* ▨ *Free* ☉ *Daily 8–5.*

Jodo Mission. Established at the turn of the 20th century by Japanese contract workers, this Buddhist mission is one of Lahaina's most popular sites, thanks to its idyllic setting and spectacular views across the channel. Although the buildings are not open to the public, you can stroll the grounds and enjoy glimpses of the 90-foot-high pagoda, as well as a great 3.5-ton copper and bronze statue of the Amida Buddha (erected in 1968). If you're nearby at 8 any evening, listen for the temple bell to toll 11 times; each peal has a specific significance. ⊠ *12 Ala Moana St., near Lahaina Cannery Mall, Lahaina, Hawaii* ☏ *808/661–4304* ▨ *Free.*

Lahaina Harbor. For centuries, Lahaina has drawn ships of all sizes to its calm harbor: King Kamehameha's conquering fleet of 800 carved *koa* canoes gave way to Chinese trading ships, Boston whalers, United States Navy frigates, and, finally, a slew of pleasure craft. The picturesque harbor is the departure point for ferries headed to nearby islands, sailing charters, deep-sea fishing trips, and snorkeling excursions. ⊠ *Wharf St., Lahaina, Hawaii* 🖅 *Free.*

FAMILY **Lahaina–Kaanapali and Pacific Railroad.** Affectionately called the Sugar Cane Train, Maui's only passenger train is an 1890s-vintage railway that once shuttled crops but now moves sightseers between Kaanapali and Lahaina. This quaint little attraction with its singing conductor is a big deal for Hawaii but probably not much of a thrill for those more accustomed to trains (though kids like it no matter where they grew up). ⊠ *Honoapiilani Hwy. at Hinau St., 1½ blocks north of Lahainaluna Rd. stoplight, Lahaina, Hawaii* 🕾 *808/661–0080* ⊕ *www.sugarcanetrain.com* 🖅 *$22.95* ⊙ *Weekdays 10:15–4.*

> ### ISLAND HOPPING
>
> If you have a week or more on Maui, consider taking a day or two for a trip to Molokai or Lanai. Tour operators such as Trilogy offer day-trip packages to Lanai that include snorkeling and a van tour. Ferries to both Islands have room for your golf clubs and mountain bike. (Avoid ferry travel on a blustery day.) If you prefer to travel to Molokai or Lanai by air and don't mind 4- to 12-seaters, you can take a small air taxi. Book with Pacific Wings *(see Air Travel in Travel Smart Hawaii). See Chapters 6 and 7 for more information.*

KAANAPALI AND NEARBY
4 miles north of Lahaina.

As you drive north from Lahaina, the first resort community you reach is Kaanapali, a cluster of high-rise hotels framing a world-class white-sand beach. This is part of West Maui's famous resort strip and a perfect destination for families and romance seekers wanting to be in the center of the action. A little farther up the road lie the condo-filled beach towns of Honokowai, Kahana, and Napili, followed by Kapalua. Each boasts its own style and flavor, though most rely on a low-key beach vibe for people wanting upscale vacation rentals.

GETTING HERE AND AROUND
Shuttles and taxis are available from Kahului and West Maui airports. Resorts offer free shuttles between properties, and some hotels also provide complimentary shuttles into Lahaina. In the Maui Bus system the Napili Islander begins and ends at Whalers Village in Kaanapali and stops at most condos along the coastal road as far north as Napili Bay.

TOP ATTRACTIONS
Kaanapali. The theatrical look of Hawaii tourism—planned resort communities where luxury homes mix with high-rise hotels, fantasy swimming pools, and a theme-park landscape—all began right here in the 1960s, when clever marketers built this sunny shoreline into a playground for the world's vacationers. Three miles of uninterrupted

MAUI SIGHTSEEING TOURS

Maui is too big to see all in one day, so companies offer specialized tours, visiting either Haleakala or Hana and its environs. A tour of Haleakala and Upcountry is usually a half-day excursion, offered in several versions by different companies for $75 and up. The trip often includes stops at Tedeschi Vineyards, Maui's only winery.

A Haleakala sunrise tour starts before dawn so that you can get to the top of the dormant volcano before the sun peeks over the horizon. Because trips offer hotel pickup around the island, many sunrise trips leave around 2:30 am.

A tour of Hana is almost always done in a van, since the winding Road to Hana isn't built for bigger buses. Tours run from $100 to $140.

The key is to ask how many stops you get and how many other passengers will be on board—otherwise you could end up on a packed bus, sightseeing through a window.

Most of the tour guides have been in the business for years, and a tip of at least $1 per person is expected but not required.

Polynesian Adventure Tours. This company uses large buses with floor-to-ceiling windows. The drivers are fun and, because they have extensive training, really know the island. Some Haleakala tours also include visits to Iao Valley and Lahaina. ✉ *Hawaii* ☎ *808/877–4242, 800/622–3011* ⊕ *www.polyadhawaiitours.com* 🖃 *From $92.*

Roberts Hawaii Tours. This is one of the state's largest tour companies and offers numerous experiences. Its staff can arrange tours with bilingual guides if requested ahead of time. Eleven-hour trips venture out to Kaupo, the wild area past Hana. ✉ *Hawaii* ☎ *808/871–6226, 866/898–2519* ⊕ *www.robertshawaii.com* 🖃 *From $63.*

Temptation Tours. An affluent older crowd is the market for this company. Tours in plush eight-passenger limo-vans explore Haleakala and Hana. The "Hana Sky-Trek" includes a return trip via helicopter. ✉ *Hawaii* ☎ *808/877–8888, 800/817–1234* ⊕ *www.temptationtours.com* 🖃 *From $219.*

Tour da Food Maui. Maui resident Bonnie Friedman (a Fodor's contributor) guides small, customized ethnic food tours through Wailuku and Upcountry that include a couple of holes-in-the-wall some locals don't even know about. Newest is her GAS-tronomy tour—yes, good eats at Island gas stations. Tours leave Tuesday, Wednesday, and Thursday morning. ✉ *Maui, Hawaii* ☎ *808/242–8383* ⊕ *www.tourdafoodmaui.com* 🖃 *From $120.*

white-sand beach and placid water form the front yard for this artificial utopia, with its 40 tennis courts and two championship golf courses.

In ancient times, this area was known for its bountiful fishing (especially lobster) and its seaside cliffs. Puu Kekaa, today incorrectly referred to as "Black Rock," was a *lele*, a place in ancient Hawaii from which souls leaped into the afterlife. (Today this site is near the Sheraton Maui.) But times changed and the sleepy fishing village was washed away by the wave of Hawaii's new economy: tourism. ✉ *Kaanapali, Hawaii.*

FAMILY **Whalers Village Museum.** The skeleton of a massive whale leads the way to the Whale Center of the Pacific on the second floor of Whalers Village. Here you can learn about the hard life of whalers during the 19th-century Moby-Dick era. A replica of their living quarters, their tools and equipment, their letters and business papers, and other artifacts are on display. Many historical photos illustrate how the whalers chased and captured these giants of the deep and how they processsed their catch while out at sea. Several short films run continuously, including one about Hawaiian turtles and the folklore surrounding them. ■ TIP➔ **During humpback-whale season, docents lead informative talks about these great migratory creatures on Thursday and Saturday at 11 and 1.** ✉ *2435 Kaanapali Pkwy., Suite H16, Kaanapali, Hawaii* ☎ *808/661–5992* ⊕ *www.whalersvillage.com/museum.htm* 🎫 *$3* ⊙ *Daily 10–6.*

WORTH NOTING

Farmers' Market of Maui–Honokowai. From pineapples to corn, the produce at this West Maui open-air market is local and flavorful. Prices are good, too. Colorful tropical flowers and handcrafted items are also available. ✉ *Honoapiilani Hwy., across from Honokowai Park, Honokowai, Hawaii* ☎ *808/669–7004* ⊙ *Mon., Wed., and Fri. 7 am–11 am.*

KAPALUA AND KAHAKULOA

Kapalua is 10 miles north of Kaanapali and 36 miles west of Kahului.

Upscale Kapalua is north of the Kaanapali resorts, past Napili, and is a hideaway for those with money who want to stay incognito. Farther along the Honoapiilani Highway, you'll find the remote village of Kahakuloa, a reminder of old Hawaii.

GETTING HERE AND AROUND

Shuttles and taxis are available from Kahului and West Maui airports. The Ritz-Carlton, Kapalua has a resort shuttle within the Kapalua Resort.

TOP ATTRACTIONS

Kahakuloa. The wild side of West Maui, this tiny village at the north end of Honoapiilani Highway is a relic of pre-jet-travel Maui. Remote villages similar to Kahakuloa were once tucked away in several valleys in this area. Many residents still grow taro and live in the old Hawaiian way. Driving this route is not for the faint of heart: the unimproved road weaves along coastal cliffs, and there are lots of blind curves; it's not wide enough for two cars to pass in places, so one of you (most likely you) will have to reverse on this nail-biter of a "highway." Watch out for stray cattle, roosters, and falling rocks. True adventurers will find terrific snorkeling and swimming along this drive, as well as some good hiking trails, a labyrinth, and excellent banana bread. ✉ *Kahakuloa, Hawaii.*

Kapalua. Beautiful and secluded, Kapalua is West Maui's northernmost, most exclusive resort community. First developed in the late 1970s, the resort now includes the Ritz-Carlton, posh residential complexes, two golf courses, and the surrounding pineapple fields. The area's distinctive shops and restaurants cater to dedicated golfers, celebrities who want to be left alone, and some of the world's richest folks. In addition to golf, recreational activities include hiking and snorkeling. Mists

Ideal for snorkeling and swimming, sheltered Kapalua Bay Beach borders the luxurious Kapalua Resort.

regularly envelop the landscape of tall Cook pines and rolling fairways in Kapalua, which is cooler and quieter than its southern neighbors. The beaches here, including Kapalua and D.T. Fleming, are among Maui's finest. ⊠ *Kapalua, Hawaii.*

NEED A BREAK?

Honolua Store. In contrast to Kapalua's many high-end retailers, the old Honolua Store still plies the groceries, household goods, and fishing nets it did in plantation times. Hefty plates of *ono* (delicious) local foods are served at the deli until 3 pm and best enjoyed on the wraparound porch. The plate lunches are the quintessential local meal. ⊠ *502 Office Rd., Kapalua, Hawaii* ☎ *808/665–9105.*

THE SOUTH SHORE

Blessed by more than its fair share of sun, the southern shore of Hale-akala was an undeveloped wilderness until the 1970s. Then the sun worshippers found it; now restaurants, condos, and luxury resorts line the coast from the world-class aquarium at Maalaea Harbor, through working-class Kihei, to lovely Wailea, a resort community rivaling its counterpart, Kaanapali, on West Maui. Farther south, the road disappears and unspoiled wilderness still has its way.

Because the South Shore includes so many fine beach choices, a trip here (if you're staying elsewhere on the island) is an all-day excursion—especially if you include a visit to the aquarium. Get active in the morning with exploring and snorkeling, then shower in a beach park, dress up a little, and enjoy the cool luxury of the Wailea resorts. At sunset, settle in for dinner at one of the area's many fine restaurants.

MAALAEA

13 miles south of Kahului; 6 miles west of Kihei; 14 miles southeast of Lahaina.

Pronounced Mah-*ah*-lye-*ah*, this spot is not much more than a few condos, an aquarium, and a wind-blasted harbor—but that's more than enough for some visitors. Humpback whales seem to think Maalaea is tops for meeting mates, and green sea turtles treat it like their own personal spa, regularly seeking appointments with cleaner wrasses in the harbor. Surfers revere this spot for "Freight Train," reportedly the world's fastest wave.

GETTING HERE AND AROUND

To reach Maalaea from Kahului Airport, take Route 380 to Route 30. The town is also a transfer point for many Maui Bus routes.

TOP ATTRACTIONS

Maalaea Small Boat Harbor. With so many good reasons to head out onto the water, this active little harbor is quite busy. Many snorkeling and whale-watching excursions depart from here. There was a plan to expand the facility, but surfers argued that would have destroyed their surf breaks. In fact, the surf here is world renowned. The elusive spot to the left of the harbor, called Freight Train, rarely breaks, but when it does, it's said to be the fastest anywhere. Shops, restaurants, and a museum front the harbor. ⊠ *101 Maalaea Boat Harbor Rd., off Honoapiilani Hwy.*

FAMILY **Maui Ocean Center.** You'll feel as though you're walking from the sea-
Fodor's Choice shore down to the bottom of the reef at this aquarium, which focuses on
★ creatures of the Pacific. Vibrant exhibits let you get close to turtles, rays, sharks, and the unusual creatures of the tide pools; allow two hours or so to explore it all. It's not an enormous facility, but it does provide an excellent (though pricey) introduction to the sea life that makes Hawaii special. The center is part of a complex of retail shops and restaurants overlooking the harbor. Enter from Honoapiilani Highway as it curves past Maalaea Harbor. ■ TIP→ The Ocean Center's gift shop is one of the best on Maui for artsy souvenirs and toys. ⊠ *192 Maalaea Rd., off Honoapiilani Hwy.* ☎ *808/270–7000* ⊕ *www.mauioceancenter.com* 🎟 *$25.95 adults; $18.95 children* ☉ *Sept.–June, daily 9–5; July–Aug., daily 9–6.*

KIHEI

9 miles south of Kahului; 20 miles east of Lahaina.

Traffic lights and shopping malls may not fit your notion of paradise, but Kihei offers dependably warm sun, excellent beaches, and a front-row seat to marine life of all sorts. Besides all the sun and sand, the town's relatively inexpensive condos and excellent restaurants make this a home base for many Maui visitors.

The county beach parks such as Kamaole I, II, and III have lawns, showers, and picnic tables. ■ TIP→ Remember: Beach park or no beach

Hawaiian Aquarium at the Maui Ocean Center: "We sat and just watched this sight. It was so calming." –Kevin J. Klitzke, Fodors.com photo contest participant

park, the public has a right to the entire coastal strand but not to cross private property to get to it.

GETTING HERE AND AROUND

Kihei is a 20-minute ride south of Kahului once you're past the heavy traffic on Dairy Road and get on the four-lane Mokulele Highway (Route 311).

TOP ATTRACTIONS

FAMILY

Fodor'sChoice
★

Hawaiian Islands Humpback Whale National Marine Sanctuary. This nature center sits in prime humpback-viewing territory beside a restored ancient Hawaiian fishpond. Whether the whales are here or not, the education center is a great stop for youngsters curious to know more about underwater life, and anyone eager to gain insight into the cultural connection between Hawaii and its whale residents. Interactive displays and informative naturalists explain it all, including the sanctuary that acts as a breeding ground for humpbacks. Throughout the year, the center hosts activities that include talks, labs, volunteer opportunities, and more. The sanctuary itself includes virtually all the waters surrounding the archipelago. ■TIP→ Just outside the visitor center is the ancient Kalepolepo fishpond (also known as the Koieie fishpond), which is a popular place for locals to bring their keikis to wade in the water. ⊠ 726 S. Kihei Rd. ☎ 808/879–2818, 800/831–4888 ⊕ www. hawaiihumpbackwhale.noaa.gov ☕ Free ⊗ Weekdays 10–3.

FAMILY

Kealia Pond National Wildlife Refuge. Natural wetlands have become rare in the Islands, and the 700 acres of this reserve attract migratory birds and other wildlife. Long-legged stilts casually dip their beaks into the shallow waters as traffic shuttles by. Sharp-eyed birders may catch sight of migratory visitors such as osprey. Interpretive signs on the boardwalk explain the journey of the endangered hawksbill turtles and how they return to the sandy dunes year after year. The boardwalk stretches along the coast by North Kihei Road; the main entrance to the reserve is on Mokulele Highway. A visitor center with the reserve headquarters and exhibits provides a good introduction. ⊠ *Mokulele Hwy., mile marker 6* ☎ *808/875–1582* ⊕ *www.fws.gov/kealiapond* ▧ *Free* ⊙ *Weekdays 7:30–4.*

WORTH NOTING

Farmers' Market of Maui–Kihei. Tropical flowers, tempting produce, massive avocadoes, and locally made preserves, banana bread, and crafts are among the bargains at this South Shore market. It's in the west end of Kihei, next to the ABC Store. ⊠ *61 S. Kihei Rd.* ☎ *808/875–0949* ⊙ *Mon.–Thu. 8–4, Fri. 8–5.*

WAILEA AND FARTHER SOUTH

15 miles south of Kahului; at the southern border of Kihei.

The South Shore's resort community, Wailea is slightly quieter and drier than its West Maui sister, Kaanapali. Many visitors cannot pick a favorite, so they stay at both. The luxury of the resorts (edging on the excessive) and the simple grandeur of the coastal views make the otherwise stark landscape an outstanding destination; take time to stroll the coastal beach path. A handful of perfect little beaches, all with public access, front the resorts.

The first two resorts were built here in the late 1970s. Soon a cluster of upscale properties sprang up, including the Four Seasons and the Fairmont Kea Lani. Check out the Grand Wailea Resort's chapel, which tells a Hawaiian love story in stained glass.

GETTING HERE AND AROUND

From Kahului Airport, take Route 311 (Mokulele Highway) to Route 31 (Piilani Highway) until it ends in Wailea. Shuttles and taxis are available at the airport. If you're traveling by Maui Bus, the Kihei Islander route runs between the Shops at Wailea and Kaahumanu Center in Kahului. There's a resort shuttle, and a paved shore path goes between the hotels.

WORTH NOTING

Coastal Nature Trail. A 1.5-mile-long paved beach walk allows you to stroll among Wailea's prettiest properties, restaurants, and rocky coves. The trail teems with joggers in the morning hours. The *makai,* or ocean side, is landscaped with rare native plants like the silvery *hinahina,* named after the Hawaiian moon goddess. In winter, keep an eye out for whales. The trail is accessible from Polo Beach as well as from the many Wailea beachfront resorts. ⊠ *Wailea Beach, Wailea Alanui Dr., south of Grand Wailea Resort.*

CENTRAL MAUI

Kahului, where you most likely landed when you arrived on Maui, is the industrial and commercial center of the island. West of Kahului is Wailuku, the county seat since 1950 and the most charming town in

Central Maui, with some good, inexpensive restaurants. Outside these towns are attractions from museums and historic sites to gardens.

You can combine sightseeing in Central Maui with some shopping at the Queen Kaahumanu Center, Maui Mall, and Maui Marketplace *(see Shopping)*. This is one of the best areas on the island to stock up on groceries and supplies, thanks to major retailers including Walmart, Kmart, and Costco. Note that grocery prices are much higher than on the mainland.

KAHULUI

3 miles west of Kahului Airport; 9 miles north of Kihei; 31 miles east of Kaanapali; 51 miles west of Hana.

With the island's largest airport and commercial harbor, Kahului is Maui's commercial hub. But it also offers plenty of natural and cultural attractions. The town was developed in the early 1950s to meet the housing needs of the large sugarcane interests here, specifically those of Alexander & Baldwin. The company was tired of playing landlord to its many plantation workers and sold land to a developer who promised to create affordable housing. The scheme worked and "Dream City," the first planned city in Hawaii, was born.

GETTING HERE AND AROUND

From the airport, take Keolani Place to Route 36 (Hana Highway), which becomes Kaahumanu Avenue, Kahului's main drag. Run by Maui Bus, the Kahului Loop route traverses all of the town's major shopping centers. The fare is $2.

TOP ATTRACTIONS

Alexander & Baldwin Sugar Museum. Maui's largest landowner, A&B was one of the "Big Five" companies that spearheaded the planting, harvesting, and processing of sugarcane. At this museum, historic photos, artifacts, and documents explain the introduction of sugarcane to Hawaii. Exhibits reveal how plantations brought in laborers from other countries, forever changing the Islands' ethnic mix. Although Hawaiian cane sugar is now being supplanted by cheaper foreign versions—as well as by sugar derived from inexpensive sugar beets—the crop was for many years the mainstay of the local economy. You can find the museum in a small, restored plantation manager's house across the street from the post office and the still-operating sugar refinery, where smoke billows up when cane is being processed. ■TIP→ Their gift shop sells excellent sugar, coffee, and a selection of history books. ⊠ *3957 Hansen Rd., Puunene* ☎ *808/871–8058* ⊕ *www.sugarmuseum.com* 💲 *$7* ⊙ *Daily 9:30–4:30; last admission at 4.*

FAMILY **Maui Nui Botanical Gardens.** Hawaiian and Polynesian species are cultivated at this fascinating 7-acre garden, including Hawaiian bananas, local varieties of sweet potatoes and sugarcane, native poppies, hibiscus, and *anapanapa*, a plant that makes a natural shampoo when rubbed between your hands. Reserve ahead for the ethnobotany tours that are offered four times a week. Self-guided tour booklets cost $4, or you can arrange a tour with a docent for $10. ⊠ *150 Kanaloa Ave., Kahului* ☎ *808/249–2798* ⊕ *www.mnbg.org* 💲 *Free* ⊙ *Mon.–Sat. 8–4.*

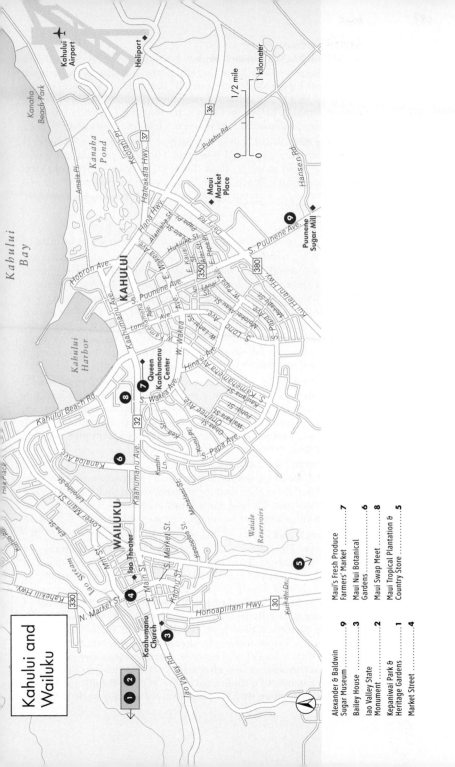

Kahului and Wailuku

Kahului Airport

Heliport

1/2 mile
1 kilometer

36

37

Keolani Pl.

Amala Pl.

Hobron Ave.

Hana Hwy.

Haleakala Hwy.

Kanaha Pond

Kanaha Beach Park

Kahului Bay

Kahului Harbor

Alamaha St.

Pulehu Pl.

Hukilike St.

E. Kuiaha St.

E. Papa Ave.

Dairy Rd.

Maui Market Place

8

Kahului Beach Rd.

KAHULUI

Kaahumanu Ave.

Lono ave.

Puunene Ave.

S. Kaahumanu Ave.

Kamehameha Ave.

E. Wakea Ave.

350

Lanai St.

Mokuhau St.

S. Kane Ave.

W. Wakea Ave.

S. Puunene Ave.

380

9

Puunene Sugar Mill

Hansen Rd.

Pulehu Rd.

Kaahumanu Ave.

Kahului Harbor

7 Queen Kaahumanu Center

S. Wakea Ave.

W. Lono Ave.

Hina Ave.

S. Papa Ave.

32

Kanaloa Ave.

6

Kuihelani Hwy.

Kailana St.

Onehee Ave.

S. Papa Ave.

S. Lono Ave.

S. Puunene Ave.

Hea Place

Lihipali St.

Lower Main St.

WAILUKU

Kaahumanu Ave.

Kunihi Ln.

Iao Theater

E. Main St.

N. Market St.

Mill St.

S. Market St.

Kahili St.

Vineyard St.

Keopuolani St.

Wells St.

Kenolio St.

Mahalani St.

Waiale Reservoirs

Kehalani Dr.

4

Kaahumanu Church

3

Iao Valley Rd.

Iao Stream

Kahekili Hwy.

330

Honoapiilani Hwy.

30

5

Alexander & Baldwin Sugar Museum **9**

Bailey House **3**

Iao Valley State Monument **2**

Kepaniwai Park & Heritage Gardens **1**

Market Street **4**

Maui's Fresh Produce Farmers' Market **7**

Maui Nui Botanical Gardens **6**

Maui Swap Meet **8**

Maui Tropical Plantation & Country Store **5**

WORTH NOTING

Maui's Fresh Produce Farmers' Market. Local purveyors showcase their fruits, vegetables, orchids, and crafts in the central courtyard at the Queen Kaahumanu Shopping Center. If "strictly local" is critical to you, it's a good idea to ask about the particular produce/flowers/items you want to purchase. ⊠ *Queen Kaahumanu Shopping Center, 275 W. Kaahumanu Ave., Kahului* ☎ *808/877–4325* ⊙ *Tues., Wed., and Fri. 8–4.*

Maui Swap Meet. Even locals get up early to go to the Maui Swap Meet for fresh produce and floral bouquets. Hundreds of stalls sell everything from quilts to didgeridoos. Enter the parking lot from the traffic light at Kahului Beach Road. ⊠ *University of Hawaii Maui, 310 Kaahumanu Ave., Kahului* ☎ *808/244–3100* ⊕ *www.mauiexposition. com* ⊙ *Sat. 7–1.*

WAILUKU

4 miles west of Kahului; 12 miles north of Kihei; 21 miles east of Lahaina.

Wailuku is peaceful now—though it wasn't always so. Its name means "Water of Destruction," after the fateful battle in Iao Valley that pitted King Kamehameha the Great against Maui warriors. Wailuku was a politically important town until the sugar industry began to decline in the 1960s and tourism took hold. Businesses left the cradle of the West Maui Mountains and followed the new market (and tourists) to the shores. Wailuku houses the county government but has the feel of a town that's been asleep for several decades.

The shops and offices now inhabiting Market Street's plantation-style buildings serve as reminders of a bygone era, and continued attempts at "gentrification," at the very least, open the way for unique eateries, shops, and galleries. Drop by on the first Friday of the month for First Friday, when Market Street is closed to traffic and turns into a festival with live music, performances, food, and more.

GETTING HERE AND AROUND

Heading to Wailuku from the airport, Hana Highway turns into Kaahumanu Avenue, the main thoroughfare between Kahului and Wailuku. Maui Bus system's Wailuku Loop stops at shopping centers, medical facilities, and government buildings. The fare is $2.

TOP ATTRACTIONS

Fodor'sChoice
★

Bailey House. This repository of the largest and best collection of Hawaiian artifacts on Maui includes objects from the sacred island of Kahoolawe. Built in 1833 on the site of the compound of Kahekili (the last ruling chief of Maui), it was occupied by the family of missionary teachers Edward and Caroline Bailey until 1888. Edward Bailey was something of a Renaissance man: beyond being a missionary, he was also a surveyor, a naturalist, and an excellent artist. The museum displays a number of Bailey's landscape paintings, which provide a snapshot of the island during his time. There is missionary-period furniture, and the grounds include gardens with native Hawaiian plants and a fine example of a traditional canoe. ■TIP➜ **The gift shop is one of the best sources on Maui for items that are actually made in Hawaii.**

⊠ *2375A Main St.* ☎ *808/244–3326* ⊕ *www.mauimuseum.org* 💴 *$7* ☉ *Mon.–Sat. 10–4.*

Fodor's Choice **lao Valley State Monument.** When Mark Twain saw this park, he dubbed
★ it the Yosemite of the Pacific. Yosemite it's not, but it is a lovely deep valley with the curious "**Iao Needle**," a spire that rises more than 2,000 feet from the valley floor. You can walk from the parking lot across Iao Stream and explore the thick, junglelike topography. This park has some lovely short strolls on paved paths, where you can stop and meditate by the edge of a stream or marvel at the native plants. Locals come to jump from the rocks or bridge into the stream—this isn't recommended. Mist often rises if there has been a rain, which makes being here even more magical. Parking is $5, when an attendant is present. ⊠ *Western end of Rte. 32* ⊕ *www.hawaiistateparks.org* 💴 *Free* ☉ *Daily 7–7.*

WORTH NOTING

FAMILY **Kepaniwai Park & Heritage Gardens.** Picnic facilities dot the landscape of this county park, a memorial to Maui's cultural roots. Among the interesting displays are an early-Hawaiian *hale* (house), a New England–style saltbox, a Portuguese-style villa with gardens, and dwellings from such other cultures as China and the Philippines. Next door, the **Hawaii Nature Center** has excellent interactive exhibits and hikes easy enough for children.

The peacefulness here belies the history of the area. In 1790, King Kamehameha the Great from the Island of Hawaii waged a successful and bloody battle against Kahekili, the son of Maui's chief. An earlier battle at the site had pitted Kahekili himself against an older Hawaii Island chief, Kalaniopuu. Kahekili prevailed, but the carnage was so great that the nearby stream became known as Wailuku (water of destruction), and the place where fallen warriors choked the stream's flow was called Kepaniwai (damming of the waters). ⊠ *870 Iao Valley Rd.* 💴 *Free* ☉ *Daily 7–7.*

Market Street. An idiosyncratic assortment of shops makes Wailuku's Market Street a delightful place for a stroll. Brown-Kobayashi and the Bird of Paradise Unique Antiques are the best shops for interesting collectibles and furnishings. Wailuku Coffee Company houses works by local artists and occasionally offers live entertainment in the evening. On the first Friday of every month Market Street closes to traffic from 5:30 to 9 for Wailuku's First Friday celebration. The fun includes street vendors, live entertainment, and food. ⊠ *Market St.*

FAMILY **Maui Tropical Plantation & Country Store.** When Maui's cash crop declined in importance, a group of visionaries opened an agricultural theme park on the site of this former sugarcane field. The 60-acre preserve offers a 30-minute tram ride with informative narration that covers the growing process and plant types. Children will enjoy such hands-on activities as coconut husking. Also here are an art gallery, a restaurant, and a store specializing in "Made in Maui" products. ⊠ *1670 Honoapiilani Hwy., Waikapu* ☎ *808/244–7643* ⊕ *www.mauitropicalplantation.com* 💴 *Free; $15 for tram ride* ☉ *Daily 9–5.*

UPCOUNTRY MAUI

The west-facing upper slope of Haleakala is considered "Upcountry" by locals and is a hidden gem by most accounts. While this region is responsible for most of Maui's produce—lettuce, tomatoes, strawberries, sweet Maui onions, and more—it is also home to innovators, renegades, artists, and some of Maui's most interesting communities. It may not be the Maui of postcards, but some say this is the real Maui and is well worth at least a day or two of exploring.

Upcountry is also fertile ranch land; cowboys still work the fields of the historic 20,000-acre Ulupalakua Ranch and the 32,000-acre Haleakala Ranch. ■ TIP→ Take an agricultural tour and learn more about the island's bounty. Lavender and wine are among the offerings. Up here you'll notice cactus thickets mingled with purple jacaranda, wild hibiscus, and towering eucalyptus trees. Keep an eye out for *pueo,* Hawaii's native owl, which hunts these fields during daylight hours.

A drive to Upcountry Maui from Wailea (South Shore) or Kaanapali (West Maui) can be an all-day outing if you take the time to visit Tedeschi Vineyards and Winery and the tiny but entertaining town of Makawao. You may want to cut these side trips short and combine your Upcountry tour with a visit to Haleakala National Park *(see Haleakala National Park feature).* It's a Maui must-see. If you leave early enough to catch the sunrise from the summit of Haleakala, you'll have plenty of time to explore the mountain, have lunch in Kula or at Ulupalakua Ranch, and end your day with dinner in Makawao.

THE KULA HIGHWAY

15 miles east of Kahului; 44 miles east of Kaanapali; 28 miles east of Wailea.

Kula: Most Mauians say it with a hint of a sigh. Why? It's just that much closer to heaven. Explore it for yourself on some of the area's agricultural tours.

On the broad shoulder of Haleakala, this is blessed country. From the Kula Highway most of Central Maui is visible—from the lava-scarred plains of Kenaio to the cruise-ship-lighted waters of Kahului Harbor. Beyond the central valley's sugarcane fields, the plunging profile of the West Maui Mountains can be seen in its entirety, wreathed in ethereal mist. If this sounds too dramatic a description, you haven't been here yet. These views, coveted by many, continue to drive real-estate prices further skyward. Luckily, you can still have them for free—just pull over on the roadside and inhale the beauty.

GETTING HERE AND AROUND

From Kahului, take Route 37 (Haleakala Highway), which runs into Route 377 (Kula Highway). Upper and Lower Kula highways are both numbered 377, but join each other at two points.

TOP ATTRACTIONS

Fodor'sChoice
★
Haleakala National Park. *See special feature for information about this park, one of Maui's top attractions.*

Keokea. More of a friendly gesture than a town, this tiny outpost is the last bit of civilization before Kula Highway becomes a winding back road. A coffee tree pushes through the sunny deck at Grandma's Maui Coffee, the morning watering hole for Maui's cowboys who work at Ulupalakua or Kaupo Ranch. Keokea Gallery next door sells cool, quirky artwork. And two tiny stores—Fong's and Ching's—are testament to the Chinese immigrants who settled the area in the late 19th Century. ■ TIP➡ **The only restroom for miles is in the public park, and the view makes stretching your legs worth it.**

Fodor'sChoice ★ **Oo Farm.** About a mile from Alii Kula Lavender are 8 acres of organic salad greens, herbs, vegetables, coffee, cocoa, fruits, and berries—all of it headed directly to restaurants in Lahaina. Oo Farm is owned and operated by the restaurateurs responsible for some of Maui's finest dining establishments, and more than 300 pounds of its produce end up on diners' plates every week. Reserve a space for the midday tours, which include an informational walk around the pastoral grounds and a pick-your-own gourmet alfresco lunch, supervised by a chef. Cap off the experience with house-grown, roasted, and brewed coffee, and some of the yummiest chocolate in the state. Reservations are necessary. ⊠ *651 Waipoli Rd.* ☎ *808/667–4341* ⊕ *www.oofarm.com* ⊠ *Lunch tours from $50* ☉ *Mon.–Thurs. 10:30–2.*

Fodor'sChoice ★ **Tedeschi Vineyards and Winery.** You can tour Maui's only winery and its historic grounds, the former Rose Ranch, and sample such wines as Ulupalakua Red and Upcountry Gold. The top seller, naturally, is the pineapple wine, Maui Blanc. The tasting room is a cottage built in the late 1800s for the frequent visits of King Kalakaua. The cottage also contains the **Ulupalakua Ranch History Room,** which tells colorful stories of the ranch's owners, the *paniolo* (Hawaiian cowboy) tradition that developed here, and Maui's polo teams. The old Ranch Store across the road may look like a museum, but in fact it's an excellent pit stop. ■ TIP➡ **The elk burgers are fantastic.** ⊠ *Ulupalakua Ranch, Kula Hwy.* ☎ *808/878–6058* ⊕ *www.mauiwine.com* ⊠ *Free* ☉ *Daily 10–5; tours at 10:30 and 1:30.*

WORTH NOTING

Alii Kula Lavender. Make time for tea and a scone at this lavender farm with a falcon's view: It's *the* relaxing remedy for those suffering from too much sun, shopping, or golf. Knowledgeable guides lead tours through winding paths of therapeutic lavender varieties, protea, succulents, and rare Maui wormwood. The gift shop is stocked with many locally made lavender products such as brownies, moisturizing lotions, and fragrant sachets. Make a reservation in advance for their group tours. ⊠ *1100 Waipoli Rd.* ☎ *808/878–3004* ⊕ *www.aklmaui.com* ⊠ *$3; $12 for walking tours* ☉ *Daily 9–4.*

FAMILY **Surfing Goat Dairy.** It takes goats to make goat cheese, and they've got plenty of both at this 42-acre farm. Tours range from "casual" to "grand," and any of them delight kids as well as adults. If you have the time, the "Evening Chores and Milking Tour" is educational and fun. The owners make more than two-dozen kinds of goat cheese, from the plain, creamy "Udderly Delicious" to more exotic varieties that include tropical ingredients. All are available in the dairy store, along with gift baskets and even goat-milk soaps. ⊠ *3651 Omaopio Rd.*

☎ *808/878–2870* ⊕ *www.surfinggoatdairy.com* ✉ *Free; tours $10–$25* ⊙ *Mon.–Sat. 9–5, Sun. 9–2.*

Upcountry Farmers' Market. Most of Maui's produce is grown Upcountry, which is why everything is fresh at this outdoor market at the football field parking lot in Kulamalu Town Center. Farmers offer fruits, vegetables, and flowers, as well as jellies and breads. Go early, as nearly everything sells out. ✉ *55 Kiopaa St., near Longs Drugs, Pukalani* ⊕ *ww.upcountryfamersmarket.com* ⊙ *Sat. 7 am–10:30 am.*

MAKAWAO

10 miles east of Kahului; 10 miles southeast of Paia.

At the intersection of Baldwin and Makawao avenues, this once-tiny town has managed to hang on to its country charm (and eccentricity) as it has grown in popularity. Its good selection of specialized shops makes Makawao a fun place to spend some time.

The district was originally settled by Portuguese and Japanese immigrants who came to Maui to work the sugar plantations and then moved Upcountry to establish small farms, ranches, and stores. Descendants now work the neighboring Haleakala and Ulupalakua ranches. Every July 4 weekend the *paniolo* set comes out in force for the Makawao Rodeo.

The crossroads of town—lined with shops and down-home eateries—reflects a growing population of people who came here just because they liked it. For those seeking greenery rather than beachside accommodations, there are secluded B&Bs around the town.

GETTING HERE AND AROUND

To get to Makawao by car, take Route 37 (Haleakala Highway) to Pukalanai, then turn left on Makawao Avenue. You can also take Route 36 (Hana Highway) to Paia and make a right onto Baldwin Avenue. Either way, you'll arrive in the heart of Makawao.

TOP ATTRACTIONS

Fodor's Choice
★

Hui Noeau Visual Arts Center. The grande dame of Maui's visual arts scene, "The Hui" hosts exhibits that are always satisfying. Located just outside Makawao, the center's main building is an elegant two-story Mediterranean-style villa designed in 1917 by the defining Hawaii architect of the era, C.W. Dickey. You can arrange a $12 tour of the lovely grounds—which feature many dozens of species of plants and trees—with at least 24 hours notice. A self-guided tour booklet is available for $6. ✉ *2841 Baldwin Ave.* ☎ *808/572–6560* ⊕ *www.huinoeau. com* ✉ *Free* ⊙ *Mon.–Sat. 10–4.*

QUICK
BITES

✕ **Komoda Store and Bakery.** One of Makawao's landmarks is Komoda Store and Bakery, a classic mom-and-pop shop that has changed little in three-quarters of a century. You can get an incredible "stick" donut or delicious cream puff if you arrive early enough. They make hundreds, but sell out everyday. ✉ *3674 Baldwin Ave.* ☎ *808/572–7261.*

THE NORTH SHORE

Blasted by winter swells and wind, Maui's North Shore draws watersports thrill seekers from around the world. But there's much more to this area of Maui than coastline. Inland, a lush, waterfall-fed Garden of Eden beckons. In forested pockets, wealthy hermits have carved out a little piece of paradise for themselves.

North Shore action centers around the colorful town of Paia and the windsurfing mecca of Hookipa Beach. It's a far cry from the more developed resort areas of West Maui and the South Shore. Paia is also a starting point for one of the most popular excursions in Maui, the Road to Hana. Waterfalls, phenomenal views of the coast and ocean, and lush rain forest are all part of the spectacular 55-mile drive into East Maui.

PAIA

9 miles east of Kahului; 4 miles west of Haiku.

Fodor'sChoice
★

At the intersection of Hana Highway and Baldwin Avenue, Paia has eclectic boutiques that supply everything from high fashion to hemp-oil candles. Some of Maui's best shops for surf trunks, Brazilian bikinis, and other beachwear are here. Restaurants provide excellent people-watching and an array of dining and takeout options from flatbread to fresh fish. The abundance is helpful because Paia is the last place to snack before the pilgrimage to Hana and the first stop for the famished on the return trip.

This little town on Maui's North Shore was once a sugarcane enclave, with a mill, plantation camps, and shops. The old sugar mill finally closed, but the town continues to thrive. In the 1970s Paia became a hippie town, as dropouts headed for Maui to open boutiques, galleries, and unusual eateries. In the 1980s windsurfers—many of them European—discovered nearby Hookipa Beach and brought an international flavor to Paia. Today this historic town is hip and happening.

GETTING HERE AND AROUND

Route 36 (Hana Highway) runs directly though Paia; 4 miles east of town, follow the sign to Haiku, a short detour off the highway. You can take the Maui Bus from the airport and Queen Kaahumanu Shopping Center in Kahului to Paia and on to Haiku.

QUICK BITES

✕ **Mana Foods.** The North Shore's natural-foods store, Mana Foods has an inspired deli with hot and cold items. ✉ *49 Baldwin Ave.* ☎ *808/579–8078* ⊕ *www.manafoodsmaui.com.*

HAIKU

13 miles east of Kahului; 4 miles east of Paia.

At one time this area vibrated around a couple of enormous pineapple canneries. Both have been transformed into rustic warehouse malls. Because of the post office next door, Old Haiku Cannery earned the title of town center. Here you can try eateries offering everything from plate lunches to vegetarian dishes to juicy burgers and fantastic sushi. Follow windy Haiku Road to Pauwela Cannery, the other defunct factory-turned-hangout. Don't fret if you get lost. This jungle hillside is a maze of flower-decked roads that seem to double back upon themselves.

The Road to Hana is a stunning drive, with plenty of lookouts to enjoy the view.

GETTING HERE AND AROUND

Haiku is a short detour off Hana Highway (Route 36) just past Hookipa Beach Park on the way to Hana. Haiku Road turns into Kokomo Road at the post office.

ROAD TO HANA

As you round the impossibly tight turn, a one-lane bridge comes into view. Beneath its worn surface, a lush forested gulch plummets toward the coast. The sound of rushing water fills the air, compelling you to search the overgrown hillside for waterfalls. This is the Road to Hana, a 55-mile journey into the unspoiled heart of Maui. Tracing a centuries-old path, the road begins as a well-paved highway in Kahului and ends in the tiny town of Hana on the island's rain-gouged windward side, spilling into a backcountry rarely visited by humans.

This drive is a Hawaii pilgrimage for those eager to experience what glossy magazines consider the "real" Hawaii. To most, the lure of Hana is its timelessness, and paired with the spectacular drive (which brings to life the old adage: The journey is the destination), this is one of Hawaii's best experiences.

The drive begs to be taken at a leisurely pace. You'll want to slow time to take in foliage-hugged ribbons of road, roadside banana bread stands, to swim beneath a waterfall, and to inhale the lush Maui tropics in all its glory. The Road to Hana is definitely one of the most beautiful drives on the planet.

TIPS ON DRIVING THE ROAD TO HANA

Despite its twists and turns, the Road to Hana is not as frightening as it may seem. You're bound to be a little nervous approaching it the first time; but afterward you'll wonder if somebody out there is making it sound tough just to keep out the hordes. The challenging part of the road takes only an hour and a half, but you'll want to stop often and let the driver enjoy the view, too.

With short stops, the drive from Paia to Hana should take you between two and three hours one way. Lunching in Hana, hiking, and swimming can easily turn the round-trip into a full-day outing, especially if you continue past Hana to Oheo Gulch and Kipahulu. If you go that far, you might consider continuing around the "back side" for the return trip. The scenery is completely different and you'll end up in beautiful Upcountry Maui.

Since there's so much scenery to take in, we recommend staying overnight in Hana. It's worth taking time to enjoy the waterfalls and beaches without being in a hurry. Try to plan your trip for a day that promises fair, sunny weather—though the drive can be even more beautiful when it's raining, the roads become more hazardous.

During high season, the Road to Hana tends to clog—well, not clog exactly, but develop little choo-choo trains of cars, with everyone in a line of six or a dozen driving as slowly as the first car. The solution: leave early (dawn) and return late (dusk). And if you find yourself playing the role of locomotive, pull over and let the other drivers pass. You can also let someone else take the turns for you—several companies offer van tours that make stops all along the way.

BASIC ROAD TIPS

■ Common courtesy in Hawaii dictates that slower drivers should pull over for faster drivers. Please don't try to zoom through this windy road.

■ When approaching one-lane bridges, it is local custom for about five cars to go in one direction at a time—so if you happen to be the sixth car, stop before entering the bridge and let drivers traveling in the other direction pass.

■ Instead of stopping in the middle of the road, or a bridge, to snap photos, park at a turnoff and carefully walk back to the waterfall to take your photos.

■ While rain makes the drive more beautiful, with gushing waterfalls and rainbows, it also makes the roads slick. Drive slowly and cautiously on wet roads.

■ Just after Haiku the mile markers start at zero again.

HUELO, KAILUA, AND NEARBY
10 miles east of Haiku.

As the Road to Hana starts its journey eastward, the slopes grow steep and the Pacific Ocean pops into view. The first waterfall you see, Twin Falls, is around mile marker 2, and farther up the road is the Koolau Forest Reserve. Embedded in the forest are two townships, Huelo and Kailua, both of which are great places to pull over and take in the dramatic landscape.

GETTING HERE AND AROUND

Just after Haiku as you travel eastward, the mile markers change back to zero. The towns of Huelo and Kailua are at mile markers 5 and 6. To reach the townships, follow the signs toward the ocean side of the road.

TOP ATTRACTIONS

The following sites are listed geographically by mile marker on route to Hana.

Twin Falls. Keep an eye out for the Twin Falls Fruit Stand just after mile marker 2 on the Hana Highway. Stop here and treat yourself to some fresh sugarcane juice. If you're feeling adventurous, follow the path beyond the stand to the paradisiacal waterfalls known as Twin Falls. Although it's still private property, the "no trespassing" signs have been replaced by colorfully painted arrows pointing toward the easily accessible falls. Several deep, emerald pools sparkle beneath waterfalls and offer excellent swimming and photo opportunities. ⊠ *Hana Hwy., past mile marker 2, Haiku.*

Huelo. When you see the colorful mailboxes on the makai (ocean) side of the road around mile marker 5 on the Hana Highway, follow the windy road to the rural area of Huelo—a funky community that includes a mix of off-the-grid inhabitants and vacation rentals. The town features two picturesque churches, including Kaulanapueo Church, constructed in 1853 out of coral blocks. If you linger awhile, you may meet local residents and learn about a rural lifestyle you might not have expected to find on the Islands. The same can be said for nearby Kailua (mile marker 6). ■TIP→ When you're back up on Hana Highway, pull into the Huelo Lookout Fruit Stand for yummy smoothies and killer views of the Pacific below. ⊠ *Hana Hwy., near mile marker 5, Huelo.*

Waikamoi Nature Trail. Just after Huelo, the road enters the Koolau Forest Reserve. This is what you expected from the Road to Hana. Vines wrap around street signs and waterfalls are so abundant that you don't know which direction to look. A good start is between mile markers 9 and 10, where the Waikamoi Nature Trail sign beckons you to stretch your car-weary limbs. A short (if muddy) trail leads through tall eucalyptus trees to a coastal vantage point with a picnic table. Signage reminds visitors: "Quiet, Trees at Work" and "Bamboo Picking Permit Required." *Awapuhi,* or Hawaiian shampoo ginger, sends up fragrant shoots along the trail. ■TIP→ The area has picnic tables and a restroom. ⊠ *Hana Hwy., between mile markers 9 and 10.*

KEANAE, WAILUA, AND NEARBY

13 miles east of Kailua.

Officially, Keanae is the halfway point to Hana, but for many, this is where the drive offers the most rewarding vistas. The greenery seems to envelop the skinny road, forcing drivers to slow to a crawl as they ooh and ah at waterfalls at every turn. Keanae itself isn't much of a stunner, save the banana bread shack at the bottom of the road, but the scenery as your car winds through these tropics makes the white-knuckle parts of the drive worth it. Around the nearby village of Wailua, one of the most fiercely native Hawaiian regions on the island, there seem to be waterfalls at every turn.

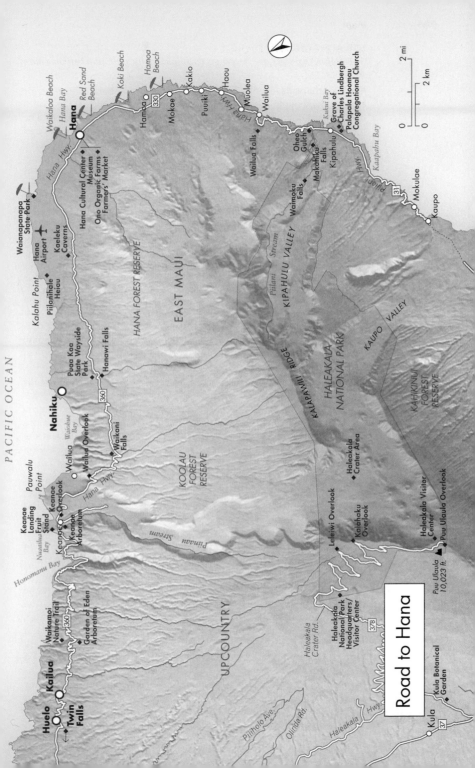

Road to Hana

TOP ATTRACTIONS

The following sites are listed geographically by mile marker on route to Hana.

Keanae Arboretum. Here you can add to your botanical education or enjoy a challenging hike into the forest. Signs help you learn the names of the many plants and trees now considered native to Hawaii. The meandering Piinaau Stream adds a graceful touch to the arboretum and provides a swimming pond. You can take a fairly rigorous hike from the arboretum if you can find the trail at one side of the large taro patch. Be careful not to lose the trail once you're on it. A lovely forest waits at the end of the 25-minute hike. ⊠ *Hana Hwy., mile marker 17* ◲ *Free* ☉ *Daily (recommended to visit only during daylight hours).*

Keanae Landing Fruit Stand. Located in the blink-and-you'll-miss-it community of Keanae, this legendary banana bread shop is just past the coral-and-lava-rock church. Aunt Sandy's sweet loaves lure locals and tourists alike, but be sure to arrive early, because once the stand runs out, you'll have to scurry back up the main road to the **Halfway to Hana Fruit Stand** to find a tasty replacement.

Keanae Overlook. Near mile marker 17 along the Hana Highway, you can stop at the Keanae Overlook. From this observation point you can take in the quiltlike effect the taro patches create against the dramatic backdrop of the ocean. In the other direction there are awesome views of Haleakala through the foliage. This is a great spot for photos. ⊠ *Hana Hwy., near mile marker 17.*

Waikani Falls. Though not necessarily bigger or taller than the other falls along the Hana Highway, these are the most dramatic—some say the best—falls you'll find in East Maui. That's partly because the water is not diverted for sugar irrigation. The taro farmers in Wailua need all the runoff. This is a particularly good spot for photos. To access the falls, park a half mile beyond mile marker 19, and follow the trail on the Hana side of the bridge to the 70-foot waterfalls. ⊠ *Hana Hwy., past mile marker 19, Wailua.*

Wailua Overlook. From the parking lot on the side of the Hana Highway near mile marker 21, you can see Wailua Canyon in one direction and Wailua Village in the other. Photos are spectacular in the morning light of the verdant expanse below. Also from your perch, you can see Wailua Village's landmark 1860 church, which was allegedly constructed of coral that washed up onto the shore during a storm. ⊠ *Hana Hwy., near mile marker 21, Wailua.*

Puaa Kaa State Wayside Park. Many believe the stretch of landscape between mile markers 19 and 25 of the Hana Highway contain the most picturesque waterfalls on Maui. While there are stunning waterfalls in all directions, perhaps the loveliest is about a half mile beyond mile marker 22. The series of waterfalls gushing into a pool below will have you snapping screen savers. To get here, park at the turnoff just over the bridge and then carefully walk west across the bridge to the waterfalls. There are hiking trails that snake up the mountain, but they are muddy and slightly dangerous. ■TIP➔ Usually in the parking lot by the waterfalls, a couple of flatbed trucks are loaded with crafts and fruit breads for sale. Look around for Dave's banana bread truck. It's some of the best on the island. ✉ *Hana Hwy., Wailua.*

HANA AND NEARBY
15 miles east of Keanae.

Even though the "town" is little more than a gas station, a post office, and a general store, the relaxed pace of life that Hana residents enjoy will have you in its grasp. Hana is one of the few places where the slow pulse of the island is still strong. The town centers on its lovely circular bay, dominated on the right-hand shore by a *puu* (volcanic cinder cone) called Kauiki. A short trail here leads to a cave, the birthplace of Queen Kaahumanu.

> ### TROPICAL DELIGHTS
>
> The drive to Hana wouldn't be as enchanting without a stop or two at one of the countless fruit (and banana bread) and flower stands by the highway. Every half mile or so a thatched hut tempts passersby with apple bananas (a smaller, firmer variety), *lilikoi* (passion fruit), avocados, or star fruit just plucked from the tree. Leave a few dollars in the can for the folks who live off the land. Huge bouquets of tropical flowers are available for a handful of change, and some farms will ship.

Two miles beyond town another *puu* presides over a loop road that passes Hana's two best beaches—Koki and Hamoa. The hill is called Ka Iwi O Pele (Pele's Bone). Offshore here, at tiny Alau Island, the demigod Maui supposedly fished up the Hawaiian Islands.

Although sugar was once the mainstay of Hana's economy, the last plantation shut down in the 1940s. In 1946 rancher Paul Fagan built the Hotel Hana-Maui (now the Travassa Hana) and stocked the surrounding pastureland with cattle. Now it's the ranch and its hotel that put food on most tables. It's pleasant to stroll around this beautifully rustic property. In the evening, while local musicians play in the lobby bar, their friends jump up to hula dance. The cross you can see on the hill above the hotel was put there in memory of Fagan.

TOP ATTRACTIONS
The following sites are listed geographically by mile marker on route to Hana.

Kaeleku Caverns. If you're interested in spelunking, take the time to explore Kaeleku Caverns (also known as Hana Lava Tube), just after mile marker 31 on the Hana Highway. The site is a mile down Ulaino Road. The friendly folks at the cave give a brief orientation and promptly send nature enthusiasts into Maui's largest lava tube, accented by colorful underworld formations. You can take a self-guided, 30- to 40-minute tour daily from 10:30 am to 4 pm for $11.95 per person. LED flashlights are provided. ✉ *Ulaino Rd., off Hana Hwy.* ☎ *808/248–7308* ⊕ *www.mauicave.com* ☉ *Daily 10:30–4.*

Piilanihale Heiau. This temple was built for a great 16th-century Maui king named Piilani and his heirs. Hawaiian families continue to maintain and protect this sacred site as they have for centuries, and they have not been eager to turn it into a tourist attraction. However, they now offer a brochure, so you can tour the property yourself, including the 122-acre **Kahanu Garden,** a federally funded research center focusing on the ethnobotany of the Pacific. To get here, turn left onto Ulaino Road at Hana Highway mile marker 31; the road turns to gravel; continue 1½ miles. ⊠ *650 Ulaino Rd.* ☎ *808/248–8912* ⊕ *www.ntbg.org* ☞ *$10* ☉ *Mon.–Sat. 9–2. Guided tour Sat. at 10, reservations required.*

Waianapanapa State Park. Home to one of Maui's only black-sand beaches and freshwater caves for adventurous swimmers to explore, this park is right on the ocean. It's a lovely spot to picnic, hike, or swim. To the left you'll find the volcanic-sand beach, picnic tables, and cave pools. To the right is an ancient trail that snakes along the ocean past blowholes, sea arches, and archaeological sites. The tide pools here turn red several times a year. Scientists say it's explained by the arrival of small shrimp, but legend claims the color represents the blood of Popoalaea, said to have been murdered in one of the caves by her husband, Chief Kakae. In either case, the dramatic landscape is bound to leave a lasting impression. ■TIP→ With a permit, you can stay in a state-run cabin for a steal. But you have to book a year in advance as these rustic spots book up quickly. ⊠ *Hana Hwy., near mile marker 32* ☎ *808/984–8109* ⊕ *www.hawaiistateparks.org* ☞ *Free.*

Hana Cultural Center Museum. If you're determined to spend some time and money in Hana after the long drive along the Hana Highway, head to the Hana Cultural Center Museum in the center of town. Besides operating a well-stocked gift shop, it displays artifacts, quilts, a replica of an authentic *kauhale* (an ancient Hawaiian living complex, with thatch huts and food gardens), and other Hawaiiana. The knowledgeable staff can explain it all to you. ⊠ *4974 Uakea Rd.* ☎ *808/248–8622* ⊕ *www.hanaculturalcenter.org* ☞ *$3* ☉ *Weekdays 10–4.*

EAST MAUI

East Maui defies definition. Part hideaway for renegades, part escape for celebrities, this funky stretch of Maui surprises at every turn. You might find a smoothie shop that powers your afternoon bike ride, or a hidden restaurant–artist gathering off a backcountry road serving organic cuisine that could have been dropped in from San Francisco. Farms are abundant, and the dramatic beauty seems to get better the farther you get from Hana. This route leads through stark ocean vistas rounding the back side of Haleakala and into Upcountry. If you plan to meander this way, be sure to check the weather and road conditions.

KIPAHULU AND NEARBY

11 miles east of Hana.

Most know Kipahulu as the resting place of Charles Lindbergh. Kipahulu devotes its energy to staying under the radar. There is not much for tourists, save an organic farm, a couple of cafés, and astounding natural landscapes. Maui's wildest wilderness might not beg for your tourist dollars, but it is a tantalizing place to escape just about everything.

GETTING HERE AND AROUND

To access Kipahulu, continue on Hana Highway, also known as 330, for 11 miles southeast. You can also reach the area from Upcountry's Highway 37, which turns into Highway 31, though this route can take up to two hours and is a bit rough on your rental car.

TOP ATTRACTIONS

Fodor'sChoice ★ **Oheo Gulch.** One branch of Haleakala National Park runs down the mountain from the crater and reaches the sea here, 10 miles past Hana at mile marker 42 on the Hana Highway, where a basalt-lined stream cascades from one pool to the next. Some tour guides still call this area "Seven Sacred Pools," but in truth there are more than seven, and they've never been considered sacred. You can park here and walk to the lowest pools for a cool swim. The place gets crowded, though, because most people who drive the Hana Highway make this their last stop. It's best to get here early to soak up the solace of these waterfalls. If you enjoy hiking, go up the stream on the 2-mile hike to **Waimoku Falls.** The trail crosses a spectacular gorge, then turns into a boardwalk that takes you through an amazing bamboo forest. You can pitch a tent in the grassy campground down by the sea. ■ TIP➜ **The $10 parking fee is good for three days and includes entry to Haleakala Volcano.** ✉ *Piilani Hwy., 10 miles south of Hana.*

Grave of Charles Lindbergh. Many people travel the mile past Oheo Gulch to see the Grave of Charles Lindbergh. The world-renowned aviator chose to be buried here because he and his wife, writer Anne Morrow Lindbergh, spent a lot of time living in the area in a home they'd built. He was buried here in 1974, next to Palapala Hoomau Congregational Church. The simple one-room church sits on a bluff over the sea, with the small graveyard on the ocean side. Since this is a churchyard, be considerate and leave everything exactly as you found it. Next to the churchyard on the ocean side is a small county park, a good place for a peaceful picnic. ✉ *Palapala Hoomau Congregational Church, Piilani Hwy., Kipahulu.*

BEACHES

Updated by Heidi Pool

Of all the beaches on the Hawaiian Islands, Maui's are some of the most diverse. You can find the pristine, palm-lined shores you've always dreamed of, with clear and inviting waters the color of green sea glass, and you can also discover rich red- and black-sand beaches, craggy cliffs with surging whitecaps, and year-round sunsets that quiet the soul. As on the other islands, all Maui's beaches are public—but that doesn't mean it's not possible to find a secluded cove where you can truly get away from the world.

The island's leeward shores (West Maui and the South Shore) have the calmest, sunniest beaches. Hit the beach early, when the aquamarine waters are calm as bathwater. In summer, afternoon winds can be a sandblasting force and can chase away even the most dedicated sun worshippers. From November through May these beaches are also great spots to watch the humpback whales that spend winter and early spring in Maui's waters.

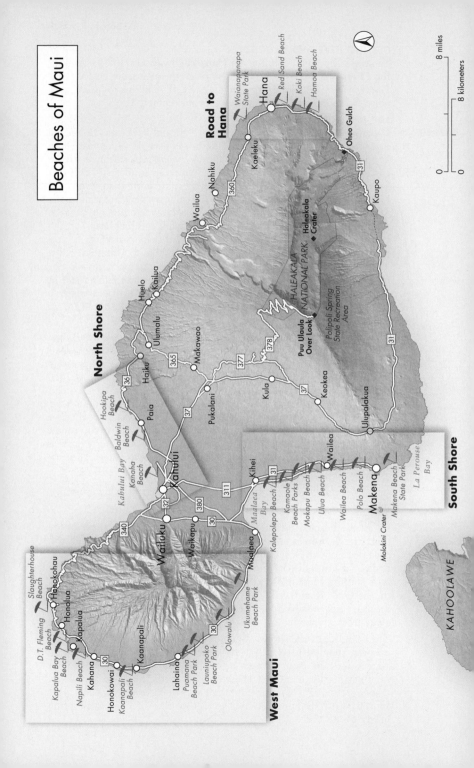

Beaches of Maui

Road to Hana

North Shore

South Shore

West Maui

Waianapanapa State Park

Red Sand Beach

Hana

Koki Beach

Hamoa Beach

Kaeleku

Nahiku

Wailua

Oheo Gulch

Kaupo

HALEAKALA NATIONAL PARK

Haleakala Crater

Polipoli Spring State Recreation Area

Puu Ulaula Over Look

Huelo

Kailua

Ulumalu

Makawao

Kula

Keokea

Haiku

Pukalani

Ulupalakua

Hookipa Beach

Paia

Baldwin Beach

Kahului

Kanaha Beach

Kahului Bay

Kihei

Wailea

Kalepolepo Beach

Kamaole Beach Parks

Mokapu Beach

Ulua Beach

Wailea Beach

Polo Beach

Makena

Makena Beach State Park

La Perouse Bay

Maalaea Bay

Molokini Crater

Wailuku

Waikapu

Maalaea

Slaughterhouse Beach

D.T. Fleming Beach

Honokohau

Honolua

Kapalua

Kapalua Bay Beach

Napili Beach

Kahana

Honokowai

Kaanapali Beach

Kaanapali

Lahaina

Puamana Beach Park

Launiupoko Beach Park

Olowalu

Ukumehame Beach Park

KAHOOLAWE

8 miles

8 kilometers

Windward shores (the North Shore and East Maui) are for the more adventurous. Beaches face the open ocean rather than other islands, and tend to be rockier and more prone to powerful swells. This is particularly true in winter, when the North Shore becomes a playground for big-wave riders and windsurfers. Don't let this keep you away, however; some of the island's best beaches are those slivers of volcanic sand found on the windward shore.

WEST MAUI

The beaches in West Maui are legendary for their glittering aquamarine waters backed by long stretches of golden sand. Reef fronts much of the western shore, making the underwater panorama something to behold. A few tips: parking can be challenging in resort areas. Look for the blue "Shoreline Access" signs to find limited parking and a public path to the beach. Watch out for *kiawe* thorns when you park off-road, because they can puncture tires—and feet.

There are a dozen roadside beaches to choose from on Route 30, of which these are the ones we like best.

The beaches listed here start in the north at Kapalua and head south past Kaanapali and Lahaina.

"Slaughterhouse" (Mokuleia) Beach. The island's northernmost beach is part of the Honolua-Mokuleia Marine Life Conservation District. "Slaughterhouse" is the surfers' nickname for what is officially Mokuleia. Weather permitting, this is a great place for bodysurfing and sunbathing. Concrete steps and a green railing help you get down the cliff to the sand. The next bay over, Honolua, has no beach but offers one of the best surf breaks in Hawaii. Competitions are often held there; telltale signs are cars pulled off the road and parked in the pineapple field. **Amenities:** none. **Best for:** sunset; surfing. ⊠ *Rte. 30, mile marker 32, Kapalua.*

D.T. Fleming Beach. Because the current can be quite strong, this charming, mile-long sandy cove is better for sunbathing than for swimming or water sports. Still, it's one of the island's most popular beaches. It's a perfect spot to watch the spectacular Maui sunsets, and there are picnic tables and grills. Part of the beach runs along the front of the Ritz-Carlton, Kapalua (*see Where to Stay*)—a good place to grab a cocktail and enjoy the view. **Amenities:** lifeguards; parking (no fee); showers; toilets. **Best for:** sunset; walking. ⊠ *Rte. 30, 1 mile north of Kapalua, Kapalua.*

Fodor's Choice ★ **Kapalua Bay Beach.** Over the years Kapalua has been recognized as one of the world's best beaches, and for good reason: it fronts a pristine bay good for snorkeling, swimming, and general lazing. Just north of Napili Bay, this lovely, sheltered shore often remains calm late into the afternoon, although currents may be strong offshore. Snorkeling is easy here, and there are lots of colorful reef fish. This popular area is bordered by the Kapalua Resort, so don't expect to have the beach to yourself. Walk through the tunnel from the parking lot at the end of Kapalua Place to get here. **Amenities:** parking (no fee); showers; toilets. **Best for:** snorkeling; sunset; swimming. ✉ *Rte. 30, turn onto Kapalua Pl., Kapalua.*

> **DON'T FORGET**
>
> All of the island's beaches are free and open to the public—even those that grace the front yards of fancy hotels. Some of the prettiest beaches are often hidden by buildings; look for the blue "Shoreline Access" signs that indicate public rights-of-way through condominiums, resorts, and other private properties.

FAMILY **Fodor's**Choice ★ **Napili Beach.** Surrounded by sleepy condos, this round bay is a turtle-filled pool lined with a sparkling white crescent of sand. Sunbathers love this beach, which is also a terrific sunset spot. The shore break is steep but gentle, so it's great for bodyboarding and bodysurfing. It's easy to keep an eye on kids here as the entire bay is visible from everywhere. The beach is right outside the Napili Kai Beach Resort (*see Where to Stay*), a popular little resort for honeymooners, only a few miles south of Kapalua. **Amenities:** showers; toilets. **Best for:** sunset; surfing; swimming. ✉ *5900 Lower Honoapiilani Hwy., look for Napili Pl. or Hui Dr., Napili.*

Kaanapali Beach. Stretching from the northernmost end of the Sheraton Maui to the Hyatt Regency Maui at its southern tip, Kaanapali Beach is lined with resorts, condominiums, restaurants, and shops. If you're looking for quiet and seclusion, this is not the beach for you. But if you want lots of action, spread out your towel here. The center section in front of Whalers Village, also called Dig Me Beach, is one of Maui's best people-watching spots: folks in catamarans and on windsurfers and stand-up paddleboarders head out from here while the beautiful people take in the scenery. A cement pathway weaves along the length of this 3-mile-long beach, leading from one astounding resort to the next.

The drop-off from Kaanapali's soft, sugary sand is steep, but waves hit the shore with barely a rippling slap. The northern section, known as Kekaa, was, in ancient Hawaii, a *lele,* or jumping-off place for spirits. It's easy to get into the water from the beach to enjoy the prime snorkeling among the lava rock outcroppings.

Throughout the resort, blue Shoreline Access signs point the way to a few free-parking stalls and public rights-of-way to the beach. Kaanapali Resort public beach parking can be found between the Hyatt and the Marriott, between the Marriott and the Kaanapali Alii, next to Whalers Village, and at the Sheraton. You can park for a fee at most of the large hotels (*see Where to Stay*) and at Whalers Village. The merchants

The sandy crescent of Napili Beach on West Maui is a lovely place to wait for sunset.

in the shopping village will validate your parking ticket if you make a purchase. **Amenities:** parking (no fee); showers; toilets. **Best for:** snorkeling; sunset; swimming; walking. ⊠ *Honoapiilani Hwy., follow any of three Kaanapali exits, Kaanapali.*

FAMILY **Launiupoko Beach Park.** This is the beach park of all beach parks: both a surf break and a beach, it offers a little something for everyone with its inviting stretch of lawn, soft white sand, and gentle waves. The shoreline reef creates a protected wading pool, perfect for small children. Outside the reef, beginner surfers will find good longboard rides. From the long sliver of beach (good for walking), you can enjoy superb views of Neighbor Islands, and, landside, of deep valleys cutting through the West Maui Mountains. Because of its endless sunshine and serenity—not to mention such amenities as picnic tables and grills—Launiupoko draws a crowd on the weekends, but there's space for everyone (and overflow parking across the street). **Amenities:** parking (no fee); showers; toilets. **Best for:** sunset; surfing; swimming; walking. ⊠ *Rte. 30, mile marker 18, Lahaina.*

Olowalu. More an offshore snorkel spot than a beach, Olowalu is also a great place to watch for turtles and whales in season. The beach is literally a pullover from the road, which can make for some unwelcome noise if you're looking for quiet. The entrance can be rocky (reef shoes help), but if you've got your snorkel gear it's a 200-yard swim to an extensive and diverse reef. Shoreline visibility can vary depending on the swell and time of day; late morning is best. Except for during a south swell, the waters are usually calm. A half mile north of mile marker 14 you can find the rocky surf break, also called Olowalu. Snorkeling here is along pathways that wind among coral heads. Note: This is a local hangout and can be unfriendly at times. **Amenities:** None. **Best for:** snorkeling. ⊠ *Rte. 30, mile marker 14, south of Olowalu General Store, Olowalu.*

THE SOUTH SHORE

Sandy beach fronts nearly the entire southern coastline of Maui. The farther south, the better the beaches get. Kihei has excellent beach parks in town, with white sand, plenty of amenities, and paved parking lots. Good snorkeling can be found along the beaches' rocky borders. As good as Kihei is, Wailea is better. The beaches are cleaner, and the views more impressive. You can take a mile-long walk on a shore path from Ulua to near Polo Beach. Look for blue "Public Shoreline Access" signs for parking along the main thoroughfare, Wailea Alanui. ⚠ **Break-ins have been reported at many parking lots, so don't leave valuables in the car.** As you head to Makena, the terrain gets wilder; bring lunch, water, and sunscreen.

The following South Shore beaches are listed from North Kihei southeast to Makena.

Kalama Park. This 36-acre beach park with plenty of shade is great for families and sports lovers. With its extensive lawns and sports fields, the park welcomes volleyball, baseball, and tennis players, and even has a playground, skateboard park, and a roller hockey rink. Stocked with grills and picnic pavilions, it's a recreational mecca. The beach itself is all but nonexistent, but swimming is fair—though you must brave the rocky steps down to the water. If you aren't completely comfortable with this entrance, stick to the burgers and bocce ball. **Amenities:** parking (no fee); showers; toilets. **Best for:** partiers. ⊠ *S. Kihei Rd., across from Kihei Kalama Village, Kihei.*

FAMILY **Kamaole I, II, and III.** Three steps from South Kihei Road are three golden stretches of sand separated by outcroppings of dark, jagged lava rocks. You can walk the length of all three beaches if you're willing to get your feet wet. The northernmost of the trio, Kamaole I (across from the ABC Store, in case you forget your sunscreen), offers perfect swimming and an active volleyball court. There's also a great lawn where you can spread out at the south end of the beach. Kamaole II is nearly identical except for the lawn, but there is no parking lot. The last beach, the one with all the people on it, is Kamaole III, perfect for throwing a disk or throwing down a blanket. This is a great family beach, complete with a playground, barbecue grills, kite flying, and, frequently, rented inflatable castles—a must at birthday parties for cool kids.

Locally—and quite disrespectfully, according to native Hawaiians— known as "Kam" I, II, and III, all three beaches have great swimming and lifeguards. In the morning the water can be as still as a lap pool. Kamaole III offers terrific breaks for beginning bodysurfers. **Amenities:** lifeguards; parking (no fee); showers; toilets. **Best for:** surfing; swimming; walking. ⊠ *S. Kihei Rd., between Alii Ke Alanui and the Hale Kamaole Condominums, Kihei.*

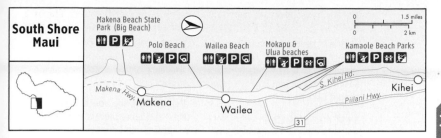

South Shore Maui

Makena Beach State Park (Big Beach)

Polo Beach   Wailea Beach

Mokapu & Ulua beaches

Kamaole Beach Parks

0   1.5 miles
0   2 km

S. Kihei Rd.

Kihei

Makena Hwy.   Makena

Wailea

Piilani Hwy.

31

3

Keawakapu Beach. Everyone loves Keawakapu, with its long stretch of golden sand, near-perfect swimming, and views of Puu Olai cinder cone. It's great fun to walk or jog this beach south into Wailea, as it's lined with over-the-top residences. It's best here in the morning—the winds pick up in the afternoon (beware of sandstorms). Keawakapu has three entrances: one is at the Mana Kai Maui resort (look for the blue "Shoreline Access" sign); the second is directly across from the parking lot on Kilohana Street (the entrance is unmarked); and the third is at the dead end of Kihei Road. Toilets are portable. **Amenities:** parking (no fee); showers; toilets. **Best for:** sunset; swimming; walking. ⊠ *S. Kihei Rd., near Kilohana St., Kihei.*

FAMILY **Mokapu and Ulua.** Look for a little road and public parking lot near the Wailea Beach Marriott Resort (*see Where to Stay*) if you are heading to Mokapu and Ulua beaches. Though there are no lifeguards, families love this place. Reef formations create tons of tide pools for kids to explore, and the beaches are protected from major swells. Snorkeling is excellent at Ulua, the beach to the left of the entrance. Mokapu, to the right, tends to be less crowded. **Amenities:** parking (free); showers; toilets. **Best for:** snorkeling; swimming. ⊠ *Wailea Alanui Dr., north of the Wailea Marriott, Wailea.*

Wailea Beach. A road near the Grand Wailea Resort takes you to Wailea Beach, a wide, sandy stretch with snorkeling and swimming. If you're not a guest at the Grand Wailea or Four Seasons (*see Where to Stay* for both hotels) the cluster of private umbrellas and chaises longues can be a little annoying, but the calm, unclouded waters and soft, white sand more than make up for this. From the parking lot, walk to the right to get to the main beach; to the left is another, smaller section that fronts the Four Seasons. There are picnic tables and grills away from the beach. **Amenities:** parking (no fee); showers; toilets. **Best for:** snorkeling; swimming. ⊠ *Wailea Alanui Dr., south of Grand Wailea Resort entrance, Wailea.*

Polo Beach. Small and secluded, this crescent fronts the Fairmont Kea Lani (*see Where to Stay*). Swimming and snorkeling are great here, and it's a good place to whale-watch. As at Wailea Beach, private umbrellas and chaises longues occupy the choicest real estate, but there's plenty of room for you and your towel. There's a nice grass picnic area, although it's a considerable distance from the beach. The pathway connecting the two beaches is a great spot to jog or to take in awesome views of nearby Molokini and Kahoolawe. Rare native plants grow along the

BEST BEACHES

Ah, Maui's beaches: it's hard to single out just a few because the island's strands are so varied. Here are some favorites for different interests from around the island.

BEST FOR FAMILIES
Baldwin Beach, the North Shore. The long, shallow, calm end closest to Kahului is safe even for toddlers—with adult supervision, of course.

Kamaole III, the South Shore. Sand, gentle surf, a playground, volleyball net, and barbecues all add up to great family fun.

Napili Beach, West Maui. Kids will love the turtles that nosh on the *limu* (seaweed) growing on the lava rocks. This intimate, crescent-shape beach offers sunbathing, snorkeling, swimming, bodysurfing, and startling sunsets.

BEST OFFSHORE SNORKELING
Olowalu, West Maui. The water remains shallow far offshore, and there's plenty to see.

Ulua, the South Shore. It's beautiful, and the kids can enjoy the tide pools while the adults experience the excellent snorkeling.

BEST SURFING
Honolua Bay, West Maui. One bay over from Slaughterhouse (Mokuleia) Beach north of Kapalua, you can find one of the best surf breaks in Hawaii.

Hookipa, the North Shore. This is the place to see great surfers and windsurfers: it's not for beginners or for swimmers, but Hookipa is great for experienced wave riders and also for anyone who wants to take in the North Shore scene.

BEST SUNSETS
Kapalua Bay, West Maui. The ambience here is as stunning as the sunset.

Keawakapu, the South Shore. Most active beachgoers enjoy this gorgeous spot before midafternoon when the wind picks up, so it's never crowded at sunset.

BEST FOR SEEING AND BEING SEEN
Kaanapali Beach, West Maui. Backed by resorts, condos, and restaurants, this is not the beach for solitude. But the sand is soft, the waters are gentle, and the action varies from good snorkeling to people-watching in front of Whalers Village—not for nothing is this section called Dig Me Beach.

Wailea Beach, the South Shore. At this beach fronting the ultraluxurious Four Seasons and Grand Wailea resorts, you never know who might be "hiding" in that private cabana.

BEST SETTING
Makena (Oneloa), South Shore. Don't forget the camera for this beauty, a state park away from the Wailea resort area. Finding it is worth the effort—a long, wide stretch of golden sand and translucent offshore water. This long beach is never crowded. Use caution for swimming, because the steep, onshore break can get big.

Waianapanapa State Park, East Maui. This rustic black-sand beach will capture your heart—it's framed by lava cliffs and backed by bright green beach *naupaka* bushes. Ocean currents can be strong, so enjoy the views and cool off in one of two freshwater pools.

ocean, or *makai,* side of the path; the honey-sweet-smelling one is *naio,* or false sandalwood. **Amenities:** parking (no fee); showers; toilets. **Best for:** snorkeling; swimming. ⊠ *Kaukahi St., south of Fairmont Kea Lani entrance, Wailea.*

Fodor's Choice ★ **Makena Beach State Park (Big Beach).** Locals successfully fought to turn Makena—one of Hawaii's most breathtaking beaches—into a state park. This stretch of deep golden sand abutting sparkling aquamarine water is 3,000 feet long and 100 feet wide. It's often mistakenly referred to as "Big Beach," but natives prefer its Hawaiian name, Oneloa. Makena is never crowded, no matter how many cars cram into the lots. The water is fine for swimming, but use caution. ■TIP→ **The shore drop-off is steep, and swells can get deceptively big.** Despite the infamous "Makena cloud," a blanket that rolls in during the early afternoon and obscures the sun, it rarely rains here. For a dramatic view of the beach, climb Puu Olai, the steep cinder cone near the first entrance you pass if you're driving south. Continue over the cinder cone's side to discover "Little Beach"—clothing optional by popular practice, although this is technically illegal. On Sunday, free spirits of all kinds crowd Little Beach's tiny shoreline for a drumming circle and bonfire. Little Beach has the island's best bodysurfing (no pun intended). Skim boarders catch air at Makena's third entrance, which is a little tricky to find (it's just a dirt path with street parking). **Amenities:** lifeguards; parking (no fee); toilets. **Best for:** surfing; swimming; walking. ⊠ *Off Wailea Alanui Dr., Makena* ⊕ *www.hawaiistateparks.org.*

THE NORTH SHORE

Many of the people you see jaywalking in Paia sold everything they owned to come to Maui and live a beach bum's life. Beach culture abounds on the North Shore. But these folks aren't sunbathers; they're big-wave riders, windsurfers, or kiteboarders, and the North Shore is their challenging sports arena. Beaches here face the open ocean and tend to be rougher and windier than beaches elsewhere on Maui—but don't let that scare you off. On calm days the reef-speckled waters are truly beautiful and offer a quieter and less commercial beachgoing experience than the leeward shore. Be sure to leave your car in a paved parking area so that it doesn't get stuck in soft sand.

Beaches below are listed from Kahului (near the airport) eastward to Hookipa.

Kanaha Beach. Windsurfers, kiteboarders, joggers, and picnicking families like this long, golden strip of sand bordered by a wide grassy area with lots of shade. The winds pick up in the early afternoon, making for the best kiteboarding and windsurfing conditions—if you know what you're doing, that is. The best spot for watching kiteboarders is at the far left end of the beach. From Kaahumanu Avenue, turn *makai* (toward the ocean) onto Hobron Street, then right onto Amala Place. Drive just over a mile through an industrial area and take any of the three entrances into Kanaha. **Amenities:** lifeguard; parking (free); showers; toilets. **Best for:** walking; windsurfing. ⊠ *Amala Pl., Kahului.*

FAMILY **Baldwin Beach.** A local favorite, this is a big stretch of comfortable golden sand that's a good place to stretch out, jog, or swim, though the waves can sometimes be choppy and the undertow strong. Don't be alarmed by those big brown blobs floating beneath the surface; they're just pieces of seaweed awash in the surf. You can find shade along the beach beneath the ironwood trees, or in the large pavilion, regularly used for local parties and community events. There are picnic tables and grills as well.

The long, shallow pool at the Kahului end of the beach is known as "Baby Beach." Separated from the surf by a flat reef wall, this is where ocean-loving families bring their kids (and sometimes puppies) to practice a few laps. Take a relaxing stroll along the water's edge from one end of Baldwin Beach to Baby Beach and enjoy the scenery. The view of the West Maui Mountains is hauntingly beautiful. **Amenities:** lifeguard; parking (free); showers; toilets. **Best for:** swimming; walking. ⊠ *Hana Hwy., 1 mile west of Baldwin Ave., Paia.*

Fodor'sChoice **Hookipa Beach.** To see some of the world's finest windsurfers, hit this
★ beach along the Hana Highway. It's also one of Maui's hottest surfing spots, with waves that can be as high as 20 feet. Hookipa is not a good swimming beach, nor the place to learn windsurfing, but it's great for hanging out and watching the pros. There are picnic tables and grills. Bust out your telephoto lens at the cliff-side lookout to capture the aerial acrobatics of board sailors and kiteboarders. **Amenities:** lifeguard; showers; toilets; parking (free). **Best for:** surfing; windsurfing. ⊠ *Rte. 36, 2 miles east of Paia, Paia.*

ROAD TO HANA

East Maui's and Hana's beaches will literally stop you in your tracks— they're that beautiful. Black and red sands stand out against pewter skies and lush tropical foliage creating picture-perfect scenes, which seem too breathtaking to be real. Rough conditions often preclude swimming, but that doesn't mean you can't explore the shoreline.

Beaches below are listed in order from the west end of Hana town eastward.

Fodor'sChoice **Waianapanapa State Park.** Small but rarely crowded, this beach will
★ remain in your memory long after your visit. Fingers of white foam rush onto a black volcanic-pebble beach fringed with green beach vines and palms. Swimming here is both relaxing and invigorating: Strong currents bump smooth stones up against your ankles while seabirds flit above a black, jagged sea arch. There are picnic tables and grills. At the

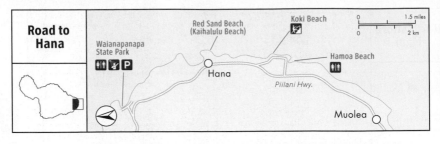

edge of the parking lot a sign tells you the sad story of a doomed Hawaiian princess. Stairs lead through a tunnel of interlocking Polynesian *hau* (a native tree) branches to an icy cave pool—the secret hiding place of the ancient princess. ■TIP→ **You can swim in this pool, but beware of mosquitoes.** In the other direction a dramatic 3-mile coastal path continues past sea arches, blowholes, cultural sites, and even a ramshackle fishermen's shelter, all the way to Hana town. **Amenities:** parking (free); showers; toilets. **Best for:** walking. ✉ *Hana Hwy., near mile marker 32* ☎ *808/984–8109* ⊕ *www.hawaiistateparks.org.*

Red Sand Beach (Kaihalulu Beach). Unmatched in its raw and remote beauty, this beach is not easy to find, but when you round the last corner of the trail and are confronted with the sight of it, your jaw is bound to drop. Earthy red cliffs tower above the deep maroon beach, and swimmers bob about in a turquoise lagoon formed by volcanic boulders. The experience is like floating in a giant natural bathtub. It's worth spending a night in Hana so you can get here early to enjoy it before anyone else shows up.

To get here you have to pass through private property—do so at your own risk. The cliff-side cinder path is slippery and constantly eroding. Hiking is not recommended in shoes without traction, or in bad weather. By popular practice, clothing on the beach is optional. The beach is at the end of Uakea Road past the baseball field. Park near the community center and walk through the grass lot to the trail below the cemetery. **Amenities:** None. **Best for:** swimming. ✉ *Uakea Rd.*

Koki Beach. You can tell from the trucks parked alongside the road that this is a favorite local surf spot. ■TIP→ **Watch conditions before swimming or bodysurfing, as riptides can be mean.** Look for awesome views of the rugged coastline and a sea arch on the left end. *Iwa,* or white-throated frigate birds, dart like pterodactyls over the offshore Alau Islet. **Amenities:** None. **Best for:** surfing. ✉ *Haneoo Loop Rd., 2 miles south of Hana town.*

Hamoa Beach. Why did James Michener describe this stretch of salt-and-pepper sand as the most "South Pacific" beach he'd come across, even though it's in the North Pacific? Maybe it was the perfect half-moon shape, speckled with the shade of palm trees. Perhaps he was intrigued by the jutting black coastline, often outlined by rain showers out at sea, or the pervasive lack of hurry he felt here. Whatever it was, many still feel the lure. The beach can be crowded but is still relaxing. Early mornings and late afternoons are best for swimming. At times the churning surf might intimidate swimmers, but the bodysurfing can be great. Hamoa is half a mile past Koki Beach on Haneoo Loop Road, 2 miles south of Hana town. **Amenities:** toilets. **Best for:** surfing; swimming. ✉ *Haneoo Loop Rd.*

WATER SPORTS AND TOURS

Updated by
Eliza Escaño-
Vasquez

Getting into (or onto) the water may well be the highlight of your Maui trip. The Valley Isle is an aquatic wonderland where you can learn to surf, stand-up paddle, or scuba dive. Vibrant snorkel sites can be explored right off the shore, or easily accessed aboard a kayak, motorized raft, or power catamaran. From December into May, whale-watching adventures are a top draw as humpbacks escaping Alaska's frigid winter arrive in Maui's warm protected waters to frolic, mate, and birth.

Along Maui's leeward coastline, from Kaanapali on the West Shore all the way down to Waiala Cove on the South Shore, you can discover great spots for snorkeling and swimming, some more crowded than others. On a good day, you might encounter dozens of green sea turtles at an underwater cleaning station, a pod of dolphins riding by the catamaran's bow, and an abundance of colorful fish hovering by bright cauliflower coral reefs. For those thrill seekers who flock to Hawaii for the wind, it's best to head out to the North Shore's Hookipa, where consistent winds keep kiteboarders flying and windsurfers jibing; or Peahi, also known as Jaws, where surfers seasonally get towed in to glide on 30- to 60-foot waves.

BODYBOARDING AND BODYSURFING

Bodysurfing and "sponging" (as bodyboarding is called by the regulars; boogie boarding is another variation) are great ways to catch some waves without having to master surfing—and there's no balance or coordination required. A bodyboard (or "sponge") is softer than a hard, fiberglass surfboard, which means you can ride safely in the rough-and-tumble surf zone. If you get tossed around (which is half the fun), you don't have a heavy surfboard nearby to bang your head on, but you do have something to hang onto. Serious spongers invest in a single short-clipped fin to help propel them into the wave.

BEST SPOTS

In West Maui, **D.T. Fleming Beach** offers great surf almost daily along with some nice amenities: ample parking, restrooms, a shower, grills, picnic tables, and a daily lifeguard. Caution is advised, especially during winter months when the current and undertow can get rough.

Between Kihei and Wailea on the South Shore, **Kamaole III** is a good spot for bodysurfing and bodyboarding. It has a sandy floor, with 1- to 3-foot waves breaking not too far out. It's often crowded late in the day, especially on weekends when local kids are out of school. Don't let that chase you away; the waves are wide enough for everyone.

If you don't mind public nudity (officially illegal but practiced nonetheless), **Little Beach** on the South Shore is the best break on the island

for bodyboarding and bodysurfing. The shape of the sandy shoreline creates waves that break a long way out and tumble into shore. Because it's sandy, you only risk stubbing a toe on the few submerged rocks. Don't try bodyboarding at neighboring Big Beach—waves will slap you onto the steep shore. To get to Little Beach, take the first entrance to Makena State Beach Park; climb the rock wall at the north end of the beach.

OUTRIGGER-CANOE RACES

Polynesians first traveled to Hawaii by outrigger canoe, and racing the traditional craft is a favorite pastime on the Islands. Canoes were revered in old Hawaii, and no voyage began without a blessing, ceremonial chanting, and a hula performance to ensure a safe journey.

On the North Shore, **Paia Bay** has waves suitable for spongers and bodysurfers. The beach is just before Paia town, beyond the large community building and grass field.

EQUIPMENT

Most condos and hotels have bodyboards available to guests—some in better condition than others (beat-up boards work just as well for beginners). You can also pick up a bodyboard from any discount shop, such as Kmart or Longs Drugs, for upward of $30.

Auntie Snorkel. You can rent decent bodyboards here for $6 a day or $18 a week, and paddleboards for $35 a day. ⊠ *2439 S. Kihei Rd., Kihei* ☎ *808/879–6263* ⊕ *www.auntiesnorkel.com.*

West Maui Sports and Fishing Supply. This old country store has been around since 1987 and has some of the best prices on the west side. Surf boards go for $15 a day or $70 a week. ⊠ *843 Wainee St., Lahaina* ☎ *808/661–6252* ⊕ *www.westmauisports.com.*

DEEP-SEA FISHING

If fishing is your sport, Maui is your island. In these waters you'll find ahi, *aku* (skipjack tuna), barracuda, bonefish, *kawakawa* (bonito), mahimahi, Pacific blue marlin, ono, and *ulua* (jack crevalle). You can fish year-round and you don't need a license. ■TIP→ **Because boats fill up fast during busy seasons, make reservations before coming to Maui.**

Plenty of fishing boats run out of Lahaina and Maalaea harbors. If you charter a private boat, expect to spend in the neighborhood of $700 to $1,000 for a thrilling half day in the swivel seat. You can share a boat for much less if you don't mind close quarters with a stranger who may get seasick, drunk, or worse—lucky! Before you sign up, you should know that some boats keep the catch. Most will, however, fillet a nice piece for you to take home. And if you catch a real beauty, you might even be able to have it professionally mounted.

You're expected to bring your own lunch and beverages in unbreakable containers. (Shop the night before; it's hard to find snacks at 6 am.) Boats supply coolers, ice, and bait. A 7% tax is added to the cost of a trip, and a 10% to 20% tip for the crew is suggested.

BOATS AND CHARTERS

Fodor's Choice ★ **Finest Kind Sportfishing.** A 1,118-pound blue marlin was reeled in by the crew aboard *Finest Kind,* a lovely 37-foot Merritt kept so clean you'd never guess the action it's seen. Captain Dave has been around these waters for about 40 years, long enough to befriend other expert fishers. This family-run company operates three boats and specializes in skilled trolling. Shared charters start at $150 for four hours and go up to $195 for a full day. Private trips go from $600 to $1,100. No bananas on board, please; the captain thinks they're bad luck for fishing. ⊠ *Lahaina Harbor, Slip 7, Lahaina* ☎ *808/661–0338* ⊕ *www.finestkindsportfishing.com.*

Kai Palena Sportfishing. Captain Fuzzy Alboro runs a highly recommended operation on the 33-foot *Die Hard.* Check-in is at 1:45 am, returning around noon. He takes a minimum of four and maximum of six people. The cost is from $150 for a shared boat to $1,175 for a private charter. ⊠ *Lahaina Harbor, Slip 10, Lahaina* ☎ *808/878–2362* ⊕ *www.diehardsportfishing.com.*

Start Me Up Sportfishing Charters. With more than 20 years in business, Start Me Up has a fleet of seven boats, all impeccably maintained. These 42-foot Bertram Sportfishers offer some of the most comfortable fishing trips around. The company provides an ice chest, tackle, and equipment. A two-hour shared boat is $99 per person, while a private charter runs from $299 for two hours to $999 for eight hours. There's a six-person maximum. ⊠ *Lahaina Harbor, Slip 12, Lahaina* ☎ *808/667–2774* ⊕ *www.sportfishingmaui.com.*

KAYAKING

Kayaking is a fantastic and eco-friendly way to experience Maui's coast up close. Floating aboard a "plastic popsicle stick" is easier than you might think, and allows you to cruise out to vibrant, living coral reefs and waters where dolphins and even whales roam. Kayaking can be a leisurely paddle or a challenge of heroic proportions, depending on your ability, the location, and the weather. ∎TIP➔ **Although you can rent kayaks independently, we recommend hiring a guide.**

An apparently calm surface can hide extremely strong ocean currents. Most guides are naturalists who will steer you away from surging surf, lead you to pristine reefs, and point out camouflaged fish, like the stalking hawkfish. Not having to schlep your gear on top of your rental car is a bonus. A half-day tour runs around $75.

If you decide to strike out on your own, tour companies will rent kayaks for the day with paddles, life vests, and roof racks, and many will meet you near your chosen location. Ask for a map of good entries and plan to avoid paddling back to shore against the wind (schedule extra time for the return trip regardless). Read weather conditions, bring binoculars, and take a careful look from the bay before heading in. For beginners, get there early in the day before the trade wind kicks in, and try sticking close to the shore. When you're ready to snorkel, secure your belongings in a dry pack on board and drag your kayak by its bowline behind you. (This isn't as hard as it sounds.)

BEST SPOTS

Makena Landing is an excellent starting point for a South Shore adventure. Enter from the paved parking lot or the small sandy beach a little south. The shoreline is lined with million-dollar mansions. The bay itself is virtually empty, but the right edge is flanked with brilliant coral heads and juvenile turtles. If you round the point on the right, you come across Five Caves, a system of enticing underwater arches. In the morning you may see dolphins, and the arches are havens for lobsters, eels, and spectacularly hued butterfly fish.

In West Maui, past the steep cliffs on the Honoapiilani Highway, there's a long stretch of inviting coastline that includes **Ukumehame Beach**. This is a good spot for beginners; entry is easy and there's much to see in every direction. Pay attention if trade winds pick up from the late morning onwards; paddling against them can be challenging. If you want to snorkel, the best visibility is farther out at Olowalu Beach. Watch for sharp kiawe thorns buried in the sand on the way into the water. Water shoes are recommended.

EQUIPMENT AND TOURS

Kelii's Kayak Tours. One of the highest-rated kayak outfitters on the island, Kelii's offers kayaking trips and combo adventures where you can also surf, snorkel, or hike to a waterfall. Leading groups of up to eight people, the guides show what makes each reef unique. Trips are available on the island's north, south, and west shores, and range from $69 to $160. ✉ *1993 S. Kihei Rd., Ste. 12, Kihei* ☎ *888/874–7652, 808/874–7652* ⊕ *www.keliiskayak.com.*

Fodor's Choice ★ **South Pacific Kayaks.** These guys pioneered recreational kayaking on Maui, so they know their stuff. Guides are friendly, informative, and eager to help you get the most out of your experience; we're talking true, fun-loving, kayak geeks who will maneuver away from crowds when exploring prime snorkel spots. South Pacific stands out as adventurous *and* environmentally responsible, plus their gear and equipment are well maintained. They offer a variety of trips leaving from both West Maui and South Shore locations. Trips range from $65 to $114. ✉ *95 Halekuai St., Kihei* ☎ *800/776–2326, 808/875–4848* ⊕ *www. southpacifickayaks.com.*

KITEBOARDING

Catapulting up to 40 feet in the air above the breaking surf, kiteboarders hardly seem of this world. Silken kites hold the athletes aloft for precious seconds—long enough for the execution of mind-boggling tricks—then deposit them back in the sea. This new sport is not for the weak-kneed. No matter what people might tell you, it's harder to learn than windsurfing. The unskilled (or unlucky) can be caught in an upwind and carried far out in the ocean, or worse—dropped smack on the shore. Because of insurance (or the lack thereof), companies are not allowed to rent equipment. Beginners must take lessons, and then purchase their own gear. Devotees swear that after your first few lessons, committing to buying your kite is easy.

BEST SPOTS

The steady tracks on **Kanaha Beach** make this North Shore spot primo for learning. Specific areas are set aside for different water activities, so launch and land only in kiteboarding zones, and kindly give way to swimmers, divers, anglers, and paddlers.

LESSONS

Aqua Sports Maui. A local favorite of kiteboarding schools, Aqua Sports is conveniently located near Kite Beach, at the west end of Kanaha Beach, and offers basic to advanced kiteboarding lessons. Rates start at $240 for a three-hour basics course taught by certified instructors. ⊠ *111 Hana Hwy., Suite 110, near Kite Beach, Kahului* ☎ *808/242–8015* ⊕ *www.mauikiteboardinglessons.com.*

Fodor'sChoice **Hawaiian Sailboarding Techniques.** Pro kiteboarder and legendary wind-
★ surfer Alan Cadiz will have you safely ripping in no time at lower Kanaha Beach Park. A "Learn to Kitesurf" package starts at $255 for a three-hour private lesson, equipment included. Instead of observing from the shore, instructors paddle after students on a chaseboard to give immediate feedback. The company is part of Hi-Tech Surf Sports, in the Triangle Square shopping center. ⊠ *Triangle Square, 425 Koloa St., Kahului* ☎ *808/871–5423, 800/968–5423* ⊕ *www.hstwindsurfing.com.*

PARASAILING

Parasailing is an easy, exhilarating way to earn your wings: just strap on a harness attached to a parachute, and a powerboat pulls you up and over the ocean from a launching dock or a boat's platform. ■TIP→ Parasailing is limited to West Maui, and "thrill craft"—including parasails—are prohibited in Maui waters during humpback whale–calving season, December 15 to May 15.

LESSONS AND TOURS

West Maui Parasail. Soar at 800 feet above the ocean for a bird's-eye view of Lahaina, or be daring at 1,200 feet for smoother rides and even better views. The captain will be glad to let you experience a "toe dip" or "freefall" if you request it. Hour-long trips departing from Lahaina Harbor and Kaanapali Beach include 8- to 10-minute flights and run from $70 for the 800-foot ride to $80 for the 1,200-foot ride. Observers pay $35 each. ⊠ *675 Wharf St., Slip 15, Lahaina* ☎ *808/661–4060* ⊕ *www.westmauiparasail.com.*

RAFTING

The high-speed, inflatable rafts you find on Maui are nothing like the raft that Huck Finn used to drift down the Mississippi. While passengers grip straps, these rafts fly, skimming and bouncing across the sea. Because they're so maneuverable, they go where the big boats can't—secret coves, sea caves, and remote beaches. Two-hour trips run around $50, half-day trips upward of $100. ■TIP→ Although safe, these trips are not for the faint of heart. If you have back or neck problems or are pregnant, you should reconsider this activity.

3

TOURS

Blue Water Rafting. One of the few ways to get to the stunning Kanaio Coast (the roadless southern coastline beyond Ahihi-Kinau), this rafting tour begins conveniently at the Kihei boat ramp on the South Shore. Dolphins, turtles, and other marine life are the highlight of this adventure, along with majestic sea caves, lava arches, and views of Haleakala. The Molokini stop is usually timed between the bigger catamarans, so you can enjoy the crater without the usual massive crowd. If conditions permit, you'll be able to snorkel the back wall, which has much more marine life than the inside. ⊠ *Kihei Boat Ramp, S. Kihei Rd., Kihei* ☎ *808/879–7238* ⊕ *www.bluewaterrafting.com* ⬚ *From $55.*

Ocean Riders. Start the day with a spectacular view of the sun rising above the West Maui Mountains, then cross the Au Au Channel to Lanai's Shipwreck Beach. After a short swim at a secluded beach, this tour circles Lanai, allowing you to view the island's 70 miles of remote coast. The "back side" of Lanai is one of Hawaii's unsung marvels, and you can expect to stop at three protected coves for snorkeling. You might chance upon sea turtles, monk seals, and a friendly reef shark, as well as rare varieties of angelfish and butterflyfish. Guides are knowledgeable and slow down long enough for you to marvel at sacred burial caves and interesting rock formations. Sit toward the back bench if you are sensitive to motion sickness. Tours include snorkel gear, a fruit breakfast, and a satisfying deli lunch. ⊠ *Mala Wharf, Front St., Lahaina* ☎ *808/661–3586* ⊕ *www.mauioceanriders.com* ⬚ *From $139.*

Fodor's Choice
★

Redline Rafting. This company offers thrilling rides along South Maui's stunning Kanaio Coast, revealing volcanic formations of sea caves, grottoes, and lava arches. There's a quick stop at La Perouse Bay, and then it's off to Molokini Crater for some snorkeling. The last stop in Makena gives you time to do more underwater exploring, spot sea turtles, and enjoy a deli lunch. Its rafts provide great seating comfort and shade. Whale-watching excursions are $50, and snorkel trips are $140. ⊠ *2800 S. Kihei Rd., Kihei* ☎ *808/757–9211* ⊕ *www.redlinerafting.com.*

SAILING

With the islands of Molokai, Lanai, Kahoolawe, and Molokini a stone's throw away, Maui waters offer visually arresting backdrops for sailing adventures. Sailing conditions can be fickle, so some operations throw in snorkeling or whale-watching, and others offer sunset cruises. *(For more sunset cruises, see Entertainment and Nightlife.)* Winds are consistent in summer but variable in winter, and afternoons are generally windier throughout the year. Prices range from around $40 for two-hour trips to $80 for half-day excursions. ■TIP➔ You won't be sheltered from the elements on the trim racing boats, so be sure to bring a hat that won't blow away, a light jacket, sunglasses, and sunscreen.

BOATS AND CHARTERS

Paragon Sailing Charters. If you want to snorkel and sail, these are your boats. Many snorkel cruises claim to sail but actually motor most of the way; Paragon is an exception. Both Paragon vessels (one catamaran in Lahaina, the other in Maalaea) are ship-shape, and crews are accommodating and friendly. Its mooring in Molokini Crater is particularly good, and tours will often stay after the masses have left. The Lanai trip includes a picnic lunch on Manele Bay, snorkeling, and a quick afternoon blue-water swim. Extras on the trips to Lanai include mai tais, sodas, dessert, and champagne. Hot and cold appetizers come with the sunset sail, which departs from Lahaina Harbor every Monday, Wednesday, and Friday. ✉ *Maalaea Harbor, Maalaea* ☎ *808/244–2087, 800/441–2087* ⊕ *www.sailmaui.com.*

Fodor's Choice
★
Trilogy Excursions. With more than 40 years of experience and some good karma from their reef-cleaning campaigns, Trilogy has a great reputation in the community. It's one of only two companies that sail, rather than motor, to Molokini Crater. A two-hour sail starts at $69. The sunset trip includes appetizers, beer, wine, champagne, margaritas, and mai tais. Boarding the catamaran from shore can be tricky—timing is everything and getting wet is inevitable, but after that it's smooth sailing. Tours depart from Lahaina Harbor; Maalaea Harbor; and, in West Maui, in front of the Kaanapali Beach Hotel. ✉ *207 Kuopohi St., Lahaina* ☎ *808/874–5649, 888/225–6284* ⊕ *www.sailtrilogy.com.*

SCUBA DIVING

Maui, just as scenic underwater as it is on dry land, has been rated one of the top 10 dive spots in the United States. It's common on any dive to see huge sea turtles, eagle rays, and small reef sharks, not to mention many varieties of angelfish, parrot fish, eels, and octopuses. Most of the species are unique to this area, making it unlike other popular dive destinations. In addition, the terrain itself is different from other dive spots. Here you can find ancient and intricate lava flows full of nooks where marine life hide and breed. Although the water tends to be a bit rougher—not to mention colder—divers are given a great thrill during humpback-whale season, when you can actually hear whales singing underwater.

Some of the finest diving spots in all of Hawaii lie along the Valley Isle's western and southwestern shores. Dives are best in the morning, when visibility can hold a steady 100 feet. If you're a certified diver, you can rent gear at any Maui dive shop simply by showing your PADI or NAUI card. Unless you're familiar with the area, however, it's probably best to hook up with a dive shop for an underwater tour. Tours include tanks and weights and start around $130. Wet suits and buoyancy compensators are rented separately, for an additional $15 to $30. Shops also offer introductory dives ($100 to $160) for those who aren't certified. ■ **TIP➔** Before signing on with any outfitter, it's a good idea to ask a few pointed questions about your guide's experience, the weather outlook, and the condition of the equipment.

Before you head out on your dive, be sure to check conditions. Check the Glenn James weather site, ⊕ *www.hawaiiweathertoday.com,* for a breakdown of the weather, wind, and visibility conditions.

BEST SPOTS

Honolua Bay, a marine preserve in West Maui, is alive with many varieties of coral and tame tropical fish, including large ulua (jack crevalle), kahala, barracuda, and manta rays. With depths of 20 to 50 feet, this is a popular summer dive spot, good for all levels. ■TIP→ **High surf often prohibits winter dives.**

On the South Shore, one of the most popular dive spots is **Makena Landing** (also called Nahuna Point, Five Graves, or Five Caves). You can revel in underwater delights—caves, ledges, coral heads, and an outer reef home to a large green-sea-turtle colony called Turtle Town. ■TIP→ **Entry is rocky lava, so be careful where you step. This area is for more experienced divers.**

Three miles offshore from Wailea on the South Shore, **Molokini Crater** is world renowned for its deep, crystal clear, fish-filled waters. A crescent-shape islet formed by the eroding top of a volcano, the crater is a marine preserve ranging from 10 to 80 feet deep. The numerous tame fish and brilliant coral within the crater make it a popular introductory dive site. On calm days, the back side of Molokini Crater (called Back Wall) can be a dramatic sight for advanced divers, with visibility of up to 150 feet. The enormous drop-off into the Alalakeiki Channel offers awesome seascapes, black coral, and chance sightings of larger fish and sharks.

Some of the southern coast's best diving is at **Ahihi Bay,** part of the Ahihi-Kinau Natural Area Reserve. The area was closed for several years to allow the coral to recover from overuse. At the time of writing, the closure was extended through July 2014. The area is best known for its "Fishbowl," a small cove right beside the road, next to a hexagonal house. Here you can find excellent underwater scenery, with many types of fish and coral. ■TIP→ **Be careful of the rocky-bottom entry (wear reef shoes if you have them).** The Fishbowl can get crowded, especially in high season. If you want to steer clear of the crowds, look for a second entry ½ mile farther down the road—a gravel parking lot at the surf spot called Dumps. Entry into the bay here is trickier, as the coastline is all lava.

Formed from the last lava flow two centuries ago, **La Perouse Bay** brings you the best variety of fish—more than any other site. The lava rock provides a protective habitat, and all four types of Hawaii's angelfish can be found here. To dive the spot called Pinnacles, enter anywhere along the shore, just past the private entrance to the beach. Wear your reef shoes, as entry is sharp. To the right, you'll be in the Ahihi-Kinau Natural Area Reserve; to the left, you're outside. Look for the white, sandy bottom with massive coral heads. Pinnacles is for experienced divers only.

EQUIPMENT, LESSONS, AND TOURS

Fodor's Choice
★ **Ed Robinson's Diving Adventures.** Ed Robinson wrote the book, literally, on Molokini. Because he knows so much, he includes a "Biology 101" talk with every dive. An expert marine photographer, he offers diving instruction and boat charters to South Maui and the back side of Molokini Crater. Night dives are available from the shoreline for $79.95. There's a discount if you book multiple dives. Prices start at $129.95, plus $20 for the gear. ✉ *165 Halekuai St., Kihei* ☎ *808/879–3584, 800/635–1273* ⊕ *www.mauiscuba.com.*

Maui Dive Shop. With seven locations island-wide, Maui Dive Shop offers scuba charters, diving instruction, and equipment rental. Excursions go to Coral Gardens, Shipwreck Beach, and Cathedrals on Lanai. The

DIVING 101

If you've always wanted gills, Hawaii is a good place to get them. Although the bulky, heavy equipment seems freakish on shore, underwater it allows you to move about freely, almost weightlessly. As you descend into another world, you slowly grow used to the sound of your own breathing and the strangeness of being able to do so 30-plus feet down.

Most resorts offer introductory dive lessons in their pools, which allow you to acclimate to the awkward breathing apparatus before venturing out into the great blue. If you aren't starting from a resort pool, no worries. Most intro dives take off from calm, sandy beaches, such as Ulua or Kaanapali. If you're bitten by the deep-sea bug and want to continue diving, you should get certified. Only certified divers can rent equipment or go on more adventurous dives, such as night dives, open-ocean dives, and cave dives.

There are several certification companies, including PADI, NAUI, and SSI. PADI, the largest, is the most comprehensive. A child must be at least 10 to be certified. Once you begin your certification process, stick with the same company. The dives you log will not apply to another company's certification. (Dives with a PADI instructor, for instance, will not count toward SSI certification.) Remember that you will not be able to fly or go to the airy summit of Haleakala within 24 hours of diving. Open-water certification will take three to four days and cost around $350. From that point on, the sky—or rather, the sea—is the limit!

manta ray dives off Molokini Crater have a 70% success rate. Night dives and customized trips are available, as are full SSI and PADI certificate programs. ⊠ *1455 S. Kihei Rd., Kihei* ☎ *808/879–3388, 800/542–3483* ⊕ *www.mauidiveshop.com.*

Mike Severns Diving. This company has been around for over 33 years and takes groups of up to 12 certified divers with two dive masters to both popular and off-the-beaten-path dive sites. Boat trips leave from Kihei Boat Ramp, and go wherever conditions are best: the Molokini Marine Life Conservation District, Molokini Crater's Back Wall, Makena, or beyond La Pérouse Bay. Rates start at $154 for a two-tank dive. A private charter costs $1,560. ⊠ *Kihei Boat Ramp, S. Kihei Rd., Kihei* ☎ *808/879–6596* ⊕ *www.mikesevernsdiving.com.*

SNORKELING

No one should leave Maui without ducking underwater to meet a sea turtle, moray eel, or the tongue-twisting humuhumunukunukuapuaa—the state fish. ■TIP➔ **Visibility is best in the morning, before the trade winds pick up.**

There are two ways to approach snorkeling—by land or by sea. Daily around 7 am, a parade of boats heads out to Lanai or to Molokini Crater, that ancient cone of volcanic cinder off the coast of Wailea. Boat trips offer some advantages—deeper water, seasonal whale-watching, crew assistance, lunch, and gear. But much of Maui's best snorkeling is found just steps from the road. Nearly the entire leeward coastline from Kapalua south to Ahihi-Kinau offers opportunities to ogle fish and turtles. If you're patient and sharp-eyed, you may glimpse eels, octopuses, lobsters, eagle rays, and even a rare shark or monk seal.

BEST SPOTS

Snorkel sites here are listed from north to south, starting at the northwest corner of the island.

Just north of Kapalua, the **Honolua Bay Marine Life Conservation District** has a superb reef for snorkeling. ■ **TIP→ Bring a fish key with you, as you're sure to see many species of triggerfish, filefish, and wrasses.** The coral formations on the right side of the bay are particularly dramatic, with pink, aqua, and orange varieties. On a lucky day, you might even be snorkeling with a pod of dolphins nearby. Take care entering the water; there's no beach and the rocks and concrete ramp can be slippery. The northeast corner of this windward-facing bay periodically gets hammered by big waves in winter. Avoid the bay then, as well as after heavy rains.

Minutes south of Honolua Bay, dependable **Kapalua Bay** beckons. As beautiful above the water as it is below, Kapalua is exceptionally calm, even when other spots get testy. Needle and butterfly fish dart just past the sandy beach, which is why it's sometimes crowded. ■ **TIP→ The sand can be particularly hot here; watch your toes!**

Black Rock, in front of the Sheraton Maui Resort & Spa at the northernmost tip of Kaanapali Beach, is great for snorkelers of any skill level. The entry couldn't be easier—dump your towel on the sand and in you go. Beginners can stick close to shore and still see lots of action. Advanced snorkelers can swim to the tip of Black Rock to see larger fish and eagle rays. One of the underwater residents here is a turtle whose hefty size earned him the name Volkswagen. He sits very still, so you have to look closely. Equipment can be rented on-site. Parking, in a small lot adjoining the hotel, is the only hassle.

Along Honoapiilani Highway there are several favorite snorkel sites, including the area just out from the cemetery at **Hanakaoo Beach Park.** At depths of 5 and 10 feet, you can see a variety of corals, especially as you head south toward Wahikuli Wayside Park.

South of Olowalu General Store, the shallow coral reef at **Olowalu** is good for a quick underwater tour, but if you're willing to venture out about 50 yards you'll have easy access to an expansive coral reef with abundant turtles and fish—no boat required. Swim offshore toward the pole sticking out of the reef. Except for during a south swell, this area is calm and good for families with small children. Boats sometimes stop here (they refer to this site as "Coral Gardens") when conditions in Honolua Bay are not ideal. During low tide, be extra cautious when hovering above the razor-sharp coral.

Excellent snorkeling is found down the coastline between Kihei and Makena on the South Shore. ■ **TIP→ The best spots are along the rocky fringes of Wailea's beaches—Mokapu, Ulua, Wailea, and Polo—off Wailea Alanui Drive.** Find one of the public parking lots sandwiched

Snorkelers can see adorable green sea turtles around Maui.

between Wailea's luxury resorts (look for a blue sign that says "Shoreline Access" with an arrow pointing to the lot), and enjoy the sandy entries, calm waters with relatively good visibility, and variety of fish. Of the four beaches, Ulua has the best reef. You may listen to snapping shrimp and parrot fish nibbling on coral.

Between Maui and neighboring Kahoolawe you'll find the world-famous **Molokini Crater.** Its crescent-shape rim acts as a protective cove from the wind and provides a sanctuary for birds and colorful marine life. Most snorkeling tour operators offer a Molokini trip, and it's not unusual for your charter to share this dormant volcano with five or six other boats. The journey to this sunken crater takes more than 90 minutes from Lahaina, an hour from Maalaea, and less than half an hour from the South Shore.

EQUIPMENT

Most hotels and vacation rentals offer free use of snorkel gear. Beachside stands fronting the major resort areas rent equipment by the hour or day. ■TIP→ Don't shy away from asking for instructions; a snug fit makes all the difference in the world. A mask fits if it sticks to your face when you inhale deeply through your nose. Fins should cover your entire foot (unlike diving fins, which strap around your heel). If you're squeamish about using someone else's gear (or need a prescription lens), pick up your own at any discount shop. Costco and Longs Drugs have better prices than ABC stores; dive shops have superior equipment.

Maui Dive Shop. You can rent pro gear (including optical masks, bodyboards, and wet suits) from seven locations island-wide. Pump these guys for weather info before heading out—they'll know better than last night's news forecaster, and they'll give you the real deal on conditions. ✉ *1455 S. Kihei Rd., Kihei* ☎ *808/873–3388* ⊕ *www.mauidiveshop.com.*

Snorkel Bob's. Here you can rent fins, masks, and snorkels, and Snorkel Bob's will throw in a carrying bag, map, and snorkel tips for as little as $9 per week. Avoid the circle masks and go for the split-level ($26 per week) or dry snorkel ($43 per week); it's worth the extra. ✉ *Napili Village Hotel, 5425 Lower Honoapiilani Hwy., Napili* ☎ *808/669–9603* ⊕ *www.snorkelbob.com.*

TOURS

Molokini Crater, a crescent about 3 miles offshore from Wailea, is the most popular snorkel cruise destination. You can spend half a day floating above the fish-filled crater for about $80. Some say it's not as good as it's made out to be, and that it's too crowded, but others consider it to be one of the best spots in Hawaii. Visibility is generally outstanding and fish are incredibly tame. Your second stop will be somewhere along the leeward coast, either Turtle Town near Makena or Coral Gardens toward Lahaina. ■TIP➔ **On blustery mornings there's a good chance the waters will be too rough to moor in Molokini Crater and you'll end up snorkeling some place off the shore, which you could have driven to for free.**

Snorkel cruises vary—some serve mai tais and steaks whereas others offer beer and cold cuts. You might prefer a large ferryboat to a smaller sailboat, or vice versa. Be sure you know where to go to board your vessel; getting lost in the harbor at 6 am is a lousy start. ■TIP➔ **Bring sunscreen, an underwater camera (they're double the price on board), a towel, and a cover-up for the windy return trip.** Even tropical waters get chilly after hours of swimming, so consider wearing a rash guard. Wet suits can usually be rented for a fee. Hats without straps will blow away, and valuables should be left at home.

Alii Nui Maui. Come as you are (with a bathing suit, of course); towels, sunblock, and all your gear are provided on this 65-foot luxury catamaran. Since the owners also operate Maui Dive Shop, snorkel and dive equipment are top-of-the-line. Wet-suit tops are available to use for sun protection or to keep extra warm in the water. The boat, which holds a maximum of 60 people, is nicely appointed. A morning snorkel sail (there's a diving option, too) heads to Turtle Town or Molokini Crater and includes a Continental breakfast, lunch, and post-snorkel alcoholic drinks. The trip includes transportation from your hotel. Videography and snuba are available for a fee. ✉ *Maalaea Harbor, Slip 56, Maalaea* ☎ *800/542–3483, 808/875–0333* ⊕ *www.aliinuimaui.com* 🎫 *From $165.*

FAMILY **Maui Classic Charters.** Hop aboard the *Four Winds II*, a 55-foot, glass-bottom catamaran (great fun for kids), for one of the most dependable snorkel trips around. You'll spend more time than other charter boats at Molokini Crater and enjoy turtle-watching on the way home. The trip includes optional snuba ($59 extra), Continental breakfast, barbecue lunch, beer, wine, and soda. With its reasonable price, the trip can be popular and crowded. The crew works hard to keep everyone happy, but if the trip is fully booked, you will be cruising with more than 100 new friends. For a more intimate experience, opt for the *Maui Magic*, Maalaea's fastest PowerCat, which holds fewer people than some of the larger vessels. ⊠ *Maalaea Harbor, Slips 55 and 80, Maalaea* ☎ *808/879–8188, 800/736–5740* ⊕ *www.mauicharters.com* 🖃 *From $98.*

Teralani Sailing Charters. Choose between a regular snorkeling trip with a deli lunch or a top-of-the-line excursion that's an hour longer and includes two snorkel sites and a barbecue-style lunch catered by Cilantro Mexican Grill, a popular local restaurant. The company's cats could hold well over 100 people, but 49 is the maximum per trip. The boats are kept in pristine condition. Freshwater showers are available, as is an open bar after the second snorkel stop. A friendly crew provides all your gear, a flotation device, and a crash course in snorkeling. Boarding is right off Dig Me Beach at Whalers Village in West Maui. ⊠ *991 Limahana Pl., Kaanapali* ☎ *808/661–1230* ⊕ *www.teralani.net.*

FAMILY
Fodor's Choice
★
Trilogy Excursions. Many people consider a trip with Trilogy Excursions to be a highlight of their vacation. Maui's longest-running operation has comprehensive offerings, with seven beautiful multihull 50- to 64-foot sailing vessels at three departure sites. All excursions are staffed by energetic crews who will keep you well fed and entertained with local stories and corny jokes. A full-day catamaran cruise to Lanai includes a Continental breakfast and barbecue lunch, a guided tour of the island, a "Snorkeling 101" class, and time to snorkel in the waters of Lanai's Hulopoe Marine Preserve (Trilogy Excursions has exclusive commercial access). The company also offers a Molokini Crater and Honolua Bay snorkel cruise that is top-notch. Tours depart from Lahaina Harbor; Maalaea Harbor; and, in West Maui, in front of the Kaanapali Beach Hotel. ⊠ *207 Kuopohi St., Lahaina* ☎ *808/874–5649, 888/225–6284* ⊕ *www.sailtrilogy.com* 🖃 *From $119.*

STAND-UP PADDLING

Also called stand-up paddle surfing or paddleboarding, stand-up paddling is the "comeback kid" of surf sports; you stand on a longboard and paddle out with a canoe oar. While stand-up paddling requires even more balance and coordination than regular surfing, it is still accessible to just about every skill level. Most surf schools now offer stand-up paddle lessons. Advanced paddlers can amp up the adrenalin with a downwind coastal run that spans almost 10 miles from North Shore's Maliko Gulch to Kahului Harbor, sometimes reaching speeds up to 30 mph.

The fun thing about stand-up paddling is that you can enjoy it whether the surf is good or the water is flat. However, as with all water sports, it's important to read the environment and be attentive. Look at the sky and assess the wind by how fast the clouds are moving. Note where the whitecaps are going and always point the nose of your board perpendicular to the wave. ■TIP→ Because of the size and speed of a longboard, stand-up paddling can be dangerous, so lessons are highly recommended especially if you intend to surf.

LESSONS

Maui Surfer Girls. Owner and bona fide waterwoman Dustin Tester is known as Mama D to the girls she mentors. The company started with surf camps, and now also offers co-ed stand-up paddle lessons. Locations vary, depending on wind conditions, but you'll most likely go to beginner-friendly Ukumehame Beach or Thousand Peaks. The lesson includes some history of the ancient sport, gear, and refreshments after the paddle. Lessons begin at $100, with an extra $20 charge for instruction by Dustin, who is accompanied by her dog, Luna. ☎ *808/214–0606* ⊕ *www.mauisurfergirls.com.*

Stand-Up Paddle Surf School. Maui's first school devoted solely to stand-up paddleboarding was founded by the legendary Maria Souza, the first woman to surf the treacherous waves of "Jaws" on Maui's North Shore. While most surf schools offer stand-up paddling, Maria's classes are in a league of their own. They include a proper warm-up with a hula-hoop and balance ball and a cool-down with some yoga. The cost is $165 for a private session. Locations vary depending on conditions. ⊠ *Lahaina* ☎ *808/579–9231* ⊕ *www.standuppaddlesurfschool.com.*

SURFING

Maui's coastline has surf for every level of waterman or -woman. Waves on leeward-facing shores (West and South Maui) tend to break in gentle sets all summer long. Surf instructors in Kihei and Lahaina can rent you boards, give you onshore instruction, and then lead you out through the channel, where it's safe to enter the surf. They'll shout encouragement while you paddle like mad for the thrill of standing on water—most will give you a helpful shove. These areas are great for beginners; the only danger is whacking a stranger with your board or stubbing your toe against the reef.

The North Shore is another story. Winter waves pound the windward coast, attracting water champions from every corner of the world. Adrenaline addicts are towed in by Jet Ski to a legendary, deep-sea break called Jaws. Waves here periodically tower upward of 40 feet. The only spot for viewing this phenomenon (which happens just a few times a year) is on private property. So, if you hear the surfers next to you crowing about Jaws "going off," cozy up and get them to take you with them.

Whatever your skill, there's a board, a break, and even a surf guru to accommodate you. A two-hour lesson is a good intro to surf culture.

You can get the wave report each day by checking page 2 of the *Maui News,* logging onto the Glenn James weather site at ⊕ *www.hawaiiweathertoday.com,* or calling ☎ *808/871–5054* (for the weather forecast) or ☎ *808/877–3611* (for the surf report).

BEST SPOTS

On the South Shore, beginners can hang 10 at Kihei's **Cove Park,** a sometimes crowded but reliable 1- to 2-foot break. Boards can easily be rented across the street, or in neighboring Kalama Park parking lot. The only bummer is having to balance the 9-plus-foot board on your head while crossing busy South Kihei Road.

For advanced wave riders, **Hookipa Beach Park** on the North Shore boasts several well-loved breaks, including "Pavilions," "Lanes," "the Point," and "Middles." Surfers have priority until 11 am, when windsurfers move in on the action. ■TIP→ Competition is stiff here. If you don't know what you're doing, consider watching.

Long- or shortboarders in West Maui can paddle out at **Launiupoko State Wayside**. The east end of the park has an easy break, good for beginners.

Also called "Thousand Peaks," **Ukumehame** is one of the better beginner spots in West Maui. You'll soon see how the spot got its name—the waves here break again and again in wide and consistent rows, giving lots of room for beginning and intermediate surfers.

Good surf spots in West Maui include "Grandma's" at **Papalaua Park,** just after the *pali* (cliff)—where waves are so easy a grandma could ride 'em; **Puamana Beach Park** for a mellow longboard day; and **Lahaina Harbor,** which offers an excellent inside wave for beginners (called Breakwall), as well as the more advanced outside (a great lift if there's a big south swell).

EQUIPMENT AND LESSONS

Surf camps are becoming increasingly popular, especially with women. One- or two-week camps offer a terrific way to build muscle and self-esteem simultaneously.

Big Kahuna Adventures. Rent soft-top longboards here for $20 for two hours, or $30 for the day. The shop also offers surf lessons starting at $60, and rents kayaks and snorkel gear. Across from Cove Park, the company has been around for years. ⊠ *1913-C S. Kihei Rd., Kihei* ☎ *808/875–6395* ⊕ *www.bigkahunaadventures.com.*

Goofy Foot. Surfing "goofy foot" means putting your right foot forward. They might be goofy, but we like the right-footed gurus here. This shop is just plain cool and only steps away from "Breakwall," a great beginner's spot in Lahaina. A two-hour class with five or fewer students is $65, and you're guaranteed to be standing by the end or it's free. Owner and "stoke broker" Tim Sherer offers private lessons for $250 and will sometimes ride alongside to record video clips and give more thorough feedback. A private two-hour lesson with another instructor is $150. ⊠ *505 Front St., Suite 123, Lahaina* ☎ *808/244–9283* ⊕ *www. goofyfootsurfschool.com.*

Hi-Tech Surf Sports. Locals hold Hi-Tech in the highest regard. It has some of the best boards, advice, and attitude around. It rents even its best surfboards—choose from longboards, shortboards, and hybrids—starting at $25 per day. All rentals come with board bags, roof racks, and wax. ⊠ *425 Koloa St., Kahului* ☎ *808/877–2111* ⊕ *www.htmaui.com.*

Maui Surfer Girls. This highly reputable company immerses adventurous young women in wave-riding wisdom during overnight one- and two-week camps. It also offers daily surf lessons that take place away from the big crowds of Lahaina or Kihei. ⊕ *www.mauisurfergirls.com.*

FAMILY **Nancy Emerson School of Surfing.** Instructors here will get even the shakiest novice riding with the school's "Learn to Surf in One Lesson" program. A two-hour group lesson (up to five students) is $78. Private lessons with the patient and meticulous instructors are $165 for two hours. The company provides boards, rash guards, and water shoes, all in impeccable condition—and it's tops in the customer-service department. ⊠ *505 Front St., Suite 201, Lahaina* ☎ *808/244–7873* ⊕ *www. mauisurfclinics.com.*

Fodor'sChoice ★

3

WHALE-WATCHING

From December into May whale-watching becomes one of the most popular activities on Maui. During the season *all* outfitters offer whale-watching in addition to their regular activities, and most do an excellent job. Boats leave the wharves at Lahaina and Maalaea in search of humpbacks, allowing you to enjoy the awe-inspiring size of these creatures in closer proximity. From November through May, the Pacific Whale Foundation sponsors the Maui Whale Festival, a variety of whale-related events for locals and visitors; check the calendar at ⊕ *www. mauiwhalefestival.org.*

As it's almost impossible *not* to see whales in winter on Maui, you'll want to prioritize: is adventure or comfort your aim? If close encounters with the giants of the deep are your desire, pick a smaller boat that promises sightings. Those who think "green" usually prefer the smaller, quieter vessels that produce the least amount of negative impact to the whales' natural environment. For those wanting to sip mai tais as whales cruise by, stick with a sunset cruise ($40 and up) on a boat with an open bar and *pupu* (Hawaiian tapas). ■TIP➔ Afternoon trips are generally rougher because the wind picks up, but some say this is when the most surface action occurs.

Every captain aims to please during whale season, getting as close as legally possible (100 yards). Crew members know when a whale is about to dive (after several waves of its heart-shape tail) but rarely can predict breaches (when the whale hurls itself up and almost entirely out of the water). Prime viewing space (on the upper and lower decks, around the railings) is limited, so boats can feel crowded even when half full. If you don't want to squeeze in beside strangers, opt for a smaller boat with fewer bookings. Don't forget to bring sunscreen, sunglasses, a light long-sleeve cover-up, and a hat you can secure. Winter weather is less predictable and at times can be extreme, especially as the wind picks up. Arrive early to find parking.

BEST SPOTS

The northern end of **Keawakapu Beach** on the South Shore seems to be a whale magnet. Situate yourself on the sand or at the nearby restaurant and watch mamas and calves. From mid-December to mid-April, the Pacific Whale Foundation has naturalists at Ulua Beach and at the scenic

Humpback whale calves are plentiful in winter; this one is breaching off West Maui.

viewpoint at **Papawai Point Lookout**. Like the commuting traffic, whales can be spotted along the pali, or cliff side, of West Maui's Honoapiilani Highway all day long. Make sure to park safely before craning your neck out to see them.

BOATS AND CHARTERS

Maui Adventure Cruises. Whale-watching from this company's raft puts you right above the water surface and on the same level as the whales. You'll forego the cocktail in your hand but you won't have to deal with crowds, even if the vessel is at max with 36 people. The whales can get up close if they like, and when they do it's absolutely spectacular. These rafts can move with greater speed than a catamaran, so you don't spend much time motoring between whales or pods. Refreshments are included. Prices are $45 for adults and $35 for kids 5–12 years old; children under 4 years old are not admitted. ⊠ *Lahaina Harbor, Slip 11, Lahaina* ☎ *808/661–5550* ⊕ *www.mauiadventurecruises.com.*

FAMILY **Pacific Whale Foundation.** With a fleet of nine boats, this nonprofit organization pioneered whale-watching back in 1979. The crew (including a certified marine biologist) offers insights into whale behavior and suggests ways for you to help save marine life worldwide. One of the best things about these trips is the underwater hydrophone that allows you to listen to the whales sing. Trips meet at the organization's store, which sells whale paraphernalia. You'll share the boat with about 100 people in stadium-style seating. If you prefer a smaller crowd, book the speedy raft cruises instead. ⊠ *612 Front St., Lahaina* ☎ *808/249–8811* ⊕ *www.pacificwhale.org.*

CLOSE UP

The Humpback's Winter Home

The humpback whales' attraction to Maui is legendary, and seeing them between December and May is a highlight for many visitors. More than half the Pacific's humpback population winters in Hawaii, especially in the waters around the Valley Isle, where mothers can be seen just a few hundred feet offshore training their young calves in the fine points of whale etiquette. Watching from shore it's easy to catch sight of whales spouting, or even breaching—when they leap almost entirely out of the sea, slapping back onto the water with a huge splash.

At one time there were thousands of the huge mammals, but a history of overhunting and marine pollution dwindled the world population to about 1,500. In 1966 humpbacks were put on the endangered-species list. Hunting or harassing whales is illegal in the waters of most nations, and in the United States boats and airplanes are restricted from getting too close. The word is still out, however, on the effects military sonar testing has on the marine mammals.

Marine biologists believe the humpbacks (much like the humans) keep returning to Hawaii because of its warmth. Having fattened themselves in subarctic waters all summer, the whales migrate south in the winter to breed, and a rebounding population of thousands cruise Maui waters. Winter is calving time, and the young whales probably couldn't survive in the frigid Alaskan waters. No one has ever seen a whale give birth here, but experts know that calving is their main winter activity, since the 1- and 2-ton youngsters suddenly appear while the whales are in residence.

The first sighting of a humpback whale spout each season is exciting for locals on Maui. A collective sigh of relief can be heard, "Ah, they've returned." In the not-so-far distance, flukes and flippers can be seen rising above the ocean's surface. It's hard not to anthropomorphize the tail waving; it looks like such an amiable gesture. Each fluke is uniquely patterned, like a human's fingerprint, and is used to identify the giants as they travel halfway around the globe and back.

Trilogy Excursions. Whale-watching trips with Trilogy Excursions consist of smaller groups of about 20 to 36 passengers and include beverages and snacks, an onboard marine naturalist, and hydrophones that detect underwater sound waves. Trips are $49, and you load at West Maui's Kaanapali Beach Hotel. ⊠ *Kaanapali Beach Hotel, 2525 Kaanapali Pkwy., Lahaina* ☎ *808/874–5649, 888/225–6284* ⊕ *www.sailtrilogy. com.*

WINDSURFING

Windsurfing, invented in the 1950s, found its true home at Hookipa on Maui's North Shore in 1980. Seemingly overnight, windsurfing pros from around the world flooded the area. Equipment evolved, amazing film footage was captured, and a new sport was born.

If you're new to the action, you can get lessons from the experts island-wide. For a beginner, the best thing about windsurfing is (unlike surfing) you don't have to paddle. Instead, you have to hold on like heck to a flapping sail, as it whisks you into the wind. Needless to say, you're going to need a little coordination and balance to pull this off. Instructors start you out on a beach at Kanaha, where the big boys go. Lessons range from two-hour introductory classes to five-day advanced "flight school."

BEST SPOTS

After **Hookipa Bay** was discovered by windsurfers three decades ago, this windy North Shore beach 10 miles east of Kahului gained an international reputation. The spot is blessed with optimal wave-sailing wind and sea conditions, and offers the ultimate aerial experience.

In summer, the windsurfing crowd heads to **Kalepolepo Beach** on the South Shore. Trade winds build in strength, and by afternoon a swarm of Dragonfly sails can be seen skimming the whitecaps, with the West Maui Mountains as a backdrop.

A great site for speed, **Kanaha Beach Park** is dedicated to beginners in the morning hours, before the waves and wind really get roaring. After 11 am, the professionals choose from their quiver of sails the size and shape best suited for the day's demands. This beach tends to have smaller waves and forceful winds—sometimes sending sailors flying at 40 knots. If you aren't ready to go pro, this is a great place for a picnic while you watch from the beach. To get here, use any of the three entrances on Amala Place, which runs along the shore just north of Kahului Airport.

EQUIPMENT AND LESSONS

Action Sports Maui. The quirky, friendly professionals here will meet you at Kanaha Beach Park on the North Shore, outfit you with your sail and board, and guide you through your first "jibe" or turn. They promise your learning time for windsurfing will be cut in half. Lessons begin at 9 am every day except Sunday and cost $89 for a 2½-hour class. Three- and five-day courses cost $240 and $395. ⊠ *96 Amala Pl., Kahului* ☎ *808/871–5857* ⊕ *www.actionsportsmaui.com.*

Fodor'sChoice **Hawaiian Sailboarding Techniques.** Considered Maui's finest windsurfing
★ school, Hawaiian Sailboarding Techniques brings you quality instruction by skilled sailors. Founded by Alan Cadiz, an accomplished World Cup Pro, the school sets high standards for a safe, quality windsurfing experience. Intro classes start at $89 for 2½ hours, gear included. The company is inside Hi-Tech Surf Sports, which offers excellent

The world's best windsurfers love the action on Maui; it's fun to watch, too.

equipment rentals. ✉ *Hi-Tech Surf Sports, 425 Koloa St., Kahului* ☎ *808/871–5423* ⊕ *www.hstwindsurfing.com.*

Second Wind. Located in Kahului, this company rents boards with two sails for $55 per day. Additional sails are $10 each. Intro classes start at $89. ✉ *111 Hana Hwy., Kahului* ☎ *808/877–7467* ⊕ *www.secondwindmaui.com.*

GOLF, HIKING, AND OUTDOOR ACTIVITIES

Updated by
Heidi Pool

We know how tempting it is to spend your entire vacation on the beach (we're tempted many days as well), but if you do, you'll miss out on the "other side of Maui"—the eerie, moonlike surface of Haleakala Crater, the lush rain forests of East Maui, and the geological wonder that is Iao Valley State Monument, to name just a few. Even playing a round of golf on one of the world-class courses provides breathtaking vistas, reminding you just why you chose to come to Maui in the first place.

AERIAL TOURS

Helicopter flight-seeing excursions can take you over the West Maui Mountains, Haleakala Crater, or the island of Molokai. This is a beautiful, thrilling way to see the island, and the *only* way to see some of its most dramatic areas and waterfalls. Tour prices usually include a DVD of your trip so you can relive the experience at home. Prices run from about $160 for a half-hour rain-forest tour, to more than $400 for a 90-minute experience that includes a midflight landing at an exclusive remote site where you can enjoy refreshments along with the view. Generally the 45- to 50-minute flights are the best value; discounts may be available online or, if you're willing to chance it, by calling at the last minute.

Air Maui Helicopters. Priding itself on a perfect safety record, this company provides 30- to 65-minute flights covering the waterfalls of the West Maui Mountains, Haleakala Crater, Hana, and the spectacular sea cliffs of Molokai. Prices range from $198 to $348, with considerable discounts available online. Charter flights are also available. ⊠ *Kahului Heliport, Hangar 110, Kahului Airport Rd. and Keolani Blvd., Kahului* ☎ *877/238–4942, 808/877–7005* ⊕ *www.airmaui.com.*

Sunshine Helicopters. Sunshine offers tours of Maui in its FXStar or WhisperStar aircraft. A pilot-narrated DVD of your actual flight is available for purchase. Prices start at $260 for 40 to 65 minutes, with discounts available online. First-class seating is available for an additional fee. Charter flights can be arranged. ⊠ *Kahului Heliport, Hangar 107, Kahului Airport Rd. and Keolani Blvd., Kahului* ☎ *808/270–3999, 866/501–7738* ⊕ *www.sunshinehelicopters.com.*

BIKING

Long distances and mountainous terrain keep biking from being a practical mode of travel on Maui. Still, painted bike lanes enable cyclists to travel all the way from Makena to Kapalua, and you'll see hardy souls battling the trade winds under the hot Maui sun.

Several companies offer guided bike tours down Haleakala. This activity is a great way to enjoy an easy, gravity-induced bike ride, but isn't for those not confident on a bike. The ride is inherently dangerous due to the slope, sharp turns, and the fact that you're riding down an actual road with cars on it. That said, the guided bike companies take every safety precaution. A few companies offer unguided (or, as they like to say, "self-guided") tours where they provide you with the bike and transportation to the mountain and then you're free to descend at your own pace. Most companies offer discounts for Internet bookings.

Haleakala National Park no longer allows commercial downhill bicycle rides within the park's boundaries. As a result, tour amenities and routes differ by company. Ask about sunrise viewing from the Haleakala summit (be prepared to leave *very* early in the morning), if this is an important feature for you. Some lower-price tours begin at the 6,500-foot elevation just outside the national park boundaries, where you will be unable to view the sunrise over the crater. Weather conditions on Haleakala vary greatly, so a visible sunrise can never be guaranteed. Sunrise is downright cold at the summit, so be sure to dress in layers and wear closed-toe shoes.

BEST SPOTS

At present there are few truly good spots to ride on Maui, though this is changing.

Thompson Road. Street bikers will want to head out to scenic Thompson Road. It's quiet, gently curvy, and flanked by gorgeous views on both sides. Because it's at a higher elevation, the air temperature is cooler and the wind lighter. The coast back down toward Kahului on the Kula Highway is worth the ride up. ⊠ *Kula Hwy., off Rte. 37, Keokea.*

EQUIPMENT AND TOURS

Fodor's Choice
★

Bike It Maui. Small and family-owned, this company offers two guided sunrise tours down Haleakala each day. The price of $144 ($134 if booked more than a week ahead) includes transfers from your hotel, a sunrise van tour of the summit, a guided 28-mile bicycle ride down the mountain, and a full sit-down breakfast at Cafe O'Lei at the Dunes in Kahului. Riders must be at least 12 and weigh no more than 260 pounds. ⊠ *Kula* ☎ *808/878–3364, 866/776–2453* ⊕ *www.bikeitmaui.com.*

Fodor's Choice
★

Cruiser Phil's Volcano Riders. In the downhill bicycle industry since 1983, "Cruiser" Phil Feliciano offers sunrise tours ($150) and morning tours ($135) that include hotel transfers, Continental breakfast, a van tour of the summit, and a guided 28-mile ride down the mountain. Participants should be between 15 and 65, taller than 5 feet, weigh less than 250 pounds, and have ridden a bicycle in the past year. Feliciano also offers independent bike tours ($99) and van-only tours ($125). Discounts are available for online bookings. ⊠ *58-A Amala Pl., Kahului* ☎ *808/893–2332, 877/764–2453* ⊕ *www.cruiserphil.com.*

Haleakala Bike Company. If you're thinking about an unguided Haleakala bike trip, consider this company. Meet at the Old Haiku Cannery and take the van shuttle to the summit. Along the way you can learn about the history of the island, the volcano, and other Hawaiiana. Food is not included, but there are several spots along the way down to stop, rest, and eat. The simple, mostly downhill route takes you right back to the cannery where you started. HBC also offers bike sales, rentals, and services, as well as van tours. Tour prices range from $75 to $125, with discounts available for online bookings. ⊠ *810 Haiku Rd., Suite 120, Haiku* ☎ *808/575–9575, 888/922–2453* ⊕ *www.bikemaui.com.*

Island Biker. Maui's premier bike shop for rentals, sales, and service offers standard front-shock bikes, road bikes, and full-suspension mountain bikes. Daily rental rates range from $50 to $75, and weekly rates are $200 to $280. The price includes a helmet, pump, water bottle, cages, tire-repair kit, and spare tube. Car racks are $5 per day (free with weekly rentals). The staff can suggest routes appropriate for mountain or road biking. ⊠ *415 Dairy Rd., Kahului* ☎ *808/877–7744* ⊕ *www.islandbikermaui.com.*

West Maui Cycles. Serving the island's west side, West Maui Cycles offers cruisers for $15 per day, hybrids for $35 per day, and performance road bikes for $60 per day. Tandems start at $30 per day. Per day rates are discounted for longer-term rentals. The shop also rents baby joggers and car racks. Sales and service are available. ⊠ *1087 Limahana Pl., No. 6, Lahaina* ☎ *808/661–9005* ⊕ *www.westmauicycles.com.*

GOLF

Maui's natural beauty and surroundings offer some of the most jaw-dropping vistas imaginable on a golf course; add a variety of challenging, well-designed courses and it's easy to explain the island's popularity with golfers. Holes run across small bays, past craggy lava outcrops, and up into cool, forested mountains. Most courses have mesmerizing ocean views, some close enough to feel the salt in the air. Although many of the courses are affiliated with resorts (and therefore a little pricier), the general-public courses are no less impressive. Discounts are often available for resort guests, for twilight tee times, and for those who book online. ∎TIP→ **Resort courses, in particular, offer more than the usual three sets of tees, so bite off as much or little challenge as you like.** Tee it up from the tips and you can end up playing a few 600-yard par 5s and see a few 250-yard forced carries.

Fodor's Choice
★

The Dunes at Maui Lani. Robin Nelson is at his minimalist best here, creating a bit of British links in the middle of the Pacific. Holes run through ancient, lightly wooded sand dunes, 5 miles inland from Kahului Harbor. Thanks to the natural humps and slopes of the dunes, Nelson had to move very little dirt and created a natural beauty. During the design phase he visited Ireland, and not so coincidentally the par-3 3rd looks a lot like the Dell at Lahinch: a white dune on the right sloping down into a deep bunker and partially obscuring the right side of the green—just one of several blind to semiblind shots here. ⊠ *1333 Maui Lani Pkwy., Kahului* ☎ *808/873–0422* ⊕ *www.dunesatmauilani.com* ☒ *$112* ⛳ *18 holes, 6841 yards, par 72.*

Kaanapali Golf Resort. The Royal Kaanapali (North) Course (1962) is one of three in Hawaii designed by Robert Trent Jones Sr., the godfather of modern golf architecture. The greens average a whopping 10,000 square feet, necessary because of the often-severe undulation. The par-4 18th hole (into the prevailing trade breezes, with out-of-bounds on the left and a lake on the right) is notoriously tough. Designed by Arthur Jack Snyder, the Kaanapali Kai (South) Course (1976) shares similar seaside-into-the-hills terrain, but is rated a couple of strokes easier, mostly because putts are less treacherous. ⊠ *2290 Kaanapali Pkwy., Lahaina* ☎ *808/661–3691, 866/454–4653* ⊕ *www.kaanapali-golf. com* ☒ *Royal Kaanapali (North) Course, $179; Kaanapali Kai (South) Course, $125* ⛳ *Royal Kaanapali (North) Course: 18 holes, 6500 yards, par 71; Kaanapali Kai (South) Course: 18 holes, 6400 yards, par 70.*

Fodor's Choice
★

Kapalua Resort. Perhaps Hawaii's best-known golf resort and the crown jewel of golf on Maui, Kapalua hosts the PGA Tour's first event each January: the Hyundai Tournament of Champions at the Plantation Course at Kapalua. Ben Crenshaw and Bill Coore (1991) tried to incorporate traditional shot values in a nontraditional site, taking into account slope, gravity, and the prevailing trade winds. The par-5 18th hole, for instance, plays 663 yards from the back tees (600 yards from the resort tees). The hole drops 170 feet in elevation, narrowing as it goes to a partially guarded green, and plays downwind and down-grain. Despite the longer-than-usual distance, the slope is great enough and the wind at your back usually brisk enough to reach the green with two well-struck shots—a truly unbelievable finish to a course that will challenge, frustrate, and reward the patient golfer.

The Bay Course (Arnold Palmer and Francis Duane, 1975) is the more traditional of Kapalua's courses, with gentle rolling fairways and generous greens. The most memorable hole is the par-3 5th hole, with a tee shot that must carry a turquoise finger of Onelua Bay. Each of the courses has a separate clubhouse. ⊠ *Kapalua* ⊕ *www.kapalua.com/golf.*

Kapalua Golf Academy. Along with 23 acres of practice turf and 11 teeing areas, an 18-hole putting course, and 3-hole walking course, the Kapalua Golf Academy also has an instructional bay with digital video analysis. ⊠ *1000 Office Rd., Kapalua* ☎ *808/665–5455, 877/527–2582* ⊕ *www.kapalua.com/golf.*

Bay Course ⊠ *300 Kapalua Dr., Kapalua* ☎ *808/669–8044, 877/527–2582* ⊕ *www.kapalua.com/golf* ⚏ *$208* ⚐ *18 holes, 6600 yards, par 72.*

Plantation Course ⊠ *2000 Plantation Club Dr., Kapalua* ☎ *808/669–8044, 877/527–2582* ⊕ *www.kapalua.com/golf* ⚏ *$278* ⚐ *18 holes, 7411 yards, par 73.*

Fodor'sChoice **Makena Beach & Golf Resort.** Robert Trent Jones Jr. designed Makena Golf
★ Course (1994) in harmony with the existing landscape: Hawaiian rock walls still stand in their original locations, and natural gullies and stream beds were left in their natural states. Sculpted from the lava flows on the western flank of Haleakala, Makena offers quick greens with lots of breaks and plenty of scenic distractions. The 4th hole is one of Hawaii's most picturesque inland par 3s, with the green guarded on the right by a duck pond. The 6th is an excellent example of option golf: the fairway is sliced up the middle by a gaping ravine, which must sooner or later be crossed to reach the green. The last three holes are relatively short par 4s, but keen accuracy is required, as the tees wind through *kiawe* trees. At this writing, Makena Golf Course is closed for renovation, with reopening scheduled for 2014. ⊠ *5415 Makena Alanui, Makena* ☎ *808/891–4000* ⊕ *www.makenagolf.com* ⚏ *$185* ⚐ *18 holes, 6567 yards, par 72.*

Pukalani Golf Course. At 1,110 feet above sea level, Pukalani (Bob E. Baldock and Robert L. Baldock, 1970) provides one of the finest vistas in all Hawaii. Holes run up, down, and across the slopes of Haleakala. The trade winds tend to come up in the late morning and afternoon. This, combined with frequent elevation change, makes club selection a test. The fairways tend to be wide, but greens are undulating and quick. ⊠ *360 Pukalani St., Pukalani* ☎ *808/572–1314* ⊕ *www.pukalanigolf.com* ⚏ *$61* ⚐ *18 holes, 6962 yards, par 72.*

Fodor'sChoice **Wailea.** This is the only Hawaii resort to offer three different courses:
★ Gold, Emerald, and Old Blue. Designed by Robert Trent Jones Jr. (Gold and Emerald) and Arthur Jack Snyder (Old Blue), these courses share similar terrain, carved into the leeward slopes of Haleakala. Although the ocean does not come into play, its beauty is visible on almost every hole. ■TIP➜ **Remember, putts break dramatically toward the ocean.**

Jones refers to the Gold Course at Wailea (1993) as the "masculine" course. It's all trees and lava, and regarded as the hardest of the three courses. The trick here is to note even subtle changes in elevation. The par-3 8th, for example, plays from an elevated tee across a lava ravine to a large, well-bunkered green framed by palm trees, the blue sea, and tiny Molokini. The course demands strategy and careful club selection. The Emerald Course (1994) is the "feminine" layout with lots of flowers and bunkering away from greens. Although this may seem to render the

Sunset views are lovely from many hotel rooms near West Maui's Kaanapali Beach.

bunker benign, the opposite is true. A bunker well in front of a green disguises the distance to the hole. Likewise, the Emerald's extensive flower beds are dangerous distractions because of their beauty. The Gold and Emerald share a clubhouse, practice facility, and 19th hole.

At Wailea's first course, the Old Blue Course (1971), judging elevation change is also key. Fairways and greens tend to be wider and more forgiving than on the Gold or Emerald, and run through colorful flora that includes hibiscus, wiliwili, bougainvillea, and plumeria. ⊠ *Wailea* ⊕ *www.waileagolf.com*

Old Blue Course ⊠ *100 Wailea Golf Club Dr., Wailea* ☎ *808/875–7450, 888/328–6284* ⊕ *www.waileagolf.com* ☏ *$180* 🏌 *18 holes, 6765 yards, par 72.*

Gold and Emerald Courses ⊠ *100 Wailea Golf Club Dr., Wailea* ☎ *808/875–7450, 888/328–6284* ⊕ *www.waileagolf.com* ☏ *Gold Course, $235; Emerald Course, $235* 🏌 *Gold Course: 18 holes, 6653 yards, par 72; Emerald Course: 18 holes, 6407 yards, par 72.*

HANG GLIDING AND PARAGLIDING

If you've always wanted to know what it feels like to fly, hang gliding or paragliding might be your perfect Maui adventure. You'll get open-air, bird's-eye views of the Valley Isle that you'll likely never forget. And you don't need to be a daredevil to participate.

BEFORE YOU HIT THE FIRST TEE . . .

Golf is golf, and Hawaii is part of the United States, but island golf nevertheless has its own quirks. Here are a few tips to make your golf experience in the Islands more pleasant.

■ All resort courses and many daily-fee courses provide rental clubs. In many cases, they're the latest lines from top manufacturers. This is true both for men and women, as well as for left-handers, which means you don't have to schlep clubs across the Pacific.

■ Come spikeless—few Hawaii courses still permit metal spikes. And most of the resort courses require a collared shirt.

■ Maui is notorious for its trade winds. Consider playing early if you want to avoid the breezes, and remember that although it will frustrate you at times and make club selection difficult, you may well see some of your longest drives ever.

■ In theory you can play golf in Hawaii 365 days a year, but there's a reason the Hawaiian Islands are so green. An umbrella and light jacket can come in handy.

■ Unless you play a muni or certain daily-fee courses, plan on taking a cart. Riding carts are mandatory at most courses and are included in the greens fee.

LESSONS AND TOURS

Hang Gliding Maui. Armin Engert will take you on an instructional powered hang-gliding trip out of Hana Airport in East Maui. With more than 13,000 hours in the air and a perfect safety record, Armin flies you 1,000 feet over Maui's most beautiful coast. A 30-minute flight lesson costs $170, a 45-minute lesson costs $230, and a 60-minute lesson is $280. Snapshots of your flight from a wing-mounted camera cost an additional $40, and a 34-minute DVD of the flight is available for $80. Reservations are required. ⊠ *Hana Airport, Alalele Pl., off Hana Hwy., Hana* ☎ *808/572–6557* ⊕ *www.hanggldingmaui.com.*

Proflyght Paragliding. This is the only paragliding outfit on Maui to offer solo, tandem, and instruction at Polipoli Spring State Recreation Area. The leeward slope of Haleakala lends itself to paragliding with breathtaking scenery and air currents that increase during the day. Polipoli creates tremendous thermals that allow you to peacefully descend 3,000 feet to land. Prices are $95 to $185, with full certification available. ⊠ *Polipoli Spring State Recreation Area, Waipoli Rd., Kula* ☎ *808/874–5433* ⊕ *www.paraglidemaui.com.*

HIKING

Hikes on Maui include treks along coastal seashore, verdant rain forest, and alpine desert. Orchids, hibiscus, ginger, heliconia, and anthuriums grow wild on many trails, and exotic fruits like mountain apple, *lilikoi* (passion fruit), and strawberry guava provide refreshing snacks for hikers. Much of what you see in lower-altitude forests is alien, brought to Hawaii at one time or another by someone hoping to improve on nature. Plants like strawberry guava and ginger may be tasty, but they grow over native plants and have become problematic weeds.

The best hikes get you out of the imported landscaping and into the truly exotic wilderness. Hawaii possesses some of the world's rarest plants, insects, and birds. Pocket field guides are available at most grocery or drug stores and can really illuminate your walk. If you watch the right branches quietly, you can spot the same honeycreepers or happy-face spiders scientists have spent their lives studying.

BEST SPOTS

Fodor's Choice
★

Haleakala Crater. Undoubtedly the best hiking on the island is at Haleakala Crater. If you're in shape, do a day hike descending from the summit along **Keoneheehee Trail** (also known as Sliding Sands Trail) to the crater floor. You might also consider spending several days here amid the cinder cones, lava flows, and all that loud silence. Entering the crater is like landing on a different planet. In the early 1960s NASA actually brought moon-suited astronauts here to practice what it would be like to "walk on the moon." On the 30 miles of trails you can traverse black sand and wild lava formations, follow the trail of blooming *ahinahina* (silverswords), and witness tremendous views of big sky and burned-red cliffs.

The best time to go into the crater is in the summer months, when the conditions are generally more predictable. Be sure to bring layered clothing—and plenty of warm clothes if you're staying overnight. It may be scorching hot during the day, but it gets mighty chilly after dark. Bring your own drinking water, as potable water is only available at the two visitor centers. Overnight visitors must get a permit at park headquarters before entering the crater. *Moderate to difficult. For detailed information on hikes in the crater, see Haleakala National Park feature.* ✉ *Haleakala Crater Rd., Makawao* ☎ *808/572–4400* ⊕ *www.nps.gov/hale.*

A branch of Haleakala National Park, **Oheo Gulch** is famous for its pools (the area is sometimes called the "Seven Sacred Pools"). Truth is, there are more than seven pools, and there's nothing sacred about them. A former owner of the Travaasa Hotel Hana started calling the area Seven Sacred Pools to attract the masses to sleepy old Hana. His plan worked and the name stuck, much to the chagrin of many Mauians.

The best time to visit the pools is in the morning, before the crowds and tour buses arrive. Start your day with a vigorous hike. Oheo has some fantastic trails to choose from, including our favorite, the Pipiwai Trail. When you're done, nothing could be better than going to the pools, lounging on the rocks, and cooling off in the freshwater reserves. (Keep in mind, however, that the park periodically closes the pools to swimming when the potential for flash flooding exists.)

You can find Oheo Gulch on Route 31, 10 miles past Hana town. All visitors must pay a $10 national park fee (per car, not per person), which is valid for three days and can be used at Haleakala's summit as well. Be sure to visit Haleakala National Park's Kipahulu Visitor Center, 10 miles past Hana, for information about scheduled orientations and cultural demonstrations. Note that there is no drinking water here.

Hoapili Trail. A challenging hike through eye-popping scenery in southwestern Maui is this 5½-mile coastal trail beyond the Ahihi-Kinau

Continued on page 256

HALEAKALA NATIONAL PARK

HALEAKALA CRATER

From the Tropics to the Moon! Two hours, 38 miles, 10,023 feet—those are the unlikely numbers involved in reaching Maui's highest point, the summit of the volcano Haleakala. Nowhere else on earth can you drive from sea level (Kahului) to 10,023 feet (the summit) in only 38 miles. And what's more shocking—in that short vertical ascent, you'll journey from lush, tropical-island landscape to the stark, moonlike basin of the volcano's enormous, otherworldly crater.

Established in 1916, Haleakala National Park covers an astonishing 27,284 acres. Haleakala "Crater" is the centerpiece of the park though it's not actually a crater. Technically, it's an erosional valley, flushed out by water pouring from the summit through two enormous gaps. The mountain has terrific camping and hiking, including a trail that loops through the crater, but the chance to witness this unearthly landscape is reason enough for a visit.

THE CLIMB TO THE SUMMIT
To reach Haleakala National Park and the mountain's breathtaking summit, take Route 36 east of Kahului to the Haleakala Highway (Route 37). Head east, up the mountain to the unlikely intersection of Haleakala Highway and Haleakala Highway. If you continue straight the road's name changes to Kula Highway (still Route 37). Instead, turn left onto Haleakala Highway—this is now Route 377. After about 6 miles, make a left onto

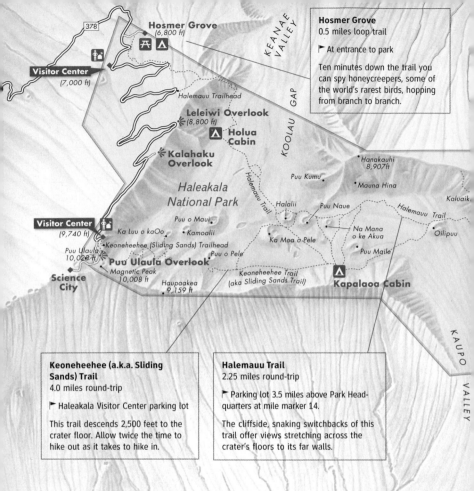

Hosmer Grove
(6,800 ft)

Visitor Center
(7,000 ft)

KEANAE VALLEY

Halemauu Trailhead

Hosmer Grove

0.5 miles loop trail

► At entrance to park

Ten minutes down the trail you can spy honeycreepers, some of the world's rarest birds, hopping from branch to branch.

KOOLAU GAP

Leleiwi Overlook
(8,800 ft)

Holua Cabin

Kalahaku Overlook

Haleakala National Park

Hanakauhi
8,907 ft

Puu Kumu

Mauna Hina

Kaluaik

Halemauu Trail

Halalii

Puu Naue

Puu o Maui

Na Mana o ke Akua

Oilipuu

Ka Luu o kaOo

Kamoalii

Ka Moa o Pele

Puu Mgile

Keoneheehee (Sliding Sands) Trailhead

Puu o Pele

Puu Ulaula
10,023 ft

Puu Ulaula Overlook

Magnetic Peak
10,008 ft

Keoneheehee Trail
(aka Sliding Sands Trail)

Kapalaoa Cabin

Science City

Haupaakea
9,159 ft

KAUPO VALLEY

Keoneheehee (a.k.a. Sliding Sands) Trail
4.0 miles round-trip

► Haleakala Visitor Center parking lot

This trail descends 2,500 feet to the crater floor. Allow twice the time to hike out as it takes to hike in.

Halemauu Trail
2.25 miles round-trip

► Parking lot 3.5 miles above Park Headquarters at mile marker 14.

The cliffside, snaking switchbacks of this trail offer views stretching across the crater's floors to its far walls.

Crater Road (Route 378). After several long switchbacks (look out for downhill bikers!) you'll come to the park entrance.

■TIP→ Before you head up Haleakala, call for the latest park weather conditions (☎ 866/944–5025). Extreme gusty winds, heavy rain, and even snow in winter are not uncommon. Because of the high altitude, the mountaintop temperature is often as much as 30 degrees cooler than that at sea level. Be sure to bring a jacket. Also make sure you have a full tank of gas. No service stations exist beyond Kula.

There's a $10 per car fee to enter the park; but it's good for three days and

can be used at Oheo Gulch (Kipahulu), so save your receipt.

6,800 feet, Hosmer Grove. Just as you enter the park, Hosmer Grove has campsites and interpretive trails (*see* Hiking & Camping *on the following pages*). Park rangers maintain a changing schedule of talks and hikes both here and at the top of the mountain. Call the park for current schedules.

7,000 feet, Park Headquarters/Visitor Center. Not far from Hosmer Grove, the Park Headquarters/Visitor Center (open daily from 6:30 am to 3:45) has trail maps and displays about the vol-

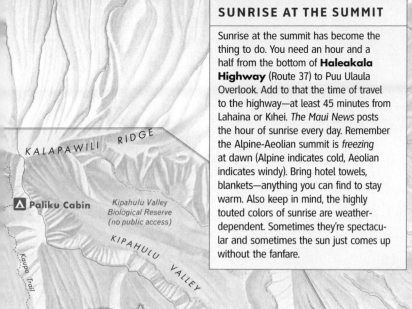

SUNRISE AT THE SUMMIT

Sunrise at the summit has become the thing to do. You need an hour and a half from the bottom of **Haleakala Highway** (Route 37) to Puu Ulaula Overlook. Add to that the time of travel to the highway—at least 45 minutes from Lahaina or Kihei. *The Maui News* posts the hour of sunrise every day. Remember the Alpine-Aeolian summit is *freezing* at dawn (Alpine indicates cold, Aeolian indicates windy). Bring hotel towels, blankets—anything you can find to stay warm. Also keep in mind, the highly touted colors of sunrise are weather-dependent. Sometimes they're spectacular and sometimes the sun just comes up without the fanfare.

cano's origins and eruption history. Hikers and campers should check-in here before heading up the mountain. Maps, posters, and other memorabilia are available at the gift shop.

8,800 feet, Leleiwi Overlook. Continuing up the mountain, you come to Leleiwi Overlook. A short walk to the end of the parking lot reveals your first awe-inspiring view of the crater. The small hills in the basin are volcanic cinder cones (called *puu* in Hawaiian), each with a small crater at its top, and each the site of a former eruption.

WHERE TO EAT

KULA LODGE (✉ Haleakala Hwy., Kula ☎ 808/878–2517) serves hearty breakfasts from 7 to 11 am, a favorite with hikers coming down from a sunrise visit to Haleakala's summit, as well as those on their way up for a late-morning tramp in the crater. Spectacular ocean views fill the windows of this mountainside lodge.

If you're here in the late afternoon, it's possible you'll experience a phenomenon called the Brocken Specter. Named after a similar occurrence in East Germany's Harz Mountains, the "specter"

10,023 feet, Puu Ulaula Overlook. The highest point on Maui is the Puu Ulaula Overlook, at the 10,023-foot summit. Here you find a glass-enclosed lookout with a 360-degree view. The building is open 24 hours a day, and this is where visitors gather for the best sunrise view. Dawn begins between 5:45 and 7, depending on the time of year. On a clear day you can see the islands of Molokai, Lanai, Kahoolawe, and Hawaii (the Big Island). On a *really* clear day you can even spot Oahu glimmering in the distance.

■**TIP**➔ The air is very thin at 10,000 feet. Don't be surprised if you feel a little breathless while walking around the summit. Take it easy and drink lots of water. Anyone who has been scuba diving within the last 24 hours should not make the trip up Haleakala.

On a small hill nearby, you can see **Science City**, an off-limits research and communications center straight out of an espionage thriller. The University of Hawaii maintains an observatory here, and the Department of Defense tracks satellites.

allows you to see yourself reflected on the clouds and encircled by a rainbow. Don't wait all day for this because it's not a daily occurrence.

9,000 feet, Kalahaku Overlook. The next stopping point is Kalahaku Overlook. The view here offers a different perspective of the crater, and at this elevation the famous silversword plant grows amid the cinders. This odd, endangered beauty grows only here and at the same elevation on the Big Island's two peaks. It begins life as a silver, spiny-leaf rosette and is the sole home of a variety of native insects (it's the only shelter around). The silversword reaches maturity between 7 and 17 years, when it sends forth a 3- to 8-foot-tall stalk with several hundred tiny sunflowers. It blooms once, then dies.

9,740 feet, Haleakala Visitor Center. Another mile up is the Haleakala Visitor Center, open daily from sunrise to 3 pm except Christmas and New Year's. There are exhibits inside, and a trail from here leads to White Hill—a short easy walk that will give you an even better view of the valley.

For more information about Haleakala National Park, contact the **National Park Service** (☎ 808/572–4400 ⊕ www.nps.gov/hale).

HIKING AND CAMPING

Exploring Haleakala Crater is one of the best hiking experiences on Maui. The volcanic terrain offers an impressive diversity of colors, textures, and shapes—almost as if the lava has been artfully sculpted. The barren landscape is home to many plants, insects, and birds that exist nowhere else on earth and have developed intriguing survival mechanisms, such as the sun-reflecting, hairy leaves of the silversword, which allow it to survive the intense climate.

Stop at park headquarters to register and pick up trail maps on your way into the park.

1-Hour Hike. Just as you enter Haleakala National Park, **Hosmer Grove** offers a short 10-minute hike and an hour-long, ¹/₂-mile loop trail that will give you insight into Hawaii's fragile ecology. Anyone can go on these hikes, whereas a longer trail through the Waikamoi Cloud Forest is accessible only with park ranger–guided hikes. Call park headquarters for the schedule. Facilities here include six campsites (no permit needed, available on a first-come, first-served basis), pit toilets, drinking water, and cooking shelters.

4-Hour Hikes. Two half-day hikes involve descending into the crater and returning the way you came. The first, **Halemauu Trail** (trailhead is between mile markers 14 and 15), is 2.25 miles round-trip. The cliffside, snaking switchbacks of this trail offer views stretching across the crater's puu-speckled floor to its far walls. On clear days you can peer through the Koolau Gap to Hana. Native flowers and shrubs grow along the trail, which is typically misty and cool (though still exposed to the sun). When you reach the gate at the bottom, head back up.

The other hike, which is 5 miles round-trip, descends down **Keoneheehee (a.k.a. Sliding Sands) Trail** (trailhead is at the Haleakala Visitor Center) into an alien landscape of reddish black cinders, lava bombs, and silverswords. It's easy to imagine life before humans in the solitude and silence of this place. Turn back when you hit the crater floor.

■TIP→ Bring water, sunscreen, and a reliable jacket. These are demanding hikes. Take it slowly to acclimate, and allow additional time for the uphill return trip.

8-Hour Hike. The recommended way to explore the crater in a single, but full day is to go in two cars and ferry yourselves back and forth between the head of **Halemauu Trail** and the summit. This way, you can hike from the summit down **Keoneheehee Trail**, cross the crater's floor, investigate the **Bottomless Pit** and **Pele's Paint Pot**, then climb out on the **switchback trail (Halemauu)**. When you emerge, the shelter of your waiting car will be very welcome (this is an 11.2-mile hike). If you don't have two cars, hitching a ride from Halemauu back to the summit should be relatively safe and easy.

■**TIP→** Take a backpack with lunch, water, sunscreen, and a reliable jacket for the beginning and end of the 8-hour hike. This is a demanding trip, but you will never regret or forget it.

Overnight Hike. Staying overnight in one of Haleakala's three cabins or two wilderness campgrounds is an experience like no other. You'll feel like the only person on earth when you wake up inside this enchanted, strange landscape. The cabins, each tucked in a different corner of the crater's floor, are equipped with 12 bunk beds, wood-burning stoves, fake logs, and kitchen gear.

Holua cabin is the shortest hike, less than 4 hours (3.7 miles) from Halemauu Trail. **Kapalaoa** is about 5 hours (5.5 miles) down Keoneheehee Trail. The most cherished cabin is **Paliku,** an eight-hour (9.3-miles) hike starting from either trail. It's nestled against the cliffs above Kaupo Gap. Cabin reservations can be made up to 90 days in advance through the Friends of Haleakala National Park's Web site (⊕ *fhnp. org/wcr*) or by calling the National Park Service (☎*808/572–4400*) between 1 and 3 pm HST. Tent campsites at Holua

and Paliku are free and easy to reserve on a first-come, first-served basis.

■**TIP→** Toilets and nonpotable water are available—bring iodine tablets to purify the water. Open fires are not allowed and packing out your trash is mandatory.

For more information on hiking or camping, contact the National Park Service (✉ Box 369, Makawao 96768 ☎808/572–4459 ⊕ www.nps.gov/hale).

OPTIONS FOR EXPLORING

If you're short on time you can drive to the summit, take a peek inside, and drive back down. But the "House of the Sun" is really worth a day, whether you explore by foot, horseback, or helicopter.

BIKING
At this writing, all guided bike tours inside park boundaries were suspended indefinitely. However, the tours continue but now start outside the boundary of the park. These can provide a speedy, satisfying downhill trip. The park is still open to individual bikes for a $5 fee. There are no bike paths, however—just the same road that is used by vehicular traffic. Whether you're on your own or with a tour, be careful!

HELICOPTER TOURS
Viewing Haleakala from above can be a mind-altering experience, if you don't mind dropping $225+ per person for a few blissful moments above the crater. Most tours buzz Haleakala, where airspace is regulated, then head over to Hana in search of waterfalls.

HORSEBACK RIDING
Several companies offer half-day, full-day, and even overnight rides into the crater. On one half-day ride you descend into the crater on Keoneheehee Trail and have lunch before you head back.

For complete information on any of these activities, ⇨ see Golf, Hiking and Outdoor Activities.

DID YOU KNOW?

You can get good views from lookouts at Haleakala National Park, or try a hiking trail to get up close to the dramatic, eerie formations in the volcanic crater. Resembling small, steep hills, cinder cones made of volcanic rock mark the sites of past eruptions.

Natural Area Reserve. Named after a bygone king, it follows the shoreline, threading through the remains of ancient villages. King Hoapili created an island-wide road, and this wide path of stacked lava rocks is a marvel to look at and walk on. (It's not the easiest surface for the ankles and feet, so wear sturdy shoes.) This is brutal territory with little shade and no facilities, and extra water is a must. To get here, follow Makena Road to La Perouse Bay. The trail can be a challenge to find—walk south along the ocean through the *kiawe* trees, where you'll encounter numerous wild goats (don't worry—they're tame), and past a scenic little bay. The trail begins just around the corner to the left. *Difficult.* ⊠ *Trailhead: La Perouse Bay, Makena Rd., Makena.*

Iao Valley Trail. Anyone (including your grandparents) can handle this short walk from the parking lot at Iao Valley State Monument. On your choice of two paved walkways, you can cross the Iao Stream and explore the junglelike area. Ascend the stairs up to the Iao Needle for spectacular views of Central Maui. Be sure to stop at the lovely Kepaniwai Heritage Gardens, which commemorate the cultural contributions of various immigrant groups. *Easy.* ⊠ *Trailhead: Iao Valley State Monument parking lot, Rte. 32, Wailuku.*

Kapalua Resort. The resort offers free access to 100 miles of hiking trails to guests and visitors as a self-guided experience. Trail information and maps are available at the Kapalua Adventure Center. Access to most trails is via a complimentary resort shuttle, which must be reserved in advance. Guided hiking tours are also available through the Jean-Michel Cousteau Ambassadors of the Environment program at the Ritz-Carlton, Kapalua. ⊠ *2000 Village Rd., corner of Office Rd., Kapalua* ☎ *808/665–4386, 877/665–4386* ⊕ *www.kapalua.com.*

Fodor's Choice **Pipiwai Trail.** This 2-mile trek upstream leads to the 400-foot Waimoku
★   Falls, pounding down in all its power and glory. Following signs from the parking lot, head across the road and uphill into the forest. The trail borders a sensational gorge and passes onto a boardwalk through a mystifying forest of giant bamboo. This stomp through muddy and rocky terrain includes two stream crossings and takes around three hours to fully enjoy. Although this trail is never truly crowded, it's best done early in the morning before the tours arrive. Be sure to bring mosquito repellent. *Moderate.* ⊠ *Hana Hwy., near mile marker 42, Hana.*

GOING WITH A GUIDE

Fodor's Choice ★ **Friends of Haleakala National Park.** This nonprofit offers day and overnight trips into the volcanic crater. The purpose of your trip, the service work itself, isn't too much—mostly native planting, removing invasive plants, and light cabin maintenance. An interpretive park ranger accompanies each trip, taking you to places you'd otherwise miss and teaching you about the native flora and fauna. ☎ *808/876–1673* ⊕ *www.fhnp.org.*

Fodor's Choice ★ **Hike Maui.** Started in 1983, the area's oldest hiking company remains extremely well regarded for waterfall, rain forest, and crater hikes led by enthusiastic, highly trained guides who weave botany, geology, ethnobotany, culture, and history into the outdoor experience. Prices range from $85 to $189 for excursions lasting 3 to 11 hours (discounts for booking online). Hike Maui supplies day packs, rain gear, mosquito repellent, first-aid supplies, bottled water, snacks, lunch for the longer trips, and transportation to and from the site. Hotel transfers are available for most hikes (extra fee may apply). ✉ *285 Hukilike St., Unit B-104, Kahului* ☎ *808/879–5270, 866/324–6284* ⊕ *www.hikemaui.com.*

Sierra Club. One great avenue into the island's untrammeled wilderness is Maui's chapter of the Sierra Club. Join one of the club's hikes into pristine forests, along ancient coastal paths, to historic sites, and to Haleakala Crater. Some outings require volunteer service, but most are just for fun. Bring your own food and water, rain gear, sunscreen, sturdy shoes, and a suggested donation of $5 for hikers over age 14. This is a true bargain. ✏ *webmaster@mauisierraclub.org* ⊕ *www.hi.sierraclub.org/maui.*

HORSEBACK RIDING

Several companies on Maui offer horseback riding that's far more appealing than the typical hour-long trudge over a dull trail with 50 other horses.

GOING WITH A GUIDE

Mendes Ranch. Family-owned and run, Mendes operates out of the beautiful ranchland of Kahakuloa on the windward slopes of the West Maui Mountains. Morning and afternoon trail rides lasting 1½ hours ($99) are available. Cowboys take you cantering up rolling pastures into the lush rain forest, and then you'll descend all the way down to the ocean for a photo op with a dramatic backdrop. Don't expect a Hawaiian cultural experience here—it's all about the horses and the ride. ✉ *3530 Kahekili Hwy., Wailuku* ☎ *808/244–7320, 800/871–5222* ⊕ *www. mendesranch.com.*

Pony Express Tours. This outfit offers horseback journeys into Haleakala Crater. The half-day ride, which descends into the crater floor for a picnic lunch ($188), is a great way to experience the majesty of the volcano without having to hike. Prior riding experience is highly recommended, as you're on horseback for at least 4 hours. The company also offers 1½- and 2-hour rides ($95 and $110) on the slopes of the Haleakala Ranch. ✉ *Kula* ☎ *808/667–2200* ⊕ *www.ponyexpresstours.com.*

TENNIS

Most courts charge by the hour but will let players continue after their initial hour for free, provided no one is waiting. Many hotels and condos charge a fee for nonguests.

Kapalua Tennis Garden. Home to the Kapalua Tennis Club, this complex has 10 courts (four lighted for night play) and a pro shop. The fee is $14 per person per day. Private and group (3-4 persons) instruction is also available. ⊠ *Kapalua Resort, 100 Kapalua Dr., Kapalua* ☎ *808/662–7730* ⊕ *www.kapalua.com.*

Lahaina Civic Center. The best free courts are the nine at the Lahaina Civic Center, near Wahikuli State Park. They all have overhead lighting for night play, and are available on a first-come, first-served basis. ⊠ *1840 Honoapiilani Hwy., Lahaina* ☎ *808/661–4685.*

Wailea Tennis Club. Featuring 11 Plexipave courts (two lighted for night play), this club also offers lessons, rentals, and ball machines. Daily clinics help you improve ground strokes, serve, volley, or doubles strategy. The daily court fee, which guarantees one hour of reserved time for singles and 1.5 hours for doubles, is $15 per player. ⊠ *131 Wailea Ike Pl., Wailea* ☎ *808/879–1958* ⊕ *www.waileatennis.com.*

ZIPLINE TOURS

Ziplining on one of Maui's several courses lets you satisfy your inner Tarzan by soaring high above deep gulches and canyons—for a price that can seem steep. A harness keeps you fully supported on each ride. Each course has its own age minimums and weight restrictions but, generally, you must be at least 10 years old and weigh a minimum of 60–80 pounds and a maximum of 250–275 pounds. You should wear closed-toe athletic-type shoes and expect to get dirty. ■**TIP→** Reconsider this activity if you are pregnant, uncomfortable with heights, or have serious back or joint problems.

Fodor's Choice ★ **Flyin' Hawaiian Zipline.** These guys have the longest line in the state (a staggering 3,600 feet), as well as the most unique course layout. You build confidence on the first line, then board a four-wheel-drive vehicle that takes you 1,500 feet above the town of Waikapu to seven more lines that carry you over 11 ridges and nine valleys. The total distance covered is more than 2½ miles, and the views are astonishing. The price of $185 includes water and snacks. You must be able to hike over steep, sometimes slippery terrain while carrying a 10-pound metal trolley. ⊠ *Waikapu* ☎ *808/463–5786* ⊕ *www.flyinhawaiianzipline.com.*

Fodor's Choice ★ **Piiholo Ranch Zipline.** This complex, on a gorgeous 900-acre family ranch, has two zipline courses. The original course consists of five lines—one quadruple, and four side by side. Access to the fifth and longest line is via a four-wheel-drive vehicle to the top of Piiholo Hill, where you are treated to stunning bicoastal views. Guides do a good job of weaving Hawaiian culture into the adventure. You must be able to climb three steep suspension bridges while hefting a 12-pound trolley over your shoulder. Prices range from $140 for four lines to $190 for five. The newer course offers a zipline canopy tour that keeps you in the trees the entire time ($90 to $165). Bring a lightweight jacket, as it can get a bit chilly at the ranch. ⊠ *Piiholo Rd., Makawao* ☎ *800/374–7050* ⊕ *www.piiholozipline.com.*

SHOPPING

Updated by
Eliza Escaño-
Vasquez

3

Whether you're searching for a dashboard hula dancer or an original Curtis Wilson Cost painting, you can find it on Front Street in Lahaina or at the Shops at Wailea. Art sales are huge in the resort areas, where artists regularly show up to promote their work. Alongside the flashy galleries are standards like Quicksilver and ABC store, where you can stock up on swim trunks, sunscreen, and flip-flops.

Beyond Lahaina and Wailea, don't miss the great boutiques lining the streets of small towns like Paia and Makawao. You can purchase boutique fashions and art while strolling through these charming, quieter communities. Notably, several local designers—Tamara Catz, Letarte, and Maui Girl—all produce top-quality island fashions. In neighboring galleries, local artisans turn out gorgeous work in a range of prices. Special souvenirs include rare hardwood bowls and boxes, prints of sea life, Hawaiian quilts, and blown glass.

Specialty food products—pineapples, coconuts, or Maui onions—and "Made in Maui" jams and jellies make great, less expensive souvenirs. Cook Kwee's Maui Cookies have gained a following, as have Maui Potato Chips. Coffee sellers now offer Maui-grown-and-roasted beans alongside the better-known Kona varieties. Remember that fresh fruit must be inspected by the U.S. Department of Agriculture before it can leave the state, so it's safest to buy a box that has already passed inspection.

Business hours for individual shops on the island are usually 9 to 5, seven days a week. Shops on Front Street and in shopping centers tend to stay open later (until 9 or 10 on weekends).

WEST MAUI

SHOPPING CENTERS

Lahaina Cannery Mall. This building, reminiscent of an old pineapple cannery, houses 50 shops. The mall hosts fabulous free events year-round like the Keiki Hula Festival and an annual ice-sculpting competition. Free ukulele lessons are available on Tuesday afternoon. Recommended stops include Na Hoku, purveyor of striking Hawaiian heirloom-quality jewelry and pearls, and Banana Wind, which carries island-inspired home decor. Whether you're searching for surf and skate threads or tropical resort wear, Crazy Shirt, Hawaiian Island Creations, Serendipity, and other retailers will give you ample selections. ⊠ *1221 Honoapiilani Hwy., Lahaina* ☎ *808/661–5304* ⊕ *www.lahainacannerymall.com.*

The Outlets of Maui. If discounted designer brands don't entice you to visit this Lahaina retail spot, the artisanal gelato most definitely will. Once you're done perusing goods at Adidas, Gap, Calvin Klein, or Maui Jim sunglasses, you can refuel with wood-fire pizzas and crafted cocktails from Pi Artisan Pizzeria, or locally spun confections from Ono Gelato. ✉ *900 Front St., Lahaina* ☎ *808/661–8277* ⊕ *www.theoutletsofmaui.com.*

Fodor's Choice ★ **Whalers Village.** Chic Whalers Village has a whaling museum and wonderful restaurants and shops. Upscale haunts include Louis Vuitton and Coach, and beautyphiles can get their fix at Sephora. Peruse elegant koa home accessories and other local gifts at Martin and MacArthur. The complex also offers fun diversions: Hawaiian artisans display their crafts on Monday; hula dancers perform on an outdoor stage some nights from 7 to 8 pm; jazz is performed every first Sunday of the month; and Polynesian rhythms resound on Saturday. If you find yourself there on the first Saturday of May, the Maui Onion Festival is a fun foodie event. ✉ *2435 Kaanapali Pkwy., Kaanapali* ☎ *808/661–4567* ⊕ *www.whalersvillage.com.*

> ### BEST MADE-ON-MAUI GIFTS
>
> ■ *Koa* jewelry boxes from **Maui Hands.**
>
> ■ Sushi platters and bamboo chopsticks from the **Maui Crafts Guild.**
>
> ■ Black pearl pendant from **Maui Divers.**
>
> ■ Handmade Hawaiian quilt from **Hana Coast Gallery.**
>
> ■ Jellyfish paperweight from **Hot Island Glass.**
>
> ■ Ukulele from **Mele Ukulele.**
>
> ■ Hawaiian spice blends from **Volcano Spice Co.**
>
> ■ Plumeria lei, made by you!

BOOKSTORES

Fodor's Choice ★ **Maui Friends of the Library Used Book Store.** Behind the Wharf Cinema Center, this nonprofit bookshop is run by volunteers who let you spend a few minutes (or hours) browsing shelves filled with mystery, sci-fi, fiction, military history, and "oddball" volumes. There's a nice section reserved for new Hawaiiana books. Finished with your vacation reading? You can donate it to benefit the island's public libraries. ✉ *658 Front St., Lahaina* ☎ *808/667–2696* ⊕ *www.mfol.org.*

CLOTHING

Honolua Surf Company. If you're in the mood for colorful print shirts and sundresses, check out this surf shop. It's popular with young women and men for surf trunks, casual clothing, and accessories. ✉ *845 Front St., Lahaina* ☎ *808/661–8848* ⊕ *www.honoluasurf.com.*

FOOD

Lahaina Square Shopping Center Foodland. This Foodland serves West Maui and is open daily from 6 am to midnight. ✉ *878 Front St., Lahaina* ☎ *808/661–0975.*

Safeway. The chain has three stores on the island open 24 hours daily. ✉ *Lahaina Cannery Mall, 1221 Honoapiilani Hwy., Lahaina* ☎ *808/667–4392.*

Take Home Maui. The folks at this colorful grocery and deli in West Maui will supply, pack, and deliver produce to the airport or your hotel. They can even ship the produce straight from the farm to your door. ✉ *121 Dickenson St., Lahaina* ☎ *808/661–8067* ⊕ *www.takehomemaui.com.*

GALLERIES

Lahaina Printsellers Ltd. Hawaii's largest selection of original antique maps and prints of Hawaii and the Pacific is available here. You can also buy museum-quality reproductions. ✉ *Whalers Village, 2435 Kaanapali Pkwy., Kaanapali* ☎ *808/667–7617* ⊕ *www.printsellers.com.*

Lik Lahaina. Fine-art photograher Peter Lik is known all over the world. It's easy to understand why when you see his exquisite and hyper-real pictures of vast Maui landscapes displayed in this Lahaina gallery. ✉ *712 Front St., Lahaina* ☎ *808/661–6623* ⊕ *www.lik.com/galleries/lahaina.html.*

Village Gallery. This gallery houses the landscape paintings of popular local artists Betty Hay Freeland, George Allan, Joseph Fletcher, Pamela Andelin, Fred KenKnight, and Macario Pascual. There's a second location in Kapalua at the Ritz-Carlton. ✉ *120 Dickenson St., Lahaina* ☎ *808/661–4402* ⊕ *www.villagegalleriesmaui.com.*

HOME FURNISHINGS

Hale Zen. If you're shopping for gifts in West Maui, don't miss this store packed with beautiful island-inspired pieces for the home. Most of the teak furniture and home accessories are imported from Bali, but local purveyors supply the inventory of clothing, jewelry, beauty products, kitchenware, and food. ✉ *180 Dickenson St., Suite 111, Lahaina* ☎ *808/661–4802* ⊕ *www.halezen.com.*

JEWELRY

Jessica's Gems. Specializing in black pearls, Jessica's Gems also has a sublime selection of Hawaiian heirloom jewelry and locally made sterling silver, including custom designs by David Welty, Dave Haake, and Cici Maui Designs. ✉ *Whalers Village, 2435 Kaanapali Pkwy., Kaanapali* ☎ *808/661–4223* ⊕ *www.jessicasgemsmaui.com.*

Lahaina Scrimshaw. Here you can buy brooches, rings, pendants, cuff links, tie tacks, and collector's items adorned with intricately carved sailors' art. The store sells a few antiques, but most pieces are modern creations. ✉ *845A Front St., Lahaina* ☎ *808/661–8820* ⊕ *www.lahainascrimshawmaui.com.*

Maui Divers. This company has been crafting pearls, coral, and traditional gemstones into jewelry for more than 55 years. ✉ *640 Front St., Lahaina* ☎ *808/661–0988* ⊕ *www.mauidivers.com.*

CENTRAL MAUI

SHOPPING CENTERS

Maui Marketplace. On the busy stretch of Dairy Road, this behemoth mall near Kahului Airport couldn't be more conveniently located. The 20-acre complex houses several outlet stores and big retailers, such as Pier One Imports, Sports Authority, and Old Navy. Sample local and ethnic cuisines at the Kau Kau Corner food court. ✉ *270 Dairy Rd., Kahului* ☎ *808/873–0400.*

Native Intelligence. This store in the heart of Wailuku champions cultural traditions and craftsmanship. It has curated Hawaiian and Polynesian works of art that include traditional wear, weaponry, photography, books, music, and even surfboards. ⊠ *1980 Main St., Wailuku* ☎ *808/249–2421* ⊕ *www.native-intel.com.*

Queen Kaahumanu Center. Maui's largest mall has 75 stores, a movie theater, and a food court. The mall's interesting rooftop, composed of a series of manta ray–like umbrella shades, is easily spotted. Stop at Camellia Seeds for what locals call crack seed, a snack made from dried fruits, nuts, and lots of sugar. Hawaii-based streetwear can be found at 180 Boardshop. Other stops include mall standards such as Macy's, Pacific Sunwear, and American Eagle Outfitters. ⊠ *275 W. Kaahumanu Ave., Kahului* ☎ *808/877–3369* ⊕ *www.queenkaahumanucenter.com.*

ARTS AND CRAFTS

Fodor's Choice ★ **Mele Ukulele.** For a professional quality, authentic ukulele, skip the souvenir shops. Mele's handcrafted beauties are made of koa or mahogany and strung and finished by the store's owner, Michael Rock. ⊠ *1750 Kaahumanu Ave., Wailuku* ☎ *808/244–3938* ⊕ *www.meleukulele.com.*

CLOTHING

Ha Wahine. At this clothing store, statement Polynesian prints are redefined in vibrantly colored blouses, *pareos* (beach wraps), dresses, and aloha shirts. All clothing is designed and made locally, as is most of the jewelry. ⊠ *53 N. Market St., Wailuku* ☎ *808/344–1642.*

Hi-Tech. Stop here immediately after deplaning to stock up on surf trunks, windsurfing gear, bikinis, or sundresses. You can also sign up for windsurfing or kitesurfing lessons while you're at it. ⊠ *425 Koloa St., Kahului* ☎ *808/877–2111* ⊕ *www.surfmaui.com.*

FLEA MARKETS

Maui Swap Meet. Crafts, souvenirs, fruit, shells, and aloha attire make this flea market in a college parking lot the island's biggest bargain. Maui's food trucks and specialty doughnuts are an added draw. ⊠ *Off Kahului Beach Rd., Kahului* ☎ *808/244–3100* ⊕ *www.mauiexposition. com* ⊡ *50¢* ⊙ *Sat. 7 am–1 pm.*

FOOD

Maui Coffee Roasters. The best stop for Kona and island coffees on Maui is this café and roasting house near Kahului Airport. Salespeople give good advice and will ship items, and you even get a free cup of joe in a signature to-go cup when you buy a pound of coffee. ⊠ *444 Hana Hwy., Kahului* ☎ *808/877–2877* ⊕ *www.mauicoffeeroasters.com.*

Safeway. If you're coming from the airport, this grocery store (one of three on the island) may be a useful stop. It's open 24 hours daily. ⊠ *170 E. Kamehameha Ave., Kahului* ☎ *808/877–3377.*

THE SOUTH SHORE

SHOPPING CENTERS

Azeka Place Shopping Center. Azeka II, on the *mauka* (toward the mountains) side of South Kihei Road, has the Coffee Store, Brazilian Beauty Boutique, and Pacific Lotus Gift Shop. Azeka I, the older half on the *makai* (toward the ocean) side of the street, has a decent Vietnamese restaurant, B&B Scuba for rentals and dive bookings, Ono Gelato, and Kihei's post office. ✉ *1280 S. Kihei Rd., Kihei* ☎ *808/879–5000.*

Fodor'sChoice ★ **Kihei Kalama Village Marketplace.** The shaded outdoor stalls at this fun place sell everything from printed and hand-painted T-shirts and sundresses to jewelry, pottery, wood carvings, fruit, and gaudily painted coconut husks—some, but not all, made by local craftspeople. ✉ *1941 S. Kihei Rd., Kihei* ☎ *808/879–6610.*

The Shops at Wailea. Stylish, upscale, and close to most of the resorts, this mall brings high fashion to Wailea. Luxury boutiques such as Gucci, Cos Bar, and Tiffany & Co. are represented, as are less-expensive chains like Gap, Guess, and Tommy Bahama's. Several good restaurants face the ocean, and regular Wednesday-night events include live entertainment, art exhibits, and fashion shows. ✉ *3750 Wailea Alanui Dr., Wailea* ☎ *808/891–6770* ⊕ *www.shopsatwailea.com.*

Wailea Gateway Center. While lunch at chef Peter Merriman's Monkeypod is reason enough to venture to Wailea Gateway Center, you might also be enticed by the artisanal confections from Sweet Paradise Chocolate, fine cheese and charcuterie from Guava, Gouda and Caviar, and a vast collection of vintage clothing from the Aloha Shirt Museum. ✉ *34 Wailea Gateway Pl., Wailea.*

CLOTHING

Cruise. Sundresses, swimwear, sandals, bright beach towels, and a few nice pieces of resort wear fill this upscale resort boutique. ✉ *Grand Wailea Resort, 3850 Wailea Alanui Dr., Wailea* ☎ *808/874–3998.*

Hilo Hattie Fashion Center. Hawaii's largest manufacturer of aloha shirts also carries brightly colored blouses, skirts, and children's clothing. You can also pick up many local gift items here. ✉ *297 Piikea Ave., Kihei* ☎ *808/875–4545* ⊕ *www.hilohattie.com.*

Sisters & Company. Opened by four sisters, this little shop has a lot to offer: casual lines like True Religion and Michael Stars, and Hard Tail loungewear. One sister, Rhonda, runs a tiny, hip hair salon in back, while another, Caroline, offers mani-pedis and waxing. ✉ *The Shops at Wailea, 3750 Wailea Alanui Dr., Wailea* ☎ *808/874–0003* ⊕ *www. sistersandco.com.*

3

Tommy Bahama's. It's hard to find a man on Maui who *isn't* wearing a TB–logo aloha shirt. For better or worse, here's where you can get yours. And just to prove you're on vacation, grab a drink or dessert on the way out at the restaurant attached to the shop. ⊠ *The Shops at Wailea, 3750 Wailea Alanui Dr., Wailea* ☎ *808/879–7828* ⊕ *www. tommybahamas.com.*

FOOD

Foodland. In Kihei town center, this is the most convenient supermarket for those staying in Wailea. It's open around the clock. ⊠ *1881 S. Kihei Rd., Kihei* ☎ *808/879–9350.*

Safeway. Open 24 hours a day, this store is a convenient place to stock up for South Maui stays. ⊠ *277 Piikea Ave., Kihei* ☎ *808/891–9120.*

UPCOUNTRY, THE NORTH SHORE, AND HANA

CLOTHING

Alice in Hulaland. While the store is famous for its vintage tees, it also carries a lovely mix of gift items and casual wear for the whole family. Best sellers include burnout T-shirts, Goorin Bros. hats, and beach-staple Havaianas slippers. ⊠ *19 Baldwin Ave., Paia* ☎ *808/579–9922* ⊕ *www.aliceinhulaland.com.*

Designing Wahine Emporium. At this Upcountry haven for Hawaiian merchandise and Balinese imports, you can find endless gift options like authentic aloha shirts, jams and jellies, children's clothes and books, bath and beauty products, and home decor crafted from wood. ⊠ *3640 Baldwin Ave., Makawao* ☎ *808/573–0990.*

Pink By Nature. Owner Desiree Martinez dresses the modern bohemian, as she keeps the rustic store stocked with local jewelry and pieces from Indah, Mother Denim, Bella Dahl, and Linea Pelle. ⊠ *3663 Baldwin Ave., Makawao* ☎ *808/572–9576.*

Fodor's Choice ★ **Tamara Catz.** This Maui designer has a worldwide following, and her superstylish threads have appeared in many fashion magazines. If you're looking for ethereal tunics, delicately embroidered maxis, or beaded wedge sandals, this is the place. Catz also has a bridal line that is elegant and beach-perfect. Her pieces cost a pretty penny, but if you visit around May or December, you might luck out on one of her sample sales. ⊠ *83 Hana Hwy., Paia* ☎ *808/579–9184* ⊕ *www.tamaracatz.com.*

FOOD

Fodor's Choice ★ **Mana Foods.** At this bustling health-food store you can stock up on local fish and grass-fed beef for your barbecue. You'll find the best selection of organic produce on the island, as well as a great bakery and deli. ⊠ *49 Baldwin Ave., Paia* ☎ *808/579–8078* ⊕ *www.manafoodsmaui. com.*

Ono Gelato. Fresh gelato made with organic fruit is the drawing card here. You'll also find jams, jellies, and dressings from Jeff Gomes; coffees from Maui Oma Roasters; and treats from the Maui Culinary Academy. There's a location in Kihei and two in Lahaina, which carry

Continued on page 268

ALL ABOUT LEI

Lei brighten every occasion in Hawaii, from birthdays to bar mitzvahs to baptisms. Creative artisans weave nature's bounty—flowers, ferns, vines, and seeds—into gorgeous creations that convey an array of heartfelt messages: "Welcome," "Congratulations," "Good luck," "Farewell," "Thank you," "I love you." When it's difficult to find the right words, a lei expresses exactly the right sentiment.

WHERE TO BUY THE BEST LEI

In Honolulu's Chinatown, you'll encounter numerous lei "stands" that offer grand arrays of gorgeous garlands. Every florist shop in the Islands sells lei; you can also treat yourself to a lei while shopping for provisions at any supermarket or box store. And you'll always find lei sellers at crafts fairs and outdoor festivals.

LEI ETIQUETTE

■ To wear a closed lei, drape it over your shoulders, half in front and half in back. Open lei are worn around the neck, with the ends draped over the front in equal lengths.

■ Pikake, ginger, and other sweet, delicate blossoms are "feminine" lei. Men opt for cigar, crown flower, and ti leaf, which are sturdier and don't emit as much fragrance.

■ Lei are always presented with a kiss, a custom that supposedly dates back to World War II when a hula dancer fancied an officer at a U.S.O. show. Taking a dare from members of her troupe, she took off her lei, placed it around his neck, and kissed him on the cheek.

■ You shouldn't wear a lei before you give it to someone else. Hawaiians believe the lei absorbs your *mana* (spirit); if you give your lei away, you'll be giving away part of your essence.

ORCHID

Growing wild on every continent except Antarctica, orchids—which range in color from yellow to green to purple—comprise the largest family of plants in the world. There are more than 20,000 species of orchids, but only three are native to Hawaii—and they are very rare. The pretty lavender vanda you see hanging by the dozens at local lei stands has probably been imported from Thailand.

MAILE

Maile, an endemic twining vine with a heady aroma, is sacred to Laka, goddess of the hula. In ancient times, dancers wore maile and decorated hula altars with it to honor Laka. Today, "open" maile lei usually are given to men. Instead of ribbon, interwoven lengths of maile are used at dedications of new businesses. The maile is untied, never snipped, for doing so would symbolically "cut" the company's success.

ILIMA

Designated by Hawaii's Territorial Legislature in 1923 as the official flower of the island of Oahu, the golden ilima is so delicate it lasts for just a day. Five to seven hundred blossoms are needed to make one garland. Queen Emma, wife of King Kamehameha IV, preferred ilima over all other lei, which may have led to the incorrect belief that they were reserved only for royalty.

PLUMERIA

This ubiquitous flower is named after Charles Plumier, the noted French botanist who discovered it in Central America in the late 1600s. Plumeria ranks among the most popular lei in Hawaii because it's fragrant, hardy, plentiful, inexpensive, and requires very little care. Although yellow is the most common color, you'll also find plumeria lei in shades of pink, red, orange, and "rainbow" blends.

PIKAKE

Favored for its fragile beauty and sweet scent, pikake was introduced from India. In lieu of pearls, many brides in Hawaii adorn themselves with long, multiple strands of white pikake. Princess Kaiulani enjoyed showing guests her beloved pikake and peacocks at Ainahau, her Waikiki home. Interestingly, pikake is the Hawaiian word for both the bird and the blossom.

KUKUI

The kukui (candlenut) is Hawaii's state tree. Early Hawaiians strung kukui nuts (which are quite oily) together and burned them for light; mixed burned nuts with oil to make an indelible dye; and mashed roasted nuts to consume as a laxative. Kukui nut lei may not have been made until after Western contact, when the Hawaiians saw black beads from Europe and wanted to imitate them.

TOMS shoes and island-inspired Nina Kuna jewelry. ✉ *115 Hana Hwy., Paia* ☎ *808/579–9201* ⊕ *www.onogelatocompany.com.*

GALLERIES

Fodor's Choice
★ **Hana Coast Gallery.** One of the best-curated galleries on the island, this 3,000-square-foot facility has handcrafted koa furniture, marble sculptures, photography, and jewelry on consignment from local artists. ✉ *Travaasa Hana, Hana Hwy., Hana* ☎ *808/248–8636, 800/637–0188* ⊕ *www.hanacoast.com.*

Fodor's Choice
★ **Maui Crafts Guild.** The island's only artist cooperative, Maui Crafts Guild is crammed with treasures. Resident artists produce lead-glazed pottery, basketry, glass and feather art, photography, ceramics, and pressed-flower art. The prices are surprisingly low. ✉ *120 Hana Hwy., Paia* ☎ *808/579–9697* ⊕ *www.mauicraftsguild.com.*

Maui Hands. This gallery shows work by hundreds of local artists, including exquisite woodwork, lovely ceramics, authentic Niihau shell lei, and famous wave photography by Clark Little. There are locations in Lahaina, Makawao, and at the Hyatt Regency in Kaanapali. ✉ *84 Hana Hwy., Paia* ☎ *808/579–9245* ⊕ *www.mauihands.com.*

Viewpoints Gallery. This friendly gallery is co-owned by six local artists and offers eclectic paintings, sculptures, photography, ceramics, and glass, along with locally made jewelry and quilts. In a courtyard across from Market Fresh Bistro, its monthly exhibits feature artists from various disciplines. ✉ *3620 Baldwin Ave., Makawao* ☎ *808/572–5979* ⊕ *www.viewpointsgallerymaui.com.*

JEWELRY

Maui Master Jewelers. The shop's exterior is as rustic as all the old buildings of Makawao, so be prepared for the elegance of the handcrafted jewelry displayed within. The store has added a diamond collection to its designs. ✉ *3655 Baldwin Ave., Makawao* ☎ *808/573–5400* ⊕ *www.mauimasterjewelers.com.*

SWIMWEAR

Fodor's Choice
★ **Maui Girl.** This is *the* place on Maui for swimwear, cover-ups, beach hats, and sandals. Maui Girl designs its own suits, which have been spotted in *Sports Illustrated* fashion shoots, and imports tinier versions from Brazil as well. Tops and bottoms can be purchased separately, increasing your chances of finding the perfect fit. ✉ *12 Baldwin Ave., Paia* ☎ *808/579–9266* ⊕ *www.maui-girl.com.*

SPAS

Updated by
Eliza Escaño-
Vasquez

Traditional Swedish massage and European facials anchor most spa menus on the island, though you can also find shiatsu, ayurveda, aromatherapy, and other body treatments drawn from cultures across the globe. It can be fun to try some more local treatments or ingredients, though. *Lomilomi,* traditional Hawaiian massage involving powerful strokes down the length of the body, is a regional specialty passed down through generations. Many treatments incorporate local plants and flowers. *Awapuhi,* or Hawaiian ginger, and *noni,* a pungent-smelling fruit, are regularly used for their therapeutic benefits. *Limu,* or seaweed, and even coffee are employed in rousing salt scrubs and soaks.

WEST MAUI

Fodor's Choice ★ **Spa Montage, Kapalua Bay.** This spa's nondescript entrance opens onto an airy, modern beach house with a panoramic view of Kapalua Bay. With amenities including a gym, a saltwater infinity pool, and outdoor hydrotherapy circuits, you can easily spend a day meandering about the spa's three floors without feeling cooped up. The menu includes some ancient Hawaiian healing practices. The *lomi* wrap, designed by Big Island resident and healer Darrell Lapulapu, begins with a special cava tea for instant relaxation, is followed by a body wrap of cacao and kukui oil, and finishes with *lomilomi* (a traditional Hawaiian massage involving strokes down the length of the body). The café and juice bar serve health potions that combine pure fruits and juiced veggies with natural additives like yogurt. Lunch can be served poolside or in the waiting areas. ⊠ *100 Bay Dr., Kapalua* ☎ *808/665–8282* ☞ *$160 60-min massage, $246 half-day spa package. Hair salon, sauna, steam room. Gym with: cardiovascular machines, free weights, weight-training equipment. Services: aromatherapy, body wraps, facials, hydrotherapy, massage. Classes and programs: free Sunday beach walk, Pilates, yoga, Zumba.*

Fodor's Choice ★ **Waihua Spa, Ritz-Carlton, Kapalua.** At this gorgeous 17,500-square-foot spa, you enter a blissful maze where floor-to-ceiling riverbed stones lead to serene treatment rooms, couples' *hales* (cabanas), and a rain forest–like grotto with a Jacuzzi, dry cedar sauna, and eucalyptus steam rooms. Hang out in the coed waiting area, where sliding-glass doors open to a whirlpool overlooking a taro-patch garden. Exfoliate any rough spots with a pineapple-papaya or coffee scrub; then wash off in a private outdoor shower garden before indulging in a *lomilomi* massage (traditional Hawaiian massage involving powerful strokes down the length of the body). High-end beauty treatments include advanced oxygen technology to tighten and nourish mature skin. The boutique has a highly coveted collection of organic, local, and high-end beauty products, fitness wear, and Maui-made jewelry and natural skin-care lines. The fitness center is handsomely appointed. ⊠ *Ritz-Carlton, Kapalua, 1 Ritz-Carlton Dr., Kapalua* ☎ *808/669–6200, 800/262–8440* ⊕ *www. ritzcarlton.com* ☞ *$165 50-min massage, $454 half-day spa packages. Hair salon, hot tubs (outdoor and indoor), sauna, steam room. Gym with: cardiovascular machines, free weights, weight-training equipment. Services: aromatherapy, body wraps, facials, massage. Classes and programs: cycling, Pilates, yoga.*

SOUTH SHORE

Awili Spa and Salon, ANdAZ Maui at Wailea. The Japanese term *omakase* means to trust the chef to create a fulfilling dining experience. The Awilii Spa and Salon uses this concept at its apothecary or blending bar (*awili* means to mix), where freshly dehydrated organic and local fruits and herbs are made into oils and blended together according to a guest's preferences. Papaya or pineapple pulp are made into powder for scrubs, and local chilis into a warming massage oil. Set aside an extra hour to fully indulge in the blending bar, or opt for ready-made concoctions like the kava, noni, and aloe combo for body exfoliation. The cool, soothing interior of this spa is an extension of the minimalist, monochromatic style of the ANdAZ Maui at Wailea. Relaxation lounges are stocked with thoughtful amenities like tea, coconut macaroons, and edamame hummus. ⊠ *ANdAZ Resort at Wailea, 3550 Wailea Alanui Dr., Wailea* ☎ *808/573–1234* ⊕ *maui.andaz.hyatt.com* ⚲ *$175 60-min massage. Heated plunge pool, dry and steam sauna, hair and nail salon. Gym with: Matrix Fitness equipment and free weights. Services: Body wraps, facials, hair trim and style services, make-up, manicure, massage, pedicure, waxing. Classes: sunrise and sunset yoga, stretch and cardio.*

Spa Grande, Grand Wailea Resort. This 50,000-square-foot spa makes others seem like well-appointed closets. Slathered in honey (fresh from the hotel's own apiary) and wrapped up in the steam room (if you go for the honey steam wrap), you'll feel like royalty. All treatments include a loofah scrub and a trip to the *termé,* a hydrotherapy circuit including five therapeutic baths with Hawaii-grown esssences. The circuit includes a Japanese Furo bath, waterfall massage, cold plunge pool, jet showers, and a large Roman hot tub. To fully enjoy the baths, plan to arrive an hour before your treatment. Free with any treatment, the *termé* is also available separately for $55 for two hours. At times—especially during the holidays—this wonderland can be crowded. When it isn't, it's difficult to pry yourself away. ⊠ *Grand Wailea Resort, 3850 Wailea Alanui Dr., Wailea* ☎ *808/875–1234, 800/888–6100* ⊕ *www. grandwailea.com* ⚲ *$160 50-min massage, $442 day-spa packages. Hair salon, hot tub, sauna, steam room. Gym with: Cardiovascular machines, free weights, weight-training equipment. Services: Aromatherapy, body wraps, facials, hydrotherapy, massage, Vichy shower. Classes and programs: Aquaerobics, cycling, Pilates, Spinning, yoga.*

Fodor's Choice ★ **The Spa at Four Seasons Resort Maui.** The resort's hawk-like attention to detail and genuine hospitality are reflected here. Thoughtful gestures like fresh flowers beneath the massage table, organic ginger tea in the relaxation room, and your choice of music eases your mind and muscles before the treatment even begins. The spa is romantic yet modern, and the therapists are superb. Thanks to an exclusive partnership, the spa offers excellent treatments created by skin guru Kate Somerville. The Lomi Mohala massage uses muscle-relaxing oils blended exclusively for the treatment. Shop for sustainable and organic beauty products like ISUN and Ola Hawaii from the Big Island, or book an appointment at the Ajne blending bar to customize a scent according to your body chemistry. For the ultimate indulgence, reserve one of the seaside open-air *hale hau* (traditional thatch-roof houses). You can have two therapists realign your body and spirit with a *lomilomi* massage (traditional Hawaiian massage involving powerful strokes down the length of the body). ⊠ *Four Seasons Resort Maui, 3900 Wailea Alanui Dr., Wailea* ☎ *808/874–8000, 800/334–6284* ⊕ *www.fourseasons.com/maui* ⚲ *$165 50-min massage. Hair salon, steam room. Gym with: Cardiovascular machines, free weights, weight-training equipment. Services: Aromatherapy, body wraps, facials, massage. Classes and programs:*

Aquaerobics, meditation, personal training, Pilates, Spinning, tai chi, yoga.

ROAD TO HANA

The Spa at Travaasa Hana. A bamboo gate opens into an outdoor sanctuary with a lava-rock basking pool and hot tub. At first glimpse, this spa seems to have been organically grown, not built. The decor can hardly be called decor—it's a sprawling garden that overlooks Hana Bay. Ferns still wet from Hana's frequent downpours nourish the spirit as you rest with a cup of Hawaiian herbal tea, or take an invigorating dip in the cold plunge pool, or have a therapist stretch your limbs as you soak in the warm waters of the aquatic therapy pool. Luxurious skin-care teatments feature organic products from Amala and essential oils from locally produced Maui Excellent. ⊠ *Travaasa Hana, 5031 Hana Hwy., Hana* ☎ *808/270–5290* ⊕ *www.travaasa.com/hana* ✆ *$130 60-min massage, $200 spa package. Outdoor hot tub, steam room. Gym with: Cardiovascular machines, free weights, weight-training equipment. Services: Aromatherapy, body wraps, facials, massage. Classes and programs: Meditation, Pilates, yoga.*

ENTERTAINMENT AND NIGHTLIFE

Updated by
Eliza Escaño-
Vasquez

Looking for wild island nightlife? We can't promise you'll always find it here—and sometimes you'll have to be the party. This island has little of Waikiki's after-hours decadence, and the club scene can be quirky, depending on the season and day of the week. But Maui will surprise you with a big-name concert or world-class DJ. Outdoor music festivals are usually held at the Maui Arts & Cultural Center, or even a randomly scouted performance space in Hana.

Block parties in each town happen on Friday, with Wailuku leading the pack. Main streets are blocked for local bands, food vendors, and street performers, and it's a family-friendly affair. Lahaina, Paia, and Kihei are your best bets for action. Outside those towns, you might be able to hit an "on" night in Paia (North Shore) or Makawao (Upcountry). Charley's in Paia is usually the go-to venue for mainland and international DJs looking to play an intimate set. But, generally, these towns are on the mellow side. Your best option? Pick up the free *Maui Time Weekly*, or Thursday's edition of the *Maui News*, where you can find a listing of all your after-dark options, island-wide.

ENTERTAINMENT

Before 10 pm there's a lot to offer by way of luau shows, dinner cruises, and tiki-lighted cocktail hours. Aside from that, you should at least be able to find some down-home DJ-spinning or the strum of acoustic guitars at your nearest watering hole or restaurant.

DINNER CRUISES AND SHOWS

There's no better place to see the sun set on the Pacific than from one of Maui's many boat tours. You can find a tour to fit your mood, as the options range from a quiet, sit-down dinner to a festive, beer-swigging booze cruise. Note, however, that many cocktail cruises have put a cap on the number of free drinks offered with open bars, instead including a limited number of drinks per ticket.

Tours leave from Maalaea or Lahaina harbors. Be sure to arrive at least 15 minutes early (count in the time it will take to park). The dinner cruises typically feature music and are generally packed—which is great if you're feeling social, but you might have to fight for a good seat. You can usually get a much better meal at one of the local restaurants, and opt instead for a different type of tour. Most non-dinner cruises offer *pupu* (appetizers) and sometimes a chocolate-and-champagne toast.

Winds are consistent in summer but variable in winter—sometimes making for a rocky ride. If you're worried about seasickness, you might consider a catamaran, which is much more stable than a monohull. Keep in mind that the boat crews are experienced in dealing with such matters. A Dramamine before the trip should keep you in tip-top shape, but if you feel seasick you should sit in the shade, place a cold rag or ice on the back of your neck, and breathe as you look at the horizon.

FAMILY

Fodor's Choice

★

Hula Girl **Dinner Cruise.** This custom catamaran is one of the slickest and best-equipped boats on the island, complete with a VIP lounge for 12 people by the captain's fly bridge. Trips are on the pricier side, mainly because the initial cost doesn't include the cooked-to-order meals. But if you're willing to splurge a little for live music, an onboard chef, and upscale service, it's absolutely worth it. From mid-December to early April the cruise focuses on whale-watching. Check-in is in front of Leilani's restaurant at Whalers Village. ⊠ *2435 Kaanapali Pkwy., Kaanapali* ☎ *808/665–0344, 808/667–5980* ⊕ *www.sailingmaui.com* ⊠ *$78* ⊙ *Tues., Thurs., and Sat. 4:30–7 pm.*

Pride of Maui **Charters.** A 65-foot catamaran built specifically for Maui's waters, the *Pride of Maui* has a spacious cabin with live entertainment, dance floor, and large upper deck for unobstructed sightseeing. Evening cruises include top-shelf cocktails and an impressive spread of baby back ribs, grilled chicken, warm artichoke dip, Maui onion tartlets, and seasonal desserts. ⊠ *Maalaea Harbor, 101 Maalaea Boat Harbor Rd., Maalaea* ☎ *877/867–7433* ⊕ *www.prideofmaui.com* ⊠ *$69.65* ⊙ *Tues., Thurs., and Sat. 5–7.*

Teralani Sailing Charters. These catamarans are modern, spotless, and laid out nicely for dining and lounging. They head back shortly after sunset, which means there's plenty of light to savor dinner and the view. During whale-watching season, the best seats are the corner booths by the stern of the boat. Catered by local fave Pizza Paradiso, the meal outdoes most dinner-cruise spreads, with ratatouille, chipotle-citrus rotisserie chicken, and potato gratin and sun-dried tomatoes. The trip departs from Kaaanapali's Dig Me Beach in front of Leilani's at Whalers Village. ⊠ *2435 Kaaanapali Pkwy., Kaanapali* ☎ *808/661–1230* ⊕ *www.teralani.net* ⊠ *$93.95* ⊙ *Daily, hrs vary.*

The popular Old Lahaina Luau surveys Hawaii's history through music, hula, chanting, and more.

FILM

In the heat of the afternoon a theater may feel like paradise. There are megaplexes showing first-run movies in Kukui Mall (Kihei), Lahaina Center, Maui Mall (Kahului), and Kaahumanu Shopping Center (Kahului).

Fodor's Choice ★ **Maui Film Festival.** From mid-December through early January, this international festival attracts big-name celebrities to Maui for cinema and elegant soirees under the stars at the Maui Arts & Cultural Center. Throughout the year, the center presents art-house films on selected evenings, often accompanied by live music, cocktails, and wine. ⊠ *1 Cameron Way, Kahului* ☎ *808/579–9244 information, 808/242–7469 box office* ⊕ *www.mauifilmfestival.com.*

LUAU

Locals still hold luau to mark milestones or as informal, family-style gatherings. For tourists, luaus are a major attraction and, for that reason, have become big business. Keep in mind—some are watered-down tourist traps just trying to make a buck; others offer a night you'll never forget. As the saying goes, you get what you pay for. ■ TIP→ **Many of the best luau book weeks or months in advance, so reserve early.** Plan your luau night early on in your trip to help you get into the Hawaiian spirit.

Fodor's Choice ★ **Feast at Lele.** This place redefines the luau by crossing it with island-style fine dining in an intimate beach setting. Each course of this succulent sit-down meal is prepared by chef James McDonald of the nearby PacificO restaurant, and coincides with the island cultures—Hawaiian, Samoan, Aotearoan, Tahitian—featured onstage. Wine, spirits, and cocktail options are copious and go beyond the usual tropical concoctions. Lahaina's gorgeous sunset serves as the backdrop to the show, which forgoes gimmicks and pageantry for an authentic expression of Polynesian chants and dances. "Lele," by the way, is a more traditional name for Lahaina. ⊠ *505 Front St., Lahaina* ☎ *808/667–5353* ⊕ *www.feastatlele.com* ✉ *$120* ⌲ *Reservations essential* ☉ *Daily. Oct.–Jan., 5:30 pm; Feb.–Apr. and Sept., 6 pm; May–Aug., 6:30 pm.*

Grand Luau at Honuaula. This show captivates with a playful interpretation of Hawaiian mythology and folklore. Indulge in pre-luau fun with Hawaiian games, lei making, and photo ops with the cast, then witness the unearthing of the *kalua* pig from the underground oven. Traditional dances share a vision of the first Polynesian voyage to the island, and there are also dancers on stilts, an iridescent aerialist suspended by silk, and many elaborate costumes. As a finale, champion fire-knife dancer Ifi Soo brings the house down with a fiery display. ⊠ *Grand Wailea Resort and Spa, 3850 Wailea Alanui Dr., Wailea* ☎ *808/875–7710* ⊕ *www.honuaula-luau.com* ✉ *$105 standard, $117 premium* ☉ *Mon. and Thurs.–Sat. 4–8 pm.*

FAMILY **Hyatt Regency Maui Drums of the Pacific Luau.** By Kaanapali Beach, this luau shines in every category—convenient parking, well-made food, smooth-flowing buffet lines, and a nicely paced program that touches on Hawaiian, Samoan, Tahitian, Fijian, Tongan, and Maori cultures. Some guests get tickled by the audience hula tutorial on stage. The finale features three fire-knife dancers. You'll feast on delicious Hawaiian delicacies like shoyu chicken, *lomilomi* (rubbed with onions and herbs) salmon, and Pacific ahi *poke* (pickled raw tuna, tossed with herbs and seasonings). The dessert spread consists of chocolate, pineapple, and coconut indulgences. An open bar offers beer, wine, and standard tropical mixes. ⊠ *Hyatt Regency Maui, 200 Nohea Kai Dr., Kaanapali* ☎ *808/667–4727* ⊕ *www.maui.hyatt.com* ✉ *$110 standard, $125 preferred, $145 VIP* ☉ *Tues., Wed., Fri., and Sat. 5:30–8:30 pm (5–8 pm, Oct.–Mar.).*

FAMILY

Fodor's Choice

★

Old Lahaina Luau. Considered the best luau on Maui, it's certainly the most traditional. Immerse yourself in making *kapa* (bark cloth), weaving *lauhala* (coconut palm fronds), and pounding *poi* at the various interactive stations. Sitting either at a table or on a *lauhala* mat, you can dine on Hawaiian cuisine such as pork *laulau* (wrapped with taro sprouts in *ti* leaves), ahi *poke* (pickled raw tuna tossed with herbs and seasonings), *lomilomi* salmon (rubbed with onions and herbs), and *haupia* (coconut pudding). At sunset, the historical journey touches on the arrival of the Polynesians, the influence of missionaries, and, later, the advent of tourism. Talented performers will charm you with beautiful music, powerful chanting, and a variety of hula styles, from *kahiko*, the ancient way of communicating with the gods, to *auana*, the modern hula. You won't see fire dancers here, as they aren't considered traditional. ■**TIP**➔ **This luau sells out regularly, so make reservations before your trip to Maui.** ⊠ *1251 Front St., near Lahaina Cannery Mall, Lahaina* ☎ *808/667–1998* ⊕ *www.oldlahainaluau.com* ✉ *$105* ⌲ *Reservations essential* ☉ *Oct.–Mar., daily 5:15 pm; Apr.–Sept., daily 5:45 pm.*

Wailea Beach Marriott Te Au Moana. Te Au Moana means "ocean tide," which is all you need to know about the simply breathtaking backdrop for this South Maui luau. The evening begins with lei making, local crafts, and an *imu* (underground oven) ceremony. The tasty buffet serves a plethora of local staples and desserts like *haupia* (coconut pudding), chocolate chip cookies, macadamia-nut brownies, and key lime squares. The performance seamlessly intertwines ancient Hawaiian stories and contemporary songs with traditional hula and Polynesian dances, concluding with a jaw-dropping solo fire-knife dance. ⊠ *Wailea Beach Marriott, 3700 Wailea Alanui Dr., Wailea* ☎ *808/879–1922* ⊕ *www.marriotthawaii.com* ⊡ *$104* ⌂ *Reservations essential* ☉ *Mon. and Thurs.–Sat. 4:30–8 pm.*

THEATER

For live theater, check local papers for events and showtimes.

Maui Academy of Performing Arts. Founded in 1974, this nonprofit performing-arts group offers fine productions, as well as dance and drama classes for children and teens. Recent shows have included *Fiddler on the Roof,* and *The Emperor and the Nightingale.* ⊠ *81 N. Church St., Wailuku* ☎ *808/244–8760* ⊕ *www.mauiacademy.org* ⊡ *$10–$35.*

FAMILY
Fodor'sChoice
★
Ulalena at Maui Theatre. One of Maui's hottest tickets, *Ulalena* is a musical extravaganza that has received accolades from audiences and Hawaiian culture experts. The powerful ensemble (20 singer-dancers and five musicians) uses creative stage wizardry to give an enchanting portrayal of island history and mythology. Native rhythms from authentic and rare instruments are blended with heart-wrenching chants and aerialist precision, making the 75-minute production seem like a whirlwind. Beer and wine are for sale at the concession stand. ∎**TIP→ Check out dinner-theater packages in conjunction with local restaurants.** ⊠ *Maui Theatre, 878 Front St., Lahaina* ☎ *808/661–9913, 877/688–4800* ⊕ *www.mauitheatre.com* ⊡ *$59.99–$79.99; $139.99 for dinner package* ⌂ *Reservations essential* ☉ *Mon.–Fri. 5 pm, check in at 4:15 pm.*

Warren & Annabelle's. This is a hearty comedy with amazing sleight of hand. Magician Warren Gibson entices guests into his swank nightclub with a gleaming mahogany bar, a grand piano, and a resident ghost named Annabelle who tickles the ivories. Servers efficiently ply you with appetizers (coconut shrimp, crab cakes), desserts (chocolate pots de crème, assorted pies and cheesecakes, crème brûlée), and cocktails, while obliging a few impromptu song requests. Then, guests are ushered into a small theater where magic hilariously ensues. Since this is a nightclub act, no one under 21 is allowed. ⊠ *Lahaina Center, 900 Front St., Lahaina* ☎ *808/667–6244* ⊕ *www.warrenandannabelles.com* ⊡ *$64 or $104.50, including food and drinks* ⌂ *Reservations essential* ☉ *Mon.–Sat. 5 and 7:30.*

NIGHTLIFE

Your best bet when it comes to bars on Maui? If you walk by and it sounds like it's happening, go in. If you want to scope out your options in advance, be sure to check the free *Maui Time Weekly,* found at most stores and restaurants, to find out who's playing where. Don't overlook the resorts and their bars and restaurants. *Maui News* also publishes an entertainment schedule in its Thursday edition of the "Maui Scene." With an open mind (and a little luck), you can usually find some fun.

WEST MAUI

Alaloa Lounge. When ambience weighs heavy on the priority list, this spot at the Ritz-Carlton might just be the ticket. Nightly performances range from jazz to island rhythms. The menu includes a fantastic seared filet mignon on a pretzel roll, and Kai Sushi's artisanal creations are available to order. Step onto the lanai for that plumeria-tinged Hawaiian air and gaze at the deep blue of the Pacific. ✉ *Ritz-Carlton, Kapalua, 1 Ritz-Carlton Dr., Kapalua* ☎ *808/669–6200* ⊕ *www.ritzcarlton.com.*

> **WHAT'S A LAVA FLOW?**
>
> Can't decide between a piña colada and strawberry daiquiri? Go with a Lava Flow—a mix of light rum, coconut and pineapple juice, and a banana, with a swirl of strawberry purée. Add a wedge of fresh pineapple and a paper umbrella, and mmm . . . good.

Cheeseburger in Paradise. A chain joint on Front Street, this place is known for—what else?—big beefy cheeseburgers, not to mention a great spinach-nut burger. It's a casual place to start your evening, as they have live music (usually classic or contemporary rock) until 10:30 pm. The second-floor balcony gives you a bird's-eye view of Lahaina's Front Street action. ✉ *811 Front St., Lahaina* ☎ *808/661–4855* ⊕ *www.cheeseburgerland.com.*

Cool Cat Café. You could easily miss this casual 1950s-style diner while strolling through Lahaina. Tucked in the second floor of the Wharf Cinema Center, its semi-outdoor area plays host to rockin' local music nightly until 10 pm. The entertainment lineup covers jazz, contemporary Hawaiian, and traditional island rhythms. It doesn't hurt that the kitchen dishes out specialty burgers, fish that's fresh from the harbor, and delicious homemade sauces from the owner's family recipes. ✉ *658 Front St., Lahaina* ☎ *808/667–0908* ⊕ *www.coolcatcafe.com.*

George Kahumoku Jr.'s Slack Key Show: Masters of Hawaiian Music. Beloved musician George Kahumoku Jr. hosts this weekly Wednesday program, which features the Islands' most renowned slack-key artists as well as other traditional forms of Hawaiian music. The setup at Aloha Pavilion is humble, but you get to enjoy Grammy-winning, legendary musicians from the genre. ✉ *Napili Kai Beach Resort, 5900 Lower Honoapiilani Rd., Lahaina* ☎ *808/669–3858* ⊕ *www.slackkeyshow.com.*

THE SOUTH SHORE

Fodor's Choice
★

Ambrosia Martini Lounge. A South Maui favorite, Ambrosia is a lively hangout for house music and old-school jams, as well as the occasional absinthe drink. It's the size of a living room, but mixology is given more consideration here than other venues. ✉ *1913 S. Kihei Rd., Kihei* ☎ *808/891–1011* ⊕ *www.ambrosiamaui.com* ☾ *5 pm–2 am.*

Fodor's Choice
★

Lobby Lounge at the Four Seasons Resort Maui at Wailea. This lofty resort's lobby lounge is perfect when you want live Hawaiian music, a bit of hula, and freshly prepared sushi all in one sitting. If you're not in the mood for a ceremonious sit-down meal but still crave something out of

Performers in colorful costumes help make luau appealing to all ages.

the ordinary, the place is perfect for a quick bite. The artisanal cocktails are well done and highlight locally distilled spirits. Gorgeous orange ceilings, stark-white stone columns, and modern wicker furnishing pull off the understated look quite well. The fiery sunset over Lanai isn't too shabby either. ⊠ *Four Seasons Resort Maui at Wailea, 3900 Wailea Alanui Dr., Wailea* ☎ *808/874–8000* ⊕ *www.fourseasons.com.*

South Shore Tiki Lounge. Good eats are paired with cool tunes in this breezy, tropical tavern. Local acts and DJs are featured most evenings; if you're craving some old-school hip-hop, Tuesday is your night. Thursday is a mix of reggaeton and Top 40 hits. Happy hour specials run from 11 am to 6 pm. ⊠ *1913 S. Kihei Rd., Kihei* ☎ *808/874–6444* ⊕ *www.southshoretikilounge.com.*

UPCOUNTRY AND THE NORTH SHORE

Casanova Italian Restaurant & Deli. Casanova brings in some big acts, including Kool and the Gang, Los Lobos, Taj Majal, and electro DJs from the mainland. Most Friday and Saturday nights attract a hip, local scene with live bands and eclectic DJs spinning house, funk, and world music. Wednesday is for Wild Wahine (code for ladies get in free), which can be on the smarmy side, but hey, a vacation is a "no judgment" zone. There's a $5 to $25 cover. ⊠ *1188 Makawao Ave., Makawao* ☎ *808/572–0220* ⊕ *www.casanovamaui.com.*

Fodor'sChoice
★
Charley's. The closest thing to country Maui has to offer, Charley's is a down-home dive bar in the heart of Paia that is also known for its great breakfasts. It hosts reggae, house, Latin soul, and jazz nights, as well as one-off events with sought-after DJs. Live bands are featured on

Friday and Saturday. ⊠ *142 Hana Hwy., Paia* ☎ *808/579–9453* ⊕ *www. charleysmaui.com.*

Stopwatch Bar & Grill. This friendly dive bar hosts karaoke nights on Thursday and Saturday, and books favorite local bands on Friday for a $4 admission. ⊠ *1127 Makawao Ave., Makawao* ☎ *808/572–1380.*

WHERE TO EAT

Updated
by Bonnie
Friedman

"Mischievous, marvelous, magical Maui," sings Israel Kamakawiwoole in *Maui Hawaiian Sup'pa Man*, his ode to the demigod. The island is all those things and more, and its restaurants try to keep up with the sophisticated palates and discriminating tastes of locals and visitors. For a place the size of Maui, there's a lot going on, from ethnic holes-in-the-wall to stunningly appointed hotel dining rooms, and from sea-food trucks to oceanfront fish houses with panoramic views. Much of the food is excellent, but some of it is overpriced and touristy. If you're coming from a "food destination" city, you may have to adjust your expectations.

Follow the locavore trend, and at casual and fine-dining restaurants choose menu items made with products that are abundant on the island, including local fish, onions, avocados, cabbage, broccoli, asparagus, hydroponic tomatoes, myriad herbs, salad greens, *kalo* (taro), bananas, papaya, guava, *lilikoi* (passion fruit), coconut, mangoes, strawberries, and Maui pineapple. You can also look for treats grown on neighboring islands, such as mushrooms, purple sweet potatoes, and watermelon.

"Local food," a specific and official cuisine designated as such in the 1920s, is an amalgam of foods brought by the ethnic groups that have come here since the mid-1800s and also blended with the foods native Hawaiians have enjoyed for centuries. Dishes to try include *lomilomi* salmon, *laulau,* poi, Portuguese bean soup, *kalbi* ribs, chicken *katsu,* chow fun, hamburger steak, and macaroni salad. For a food adventure, take a drive into Central Maui and have lunch or dinner at one of the "local" spots recommended here. Or get even more adventurous and take a drive around Wailuku or Kahului and find your own hidden gem. There are plenty out there.

Prices in the reviews are the average cost of a main course at dinner or, if dinner is not served, at lunch.

WEST MAUI

OLOWALU

$
AMERICAN

✕ **Leoda's Kitchen and Pie Shop.** Slow down as you drive through the little roadside village of Olowalu, about 15 minutes before Lahaina town if you're coming from the airport, so you don't miss this adorable farmhouse-chic restaurant and pie shop where everything is prepared with care. Old photos of the area, distressed wood, and muted colors set the mood. Try the signature ahi Benedict for breakfast. For lunch, have a sandwich or a burger with Kula onions. All the breads are home baked and excellent, and most ingredients are sourced locally. Don't get too full: you must try the pie. The banana cream is out of this world, or dig into the Olowalu lime tart. $ *Average main: $15* ✉ *820 Olowalu Village Rd., Olowalu* ☎ *808/662–3600* ⊕ *www.leodas.com.*

LAHAINA

$ ✕ **Aloha Mixed Plate.** From the wonderful folks who bring you Maui's
HAWAIIAN best luau—the Old Lahaina Luau—comes this extremely casual, multi-award-winning, oceanfront eatery. If you've yet to indulge in a "plate lunch" (a protein—usually in an Asian-style preparation—two scoops of rice, and a scoop of potato-macaroni salad), this is a good place to try one. The menu features fresh local fish preparations, lots of local produce, and such favorites as dry mein, saimin, Asian-style pickle platters, and poi beef stew made with poi from the restaurant's own farm. Take your plate to a table so close to the ocean you just might get wet. Oh, and don't forget the mai tai! $ *Average main: $10* ✉ *1285 Front St., Lahaina* ☎ *808/661–3322* ⊕ *www.AlohaMixedPlate.com.*

$$$$ ✕ **Gerard's.** For three decades, classically trained French chef Gerard
FRENCH Reversade—he started as an apprentice in acclaimed Paris restaurants when he was just 14—has remained true to his Gascony roots. His exacting standards—in the dining room as well as in the kitchen—have always been the hallmarks of his charming eponymous restaurant. He cooks *his* way, utilizing island ingredients in such classic dishes as Hamakua mushrooms in puff pastry, escargots *forestière,* Molokai shrimp consommé, terrine of foie gras, and confit of duck. The wine list is first-class. Floral fabrics and white tablecloths echo the look of a French country inn. $ *Average main: $45* ✉ *Plantation Inn, 174 Lahainaluna Rd., Lahaina* ☎ *808/661–8939* ⊕ *www.gerardsmaui. com* ☾ *No lunch.*

$$$$ ✕ **Honu.** Right next door to their popular Mala Ocean Tavern, celebrity
ECLECTIC chef Mark Ellman and Judy Ellman have brought an excellent addition to the Maui dining scene with this oceanfront fish house and pizza restaurant. Much of the seafood comes from the East Coast and Pacific Northwest: clams, crabs, mussels—and, finally, Maui has lobster rolls. The pizzas are cooked in a wood-fired brick oven (is there any other way?). The wine and cocktail lists are fabulous. Judy designed the sleek, bright interior with white walls, abundant use of wood, and large windows: Honu makes the best of an unparalled ocean view. $ *Average main: $36* ✉ *1295 Front St., Lahaina* ☎ *808/667–9390* ⊕ *www. honumaui.com.*

$$$$ ✕ **Lahaina Grill.** At the top of many best-restaurants lists, this expensive,
AMERICAN upscale bistro is about as fashionably chic as it gets on Maui. The food and service are consistently excellent and the place is abuzz with beautiful people every night of the week. The Cake Walk (little samples of Kona lobster crab cake, sweet Louisiana rock-shrimp cake, and seared ahi cake), toy-box tomato salad, and Kona-coffee-roasted rack of lamb are a few of the classics customers demand. Newer items include Marcho Farms center cut all-natural veal osso bucco and seared California lion-paw scallops. The full menu—including dessert—is available at the bar. The interior is as pretty as the patrons. $ *Average main: $45* ✉ *127 Lahainaluna Rd., Lahaina* ☎ *808/667–5117* ⊕ *www.lahainagrill. com* ☾ *No lunch.*

BEST BETS FOR MAUI DINING

Fodor'sChoice★

Ba-Le Sandwiches & Plate Lunch, $, p. 291

Café des Amis, $, p. 294

Cafe Mambo, $, p. 294

Colleen's at the Cannery, $$, p. 293

Da Kitchen, $, p. 290

Hana Fresh Market, $, p. 295

Ka'ana Kitchen, $$$$, p. 288

Mala Ocean Tavern, $$$, p. 280

Morimoto Maui, $$$$, p. 289

Paia Fishmarket Restaurant, $, p. 294

Pita Paradise Mediterranean Bistro, $$, p. 290

Roy's Kaanapali Bar & Grill, $$$$, p. 284

Sam Sato's, $, p. 292

Sangrita Grill & Cantina, $$$, p. 284

Sansei Seafood Restaurant & Sushi Bar, $$, p. 286

Star Noodle, $$, p. 281

Tokyo Tei, $, p. 292

Tommy Bahama, $$$, p. 290

By Price

$

Ba-Le Sandwiches & Plate Lunch, p. 291

Café des Amis, p. 294

Cafe Mambo, p. 294

Da Kitchen, p. 290

Hana Fresh Market, p. 295

Paia Fishmarket, p. 294

Sam Sato's, p. 292

Tokyo Tei, p. 292

$$

Pita Paradise Mediterranean Bistro, $$, p. 290

Sansei Seafood Restaurant & Sushi Bar, p. 286

Star Noodle, p. 281

Tiki Terrace, p. 285

$$$

Mala Ocean Tavern, p. 280

Market Fresh Bistro, p. 293

Sangrita Grill & Cantina, p. 284

Tommy Bahama, p. 290

$$$$

Ka'ana Kitchen, p. 288

Morimoto Maui, p. 289

Roy's Kaanapali Bar & Grill, p. 284

Spago, p. 290

$$$
ITALIAN

✕**Longhi's.** A Lahaina landmark created by Bob Longhi—"a man who loves to eat"—Longhi's has been serving pasta and other Italian fare to throngs of visitors since 1976. Although Bob's children run the restaurants now, his influence is still strong. Many of the classic dishes on the menu are his—prawns Amaretto, steak Longhi, and the signature lobster Longhi for two. The wine list is award winning and gigantic. Before the rest of Lahaina (or Wailea) wakes up, have yourself a cup of freshly squeezed orange juice and some good, strong coffee to start the day. Breakfast pastries are made in-house. There are two spacious, open-air dining levels; and there's a second Maui restaurant at the Shops at Wailea. $ *Average main: $34 ⊠ 888 Front St., Lahaina ☎ 808/667-2288 ⊕ www.longhis.com.*

$$$
MODERN
HAWAIIAN
Fodor's Choice
★

✕**Mala Ocean Tavern.** Chef-owner Mark Ellman started Maui's culinary revolution of the late '80s with his restaurant Avalon, but Mala is a more than satisfactory successor. The place is adorable; the best tables are on the lanai, which actually juts out over the water. The menu reflects Mark's and his wife Judy's world travels with dishes influenced by the Middle East, the Mediterranean, Italy, Bali, and Thailand. Every item on the menu is delicious, and there's a focus on ingredients that promote local sustainability. The cocktails and wine list are great, too. Another location of Mala is at the Wailea Beach Marriott Resort, but the Lahaina original is highly recommended. $ *Average main: $30* ✉ *1307 Front St., Lahaina* ☎ *808/667–9394* ⊕ *www.malaoceantavern.com.*

$$$$ ✕ **PacificO.** Sophisticated outdoor dining on the beach (no, really *on* the
MODERN beach) and creative island cuisine using local, fresh-caught fish and greens
HAWAIIAN and veggies grown in the restaurant's own Upcountry O'o Farm (and,
quite possibly, picked that very morning)—this is the Maui dining experience you've been dreaming about. Start with the award-winning appetizer of prawn and basil wontons, move on to any of the fantastic fresh fish dishes, and for dessert, finish with the banana pineapple *lumpia* served hot with homemade banana ice cream. $ *Average main: $38* ✉ *505 Front St., Lahaina* ☎ *808/667–4341* ⊕ *www.pacificomaui.com.*

$$ ✕ **Star Noodle.** In a very short time this wonderful spot has become
ASIAN one of Maui's best restaurants. It's way up above the highway in a
Fodor's Choice light industrial park, but don't be discouraged by the location. Take
★ the drive and you'll find a hip place and a welcoming staff that knows the meaning of aloha. There's a communal table in the center of the room, smaller tables around the perimeter, and comfortable stools for those who like to eat at a bar. Menu musts include the Ahi Avo, pan-roasted brussels sprouts with bacon and kim chee purée, and really any of the noodle dishes, especially the Lahaina fried soup (fat chow fun, pork, bean sprouts). The cocktail list is fabulous and the lychee martinis served here may be the best on Maui. $ *Average main: $18* ✉ *286 Kupuohi St., Lahaina* ☎ *808/667–5400* ⊕ *www.starnoodle.com.*

KAANAPALI

$ ✕ **CJ's Deli & Diner.** Chef Christian Jorgensen left fancy hotel kitchens
AMERICAN behind to open a casual place serving simple, delicious food at reasonable prices. The mango-glazed ribs, burgers, and classic Reuben sandwich are good choices, and the pineapple fried rice is *ono* (delicious); just order and pick up at the counter, and take your food to a table. If you're traveling to Hana or the Haleakala Crater, buy a box lunch and you're set. If you're staying in a condo, the "Chefs to Go" service is a great alternative to picking up (run of the mill and usually lousy) fast food. Everything is prepped and comes with easy cooking instructions. And if you decide, even on the spur of the moment, that Maui is a nice place for a wedding, CJ's can cater it. $ *Average main: $12* ✉ *Fairway Shops, 2580 Kekaa Dr., Kaanapali* ☎ *808/667–0968* ⊕ *www.cjsmaui.com.*

$$$ ✕ **Hula Grill.** A bustling and family-oriented spot on Kaanapali Beach
MODERN at Whalers Village shopping center, this restaurant designed to look
HAWAIIAN like a sprawling '30s beach house represents a partnership between
FAMILY TS Restaurants group and Hawaii Regional Cuisine pioneer chef Peter Merriman. They serve up large dinner portions with an emphasis on fresh local fish—try the macadamia nut–crusted catch, fire-grilled ahi steak, coconut seafood chowder—as well as USDA Prime steaks. Just in the mood for an umbrella-adorned cocktail and some pupu? Go to the Barefoot Bar, where you can wiggle your toes in the sand while you sip. The beach is called Dig Me—you'll understand why after just a few

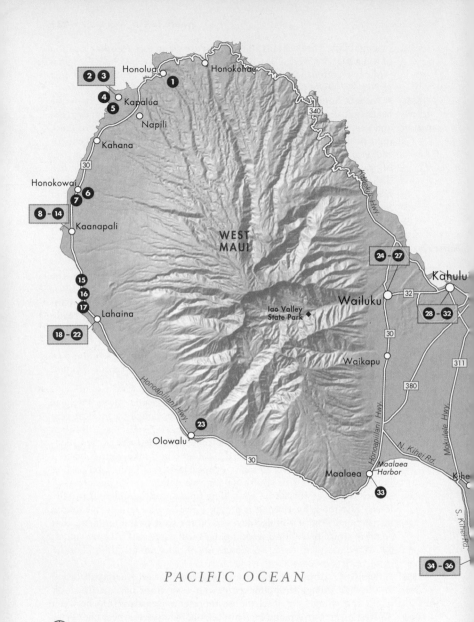

PACIFIC OCEAN

Where to Eat on Maui

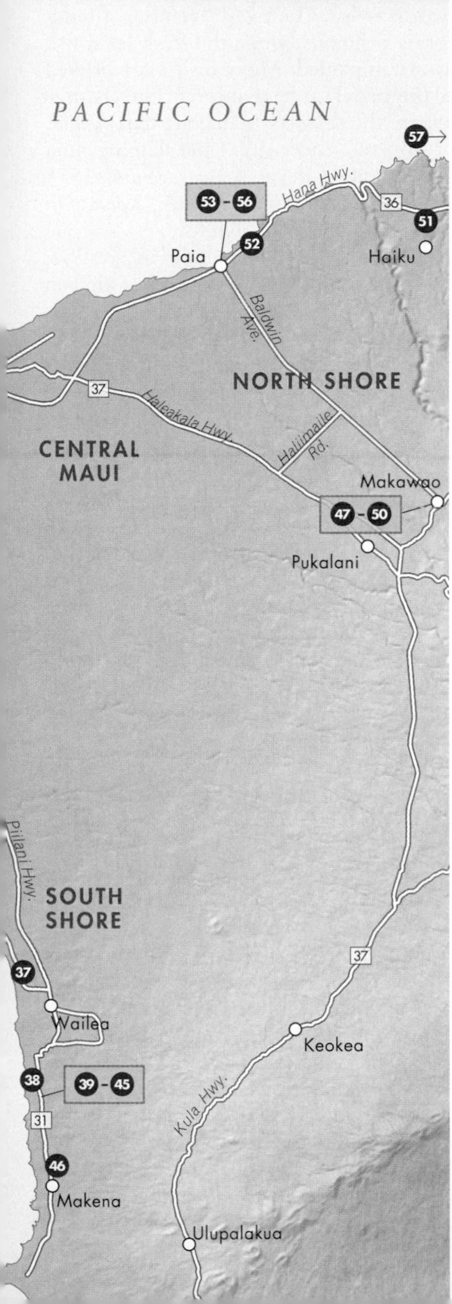

PACIFIC OCEAN

Paia

Haiku

NORTH SHORE

CENTRAL MAUI

Makawao

Pukalani

SOUTH SHORE

Wailea

Keokea

Makena

Ulupalakua

moments. [$] *Average main: $29* ✉ *Whalers Village, 2435 Kaanapali Pkwy., Kaanapali* ☎ *808/667–6636* 🌐 *www.hulagrillkaanapali.com.*

$$$$ ASIAN 🍴 **Japengo.** This nicely appointed open-air restaurant gives hotel dining a better name. The ocean views are stunning, and the gentle trade winds cool the night air. The glassed-in sushi bar is gorgeous. But it's the food that makes Japengo worth a visit. The award-winning sashimi-style hamachi and watermelon is delicious, while the fresh local fish is well prepared and perfectly accompanied. Many dishes are offered in half portions at half price, the better to taste more of the creative menu. Perhaps most surprising are the desserts, which are crazy good. Even if dessert translates for you to "chocolate," the flaming piña colada crème here will change your mind forever. [$] *Average main: $38* ✉ *Hyatt Regency Maui Resort & Spa, 200 Nohea Kai Dr., Kaanapali* ☎ *808/667–4909* 🌐 *www.japengomaui.com* 🕒 *No lunch.*

$$$ ITALIAN 🍴 **Pulehu, an Italian Grill.** If you need proof that Italian plays in paradise, you'll find it here. Chef Wesley Holder and his merry band of kitchen innovators are using 80% local Maui products to do what the Italians do best: craft simple, delicious food that lets the ingredients shine. Must-haves include the Hoopono Farms Caprese salad, Molokai sweet potato gnocchi, and Chianti-braised short ribs. The wine list is excellent. As if great food and drink weren't enough, the service is stellar, and the glassed-in exhibition kitchen provides an eyeful of culinary entertainment. [$] *Average main: $32* ✉ *The Westin Kaanapali Ocean Resort Villas, 6 Kai Ala Dr., Kaanapali* ☎ *808/667–3254* 🌐 *www.pulehurestaurantmaui.com* 🕒 *Closed Tues. and Wed.*

$$$$ MODERN HAWAIIAN Fodor's Choice ★ 🍴 **Roy's Kaanapali.** Roy Yamaguchi is a James Beard award-winning chef and the granddaddy of East-meets-West cuisine. He has restaurants all over the world, but his eponymous Maui restaurant was one of the first, and it's still one of the best. It's loud and brassy with a young vibe, but come for the great food, even if the atmosphere isn't quite your thing. Signatures like fire-grilled, Szechuan-spiced baby back pork ribs, Roy's original blackened ahi tuna, hibachi-style grilled salmon, and the to-die-for hot chocolate soufflé have been on the menu from the beginning, and with good reason. Roy's wine list is exceptionally user-friendly. The service here is welcoming and professional. [$] *Average main: $36* ✉ *2990 Kaanapali Pkwy., Kaanapali* ☎ *808/669–6999* 🌐 *www.roysrestaurant.com.*

$$$ MEXICAN Fodor's Choice ★ 🍴 **Sangrita Grill & Cantina.** Maui, at last, has excellent Mexican food. The menu categories at Sangrita may be familiar, but the authentic ingredients and deep flavors are new. The guacamoles and salsas—all house-made from scratch—come with a bottomless basket of corn and flour chips. The duck *carnitas* tacos with fig *mole*, jicama slaw, and avocado are stellar, and the avocado fries with cilantro pesto aioli are addictive accompaniments. Save room for the unique *flan de elote* for dessert. The cocktails prominently feature tequila and mezcal, and the wine list is affordable. The partially painted wooden tables and chairs are intriguing, and the service is delightful. [$] *Average main: $30* ✉ *The Fairway Shops, 2580 Kekaa Dr., Kaanapali* ☎ *808/662–6000* 🌐 *www.sangritagrill.com.*

$$$$ MEDITERRANEAN 🍴 **Son'z at Swan Court.** If you're celebrating a special occasion and want to splurge, this just might be the place for you. You'll descend a grand

Pineapple and shrimp add local flavors to tasty grilled skewers.

staircase into an amber-lighted dining room with soaring ceilings and a massive artificial lagoon complete with swans, waterfalls, and tropical gardens. Must-haves on Chef Geno Sarmiento's contemporary, Mediterranean-influenced menu include *tre formaggi gnocchi Caprese* with Olowalu tomatoes and mozzarella *di buffala*; and grilled beef tenderloin marinated in coffee and served with Parmesan-garlic fries. The restaurant claims the largest wine cellar in Hawaii, with 3,000 bottles. [$] *Average main: $40* ✉ *Hyatt Regency Maui, 200 Nohea Kai Dr., Kaanapali* ☎ *808/667–4506* 🌐 *sonzrestaurant.com* 🕑 *No lunch.*

$$ MODERN HAWAIIAN 🍴 **Tiki Terrace.** Executive chef Tom Muromoto is a local boy who loves to cook modern, upscale Hawaiian food. He augments the various fresh fish dishes on his menu with items influenced by Hawaii's ethnic mix. This casual, open-air restaurant is the only place on Maui—maybe in Hawaii—where you can have a Native Hawaiian combination plate that is as healthful as it is authentic. Sunday brunch, complete with strolling Hawaiian musicians and hula dancers, is renowned here; and if you're around for any holiday, chow down at the amazing holiday brunch buffets. [$] *Average main: $26* ✉ *Kaanapali Beach Hotel, 2525 Kaanapali Pkwy., Kaanapali* ☎ *808/667–0124* 🌐 *www.kbhmaui.com* 🕑 *No lunch.*

KAPALUA AND VICINITY

$ DINER 🍴 **The Gazebo Restaurant.** Breakfast is the reason to seek out this restaurant located poolside at the Napili Shores Resort. The ambience is a little funky but the oceanfront setting and views are spectacular—including the turtle, spinner dolphin, and, in winter, humpback-whale sightings. The food is standard diner fare and portions are big. Many folks think the Gazebo serves the best pancakes on West Maui. Have them with pineapple, bananas, macadamia nuts, or chocolate chips, or make up your own combination. You will almost certainly have to wait for a table, sometimes for quite a while, but at least it's a pleasant place to do so. $ *Average main: $11* ✉ *Napili Shores Resort, 5315 Lower Honoapiilani Hwy., Napili* ☎ *808/669–5621* ☽ *No dinner.*

$$$ ✗ **Kai Sushi.** For a quiet, light dinner, or to meet friends for a cock-
JAPANESE tail and some ultrafresh sushi, head to this handsome restaurant on the lobby level of the Ritz-Carlton Kapalua. You have your choice of sushi, sashimi, and a list of rolls. The especially good Kai special roll combines spicy tuna, yellowtail, and green onion. In keeping with the hotel's commitment to the culture, the restaurant's design was inspired by the story of Native Hawaiians' arrival by sea; the hand-carved ceiling beams resemble outrigger canoes. $ *Average main: $30* ✉ *Ritz-Carlton, Kapalua, 1 Ritz-Carlton Dr., Kapalua* ☎ *808/669–7385* ⊕ *www.ritzcarlton.com/kapalua* ☽ *Closed Tues. and Wed. No lunch.*

$$$$ ✗ **Pineapple Grill.** High on the hill overlooking the Kapalua Resort, this
MODERN casual restaurant offers ocean, mountain, and resort views. The kitchen
HAWAIIAN crew makes good use of the island's bounty, with dishes featuring greens and vegetables from Waipoli and Nalo farms, local, sustainable fish, Maui pineapple, and Roselani ice cream. Menu item descriptions detail where almost every ingredient is sourced. $ *Average main: $38* ✉ *200 Kapalua Dr., Kapalua* ☎ *808/669–9600* ⊕ *www.cohnrestaurants.com/pineapplegrill.*

$ ✗ **Pizza Paradiso.** When it opened in 1995, this was an over-the-counter
ITALIAN pizza place. It has evolved over the years into a local favorite serving Italian, Mediterranean, and Middle Eastern comfort food as well as pizza. The pies are so popular because of the top ingredients—100% pure Italian olive oil, Maui produce whenever possible, and Maui Cattle Company beef. The menu also features gyros, falafel, grilled fish, rotisserie chicken, and tiramisu. $ *Average main: $14* ✉ *Honokowai Marketplace, 3350 Lower Honoapiilani Rd., Honokowai* ☎ *808/667–2929* ⊕ *www.pizzaparadiso.com.*

$$$$ ✗ **Plantation House Restaurant.** It's a bit of a drive, but when you get
MODERN there you'll find a beautiful and comfortable restaurant with expan-
HAWAIIAN sive views of the ocean below and the majestic mountains above. Chef JoJo Vasquez recently turned the menu upside down and infused his own particular style. He calls his cuisine "Hawaiian Eclectic," and is known for local sourcing of as many ingredients as possible. $ *Average main: $40* ✉ *Plantation Course Clubhouse, 2000 Plantation Club Dr., Kapalua* ☎ *808/669–6299* ⊕ *www.theplantationhouse.com.*

$$ ✗ **Sansei Seafood Restaurant & Sushi Bar.** If you are a fish or shellfish lover,
ASIAN then this is the place for you. One of the most wildly popular restaurants
Fodor'sChoice in Hawaii with locations on three islands, Sansei takes sushi, sashimi, and
★ contemporary Japanese food to a new level. Favorite dishes include the mango-and-crab-salad handroll, panko-crusted-ahi sashimi roll, Asian shrimp cake, Japanese calamari salad, and Dungeness crab ramen with Asian-truffle broth. There are great deals on sushi and small plates for early birds and night owls. This busy restaurant has several separate dining areas, a sushi bar, and a bar area, but the focus is squarely on excellent food and not the ambience. There's another branch in Kihei

Town Center (✉ *1881 S. Kihei Rd.* ☎ *808/879–0004*). [$] *Average main: $26* ✉ *600 Office Rd., Kapalua* ☎ *808/669–6286* 🌐 *www.sanseihawaii.com* 🕓 *No lunch.*

THE SOUTH SHORE

KIHEI AND MAALAEA

$ AMERICAN 🍴 **Kihei Caffe.** This small, unassuming place across the street from Kalama Beach Park has a breakfast menu that runs the gamut from healthy yogurt-filled papaya to the local classic, *loco moco*—two eggs, ground beef patty, rice, and brown gravy—and everything in between. And the best thing about it is that the breakfast menu is served all day long. Prices are extremely reasonable and it's a good spot for people-watching. This is a popular place with locals, so you may have to wait for a table, depending on the time and day. [$] *Average main: $8* ✉ *1945 S. Kihei Rd., Kihei* ☎ *808/879–2230* 🌐 *www.kiheicaffe.net* 🕓 *No dinner.*

$$$$ ITALIAN 🍴 **Sarento's on the Beach.** This upscale Italian restaurant's setting right on spectacular Keawakapu Beach, with views of Molokini and Kahoolawe, is irresistible. After years of serving dinner only, it now offers breakfast service so diners can enjoy the extraordinary view in the morning, too. The breakfast menu offers all the regular fare; dinner has a decidedly Italian bent, with dishes like linguine with clams, penne Bolognese, and portobello Napoleon with local eggplant, mozzarella, tomatoes, and arugula pesto. The food is very good, if a bit old-fashioned, and the portions may be too big for some. [$] *Average main: $38* ✉ *2980 S. Kihei Rd., Kihei* ☎ *808/875–7555* 🌐 *www.sarentosonthebeach.com* 🕓 *No lunch.*

$ SEAFOOD FAMILY 🍴 **Seascape Maalaea.** A good choice for a seafood lunch, the Maui Ocean Center's signature restaurant (aquarium admission is not required to dine here) offers harbor and ocean views from its open-air perch. The restaurant promotes heart-healthy cuisine, using sustainable seafood and trans-fat-free items. Fresh fish entree, lunch-size salads, sandwiches, burgers, fish tacos, teriyaki tofu, fish-and-chips, chicken, ribs, and a full kids' menu are on offer. There's something for everyone here, and the view isn't bad either. [$] *Average main: $15* ✉ *Maui Ocean Center, 192 Maalaea Rd., Maalaea* ☎ *808/270–7068* 🌐 *www.mauioceancenter.com* 🕓 *No dinner.*

$ AMERICAN 🍴 **South Shore Tiki Lounge.** Come on, how can you come to Hawaii and *not* go to a tiki bar? And this one—tucked into Kihei Kalama Village—is consistently voted "Best Bar" (and best pizza) by locals. During the day, sit on the shaded lanai to enjoy a burger, sandwich, or, better yet, one of those delicious specialty pizzas, crafted from scratch with sauces made from fresh Roma tomatoes and Maui herbs. Seven nights a week, the tiny bar area lights up with a lively crowd, as DJs spin dance tunes under the glowing red eyes of the lounge's namesake tiki. And you can order food right up until midnight. [$] *Average main: $15* ✉ *Kihei Kalama Village, 1913-J S. Kihei Rd., Kihei* ☎ *808/874–6444* 🌐 *www.southshoretikilounge.com.*

$ THAI 🍴 **Thailand Cuisine.** Fragrant tea and coconut-ginger chicken soup begin a satisfying meal at this excellent Thai restaurant, set unassumingly in the middle of a shopping mall. The care and expense that has gone into the interior—glittering Buddhist shrines, elaborate hardwood facades, fancy napkin folds, and matching blue china—also applies to the cuisine. Take an exotic journey with the fantastic pad thai, special house noodles, curries, and crispy fried chicken. Can't decide? Try the family dinners for two or four. The fried bananas with ice cream are wonderful. There's a second location in Kahului's Maui Mall, a perfect choice before or after a movie at the megaplex. $ *Average main: $15* ✉ *Kukui Mall, 1819 S. Kihei Rd., Kihei* ☎ *808/875–0839* ⊕ *www. thailandcuisinemaui.net* ⊗ *No lunch Sun.*

WAILEA AND SOUTH SHORE (MAKENA)

$$$$
INTERNATIONAL

✕ **Alan Wong's Amasia.** This big, labyrinthine restaurant offers a slew of seating and menu options. There's a sushi bar, a *robata* (Japanese grill) bar, tatami rooms, private dining rooms, and regular restaurant tables. On first visit, it can be a little confusing. But Alan Wong is definitely Hawaii's biggest culinary name and Maui had been wanting him to open a restaurant here for years. Small plates are the way to go, and you can choose from local ingredients prepared in many ways—fried, griddled or baked, steamed, grilled, and, of course, raw. Szechuan chicken wings, pork adobo empanadas, shoyu duck bao buns, and soy-braised short ribs are just a few of the internationally flavored offerings. $ *Average main: $40* ✉ *Grand Wailea, 3850 Wailea Alanui, Wailea* ☎ *808/891–3954* ⊕ *www.alanwongamasia.com* ⊗ *No lunch.*

$$$$
ITALIAN

✕ **Ferraro's Bar e Ristorante.** Overlooking the ocean from a bluff above Wailea Beach, this outdoor Italian restaurant at the Four Seasons Resort Maui at Wailea is beautiful both day and night. For lunch, indulge in a lobster sandwich or one of a variety of stone-baked pizzas. At dinner, try the Italian-inspired salads and a house-made pasta. Not surprisingly, the wine list includes excellent Italian choices. Live classical music often adds to the atmosphere, and occasionally you can spot celebrities at the bar. $ *Average main: $40* ✉ *Four Seasons Resort Maui at Wailea, 3900 Wailea Alanui Dr., Wailea* ☎ *808/874–8000* ⊕ *www.fourseasons. com/maui.*

$$$$
MODERN
HAWAIIAN

✕ **Gannon's.** You'll love the amazing ocean and mountain views at this outpost of acclaimed chef Beverly Gannon, as well as the splashy Red Bar. Here you'll find Beverly's style of food, which consists of local ingredients prepared with international flavors. For a starter, try something from the raw bar and follow that with fennel-chili-crusted ahi with lemon beurre blanc or the Hawaiian salt-crusted rib eye. Breakfast is especially nice here. The outdoor lanai seating is cool in the morning and overlooks the parade of boats heading out to Molokini. $ *Average main: $38* ✉ *100 Wailea Golf Club Dr., Wailea* ☎ *808/875–8080* ⊕ *www.gannonsrestaurant.com.*

$$$$
MODERN
HAWAIIAN
Fodor's Choice
★

✕ **Ka'ana Kitchen.** This signature restaurant at the island's newest luxury resort, ANdAZ Maui at Wailea, has it all. The farm-to-table menu is truly market based, with almost every ingredient sourced within the Islands. The wine list is marvelous, the service is stellar, and the views spectacular from every table thanks to the tiered layout. But wait, there's still more. The whole space has been masterfully designed—there are dining seats available at the cocktail bar and at strategic locations around the gorgeous exhibition kitchen "counters." All guests are encouraged to walk around, see what the cadre of cooks are up

Dig into *pupu*—Hawaiian appetizers—such as seaweed salad and ahi (yellowfin tuna).

to, ask questions, get interactive. It's better than a beautiful restaurant with creative and carefully prepared food—it's fun. $ *Average main: $40* ✉ *ANdAZ Maui at Wailea, 3550 Wailea Alanui Dr., Wailea* ☎ *808/243–4750* ⊕ *www.maui.andaz.hyatt.com.*

$$
MODERN
HAWAIIAN

✕ **Migrant.** For those wondering where one of Bravo's Top Chefs, Sheldon Simeon, would land, the answer is Wailea. Simeon invites you to Migrant with the phrase, "Come my house. Eat." The place is casual and comfortable with outdoor, indoor, bar, and communal table seating. South Shore sunsets provide the backdrop. The food is definitely the main event—modern local cuisine that is tasty and comforting. How about ramen with a French-onion-soup base instead of broth? It's here, and it's delicious. Other must-try dishes are the street corn and the outrageously good Korean fried chicken. $ *Average main: $19* ✉ *Wailea Beach Marriott Resort & Spa, 3700 Wailea Alanui Dr., Wailea* ☎ *808/875–9394* ⊕ *www.migrantmaui.com* ☾ *No lunch.*

$$$$
MODERN ASIAN
Fodor's Choice
★

✕ **Morimoto Maui.** If you're a fan of Iron Chef and Iron Chef America, rejoice. Maui now has an outpost of Masaharu Morimoto's eponymous restaurant. Located at the new ANdAZ Maui resort, it's as hip as hip can be, in every way. Outdoor tables, a bustling dining room, and a sushi bar all make it a lively choice. But the reason to go is for the food. There's a long sushi-sashimi menu and the fish is the freshest. The tuna pizza is scrumptious, the fresh fish, prime steak, and lobster dishes are big enough to share, and just one bite will have you dreaming about the the 10-hour braised pork belly in rice congee. $ *Average main: $43* ✉ *ANdAZ Maui at Wailea, 3550 Wailea Alanui Dr., Wailea* ☎ *808/243–4766* ⊕ *www.maui.andaz.hyatt.com/en/hotel/dining/morimoto-maui.html.*

$$ MEDITERRANEAN Fodor's Choice ★ 🍴 **Pita Paradise Mediterranean Bistro.** The more upscale and newer outpost of the Pita Paradise in Kihei Kalama Village is beautiful and welcoming, and the staff is knowledgeable and friendly. But it's the food that's the main event here. The owner is a fisherman so you know the fish here is the freshest available. Lunch features affordable and delicious Greek/Mediterranean appetizers, fresh salads, and, of course, the signature pita sandwiches. The spicy falafel and Greek burgers are standouts. In the evening it's transformed into an Italian/Greek bistro with entrées like chicken fettucine and moussaka. Save room for the award-winning baklava ice-cream pie—yes, that's right!—made with Maui's own Roselani Hawaiian vanilla-bean ice cream. [$] *Average main: $20* ✉ *Wailea Gateway Center, 34 Wailea Gateway Center, Wailea* ☎ *808/879–7177* 🌐 *www.pitaparadisehawaii.com.*

$$$$ MODERN HAWAIIAN 🍴 **Spago.** It's a marriage made in Hawaii heaven. The California cuisine of celebrity-chef Wolfgang Puck is combined with Maui flavors and served lobby level and oceanfront at the luxurious Four Seasons Resort. Try the spicy ahi tuna *poke* in sesame-miso cones to start, and then see what the chefs-in-residence can do with some of Maui's fantastic local fish. Finish with a little wild *lilikoi* (passion fruit) crème brûlée with white chocolate–macadamia nut biscotti. Oh, it'll cost you, but the service is spot-on and the smooth, Asian-inspired interior allows the food to claim the spotlight. [$] *Average main: $42* ✉ *Four Seasons Resort Maui at Wailea, 3900 Wailea Alanui Dr., Wailea* ☎ *808/879–2999* 🌐 *www.wolfgangpuck.com* 🕒 *No lunch.*

$$$ MODERN AMERICAN Fodor's Choice ★ 🍴 **Tommy Bahama.** It's more island style than Hawaii, and yes, it's a chain, but the food is consistently great, the service is filled with aloha, and the ambience is just so island refined. Try the ahi *poke* napoleon (with capers, sesame, guacamole, and flatbread), the *kalua* pork or blackened fish sandwich, any of the generous salads, or the local fish preparations. The crab bisque is worthy of a cross-island drive, as are the desserts. The cocktails are among the best and most creative on the island. [$] *Average main: $35* ✉ *The Shops at Wailea, 3750 Wailea Alanui Dr., Wailea* ☎ *808/875–9983* 🌐 *www.tommybahama.com.*

CENTRAL MAUI

KAHULUI

$ ECLECTIC FAMILY Fodor's Choice ★ 🍴 **Da Kitchen.** After a floor-to-ceiling renovation in late 2013, this extremely popular purveyor of all food "local" is bright, shiny, comfortable, and able to accommodate at least 30 more hungry diners than before. But don't worry, the food is every bit as good as it's ever been. Try the signature mahimahi tempura, loco moco, Hawaiian plate, chicken katsu, and daily mixed bentos; and be assured everything on the menu is delicious and the portions are gigantic. The upbeat ambience is reflected in the service as well as the food. There's an "express" location in Kihei, but we recommend the happy, always-crowded Kahului location. [$] *Average main: $14* ✉ *425 Koloa St., Kahului* ☎ *808/871–7782* 🌐 *www.da-kitchen.com* 🕒 *Closed Sun.*

$ CHINESE 🍴 **Dragon Dragon.** Whether you're a party of 10 or 2, this is the place to stop for what is arguably the best Chinese food on Maui. Dim sum is available only during lunch, but for a real treat, try some of the house specialties like the honey walnut prawns, spicy crab Singapore-style, and the sizzling platter of fish with basil leaves. Top it all off with Maui's own Roselani lychee sherbet. $ *Average main: $16* ⊠ *Maui Mall, 70 E. Kaahumanu Ave., Kahului* ☎ *808/893–1628.*

$$ ✕**Marco's Grill & Deli.** One of the go-to places for airport comers and ITALIAN goers, this popular Italian restaurant also draws a steady crowd of local residents, mostly for business lunches. Meatballs, sausages, and sauces are all made in-house; the owner was a butcher in his former life. There's a long list of sandwiches that are available all day, and the salads are big enough to share. Note that food substitutions or special requests are not appreciated here. $ *Average main: $18* ⊠ *444 Hana Hwy., Kahului* ☎ *808/877–4446.*

$ ✕**Ramen Ya.** Part of a Japanese chain, this outpost in a mall is the JAPANESE first and only location in Maui. All the ramen combinations are slurp-worthy, and the *gyoza* (dumplings) and local-style curries are reason enough to dine here. The portions are gigantic—seriously gigantic—so if you're not that hungry or just have a small appetite, you can order kid-size portions. The service is quick and friendly, and the prices are right. $ *Average main: $9* ⊠ *Queen Kaahumanu Center, 275 W. Kaahumanu Ave, Kahului* ☎ *808/873–9688.*

$ ✕**Zippy's.** Hawaii's favorite casual, eat-in, or take-out restaurant, Zip-ECLECTIC py's was founded more than 45 years ago. Today Oahu has more than FAMILY two dozen locations from which to choose, and Maui waited a long time to get one. It's a 24-hour-a-day (takeout only after midnight Sun.–Thurs.), diner-type place with a big menu. Spaghetti with chili, oxtail soup, Korean chicken, chicken katsu, noodles, burgers, and burritos are just a few of the tasty menu options. Napoleon's Bakery counter up front serves its only-in-Hawaii-style turnovers, pies, cakes, and pastries, as well as made-to-order malasadas and andagi. $ *Average main: $10* ⊠ *15 Hookele St., Kahului* ☎ *808/856–7599* ⊕ *www.zippys.com.*

WAILUKU

$$ ✕**Asian Star.** This restaurant in Wailuku's Millyard (a light industrial VIETNAMESE area) is the best choice for Vietnamese food on Maui. Owner Jason Chau grows his own Hawaiian chili peppers, mint, basil, chives, lemongrass, and green onions around the perimeter of the parking lot, and these seasonings add robust and concentrated flavors to his dishes. Try the lemongrass chicken or tofu, the garlic beef or green papaya salad, the crispy sesame or orange beef, the clay pots with crunchy, charred rice bits on the bottom, and the *bun,* bowls brimming with cold vermicelli noodles and topped with chicken, beef, or pork. $ *Average main: $18* ⊠ *The Millyard, 1764 Wili Pa Loop, Wailuku* ☎ *808/244–1833.*

$ ✕**Ba-Le Sandwiches & Plate Lunch.** It began as a French-Vietnamese bakery VIETNAMESE on Oahu and has branched into popular small restaurants sprinkled Fodor'sChoice throughout the Islands. Some are kiosks in malls; others are stand-★ alones with some picnic tables out front, as is the case at this location, which is one of four on Maui. Vietnamese *pho* (the famous soups laden with seafood or rare beef, fresh basil, bean sprouts, and lime) share menu space with local-style *saimin* and plates of barbecue or spicy chicken, beef, pork, or local fish served with jasmine rice. The delicious sandwiches—*banh mi* in Vietnamese—are perfect for lunch to stay or to go. There are a slew of tapioca flavors for dessert. [$] *Average main: $9* ✉ *1824 Oihana St., Wailuku* ☎ *808/249–8833* 🌐 *www.balemaui.com.*

$ HAWAIIAN Fodor's Choice ★ 🍴 **Sam Sato's.** Every island has its noodle shrine, and this is Maui's. Dry mein, *saimin,* chow fun—they all come in different-size portions and with add-ins to satisfy every noodle craving. While you wait for your bowl, be sure to try a teriyaki beef stick or two. Save room for the popular turnovers—pineapple, coconut, apple, or peach—and traditional Japanese manju filled with either lima or azuki beans. At busy times, which is almost always, you will likely have to wait for a table or a stool at the counter. Be sure to write your name on the little yellow pad at the take-out window. [$] *Average main: $8* ✉ *The Millyard, 1750 Wili Pa Loop, Wailuku* ☎ *808/244–7124* 💳 *No credit cards* 🕒 *No dinner. Closed Sun.*

$ JAPANESE Fodor's Choice ★ 🍴 **Tokyo Tei.** Getting there is half—well, maybe a quarter—of the fun. Tucked in the back corner of a covered parking garage, Tokyo Tei is worth seeking out for wonderful local-style Japanese food. At lunch you'll rub elbows with bankers and construction workers; at dinner, three generations might be celebrating *Tutu's* (grandma's) birthday at the next table. This is a bona fide local institution where for more than six decades people have come for the food and the comfort of familiarity. You'll find the freshest sashimi, feather-light yet crispy shrimp and vegetable tempura, and local-style bentos and plate lunches. [$] *Average main: $12* ✉ *1063 Lower Main St., Wailuku* ☎ *808/242–9630* 🌐 *www.tokyotei.com* 🕒 *No lunch Sun.*

UPCOUNTRY

$$$ ITALIAN 🍴 **Casanova Italian Restaurant & Deli.** An authentic Italian dinner house and nightclub, this place is smack in the middle of Maui's *paniolo* (cowboy) town of Makawao. The brick wood-burning oven, imported from Italy, has been turning out perfect pies and steaming hot focaccia for more than 20 years. You can pair a pie with a salad (they're all big enough to share) and a couple of glasses of wine without breaking the bank. The daytime deli is fabulous for breakfast, cappuccino, croissants, and people-watching. The place turns positively raucous—in a good way—on Wednesday, Friday, and Saturday nights. [$] *Average main: $28* ✉ *1188 Makawao Ave., Makawao* ☎ *808/572–0220* 🌐 *www.casanovamaui.com.*

$ AMERICAN 🍴 **Grandma's Maui Coffee.** If you're taking a drive through gorgeous Upcountry Maui, this is a great place to stop for a truly homegrown cup of coffee and snack. All of the coffee is grown right on the slopes of Haleakala and roasted on the premises in a 100-year-old roaster proudly on display. The baked goods are fabulous—particularly the lemon bars—and the variety of menu items for breakfast and lunch is vast. Eggs, omelets, crepes, and fantastic home fries are served for breakfast; salads, sandwiches, lasagna, and more can be ordered at lunch. Enjoy your coffee and goodies on the lovely deck; sometimes a Hawaiian musician is there playing a tune. A dinner menu featuring fresh local fish, pasta, and more is now served Wednesday through Saturday. [$] *Average main: $9* ✉ *9232 Kula Hwy., Kula* ☎ *808/878–2140* 🌐 *www.grandmascoffee.com* 🕒 *No dinner Sun.–Tues.*

$$$$ ✗**Haliimaile General Store.** Chef-restaurateur Beverly Gannon's first restau-
MODERN rant remains a culinary destination after more than a quarter century.
HAWAIIAN The big, rambling former plantation store has two dining rooms: sit in
the front to be seen and heard; head on back for some quiet and privacy. Classic dishes like Bev's "Famous" Crab Pizza, Asian duck tostada,
grilled rack of lamb, and many more are complemented with daily and
nightly specials. To get here, take the exit on the left halfway up Haleakala Highway. $ *Average main: $38* ✉ *900 Haliimaile Rd., Haliimaile*
☎ *808/572–2666* ⊕ *www.bevgannonrestaurants.com/haliimaile.*

$$$ ✗**Market Fresh Bistro.** This hard-to-find restaurant tucked into a court-
MODERN yard serves farm-to-table food prepared by chef Justin Pardo, for-
HAWAIIAN merly of Union Square Café in New York City. In addition to locally
grown and produced ingredients, he nods to healthful eating by using
reductions and infused oils rather than butter. Representative dishes
include the Upcountry vegetable salad and creative fresh fish prepara-
tions. Brunch is served on Sunday only; prix-fixe farm dinners ($60)
are held Thursday night and reservations are required. $ *Average*
main: $30 ✉ *3620 Baldwin Ave., Makawao* ☎ *808/572–4877* ⊕ *www.*
marketfreshbistro.com ☉ *Closed Mon. No dinner Fri.–Wed.*

THE NORTH SHORE

HAIKU

$$ ✗**Colleen's at the Cannery.** From the nondescript exterior and the location
AMERICAN in an old pineapple cannery-cum-strip mall, you'd never anticipate what's
Fodor'sChoice inside. Colleen's is one of the most overlooked restaurants on Maui. It's
★ popular with locals for breakfast and lunch, but try it at dinner when
the candles come out and it's time for martinis and fresh fish. The food
is excellent, in particular the huge salads made with Upcountry's best
produce, the fish specials, the burgers, and the simple roast chicken.
When eating here, you'll feel like you're at a hip, urban eatery. $ *Aver-*
age main: $20 ✉ *Haiku Cannery Marketplace, 810 Haiku Rd., Haiku*
☎ *808/575–9211* ⊕ *www.colleensinhaiku.com.*

KUAU

$$$$ ✗**Mama's Fish House.** For almost four decades, Mama's has been *the* Maui
SEAFOOD destination for special occasions. A path of gecko-shaped stones leads
through the coconut grove past the giant clamshell and under the banyan arch to an ever-changing fantasyland of Hawaiiana kitsch. True,
the setting couldn't be more spectacular, and yes, the menu names the
angler that reeled in your fresh catch (do we know he *really* caught it?),
but the dishes are a bit dated in terms of preparation and presentation—
and the prices are extremely high. But if you're looking for an overall
experience, make a reservation and celebrate your special occasion here.
$ *Average main: $50* ✉ *799 Poho Pl., Kuau* ☎ *808/579–8488* ⊕ *www.*
mamasfishhouse.com.

PAIA

$
ECLECTIC
Fodor'sChoice
★

✕ Café des Amis. The menu is a little neurotic—in a good way—featuring Mediterranean and Indian dishes, but the food is fresh and tasty. This budget-friendly café offers flavors and preparations not easily obtainable at other island eateries, with a nice selection of sweet and savory crepes, Indian wraps, and salads. Now, you can have a cocktail, wine, and beer, too. All in all, you get delicious, good-value food, as well as excellent people-watching from the umbrella-shaded tables outside. $ Average main: $16 ⊠ 42 Baldwin Ave., Paia ☎ 808/579–6323 ⊕ www.cdamaui.com ⊟ No credit cards.

$
ECLECTIC
Fodor'sChoice
★

✕ Cafe Mambo. Paia is one of Maui's most interesting food towns, and this Mediterranean-inspired joint is right in the thick of things. It's kind of frenetic in every way, from the menu to the style and the service. But the food is great and well priced, and the people-watching is fascinating. The husband-and-wife owners, from England and Spain respectively, decorated the place with Moroccan clay pieces; teak and coconut-wood tables are set in the middle of benches with Middle Eastern pillows. The menu goes all over the place, too, with all-American burgers, island fish, falafel and hummus, Spanish tapas, and paella. $ Average main: $15 ⊠ 30 Baldwin Ave., Paia ☎ 808/579–8021 ⊕ www.cafemambomaui.com.

$$
PIZZA
FAMILY

✕ Flatbread Company. This Vermont-based company marched right in to Paia in 2007 and instantly became a popular restaurant and a valued addition to the community. As part of the company's mission, they started "giving back" to local nonprofits immediately. Happily, along with the altruism, the food is fantastic. There's a big, primitive-looking, earthen, wood-fired oven from which emerge utterly delicious flatbread pizzas. They use organic, local, sustainable products, including 100% organically grown wheat for the dough, which is made fresh daily. The place is a good spot to take the kids. There's a no reservations policy but they do have "call ahead seating" so you can put your name on the wait list before you arrive. $ Average main: $22 ⊠ 89 Hana Hwy., Paia ☎ 808/579–8989 ⊕ www.flatbreadcompany.com ⚑ Reservations not accepted.

$
SEAFOOD
Fodor'sChoice
★

✕ Paia Fishmarket Restaurant. If you're okay with communal picnic tables, or taking your meal to a nearby beach, this place in funky Paia town serves, arguably, the best fresh fish for the best prices on this side of the island. Four preparations are offered and, on any given day, there are at least four fresh fishes from which to choose. For the non-fish fans, there are burgers, chicken, and pasta. The side dishes—Cajun rice, home fries, and the amazing hand-cut crunchy cole slaw—are all as delectable as the main event. You can have a beer or a glass of wine, too, as long as you stay inside, of course. $ Average main: $15 ⊠ 100 Hana Hwy., Paia ☎ 808/579–8030 ⊕ www.paiafishmarket.com.

ROAD TO HANA

HANA

$ 🍴 **Hana Fresh Market.** Directly in front of (and associated with) Hana
AMERICAN Health, you'll find rows of tables laden with delicious and organic
Fodor's Choice ★ fresh salads and entrées worthy of any chic farm-to-table restaurant anywhere. Chicken salad with dates, red bell pepper, hard-boiled egg, peanuts, yellow beets, greens, and dried cranberries; soba noodles with salmon; peppercorn-brined pork chop with braised cabbage, green beans, and sweet potato cake are just a few of the always-changing choices. Early birds can enjoy made-to-order omelets and waffles. Best of all, the produce comes from its farm, directly behind the health center. If your accommodations include a kitchen, stock up here on bags of fresh veggies at incredibly reasonable prices. [$] *Average main: $10* ✉ *4590 Hana Hwy., Hana* ☎ *808/248–7515* 🌐 *www.hanafresh.org.*

WHERE TO STAY

Updated by Michele Bigley

Maui's accommodations run the gamut from rural bed-and-breakfasts to superopulent megaresorts. In between the extremes, there's something for every vacation style and budget. The large resorts, hotels, and condominiums for which Maui is noted are on the sunny, leeward, southern and western shores. They bustle with activity and are near plenty of restaurants, shopping, golf, and water sports. Those seeking a different experience can try the inns, B&Bs, and rentals in the small towns and quieter areas along the North Shore and Upcountry on the verdant slopes of Haleakala.

If the latest and greatest is your style, be prepared to spend a small fortune. Properties like the Ritz-Carlton, Kapalua, the Four Seasons Resort Maui at Wailea, the sparkling ANdAZ Maui at Wailea, and condo complexes such as the luxe Wailea Beach Villas may set you back at least $600 a night.

Although there aren't many of them, small B&Bs are charming. They tend to be in residential or rural neighborhoods around the island, sometimes beyond the resort areas of West Maui and the South Shore. The B&Bs offer both a personalized experience and a window onto authentic local life. The prices tend to be the lowest available on Maui, sometimes less than $200 per night.

WHERE TO STAY IN MAUI

	LOCAL VIBE	PROS	CONS
West Maui	Popular and busy, the West Side includes the picturesque, touristy town of Lahaina and the upscale resort areas of Kaanapali and Kapalua.	A wide variety of shopping, water sports, and historic sites provide plenty to do. To relax, there are great beaches and brilliant sunsets.	Traffic is usually congested; parking is hard to find; beaches can be crowded.
South Shore	The protected South Shore of Maui offers diverse experiences, and accommodations, from comfortable condos to luxurious resorts—and golf, golf, golf.	Many beautiful beaches; sunny weather; great snorkeling.	Numerous strip malls; crowded with condos; there can be lots of traffic.
Upcountry	Country and chic come together in farms, ranches, and trendy towns on the cool, green slopes of Haleakala.	Cooler weather at higher elevations; panoramic views of nearby Islands; distinctive shops, boutiques, galleries, and restaurants.	Fewer restaurants; no nightlife; can be very dark at night and difficult to drive for those unfamiliar with roads and conditions.
North Shore	The North Shore is a mecca for surfing, windsurfing, and kite sailing. When the surf's not up, the focus is on shopping: Paia is full of galleries, shops, and hip eateries.	Wind and waves are terrific for water sports; colorful small towns to explore without the intrusion of big resorts.	Weather may not be as sunny as other parts of the island; no nightlife; most stores in Paia close early.
Road to Hana and East Maui	Remote and rural, laid-back and tropical Hana and East Maui are special places to unwind.	Natural experience; rugged coastline and lush tropical scenery; lots of waterfalls.	Accessed by a long and winding road; no nightlife; few places to eat or shop.

Apartment and condo rentals are ideal for families, groups of friends, and those traveling on modest budgets. Not only are the nightly rates lower than hotel rooms, but "eating in" (all have kitchens of some description) is substantially less expensive than dining out. There are literally hundreds of these units all over the island, ranging in size from studios to luxurious four-bedroom properties with multiple baths. The vast majority are found along the sunny coasts, from Makena to Kihei on the South Shore and Lahaina up to Kapalua in West Maui. Prices depend on the size of the unit and its proximity to the beach, as well as the amenities and services offered. For about $250 a night, you can get a lovely one-bedroom apartment without many frills or flourishes, close to but probably not on the beach. Many rentals have minimum stays (usually three to five nights).

Most of Maui's resorts—several are megaresorts—have opulent gardens, fantasy swimming pools, championship golf courses, and full-service fitness centers and spas. Expect to spend at least $350 a night at the less posh resort hotels; they are all in the Wailea and Makena resort area on the South Shore and Kaanapali and Kapalua in West Maui. At all lodgings, ask about discounts and deals (free nights with longer stays, for example), which have proliferated.

Prices in the reviews are the lowest cost of a standard double room in high season or, for rentals, the lowest per-night cost of a one-bedroom unit in high season. For expanded hotel reviews, visit Fodors.com.

WEST MAUI

LAHAINA

$$$ B&B/INN Fodor's Choice ★ **Hooilo House.** If you want to treat yourself to a luxurious but intimate getaway and don't require resort facilities, this stunning Bali-inspired B&B, in the foothills of the West Maui Mountains, just south of Lahaina town, exemplifies quiet perfection. **Pros:** friendly on-site hosts Amy and Dan Martin are an asset; beautiful furnishings. **Cons:** not good for families with younger children; three-night minimum; beaches are a short drive away. [$] *Rooms from: $329* ✉ *138 Awaiku St., Lahaina* ☎ *808/667–6669* 🌐 *www.hooilohouse.com* 🛏 *6 rooms* 🍴 *Breakfast.*

$ B&B/INN **Lahaina Inn.** An antique jewel in the heart of town, this two-story timbered building will transport romantics back to the turn of the 20th century. **Pros:** a half block off Front Street, the location is within easy walking distance of shops, restaurants, and attractions; lovely antique style; the price is right. **Cons:** rooms are small, bathrooms particularly so; some street noise; two stories, no elevator. [$] *Rooms from: $99* ✉ *127 Lahainaluna Rd., Lahaina* ☎ *808/661–0577, 800/222–5642* 🌐 *www.lahainainn.com* 🛏 *9 rooms, 3 suites* 🍴 *No meals.*

$$ RENTAL **Lahaina Shores Beach Resort.** You really can't get any closer to the beach than this lofty (by Lahaina standards), seven-story rental property that offers panoramic ocean and mountain views and fully equipped kitchens. **Pros:** right on the beach; historical sites, attractions, and activities are a short walk away. **Cons:** older property; no posh resort-type amenities. [$] *Rooms from: $225* ✉ *475 Front St., Lahaina* ☎ *808/661–4835, 866/934–9176* 🌐 *www.lahainashores.com* 🛏 *199 rooms* 🍴 *No meals.*

KAANAPALI AND NEARBY

$$$$ RESORT **Hyatt Regency Maui Resort and Spa.** Fantasy landscaping with splashing waterfalls, swim-through grottoes, a lagoonlike swimming pool, and a 150-foot waterslide wow guests of all ages at this bustling Kaanapali resort in the midst of the Kaanapali Beach action. **Pros:** nightly on-site luau; home of Astronomy Tour of the Stars; contemporary restaurant and bar. **Cons:** can be difficult to find a space in self-parking; popular resort might not offer the most peaceful escape. [$] *Rooms from: $429* ✉ *200 Nohea Kai Dr., Kaanapali* ☎ *808/661–1234* 🌐 *www.maui.hyatt.com* 🛏 *806 rooms* 🍴 *No meals.*

$$$$ RENTAL **Kaanapali Alii.** Amenities like daily maid service, an activities desk, small store with complimentary DVDs for guests to borrow, and 24-hour front-desk service—and no pesky resort fees—make this a winning choice for families and those wanting to play house on Maui's most stunning shores. **Pros:** large, comfortable units on the beach; good location in the heart of the action in Kaanapali Resort. **Cons:** elevators

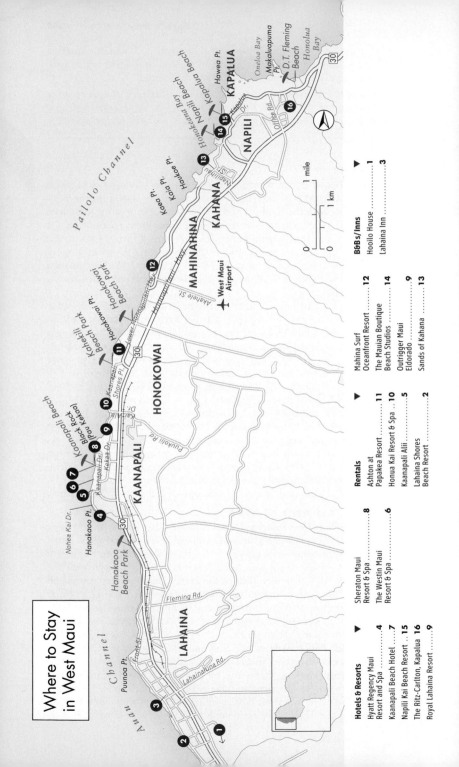

Where to Stay in West Maui

Hotels & Resorts ▶

Hyatt Regency Maui Resort and Spa **4**
Kaanapali Beach Hotel **7**
Napili Kai Beach Resort **15**
The Ritz-Carlton, Kapalua **16**
Royal Lahaina Resort **9**

Sheraton Maui Resort & Spa **8**
The Westin Maui Resort & Spa **6**

Rentals ▶

Ashton at Papakea Resort **11**
Honua Kai Resort & Spa .. **10**
Kaanapali Alii **5**
Lahaina Shores Beach Resort **2**

Mahina Surf Oceanfront Resort **12**
The Mauian Boutique Beach Studios **14**
Outrigger Maui Eldorado **9**
Sands of Kahana **13**

B&Bs/Inns ▶

Hooilo House **1**
Lahaina Inn **3**

BEST BETS FOR MAUI LODGING

Fodor's Choice★

ANdAZ Maui at Wailea, $$$$, p. 303

Fairmont Kea Lani Maui, $$$$, p. 304

Four Seasons Resort Maui at Wailea, $$$$, p. 304

Hale Hookipa Inn, $, p. 309

Hana Kai-Maui Resort Condominiums, $$, p. 310

Hooilo House, $$$, p. 297

The Inn at Mama's Fish House, $, p. 309

Kaanapali Beach Hotel, $, p. 299

Luana Kai, $, p. 302

Napili Kai Beach Resort, $$$, p. 301

The Old Wailuku Inn at Ulupono, $, p. 308

Outrigger® Maui Eldoradosm, $$$, p. 299

The Ritz-Carlton, Kapalua, $$$$, p. 301

By Price

$

Banyan Tree House, p. 308

Hale Hookipa Inn, p. 309

Kaanapali Beach Hotel, p. 299

Luana Kai, p. 302

The Old Wailuku Inn at Ulupono, p. 308

Puu Koa Maui Rentals, p. 310

Royal Lahaina Resort, p. 300

$$

Hale Hui Kai, p. 301

Paia Inn Hotel, p. 310

$$$

Hooilo House, p. 297

Outrigger® Maui Eldoradosm, p. 299

$$$$

ANdAZ Maui at Wailea, p. 303

Four Seasons Resort Maui at Wailea, p. 304

Grand Wailea Resort Hotel & Spa, p. 304

Makena Surf, p. 304

Polo Beach Club, p. 304

The Ritz-Carlton, Kapalua, p. 301

The Westin Maui Resort & Spa, $$$$, p. 300

---

are notoriously slow; parking can be crowded during high season; no on-site restaurant. $ *Rooms from: $495* ⊠ *50 Nohea Kai Dr., Kaanapali* ☎ *808/667–1400, 800/642–6284* ⊕ *www.kaanapalialii.com* ⌐ *264 units* ❍| *No meals.*

$
HOTEL
Fodor's Choice
★
🗃 **Kaanapali Beach Hotel.** From the Hawaiian artifacts in the garden to the tropical interiors, this charming beachfront hotel is full of aloha— locals say it's one of the few resorts on the island where you can get a true Hawaiian experience. **Pros:** exceptional Hawaiian culture program; friendly staff; great price; Tiki Terrace restaurant serves delicious meals and one of the most bountiful Sunday brunches on the island. **Cons:** the property is older than neighboring modern resorts; fewer amenities than other places along this beach. $ *Rooms from: $159* ⊠ *2525 Kaanapali Pkwy., Kaanapali* ☎ *808/661–0011, 800/262–8450* ⊕ *www.kbhmaui. com* ⌐ *432 rooms* ❍| *No meals.*

$$$
RENTAL
Fodor's Choice
★
🗃 **Outrigger® Maui EldoradoSM.** The Kaanapali Golf Course's fairways wrap around this fine, well-priced condo complex that boasts spacious studios, one- and two-bedroom units with fully equipped kitchens, no resort fee, and access to a stocked beach cabana on a semiprivate beach. **Pros:** privileges at the Kaanapali Golf Courses; Wi-Fi in all units; friendly staff. **Cons:** not right on beach; some distance from attractions of the Kaanapali Resort; two-story buildings have no elevator. $ *Rooms from:*

$330 ✉ 2661 Kekaa Dr., Kaanapali ☎ 808/661–0021 🌐 www.outriggermauieldorado.com ⇆ 204 units 🍴 No meals.

> **KEEP IN MIND**
>
> Most resorts now charge parking and facility fees. What once was complimentary is now tacked on as a "resort fee." Thankfully, condos haven't followed suit just yet—sometimes local calls are still free.

$ RESORT 🏨 **Royal Lahaina Resort.** Built in 1962 as the first hotel in the Kaanapali Resort, this grand property toward the northern end of Kaanapali has hosted millionaires and Hollywood stars, and today pleases families, budget seekers, and luxury travelers with its variety of lodging styles. **Pros:** on-site luau nightly; variety of lodgings and rates; tennis ranch with 11 courts and a pro shop. **Cons:** older property still in need of updating. [$] *Rooms from: $179 ✉ 2780 Kekaa Dr., Kaanapali ☎ 808/661–3611, 800/447–6925 🌐 www.hawaiihotels.com ⇆ 511 rooms 🍴 No meals.*

$$$$ RESORT 🏨 **Sheraton Maui Resort & Spa.** Set among dense gardens on Kaanapali's best stretch of beach, the Sheraton offers a quieter, more low-key atmosphere than its neighboring resorts and sits next to and on top of the 80-foot-high Puu Kekaa, from which divers leap in a nightly torch-lighting and cliff-diving ritual. **Pros:** luxury resort with terrific beach location; great snorkeling right off the beach. **Cons:** extensive property can mean a long walk from your room to the lobby, restaurants, and beach. [$] *Rooms from: $639 ✉ 2605 Kaanapali Pkwy., Kaanapali ☎ 808/661–0031, 866/500-8313 🌐 www.sheraton-maui.com ⇆ 464 rooms, 44 suites 🍴 No meals.*

$$$$ RESORT FAMILY 🏨 **The Westin Maui Resort & Spa.** The cascading waterfall in the lobby of this hotel—a great choice for an active vacation—gives way to an "aquatic playground" with five heated swimming pools, abundant waterfalls (15 at last count), lagoons complete with pink flamingos and swans, and a premier beach. **Pros:** complimentary shuttle to Westin Kaanapali Ocean Resort Villas and to Lahaina, where parking can be difficult; activity programs for all ages; one pool just for adults. **Cons:** you could end up with fantasy overload; resort fee and "extras" can be expensive for some. [$] *Rooms from: $560 ✉ 2365 Kaanapali Pkwy., Kaanapali ☎ 808/667–2525, 866/716–8112 🌐 www.westinmaui.com ⇆ 731 rooms, 28 suites 🍴 No meals.*

KAPALUA AND NEARBY

$$ RENTAL FAMILY 🏨 **Aston at Papakea Resort.** All studios and one- and two-bedroom units at this casual, oceanfront condominium complex face the ocean and, because its units are spread out among 11 low-rise buildings on about 13 acres of land, Papakea has built-in privacy. **Pros:** units have large rooms; lovely garden landscaping; complimentary swimersize, yoga, and tennis lessons. **Cons:** no beach in front of property; pool can get crowded. [$] *Rooms from: $255 ✉ 3543 Lower Honoapiilani Hwy., Honokowai ☎ 808/669–4848, 866/774–2924 🌐 www.astonhotels.com ⇆ 364 units 🍴 No meals.*

$$$ RENTAL FAMILY 🏨 **Honua Kai Resort & Spa.** Two high-rise towers contain these individually owned, eco-friendly (and family-friendly) units combining the conveniences of a condo with the full service of a hotel. **Pros:** large units;

upscale appliances and furnishings. **Cons:** can be windy here. [$] *Rooms from: $339* ✉ *130 Kai Malina Pkwy., Honokowai* ☎ *808/662–2800, 855/718–5789* 🌐 *www.honuakai.com* 🛏 *628 units* 🍴 *No meals.*

$ RENTAL 🏨 **Mahina Surf Oceanfront Resort.** Of the many condo complexes lining the ocean-side stretch of Honoapiilani Highway, this one offers affordable units, friendly service, and a saline oceanfront pool. **Pros:** oceanfront barbecues; resident turtles hang out on the rocks below; no "hidden" fees. **Cons:** oceanfront but with rocky shoreline rather than a beach. [$] *Rooms from: $180* ✉ *4057 Lower Honoapiilani Hwy., Mahinahina* ☎ *808/669–6068, 800/367–6068* 🌐 *www.mahina-surf.com* 🛏 *56 units* 🍴 *No meals.*

$$ RENTAL 🏨 **The Mauian Boutique Beach Studios.** If you're looking for a quiet place to stay, this small, delightful property, with landscaped 2-acre grounds opening out onto lovely Napili Bay, may be for you. **Pros:** reasonable rates; friendly staff. **Cons:** older building; few amenities. [$] *Rooms from: $203* ✉ *5441 Lower Honoapiilani Hwy., Napili* ☎ *808/669–6205, 800/367–5034* 🌐 *www.mauian.com* 🛏 *44 rooms* 🍴 *Breakfast.*

$$$ RESORT FAMILY Fodor's Choice ★ 🏨 **Napili Kai Beach Resort.** Spread across 10 beautiful acres along one of the best beaches on Maui, the Napili Kai draws a loyal following to its Hawaiian-style rooms that open onto private lanai. **Pros:** kids' hula performance and Hawaiian slack-key guitar concert every week; fantastic swimming and sunning beach; old-Hawaii feel; no resort fees. **Cons:** not as modern as other resorts in West Maui. [$] *Rooms from: $280* ✉ *5900 Lower Honoapiilani Hwy., Napili* ☎ *808/669–6271, 800/367–5030* 🌐 *www.napilikai.com* 🛏 *163 units* 🍴 *No meals.*

$$$$ RESORT Fodor's Choice ★ 🏨 **The Ritz-Carlton, Kapalua.** One of Maui's most notable resorts, this elegant hillside property features luxurious service, upscale accommodations, a spa, restaurants, and pool, along with an education center and an enhanced Hawaiian sense of place. **Pros:** luxury and service you'd expect from a Ritz; many cultural and recreational programs. **Cons:** expensive; can be windy on the grounds and at the pool; not on the beach and far from major attractions such as Haleakala. [$] *Rooms from: $479* ✉ *1 Ritz-Carlton Dr., Kapalua* ☎ *808/669–6200, 800/262–8440* 🌐 *www.ritzcarlton.com* 🛏 *463 rooms* 🍴 *No meals.*

$ RENTAL 🏨 **Sands of Kahana.** Meandering gardens, spacious rooms, and an on-site restaurant distinguish this large condominium complex that's primarily a time-share property, with a few units available as vacation rentals—those on the upper floors benefit from the height, with matchless ocean views stretching away from private lanai. **Pros:** spacious units at reasonable prices; restaurant on the premises. **Cons:** you may be approached about buying a unit; street-facing units may get a bit noisy. [$] *Rooms from: $150* ✉ *4299 Lower Honoapiilani Hwy., Kahana* ☎ *808/669–0400 property phone, 800/332–1137 vacation rentals (Sullivan properties)* 🌐 *www.mauiresorts.com* 🛏 *196 units* 🍴 *No meals.*

THE SOUTH SHORE

KIHEI

$$ RENTAL 🏨 **Hale Hui Kai.** Bargain hunters who stumble across this small three-story condo complex of mostly two-bedroom units, just steps away from the sea, will think they've died and gone to heaven. **Pros:** far

enough from the noise and tumult of "central" Kihei; a hidden gem; close enough to all the conveniences; guest discounts at neighboring restaurants. **Cons:** nondescript 1970s architecture; a private home next door blocks the ocean view from some units. [$] *Rooms from: $185* ✉ *2994 S. Kihei Rd., Kihei* ☎ *808/879–1219, 800/809–6284* 🌐 *www.halehuikaimaui.com* 🛏 *40 units* 🍴 *No meals.*

$ RENTAL FAMILY 🏨 **Kamaole Sands.** At this south Kihei property, a good choice for active families, there are swimming pools, tennis courts for a friendly game, and the ideal family beach (Kamaole III) is just across the street. **Pros:** in the seemingly endless strip of Kihei condos, this stands out for its pleasant grounds and well-cared-for units. **Cons:** the complex of buildings may seem a bit too "citylike"; all buildings look the same, so remember a landmark to help you find your unit. [$] *Rooms from: $180* ✉ *2695 S. Kihei Rd., Kihei* ☎ *808/874–8700, 800/367–5004* 🌐 *www.castleresorts.com* 🛏 *205 units* 🍴 *No meals.*

$ RENTAL Fodor's Choice ★ 🏨 **Luana Kai.** If you don't need everything to be totally modern, consider setting up house at this North Kihei condominium-by-the-sea with individually owned units offered in two categories: standard and deluxe. **Pros:** great value; meticulously landscaped grounds; excellent management team. **Cons:** three stories with no elevator; no maid service. [$] *Rooms from: $159* ✉ *940 S. Kihei Rd., Kihei* ☎ *808/879–1268, 800/669–1127* 🌐 *www.luanakai.com* 🛏 *113 units* 🍴 *No meals.*

$$ RENTAL FAMILY 🏨 **Mana Kai Maui.** An unsung hero of South Shore hotels, with both renovated hotel rooms and condos that may be older than its competitors, but you simply cannot get any closer to gorgeous Keawakapu Beach than this. **Pros:** arguably the best beach on the South Shore; great value; Maui Yoga Path is on the property and offers classes at an additional cost. **Cons:** older property; interior design might not appeal to discerning travelers; this part of Kihei can get gusty winds. [$] *Rooms from: $200* ✉ *2960 S. Kihei Rd., Kihei* ☎ *808/879–2778, 800/367–5242* 🌐 *www.crhmaui.com* 🛏 *98 units* 🍴 *No meals.*

$$$ HOTEL 🏨 **Maui Coast Hotel.** You may never notice this lovely hotel because it's set back off the street, but it's worth a look for its proximity to Kamaole Beach I, II, III, the helpful staff, and simple rooms offered at the right price. **Pros:** closest thing to a boutique hotel on the South Shore; Spices restaurant on property is open for breakfast, lunch, and dinner; free use of bicycles. **Cons:** right in the center of Kihei, so traffic and some street noise are issues. [$] *Rooms from: $295* ✉ *2259 S. Kihei Rd., Kihei* ☎ *808/874–6284, 800/895–6284* 🌐 *www.mauicoasthotel.com* 🛏 *151 rooms, 114 suites* 🍴 *No meals.*

$ RENTAL 🏨 **Maui Sunseeker Resort.** Particularly popular with a gay and lesbian clientele, this small, private, and relaxed North Kihei property is a great value for the area, especially since the addition of the new building that houses an on-site café. **Pros:** impeccably maintained; webcam on building videos panoramic ocean views and whales in winter months; good for romance as no kids are allowed. **Cons:** no frills. [$] *Rooms from: $175* ✉ *551 S. Kihei Rd., Kihei* ☎ *808/879–1261, 800/532–6284* 🌐 *www.mauisunseeker.com* 🛏 *23 units* 🍴 *No meals.*

CONDO COMFORTS

Condo renters in search of food and take-out meals should try these great places around Maui.

WEST MAUI

Foodland Farms. This large supermarket combines the best of gourmet selections with all the familiar staples you need to stock your vacation kitchen. They also make a mean *poke* (seafood salad). ✉ *Lahaina Gateway Shopping Center, 345 Keawe St., Lahaina* ☎ *808/662–7088.*

The Maui Fish Market. It's worth stopping by this little fish market for oysters or a cup of fresh fish chowder. You can also get live lobsters and marinated fish to grill up on your barbecue. ✉ *3600 Lower Honoapiilani Hwy., Honokowai* ☎ *808/665–9895* 🌐 *www.fishmarketmaui.com.*

SOUTH SHORE

Safeway. Find everything you could possibly need at this huge supermarket. ✉ *277 Piikea Ave., Kihei* ☎ *808/891–9120.*

CENTRAL MAUI

Safeway. This supermarket has a deli, prepared-foods section, and bakery that are all fantastic. There's a good wine selection, tons of produce, and a flower shop where you can treat yourself to a fresh lei. ✉ *170 E. Kaahumanu Ave., Kahului* ☎ *808/877–3377.*

UPCOUNTRY

Pukalani Terrace Center. Come here if you're looking for pizza, a bank, post office, hardware store, Laundromat, or Starbucks. ✉ *55 Pukalani St., Pukalani.*

Foodland. This member of a local supermarket chain is at Pukalani Terrace Center; it has fresh sushi and a good seafood section in addition to the usual fare. ✉ *55 Pukalani St., Pukalani* ☎ *808/572–0674.*

NORTH SHORE

Haiku Cannery. This marketplace is home to the Haiku Grocery, a Laundromat, and a few other small stores. The post office is across the street. ✉ *810 Haiku Rd., Haiku.*

Haiku Grocery. You can find the basics, such as veggies, meats, wine, snacks, and ice cream, at this local store in the Haiku Cannery. ✉ *810 Haiku Rd., Haiku* ☎ *808/575–9291.*

3

WAILEA

$$$$ RESORT Fodor's Choice ★ 🏨 **ANdAZ Maui at Wailea.** Maui's newest luxury (and eco-friendly) beachfront resort has the world talking about its sleek island style, five infinity pools, and hyperlocal approach to everything from its cocktail program to the designer clothes worn by iPad-toting staff. **Pros:** outstanding service; no resort fee; free Wi-Fi; shuttle service around Wailea; use of the spa's wet rooms. **Cons:** expensive; can be loud in the evenings; slick design style might feel cold to some. [$] *Rooms from: $799* ✉ *3550 Wailea Alanui Dr., Wailea* ☎ *808/879–1234* 🌐 *maui.andaz.hyatt.com* 🛏 *255 rooms, 7 villas, 35 suites* 🍴 *No meals.*

$$$$ RESORT FAMILY Fodor's Choice ★ 🏨 **Fairmont Kea Lani Maui.** Gleaming white spires and tiled archways are the hallmark of this stunning resort that's particularly good for families. **Pros:** for families, this is the best of the South Shore luxury resorts; on-site deli good for picnic fare. **Cons:** some feel the architecture and design scream anything *but* Hawaii; great villas but price puts them out of range for many. [$] *Rooms from: $549* ✉ *4100 Wailea Alanui Dr., Wailea* ☎ *808/875–4100, 866/540–4456* 🌐 *www.fairmont.com/kealani* 🛏 *413 suites, 37 villas* 🍴 *No meals.*

$$$$ RESORT Fodor's Choice ★ 🏨 **Four Seasons Resort Maui at Wailea.** *Impeccably stylish, subdued, and relaxing* describe most Four Seasons properties, and this one fronting award-winning Wailea Beach is no exception, with thoughtful luxuries like Evian spritzers poolside and twice-daily housekeeping making it a Maui favorite. **Pros:** no resort fee; children's program, poolside cabanas, tennis, and other activities are complimentary; the most low-key elegance on Maui; exceptional service. **Cons:** expensive; a bit pretentious for some. [$] *Rooms from: $595* ✉ *3900 Wailea Alanui Dr., Wailea* ☎ *808/874–8000, 800/332–3442* 🌐 *www.fourseasons.com/maui* 🛏 *305 rooms, 75 suites* 🍴 *No meals.*

$$$$ RESORT FAMILY 🏨 **Grand Wailea Resort Hotel & Spa.** "Grand" is no exaggeration for this opulent, sunny, 40-acre resort—either astounding or over the top, depending on your point of view—with elaborate water features such as a "canyon riverpool" with slides, caves, a Tarzan swing, and a water elevator. **Pros:** you can meet every vacation need without ever leaving the property; many shops. **Cons:** at these prices, service should be extraordinary, but isn't always up to par; extra charges for resort fee, parking, and more; sometimes too much is too much. [$] *Rooms from: $369* ✉ *3850 Wailea Alanui Dr., Wailea* ☎ *808/875–1234, 800/888–6100* 🌐 *www.grandwailea.com* 🛏 *728 rooms, 52 suites* 🍴 *No meals.*

$$$$ RENTAL 🏨 **Makena Surf.** For travelers who've done all there is to do on Maui and just want simple but luxurious relaxation at a condo that spills onto a private beach, this is the spot. **Pros:** away from it all, yet still close enough to "civilization"; laundry facilities in every unit. **Cons:** too secluded and "locked-up" for some; check-in is at a different location (✉ *34 Wailea Gateway Plaza*); Hawaiian legend has it that spirits may have been disturbed here. [$] *Rooms from: $449* ✉ *128 Kio Loop, Kihei* ☎ *808/891–6249, 800/367–5246* 🌐 *www.destinationresortshawaii.com* 🛏 *39 units* 🍴 *No meals.*

$$$$ RENTAL 🏨 **Polo Beach Club.** Lording over a hidden section of Polo Beach, this wonderful older eight-story rental property's charm somehow manages to stay under the radar. **Pros:** you can pick fresh herbs for dinner out of the garden; the beach fronting the building is a beautiful, private crescent of sand. **Cons:** some may feel isolated; check-in is at a different location (✉ *34 Wailea Gateway Plaza*). [$] *Rooms from: $709* ✉ *4400 Makena Rd., Kihei* ☎ *808/891–6249, 800/367–5246* 🌐 *www.destinationresortshawaii.com* 🛏 *71 units* 🍴 *No meals.*

$$$$ RESORT 🏨 **Wailea Beach Marriott Resort & Spa.** Built before current construction laws, the Marriott's rooms sit much closer to the crashing surf than at most resorts and a stay here promises luxurious amenities, spacious accommodations, and golf and tennis privileges nearby. **Pros:** spa is one of the most fanciful in Hawaii; near good shopping; luau four

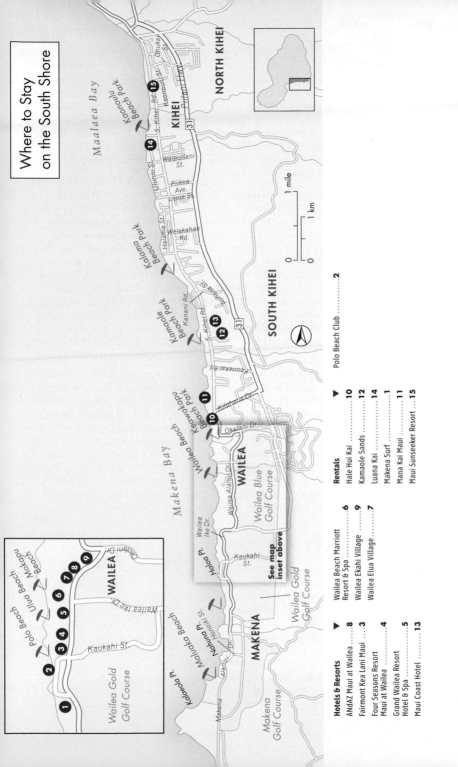

Where to Stay on the South Shore

Maalaea Bay

NORTH KIHEI

KIHEI

SOUTH KIHEI

Kaonoulu Beach Park

Kalama Beach Park

Kamaole Park Beach Park

Makena Bay

Wailea Beach

Keawakapu Beach Park

WAILEA

Wailea Blue Golf Course

Wailea Gold Golf Course

MAKENA

Makena Golf Course

Polo Beach

Ulua Beach

Mokapu Beach

Maluaka Beach

WAILEA

Wailea Gold Golf Course

See map inset above

Hotels & Resorts ▶

ANdAZ Maui at Wailea	**8**
Fairmont Kea Lani Maui	**3**
Four Seasons Resort Maui at Wailea	**4**
Grand Wailea Resort Hotel & Spa	**5**
Maui Coast Hotel	**13**
Wailea Beach Marriott Resort & Spa	**6**
Wailea Ekahi Village	**9**
Wailea Elua Village	**7**

Rentals ▶

Hale Hui Kai	**10**
Kamaole Sands	**12**
Luana Kai	**14**
Makena Surf	**1**
Mana Kai Maui	**11**
Maui Sunseeker Resort	**15**
Polo Beach Club	**2**

0   1 mile
0   1 km

VACATION RENTAL COMPANIES

There are many real-estate companies that specialize in short-term vacation rentals. They may represent an entire resort property, most of the units at one property, or even individually owned units. The companies listed here have a long history of excellent service to Maui visitors.

AA Oceanfront Rentals and Sales. As the name suggests, the specialty is "oceanfront." With rental units in more than 25 condominium complexes on the South Shore from the northernmost reaches of Kihei all the way to Wailea, there's something for everyone at prices that range from $90 to $450 a night. ⊠ *1279 S. Kihei Rd., No. 107, Kihei* ☎ *808/879–7288, 800/488–6004* ⊕ *www.aaoceanfront.com.*

Chase 'n Rainbows. Family-owned and -operated, this is the largest property management company on West Maui, with the largest selection of rentals, from studios to three bedrooms. Rentals are everywhere from Lahaina town to Kapalua. Prices range from about $100 to $1,500 per night. The company has been in business since 1980, and is good at what it does. ⊠ *118 Kupuohi St., Lahaina* ☎ *808/667–7088, 800/367–6092* ⊕ *www.westmauicondos.com.*

Destination Resorts Hawaii. If it's the South Shore luxury of Wailea and Makena you seek, look no further. This company has hundreds of condominiums and villas ranging in size from studios to five bedrooms, and in price from $279 a night for a studio at Wailea Grand Champions Villas, to more than $4,000 (yes, a night) for the splashy Wailea Beach Villas. The company offers excellent personalized service (including grocery discount cards, Wi-Fi, and parking, all included in the price) and is known for particularly fine housekeeping services. ⊠ *34 Wailea Gateway Pl., Suite A102, Wailea* ☎ *808/891–6249, 800/367–5246* ⊕ *www. destinationresortshawaii.com.*

Maalaea Bay Realty and Rentals. A little strip of condominiums within the isthmus that links Central and West Maui, Maalaea is often overlooked, but it shouldn't be. This company has more than 100 one- and two-bedroom units from $100 to $300 per night. The wind is usually strong here, but there's a nice beach, a harbor, and some good shopping and decent restaurants. ⊠ *280 Hauoli St., Maalaea* ☎ *808/244–5627, 800/367–6084* ⊕ *www.maalaeabay.com.*

Maui Condo & Home Vacations. This Maui-based agency manages more than 3,000 individually owned condos. Most of the units are near the beach or golf courses, and are located throughout Maui. Studios to three-bedroom units range in price from $100 to $450 per night. ⊠ *1819 S. Kihei Rd., Suite D103, Kihei* ☎ *808/879–5445, 800/822–4409* ⊕ *www.mauicondo.com.*

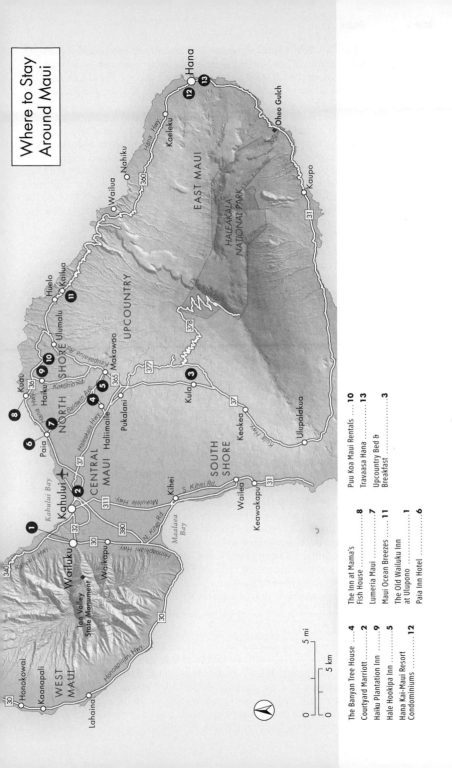

Where to Stay Around Maui

The Banyan Tree House **4**
Courtyard Marriott **2**
Haiku Plantation Inn **9**
Hale Hookipa Inn **5**
Hana Kai-Maui Resort
Condominiums **12**

The Inn at Mama's
Fish House **8**
Lumeria Maui **7**
Maui Ocean Breezes **11**
The Old Wailuku Inn
at Ulupono **1**
Paia Inn Hotel **6**

Puu Koa Maui Rentals **10**
Travaasa Hana **13**
Upcountry Bed &
Breakfast **3**

nights a week. **Cons:** not quite beachfront and has a rocky shore, so you must walk left or right to sit on the sand; there can be a lot of foot traffic on the beach walk along the coast. [$] *Rooms from: $595* ✉ *3700 Wailea Alanui Dr., Wailea* ☎ *808/879–1922* 🌐 *www.waileamarriott.com* 🛏 *497 rooms, 47 suites* 🍴 *No meals.*

$$$$ RESORT 🏨 **Wailea Ekahi Village.** Overlooking Keawakapu Beach, this family-friendly vacation resort features studios and one- and two-bedroom suites in low-rise buildings that span 34 acres of tropical gardens and won't cost your child's entire college fund. **Pros:** convenient access to a great beach; kitchen and laundry facilities in-suite. **Cons:** the large complex can be tricky to find your way around; check-in is at a different location (✉ *34 Wailea Gateway Plaza*). [$] *Rooms from: $350* ✉ *3300 Wailea Alanui Dr., Wailea* ☎ *808/891–6249, 800/357–5246* 🌐 *www.destinationresortshawaiicom* 🛏 *289 units* 🍴 *No meals.*

$$$$ RESORT 🏨 **Wailea Elua Village.** Located on Ulua Beach, one of the island's most beloved snorkeling spots, these upscale one-, two-, and three-bedroom condo suites have spectacular views and 24 acres of manicured lawns and gardens. **Pros:** easy access to the designer boutiques and upscale restaurants at the Shops at Wailea; for a nominal fee, the concierge will stock your refrigerator with groceries, even hard-to-find items for those with dietary restrictions. **Cons:** large complex; hard to find your way around; check-in is at a different location (✉ *34 Wailea Gateway Plaza*). [$] *Rooms from: $429* ✉ *3600 Wailea Alanui Dr., Wailea* ☎ *808/891–6249, 800/367–5246* 🌐 *www.destinationresortshawaii.com* 🛏 *152 suites* 🍴 *No meals.*

CENTRAL MAUI

$$ HOTEL 🏨 **Courtyard Marriott.** Conveniently located near Kahului Airport, this hotel offers many amenities for business travelers as well as tourists. **Pros:** recent construction; central location; no resort fee. **Cons:** not on—or even really near—any good beaches; airport and city noise. [$] *Rooms from: $189* ✉ *532 Keolani Place, Kahului* ☎ *808/871–1800, 877/852–1880* 🌐 *www.marriotthawaii.com* 🛏 *138 rooms* 🍴 *No meals.*

$ B&B/INN Fodor's Choice ★ 🏨 **The Old Wailuku Inn at Ulupono.** Built in 1924 and listed on the State of Hawaii Register of Historic Places, this home may be the ultimate Hawaiian B&B. **Pros:** the charm of old Hawaii; knowledgeable innkeepers; walking distance to Maui's best ethnic restaurants; free Wi-Fi and parking; no resort fees. **Cons:** closest beach is a 20-minute drive away; you may hear some traffic at certain times. [$] *Rooms from: $165* ✉ *2199 Kahookele St., Wailuku* ☎ *808/244–5897, 800/305–4899* 🌐 *www.mauiinn.com* 🛏 *10 rooms* 🍴 *Breakfast.*

UPCOUNTRY

$ B&B/INN FAMILY 🏨 **The Banyan Tree House.** If a taste of rural Hawaii life in plantation days is what you crave, you can find it at this pastoral two-acre property awash in tropical foliage, huge monkeypod, and banyan trees. **Pros:** two cottages and the pool are outfitted for travelers with disabilities; you can walk to Makawao town for dining and shopping. **Cons:** the furniture in the cottages is pretty basic; few amenities. [$] *Rooms from:*

$155 ✉ *3265 Baldwin Ave., Makawao* ☎ *808/572–9021* 🌐 *www.bed-breakfast-maui.com* 🛏 *7 rooms* 🍴 *Breakfast.*

$ B&B/INN Fodor's Choice ★ 🏨 **Hale Hookipa Inn.** A handsome 1924 Craftsman-style house in the heart of Makawao town is on both the Hawaii and the National Historic Registers, and provides a great base for excursions to Haleakala, Hana, or North Shore beaches. **Pros:** genteel rural setting; price includes buffet breakfast with organic fruit from the garden. **Cons:** a 20-minute drive to the nearest beach; this is not the sun, sand, and surf surroundings of travel posters. [$] *Rooms from: $140* ✉ *32 Pakani Pl., Makawao* ☎ *808/572–6698, 877/572–6698* 🌐 *www.maui-bed-and-breakfast.com* 🛏 *3 rooms, 1 suite* 🍴 *Breakfast.*

$$$ B&B/INN 🏨 **Lumeria Maui.** Peace, tranquillity, and a healthful experience are what you will find at this beautifully restored historic property. **Pros:** organic and healthy; peaceful and restful setting. **Cons:** bathrooms have shower only; not near the beach. [$] *Rooms from: $329* ✉ *1813 Baldwin Ave., Makawao* ☎ *808/579–8877, 855/579–8877* 🌐 *www.lumeriamaui.com* 🛏 *24 rooms* 🍴 *Breakfast.*

$ B&B/INN 🏨 **Upcountry Bed & Breakfast.** Spacious rooms and unobstructed views are two reasons to experience Upcountry Maui at this B&B, into which owner Michael Sullivan has put a lot of heart and soul. **Pros:** at 3,000 feet above sea level, it's closer to Haleakala than most accommodations; two rooms are ADA accessible; local store and restaurant nearby; rates include taxes. **Cons:** can be cool in Kula; far from beach; not everyone may enjoy the mellow and friendly resident dog, Gabby. [$] *Rooms from: $150* ✉ *4925 Lower Kula Rd., Kula* ☎ *808/878–8083* 🌐 *www.upcountrybandb.com* 🛏 *4 rooms* 🍴 *Breakfast.*

THE NORTH SHORE

HAIKU

$ B&B/INN 🏨 **Haiku Plantation Inn.** Water lilies and a shade tree bedecked in orchids greet you at this forested bend in the road, where a gracious estate, built in 1870 for the plantation company doctor, continues the healing tradition with its wellness programs. **Pros:** quiet setting; close to restaurants, gas station, and post office; opportunities to experience authentic Hawaiian culture. **Cons:** no resort amenities; 10-minute drive to closest beach. [$] *Rooms from: $119* ✉ *555 Haiku Rd., Haiku* ☎ *808/575–7500* 🌐 *www.haikuleana.net* 🛏 *4 rooms* 🍴 *Breakfast.*

KUAU

$ RENTAL FAMILY Fodor's Choice ★ 🏨 **The Inn at Mama's Fish House.** Nestled in gardens adjacent to one of Maui's most popular dining spots (Mama's Fish House) and fronting a small beach known as Kuau Cove, these well-maintained one- and two-bedroom cottages have a retro-Hawaiian style with rattan furnishings and local artwork. **Pros:** daily maid service; free parking; next to Hookipa Beach. **Cons:** three-night minimum stay; Mama's Fish House is popular, so there can be many people around in the evenings (it's more mellow during the day). [$] *Rooms from: $175* ✉ *799 Poho Pl., Kuau* ☎ *808/579–9764, 800/860–4852* 🌐 *www.mamasfishhouse.com* 🛏 *12 units* 🍴 *No meals.*

3

$ RENTAL 🏨 **Maui Ocean Breezes.** The cool ocean breeze rolls through these pretty eco-friendly rentals, making this a perfect spot to relax and enjoy the gorgeous scenery along the ocean side of the famed Road to Hana. **Pros:** one of few licensed rentals in area; expansive lawn with ocean views; meditation hut. **Cons:** you have to drive to the beach; the owner prefers stays of seven nights or longer, though will negotiate depending on availability. [$] *Rooms from: $155* ✉ *240 N. Holokai Rd., Haiku* ☎ *808/283–8526* 🌐 *www.mauivacationhideaway.com* 🛏 *3 units* 🍴 *No meals.*

$$ B&B/INN 🏨 **Paia Inn Hotel.** Despite the location sandwiched between the bustling Paia town along Hana Highway and the sandy Paia Bay, this stylish inn is refreshingly quiet and includes oceanfront and ocean-view accommodations. **Pros:** friendly and knowledgeable staff; no minimum stay required; guests receive a complimentary membership at Upcountry Fitness in Haiku and free coffee and tea throughout the day. **Cons:** no elevator; standard rooms are extraordinarily small and have no closets. [$] *Rooms from: $199* ✉ *93 Hana Hwy., Paia* ☎ *808/579–6000, 800/721–4000* 🌐 *www.paiainn.com* 🛏 *15 rooms* 🍴 *No meals.*

$ RENTAL 🏨 **Puu Koa Maui Rentals.** Off a peaceful cul-de-sac in a residential area, these two well-maintained and immaculately clean homes offer studio and one-bedroom accommodations. **Pros:** very clean; reasonable rates; good spot for a group. **Cons:** 10-minute drive to the beach; set in quiet residential area. [$] *Rooms from: $90* ✉ *66 Puu Koa Pl., Haiku* ☎ *808/573–2884* 🌐 *www.puukoa.com* 🛏 *7 rooms* 🍴 *No meals.*

ROAD TO HANA

$$ RENTAL Fodor's Choice ★ 🏨 **Hana Kai-Maui Resort Condominiums.** Perfectly situated on Hana Bay, this resort complex has a long history (it opened in 1970) and an excellent reputation for visitor hospitality—and the ocean views are stunning. **Pros:** it's a stone's throw to Hana Bay, where you can take a swim or have a Roselani mac-nut ice-cream cone at Tutu's; one-night rentals are accepted; daily housekeeping. **Cons:** early to bed and early to rise—no nightlife or excitement here; no elevator. [$] *Rooms from: $210* ✉ *4865 Uakea Rd., Hana* ☎ *808/248–8426, 800/346–2772* 🌐 *www.hanakaimaui.com* 🛏 *18 units* 🍴 *No meals.*

$$$$ RESORT 🏨 **Travaasa Hana.** A destination in itself, the former Hotel Hana-Maui might have a new name, but this secluded and quietly luxurious property still delivers the tropical Hawaii of your dreams, complete with a decadent spa, an adults-only section, unobstructed views of the Pacific, and a restaurant that's a local celeb hot spot. **Pros:** for getting away from it all, there's no better or more beautiful place; spa is incredibly relaxing. **Cons:** everything moves slowly; if you can't live without your iPhone, this is not the place for you; it's oceanfront but doesn't have a sandy beach (though red- and black-sand beaches are nearby). [$] *Rooms from: $400* ✉ *5031 Hana Hwy., Hana* ☎ *808/248–8211, 855/868–7282* 🌐 *www.travaasa.com/hana* 🛏 *47 cottages, 27 suites* 🍴 *Multiple meal plans.*

4

THE BIG ISLAND

WELCOME TO THE BIG ISLAND

TOP REASONS TO GO

★ **Hawaii Volcanoes National Park:** Catch the lava fireworks at night and explore newly made land, lava tubes, steam vents, and giant craters.

★ **Waipio Valley:** Experience a real-life secret garden, the remote spot known as the Valley of the Kings.

★ **Kealakekua Bay:** Watch spinner dolphins near the Captain Cook Monument, then go snorkeling over the fabulous coral reefs.

★ **The Heavens:** Stargaze through gigantic telescopes on snow-topped Mauna Kea.

★ **Hidden Beaches:** Discover one of the Kohala Coast's lesser-known gems.

1 Kailua-Kona. This seaside town is packed with restaurants, shops, and a busy waterfront bustling with tourists along the main street, Alii Drive.

2 The Kona Coast. This area stretches a bit north of Kailua-Kona and much farther south, including gorgeous Kealakekua Bay. It's the place to take farm tours and taste samples of world-famous Kona Coffee.

3 The Kohala Coast. The sparkling coast is home to all those long, white-sand beaches, and the expensive resorts that go with them.

4 Waimea. Ranches sprawl across the cool, upland meadows of the area, known as *paniolo* (cowboy) country.

5 Mauna Kea. Climb (or drive) this 13,796-foot mountain for what's considered the world's best stargazing, with 13 telescopes perched on top.

6 The Hamakua Coast. Waterfalls, dramatic cliffs, ocean views, ancient hidden valleys, rain forests, and the stunning Waipio Valley are just a few of the treats here.

7 Hilo. Known as the City of Rainbows for all its rain, Hilo is often skipped by tourists in favor of the sunny

Kohala Coast. But for what many consider the "real" Hawaii, as well as incredible rain forests, waterfalls, and the island's best farmers' market, Hilo can't be beat.

8 Puna. This is where the most recent lava flows are happening, so it has brand-new jet-black beaches with volcanic hot springs.

9 Hawaii Volcanoes National Park and vicinity. The land around the park is continually expanding, as the active Kilauea Volcano sends lava spilling into the ocean. The nearby town of Volcano Village provides a great base for exploring the park.

10 Kau and Ka Lae (South Point). Round the southernmost part of the island for two of the Big Island's most unusual beaches: Papakolea (Green Sands) Beach, and Punaluu Black Sand Beach.

GETTING ORIENTED

You could fit all the other Hawaiian Islands into the Big Island and still have a little room left over—hence the name. Locals refer to the island by side: the Kona (leeward) side to the west and Hilo side to the east. Most of the resorts, condos, attractions, and restaurants are located along 30 miles of the sunny Kona side, while the rainy, windward Hilo side offers a much more local and "old Hawaii" experience.

4

Map of the Big Island of Hawaii showing regions and locations

HAMAKUA COAST

240 Honokaa
19 (Mamalahoa Hwy.) 6
Hawaii Belt Rd.

aimea / amuela
amuela airport 4
Saddle Rd.

HAMAKUA

Mauna Kea 13,796 ft.

200 5

19

Hilo Bay

200 Saddle Rd.
HILO 7 Hilo
11 Hilo International Airport (General Lyman Field)

Stainback Hwy.

Kulani Honor Camp
Ola'a Rain Forest
Hawaii Belt Rd.

130
Pahoa
Cape Kumukahi
132

PUNA
8
130

auna Loa 3,679 ft.
Volcano Village
Kilauea Crater
Kilauea 4,069 ft. 9
11

Hawaii Volcanoes National Park

Kalapana

KAU
10

Hawaii Belt Rd.

Punaluu

0   15 mi
0   15 km

Honuapo Bay

Waikapuna Bay

Puu Nahaha Point

a Lae (Souh Point)

GREAT ITINERARIES

Yes, the Big Island is big, and yes, there's a lot to see. If you're short on time, consider flying into one airport and out the other. That will give you the opportunity to see both sides of the island without ever having to backtrack. Decide what sort of note you'd rather end on to determine your route—if you'd prefer to spend your last few days near the beach, go from east to west; if hiking through rain forests and showering in waterfalls sounds like a better way to wrap up the trip, move from west to east. If you're short on time, head straight for Hawaii Volcanoes National Park and briefly visit Hilo before traveling the Hamakua Coast route and making your new base in Kailua-Kona.

Hike Volcanoes

Devote a full day (at least) to exploring Hawaii Volcanoes National Park. Head out on the Kilauea Iki trail—a 4-mile loop near Thurston Lava Tube—by late morning. Leave the park to grab lunch at nearby restaurants in Volcano Village just a few minutes away, or plan ahead and pack your own picnic before you start your morning hike. Later you can take a stroll past the steam vents and sulfur banks, and then hit the Jaggar Museum, which offers great views of Halemaumau Crater's glow at night.

Black and Green Sand

Check out some of the unusual beaches you'll find only on the Big Island. Start with a hike into Green Sands Beach near South Point and plan to spend some time sitting on the beach, dipping into the bay's turquoise waters, and marveling at the surreal beauty of this spot.

When you've had your fill, hop back in the car and head south about half an hour to Punaluu Black Sand Beach, the favorite nesting place of the endangered Hawaiian hawksbill turtle. Although the surf is often too rough to go swimming with green sea turtles, there are typically at least two or three napping on the beach at any given time.

Majestic Waterfalls and Valley of the Kings

Take a day to enjoy the splendors of the Hamakua Coast—any gorge you see on the road is an indication of a waterfall waiting to be explored. For a sure bet, head to beautiful Waipio Valley. Book a horseback, hiking, or four-wheel-drive tour, or walk on in yourself (just keep in mind that it's an arduous hike back up—a 25% grade for a little over a mile).

Once in the valley, take your first right to get to the black-sand beach. Take a moment to sit here—the ancient Hawaiians believed this was where souls crossed over to the afterlife. Whether you believe it or not, there's something unmistakably special about this place.

Sun and Stars

Spend the day lounging on a Kohala Coast beach (Hapuna, Kaunaoa—also known as Mauna Kea—or Kua Bay), but throw jackets and boots in the car because you'll be catching the sunset from Mauna Kea's summit. Bundle up and stick around after darkness falls for some of the world's best stargazing.

For the safest, most comfortable experience, book a summit tour or stop in at the Onizuka Center for International Astronomy, a visitor center located at about 9,000 feet, or join the free summit tour at 1 pm on Saturday or Sunday, and return to the center to use the telescopes for evening stargazing.

4

Nicknamed "The Big Island," Hawaii Island is a microcosm of Hawaii the state. From long white-sand beaches and crystal clear bays to rain forests, waterfalls, valleys, exotic flowers, and birds, all things quintessentially Hawaii are well represented here. An assortment of happy surprises also distinguishes the Big Island from the rest of Hawaii — an active volcano (Kilauea) oozing red lava and creating new earth every day, the clearest place in the world to view stars in the night sky (Mauna Kea), and some seriously good coffee from the famous Kona district and also from neighboring Kau.

GEOLOGY

Home to eight of the world's 13 sub-climate zones, this is the land of fire (thanks to active Kilauea volcano) and ice (compliments of not-so-active Mauna Kea, topped with snow and expensive telescopes). At just under a million years old, Hawaii is the youngest of the main Hawaiian Islands. Three of its five volcanoes are considered active: Mauna Loa, Hualalai, and Kilauea. The southeast rift zone of Kilauea has been spewing lava regularly since January 3, 1983; another eruption began at Kilauea's summit caldera in March 2008, the first since 1982. Back in 1984, Mauna Loa's eruptions crept almost to Hilo, and it could fire up again any minute—or not for years. Hualalai last erupted in 1801, and geologists say it will definitely do so again within 100 years. Mauna Kea is currently considered dormant but may very well erupt again. Kohala, which last erupted some 120,000 years ago, is inactive, but on volatile Hawaii Island, you can never be sure.

AGRICULTURE

In the 19th- and mid-20th centuries sugar was the main agricultural and economic staple of all the Islands, but especially the Big Island. The drive along the Hamakua Coast, from Hilo or Waimea, illustrates

The Big Island of Hawaii

↖
TO MAUI

THE KOHALA COAST AND WAIMEA

UPOLU PT.

Pololu Valley
Pololu Beach

Kohala Forest Reserve

Hawi
Kapaau
Kapaa Beach Park
Mahukona Beach Park
Mahukona
Lapakahi State Historical Park

NORTH KOHALA

KOHALA MOUNTAINS

Kohala Mountain Rd.

Akoni Pule Hwy.

250

270

Kawaihae

Waika

Waioka

Kawaihae Rd.

Puukohola Heiau National Historic Site, Mailekini Heiau
Spencer Beach Park
Kaunaoa Beach
Hapuna Beach State Park

Puako

SOUTH KOHALA

Waikoloa

Anaehoomalu

Anaehoomalu Bay

19

MAUNA KEA AND THE HAMAKUA COAST

HAMAKUA COAST

WAIPIO VALLEY OVERLOOK

Waipio Valley

240

Honokaa

19 (Mamalahoa Hwy.)

Paquilo

Kukaiau

Ookala

Kalopa State Rec. Area

Hilo Forest Reserve

Laupahoehoe
Papaaloa
Weloka

Ninole

Honohina

Akaka Falls State Park

Hakalau

Honomu

Kolekole Beach Park

Wailea

19

HAMAKUA

Mauna Kea
13,796 ft

Kawainui

Papaikou

Hilo Bay

Reeds Bay Beach Park
LELEIWI POINT

Hilo International Airport (General Lyman Field)

Onekahakaha Beach Park

Kapoho

HILO

Wainaku

NORTH HILO

SOUTH HILO

11

Keaau

Kurtistown

130

Mountain View

Kukui

Kulani Honor Camp

Saddle Rd.

Stainback Hwy.

200

Waimea (Kamuela)

Saddle Rd.

Waikii

200

Hawaii Belt Rd.

NORTH KONA

Puuanahulu

Mamalahoa Hwy.

190

Queen Kaahumanu Hwy.

Huehue Ranch

Mount Hualalai
8,271 ft

Kalaoa

Kiholo Bay

Kua Bay

Kekaha Kai State Park

Kona International Airport

Kaloko-Honokohau National Historical Park

Honokohau

19

Holualoa

KAILUA-KONA

Kailua Bay

White Sands Beach Park

Kahaluu

Kealakekua

11

Mamalahoa Hwy.

Mauna Loa

KOHALA COAST

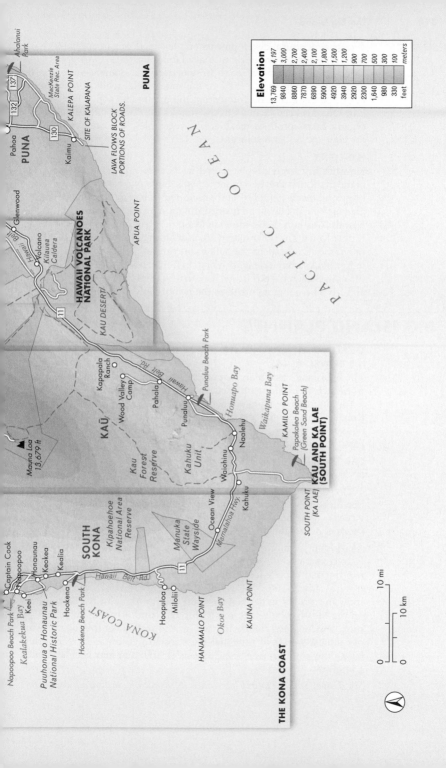

THE KONA COAST

SOUTH KONA

Napoopoo Beach Park
Kealakekua Bay
Captain Cook
Napoopoo
Keei
Honaunau
Puuhonua o Honaunau
National Historic Park
Keokea
Kealia
Hookena
Hookena Beach Park

KONA COAST

Hawaii Belt Rd.

Kipahoehoe
National Area
Reserve

Manuka
State
Wayside

Hoopuloa
Miloii

HANAMALO POINT

Okoe Bay

KAUNA POINT

Ocean View

Mamalahoa Hwy.

Kahuku

KAU

Kau Forest
Reserve

Kahuku
Unit

Waiohinu

Naalehu

SOUTH POINT
(KA LAE)

KAU AND KA LAE
(SOUTH POINT)

KAMILO POINT

Papakolea Beach
(Green Sand Beach)

Waikapuna Bay

Honuapo Bay

Punaluu Beach Park
Punaluu

Pahala

Wood Valley
Camp

Kapapala
Ranch

Hawaii Belt Rd.

Mauna Loa
13,679 ft

HAWAII VOLCANOES
NATIONAL PARK

KAU DESERT

Kilauea
Caldera
Volcano
Glenwood

Hawaii Belt Rd.

APUA POINT

PACIFIC OCEAN

LAVA FLOWS BLOCK
PORTIONS OF ROADS.

SITE OF KALAPANA
Kaimu

130

PUNA
Pahoa

132

137

MacKenzie
State Rec. Area

KALEPA POINT

Ahalanui
Park

PUNA

Elevation

	feet	meters
	13,769	4,197
	9840	3,000
	8860	2,700
	7870	2,400
	6890	2,100
	5900	1,800
	4920	1,500
	3940	1,200
	2920	900
	2300	700
	1,640	500
	980	300
	330	100
	feet	meters

0   10 mi

0   10 km

diverse agricultural developments on the island. Sugarcane stalks have been replaced by orchards of macadamia-nut trees, eucalyptus, and specialty crops from lettuce to strawberries. Macadamia-nut orchards on the Big Island supply 90% of the state's yield, while coffee continues to be big business, dominating the mountains above Kealakekua Bay. Orchids keep farmers from Honokaa to Pahoa afloat, and small organic farms produce meat, fruits, vegetables, and even goat cheese for high-end resort restaurants.

HISTORY

Hawaii's history is deeply rooted in its namesake island, which was home to the first Polynesian settlements and now boasts the state's best-preserved *heiau* (temples) and *puuhonua* (refuges). Kamehameha, the greatest king in Hawaiian history and the man credited with uniting the Islands, was born here, raised in Waipio Valley, and died peacefully in Kailua-Kona. The other man who most affected Hawaiian history, Captain James Cook, spent the bulk of his time in the Islands here, docked in Kealakekua Bay. (He landed first on Kauai, but had little contact with the natives there.) Thus it was here that Western influence was first felt, and from here that it spread to the rest of Hawaii.

BIG ISLAND PLANNER

GETTING HERE AND AROUND

AIR TRAVEL

The Big Island's two main airports are almost directly across the island from each other. Kona International Airport, on the west side, is about a 10-minute drive from Kailua-Kona and 30 to 45 minutes from the Kohala Coast. On the east side, Hilo International Airport, 2 miles from downtown Hilo, is about 40 minutes from Hawaii Volcanoes National Park. A 2½-hour drive connects Hilo and Kailua-Kona.

CAR TRAVEL

It's essential to rent a car when visiting the Big Island. As the name suggests, it's a big island, and it takes a while to get from point A to point B.

For those who want to travel from the west side to the east side, or vice versa, the newly rerouted and repaved Saddle Road creates a nice shortcut across the middle of the island.

As a result of multiple microclimates and varying elevations, the Big Island experiences its share of diverse weather. On one circle-the-island trip you may experience combinations of the following: intensely heavy tropical downpours; cool, windy conditions; searing heat; and even snow flurries if you happen to be driving up Mauna Kea. Be cautious on the mostly single-lane roads through rural areas, as these can be slick, winding, and poorly lit. Pull over to the side of the road to wait out intense bursts of rain that may obscure vision and create other hazardous conditions. These are usually brief and may even end with a rainbow.

See Travel Smart Hawaii for more information on renting a car and driving.

ISLAND
DRIVING TIMES
Before you embark on your day trip, it's a good idea to know how long it will take you to get to your destination. Some areas, like downtown Kailua-Kona and Waimea, can become congested at certain times of day. For those traveling to South Kona, the county has opened a long-awaited bypass road between Keauhou and Kealakekua, which has alleviated congestion considerably during rush hour. In general, you can expect the following average driving times:

ISLAND DRIVING TIMES	
Kailua-Kona to Kealakekua Bay	14 miles/25 mins
Kailua-Kona to Kohala Coast	32 miles/40 mins
Kailua-Kona to Waimea	40 miles/1 hr mins
Kailua-Kona to Hamakua Coast	53 miles/1 hr, 40 mins
Kailua-Kona to Hilo	75 miles/2½ hrs
Kohala Coast to Waimea	16 miles/20 mins
Kohala Coast to Hamakua Coast	29 miles/55 mins
Hilo to Volcano	30 miles/40 mins

RESTAURANTS

Hawaii is a melting pot of cultures, and nowhere is this more apparent than in its cuisine. From luau and "plate lunches" to sushi and steak, there's no shortage of interesting flavors and presentations. The "grow local, buy local" movement is in full force on the Big Island. This is a welcome shift from years past, in which many foods were imported, and it's a happy trend for visitors, who get to taste juicy, flavorful Waimea tomatoes, handmade Hamakua goat cheese, locally raised beef, or even island-grown wine. Whether you're looking for a quick snack or a multicourse meal, you can find the best that the island has to offer at farmers' markets, restaurants, and cafés.

Prices in the reviews are the average cost of a main course at dinner or, if dinner is not served, at lunch.

HOTELS

Consider spending part of your vacation at a resort and part of it at a small inn or bed-and-breakfast. The big resorts sit squarely on some of the best beaches on the Big Island, and they have a lot to offer—spas, golf, and great restaurants for starters. The B&Bs provide a more intimate experience in settings as diverse as an Upcountry ranch, a rain-forest tree house, and a Victorian mansion perched on a dramatic sea cliff. Several romantic B&Bs nestle in the rain forest surrounding Hawaii Volcanoes National Park—very convenient (and romantic) after a nighttime lava hike.

Prices in the reviews are the lowest cost of a standard double room in high season.

For expanded hotel reviews, visit www.Fodors.com

WILL I SEE FLOWING LAVA?

Without question, the best time to see lava is at night. Nevertheless, you may not know until the day of your visit whether the lava flow will be in an accessible location, or even visible from a distance. Your best bet is to call the visitor center at Hawaii Volcanoes National Park before you head out. No matter what's happening at the active lava flows, there's plenty to see and do inside the national park, where the Halemaumau Crater is located. The nighttime glow of the crater, located below the Jaggar Museum and Halemaumau Overlook, is a jaw-dropping sight and one that should not be missed. Plan your trip to the volcano so that you can be near the crater at dusk. Fortunately, the park is open 24 hours a day, and night visits are allowed.

In recent years, active lava flows have been taking place outside the park in lower Puna. When lava is flowing outside the park boundaries, hiking is sometimes regulated because trails pass through private land. Pay attention to all warning signs, and take safety advice from park rangers seriously. ■TIP→ Bring a flashlight, water, and sturdy shoes, and be prepared for some rough going over the lava fields at night.

For more information about visiting Hawaii Volcanoes National Park, see Hawaii National Park.

VISITOR INFORMATION

Before you go, contact the Big Island Visitors Bureau to request a free official vacation planner. The Hawaii Island Chamber of Commerce also has links to dozens of museums, attractions, bed-and-breakfasts, and parks on its website. The Kona-Kohala Chamber of Commerce also has resources for the west side of the island.

Contacts Big Island Visitors Bureau ☎ *808/961–5797, 800/648–2441* ⊕ *www.bigisland.org.* **Hawaii Island Chamber of Commerce** ☎ *808/935–7178* ⊕ *www.hicc.biz.*

EXPLORING

KAILUA-KONA

7 miles south of the Kona airport.

A fun and quaint seaside town, Kailua-Kona has the souvenir shops and open-air restaurants you'd expect in a small tourist hub, plus a surprising number of historic sites. Quite a few nice oceanfront restaurants here offer far more affordable fare than those at the resorts on the Kohala Coast and in Waimea.

Except for the rare deluge, the sun shines year-round. Mornings offer cooler weather, smaller crowds, and more birds singing in the banyan trees; you'll see tourists and locals out running on Alii Drive, the town's main drag, by about 5 am every day. Afternoons sometimes bring clouds and soft rain, but evenings often clear up for cool drinks, brilliant

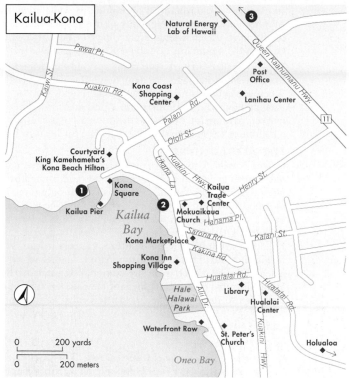

sunsets, gentle trade winds, and lazy hours spent gazing out over the ocean. Though there are better beaches north of town on the Kohala Coast, Kailua-Kona is home to a few gems, including a fantastic snorkeling beach (Kahaluu) and a tranquil bay perfect for kids (Kamakahonu Beach, in front of the Courtyard King Kamehameha hotel).

Scattered among the shops, restaurants, and condo complexes of Alii Drive are Ahuhena Heiau, a temple complex restored by King Kamehameha the Great and the spot where he spent his last days (he died here in 1819); the last royal palace in the United States (Hulihee Palace); and a battleground dotted with the graves of ancient Hawaiians who fought for their way of life and lost. It was also here in Kailua-Kona that Kamehameha's successor, King Liholiho, broke and officially abolished the ancient *kapu* (roughly translated as "forbidden," it was the name for the strict code of conduct that islanders were compelled to follow) system by publicly sitting and eating with women. The following year, on April 4, 1820, the first Christian missionaries came ashore here, changing life in the Islands forever.

GETTING HERE AND AROUND

Half a day is plenty of time to explore Kailua-Kona, as most of the town's sights are located in or near the downtown area. Still, if you add in a beach trip (Kahaluu Beach has some of the best and easiest snorkeling on the island), it's tempting to while away the day here. Another option for making a day of it is to tack on a short trip up a small hill to the charming, artsy village of Holualoa or to the coffee farms in the mountains just above Kealakekua Bay.

The easiest place to park your car is at Courtyard King Kamehameha's Kona Beach Hotel ($15 per day). Some free parking is also available: When you enter Kailua via Palani Road (Highway 190), turn left onto Kuakini Highway, drive for a half block, and turn right into the small marked parking lot. Walk *makai* (toward the ocean) on Likana Lane a half block to Alii Drive, and you'll be in the heart of Kailua-Kona.

TOP ATTRACTIONS

Fodor'sChoice ★ **Hulihee Palace.** A lovely two-story oceanfront home surrounded by jewel green grass and elegant coco palms and fronted by an elaborate wrought-iron gate, Hulihee Palace is one of only three royal palaces in America (the other two are in Honolulu). The royal residence was built by Governor John Adams Kuakini in 1838, a year after he completed Mokuaikaua Church. During the 1880s, it served as King David Kalakaua's summer palace. Built of lava rock, it features vintage koa furniture, weaving, portraits, tapa cloth, feather work, and Hawaiian quilts. The palace is on the National Register of Historic Places and is operated by the Daughters of Hawaii, a nonprofit organization dedicated to preserving the culture and royal heritage of the Islands. ⊠ *75-5718 Alii Dr.* ☏ *808/329–1877* ⊕ *www.daughtersofhawaii.org* 🖃 *$8–$10* ☉ *Tues.–Sat. 9–4.*

WORTH NOTING

Kaloko–Honokohau National Historical Park. The trails at this sheltered 1,160-acre coastal park near Honokohau Harbor, just north of Kailua-Kona, are popular with walkers and hikers. The park is a good place to observe Hawaiian archaeological history and intact ruins, including a heiau, house platforms, ancient fishponds, and numerous petroglyphs, along the newly installed boardwalk. The park's wetlands provide refuge to a number of waterbirds, including the endemic Hawaiian stilt and coot. Two beaches here are good for swimming, sunbathing, and sea turtle spotting: **Aiopio**, a few yards north of the harbor, is a small beach with calm, protected swimming areas (good for kids) near the archaeological site of Puu Oina heiau, while **Honokohau Beach** is a ¾-mile stretch with ruins of ancient fishponds, also north of the harbor. Of the park's three entrances, the middle one leads to a visitor center with helpful rangers and lots of information. To go directly to the beaches, take the harbor road past the Kona Sailing Club, park in the gravel lot, and walk the sandy path to the water. ⊠ *74-425 Kealakehe Pkwy., off Hwy. 19 near airport* ☏ *808/329–6881* ⊕ *www.nps.gov/kaho* 🖃 *Free* ☉ *Kaloko Rd. gate daily 8–5.*

Kamakahonu and Ahuena Heiau. In the early 1800s, King Kamehameha the Great built a royal compound at Kamakahonu, the bay fronting what is now the Courtyard King Kamehameha's Kona Beach Hotel. It was a four-acre homestead, complete with several houses and religious sites. In 1813, he rebuilt Ahuena Heiau, a stunning temple dedicated to Lono, the Hawaiian god of peace and prosperity, which was also used as a seat of government. Today it's on the National Register of Historic Places and a National Historic Landmark. One of the most revered and historically significant in all of Hawaii, the site sustained damage in the 2011 tsunami and is currently being repaired. ✉ *75-5660 Palani Rd.* ⊕ *www.ahuena.net.*

THE KONA COAST

South of Kailua-Kona, Highway 11 hugs splendid coastlines and rural towns, leaving busy streets behind. The winding, Upcountry road takes you straight to the heart of coffee country, where fertile plantations and jaw-dropping views offer a taste of what Hawaii was like before the resorts took over. Tour one of the coffee farms to find out what the big deal is about Kona coffee, and enjoy a free sample while you're at it.

A half-hour drive off the highway from Kailua-Kona leads to beautiful Kealakekua Bay, where Captain James Cook arrived in 1778, dying here not long after. Hawaiian spinner dolphins frolic in the bay, now a Marine Life Conservation District, nestled alongside immensely high green cliffs that jut dramatically out to sea. Snorkeling is superb here, so you may want to bring your gear and spend an hour or so exploring the coral reefs. This is also a nice kayaking spot; the bay is normally extremely calm. ■**TIP→** One of our favorite ways to spend a morning is to kayak in the pristine waters of Kealakekua Bay, paddling over to see the spot where Cook died. Guided tours are your best bet, and you'll likely see plenty of dolphins along the way.

North of Kona International Airport, along Highway 19, brightly colored bougainvillea stand out in relief against miles of jet-black lava fields stretching from the mountain to the sea. The dry, barren landscape may not be what you'd expect to find on a tropical island, but it's a good reminder of the island's evolving volcanic nature.

SOUTH KONA AND KEALAKEKUA BAY
14 miles south of Kailua-Kona.

Between its coffee plantations, artsy havens, and Kealakekua Bay—one of the most beautiful spots on the Big Island—South Kona has plenty of activities to occupy a day. Bring a swimsuit and snorkel gear, and hit Kealakekua Bay first thing in the morning. You'll beat the crowds, have a better chance of a dolphin sighting, and see more fish. After a morning of swimming or kayaking, head to one of the great cafés in nearby Kainaliu to refuel.

GETTING HERE AND AROUND
Between the coffee plantations, artsy towns, and Kealakekua Bay, South Kona has plenty of activities to keep you occupied for a day. Bring a swimsuit and snorkel gear, and hit Kealakekua Bay first thing in the morning. You'll have a better chance of a dolphin sighting, and you'll beat the large snorkel cruise groups. To get to Kealakekua Bay, follow the signs off Highway 11 and park at Napoopoo Beach. It's not much of a beach, but it provides easy access into the water.

COFFEE FARMS

Several coffee farms around the Kona coffee-belt area welcome visitors to watch all or part of the coffee-production process, from harvest to packaging. Some tours are self-guided and most are free, with the exception of the Kona Coffee Living History Farm.

FAMILY **Greenwell Farms.** The Greenwell family played a significant role in the cultivation of the first commercial coffee in the Kona area. Depending on the season, the 20-minute walking tour of this working farm takes in various stages of coffee production, but it always includes a sample of Greenwell Farms' Kona coffee at the end and the opportunity to buy some from the gift shop. ⊠ *81-6581 Mamalahoa Hwy., between mile markers 112 and 111, Kealakekua* ☎ *808/323–2295* ⊕ *www. greenwellfarms.com* ▤ *Free* ⊙ *Daily 8:30–4.*

Hula Daddy. On a walking tour of this working coffee orchard, visitors can learn the history of the farm, pick and pulp their own coffee beans, see a roasting demonstration, and have a tasting. And of course there's a gift shop. ⊠ *74-4944 Mamalahoa Hwy., Holualoa* ☎ *808/327–9744, 888/553–2339* ⊕ *www.huladaddy.com* ▤ *Free* ⊙ *Mon.–Sat. 10–4.*

Kona Coffee Living History Farm (D. Uchida Farm). On the National Register of Historic Places, this perfectly preserved farm was completely restored by the Kona Historical Society. It includes a 1913 farmhouse surrounded by coffee trees, a Japanese bathhouse, *kuriba* (coffee-processing mill), and *hoshidana* (traditional drying platform). Caretakers still grow, harvest, roast, and sell the coffee exactly as they did 100 years ago. ⊠ *82-6199 Mamalahoa Hwy., mile marker 110, Captain Cook* ☎ *808/323–2006* ⊕ *www.konahistorical.org* ▤ *$15* ⊙ *Tours weekdays 10–2.*

Mountain Thunder. This is the largest coffee grower and the most extensive organic coffee producer in Hawaii. Hourly "bean to cup" tours include a tasting and access to the processing plant, which shows dry milling, sizing, coloring, sorting, and roasting. Private VIP tours (small fee) let you be roast master for a day. Hawaiian teas, handmade chocolate, and macadamia nuts grown on-site are also available. ⊠ *73-1944 Hao St., Kailua-Kona* ☎ *888/414–5662* ⊕ *www.mountainthunder.com* ▤ *Free* ⊙ *Tours daily 10–4.*

Royal Kona Coffee Museum & Coffee Mill. Take an easy self-guided tour by following the descriptive plaques located around the coffee mill. Then stop off at the small museum to see coffee-making relics and watch an informational film. ⊠ *83-5427 Mamalahoa Hwy., next to tree house, Captain Cook* ☎ *808/328–2511* ⊕ *www.royalkonacoffee.com* ▤ *Free* ⊙ *Daily 7:30–5.*

COFFEE **Kona Coffee Cultural Festival.** This annual community-wide festival runs
FESTIVAL for 10 days in November and includes recipe competitions, parades with Miss Kona Coffee, concerts, special tours, an art stroll and coffee tasting in Holualoa, and the Gevalia Kona Cupping Competition (a judged tasting). ⊕ *www.konacoffeefest.com.*

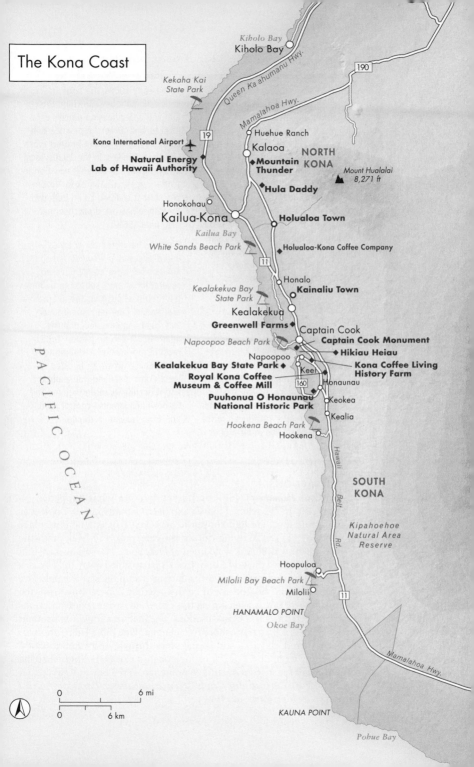

The Kona Coast

Kiholo Bay
Kiholo Bay

Kekaha Kai State Park

190

Queen Ka ahumanu Hwy.

Mamalahoa Hwy.

Kona International Airport ✈
Natural Energy Lab of Hawaii Authority

Huehue Ranch
Kalaoa
Mountain Thunder ◆

NORTH KONA

▲ Mount Hualalai
8,271 ft

Hula Daddy ◆

Honokohau
Kailua-Kona

Holualoa Town ◆

Kailua Bay
White Sands Beach Park

Holualoa-Kona Coffee Company ◆

11

Honalo
Kainaliu Town ◆

Kealakekua Bay State Park

Kealakekua
Greenwell Farms ◆

Captain Cook
Captain Cook Monument

Napoopoo Beach Park

Napoopoo
Kealakekua Bay State Park ◆
Royal Kona Coffee Museum & Coffee Mill
Puuhonua O Honaunau National Historic Park

Hikiau Heiau ◆
Kona Coffee Living History Farm

Keei
160
Honaunau

Keokea

Kealia

Hookena Beach Park
Hookena

Hawaii Belt Rd.

SOUTH KONA

Kipahoehoe Natural Area Reserve

Hoopuloa
Milolii Bay Beach Park
Milolii

11

HANAMALO POINT
Okoe Bay

P A C I F I C   O C E A N

Mamalahoa Hwy.

0   6 mi
0   6 km

KAUNA POINT

Pohue Bay

CLOSE UP

Kona Coffee

The Kona Coffee belt, some 16 miles long and about a mile wide, has been producing smooth, aromatic coffee for more than a century. The slopes of massive Mauna Loa at this elevation provide the ideal conditions for growing coffee: sunny mornings; cloudy, rainy afternoons; and rich, rocky, volcanic soil. More than 600 farms, most just three to seven acres in size, grow the delicious—and luxurious, at generally more than $25 per pound—gourmet beans. Only coffee from the North and South Kona districts can be called Kona, and Hawaii is the only U.S. producer of commercially grown coffee.

In 1828 Reverend Samuel Ruggles, an American missionary, brought a cutting over from the Oahu farm of Chief Boki, Oahu's governor. That coffee plant was a strain of Ethiopian coffee called Arabica, which is still produced today, although a Guatemalan strain of Arabica introduced in the late 1800s is produced in far higher quantities.

In the early 1900s, the large Hawaiian coffee plantations subdivided their lots and began leasing parcels to local tenant farmers, a practice that continues. Many tenant farmers were Japanese families. In the 1930s, local schools switched summer vacation to "coffee vacation," August to November, so that children could help with the coffee harvest, a practice that held until 1969.

Coffee is harvested as "cherries"— beans encased in a sweet, red shell. Kona coffee trees are handpicked several times each season to guarantee the ripest product. The cherries are shelled, their parchment layer sun-dried and removed, and the beans roasted to perfection. Today most farms—owned and operated by Japanese-American families, West Coast mainland transplants, and descendants of Portuguese and Chinese immigrants—control production from cultivation to cup.

TOP ATTRACTIONS

Fodor's Choice
★
Captain Cook Monument. No one knows for sure what happened on February 14, 1779, when English explorer Captain James Cook was killed on this spot. He had chosen Kealakekua Bay as a landing place in November 1778. Arriving during the celebration of Makahiki, the harvest season, Cook was welcomed at first. Some Hawaiians saw him as an incarnation of the god Lono. Cook's party sailed away in February 1779, but a freak storm forced his damaged ship back to Kealakekua Bay. Believing that no god could be thwarted by a mere rainstorm, the Hawaiians were not so welcoming this time, and various confrontations arose between them and Cook's sailors. The theft of a longboat brought Cook and an armed party ashore to reclaim it. One thing led to another: shots were fired, daggers and spears were thrown, and Captain Cook fell, mortally wounded. A 27-foot-high obelisk marks the spot where he died. You can see it from a vantage point across the bay at Kealakekua Bay State Park. ⊠ *Captain Cook* ⊕ *www.hawaiistateparks.org/parks/ hawaii/index.cfm?park_id=46.*

Kealakekua Bay is one of the most beautiful spots on the Big Island.

Kainaliu Town. This is the first town you encounter to the south heading Upcountry from Kailua town. In addition to a ribbon of funky old stores, coffee bars, and bistros, a handful of galleries and shops have sprung up in the last few years. Browse around Oshima's, established in 1926, and Kimura's, founded in 1927, to find fabrics and Japanese goods beyond tourist trinkets. Pop into a local café for everything from burgers to authentic Italian. Peek into the 1932-vintage Aloha Theatre, where a troupe of community-theater actors might be practicing a Broadway revue. ⊠ *Hwy. 11, mile markers 112–114, Kainaliu.*

Fodor's Choice ★ **Kealakekua Bay State Park.** This underwater marine reserve is one of the most beautiful spots in the state. Dramatic cliffs surround super-deep, crystal clear, turquoise water chock-full of stunning coral pinnacles and tropical fish. The dolphins that frequent the sanctuary should not be disturbed, as they use the bay to escape predators and sleep. The brown sand at west-facing **Napoopoo Beach,** washed away during Hurricane Iniki in 1992, is slowly returning. This is a nice, easy place to enter the water and swim, as it's well protected from currents. ⚠ No lifeguards; at times, you may feel tiny jellyfish stings. ⊠ *Beach Rd., off Government Rd. from Puuhonua Rd. (Hwy. 160), Captain Cook* ⊕ *www. hawaiistateparks.org/parks/hawaii/index.cfm?park_id=46.*

Fodor's Choice ★ **Puuhonua O Honaunau National Historical Park** (*City of Refuge or Place of Refuge*). This 420-acre National Historical Park houses the best-preserved *puuhonua* (place of refuge) in the state. Providing a safe haven for noncombatants, *kapu* (taboo) breakers, defeated warriors, and others, the puuhonua offered protection and redemption for anyone who could reach its boundaries, by land or sea. The oceanfront,

960-foot stone wall still stands and is one of the park's most prominent features. A number of ceremonial temples, including the restored **Hale o Keawe Heiau** (circa 1700) have served as royal burial chambers. An aura of ancient sacredness and serenity still embues the place. ⊠ *Rte. 160, about 20 miles south of Kailua-Kona, Honaunau* ☎ *808/328–2288* ⊕ *www.nps.gov/puho* ⌨ *$5 per vehicle* ☉ *Park daily 7 am–sunset; visitor center daily 8–4:30.*

WORTH NOTING

Holualoa Town. Hugging the hillside along the Kona Coast, the artsy village of Holualoa is 3 miles up winding Hualalai Road from Kailua-Kona. Galleries here feature all types of artists—from painters, woodworkers, and jewelers to gourd makers and potters—working in their studios in back and selling their wares up front. Formerly the exclusive domain of coffee plantations, Holualoa still has quite a few coffee farms offering free tours and inviting cups of joe. ⊠ *Holualoa* ⊕ *www. holualoahawaii.com.*

NORTH KONA

Most of the lava flows in North Kona originate from the last eruptions of Hualalai, in 1800 and 1801, although some flows by the resorts hail from Mauna Loa. You will no doubt notice the white graffiti dotting the vast lava fields. This has been going on for decades, and locals still get a kick out of it, as do visitors. The first thing everyone asks is "where do the white rocks come from?" The answer is that they're bits of coral from the ocean, and if you want to write a message, you've got to use the coral that's already out there. This means that messages don't last long, but that's all part of the fun. Some local couples write their names in the same spot on the lava fields every anniversary. Other people greet friends as they arrive or depart Kona.

GETTING HERE AND AROUND

Head north from Kona International Airport and follow Highway 19 along the coast. Take caution driving at night between the airport and where resorts begin on the Kohala Coast; it's extremely dark and there are few road signs or traffic lights on this two-lane road.

TOP ATTRACTIONS

Natural Energy Lab of Hawaii Authority. Just south of Kona International Airport, a large mysterious group of buildings with an equally large and mysterious photovoltaic (solar) panel installation looks like some sort of top-secret military station. It's really the site of the Natural Energy Lab of Hawaii Authority, NELHA for short. Here, scientists, researchers, and entrepreneurs make use of a cold, deep-sea pipeline to develop and market everything from desalinated, mineral-rich drinking water and super-nutritious algae products to energy-efficient air-conditioning systems and environmentally friendly aquaculture techniques. Three types of facility tours are offered most days. ⊠ *73-4460 Queen Kaahumanu Hwy., Kailua-Kona* ☎ *808/329–8073* ⊕ *www.energyfuturehawaii.org* ⌨ *$8 donation for tours* ☉ *Tours weekdays at 10 am.*

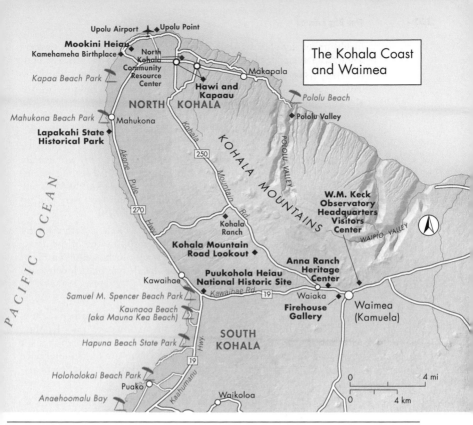

The Kohala Coast
and Waimea

THE KOHALA COAST

32 miles north of Kailua-Kona.

If you had only a weekend to spend on the Big Island, this is probably
where you'd want to be. The Kohala Coast is a mix of the island's best
beaches and swankiest hotels not far from ancient valleys and temples,
waterfalls, and funky artist enclaves.

The resorts on the Kohala Coast lay claim to some of the island's finest
restaurants, golf courses, and destination spas. But the real attraction
here is the island's glorious beaches. On a clear day, you can see Maui,
and during the winter months, numerous glistening humpback whales
cleave the waters just offshore.

Rounding the northern tip of the island, the arid coast shifts rather
suddenly to green villages and hillsides, leading to lush Pololu Valley in
North Kohala, as the hot sunshine along the coast gives way to cooler
temperatures.

As you drive north, you'll find the quaint sugar-plantation-towns-
turned-artsy-villages of Hawi and Kapaau. New galleries are inter-
spersed with charming reminders of old Hawaii—wooden boardwalks,
quaint local storefronts, delicious neighborhood restaurants, friendly

locals, and a delightfully slow pace. There's great shopping for everything from designer beachwear to authentic Hawaiian crafts.

GETTING HERE AND AROUND

Two days is sufficient time for experiencing each unique side of Kohala—one day for the resort perks: the beach, the spa, the golf, the restaurants; one day for hiking and admiring the waterfalls and valleys of North Kohala, coupled with a wander around Hawi and Kapaau.

Diving and snorkeling are primo along the Kohala Coast, so bring or rent equipment. If you're staying at one of the resorts, they will usually have any equipment you could possibly want. If you're feeling adventurous, get your hands on a four-wheel-drive vehicle and head to one of the unmarked beaches along the Kohala Coast—you may end up with a beach to yourself.

The best way to explore the valleys of North Kohala is with a hiking tour. Look for one that includes lunch and a dip in one of the area's waterfall pools. There are a number of casual lunch options in Hawi and Kapaau (sandwiches, sushi, seafood, local-style plate lunch), and a few good dinner spots.

WORTH NOTING

Hawi and Kapaau. Near the birthplace of King Kamehameha, these North Kohala towns thrived during the plantation days, once bustling with hotels, saloons, and theaters—even a railroad. They took a hit when "Big Sugar" left the island, but both towns are blossoming once again, thanks to strong local communities, tourism, and an influx of artists keen on honoring the towns' past. They are full of lovingly restored vintage buildings housing fun and funky shops, galleries, and eateries.

Ackerman Gift Gallery. In Kapaau, browse through this longtime gallery's collections of local art, including glass, woodworks, bowls, fine art photography, and paintings. There's also a gift shop a couple of doors away. ✉ *54-3897 Akoni Pule Hwy., Hwy. 270, North Kohala* ☎ *808/889–5971 gallery, 808/889–5138 gift shop* ⊕ *www. ackermangalleries.com*

Kohala Mountain Road Lookout. The road between North Kohala and Waimea is one of the most scenic drives in Hawaii, passing Parker Ranch, open pastures, and tree-lined mountains. There are a few places to pull over and take in the view; the lookout at mile marker 8 provides a splendid vista of the Kohala Coast and Kawaihae Harbor far below. On clear days, you can see well beyond the resorts to Maui, while other times an eerie, thick mist drifts over the view. ✉ *Kohala Mountain Rd. (Hwy. 250), Kamuela.*

Lapakahi State Historical Park. A self-guided, 1-mile walking tour leads through the ruins of the once-prosperous fishing village Koaie, which dates as far back as the 15th century. Displays illustrate early Hawaiian fishing and farming techniques, salt gathering, games, and legends. Because the shoreline near the state park is an officially designated Marine Life Conservation District (and part of the site itself is considered sacred), swimming, swim gear, and sunscreen are not allowed in the water. Restrooms are available but not drinking water. ✉ *Hwy.*

Take a tour of one of the many Kona coffee farms on the Big Island.

270, mile marker 14 between Kawaihae and Mahukona, North Kohala ☎ 808/327–4958 ⊕ www.hawaiistateparks.org ✉ Free ☉ Daily 8–4.

Mookini Heiau. This isolated National Historic Landmark is so impressive in size and atmosphere that it may give you what locals call "chicken skin" (goose bumps). Its foundations date to about AD 480, but the high priest Paao from Tahiti expanded the *heiau* (temple) several centuries later and it continued to be used by Hawaiian religious leaders. You can still see the lava slab where hundreds of people were sacrificed, giving this place a truly haunted feel. Visit with utmost care and respect. Nearby is Kamehameha Akahi Aina Hanau, the birthplace of Kamehameha the Great. ⚠ **Check conditions in the area before venturing. The access road is unpaved. When it's dry, it's not bad, but with pooled rainwater, it can be difficult, if not impossible, to traverse. Even with four-wheel drive, you could easily get stuck in the mud.** ✉ *Off Hwy. 270, turn at sign for Upolu Airport, near Hawi, and hike or drive 1½ miles southwest, North Kohala* ☎ 808/974–6200

Fodor's Choice
★   **Puukohola Heiau National Historic Site.** Quite simply, this is one of the most historic sites in all of Hawaii. It was here in 1810, on top of Puukohala (Hill of the Whale), that Kamehameha the Great built the war *heiau* (temple) that would serve to unify the Hawaiian Islands. The oceanfront, fortress-like site is foreboding and impressive. A paved ½-mile, looped trail runs from the visitor center to the main temple sites. An even older temple, dedicated to the shark gods, lies submerged just offshore, where sharks can be seen circling. A new museum displays ancient Hawaiian weapons, including clubs, spears, and a replica of a bronze cannon that warriors dragged into battle on an ancient

Hawaiian sled. Stop on the lanai for a cool breeze and a spectacular view. A free audio tour can be heard on your cell phone. ✉ 62-3601 *Kawaihae Rd., Kawaihae* ☎ *808/882–7218* ⊕ *www.nps.gov/puhe/ index.htm* 🔊 *Free* ⊙ *Daily 8–4:45.*

WAIMEA

40 miles northeast of Kailua-Kona; 10 miles east of the Kohala Coast.

Thirty minutes over the mountain from Kohala, Waimea offers a completely different experience from the rest of the island. Rolling green hills, large open pastures, light rain, cool evening breezes and morning mists, abundant cattle, horses, and regular rodeos are just a few of the surprises you'll stumble upon here in *paniolo* (Hawaiian for "cowboy") country.

Waimea is also where some of the island's top Hawaii regional-cuisine chefs practice their art using local ingredients, which makes it an ideal place to find yourself at dinnertime. In keeping with the recent Big Island restaurant trend toward featuring locally farmed ingredients, a handful of Waimea farms and ranches supply most of the restaurants on the island, and many sell to the public as well. With its galleries, restaurants, beautiful countryside, and *paniolo* culture, Waimea is well worth a stop if you're heading to Hilo or Mauna Kea. ■**TIP→** And the short highway, or mountain road, that connects Waimea to North Kohala (Highway 250) affords some of our favorite Big Island views.

GETTING HERE AND AROUND

You can see most of what Waimea has to offer in one day, but if you're heading up to Mauna Kea for stargazing (which you should), it could easily be stretched to two. If you stay in Waimea overnight (there are a few bed-and-breakfast options), spend the afternoon browsing through town or touring some of the area's ranches and historic sites. Then indulge in a gourmet dinner before heading up Saddle Road for world-renowned stargazing atop Mauna Kea.

A word to the wise—there are no services or gas stations on Saddle Road, the only way to reach the summit of Mauna Kea. Fill up on gas and bring water, snacks, and warm clothes with you (there are plenty of gas stations, cafés, and shops in Waimea).

TOP ATTRACTIONS

Fodor'sChoice
★
Anna Ranch Heritage Center. This stunning heritage property, on the National Register of Historic Places, belonged to the "first lady" of Hawaii ranching, Anna Lindsey Perry-Fiske. Here is a rare opportunity to see a fully restored cattle ranch compound and learn about the life of this fascinating woman, who butchered cattle by day and threw lavish parties by night. Wander the picturesque grounds and gardens on a self-guided walk, watch a master saddle maker and an ironsmith in action, and take a tour of the historic house, where Anna's furniture, gowns, and elaborate *pau* (parade riding) costumes are on display. The knowledgeable staff shares anecdotes about Anna's amazing life. ✉ 65-1480 Kawaihae Rd. ☎ 808/885–4426 ⊕ *www.annaranch.org* 🔊 *Guided tours $10* ⊙ *Tues.–Fri. 10–3; guided tours by appointment.*

WORTH NOTING

Firehouse Gallery. Local Big Island artwork is featured at this historic gallery, an 80-year-old fire station at the intersection of Lindsey Road and old Mamalahoa Highway. Supporting the Waimea Arts Council, the gallery is home to annual juried shows as well as solo and group exhibitions by its many award-winning multimedia artists and artisans. ⊠ *67-1201 Mamalahoa Hwy., across from Waimea Chevron* ☎ *808/887–1052* ⊕ *www.waimeaartscouncil.org* ⊗ *Wed.–Sat. 11–3.*

W. M. Keck Observatory Headquarters Vistors Center. If you are keen on astronomy but don't have time to go all the way to the summit, visit Keck Observatory headquarters right in Waimea, with its educational exhibits and informed staff. You can see models and images taken from the twin 10-meter Keck telescopes on Mauna Kea and learn about the latest discoveries. ⊠ *65-1120 Mamalahoa Hwy, across from hospital* ☎ *808/885–7887* ⊕ *www.keckobservatory.org* ⊗ *Tues.–Fri. 10–2 (docent program).*

MAUNA KEA

18 miles southeast of Waimea; 34 miles northwest of Hilo.

Mauna Kea ("white mountain") is the antithesis of the typical island experience. Freezing temperatures and arctic conditions are common at the summit, and snow can fall year-round.

Mauna Kea's summit—at 13,796 feet—is the best place in the world for viewing the night sky. For this reason, the summit is home to the largest and most productive astronomical observatories in the world—and $1 billion (with a "B") worth of equipment. Research teams from 11 different countries operate 13 telescopes on Mauna Kea, several of which are record holders: the world's largest optical–infrared telescopes (the dual Keck telescopes), the world's largest dedicated infrared telescope (UKIRT), and the largest submillimeter telescope (the JCMT). A still-larger 30-meter telescope has been cleared for construction and is slated to open its record-breaking eye to the heavens in 2018.

GETTING HERE AND AROUND

The summit of Mauna Kea isn't terribly far, but the drive takes about an hour and a half from Hilo and an hour from Waimea thanks to the steep road. Between the ride there, sunset on the summit, and stargazing, allot at least five hours for a Mauna Kea visit.

To reach the summit, you must take Saddle Road (Highway 200), which has been rerouted and repaved and is now a beautiful shortcut across the middle of the island. At mile marker 28, John A. Burns Way, the access road to the visitor center (9,200 feet), is fine, but the road from there to the summit is a lot more precarious because it's unpaved washboard and very steep. Only four-wheel-drive vehicles with low range should attempt this journey. Two-wheel-drive cars are unsafe, especially in winter conditions, and their lack of traction tears up the road. Rental car companies do not permit them to go to the summit; even if you rent a four-wheel-drive vehicle, make sure you are allowed to take it to the top. If you aren't and you go anyway, your contract will be void and you'll be responsible for any damages. This happens more often than you think. And if you're driving back down in the dark, slow and cautious is the name of the game.

Another factor to consider is altitude. ■TIP→ Take the change in altitude seriously—stop at the visitor center for at least an hour, and don't overexert yourself, especially at the top. The extreme altitude can cause disorientation, headaches, and light-headedness. Keeping hydrated is crucial. Scuba divers must wait at least 24 hours before travel-

WAIMEA OR KAMUELA?

Both, actually. Everyone knows it as Waimea, but the sign on the post office says "Kamuela," which is Hawaiian for "Samuel," referring to Samuel Parker, the son of the founder of Parker Ranch. That designation is used to avoid confusion with communities named Waimea on the islands of Kauai and Oahu. But the official name of the town is Waimea.

ing to the summit. Children under 16, pregnant women, and those with heart, respiratory, or weight problems should not go higher than the visitor center. And yes, you can park there and hike to the summit if you are in good shape, but the trip takes approximately six hours one way, and no camping is allowed. That means you must leave early and obtain a permit to hike, and remember that this is a wilderness area with no services.

The last potential obstacle: it's cold, as in freezing, usually with significant wind chill. Most summit tours provide parkas, but it's difficult to find cold-weather clothing in Hawaii, so if you plan to visit Mauna Kea, bring your favorite warm things from home.

ONIZUKA VISITOR CENTER

Fodor'sChoice **Onizuka Center for International Astronomy Visitor Information Station.** At
★ 9,200 feet, this excellent amateur observation-site has a handful of telescopes and a knowledgeable staff. You can enjoy the nightly stargazing sessions from 6 to 10, or just stop here to acclimate to the altitude if you're heading for the summit. Fortunately, it's a pleasure to do so. Sip hot chocolate and peruse exhibits on ancient Hawaiian celestial navigation, about the mountain's significance as a quarry for the best basalt in the Hawaiian Islands and as a revered spiritual destination, on modern astronomy, and about ongoing projects at the summit.

On weekends, the center offers free escorted caravan-style summit tours. Participants must arrive by 1 pm with their *own* low-range four-wheel-drive vehicle. Keep in mind that most summit telescope facilities are not open to the public, so your best bet for actual stargazing is at the visitor center. Nights are clear 90% of the year. ⊠ *Mauna Kea* ☎ *808/961–2180* ⊕ *www.ifa.hawaii.edu/info/vis* ☞ *Donations welcome* ☉ *Daily 9 am–10 pm.*

THE SUMMIT

Head to the summit before dusk so you can witness the stunning sunset and emerging star show. Only the astronomers are allowed to use the telescopes and other equipment, but the scenery is available to all. After the sun sinks, head down to the visitor center to warm up and stargaze, or do your stargazing first and then head up here. If you were blown away by the number of stars crowding the sky over the visitor center, this vantage point will make you speechless.

GOING WITH A GUIDE

If you haven't rented a four-wheel-drive vehicle, don't want to deal with driving to the summit, or don't want to wait in line to use the handful of telescopes at the visitor center, consider booking a tour. Operators provide transportation to and from the summit along with expert guides; some also provide parkas, gloves, telescopes, dinner, hot beverages, and snacks. Excursion fees range from $90 to $212.

Arnott's Lodge & Hiking Adventures. This Mauna Kea summit tour focuses more on the experience of the mountain than on astronomy. Guides use laser lights to provide an informative lesson on major celestial objects and Polynesian navigational stars. The excursion departs from Hilo and costs $180 per person, including parkas and hot beverages. The outfitter also offers lava and waterfall tours. ⊠ *98 Apapane Rd., Hilo* ☎ *808/969–7097, 808/339–0921* ⊕ *www.arnottslodge.com.*

Fodor'sChoice ★ **Hawaii Forest & Trail.** This comfortable, highly educational tour packs a lot of fun into a few hours. Guides are knowledgeable about astronomy and Hawaii's geologic and cultural history, and the small group size (max of 14) encourages camaraderie. Included in the tour are dinner at an old ranching station, catered by a favorite local restaurant; sunset on the summit; and a fantastic private star show mid-mountain. The company's powerful 11-inch Celestron Schmidt-Cassegrain telescope reveals lots of interesting celestial objects, including seasonal stars, galaxies, and nebula. The moon alone, if present, will knock your socks off. Everything from water bottles, parkas, and gloves to hot chocolate and brownies is included for $199. ⊠ *74-5035 Queen Kaahumanu Hwy., 3 miles south of Kona airport, Kailua-Kona* ☎ *808/331–8505, 800/464–1993* ⊕ *www.hawaii-forest.com.*

Mauna Kea Summit Adventures. As the first company to specialize in tours to the mountain, Mauna Kea Summit Adventures focuses on stars. Cushy vans with panoramic windows go first to the visitor center, where participants eat dinner and acclimate for an hour before donning hooded arctic-style parkas and ski gloves for the sunset trip to the 14,000-foot summit. Stargazing through a powerful Celestron telescope happens mid-mountain with the help of knowledgeable guides. Tour, dinner, and west-side pickup cost $212 and run 364 days year, weather permitting. ■TIP➔ You can save 15% by booking online. ⊠ *Kailua-Kona* ☎ *808/322–2366, 888/322–2366* ⊕ *www.maunakea.com.*

THE HAMAKUA COAST

25 miles east of Waimea.

The spectacular waterfalls, mysterious jungles, emerald fields, and stunning ocean vistas along Highway 19 northwest of Hilo are collectively referred to as the Hilo–Hamakua Heritage Coast. Brown signs featuring a sugarcane tassel reflect the area's history: thousands of former acres of sugarcane are now idle, with little industry to support the area since "King Sugar" left the island in the early 1990s.

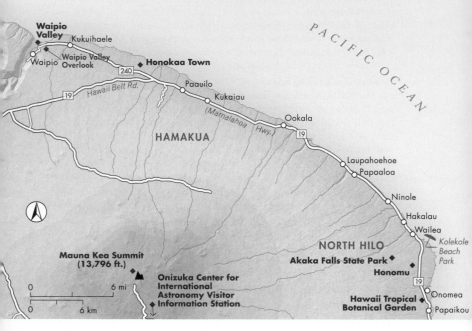

This is a great place to wander off the main road and see "real" Hawaii—untouched valleys, overgrown banyan trees, tiny coastal villages, and little plantation towns, Papaikou, Laupahoehoe, and Paauilo among them. Some small communities are still hanging on quite nicely, well after the demise of the big sugar plantations that first engendered them. They have homey cafés, gift shops, galleries, and a way of life from a time gone by.

The dramatic Akaka Falls is only one of hundreds of waterfalls here, many of which tumble into refreshing swimming holes, so bring your swimsuit when you explore this area. The pristine Waipio Valley was once a favorite getaway spot for Hawaiian royalty. The isolated valley floor has maintained the ways of old Hawaii, with taro patches, wild horses, and a handful of houses. The view from the lookout is breathtaking.

GETTING HERE AND AROUND

Though Highway 19 is the fastest route through the area, any turnoff along this coast could lead to an incredible view, so take your time and go exploring up and down the side roads. If you're driving from Kailua-Kona, rather than around the northern tip of the island, cut across on the Mamalahoa Highway (Highway 190) to Waimea, and then catch Highway 19 to the coast. It takes a little longer but is worth it.

■**TIP→** The "Heritage Drive," a 4-mile loop just off the main highway, is well worth the detour. Signs mark various sites of historical interest, as well as scenic views along the 40-mile stretch of coastline. Keep an eye out for them and try to stop at the sights mentioned—you won't be disappointed

Once back on Highway 19, you'll pass the road to Honokaa, which leads to the end of the road bordering Waipio Valley.

If you've stopped to explore the quiet little villages with wooden boardwalks and dogs dozing in backyards, or if you've spent several hours in Waipio Valley, night will undoubtedly be falling. Don't worry: the trip to Hilo via Highway 19 only takes about an hour, or you can go in the other direction to stop for dinner in Waimea before heading to the Kohala Coast (another 25 to 45 minutes). Although you shouldn't have any trouble exploring the Hamakua Coast in a day, a handful of romantic bed-and-breakfasts are available if you want to spend more time.

TOURS

A guided tour is the best way to see Waipio Valley. You can walk down and up the steep narrow road yourself, but you won't see as much. Costs range from about $50 to $150, depending on the company and the transport mode.

Naalapa Stables. Friendly horses and friendly guides take guests on tours of the valley floor. The 2½-hour tours run Monday through Saturday (the valley rests on Sunday) with check-in times of 9 am and 12:30 pm. Cost is $88.50 per person. ⊠ *48-5416 Kukuihale Rd., Waipio Valley Artworks building, Honokaa* ☎ *808/775–0419* ⊕ *www.naalapastables.com.*

Waipio on Horseback and ATV Ranch Ride. This outfit offers guided horseback-riding trips on the valley floor for $88.54 and two- to three-hour ATV ranch tours up top (ages 16 and older), with awesome views of the valley and surrounding areas, for $104. Trips run every day but Sunday, and reservations are highly recommended. ⊠ *Hwy. 240, mile marker 7.5, northwest of Honokaa* ☎ *808/775–7291, 877/775–7291* ⊕ *www.waipioonhorseback.com.*

Waipio Valley Shuttle. These informative, 1½–2-hour four-wheel-drive tours explore the valley with lots of stops and run Monday through Saturday. The windows on the van are removed, allowing guests to snap unobstructed photos. The cost is $57.29. ⊠ *48-5416 Kukuihaele Rd., Honokaa* ☎ *808/775–7121* ⊕ *www.waipiovalleyshuttle.com.*

TOP ATTRACTIONS

Fodor'sChoice **Akaka Falls State Park.** An easy, meandering 10-minute loop trail (approx-
★ imately 4/10-mile) takes you to the best spots to see the spectacular cascades of Akaka. The majestic upper Akaka Falls drops more than 442 feet, tumbling far below into a pool drained by Kolekole Stream amid a profusion of fragrant white, yellow, and red torch ginger and other tropical foliage. Another 400-foot falls is on the lower end of the trail. ⊠ *Off Hwy. 19, 4 miles inland, near Honomu* ☎ *808/974–6200* 🖃 *$5 per vehicle (non-residents); $1 for walk-ins* ☉ *Daily 7–7.*

Hawaii Tropical Botanical Garden. Eight miles north of Hilo, stunning coastline views appear around each curve of the 4-mile scenic jungle

drive that accesses this privately owned nature preserve beside Onomea Bay. Paved pathways in the 17-acre botanical garden lead past ponds, waterfalls, and more than 2,000 species of plants and flowers, including palms, bromeliads, ginger, heliconia, orchids, and ornamentals. ✉ *27-717 Old Mamalahoa Hwy., Papaikou* ☎ *808/964–5233* ⊕ *www.hawaiigarden.com* 🖃 *$15* ⊙ *Daily 9–4.*

Fodor's Choice
★
Waipio Valley. Bounded by 2,000-foot cliffs, the "Valley of the Kings" was once a favorite retreat of Hawaiian royalty. Waterfalls drop 1,200 feet from the Kohala Mountains to the valley floor, and the sheer cliff faces make access difficult. Though completely off the grid today, Waipio was once a center of Hawaiian life; somewhere between 4,000 and 20,000 people made it their home between the 13th and 17th centuries.

To preserve this pristine part of the island, commercial-transportation permits are limited—only four outfitters offer organized valley trips and they're not allowed to take visitors to the beach: environmental laws protect the swath of black sand. On Sunday the valley rests.

A road leads down from the **Waipio Valley Overlook**, but only four-wheel-drive vehicles may attempt the *very* steep, treacherous road. (Check your rental contract to see if it is allowed.) An information booth at the lookout is staffed by volunteers who can answer questions. There are no roads on the valley floor, and the going is often muddy. The walk down into the valley is less than a mile from the lookout point—just keep in mind the climb back gains 1,000 feet in elevation and is strenuous. If you do visit here, please respect this area, as it is considered highly sacred to Hawaiians. ✉ *Hwy. 240, 8 miles northwest of Honokaa.*

WORTH NOTING

Honokaa Town. This quaint, cliff-top village fronting the ocean was built in the 1920s and 1930s by Japanese and Chinese workers who quit the nearby plantations to start businesses that supported the sugar economy. The intact historic character of the buildings, bucolic setting, and friendliness of the residents provide a nice reason to stop and stroll. Cool antiques shops, a few interesting galleries, and good cafés abound. Most restaurants close by 8 pm. ✉ *Hwy. 240, Honokaa* ⊕ *www.honokaa.org.*

Honomu. Honomu did not die when sugar did. Its sugar-plantation past is reflected in the wooden boardwalks and metal-roofed buildings of this tiny town, which borders Akaka Falls State Park. It's fun to poke through old dusty shops filled with little treasures, check out homemade baked goods, or browse the local art at one of the fine galleries. ✉ *1 mile inland from Hwy. 19 en route to Akaka Falls State Park.*

HILO

55 miles southeast of Waimea; 95 miles northeast of Kailua-Kona, and north of the Hilo Airport.

In comparison to Kailua-Kona, Hilo is often described as "the old Hawaii." With significantly fewer visitors than residents, more historic

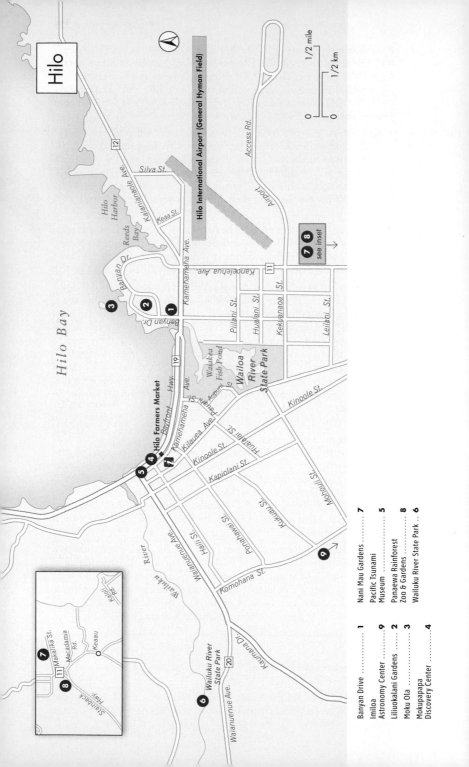

Hilo

Hilo Bay

Hilo Harbor

Reeds Bay

Banyan Dr.

Silva St.

Keaa St.

Kalanianaole Ave.

Hilo International Airport (General Hyman Field)

Access Rd.

Airport

Kamehameha Ave.

Kanoelehua Ave.

Pillani St.

Hualani St.

Kekuanaoa St.

Leilani St.

3

2

1

7

8

see inset

Waiakea Fish Pond

Wailoa River State Park

Waianuenue Ave.

Keawe St.

Banyan Dr.

Bayfront Hwy.

Kamehameha Ave.

Hilo Farmers Market

5

4

1

Kilauea Ave.

Kinoole St.

Huatatai St.

Kapiolani St.

Kinoole St.

Kukuau St.

Mohouli St.

Kinoole St.

Ponahawai St.

Halili St.

Waianuenue Ave.

Komohana St.

Kaumana Dr.

9

Wailuku River State Park

6

Waianuenue Ave.

Wailuku River

1/2 mile

1/2 km

0

0

Inset

Makalika St.

Macadamia Rd.

Keaau

Stainback Hwy.

Keaau

7

8

Legend

Banyan Drive **1**
Imiloa
Astronomy Center **9**
Liliuokalani Gardens **2**
Moku Ola **3**
Mokupapapa
Discovery Center **4**

Nani Mau Gardens **7**
Pacific Tsunami
Museum **5**
Panaewa Rainforest
Zoo & Gardens **8**
Wailuku River State Park .. **6**

buildings, and a much stronger identity as a long-established community, this quaint, traditional town does seem more authentic. It stretches from the banks of the Wailuku River to Hilo Bay, where a few hotels line stately Banyan Drive. The characteristic old buildings that make up Hilo's downtown have been spruced up as part of a revitalization effort.

One of the main reasons visitors have tended to steer clear of the east side of the island is its weather. With an average rainfall of 130 inches per year, it's easy to see why Hilo's yards are so green and its buildings so weatherworn. Outside town, the Hilo District has rain forests and waterfalls, a terrain unlike the hot and dry white-sand beaches of the Kohala Coast. But when the sun does shine—usually part of nearly every day—the town sparkles, and, during winter, the snow glistens on Mauna Kea, 25 miles in the distance. Best of all is when the mists fall and the sun shines at the same time, leaving behind the colorful arches that earn Hilo its nickname: "the City of Rainbows."

GETTING HERE AND AROUND

Hilo is a great base for exploring the eastern and southern parts of the island—just be sure to bring an umbrella for sporadic showers. If you're just passing through town or making a day trip, make the first right turn into the town off Highway 19 (it comes up fast) and grab a parking spot in the lot on your left or on any of the surrounding streets. Downtown Hilo is best experienced on foot.

There are plenty of gas stations and restaurants in the area. Hilo is a good spot to load up on food and supplies—just south of downtown there are several large budget chains. If you're here on Wednesday or Sunday, be sure to stop by the expansive Hilo Farmers' Market. The Merrie Monarch Hula Festival takes place in Hilo every year during the second week of April, and dancers and admirers flock to the city from all over the world. If you're planning a stay in Hilo during this time, be sure to book your room well in advance.

TOP ATTRACTIONS

Fodor's Choice ★ **Imiloa Astronomy Center.** Part Hawaiian cultural center, part astronomy museum, this center provides an educational and cultural complement to the research being conducted atop Mauna Kea. Although visitors are welcome at Mauna Kea, its primary function is as a research center—not observatory, museum, or education center. Those roles have been taken on by Imiloa in a big way. With its interactive exhibits, full-dome planetarium shows, and regularly scheduled talks and events, the center is a must-see for anyone interested in the stars, the planets, or Hawaiian culture and history. Five minutes from downtown Hilo, the center also provides an important link between the scientific research being conducted at Mauna Kea and its history as a sacred mountain for the Hawaiian people. Admission includes one planetarium show and an all-day pass to the exhibit hall, which features more than 100 interactive displays. The lunch buffet at the adjoining Sky Garden Cafe is popular and affordable. ✉ *600 Imiloa Pl., at the UH Hilo Science & Technology Park, off Nowelo and Komohana* ☎ *808/969–9700* ⊕ *www.imiloahawaii.org* ▲ *$17.50* ☉ *Tues.–Sun. 9–5.*

Liliuokalani Gardens. Designed to honor Hawaii's first Japanese immigrants, Liliuokalani Gardens' 30 acres of fish-filled ponds, stone lanterns, half-moon bridges, elegant pagodas, and a ceremonial teahouse make it a favorite Sunday destination. The surrounding area, once a busy residential neighborhood, was destroyed by a 1960 tsunami that caused widespread devastation and killed 61 people. ⊠ *Banyan Dr. at Lihiwai St.*

FAMILY **Panaewa Rainforest Zoo & Gardens.** Billed as "the only natural tropi-
Fodor'sChoice cal rainforest zoo in the United States," this sweet zoo is the home of
★ white Bengal tiger Namaste, whose daily 3:30 feeding is quite a sight. Among the other animals here are such native Hawaiian species as the state bird, the nene goose, and the *io* (hawk), as well as lots of other rare birds, monkeys, and lemurs. To get here, turn left on Mamaki off Highway 11; it's just past the "Kulani 19, Stainback Hwy." sign. ⊠ *800 Stainback Hwy.* ☎ *808/959-7224* ⊕ *www.hilozoo.com* ⊒ *Donations encouraged* ⊙ *Daily 9–4.*

Wailuku River State Park (Rainbow Falls). After a hard rain, these falls thunder into the Wailuku River gorge, often creating magical rainbows in the mist. Sometimes known as the "Hilo Town Falls," they are located just above downtown Hilo. Take Waianuenue Avenue west for a mile; when the road forks, stay right and look for the Hawaiian warrior sign. Open daylight hours. ⊠ *Rainbow Dr.* ⊕ *www.hawaiistateparks.org/ parks/hawaii/index.cfm?park_id=57* ⊙ *Daily dawn–dusk.*

Wailuku River State Park (Boiling Pots). Four separate streams fall into a series of circular pools here, forming the Peepee Falls. The resulting turbulent action—best seen after a good rain—has earned this stretch of the Wailuku River the nickname Boiling Pots. ⚠ **There's no swimming allowed at Peepee Falls or anywhere in the Wailuku river, due to dangerous currents and undertows.** The falls are 3 miles northwest of Hilo off Waianuenue Avenue; keep to the right when the road splits and look for the sign. Open daylight hours. ⊠ *Peepee Falls Dr.* ⊕ *www. hawaiistateparks.org/parks/hawaii/Index.cfm?park_id=57* ⊙ *Daily dawn–dusk.*

WORTH NOTING

Banyan Drive. More than 50 enormous banyan trees with aerial roots dangling from their limbs were planted some 60 to 70 years ago by visiting celebrities. Names such as Amelia Earhart and Franklin Delano Roosevelt can be seen on plaques affixed to the trees. A scenic loop beginning at the Hawaii Naniloa Resort makes a nice walk. ⊠ *93 Banyan Dr.* ⊕ *downtownhilo.com.*

Moku Ola (*Coconut Island*). This small island, just offshore from Liliuokalani Gardens, is accessible via a footbridge. It was considered a place of healing in ancient times. Today children play in the tide pools while fisherfolk try their luck. ⊠ *Banyan Dr.*

FAMILY **Mokupapapa Discovery Center.** This informative center teaches about the Papahanaumokuakea Marine National Monument, which encompasses about 140,000 square miles in the waters northwest of the main Hawaiian Islands and is a UNESCO World Heritage site. Giant graphics, murals, and 3-D maps depict the monument's extensive coral reefs and the more than 7,000 marine species that live there, one in four of which are found only in the Hawaiian archipelago. Knowledgeable staff or volunteers are on hand to answer questions. Interactive programs, a new aquarium, and short films give insight into marine life and environmental impact. It's worth a stop just to get an up-close look at the center's huge stuffed albatross, with wings outstretched. ⊠ *Old Koehnen's Building, 76 Kamehameha Ave.* ☎ *808/933–8195* ⊕ *www. papahanaumokuakea.gov/education/center.html* ☒ *Free* ⊗ *Tues.–Sat. 9–4.*

Nani Mau Gardens. The name means "forever beautiful" in Hawaiian, and that's a good description of this 20-acre botanical garden filled with several varieties of fruit trees and hundreds of varieties of ginger, orchids, anthuriums, and other exotic plants. The restaurant has a lunch buffet. ⊠ *421 Makalika St., off Hwy. 11* ☎ *808/959–3500* ⊕ *www. nanimaugardens.com* ☒ *$5* ⊗ *Daily 10–3.*

FAMILY **Pacific Tsunami Museum.** In downtown Hilo, businesses tend to be far from the bayfront. There's a reason for this. Tsunamis have killed more people in Hawaii than any other natural event, especially in Hilo. A small but informative museum in a 1931 building provides tsunami education and scientific information, and chronicles the poignant history of these devastating disasters, with accounts taken from tsunami survivors from Hawaii and worldwide. Exhibits include a wave machine and tsunami warning center simulation as well as detailing recent tsunamis in Japan, Alaska, and Indonesia. ⊠ *130 Kamehameha Ave.* ☎ *808/935– 0926* ⊕ *www.tsunami.org* ☒ *$8* ⊗ *Mon.–Sat. 9–4.*

PUNA

6 miles south of Hilo.

The Puna District is wild in every sense of the word. The jagged black coastline is changing all the time; the trees are growing out of control, forming canopies over the few paved roads; the land is dirt cheap and there seem to be no building codes; and the people—well, there's something about living in an area that could be destroyed by lava at any moment (as Kalapana was in 1990) that makes the laws of modern society seem silly. So it is that Puna has its well-deserved reputation as an "outlaw" region of the Big Island.

That said, it's well worth a detour, especially if you're near this part of the island anyway. Volcanically heated springs and tide pools burst with interesting sea life, and some mighty fine people-watching opportunities exist in Pahoa, a funky little town that the "Punatics" call home.

When dusk falls here, the air fills with the high-pitched symphony of thousands of coqui frogs. Though they look cute on the signs and seem harmless, the invasive frogs are pests both to local crops and to locals tired of their shrieking, all-night calls.

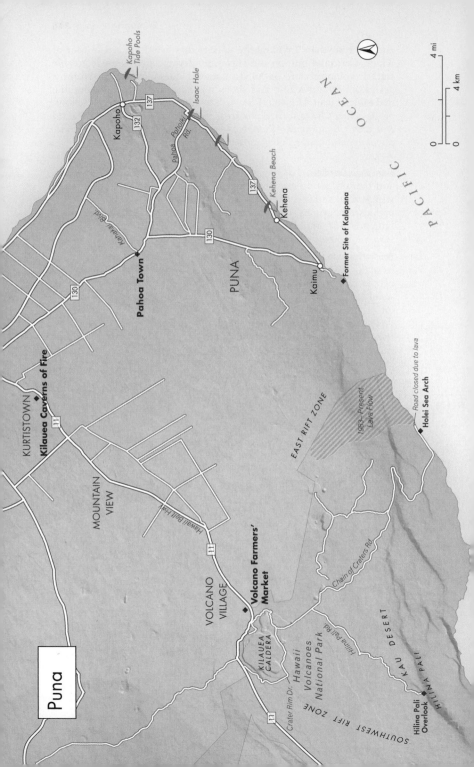

Puna

PACIFIC OCEAN

Kapoho Tide Pools

137

Kapoho
132

Pahoa – Pahoiki Rd.

Isaac Hale

137

Kehena Beach

Kehena

Kaimu

Former Site of Kalapana

130

PUNA

Pahoa Town

Kahakai Blvd.

130

KURTISTOWN
Kilauea Caverns of Fire
11

MOUNTAIN VIEW

Hawaii Belt Hwy.

11

EAST RIFT ZONE

1983–Present Lava Flow

Road closed due to lava

Holei Sea Arch

Chain of Craters Rd.

VOLCANO VILLAGE

Volcano Farmers' Market

KILAUEA CALDERA

Hawaii Volcanoes National Park

Crater Rim Dr.

Hilina Pali Rd.

KAU DESERT

SOUTHWEST RIFT ZONE

HILINA PALI

Hilina Pali Overlook

11

4 mi

4 km

0   0

GETTING HERE AND AROUND

The sprawling Puna District includes part of the volcano area and stretches northeast down to the coast. If you're staying in Hilo for the night, driving around wild lower Puna is a great way to spend a morning.

The roads connecting Pahoa to Kapoho and the Kalapana Coast form a loop that's about 25 miles long; driving times are from two to three hours, depending on the number of stops you make and the length of time at each stop. There are restaurants, stores, and gas stations in Pahoa, but services elsewhere in the region are spotty. Long stretches of the road may be completely isolated at any given point; this can be a little scary at night but beautiful and tranquil during the day.

Compared to big-city living, it's pretty tame, but there is a bit of a "locals-only" vibe in parts of Puna, and some areas have crime and drug problems. Don't wander around alone at night or get lost on backcountry roads.

WORTH NOTING

Pahoa Town. This eclectic little town is reminiscent of the Wild West, with its wooden boardwalks and vintage buildings—not to mention a reputation as a pot growers' haven. A throwback to the '60s, and '70s, it attracts plenty of hippies, gurus, woofers (workers on organic farms), yoga students, and other colorful characters pursuing alternative lifestyles. Secondhand stores, tie-dye/hemp clothing boutiques, smoke shops, and art galleries add to the "trippy" experience. Pahoa's main street boasts a handful of local-style eateries. To get here, turn southeast onto Highway 130 at Keaau, and drive 11 miles to a marked right turn. ⊠ *Pahoa.*

HAWAII VOLCANOES NATIONAL PARK AND VICINITY

22 miles southwest from the start of the Puna district; 27 miles southwest of Hilo.

Few visitors realize that in addition to "the volcano" (Kilauea)—that mountain oozing new layers of lava onto its flanks—there's also Volcano, the village. Conveniently located next to Hawaii Volcanoes National Park, Volcano Village is a charming little hamlet in the woods that offers a dozen or so excellent inns and bed-and-breakfasts, a decent (although strangely expensive) Thai restaurant, and a handful of things to see and do that don't include the village's namesake.

GETTING HERE AND AROUND

There is a handful of dining options, a couple of stores, and gas stations available in Volcano, so most of your needs should be covered. Kilauea Military Camp, inside the park, also runs a good general store and sells gas. If you can't find what you're looking for, Hilo is about a 35-minute drive away, and the Keaau grocery store and fast-food joints are 25 minutes away.

Many people choose to stay the night in Volcano to see the dramatic glow at the summit vent and to drive to the coast to see the lava flow

Continued on page 352

HAWAII VOLCANOES NATIONAL PARK

Exploring the surface of the world's most active volcano—from the moonscape craters at the summit to the red-hot lava flows on the coast to the kipuka, pockets of vegetation miraculously left untouched—is the ultimate ecotour and one of Hawaii's must-dos.

The park sprawls over 520 square miles and encompasses Kilauea and Mauna Loa, two of the five volcanoes that formed the Big Island nearly half a million years ago. Kilauea, youngest and most rambunctious of the Hawaiian volcanoes, erupted at its summit from the 19th century through 1982. Since then, the top of the volcano had been more or less quiet, frequently shrouded in mist; an eruption in the Halemaumau Crater in 2008 ended this period of relative inactivity.

Kilauea's eastern side sprang to life on January 3, 1983, shooting molten lava four stories high. This eruption has been ongoing, and lava flows are generally steady and slow, appearing and disappearing from view. Over 500 acres have been added to Hawaii's eastern coast since the activity began, and scientists say this eruptive phase is not likely to end anytime soon.

If you're lucky, you'll be able to catch creation at its most elemental—when molten lava meets the ocean, cools, and solidifies into brand-new stretches of coastline. Even if lava-viewing conditions aren't ideal, you can hike 150 miles of trails and camp amid wide expanses of *aa* (rough) and *pahoehoe* (smooth) lava. There's nothing quite like it.

⌂ P.O. Box 52, Hawaii Volcanoes National Park, HI 96718

☎ 808/985–6000

⊕ www.nps.gov/havo

🎟 $10 per vehicle; $5 for pedestrians and bicyclists. Ask about passes. Admission is good for seven consecutive days.

🕐 The park is open daily, 24 hours. Kilauea Visitor Center: 7:45 am–5 pm. Thomas A. Jaggar Museum: 8:30–5. Volcano Art Center Gallery: 9–5.

(top) Kilauea Iki Trail
(left) Fuming rim of Puu Oo, source of the current eruption

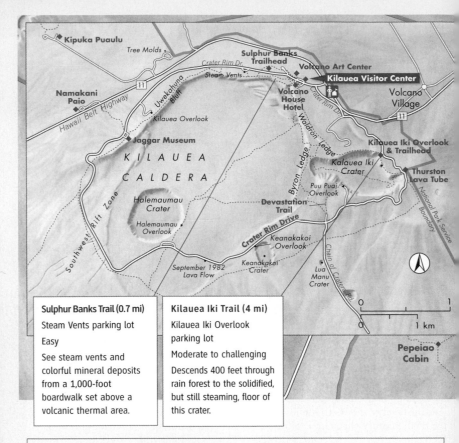

Sulphur Banks Trail (0.7 mi)

Steam Vents parking lot

Easy

See steam vents and colorful mineral deposits from a 1,000-foot boardwalk set above a volcanic thermal area.

Kilauea Iki Trail (4 mi)

Kilauea Iki Overlook parking lot

Moderate to challenging

Descends 400 feet through rain forest to the solidified, but still steaming, floor of this crater.

SEEING THE SUMMIT

The best way to explore the summit of Kilauea is to cruise along Crater Rim Drive to Kilauea Overlook. From Kilauea Overlook you can see all of Kilauea Caldera and Halemaumau Crater, an awesome depression in Kilauea Caldera measuring 3,000 feet across and nearly 300 feet deep. It's a huge and breathtaking view with pluming steam vents. At this writing, lava flows in the Southwest Rift Zone have closed parts of the 11-mile loop road indefinitely, including Halemaumau Overlook.

Near Kilauea Overlook is the Thomas A. Jaggar Museum, which offers simi-lar views, plus geologic displays, video presentations of volcanic eruptions, and exhibits of seismographs once used by volcanologists at the adjacent Hawaiian Volcano Observatory (not open to the public).

Other Highlights along Crater Rim Drive include sulfur and steam vents, a walk-through lava tube, and deep fissures, fractures, and gullies along Kilauea's flanks. Kilauea Iki Crater, on the way down to Chain of Crater's Road, is smaller, but just as fascinating when seen from Puu Pai Overlook.

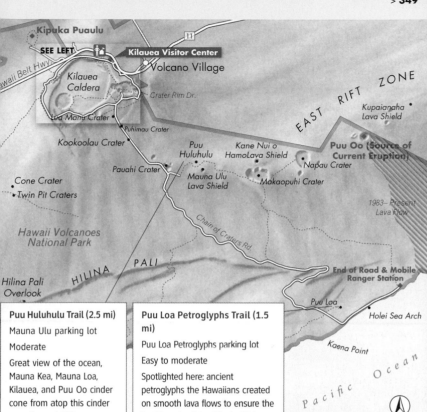

Kipuka Puaulu

SEE LEFT

Kilauea Visitor Center

Hawaii Belt Hwy

Volcano Village

11

Kilauea
Caldera

Crater Rim Dr.

EAST RIFT ZONE

Kupaianaha
Lava Shield

Loa Manu Crater

Puhimau Crater

Kookoolau Crater

Puu
Huluhulu

Kane Nui o
HamoLava Shield

Puu Oo (Source of
Current Eruption)

Napau Crater

Pauahi Crater

Mauna Ulu
Lava Shield

Makaopuhi Crater

Cone Crater

Twin Pit Craters

1983– Present
Lava Flow

Hawaii Volcanoes
National Park

Chain of Craters Rd.

HILINA PALI

Hilina Pali
Overlook

End of Road & Mobile
Ranger Station

Puu Loa

Holei Sea Arch

Kaena Point

Pacific Ocean

Puu Huluhulu Trail (2.5 mi)

Mauna Ulu parking lot

Moderate

Great view of the ocean, Mauna Kea, Mauna Loa, Kilauea, and Puu Oo cinder cone from atop this cinder cone formed 400 years ago.

Puu Loa Petroglyphs Trail (1.5 mi)

Puu Loa Petroglyphs parking lot

Easy to moderate

Spotlighted here: ancient petroglyphs the Hawaiians created on smooth lava flows to ensure the health and safety of their children.

SEEING LAVA

Before you head out to find flowing lava, pinpoint the safe viewing spots at the Visitor Center. One of the best places usually is at the end of 18-mile Chain of Craters Road. Magnificent plumes of steam rise where the rivers of liquid fire meet the sea.

There are three guarantees about lava flows in HVNP. First: They constantly change. Second: Because of that, you can't predict when and where you'll be able to see them. Third: New land formed when lava meets the sea is highly unstable and can collapse at any time. Never go into areas that have been closed.

■ TIP➔ The view of brilliant red-orange lava flowing from Kilauea's east rift zone is most dramatic at night.

People watching lava flow at HVNP

4

IN FOCUS HAWAII VOLCANOES NATIONAL PARK

PLANNING YOUR TRIP TO HVNP

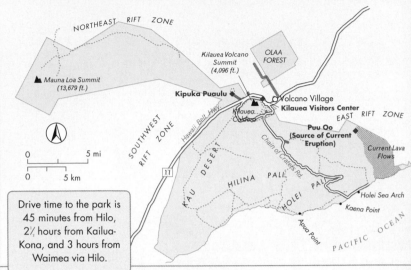

NORTHEAST RIFT ZONE

Kilauea Volcano Summit (4,096 ft.)

OLAA FOREST

Mauna Loa Summit (13,679 ft.)

Kipuka Puaulu

Volcano Village
Kilauea Visitors Center

EAST RIFT ZONE

Kilauea Caldera

Puu Oo (Source of Current Eruption)

Current Lava Flows

SOUTHWEST RIFT ZONE

Hawaii Belt Hwy.

Chain of Craters Rd.

0   5 mi
0   5 km

11

KAU DESERT

HILINA PALI

HOLEI PALI

Holei Sea Arch

Kaena Point

Apua Point

PACIFIC OCEAN

Drive time to the park is 45 minutes from Hilo, 2¼ hours from Kailua-Kona, and 3 hours from Waimea via Hilo.

Lava entering the ocean

WHERE TO START

Begin your visit at the Visitor Center, where you'll find maps, books, and DVDs; information on trails, ranger-led walks, and special events; and current weather, road, and lava-viewing conditions. Free volcano-related film showings, lectures, and other presentations are regularly scheduled.

WEATHER

Weather conditions fluctuate daily, sometimes hourly. It can be rainy and chilly even during the summer; the temperature usually is 14° cooler at the 4,000-foot-high summit of Kilauea than at sea level.

Expect hot, dry, and windy coastal conditions at the end of Chain of Craters Road. Bring rain gear, and wear layered clothing, sturdy shoes, sunglasses, a hat, and sunscreen.

Photographer on lava table filming lava flow into ocean

FOOD
It's a good idea to bring your own favorite snacks and beverages; stock up on provisions in Volcano Village, 1½ miles away.

PARK PROGRAMS
Rangers lead daily walks at 10:30 and 1:30 into different areas; check with the Visitor Center for details as times and destinations depend on weather conditions and eruptions.

Over 60 companies hold permits to lead hikes at HVNP. Good choices are Hawaii Forest & Trail (www.hawaii-forest.com), Hawaiian Walkways (www.hawaiianwalkways.com), and Native Guide Hawaii (www.nativeguide hawaii.com).

CAUTION
"Vog" (volcanic smog) can cause headaches; breathing difficulties; lethargy; irritations of the skin, eyes, nose, and throat; and other health problems. Pregnant women, young children, and people with asthma and heart conditions are most susceptible, and should avoid areas such as Halemaumau Crater where fumes are thick.

Wear long pants and boots or closed-toe shoes with good tread for hikes on lava. Stay on marked trails and step carefully. Lava is composed of 50% silica (glass) and can cause serious injury if you fall.

Carry at least 2 quarts of water on hikes. Temperatures near lava flows can rise above 100°F, and dehydration, heat exhaustion, and sunstroke are common consequences of extended exposure to intense sunlight and high temperatures.

Remember that these are active volcanoes, and eruptions can cause parts of the park to close at any time. Check the park's website or call ahead for last-minute updates before your visit.

Volcanologists inspecting a vent in the East Rift Zone

"I learned that the best viewing area was at the end of the Pahoa Kalapana Road past the Keauohana Forest Reserve." —NickiGgert, Fodors.com photo contest participant

into the sea. (If you do, bring a fleece or sweater, as temperatures drop at night and mornings are usually cool and misty.) ⚠ Chain of Craters Road is currently closed about 8 miles below the summit, however, so you will have to travel outside the boundaries of the park to see lava flows.

In recent years, lava flows to the sea have taken place across private land and outside the park boundaries. This means you may drive way past the park and all the way to the end of the road at Kalapana to see flows and then find access restricted. You can, however, book a lava flow trek with a local outfitter.

TOP ATTRACTIONS

For information on the park, see Hawaii Volcanoes National Park feature in this chapter.

Kilauea Caverns of Fire. This way-out adventure explores the underbelly of the world's most active volcano via the Kazamura Lava Tube system. The largest lava tube system in the world—40 miles long, 80 feet wide, and 80 feet tall, it comprises four main tubes, each 500–700 years old and filled with bizarre lava formations and mind-blowing colors. Customized to groups' interest and skill level, tours through fascinating caves and lava tubes must be arranged in advance but are well worth the extra planning. Equipment is included. ⊠ *Hawaiian Acres, off Hwy. 11, between Kurtistown and Mountain View* ☎ *808/217–2363* ⊕ *www. kilaueacavernsoffire.com* ✉ *$29 for walking tour, $89 for adventure tour* ☉ *By appointment only.*

Volcano Farmers' Market. Local produce, flowers, crafts, and food products, including fresh-baked breads, pastries, coffee, and homemade Thai specialties, are available every Sunday morning at one of the better farmers' markets on the island. It's best to get there early, before 7 am, as vendors tend to sell out of the best stuff quickly. There's also a great bookstore (paperbacks 50¢, hardbacks $1, and magazines 10¢) and a thrift store with clothes and knickknacks. ✉ *Cooper Center, 19-4030 Wright Rd., Volcano* ☎ *808/936–9705* ⊕ *www.thecoopercenter.org* ☉ *Sun. 6–10 am.*

KAU AND KA LAE

50 miles south of Kailua-Kona.

The most desolate region of the island, Kau, is nevertheless home to spectacular sights. Mark Twain wrote some of his finest prose here, where macadamia-nut farms, remote green-sand beaches, and tiny communities offer rugged, largely undiscovered beauty. The drive from Kailua-Kona to windswept Ka Lae (South Point) winds away from the ocean through a surreal moonscape of lava plains and patches of scrub forest. Coming from Volcano, as you near South Point, the barren lavascape gives way to lush vistas from the ocean to the hills.

At the end of the 12-mile two-lane road to Ka Lae, you can park and hike about an hour to Papakolea Beach (Green Sands Beach). Back on the highway, the coast passes verdant cattle pastures and sheer cliffs and the village of Naalehu on the way to the black-sand beach of Punaluu, a common nesting place of the Hawaiian green sea turtle.

GETTING HERE AND AROUND

Kau and Ka Lae are destinations usually combined with a quick trip to the volcano from Kona. This is probably cramming too much into one day, however. The volcano fills up at least a day (two is better), and the sights of this southern end of the island are worth more than a cursory glance.

Instead make Green Sands Beach or Punaluu a beach day, and see some of the other sights on the way there or back. Bring sturdy shoes, water, and a sun hat if Green Sands Beach is your choice (reaching the beach requires a hike). And be careful in the surf here. Don't go in unless you're used to ocean waves. There are no lifeguards at this remote beach. It's decidedly calmer and you can sometimes snorkel at Punaluu, but use caution at these and all Hawaii beaches.

The drive from Kailua-Kona to Ka Lae is a long one (roughly 2½ hours); from Volcano it's approximately 45 minutes. You can fill up on gas and groceries in Ocean View, or you can eat, fuel up, and get picnic fixings in Naalehu. Weather tends to be warm, dry, and windy.

TOP ATTRACTIONS

Fodor's Choice ★ **Ka Lae (South Point).** It's thought that the first Polynesians came ashore at this southernmost point of land in the United States, also a National Historic Landmark. Old canoe-mooring holes, visible today, were carved through the rocks, possibly by settlers from Tahiti as early as AD 750. To get here, drive 12 miles on the turnoff road, past rows of giant electricity-producing windmills powered by the nearly constant winds sweeping across this coastal plain. Bear left when the road forks, and park in the lot at the end. Walk past the boat hoists toward the little lighthouse. South Point is just past the lighthouse at the southernmost cliff. You may see brave locals jumping off the cliffs and then climbing up rusty old ladders, but swimming here is not recommended. ■ TIP➜ Don't leave anything of value in your car. ✉ *South Point Rd., off Mamalahoa Hwy. at around mile marker 70, Kau* 💲 *Free.*

BEACHES

Don't believe anyone who tells you that the Big Island lacks beaches. It's just one of the myths about Hawaii's largest island that has no basis in fact. It's not so much that the Big Island has fewer beaches than the other islands, just that there's more island, so getting to the beaches can be slightly less convenient.

That said, there are plenty of those perfect white-sand stretches you think of when you hear "Hawaii," and the added bonus of black- and green-sand beaches, thanks to the relative young age of the island and its active volcanoes. New beaches appear and disappear regularly, created and destroyed by volcanic activity. In 1989, a black-sand beach, Kamoamoa, formed when molten lava shattered as it hit cold ocean waters; it was enjoyed for a few years before it was closed by new lava flows in 1992. It's part of the ongoing process of the volcano's creation-and-change dynamic.

Hawaii's largest coral reef systems lie off the Kohala Coast. Waves have battered them over millennia to create abundant white-sand beaches on the northwest side of the island. Black-sand and green-sand beaches lie in the southern regions, along the coast nearest the volcano. On the eastern side of the island, beaches tend to be of the rocky-coast–surging-surf variety, but there are still a few worth visiting, and this is where the Hawaiian shoreline is at its most picturesque.

KAILUA-KONA

There are a few good sandy beaches near town. However, the coastline is generally rugged black lava rock, so don't expect long stretches of white sand. The beaches in Kailua-Kona get lots of use by local residents, and visitors enjoy them, too. Excellent opportunities for snorkeling, scuba diving, swimming, kayaking, and other water sports are easy to find.

FAMILY **Kahaluu Beach Park.** This shallow and easily accessible salt-and-pepper beach is one of the Big Island's most popular swimming and snorkeling

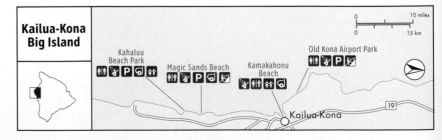

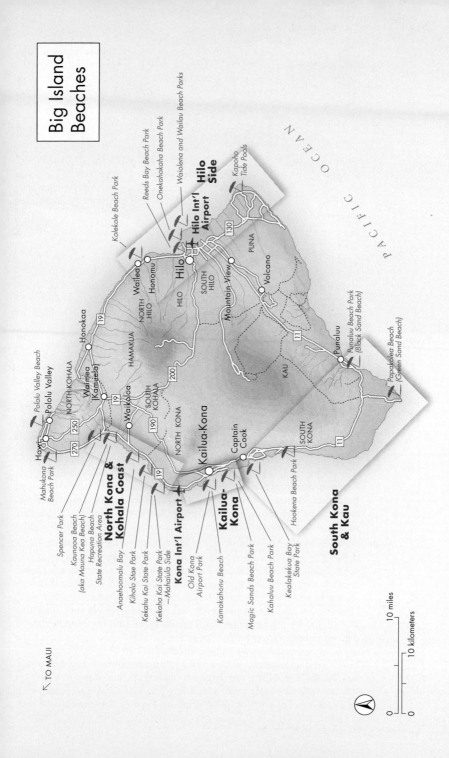

Big Island
Beaches

TO MAUI

PACIFIC OCEAN

Pololu Valley Beach
Pololu Valley
NORTH KOHALA
Honokaa
Hawi
270
250
Mahukona
Beach Park
Spencer Park
Kaunaoa Beach
(aka Mauna Kea Beach)
Hapuna Beach
State Recreation Area
North Kona &
Kohala Coast
Anaehoomalu Bay
Kiholo Stae Park
Kekahu Kai State Park
Kekaha Kai State Park
—Mahaiula Side
Kona Int'l Airport
Old Kona
Airport Park
Kamakahonu Beach
Kailua-
Kona
Magic Sands Beach Park
Kahaluu Beach Park
Kealakekua Bay
State Park
Hookena Beach Park
South Kona
& Kau

Waimea
(Kamuela)
Waikoloa
190
19
200
19
HAMAKUA
NORTH
KOHALA
SOUTH
KOHALA
NORTH
KONA
SOUTH
KONA
Kailua-Kona
Captain
Cook
11

Wailea
Honomu
Hilo
NORTH
HILO
HILO
SOUTH
HILO
Mountain-View
PUNA
Volcano
130
KAU
Punaluu
11
Punaluu Beach Park
(Black Sand Beach)
Papakolea Beach
(Green Sand Beach)

Kolekole Beach Park
Reeds Bay Beach Park
Onekahakaha Beach Park
Waiolena and Wailau Beach Parks
Hilo Int'l
Airport
Hilo
Side
Kapoho
Tide Pools

PACIFIC OCEAN

0   10 miles
0   10 kilometers

Kua Bay is protected from wind by the rocky shores that surround it.

sites, thanks to the fringing reef that helps keep the waters calm, visibility high, and reef life—especially turtles and colorful fish—plentiful. Because it is so protected, it's great for first-time snorkelers, but outside the reef, very strong rip currents can run, so caution is advised. Never chase turtles or hand-feed the unusually tame reef fish here; it upsets the balance of the reef. ■TIP➜ Experienced surfers find good waves beyond the reef, and scuba divers like the shore dives—shallow ones inside the breakwater, deeper ones outside. Snorkel equipment and boards are available for rent nearby, and surf schools operate here. Kahaluu was a favorite of the Hawaiian royal family, especially King Kalakaua. **Amenities:** food and drink; lifeguards; parking; showers; toilets. **Best for:** snorkeling; swimming. ✉ *78-6720 Alii Dr., 5½ miles south of Kailua-Kona, across from the Beach Villas* ☎ *808/961–8311.*

FAMILY **Kamakahonu Beach.** This is where King Kamehameha spent his final days—the restored Ahuena Heiau sits on a platform across from the sand. Fronting the Courtyard King Kamehameha's Kona Beach Hotel and adjacent to Kailua Pier, this scenic crescent of white sand is one of few beaches in downtown Kailua-Kona. The water here is almost always calm and the beach clean, making this a perfect spot for kids. For adults, it's a great place for a swim, some stand-up paddleboarding, watching outrigger teams practice, or enjoying a lazy beach day. It can get crowded on weekends. Snorkeling can be good north of the beach, and snorkeling, SUP, and kayaking equipment can be rented nearby. ■TIP➜ A little family of sea turtles likes to hang out next to the seawall, so keep an eye out. There's lots of grass and shade, and free parking in county lots are a short stroll away. **Amenities:** food and

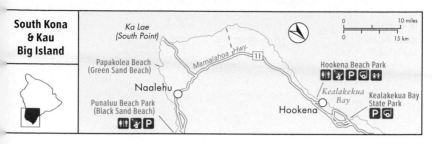

drink; showers; toilets; water sports. **Best for:** snorkeling; swimming. ⊠ *75-5660 Palani Rd., at Alii Dr.*

THE KONA COAST

The rugged beauty of this coastline harbors a couple of scenic beaches that take you off the beaten track.

Fodor's Choice ★ **Kekaha Kai State Park—Mahaiula Side.** It's slow going, down a 1.8-mile, bumpy, mostly unpaved road off Highway 19 to this beach park, but it's worth it. This state park encompasses three beaches (from south to north, Mahaiula, Makalawena, and Kua Bay, which has its own entrance). Mahaiula and Makalawena are beautiful, wide expanses of white-sand beach with dunes; there's a lot of space so you won't feel crowded. Makalawena has great swimming and bodyboarding. From there, a historic 4½-mile trail leads to Kua Bay. If you're game, work your way to the top of Puu Kuili, a 342-foot-high cinder cone whose summit offers a fantastic view of the coastline. However, be prepared for the heat and bring lots of water. Gates close promptly at 7 pm, so you need to leave the lot by 6:30. ⚠ **Watch out for rough surf and strong currents. Amenities:** toilets. **Best for:** sunset; swimming; walking. ⊠ *Hwy. 19, turnoff is about 2 miles north of Keahole–Kona International Airport, Kailua-Kona* ☎ *808/327–4958, 808/974–6200* ⊕ *www.hawaiistateparks.org.*

Kekaha Kai State Park—Kua Bay Side. This lovely beach is on the northernmost stretch of the park's coastline on an absolutely beautiful bay. The water is crystal clear, deep aquamarine, and peaceful in summer, but the park's paved entrance, amenities, and parking lot make it very accessible and, as a result, often crowded. Fine white sand sits amid black lava with little shade—bring umbrellas, as it can get hot. Rocky shores on either side protect the beach from winds in the afternoon. Gates close daily at 7 pm. ⚠ **In winter, surf can get very rough, and often the sand washes away. Amenities:** parking (no fee); showers; toilets. **Best for:** surfing; swimming. ⊠ *Hwy. 19, north of mile marker 88, across from the Veterans Cemetery, Kailua-Kona.*

Fodor's Choice ★ **Kealakekua Bay State Historical Park.** When Hurricane Iniki slammed into Hawaii in 1992, this park lost all of its sand, which is slowly returning decades later. The shoreline is rocky but don't let that deter you. The area is surrounded by high green cliffs, creating calm conditions for superb swimming, snorkeling, and diving. Among the variety of marine life are dolphins, which come to rest and escape predators during the

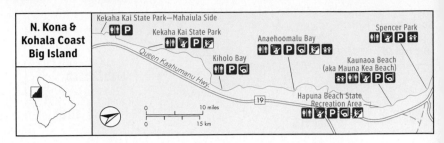

day. They are protected from harassment by federal law, so don't disturb them. This popular spot is also historically significant. Captain James Cook first landed in Hawaii here in 1778. When he returned a year later, he was killed in a skirmish with Hawaiians, now marked by a monument on the north end of the bay. Rocky but walkable trails lead to Hikiau Heiau, a sacred place for the Hawaiian people. Do not walk on or enter it. Parking is limited. △ **Be aware of the off-limits area (in case of rockfalls) marked by orange buoys. Amenities:** parking (no fee); toilets. **Best for:** snorkeling; swimming. ✉ *Napoopoo Rd., off Hwy. 11, just south of mile marker 111, Kealakekua* ☎ *808/961–9544.*

THE KOHALA COAST

Most of the Big Island's white sandy beaches are found on the Kohala Coast, which is also called the Gold Coast, and is, understandably, home to the majority of the island's world-class resorts. Hawaii's beaches are public property and the resorts are required to provide public access, so don't be frightened off by a guard shack and a fancy sign. There is some limited public parking as well. Resort beaches aside, there are some real hidden gems, accessible only by boat, four-wheel drive, or a 15- to 20-minute hike. It's well worth the effort to get to at least one of these. ■**TIP**→ The west side of the island tends to be calmer, but the surf still gets rough in winter.

FAMILY   **Anaehoomalu Bay** (*A-Bay*). Also known as A-Bay, this expansive stretch
Fodor's Choice   of white sand fronts the Waikoloa Beach Marriott and is a perfect
★   spot for swimming, windsurfing, snorkeling, and diving. Unlike some Kohala Coast beaches near hotel properties, this one is very accessible to the public and offers plenty of free parking. The bay is well protected, so even when surf is rough or trades are blasting, it's fairly calm here. (Mornings are calmest.) Snorkel gear, kayaks, and bodyboards are available for rent at the north end. Behind the beach are two ancient Hawaiian fishponds, **Kuualii** and **Kahapapa**, that once served ancient Hawaiian royalty. A walking trail follows the coastline to the Hilton Waikoloa Village next door, passing by tide pools, ponds, and a turtle sanctuary where sea turtles can often be spotted sunbathing on the sand. Footwear is recommended for the trail. **Amenities:** food and drink; parking (no fee); showers; toilets; water sports. **Best for:** snorkeling; swimming; walking. ✉ *69-275 Waikoloa Beach Dr., just south of Waikoloa Beach Marriott; turn left at Kings' Shops, Kohala Coast.*

Calm Kailua Bay is an excellent spot for outrigger paddling, snorkeling, and swimming.

FAMILY
Fodor's Choice
★

Hapuna Beach State Recreation Area. One of Hawaii's finest beaches, Hapuna is a ½-mile-long stretch of white perfection. The turquoise water is calm in summer with just enough rolling waves to make body-surfing and bodyboarding fun. Watch for the undertow; in winter it can be rough. There is excellent snorkeling around the jagged rocks that border the beach on either side, but high surf brings strong currents. Known for awesome sunsets, this is one of the best places on the island to see the "green flash" as the sun dips below a clear horizon. The north end of the beach fronts the Hapuna Beach Prince Hotel, which rents water-sports equipment and has a food concession with shaded picnic tables. There is ample parking, although the lot can fill up by midday and the beach can get crowded on holidays. Lifeguards, on duty during peak hours, only cover the state park section, not areas north of the rocky cliff that juts out near the middle of the beach. **Amenities:** food and drink; lifeguards; parking (fee); showers; toilets; water sports. **Best for:** sunset; surfing; swimming; walking. ⊠ *Hwy. 19, near mile marker 69, just south of the Hapuna Beach Prince Hotel, Kohala Coast* ☎ *808/961–9544.*

FAMILY
Fodor's Choice
★

Kaunaoa Beach (*Mauna Kea Beach*). Hands-down one of the most beautiful beaches on the island, if not the whole state, Kaunaoa features a long crescent of pure white sand. The beach, which fronts the Mauna Kea Beach Hotel, slopes very gradually, and there's great snorkeling along the rocks. Classic Hawaii postcard views abound, especially in winter, when snow tops Mauna Kea. When conditions permit, waves are good for body- and board surfing also. Currents can be strong and powerful in winter, so be careful. ■TIP→ Public parking is limited to a few spaces, so arrive before 10 am or after 3 pm. If the lot is full, head to nearby Hapuna Beach, where there's a huge parking lot ($5 per vehicle). Try this spot again another day—it's worth it! **Amenities:** parking (no fee); showers; toilets; water sports. **Best for:** sunset; swimming; walking. ⊠ *62-100 Mauna Kea Beach Dr., entry through gate to Mauna Kea Beach Hotel, Kohala Coast.*

Pololu Valley Beach. On the North Kohala peninsula, this is one of the Big Island's most scenic black-sand beaches. After about 8 miles of lush, winding road past Hawi Town, Highway 270 ends at the overlook of Pololu Valley. Snap a few photos of the stunning view, then take the 15-minute hike down (twice as long back up) to the beach. The trail is steep and rocky; it can also be muddy and slippery, so watch your step. The beach itself is a wide expanse of fine black sand surrounded by sheer green cliffs and backed by high dunes and ironwood trees. A gurgling stream leads from the beach to the back of the valley. ⚠ **This is not a safe swimming beach even though locals do swim, bodyboard, and surf here. Dangerous rip currents and usually rough surf pose a real hazard.** And because this is a remote, isolated area far from emergency help, extreme caution is advised. **Amenities:** none. **Best for:** hiking. ⊠ *Hwy. 270, end of the road, Kapaau.*

FAMILY **Spencer Park at Ohaiula Beach.** This white-sand beach is popular with local families because of its reef-protected waters. ■**TIP➔** It's probably the safest beach in West Hawaii for young children. It's also safe for swimming year-round, which makes it a reliable spot for a lazy day at the beach. There is a little shade, plus a volleyball court and pavilion, and the soft sand is perfect for sand castles. It does tend to get crowded with families and campers on weekends, but the beach is generally clean. Although you won't see a lot of fish if you're snorkeling here, in winter you can usually catch sight of a breaching whale or two. The beach park lies just below Puukohola Heiau National Historic Park, site of the historic war temple built by King Kamehameha the Great in 1810 after uniting the Islands. **Amenities:** lifeguards (weekends and holidays only); parking (no fee); showers; toilets. **Best for:** sunset; swimming. ⊠ *Hwy. 270, toward Kawaihae Harbor, just after the road forks from Hwy. 19, Kawaihae* ☎ *808/961–8311.*

HILO

Hilo isn't exactly known for its beautiful white beaches, but there are a few in the area that provide good swimming and snorkeling opportunities, and most are surrounded by lush rain forest.

FAMILY **Onekahakaha Beach Park.** Shallow, rock-wall-enclosed tide pools and an adjacent grassy picnic area make this park a favorite among Hilo families with small children. The protected pools are great places to look for Hawaiian marine life like sea urchins and anemones. There isn't much white sand, but access to the water is easy. The water is usually rough beyond the line of large boulders protecting the inner tide pools, so be careful if the surf is high. This beach gets crowded on weekends. **Amenities:** lifeguards (weekends, holidays, and summer only); parking

4

(no fee); showers; toilets. **Best for:** swimming. ⊠ *Onekahakaha Rd. and Kalanianaole Ave., via Kanoelehua St., 3 miles east of Hilo, Hilo* ☎ *808/961–8311.*

FAMILY **Waiolena and Wailua Beach Parks and Richardson Ocean Center.** Just east of Hilo, almost at the end of the road, three adjacent parks make up one beautiful spot with a series of bays, protected inlets, lagoons, and pretty parks. This is one of the best snorkeling sites on this side of the island, as rocky outcrops provide shelter for schools of reef fish, sea turtles, and dolphins. Local kids use the small black-sand pocket beach for bodyboarding. The shaded grassy areas are great for picnics. Be warned, this place is very crowded on weekends. **Amenities:** lifeguards (weekends, holidays, and summer only); parking (no fee); showers; toilets. **Best for:** snorkeling; walking. ⊠ *2349 Kalanianaole Ave., 4 miles east of Hilo, Hilo* ☎ *808/961–8311.*

PUNA

Puna's few beaches have some unusual attributes—swaths of new black sand, volcano-heated springs, and a coastline that is beyond dramatic (sheer walls of lava rock dropping into a dramatic blue ocean).

Fodor's Choice **Kapoho Tide Pools.** Snorkelers find tons of coral and the fish that feed off
★ it in this large network of tide pools at the end of Kapoho-Kai Road. This is a great place for getting close-up looks at Hawaii's interesting marine life. Some of the pools have been turned into private swimming pools in this residential area; those closest to the ocean are open to all. The pools are usually very calm, and some are volcanically heated and divine to soak in. It's best to come during the week, as the pools can get crowded on the weekend. Note: there is no real sandy beach here. Take the road to the end, turn left, and park. **Amenities:** none. **Best for:** snorkeling. ⊠ *Kapoho-Kai Rd., off Hwy. 13, about 9 miles southeast of Pahoa Town, Puna.*

KAU

You shouldn't expect to find sparkling white-sand beaches on the rugged and rocky coasts of Kau, and you won't. What you will find is something a bit rarer and well worth the visit: black- and green-sand beaches. And there's the chance to see the endangered Hawaiian green sea turtles close up.

Papakolea Beach (*Green Sands Beach*). Tired of the same old gold-, white-, or black-sand beach? Then how about a green-sand beach? You'll need good hiking shoes or sneakers to get to this olive-green crescent, one of the most unusual beaches on the island. It lies at the base of Puu O Mahana, at Mahana Bay, where a cinder cone formed during an early eruption of Mauna Loa. The greenish tint is caused by an accumulation of olivine crystals that form in volcanic eruptions. The dry, barren landscape is totally surreal but stunning, as aquamarine waters lap on green sand against reddish cliffs. The surf is often rough, and swimming is hazardous due to strong currents, so caution is advised. Drive down to Ka Lae (South Point); at the end of the 12-mile paved road, take the road to the left and park at the end. ■TIP➔ Anyone trying to charge for parking is running a scam. To reach the beach, follow the 2¼-mile coastal trail, which ends in a steep and dangerous descent down the cliff side on an unimproved trail. The hike takes about two hours each way and it can get windy, so bring lots of drinking water. Four-wheel-drive vehicles are no longer permitted on the trail. **Amenities:** none. **Best for:** solitude. ⊠ *Hwy. 11, 2½ miles northeast of South Point, Naalehu.*

Fodor's Choice ★ **Punaluu Black Sand Beach Park.** A great stop on a southeast–bound trip to the volcano, this easily accessible black-sand beach is backed by low dunes, brackish ponds, and tall coco palms. The shoreline is jagged, reefed, and rocky. Most days, large groups of sea turtles nap on the sand—a stunning sight. Resist the urge to get too close or disturb them; they're protected by federal and state law and fines for harassment can be hefty. Removing black sand is also prohibited. ⚠ Extremely strong rip currents prevail, so only experienced ocean swimmers should consider getting in the water here. Popular with locals and tour buses alike, this beach park can get very busy, especially on weekends (the north parking lot is usually quieter). Shade from palm trees provides an escape from the sun, and at the northern end of the beach, near the boat ramp, lie the ruins of Kaneeleele Heiau, an old Hawaiian temple. The area was a sugar port until the 1946 tsunami destroyed the buildings. Developers tried to bring a resort experience here in the early 1990s, but that has mostly failed. (You'll drive by a few abandoned resort buildings on your way to the beach.) ■TIP➔ Bring your camera and a picnic lunch. **Amenities:** parking (no fee); showers; toilets. **Best for:** walking. ⊠ *Hwy. 11, 27 miles south of Hawaii Volcanoes National Park between mile markers 55 and 56, Naalehu* ☎ *808/961–8311.*

WATER SPORTS AND TOURS

Updated by Kristina Anderson

From any point on the Big Island, the ocean is nearby. From bodyboarding and snorkeling to kayaking and surfing, there is a water sport for everyone. For most activities, you can rent gear and go it alone or with a group excursion with an experienced guide, who can offer security as well as special insights into Hawaiian marine life and culture. Want to try surfing? You can take lessons that promise to have you standing the first day out.

The Kona and Kohala coasts of West Hawaii boast the largest number of ocean sports outfitters and tour operators. They operate from the small-boat harbors and piers in Kailua-Kona, Keauhou, Kawaihae, and at the Kohala Coast resorts. There are also several outfitters in the East Hawaii and Hilo areas.

BODYBOARDING AND BODYSURFING

According to the movies, in the Old West there was always friction between cattle ranchers and sheep ranchers. A somewhat similar situation exists between surfers and bodyboarders (and between surfers and stand-up paddleboarders). That's why they generally keep to their own separate areas. Often the bodyboarders, who lie on their stomachs on shorter boards, stay closer to shore and leave the outside breaks to the board surfers. Or the board surfers may stick to one side of the beach and the bodyboarders to the other. The truth is, bodyboarding (often called "boogie boarding," in homage to the first commercial manufacturer of this slick, little, flexible-foam board) is a blast. Most surfers also sometimes carve waves on a bodyboard, no matter how much of a purist they claim to be. ■TIP➜ Novice bodyboarders should catch shore-break waves only. Ask lifeguards or locals for the best spots. You'll need a pair of short fins to get out to the bigger waves offshore (not recommended for newbies). As for bodysurfing, just catch a wave and make like Superman going faster than a speeding bullet.

BEST SPOTS

Fodor's Choice ★ **Hapuna Beach State Recreation Area.** Often considered one of the top 10 beaches in the world, Hapuna Beach State Recreation Area offers fine white sand, turquoise water, and easy rolling surf on most days, making it great for bodysurfing and bodyboarding at all levels. Ask the lifeguards—who only cover areas south of the rocky cliff that juts out near the middle of the beach—about conditions before heading into the water, especially in winter. Sometimes northwest swells create a dangerous undertow. Parking costs $5. ✉ *Hwy. 19, near mile marker 69, just south of Mauna Kea Hotel, Kohala Coast* ⊕ *www.hawaiistateparks. org/parks/hawaii/hapuna.cfm.*

Honolii Cove. North of Hilo, this is the best bodyboarding spot on the east side of the island. ✉ *Off Hwy. 19, near mile marker 4, Hilo.*

Magic Sands Beach Park (*White Sands Beach*). This white-sand, shore-break cove is great for beginning to intermediate bodysurfing and bodyboarding. Sometimes in winter, much of the sand here washes out to sea and forms a sandbar just offshore, creating fun wave conditions. Also known as White Sands, it's popular and can get crowded with locals, especially when school is out. Watch for nasty rip currents at high tide. ■TIP➜ If you're not using fins, wear reef shoes for protection against sharp rocks. ✉ *Alii Dr., just north of mile marker 4, Kailua-Kona.*

EQUIPMENT

Equipment-rental shacks are located at many beaches and boat harbors, along the highway, and at most resorts. Bodyboard rental rates are around $12–$15 per day and around $60 per week. Ask the vendor to throw in a pair of fins—some will for no extra charge.

Orchid Land Surf Shop. This shop has a wide variety of surf and other water-sports equipment for sale or rent. It stocks professional custom surfboards, body boards, and surf apparel, and also does repairs. You can rent a bodyboard for $12 a day, a surfboard for $20 a day. ⊠ *262 Kamehameha Ave., Hilo* ☎ *808/935–1533* ⊕ *www.orchidlandsurf.com.*

Pacific Vibrations. This family-owned surf shop—in business 35 years—holds the distinction of being the oldest, smallest surf shop in the world. Even at a compact 400 square feet, this place stocks tons of equipment, surf wear, surf gear, and GoPro cameras. You can rent a surfboard (under $20), stand-up paddleboard, or bodyboard—$5 a day but you have to buy or bring your own fins. Right in the heart of downtown Kailua Town, it's worth a stop for the authentic Hawaii surf vibe. ⊠ *75-5702 Likana La. #B, at Alii Dr., Kailua-Kona* ☎ *808/329–4140.*

DEEP-SEA FISHING

The Kona Coast has some of the world's most exciting "blue-water" fishing. Although July, August, and September are peak months, with the best fishing and a number of tournaments, charter fishing goes on year-round. You don't have to compete to experience the thrill of landing a Pacific blue marlin or other big-game fish. Some 60 charter boats, averaging 26 to 58 feet, are available for hire, all of them out of **Honokohau Harbor,** north of Kailua-Kona.

For an exclusive charter, prices generally range from $600 to $950 for a half-day trip (about four hours) and $800 to $1,600 for a full day at sea (about eight hours). For share charters, rates are about $100 to $140 per person for a half day and $200 for a full day. If fuel prices increase, expect charter costs to rise. Most boats are licensed to take up to six passengers, in addition to the crew. Tackle, bait, and ice are furnished, but you usually have to bring your own lunch. You won't be able to keep your catch, although if you ask, many captains will send you home with a few fillets.

Honokohau Harbor's Fuel Dock. Show up around 11:30 am and watch the weigh-in of the day's catch from the morning charters, or around 3:30 pm for the afternoon charters. Weigh-ins are fun when the big ones come in, but it's not a sure thing. ■ TIP→ On Kona's Waterfront Row, look for the "Grander's Wall" of anglers with their 1,000-pound-plus prizes. ⊠ *Honokohau Harbor, Kealakehe Pkwy. at Hwy. 11, Kailua-Kona.*

BOATS AND CHARTERS

Bwana Sportfishing. Full-, half-, quarter-, three-quarter-day, and overnight charters are available on the 46-foot *Bwana.* The boat features the latest electronics, top-of-the-line equipment, and air-conditioned cabins. Captain Teddy comes from a fishing family; father Peter is retired but still affiliated with the Kona Charter Skippers Association. ⊠ *Honokohau Harbor, Slip H-17, 74-381 Kealakehe Pkwy., just south of Kona airport, Kailua-Kona* ☎ *808/936–5168* ⊕ *www.teddyhoogs. com* ✉ *From $1,250.*

Charter Locker. This company offers half- and full-day charter fishing trips on 30- to 52-foot vessels. The luxurious *Blue Hawaii* has air-conditioned staterooms for overnight trips. Rates depend on the boat. ⊠ *Honokohau Harbor No. 16, 74-381 Kealakehe Pkwy., just south of Kona airport, Kailua-Kona* ☎ *808/326–2553* ⊕ *www.charterlocker. com.*

Humdinger Sportfishing. This game-fisher guide has more than three decades of fishing experience in Kona waters, and the expert crew are marlin specialists. The 37-foot *Humdinger* has the latest in electronics and top-line rods and reels. ⊠ *Honokohau Harbor, Slip B-4, 74-381 Kealakehe Pkwy., Kailua-Kona* ☎ *808/936–3034, 800/926–2374* ⊕ *www.humdingersportfishing.com* ✉ *From $600.*

Illusions Sportfishing. Captain Tim Hicks is one of Kona's top fishing-tourney producers, with 20 years of experience. The 39-foot *Illusions* is fully equipped with galley, restrooms, an air-conditioned cabin, plus the latest in fishing equipment. ⊠ *Honokohau Harbor, 74-381 Kealakehe Pkwy., just south of Kona airport, Kailua-Kona* ☎ *808/960–7371* ⊕ *www.illusionssportfishing.com* ✉ *From $550.*

KAYAKING

The leeward west coast areas of the Big Island are protected for the most part from the northeast trade winds, making for ideal, near-shore kayaking conditions. There are miles and miles of uncrowded Kona and Kohala coastline to explore, presenting close-up views of stark, raw, lava-rock shores and cliffs; lava-tube sea caves; pristine, secluded coves; and deserted beaches.

BEST SPOTS

Hilo Bay. This is a favorite kayak spot. The best place to put in is at **Reeds Bay Beach Park.** Parking is plentiful and free at the bayfront. Most afternoons you'll share the bay with local paddling clubs. Stay inside the breakwater unless the ocean is calm (or you're feeling unusually adventurous). Conditions range from extremely calm to quite choppy. ⊠ *Banyan Way and Banyan Dr., 1 mile from downtown Hilo.*

Kailua Bay and Kamakahonu Beach. The small, sandy beach that fronts the Courtyard King Kamehameha's Kona Beach Hotel is a nice place to rent or launch kayaks. You can unload in the cul-de-sac and park in nearby free lots. The water here is especially calm and the surroundings are historic and scenic. ⊠ *Alii Dr., next to Kailua Pier, Kailua-Kona.*

Kealakekua Bay State Historical Park. The excellent snorkeling and likelihood of seeing dolphins (morning is best) make Kealakekua Bay one of the most popular kayaking spots on the Big Island. An ocean conservation district, the bay is usually calm and tranquil. (Use caution and common sense during surf advisories.) Tall coral pinnacles and clear visibility surrounding the monument also make for stupendous snorkeling.

Because of new regulations, only a few operators have permits to lead kayak tours in the park. ⊠ *Napoopoo Rd and Manini Bch. Rd., Captain Cook* ⊕ *www.hawaiistateparks.org/parks/hawaii.*

Oneo Bay. Right downtown, this is usually a placid place to kayak. It's fairly easy to get to. If you can't find parking along the road, there's a free lot across the street from the library and farmers' market. ⊠ *Alii Dr., Kailua-Kona.*

EQUIPMENT, LESSONS, AND TOURS

There are several rental outfitters on Highway 11 between Kainaliu and Captain Cook, but only a few are specially permitted to lead kayak trips in Kealakekua Bay.

Aloha Kayak Co. This outfitter is one of the few that is permitted to guide tours to the stunningly beautiful Kealakekua Bay, leaving from Napoopoo, including about 1½ hours at the Captain Cook Monument. The 3½-hour morning and afternoon tours ($99) include snacks and drinks. Local guides tell about the area's cultural, historical, and natural significance. You may see dolphins, but you must watch them from a distance only, as this is a protected marine reserve. Keauhou Bay tours are also offered: a four-hour morning tour for $89, a 2½-hour afternoon version for $69, and a two-hour evening manta ray tour, $89. Kayak rentals are $35 for a single, $60 for a double, and $85 for a triple. Stand-up paddleboard lessons at Keauhou Bay cost $75. ⊠ *79-7248 Mamalahoa Hwy., across from Teshima's Restaurant, Honalo* ☎ *808/322–2868, 877/322–1444* ⊕ *www.alohakayak.com.*

Fodor's Choice **Kona Boys.** On the highway above Kealakekua Bay, this full-service, ★ environmentally conscious outfitter handles kayaks, bodyboards, surfboards, stand-up paddleboards, and snorkeling gear. Single-seat and double kayaks are offered. Surfing and stand-up paddling lessons are available for private or group instruction. Tours such as their Morning Magic and Midday Meander include two half-day guided kayaking and snorkeling trips with gear, lunch, snacks, and beverages. Kona Boys also run a beach shack fronting the King Kamehameha's Kona Beach Hotel and are happy to give advice on the changing regulations regarding South Kona bay usage. ■TIP→ The town location offers Hawaiian outrigger canoe rides, SUP lessons, and rentals of beach mats, chairs, and other gear. ⊠ *79-7539 Mamalahoa Hwy., Kealakekua* ☎ *808/328–1234, 808/329–2345* ⊕ *www.konaboys.com* ⊡ *Tours from $99; kayaks from $47; surf/paddle lessons from $75* ⊠ *75–5660 Palani Rd., Kailua-Kona.*

Ocean Safari's Kayak Adventures. On the guided 3½-hour morning sea-cave tour that begins in Keauhou Bay, you can visit lava-tube sea caves along the coast, then swim ashore for a snack. The kayaks will already be on the beach, so you won't have to hassle with transporting them. The cost is $68.50 per person. A two-hour, dolphin-spotting tour costs $35 per person. Kayak daily rental rates are $25 for singles and $40 for doubles. Stand-up boards are $25 for two hours. If you want a lesson, it's $60 including the board (two-person minimum). ⊠ *End of Kamehameha III Rd., next to Sheraton Kona Resort & Spa at Keauhou Bay, Kailua-Kona* ☎ *808/326–4699* ⊕ *www.oceansafariskayaks.com.*

SAILING

For old salts and novice sailors alike, there's nothing like a cruise on the Kona or Kohala Coast. Calm waters, serene shores, and the superb scenery of Mauna Kea, Mauna Loa, and Hualalai, the Big Island's primary volcanic peaks, make for a great sailing adventure. You can drop a line over the side and try your luck at catching dinner, or grab some snorkel gear and explore when the boat drops anchor in one of the quiet coves and bays. A cruise may well be the most relaxing and adventurous part of a Big Island visit.

BOATS AND CHARTERS

Maile Charters. Private sailing charters for two to 16 passengers are available on the *Maile*, a 50-foot GulfStar sloop. You choose the itinerary, whether it's watching for dolphins and whales, snorkeling around coral reefs, or enjoying appetizers as the sun sinks below the horizon. Morning snorkels, sunset sails, and overnight trips are offered. Snorkeling equipment is provided, and food can be catered. ✉ *Kawaihae Harbor, Hwy. 270, on the dock, Kawaihae* ☎ *808/960–9744* ⊕ *www.adventuresailing.com* 🖃 *From $997.*

SCUBA DIVING

The Big Island's underwater world is the setting for a dramatic diving experience. With generally warm and calm waters, vibrant coral reefs and rock formations, and plunging underwater drop-offs, the Kona and Kohala coasts offer some premier scuba diving. There are also some good dive locations in East Hawaii, not far from the Hilo area. Divers find much to occupy their time, including marine reserves teeming with tropical reef fish, Hawaiian green sea turtles, an occasional and critically endangered Hawaiian monk seal, and even some playful spinner dolphins. On special night dives to see manta rays, divers descend with bright underwater lights that attract plankton, which in turn attract these otherworldly creatures. The best spots to dive are all on the west coast.

BEST SPOTS

Garden Eel Cove. Only accessible by boat, this is a great place to see manta rays somersaulting overhead as they feast on a plankton supper. It's also home to hundreds of tiny garden eels darting out from their sandy homes. There's a steep drop-off and lots of marine life. ✉ *Rte. 19, near Kona airport, Kailua-Kona.*

Manta Village. Booking with a night-dive operator is required for the short boat ride to this area, one of Kona's best night-dive spots. If you're a diving or snorkeling fanatic, it's well worth it to experience manta rays drawn by the lights of the hotel. ■TIP→ If night swimming isn't your cup of tea, you can catch a glimpse of the majestic creatures from the Sheraton's deck. ✉ *78-128 Ehukai St., off Sheraton Kona Resort & Spa at Keauhou Bay, Kailua-Kona.*

Pawai Bay Marine Preserve. Clear waters, abundant reef life, and interesting coral formations make Pawai Bay Marine Preserve ideal for diving. Explore sea caves, arches, and rock formations. Located one half mile north of Old Kona Airport Park, it can be busy with snorkel boats, but is an easy dive spot. ⊠ *Kuakini Hwy., north of Old Kona Airport Park, Kailua-Kona.*

Puako. Just south of Hapuna Beach State Recreation Area, beautiful Puako offers easy entry to some fine reef diving. Deep chasms, sea caves, and rock arches abound with varied marine life. ⊠ *Puako Rd., off Hwy. 19, Kohala Coast.*

EQUIPMENT, LESSONS, AND TOURS

There are quite a few good dive shops along the Kona Coast. Most are happy to take on all customers, but a few focus on specific types of trips. Trip prices vary, depending on whether you're already certified and whether you're diving from a boat or from shore. Instruction with PADI, SDI, or TDI certification in three to five days costs $600 to $850. Most instructors rent dive equipment and snorkel gear, as well as underwater cameras. Most organize otherworldly manta ray dives at night and whale-watching cruises in season.

Jack's Diving Locker. Good for novice and intermediate divers, Jack's has trained and certified tens of thousands of divers since 1981, with classrooms and a dive pool for instruction. Four boats that accommodate 10 to 24 divers (boats at capacity can feel cramped) visit more than 80 established dive sites along the Kona Coast, yielding sightings of turtles, manta rays, garden eels, and schools of barracuda. Snorkelers can choose from morning trips and manta night trips, and dolphin-watch and reef snorkels. Combined sunset/night manta ray dives are offered as well. ■TIP➔ Kona's best deal for scuba newbies is Jack's two-part introductory dive from Kailua Pier: pool instruction plus a one-tank beach dive, or a two-tank boat dive is offered as well. ⊠ *75-5813 Alii Dr., Kailua-Kona* ☎ *808/329–7585, 800/345–4807* ⊕ *www.jacksdivinglocker.com* ◪ *Snorkel trips from $65.*

Nautilus Dive Center. Across from Hilo Bay, Nautilus Dive Center is the oldest and most experienced dive shop on the island. It offers a broad range of services for both beginners and experienced divers. Owner Bill De Rooy has been diving around the Big Island for 30 years, and can provide you with underwater maps and show you the best dive spots in Hilo. He also provides PADI instruction and likes to repair gear. ⊠ *382 Kamehameha Ave., Hilo* ☎ *808/935–6939* ⊕ *www.nautilusdivehilo.com* ◪ *Dive-equipment rentals from $35 per day.*

Ocean Eco Tours and Harbor Dive Center. This eco-friendly outfitter is eager to share a wealth of ocean knowledge with beginners and advanced divers alike. Six to 10 divers and snorkelers head out on one of two 30-foot crafts, and the day's destination—from among 80 sites, both north and south, that feature good reefs and other prime underwater spots—varies based on ocean conditions. Four-hour daytime dives or a nighttime dive to swim with manta rays are offered. PADI open-water certification can be completed in three or four days. Seasonal whale-watch tours are also offered. Ride-alongs are welcome on all charters. ⊠ *Honokohau Harbor, 74-425 Kealakehe Pkwy., Kailua-Kona* ☎ *808/324–7873, 808/331–2121* ⊕ *www.oceanecotours.com* ◪ *Excursions from $129; PADI open-water certification $650; whale-watch tours $95.*

The Kona Coast's relatively calm waters and colorful coral reefs are excellent for scuba diving.

SNORKELING

A favorite pastime on the Big Island, snorkeling is perhaps one of the easiest and most enjoyable water activities for visitors. By floating on the surface, peering through your mask, and breathing through your snorkel, you can see lava rock formations, sea arches, sea caves, and coral reefs teeming with colorful tropical fish. While the Kona and Kohala coasts boast more beaches, bays, and quiet coves to snorkel, the east side around Hilo and at Kapoho are also great places to get in the water.

If you don't bring your own equipment, you can easily rent all the gear needed from a beach activities vendor, who will happily provide directions to the best sites for snorkeling in the area. For access to deeper water and assistance from an experienced crew, you can opt for a snorkel cruise. Excursions generally range from two to five hours; be sure you know what equipment and food is included.

BEST SPOTS

Kahaluu Beach Park. Since ancient times, the waters around Kahaluu Beach have provided traditional throw net–fishing grounds. With super-easy access, the bay offers good swimming and outstanding snorkeling, revealing turtles, angelfish, parrot fish, needlefish, puffer fish, and many types of tang. ■ TIP→ **Stay inside the breakwater and don't stray too far, as dangerous and unpredictable currents swirl outside the bay.** ⊠ *Alii Dr., Kailua-Kona.*

Kapoho Tide Pools. Here you'll find the best snorkeling on the Hilo side. Fingers of lava from the 1960 flow that destroyed the town of

Kapoho jut into the sea to form a network of tide pools. Conditions near the shore are excellent for beginners, while farther out is challenging enough for experienced snorkelers. ⊠ *End of Kapoho-Kai Rd., off Hwy. 137, Hilo.*

Fodor'sChoice
★
Kealakekua Bay State Historical Park. This protected Marine Life Conservation District is hands-down one of the best snorkeling spots on the island, thanks to clear visibility, fabulous coral reefs, and generally calm waters. Pods of dolphins can be abundant, but they're protected under federal law and may not be disturbed or approached. Access to the area has been restricted in recent years, but a few companies are permitted to escort tours to the bay. ■TIP→ Overland access is difficult, so opt for one of the guided snorkel cruises permitted to moor here. ⊠ *Napoopoo, at end of Beach Rd. and Hwy. 160, Kailua-Kona* ⊕ *www.hawaiistateparks.org.*

Magic Sands Beach Park. Also known as White Sands or Disappearing Sands Beach Park, this is a great place for beginning and intermediate snorkelers. In winter, it's also a prime spot to watch for whales. ⊠ *Alii Dr., Kailua-Kona.*

Puuhonua O Honaunau. There is no swimming inside the national historical park here, but just to the north is a boat launch where the snorkeling is almost as good as at Kealakekua Bay. Parking is very limited. Be respectful of local fishermen who use the area. ⊠ *Hwy. 160, 20 miles south of Kailua-Kona.*

EQUIPMENT, LESSONS, AND TOURS

FAMILY
Body Glove Cruises. This operator is a good choice for families; kids love the waterslide and the high-dive platform, and parents appreciate the reasonable prices and good food. The 65-foot catamaran sets off for Red Hill from Kailua-Kona pier daily for a morning snorkel cruise that includes breakfast and a lunch buffet. A three-hour dinner cruise to Kealakekua Bay is a great way to relax, watch the sunset, and learn about Kona's history. It includes a buffet and live music. Seasonal whale-watch cruises are available, too. ⊠ *75-5629 Kuakini Hwy., Kailua-Kona* 🕾 *808/326–7122, 800/551–8911* ⊕ *www.bodyglovehawaii.com* 🖃 *Snorkeling $128; dinner cruise $108; whale-watch cruises $88.*

Captain Zodiac Raft Expedition. A four-hour trip on a rigid-hull inflatable Zodiac raft takes you along the Kona Coast to explore gaping lava-tube caves, search for dolphins and turtles, and snorkel around Kealakekua Bay. Captains entertain you with Hawaiian folklore and Kona history. Trips depart at 8:15 am, 10 am, and 1 pm. A seasonal three-hour whale-watching cruise is offered. All equipment, such as Rx masks and flotation devices, are included. ⊠ *Honokohau Harbor, 74-425 Kealakehe Pkwy. No. 16, Kailua-Kona* 🕾 *808/329–3199* ⊕ *www.captainzodiac. com* 🖃 *From $99 per person; whale-watching cruise $74.*

FAMILY
Fodor'sChoice
★
Fair Wind Cruises. In business since 1971, Fair Wind offers morning and afternoon snorkel trips that are great for families with small kids. The custom-built 60-foot catamaran has two 15-foot waterslides, freshwater showers, and a staircase descending directly into the water for easy access. Snorkel gear is included, with lots of pint-size flotation

Continued on page 376

SNORKELING IN HAWAII

The waters surrounding the Hawaiian Islands are filled with life—from giant manta rays cruising off the Big Island's Kona Coast to humpback whales giving birth in the warm waters surrounding Maui. Dip your head beneath the surface to experience a spectacularly colorful world: pairs of milletseed butterflyfish dart back and forth, redlipped parrotfish snack on coral algae, and spotted eagle rays flap past like silent spaceships. Sea turtles bask at the surface while tiny wrasses give them the equivalent of a shave and a haircut. The water quality is typically outstanding; many sites afford 30-foot-plus visibility. On snorkel cruises, you can often stare from the boat rail right down to the bottom.

Certainly few destinations are as accommodating to every level of snorkeler as Hawaii. Beginners can tromp in from sandy beaches while more advanced divers descend to shipwrecks, reefs, craters, and sea arches just offshore. Because of Hawaii's extreme isolation, the island chain has fewer fish species than Fiji or the Caribbean—but many of the fish that are here exist nowhere else. The Hawaiian waters are home to the highest percentage of endemic fish in the world.

The key to enjoying the underwater world is slowing down. Look carefully. Listen. You might hear the strange crackling sound of shrimp tunneling through coral, or you may hear whales singing to one another during winter. A shy octopus may drift along the ocean's floor beneath you. If you're hooked, pick up a waterproof fishkey from Long's Drugs. You can brag later that you've looked the Hawaiian turkeyfish in the eye.

Picasso Triggerfish	Milletseed Butterflyfish*	Yellow Tang
Moorish Idol	Hawaiian Whitespotted Toby*	Saddleback Wrasse*
Redlip Parrotfish	Hawaiian Turkeyfish*	Zebra Moray Eel
Stocky Hawkfish	Green Sea Turtle (Honu)	Spotted Eagle Ray

*endemic to Hawaii

4

IN FOCUS SNORKELING IN HAWAII

POLYNESIA'S FIRST CELESTIAL NAVIGATORS: HONU

Honu is the Hawaiian name for two native sea turtles, the hawksbill and the green sea turtle. Little is known about these dinosaur-age marine reptiles, though snorkelers regularly see them foraging for *limu* (seaweed) and the occasional jellyfish in Hawaiian waters. Most female honu nest in the uninhabited Northwestern Hawaiian Islands, but a few sociable ladies nest on Maui and Big Island beaches. Scientists suspect that they navigate the seas via magnetism—sensing the earth's poles. Amazingly, they will journey up to 800 miles to nest—it's believed that they return to their own birth sites. After about 60 days of incubation, nestlings emerge from the sand at night and find their way back to the sea by the light of the stars.

SNORKELING

Many of Hawaii's reefs are accessible from shore.

The basics: Sure, you can take a deep breath, hold your nose, squint your eyes, and stick your face in the water in an attempt to view submerged habitats . . . but why not protect your eyes, retain your ability to breathe, and keep your hands free to paddle about when exploring underwater? That's what snorkeling is all about.

Equipment needed: A mask, snorkel (the tube attached to the mask), and fins. In deeper waters (any depth over your head), life jackets are advised.

Steps to success: If you've never snorkeled before, it's natural to feel a bit awkward at first, so don't sweat it. Breathing through a mask and tube, and wearing a pair of fins take getting used to. Like any activity, you build confidence and comfort through practice.

If you're new to snorkeling, begin by submerging your face in shallow water or a swimming pool and breathing calmly through the snorkel while gazing through the mask.

Next you need to learn how to clear water out of your mask and snorkel, an essential skill since splashes can send water into tube openings and masks can leak. Some snorkels have built-in drainage valves, but if a tube clogs, you can force water up and out by exhaling through your mouth. Clearing a mask is similar: lift your head from water while pulling forward on mask to drain. Some masks have built-in purge valves, but those without can be cleared underwater by pressing the top to the forehead and blowing out your nose (charming, isn't it?), allowing air to bubble into the mask, pushing water out the bottom. If it sounds hard, it really isn't. Just try it a few times and you'll soon feel like a pro.

Now your goal is to get friendly with fins—you want them to be snug but not too tight—and learn how to propel yourself with them. Fins won't help you float, but they will give you a leg up, so to speak, on smoothly moving through the water or treading water (even when upright) with less effort.

Flutter stroking is the most efficient underwater kick, and the farther your foot bends forward the more leg power you'll be able to transfer to the water and the farther you'll travel with each stroke. Flutter kicking movements involve alternately separating the legs and then drawing them back together. When your legs separate, the leg surface encounters drag from the water, slowing you down. When your legs are drawn back together, they produce a force pushing you forward. If your kick creates more forward force than it causes drag, you'll move ahead.

Submerge your fins to avoid fatigue rather than having them flailing above the water when you kick, and keep your arms at your side to reduce drag. You are in the water—stretched out, face down, and snorkeling happily away—but that doesn't mean you can't hold your breath and go deeper in the water for a closer look at some fish or whatever catches your attention. Just remember that when you do this, your snorkel will be submerged, too, so you won't be breathing (you'll be holding your breath). You can dive head-first, but going feet-first is easier and less scary for most folks, taking less momentum. Before full immersion, take several long, deep breaths to clear carbon dioxide from your lungs.

If your legs tire, flip onto your back and tread water with inverted fin motions while resting. If your mask fogs, wash condensation from lens and clear water from mask.

TIPS FOR SAFE SNORKELING

■ Snorkel with a buddy and stay together.

■ Plan your entry and exit points prior to getting in the water.

■ Swim into the current on entering and then ride the current back to your exit point.

■ Carry your flippers into the water and then put them on, as it's difficult to walk in them.

■ Make sure your mask fits properly and is not too loose.

■ Pop your head above the water periodically to ensure you aren't drifting too far out, or too close to rocks.

■ Think of the water as someone else's home—don't take anything that doesn't belong to you, or leave any trash behind.

■ Don't touch any sea creatures; they may sting.

■ Wear a T-shirt over your swimsuit to help protect you from being fried by the sun.

■ When in doubt, don't go without a snorkeling professional; try a guided tour.

Green sea turtle (Honu)

equipment and prescription masks available. The company is known for its delicious meals. Cruises last 4½ hours; 3½-hour snack cruises are offered, too. For ages seven and older, the company operates the *Hula Kai* snorkel cruise, a 55-foot luxury hydrofoil catamaran with theater-style seats for panoramic views. Their five-hour morning snorkel cruise includes a gourmet breakfast buffet and barbecue lunch. ⊠ *Keauhou Bay, 78-7130 Kaleiopapa St., Kailua-Kona* ☏ *808/322–2788, 800/677–9461* ⊕ *www.fair-wind.com* ☑ *Cruises from $75.*

STAND-UP PADDLING

Stand-up paddling (or SUP for short), a sport with roots in the Hawaiian Islands, has grown popular worldwide in recent years. It's available for all skill levels and ages, and even novice stand-up paddleboarders can get up, stay up, and have a great time paddling around a protected bay or exploring the gorgeous coastline. All you need is a large body of water, a board, and a paddle. The workout tests your core strength as well as your balance, and offers an unusual vantage point from which to enjoy the beauty of island and ocean.

BEST SPOTS

Anaehoomalu Bay Beach (*A-Bay*). In this well-protected bay, even when surf is rough on the rest of the island, it's usually fairly calm here, though trades pick up in the afternoon. Boards are available for rent at the north end, and the safe area for stand-up paddling is marked by buoys. ⊠ *Off Waikoloa Beach Dr., south of Waikoloa Beach Marriott, Kohala Coast.*

Hilo Bay. At this favorite among locals, the best place to put in is at **Reeds Bay Beach Park.** Most afternoons you'll share the bay with local paddling clubs. Stay inside the breakwater unless the ocean is calm (or you're feeling unusually adventurous). Conditions range from extremely calm to quite choppy. ⊠ *Banyan Way and Banyan Dr., 1 mile from downtown Hilo.*

FAMILY **Kailua Bay and Kamakahonu Beach.** The small, sandy beach that fronts the Courtyard King Kamehameha's Kona Beach Hotel is great for kids; the water here is especially calm and gentle. If you're more daring, you can easily paddle out of the bay and along the coast for some great exploring. ⊠ *Alii Dr., next to Kailua Pier, Kailua-Kona.*

EQUIPMENT AND LESSONS

Ocean Sports. This outfitter rents equipment, offers lessons, and has the perfect location for easy access to the bay. Ocean Sports also operates rental shacks at the Hilton Waikoloa Village, Mauna Kea Beach Hotel, Whale Center Kawaihae, and Queens' MarketPlace. ⊠ *Waikoloa Beach Marriott, 69-275 Waikoloa Beach Dr., Waikoloa* ☏ *808/886–6666* ⊕ *www.hawaiioceansports.com* ☑ *Stand-up paddleboard rentals $30 per hour.*

SUBMARINE TOURS

FAMILY **Atlantis Submarines.** Want to stay dry while exploring the undersea world? Climb aboard the 48-passenger *Atlantis X* submarine, anchored off Kailua Pier, across from Courtyard King Kamehameha's Kona Beach Hotel. A large glass dome in the bow and 13 viewing ports on each side allow clear views of the aquatic world more than 100 feet down. This is a great trip for kids and nonswimmers. ■**TIP→** A $10 discount is available if you book online. ✉ *75-5669 Alii Dr., Kailua-Kona* ☎ *808/326–7939, 800/381–0237* ⊕ *www.atlantisadventures.com* ☞ *$109.*

SURFING

The Big Island does not have the variety of great surfing spots found on Oahu or Maui, but it does have decent waves and a thriving surf culture. Local kids and avid surfers frequent a number of places up and down the Kona and Kohala coasts of West Hawaii. Expect high surf in winter and much calmer activity during summer. The surf scene is much more active on the Kona side.

BEST SPOTS

Honolii Cove. North of Hilo, this is the best surfing spot on the eastern side of the island. It hosts many exciting surf contests. ✉ *Off Hwy. 19, near mile marker 4, Hilo.*

Kahaluu Beach Park. Slightly north of this beach park and just past the calm lagoon filled with snorkelers, beginning and intermediate surfers can have a go at some nice waves. ✉ *Alii Dr., Kailua-Kona.*

Old Kona Airport Park. This park is a good place for catching wave action. A couple of the island's outfitters conduct surf lessons here, as the break is far away from potentially dangerous rocks and reefs. ✉ *Kuakini Rd., Kailua-Kona.*

Pine Trees. Also known as Kohanaiki, this community beach park is among the best places to catch waves. Keep in mind that it's a very popular local surf spot on an island where there aren't all that many surf spots, so be respectful. ✉ *Off Hwy. 11, Kohanaiki entrance gate, about 2 miles south of Kona airport, Kailua-Kona.*

EQUIPMENT AND LESSONS

Hawaii Lifeguard Surf Instructors. This family-owned, lifeguard-certified school helps novices become wave riders and offers tours that take more experienced riders to Kona's top surf spots. A 1½-hour introductory lesson has one instructor per three students. Private instruction is available as well. If the waves are on the smaller side, they convert to stand-up paddleboard lessons for the same prices as surfing. ✉ *75-5909 Alii Dr., Kailua-Kona* ☎ *808/324–0442, 808/936–7873* ⊕ *www.surflessonshawaii.com* ☞ *$75 per person (group), $110 (private).*

Fodor'sChoice **Ocean Eco Tours Surf School.** Family owned and operated, Kona's oldest
★ surf school emphasizes the basics and specializes in beginners. It's one of a handful of operators permitted to conduct business in Kaloko-Honokohau National Historical Park, which gets waves even when other spots on the island are flat. All lessons are taught by certified

instructors, and the school guarantees that you will surf. If you're hooked, sign up for a three-day package. There's an authentic soul surfer's vibe to these folks, and they are equally diehard about teaching you about the ocean and having you standing up riding waves on your first day. ⊠ *Honokohau Harbor, 74-425 Kealakehe Pkwy., Kailua-Kona* ☎ *808/324–7873* ⊕ *www.oceanecotours.com* ⊠ *From $95 per person; $270 for three-day package.*

Orchid Land Surf Shop. The shop has a wide variety of water sports and surf equipment for sale or rent. It stocks custom surfboards, bodyboards, and surf apparel. The staff also handles repairs. ⊠ *262 Kamehameha Ave., Hilo* ☎ *808/935–1533* ⊕ *www.orchidlandsurf.com.*

WHALE-WATCHING

Each winter, some two-thirds of the North Pacific humpback whale population (about 4,000–5,000 animals) migrate over 3,500 miles from the icy Alaska waters to the warm Hawaiian ocean to mate and, the following year, give birth to and nurse their calves. Recent reports indicate that the whale population is on the upswing—a few years ago one even ventured into the mouth of Hilo Harbor, which marine biologists say is quite rare. Humpbacks are spotted here from early December through the end of April, but other species, like sperm, pilot, and beaked whales as well as spinner, spotted, and bottlenose dolphins, can be seen year-round. ■TIP→ If you take a morning cruise, you're more likely to see dolphins. *See Snorkeling for additional outfitters that offer whale-watching cruises.*

Blue Sea Cruises. The 46-foot *Makai* and the 70-foot *Spirit of Kona* cruise along the Kona Coast catching sight of dolphins, whales, and manta rays. Their "dry" cruise on a glass-bottom boat is good for kids. Both boats have snack bars and restrooms, and the double-decker *Spirit of Kona* also has a glass bottom. Their sunset dinner cruise has an open bar, gourmet meal, luau show, and dancing. ⊠ *Kailua-Kona Pier, 75-5660 Palani Rd., Kailua-Kona* ☎ *808/331–8875* ⊕ *www. blueseacruisesinc.com* ⚏ *From $84.*

Captain Dan McSweeney's Whale Watch Learning Adventures. This is probably the most experienced small operation on the island. Captain Dan McSweeney offers three-hour trips on his double-decker, 40-foot cruise boat. In addition to humpbacks (in winter), he'll try to show you dolphins and some of the six other whale species that live off the Kona Coast throughout the year. McSweeney guarantees you'll see whales or he'll take you out again for free. ⊠ *Honokohau Harbor, 74-381 Keal-akehe Pkwy., Kailua-Kona* ☎ *808/322–0028, 888/942–5376* ⊕ *www. ilovewhales.com* ⚏ *$110.*

GOLF, HIKING, AND OUTDOOR ACTIVITIES

Updated by Kristina Anderson

With the Big Island's predictably mild year-round climate, it's no wonder you'll find an emphasis on outdoor activities. After all, this is the home of the annual Ironman World Championship triathlon. Whether you're an avid hiker or a beginning bicyclist, a casual golfer or a tennis buff, you'll find plenty of land-based activities to lure you away from the sun and surf.

You can explore by bike, helicopter, ATV, zipline, or horse, or you can put on your hiking boots and use your own horsepower. No matter how you get around, you'll be treated to breathtaking backdrops along the Big Island's 266-mile coastline and within its 4,028 square miles (and still growing!). Aerial tours take in the latest eruption activity and lava flows, as well as the island's gorgeous tropical valleys, gulches, and coastal areas. Trips into the backcountry wilderness explore the rain forest, private ranch lands, coffee farms, and old sugar-plantation villages that offer a glimpse of Hawaii's earlier days.

AERIAL TOURS

There's nothing quite like the aerial view of a waterfall crashing down a couple of thousand feet into cascading pools, or watching lava flow to the ocean as exploding clouds of steam billow into the air. You can get this bird's-eye view from a helicopter or a small plane. All operators pay strict attention to safety. So how to get the best experience for your money? ■TIP➜ Before you choose a company, be a savvy traveler and ask the right questions. What kind of aircraft do they fly? What is their safety record?

Blue Hawaiian Helicopters. Hawaii's most comfortable ride is on the roomy, $3-million Eco-Star helicopter—so quiet you hardly realize you're taking off and with great views from every seat. Pilots are knowledgeable about the island but not overly chatty. In the Waimanu Valley, the craft hovers next to 2,500-foot cliffs and dramatic, cascading waterfalls. The two-hour Big Island Spectacular also takes in Kilauea Volcano lava flows. Prices range from $196.02 to $495 per person, depending on type of craft. Most flights leave from a private helipad in Waikoloa, but the 50-minute Circle of Fire tour departs Hilo for the volcano's wonders. ⊠ *Waikoloa Heliport, Hwy. 19, Waikoloa* ☎ *808/961–5600* ⊕ *www.bluehawaiian.com.*

Fodor's Choice **Paradise Helicopters.** This friendly company offers great options no one
★ else does. On three landing tours, departing from Kona's airport, you can either touch down for a hike in a remote Kohala valley, experience a Hilo zipline, or spend a few hours exploring downtown Hilo. After flying over active lava flows, aircraft easily maneuver near the sheer valley walls of the east side. In a "doors off" adventure, four-passenger MD 500 helicopters (Hilo only) get so close, you can feel heat from the lava. Flights start at $200 for 50 minutes to $495 for three-hour landing tours. Pilots, many of whom have military backgrounds, are fun and knowledgeable. Free hotel shuttles run to and from the Kona and Hilo airports, where tours are based. ☎ *808/969–7392, 866/876–7422* ⊕ *www.paradisecopters.com.*

ATV TOURS

A fun way to experience the Big Island's rugged coastline and wild ranch lands is through an off-road adventure—a real backcountry experience. At higher elevations, the weather gets nippy and rainy, but views can be awesome. Protective gear is provided, and everyone gets a mini driving lesson. Generally, you must be 16 or older to ride your own ATV; some outfitters allow children seven and older as passengers.

Fodor's Choice **Waipio Ride the Rim.** A fabulous way to experience the extraordinary
★ beauty atop lush Waipio Valley, the tour is led by fun and knowledgeable guides along private trails to the headwaters of the twin Hiilawe Falls, Hawaii's highest single-fall waterfalls. You stop for a swim in a ginger-laden grotto with a refreshing waterfall (disclaimer: it's cold!) and travel to a series of lookouts—at times crossing the still-active Kohala Ditch—where you can observe the valley and its black-sand beach from all angles. Bring a bathing suit and be prepared to get wet and muddy. Beginners are welcome. It's teen-tastically fun. (To drive your own ATV, you must be over 16.) Prices start at $179, or take the guided buggy tour if you're not up to driving. ⊠ *Waipio Valley Artworks Bldg., 48-5416 Kukuihaele Rd., Kukuihaele* ☎ *808/775–1450, 877/775–1450* ⊕ *www.ridetherim.com.*

BIKING

The Big Island's biking trails and road routes range from easy to moderate coastal rides to rugged backcountry wilderness treks that challenge the most serious cyclists. You can soak up the island's storied scenic vistas and varied geography—from tropical rain forest to rolling ranch country, from high-country mountain meadows to dry lava deserts. It's dry, windy, and hot on Kona's and Kohala's coastal trails and cool, wet,

The rainy Hilo side of the Big Island means lush hills and valleys and many waterfalls.

and muddy in the Upcountry Waimea and Volcano areas, as well as in lower Puna. There are long distances between towns, few bike lanes, narrow single-lane highways, and scanty services in the Kau, Puna, South Kona, and Kohala Coast areas, so plan accordingly for weather, water, food, and lodging before setting out.

BEST SPOTS

Fodor's Choice ★ **Kulani Trails.** This has been called the best ride in the state—if you really want to get gnarly. The technically demanding ride, which passes majestic eucalyptus trees, is for advanced cyclists. To reach the trailhead from the intersection of Highway 11 and Highway 19, take Highway 19 south about 4 miles, turn right on Stainback Highway, continue 2½ miles, turn right at the Waiakea Arboretum, and park near the gate. A permit is required, available from the Department of Land and Natural Resources at Kawili Street and Kilauea Avenue in Hilo. ⊠ *Stainback Hwy., Hilo.*

Old Puna Trail. A 10½-mile ride through the subtropical jungle in Puna, this trail leads into one of the island's most isolated areas. It starts on a cinder road, which becomes a four-wheel-drive trail. If it's rained recently, you'll have to deal with puddles—the first few of which you'll gingerly avoid until you give in and go barreling through the rest for the sheer fun of it. This is a great ride for all abilities and takes about 90 minutes. To get to the traihead from Highway 130, take Kaloli Road to Beach Road. ⚠ Ride at your own risk; this is not a maintained trail. ⊠ *Kaloli Rd. at Hwy. 130, Puna.*

EQUIPMENT AND TOURS

There are several rental shops in Kailua-Kona and a couple in Waimea and Hilo. Many resorts rent bicycles that can be used around the properties. Most outfitters can provide a bicycle rack for your car, and all offer reduced rates for rentals longer than one day.

BikeVolcano.com. This outfitter leads three- or five-hour bike rides through Hawaii Volcanoes National Park, mostly downhill, that take in fantastic sights, from rain forests to craters. The three-hour tour costs $105, five hours $129. There's also a spectacular seven-hour sunset tour that goes to the active lava flows (volcano depending). Equipment, support van, and food are included. ⊠ *Kilauea General Store, 19-3972 Old Volcano Rd., Volcano* ☎ *808/934–9199, 888/934–9199* ⊕ *www. bikevolcano.com.*

Fodor'sChoice
★
Cycle Station. This shop, with exceptionally nice proprietors, has a variety of bikes for rent, from hybrids to racing models. Rentals run from $20 to $75 per day and can be delivered to your hotel. Island-wide trips are also available. ⊠ *73-4976 Kamanu St., Kailua-Kona* ☎ *808/327–0087* ⊕ *www.konabikerentals.com.*

Mid Pacific Wheels. This downtown shop carries a full line of bikes and accessories and rents mountain bikes for exploring the Hilo area starting at $30 per day. The staff provides current trail information as well as expert advice on where to go and what to see and do on a self-guided tour. ⊠ *1133C Manono St., Hilo* ☎ *808/935–6211* ⊕ *www. midpacificwheelsllc.com.*

CAVING

The Kanohina Lava Tube system is about 1,000 years old and was used by the ancient Hawaiians for water collection and for shelter. More than 40 miles of these braided lava tubes have been mapped so far in the Kau District of the Big Island, near South Point. About 45 miles south of Kailua-Kona, these lava tubes are a great experience for cavers of all age levels and abilities.

Fodor'sChoice
★
Kula Kai Caverns. Expert cave guides lead groups into the fantastic underworld of these caverns near South Point. The braided lava-tube system attracts scientists from around the world, who come to study and map them (almost 40 miles so far). Tours start at $20 and range from The Crawl ($60) to the Two Hour, a deep-down-under spelunking adventure for $95. (Longer, customized tours are also available.) Programs are tailored to each group's interest and abilities, and all gear is provided. Tours start at an Indiana Jones-style expedition tent and divulge fascinating details about the caves' geologic and cultural history. Reservations are required. ⊠ *Kula Kai Estates, Lauhala Dr. at Kona Kai Blvd.* ☎ *808/929–9725* ⊕ *www.kulakaicaverns.com.*

GOLF

For golfers, the Big Island is a big deal—starting with the Mauna Kea Golf Course, which opened in 1964 and remains one of the state's top courses. Black lava and deep blue sea are the predominant themes on

Most of the Big Island's top golf courses are located on the sunny Kona Coast.

the island. In the roughly 40 miles from the Kona Country Club to the Mauna Kea resort, nine courses are carved into sunny seaside lava plains, with four more in the hills above. Indeed, most of the Big Island's best courses are concentrated along the Kohala Coast, statistically the sunniest spot in Hawaii. Vertically speaking, although the majority of courses are seaside or at least near sea level, three are located above 2,000 feet, another one at 4,200 feet. This is significant because in Hawaii temperatures drop 3°F for every 1,000 feet of elevation gained.

Greens Fee: Greens fees listed here are the highest course rates per round on weekdays for U.S. residents. Courses with varying weekend rates are noted in the individual listings. (Some courses charge non–U.S. residents higher prices.) ■TIP➜ Discounts are often available for resort guests and for those who book tee times on the Web, as well as for those willing to play in the afternoon. Twilight fees are also usually offered.

KAILUA-KONA

Big Island Country Club. Set 2,000 feet above sea level on the slopes of Mauna Kea, this course is out of the way but well worth the drive. In 1997, Pete and Perry Dye created a gem that plays through upland woodlands—more than 2,500 trees line the fairways. On the par-5 15th, a giant tree in the middle of the fairway must be avoided with the second shot. Five lakes and a meandering natural mountain stream bring water into play on nine holes. The most dramatic is the par-3 17th, where Dye created a knockoff of his infamous 17th at the TPC at Sawgrass. ⊠ *71-1420 Hawaii Belt Rd., Kailua-Kona* ☎ *808/325–5044* ⊕ *www.bigislandcountryclub.com* ⏃ *18 holes. 7075 yds. Par 72* ⊠ *$89*

☞ *Facilities: Driving range, putting green, golf carts, rental clubs, pro shop, lessons.*

THE KOHALA COAST

Hapuna Golf Course. Hapuna's challenging play and environmental sensitivity make it one of the island's most unusual courses. Designed by Arnold Palmer and Ed Seay, it is nestled into the natural contours of the land from the shoreline to about 700 feet above sea level. There are spectacular views of mountains and sea (Maui is often visible in the distance). Holes wind through kiawe scrub, beds of jagged lava, and tall fountain grasses. Hole 12 is favored for its beautiful views and challenging play. ✉ *62-100 Kanunaoa Dr., Kamuela* ☎ *808/880–3000* ⊕ *www.princeresortshawaii.com/hapuna-golf* ⅃ *18 holes. 6875 yds. Par 72* ⌷ *$125* ☞ *Facilities: Driving range, putting green, chipping green, golf carts, rental clubs, rental shoes, pro shop, lessons, restaurant.*

Fodor's Choice **Mauna Kea Golf Course.** Originally opened in 1964, this golf course is
★ one of the most revered in the state. It underwent a tee-to-green renovation by Rees Jones, son of the original architect, Robert Trent Jones, Sr. Hybrid grasses were planted, the number of bunkers increased, and the overall yardage was expanded. The par-3 3rd is one of the world's most famous holes—and one of the most photographed. You play from a cliff-side tee across a bay to a cliff-side green. Getting across the ocean is just half the battle because the green is surrounded by seven bunkers, each one large and undulated. The course is a shot-maker's paradise and follows Jones's "easy bogey, tough par" philosophy. ✉ *62-100 Kaunaoe Dr., Kamuela* ☎ *808/882–5400* ⊕ *www.maunakeagolf.com* ⅃ *18 holes. 7250 yards. Par 72* ⌷ *$250* ☞ *Facilities: Driving range, putting green, chipping green, golf carts, rental clubs, pro shop, lessons, restaurant.*

Fodor's Choice **Mauna Lani Resort.** Black lava flows, lush green turf, white sand, and
★ the Pacific's multihues of blue define the 36 holes at Mauna Lani. The South Course includes the par-3 15th across a turquoise bay, one of the most photographed holes in Hawaii. But it shares "signature hole" honors with the 7th, a long par 3, which plays downhill over convoluted patches of black lava, with the Pacific immediately to the left and a dune to the right. The North Course plays a couple of shots tougher. Its most distinctive hole is the 17th, a par 3 with the green set in a lava pit 50 feet deep. The shot from an elevated tee must carry a pillar of lava that rises from the pit and partially blocks a view of the green. ✉ *68-1310 Mauna Lani Dr., Kohala Coast* ☎ *808/885–6655* ⊕ *www. maunalani.com* ⅃ *North Course: 18 holes. 6057 yds. Par 72* ⌷ *$215. South Course: 18 holes. 6025 yds. Par 72* ⌷ *$215* ☞ *Facilities: Driving range, putting green, golf carts, rental clubs, pro shop, lessons, restaurant, bar.*

Fodor's Choice **Waikoloa Beach Resort.** Robert Trent Jones Jr. built the Beach Course at
★ Waikoloa (1981) on an old flow of crinkly *aa* lava, which he used to create holes that are as artful as they are challenging. The par-5 12th hole is one of Hawaii's most picturesque and plays through a chute of black lava to a seaside green. At the Kings' Course (1990), Tom Weiskopf and Jay Morrish built a links-esque track. It turns out lava's natural humps and declivities replicate the contours of seaside Scotland.

But there are a few island twists—such as seven lakes. This is "option golf," as Weiskopf and Morrish provide different risk-reward tactics on each hole. Beach and Kings' have separate clubhouses. ⊠ *600 Waikoloa Beach Dr., Waikoloa* ☏ *808/886–7888* ⊕ *www.waikoloagolf.com* 🏌 *Beach Course: 18 holes. 6566 yds. Par 70* 🏷 *$135 for guests, $165 for nonguests. Kings' Course: 18 holes. 7074 yds. Par 72* 🏷 *$135 for guests, $165 for nonguests* ☞ *Facilities: Driving range, putting green, golf carts, rental clubs, lessons, restaurant, bar.*

HAWAII VOLCANOES NATIONAL PARK AND VICINITY

Volcano Golf & Country Club. Just outside Hawaii Volcanoes National Park—and barely a stone's throw from Halemaumau Crater—this is by far Hawaii's highest course. At 4,200-feet elevation, shots tend to fly a bit farther than at sea level, even in the often cool, misty air. Because of the elevation and climate, it's one of the few Hawaii courses with bent-grass putting greens. The course is mostly flat, and holes play through stands of Norfolk pines, flowering *lehua* trees, and multitrunk *hau* trees. The uphill par-4 15th doglegs through a tangle of hau. ⊠ *Pii Mauna Dr., off Hwy. 11, Volcanoes National Park* ☏ *808/967–7331* ⊕ *www. volcanogolfshop.com* 🏌 *18 holes. 6106 yds. Par 72* 🏷 *$56* ☞ *Facilities: Driving range, putting green, golf carts, rental clubs, restaurant/ bar (lunch only).*

HILO

Hilo Municipal Golf Course. Hilo Muni is proof that you don't need sand bunkers to create a challenging course. Trees and several meandering creeks are the danger here. The course, which offers views of Hilo Bay from most holes, has produced many of the island's top players over the years. Taking a divot reminds you that you're playing on a volcano—the soil is dark black crushed lava. ⊠ *340 Haihai St., Hilo* ☏ *808/959–7711* 🏌 *18 holes. 6325 yds. Par 71* 🏷 *$35 weekdays, $40 weekends* ☞ *Facilities: Driving range, putting green, golf carts, pull carts, rental clubs, pro shop, lessons, restaurant, bar.*

HIKING

Ecologically diverse, Hawaii Island has four of the five major climate zones and 8 of 13 sub-climate zones—a lot of variation for one island—and you can experience them all by foot. The ancient Hawaiians cut trails across the lava plains, through the rain forests, and up along the mountain heights. Many of these paths are still in use today. Part of the King's Trail at Anaehoomalu winds through a field of lava rocks covered with ancient carvings called petroglyphs. Many other trails, historic and modern, crisscross the huge Hawaii Volcanoes National Park and other parts of the island. Plus, the serenity of remote beaches, such as Papakolea Beach (Green Sands Beach), is accessible only to hikers.

Department of Land and Natural Resources, State Parks Division. The division provides information on all the Big Island's state parks. ⊠ *75 Aupuni St., Hilo* ☏ *808/961–9544* ⊕ *www.hawaiistateparks.org.*

Keep an eye out for flora and fauna unique to the Big Island while hiking through the island's varied microclimates.

BEST SPOTS

Hawaii Volcanoes National Park. Perhaps the Big Island's premier area for hikers, the park has 150 miles of trails providing close-up views of fern and rain-forest environments, cinder cones, steam vents, lava fields, rugged coastline, and current lava-flow activity. Day hikes range from easy to moderately difficult, and from one or two hours to a full day. For a bigger challenge, consider an overnight or multiday backcountry hike with a stay in a park cabin (available by a remote coast, in a lush forest, or atop frigid Mauna Loa). To do so, you must first obtain a free permit at the backcountry permit office in the Visitor Emergency Operations Center. Daily guided hikes are led by knowledgeable, friendly park rangers. The bulletin board outside the visitor center has the day's schedule. ⊠ *Hwy. 11, 30 miles south of Hilo, Volcanoes National Park* ☎ *808/985–6000* ⊕ *www.nps.gov/havo/index.htm.*

Kekaha Kai State Park. A 1.8-mile unimproved road leads to Mahaiula Bay, a gorgeous little piece of paradise, while on the opposite end of the park is lovely Kua Bay. Connecting the two is the 4½-mile Ala Kahakai historic coastal trail. Mahaiula has picnic tables and *lua* (porta potties). Midway between the two white-sand beaches, you can hike to the summit of Puu Kuili, a 342-foot-high cinder cone with an excellent view of the coastline. It's dry and hot with no drinking water, so pack sunblock and water. Gates close at 7 pm sharp. ⊠ *Trailhead on Hwy. 19, about 2 miles north of Kona airport.*

GUIDED HIKES

To get to some of the best trails and places, it's worth going with a skilled guide. Costs range from $95 to $165, and some hikes include picnic meals or refreshments, and gear, such as binoculars, ponchos, and walking sticks. The outfitters mentioned here also offer customized adventure tours.

Fodor'sChoice **Hawaii Forest & Trail.** Since 1993, this locally owned and operated outfit
★ has had a reputation for high-quality nature tours and eco-adventures. The company has access to thousands of acres of restricted or private lands and employs expert, certified guides. Its variety of programs includes a Hakalau Forest National Wildlife Refuge birdwatching tour, Kilauea Volcano excursion, Kohala waterfall trip, and the super-fun Kona Coffee & Craters adventure. The Twilight Volcano Adventure stays in the national park after dark to see the glowing red stuff. ✉ 74-5035B Queen Kaahumanu Hwy., Kailua-Kona ☎ 808/331–8505, 800/464–1993 ⊕ www.hawaii-forest.com.

Kapoho Kine Adventures. This outfitter offers several hiking adventures in Hawaii Volcanoes National Park and surrounding areas, including a 12-hour tour that explores the region by day and sees the lava at night, a shorter day tour, and an evening tour complete with Hawaiian-style barbecue dinner. The Gold Coast/Cloud Forest Tour contrasts a hot day at a historic beach with misty hikes in a cool and endangered cloud forest teeming with birds. Tours depart from both Hilo and Kona. ✉ 224 Kamehameha Ave. #106, next to Palace Theatre, on Haili St., Hilo ☎ 808/964–1000, 866/965–9552 ⊕ www.kapohokine.com ✉ From $99 per person.

HORSEBACK RIDING

With its *paniolo* (cowboy) heritage and the ranches it spawned, the Big Island is a great place for equestrians. Riders can gallop through green pastures, or saunter through Waipio Valley for a taste of old Hawaii. *For Waipio Valley rides, see Tours in the Hamakua Coast Exploring section.*

Hamakua Adventures. One-and-a-half-hour, morning and afternoon horseback rides ($79) travel through private ranchlands in the lush Onomea area near Hilo, stopping at the base of the 80-foot, twin Waikahalulu Falls. Refreshments are provided, with an optional ($20) barbecue lunch. ✉ 27-2668 Hawaii Belt Rd., Pepeekeo ☎ 808/871–5222 ⊕ www.hamakuaadventures.com.

King's Trail Rides. A four-hour excursion ($135) down an old Hawaiian trail leads to a scenic, uncrowded spot near Kealakekua Bay for snorkeling and lunch. A mask and snorkel are provided. ✉ Hwy. 11, mile marker 111, Kealakekua ☎ 808/323–2388 ⊕ www.konacowboy.com.

ZIPLINE TOURS

One of the few ways to really see the untouched beauty of the Big Island is to fly over its lush forests, dense tree canopies, and glorious rushing waterfalls on a zipline. You strap into a harness, get clipped

The Kohala Coast along the east side of Big Island is known for its shimmering blue water, beaches, and sunshine.

to a cable, step off a platform, and then zip, zip, zip your way through paradise. Most companies start you out easy on a slower, shorter line and graduate you to faster, longer zips. It's an exhilarating adventure for all ages and, between the zipping, rappelling, and suspension bridges, has been known to help some put aside their fear of heights (at least for a few minutes).

Big Island Eco Adventures II and Kona Zip. This company knows ziplines—it built the first one on the Big Island. For $169, the three-hour tour takes you on eight ziplines and a 200-foot suspension bridge. You experience exhilarating, crisscrossing thrills over the mountains and gulches of historic North Kohala, including the enormous Waianae Gulch. Along the way you get awesome views of the Pacific Ocean, and, on clear days, Maui. The eight-line Kona treetop zip is nestled in a pristine Upcountry ohia forest, accompanied by the calls of rare native birds who live high in the canopy. ⊠ *53-496 Iole Rd., Kapau* ☏ *808/889–5111* ⊕ *www. thebigislandzipline.com.*

Kohala Zipline. This company features nine zips and five suspension bridges for a thrilling, above-the-canopy adventure in the forest. You'll bounce up to the site in a six-wheel-drive, military-style vehicle. Two certified guides accompany each small group. Designed for all ability levels, the Kohala Zipline focuses on fun and safety, offering a dual line for easy, confident braking. You'll soar hundreds of feet above the ground and feel like a pro by the last platform. Zip and Dip tours (combining zipline, nature walk, snacks, and swim) cost $169. ⊠ *54-3676 Akoni Pule Hwy., Kapaau* ☏ *808/331–3620, 800/464–1993* ⊕ *www. kohalazipline.com.*

Continued on page 392

BIRTH OF THE ISLANDS

How did the volcanoes of the Hawaiian Islands evolve here, in the middle of the Pacific Ocean? The ancient Hawaiians believed that the volcano goddess Pele's hot temper was the key to the mystery; modern scientists contend that it's all about plate tectonics and one very hot spot.

Plate Tectonics & the Hawaiian Question: The theory of plate tectonics says that the Earth's surface is comprised of plates that float around slowly over the planet's molten interior. The vast majority of earthquakes and volcanic eruptions occur near plate boundaries—the San Francisco earthquakes in 1906 and 1989, for example, were the result of activity along the nearby San Andreas Fault, where the Pacific and North American plates meet. Hawaii, more than 1,988 miles from the nearest plate boundary, is a giant exception. For years scientists struggled to explain the island chain's existence—if not a fault line, what caused the earthquakes and volcanic eruptions that formed these islands?

What's a hotspot? In 1963, J. Tuzo Wilson, a Canadian geophysicist, argued that the Hawaiian volcanoes must have been created by small concentrated areas of extreme heat beneath the plates. Wilson hypothesized that there is a hotspot beneath the present-day position of the Big Island. Its heat produced a persistent source of magma by partly melting the Pacific Plate above it. The magma, lighter than the surrounding solid rock, rose through the mantle and crust to erupt onto the sea floor, forming an active seamount. Each flow caused the seamount to grow until it finally emerged above sea level as an island volcano. Plausible so far, but why then, is there not one giant Hawaiian island?

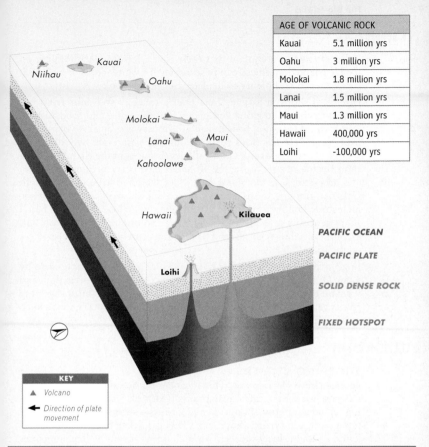

AGE OF VOLCANIC ROCK	
Kauai	5.1 million yrs
Oahu	3 million yrs
Molokai	1.8 million yrs
Lanai	1.5 million yrs
Maui	1.3 million yrs
Hawaii	400,000 yrs
Loihi	-100,000 yrs

PACIFIC OCEAN

PACIFIC PLATE

SOLID DENSE ROCK

FIXED HOTSPOT

KEY
▲ Volcano
← Direction of plate movement

Volcanoes on the Move: Wilson further suggested that the movement of the Pacific Plate itself eventually carries the island volcano beyond the hotspot. Cut off from its magma source, the island volcano becomes dormant. As the plate slowly moved, one island volcano would become extinct just as another would develop over the hotspot. After several million years, there is a long volcanic trail of islands and seamounts across the ocean floor. The oldest islands are those farthest from the hotspot. The exposed rocks of Kauai, for example, are about 5.1 million years old, but those on the Big Island are less than .5 million years old, with new volcanic rock still being formed.

An Island on the Way: Off the coast of the Big Island, the volcano known as Loihi is still submerged but erupting. Scientists long believed it to be a retired seamount volcano, but in the 1970s they discovered both old and new lava on its flanks, and in 1996 it erupted with a vengeance. It is believed that several thousand years from now, Loihi will be the newest addition to the Hawaiian Islands.

SHOPPING

Updated
by Kristina
Anderson

Residents like to complain that there isn't a lot of great shopping on the Big Island, but unless you're searching for winter coats or high-tech toys, you can find plenty to deplete your pocketbook.

Dozens of shops in Kailua-Kona offer a range of souvenirs from far-flung corners of the globe and plenty of local coffee and foodstuffs to take home to everyone you left behind. Housewares and artworks made from local materials (lava rock, coconut, koa, and milo wood) fill the shelves of small boutiques and galleries throughout the island. Upscale shops in the resorts along the Kohala Coast carry high-end clothing and accessories, as do a few boutiques scattered around the island. Galleries and gift shops, many showcasing the work of local artists, fill historic buildings in Waimea, Kainaliu, Holualoa, and Hawi. Hotel shops generally offer the most attractive and original resort wear, but, as with everything else at resorts, the prices run higher than elsewhere on the island.

In general, stores on the Big Island open at 9 or 10 am and close by 6 pm. Hilo's Prince Kuhio Plaza stays open until 8 pm on weekdays and 9 pm on Friday and Saturday. In Historic Kona Village, most shopping plazas geared to tourists remain open until 9 pm. Grocery stores such as KTA Superstore are open until 11 pm.

KAILUA-KONA

SHOPPING CENTERS

Coconut Grove Marketplace. This meandering oceanfront marketplace includes gift shops, cafés, restaurants (Outback Steakhouse, Humpy's Big Island Alehouse, Bongo Ben's, Lu Lu's), sports bars, sushi, boutiques, a frozen-yogurt shop, Jack's Diving Locker, and several art galleries. At night, locals gather to watch outdoor sand volleyball games held in the courtyard or grab a beer and enjoy live music. This place is always hopping, and it has the biggest free parking lot in downtown Kailua-Kona. ⊠ 75-5795–75-5825 Alii Dr..

Crossroads Shopping Center. This in-town shopping center includes a Safeway with an excellent deli section for on-the-go snacks, as well a Wal-Mart, where visitors can find affordable Hawaiian souvenirs including discounted Kona coffee and macadamia nuts. For a cheap meal, there's also a Denny's plus several fast-food joints. ⊠ 75-1000 Henry St. ☎ 808/329–4822.

Kaloko Light Industrial Park. This large retail complex near the airport includes Costco, the best place to stock up on food if you're staying at a vacation rental. Cycle Station has bikes to rent, and Mrs. Barry's Kona Cookies sells beautifully packaged, delicious "souvenirs." ⊠ Off Hwy. 19 and Hina Lani St., near Kona airport.

Keauhou Shopping Center. About 5 miles south of Kailua Village, this neighborhood shopping center includes KTA Superstore, Longs Drugs, Kona Stories bookstore, and a multiplex movie theater. Kenichi Pacific, a great sushi restaurant, and Peaberry & Galette, a café that serves excellent crêpes, are favorite eateries joined by Bianelli's Pizza and Sam Choy's Kai Lanai. You can also grab a quick bite at Los Habaneros, Subway, or L&L Hawaiian Barbecue. ⊠ *78-6831 Alii Dr.* ☎ *808/322–3000* ⊕ *www.keauhoushoppingcenter.com.*

Kona Commons. This downtown center features big-box retailers, such as Sports Authority (for snorkel and swim gear), and Ross Dress for Less (for suitcases, shoes, swimsuits, and aloha wear). Food and drink options include fast-food standbys like Dairy Queen, Subway, Taco Del Mar, and Panda Express; Ultimate Burger, for local beef and delicious homemade fries; Genki Sushi, where the goods are delivered via conveyer belt; and Kona Wine Market, which has a great selection of wines and spirits along with gourmet gift items. ■**TIP→** Target has fresh-flower leis for a fraction of the cost that local florists charge. ⊠ *75-5450 Makala Blvd.*

Kona Inn Shopping Village. Originally a hotel, the Kona Inn was built in 1928 to woo a new wave of wealthy travelers. As newer condos and resorts opened along the Kona and Kohala coasts, it was transformed into a low-rise, outdoor shopping village with dozens of clothing boutiques, art galleries, gift shops, and island-style eateries. Broad lawns with coconut trees on the ocean side provide a lovely setting for an afternoon picnic. The open-air Kona Inn Restaurant is a local favorite for evening mai tais. ⊠ *75-5744 Alii Dr.*

ARTS AND CRAFTS

Eclectic Craftsman. This longtime favorite brimming with handmade Hawaiian collectibles focuses on local art and crafts. The 60 Big Island artists represented here include renowned local painters and woodworkers. Affordable gifts range from bookmarks to salad servers to wine-bottle toppers. You won't find these items anywhere else, and they're all made in Hawaii. ⊠ *Kona Inn Shopping Village, 75-5744 Alii Dr.* ☎ *808/334–0562.*

Fodor'sChoice ★ **Hula Lamps of Hawaii.** Located in Kailua-Kona's Old Industrial complex, this one-of-a-kind shop features the bronze creations of Charles Moore. Inspired by the vintage hula-girl lamps of the 1930s, Moore creates art pieces sought by visitors and residents alike. Mix and match with an array of hand-painted lamp shades. ⊠ *74-5599 Luhia St., Unit F-5* ☎ *808/326–9583* ⊕ *www.hulalamps.com.*

Just Ukes. As the name suggests, this place is all about ukeleles—from music books to T-shirts to accessories like cases and bags. The independently owned shop carries a variety of ukuleles ranging from low-priced starter instruments to high-end models made of koa and mango. There's another Just Ukes at the Shops at Mauna Lani. ⊠ *Kona Inn Shopping Village, 75-5744 Alii Dr.* ☎ *808/769–5101.*

CLOTHING

Hilo Hattie. The well-known Hawaii clothier offers his-and-her aloha wear and carries a huge selection of casual clothes, local art, books, music, jewelry, local gourmet items, coffee, and souvenirs. ■**TIP→** Call for free transportation from nearby hotels. ⊠ *75-5597 Palani Rd.* ☎ *808/329–7200* ⊕ *www.hilohattie.com.*

FOOD AND WINE

Fodor's Choice ★ **Keauhou Store.** This historic roadside store has been transformed into a combination convenience store, bakeshop, lunch stop, gift shop, and museum. When Kurt and Thea Brown purchased the property in 2010, they discovered a treasure trove of untouched inventory dating to the 1920s. These artifacts are on display, along with such gift items as koa bowls, cool retro T-shirts, and Kona coffee grown on-site. Stop by for fresh produce, beverages, spirits, ice cream, Thea's yummy fresh-baked cookies, or a burger or sandwich enjoyed on the outdoor lanai overlooking the coffee trees. ⊠ *78-7010 Mamalahoa Hwy., Holualoa* ☎ *808/322–5203* ⊕ *www.keauhoustore.com.*

Kona Wine Market. This wine shop carries both local and imported varietals (with more than 600 high-end wines), specialty liquors, 150 specialty beers, gourmet foods, and even cigars. As a bonus, the market delivers wine and gift baskets to hotels. ⊠ *Kona Commons, 74-5450 Makala Blvd.* ☎ *808/329–9400* ⊕ *www.konawinemarket.com.*

FAMILY **Mrs. Barry's Kona Cookies.** For 30 years, Mrs. Barry and her family have been serving yummy home-baked cookies, including mac nut, white chocolate–mac nut, oatmeal raisin, and coffee crunch. Packaged in beautiful gift boxes or bags, the cookies make excellent gifts for family back home. Stop by on your way to Costco or the airport and pick up a bag or two or three. Ah heck, just ask Mrs. Barry to ship your stash instead. ⊠ *73-5563 Maiau St., below Costco* ☎ *808/329–6055* ⊕ *www. konacookies.com.*

Fodor's Choice ★ **Westside Wines.** Tucked away in a small downtown Kona retail center below Longs, this nifty gourmet wine and spirits shop offers restaurant-quality "wine list" wines at affordable prices. It's also the place to find large-format craft beers, French Champagne, single-malt scotches, organic vodka, small-batch bourbon, rye whiskey, fresh bread, and artisan cheese from around the world. George Clooney's Casaamigos tequila is the store's house tequila. A certified wine specialist, proprietor Alex Thropp was one of the state's top wholesale wine reps for decades. Wine and tequila tastings take place Friday and Saturday afternoons from 3 to 6. ⊠ *75-5660 Kopiko St. No. 4* ☎ *808/329–1777.*

MARKETS

Alii Gardens Marketplace. This mellow, parklike market, open Tuesday to Sunday 10 to 5, features outdoor stalls offering tropical flowers, produce, soaps, kettle corn, coffee, cookies, jewelry, koa wood, clothing, and kitschy crafts. A food kiosk serves shave ice, fish tacos, coconut water, fresh-fruit smoothies, and hamburgers, and you can also book surf lessons and kayak tours here. ⊠ *75-6129 Alii Dr., 1½ mile south of Kona Inn Shopping Village.*

Keauhou Farmers Market. In the parking lot at Keauhou Shopping Center, this cheerful market is the place to go on Saturday morning, and for good reason: live music, local produce (much of it organic), goat cheese, honey, meat, flowers, macadamia nuts, fresh-baked pastries, Kona coffee, and plenty of local color. ⊠ *Keauhou Shopping Center, 78-6831 Alii Dr.* ⊕ *www.keauhoufarmersmarket.com.*

Kona Inn Farmers' Market. An awesome florist creates custom arrangements while you wait at this touristy farmers' market. There are more than 40 vendors with lots of crafts for sale as well as the best prices on fresh produce and orchids in Kona. The market is held in a parking lot at the corner of Hualalai Road and Alii Drive, Wednesday to Sunday 7 to 4. ⊠ *75-7544 Alii Dr.*

Kona International Market. This breezy, indoor-outdoor marketplace features coffee, Hawaii-made goods, and imported collectibles, novelty items, and clothing. There's also a shaded food court; try some authentic Filipino specialities at Trini's Mixed Plate Catering. The market is open daily 9 to 5, and a free shuttle from Kailua Pier runs on Wednesdays. ⊠ *74-5533 Luhia St.* ☎ *808/329–6262* ⊕ *www. konainternationalmarket.com.*

THE KOHALA COAST

SHOPPING CENTERS

Kawaihae Harbor Shopping Center. This almost-oceanfront shopping plaza houses the exquisite Harbor Gallery, which represents more than 200 Big Island artists. Stroll inside before or after your meal at the acclaimed Café Pesto, Kohala Burger and Taco, or Kawaihae Kitchen. Try the Big Island–made ice cream and shave ice (the best in North Hawaii) at local favorite Anuenue. Also here are Mountain Gold Jewelers and Kohala Divers. ⊠ *Hwy. 270, Kawaihae* ⊕ *www.kawaihaeshopping.com.*

Kings' Shops at Waikoloa Beach Resort. Stores here include Martin & MacArthur, featuring koa furniture and accessories, and Cariloha, which offers bamboo clothing items, as well as a small Macy's and high-end chains: Coach, Tiffany, L'Occitane, and Louis Vuitton. Gourmet offerings include Merriman's Mediterranean Café, Roy's Waikoloa Bar & Grill, and Three Fat Pigs. Stock your hotel fridge with fresh local produce from the Kings' Shops Farmers Market, held Wednesdays 8:30 to 2. ⊠ *Waikoloa Beach Resort, 250 Waikoloa Beach Dr., Waikoloa* ☎ *808/886–8811* ⊕ *www.kingsshops.com.*

Queens' MarketPlace. The largest shopping complex on the Kohala Coast, Queens' MarketPlace houses fashionable clothing stores, jewelry boutiques, galleries, gift shops, and restaurants, including Sansei Seafood Restaurant & Sushi Bar and Romano's Macaroni Grill. Island Gourmet Markets and Starbucks are also here, as is an affordable food court. ⊠ *Waikoloa Beach Resort, 201 Waikoloa Beach Dr., Waikoloa* ☎ *808/886–8822* ⊕ *www.queensmarketplace.net.*

The Shops at Mauna Lani. The best part about this complex is its roster of restaurants, which includes Tommy Bahama Tropical Café, Ruth's Chris Steakhouse, Just Tacos Mexican Grill and Cantina, and Monstera, for noodles and sushi. You can find tropical apparel at Jams World, high-end housewares at Oasis Lifestyle, and original art at a number of galleries. Kids love the "adventure ride" theater, with the only "4-D" screens in Hawaii. ⊠ *68-1330 Mauna Lani Dr., Kohala Coast* ☎ *808/885–9501* ⊕ *www.shopsatmaunalani.com.*

ARTS AND CRAFTS

Elements Jewelry & Fine Crafts. The beautiful little shop carries lots of original, handmade jewelry made by local artists as well as carefully chosen gifts, including unusual ceramics, paintings, prints, glass items, baskets, fabrics, bags, and toys. ⊠ *55-3413 Akoni Pule Hwy., next to Bamboo Restaurant, Hawi* ☏ *808/889–0760* ⊕ *www.elementsjewelryandcrafts. com.*

Hawaiian Quilt Collection. The Hawaiian quilt is a work of art that is prized and passed down through generations. At this store, you'll find everything from hand-quilted purses and bags to wall hangings and blankets. You can even get a take-home kit and sew your very own Hawaiian quilt. ⊠ *Queens' MarketPlace, 201 Waikoloa Beach Dr., Waikoloa* ☏ *808/886–0494* ⊕ *www.hawaiian-quilts.com.*

Island Pearls by Maui Divers. Among the fine jewelry at this boutique is a wide selection of high-end pearl jewelry, including Tahitian black pearls, South Sea white and golden pearls, and chocolate Tahitian pearls. Also here are freshwater pearls in the shell, black coral (the Hawaii state gemstone), and diamonds. Prices are high but so is the quality. ⊠ *Queens' MarketPlace, 201 Waikoloa Beach Dr., Waikoloa* ☏ *808/886–4817* ⊕ *www.mauidivers.com.*

CLOTHING

As Hawi Turns. This North Kohala shop, housed in the historic 1932 Toyama Building, adds a sophisticated touch to resort wear with items made of hand-painted silk in tropical designs by local artists. There are plentiful vintage treasures, jewelry, gifts, hats, bags, and toys, plus handmade ukuleles by local luthier David Gomes. ⊠ *55-3412 Akoni Pule Hwy., Hawi* ☏ *808/889–5023.*

Blue Ginger. The Waikoloa branch of this fashion veteran offers really sweet matching aloha outfits for the entire family. There are also handbags, shoes, robes, jewelry, and lotions. ⊠ *Queens' MarketPlace, 201 Waikoloa Beach Dr., Waikoloa* ☏ *808/886–0022* ⊕ *www.blueginger. com.*

GALLERIES

Ackerman Fine Art Gallery. This gallery is truly a family affair. Painter Gary Ackerman's daughter, Alyssa, and her husband, Ronnie, run the gallery that showcases Gary's art. Down the block is a second gallery, which features art by several of Gary's family members as well as gifts. The side-by-side gallery, café, and gift shop are near the King Kamehameha Statue. ⊠ *54-3897 Akoni Pule Hwy., Kapaau* ☏ *808/889–5971* ⊕ *www.ackermangalleries.com.*

Harbor Gallery. Since 1990, this gallery has been enticing visitors with a vast collection of paintings and sculptures by more than 200 Big Island artists. There are also antique maps and prints, wooden bowls, paddles, koa furniture, jewelry, and glasswork. Chosen best art gallery by readers of *North Hawaii News* in 2013, the shop hosts two annual wood shows. ⊠ *Kawaihae Harbor Shopping Center, 61-3665 Akoni Pule Hwy., Kawaihae* ☏ *808/882–1510* ⊕ *www.harborgallery.biz.*

Rankin Gallery. Watercolorist and oil painter Patrick Louis Rankin show-cases his own work in his shop in a restored plantation store next to the bright-green Chinese community and social hall, on the way to Pololu Valley. The building sits right at a curve in the road, in the Palawa *ahupuaa* (land division) past Kapaau. ✉ *53-4380 Akoni Pule Hwy., Kapaau* ☎ *808/889–6849* ⊕ *www.patricklouisrankin.net.*

WAIMEA

SHOPPING CENTERS

Parker Ranch Center. With a snazzy ranch-style motif, this shopping hub includes a supermarket, some great local eateries (Village Burger and Lilikoi Café), a coffee shop, natural foods store, galleries, and clothing boutiques. The Parker Ranch Store and Parker Ranch Visitors Center and Museum are also here. ✉ *67-1185 Mamalahoa Hwy.* ⊕ *www.parkerranchcenterads.com.*

Parker Square. Although the Gallery of Great Things is this center's star attraction, it's also worth looking in at the Waimea General Store; Sweet Wind, for books, chimes, and beads; and Kamuela Goldsmiths, which sells locally crafted gold jewelry. Waimea Coffee Company satisfies with salads, sandwiches, and Kona coffee. ✉ *65-1279 Kawaihae Rd.*

ARTS AND CRAFTS

Fodor's Choice ★ **Gallery of Great Things.** You might lose yourself exploring the trove of fine art and collectibles in every price range at this gallery, which represents hundreds of local artists and has a low-key, unhurried atmosphere. The "things" include hand-stitched quilts, ceramic sculptures, vintage kimonos, original paintings, koa-wood bowls and furniture, etched glassware, Niihau shell lei, and feather art by local artist Beth McCormick. ✉ *Parker Square, 65-1279 Kawaihae Rd.* ☎ *808/885–7706* ⊕ *www.galleryofgreatthingshawaii.com.*

Wishard Gallery. A Big Island–born artist whose verdant landscapes and *paniolo* (cowboy)-themed paintings have become iconic throughout the Islands, Harry Wishard showcases his original oils at this gallery, along with works by other renowned local artists like Kathy Long, Edward Kayton, and Lynn Capell. There's a second gallery location at Queens' MarketPlace. ✉ *Parker Ranch Center, 67-1185 Mamalahoa Hwy.* ☎ *808/937–8772* ⊕ *www.wishardgallery.com.*

FOOD AND WINE

Fodor's Choice ★ **Kamuela Liquor Store.** From the outside it doesn't look like much, but this historic store sells the best selection of premium spirits, wines, and gourmet items on the island. Alvin, the owner, is a collector of fine wines, as evidenced by his multiple cellars. Wine-and-cheese tastings take place Friday afternoons—the store offers an extensive selection of artisanal cheeses from around the world. Favorites like duck mousse round out the inventory, and everything is priced within reason. ✉ *64-1010 Mamalahoa Hwy.* ☎ *808/885–4674.*

Waimea General Store. Since 1970, this Waimea landmark has been a favorite of locals and visitors alike. Although specialty kitchenware takes center stage, the shop brims with local gourmet items, books, kimonos, and Hawaiian gifts and souvenirs. ⊠ *Parker Square, 65-1279 Kawaihae Rd., Suite 112* ☎ *808/987–1565* ⊕ *www.waimeageneralstore. com.*

THE HAMAKUA COAST

ARTS AND CRAFTS

Glass from the Past. Near Akaka Falls, this is a fun place to shop for a quirky gift or just to poke around. The store is chock-full of old Hawaiian bottles, antiques, vintage clothing, Japanese collectibles, and interesting ephemera. There's often even a "free" table out front to add to the discovery. ⊠ *28-1672 Old Mamalahoa Hwy., Honomu* ☎ *808/963–6449.*

GALLERIES

Waipio Valley Artworks. In this quaint gallery in a vintage home, you can find finely crafted wooden bowls, koa furniture, paintings, and jewelry—all made by local artists. There's also a great little café where you can pick up a sandwich or ice cream before descending into Waipio Valley. ⊠ *Off Hwy. 240, Kukuihaele* ☎ *808/775–0958* ⊕ *www. waipiovalleyartworks.com.*

Woodshop Gallery. Run by local artists Peter and Jeanette McLaren, this Honomu gallery showcases their woodwork and photography collections along with beautiful ceramics, photography, glass, and paintings from other Big Island artists. The McLarens also serve up plate lunches, shave ice, homemade ice cream, and espresso to hungry tourists in the adjoining café. Their shop next door, called Same-Same, But Different, features made-in-Hawaii clothing and small gifts. The historic building still has a working soda fountain dating from 1935. ⊠ *28-1690 Old Government Rd., Honomu* ☎ *808/963–6363* ⊕ *www.woodshopgallery.com.*

HILO

SHOPPING CENTERS

Hilo Shopping Center. Among this shopping plaza's 40 shops are a day spa, a pharmacy, a trendy boutique, and popular Lanky's Pastries and Island Naturals Market and Deli, plus Sunlight Cafe and Restaurant Miwa. There's plenty of free parking. ⊠ *1261 Kilauea Ave.*

Prince Kuhio Plaza. The Big Island's most comprehensive mall has indoor shopping, entertainment (a multiplex), and dining, including KFC, Hot Dog on a Stick, Cinnabon, the island's only IHOP, and Maui Tacos. The kids might like the arcade (near the food court), while you enjoy the stores, anchored by Macy's, Sports Authority, and Sears. ⊠ *111 E. Puainako St., at Hwy. 11* ☎ *808/959–3555* ⊕ *www. princekuhioplaza.com.*

ARTS AND CRAFTS

Most Irresistible Shop. This place lives up to its name by stocking unique gifts from around the Pacific, be it pure Hawaiian ohia lehua honey, Kau coffee, aloha wear, or tinkling wind chimes. ⊠ *256 Kamehameha Ave.* ☎ *808/935–9644.*

BOOKS AND MAGAZINES

FAMILY

Fodor's Choice

★

Basically Books. More than a bookstore, this bayfront shop stocks one of Hawaii's largest selections of maps, including topographical and relief maps, and Hilo's largest selection of Hawaiian music. Of course, it also has books about Hawaii, including great choices for children. ✉ *160 Kamehameha Ave.* ☎ *808/961–0144, 800/903–6277* ⊕ *www. basicallybooks.com.*

CLOTHING AND SHOES

Hilo Hattie. Set in an indoor mall, the east-side outlet of the well-known clothier is slightly smaller than its Kailua-Kona cousin, but offers plenty of the same his-and-her aloha wear, casual clothes, slippers, jewelry, and souvenirs. ✉ *Prince Kuhio Plaza, 111 E. Puainako St.* ☎ *808/961–3077* ⊕ *www.hilohattie.com.*

Sig Zane Designs. This acclaimed boutique sells distinctive island wearables with bold colors and motifs designed by the legendary Sig Zane, known for his artwork honoring native flora and fauna. All apparel is handcrafted in Hawaii, and is often worn by local celebrities and businesspeople. ✉ *122 Kamehameha Ave.* ☎ *808/935–7077* ⊕ *www. sigzane.com.*

FOOD

Big Island Candies. A local legend in the cookie- and chocolate-making business, Big Island Candies is a must-see if you have a sweet tooth. Enjoy a free cookie sample and a cup of Kona coffee as you watch sweets being made through a window. The store has a long list of interesting and tasty products, but it is best known for its chocolate-dipped shortbread cookies. ✉ *585 Hinano St., two blocks from Hilo airport* ☎ *808/935–8890* ⊕ *www.bigislandcandies.com.*

Two Ladies Kitchen. This hole-in-the-wall confections shop has made a name for itself thanks to its pillowy *mochi* (Japanese rice pounded into a sticky paste and molded into shapes). The proprietors are best known for their huge ripe strawberries wrapped in a white mochi covering, which won't last as long as a box of chocolates—most mochi items are only good for two or three days. To guarantee you get your fill, call and place your order ahead of time. It's closed Sunday and Monday. ✉ *274 Kilauea Ave.* ☎ *808/961–4766.*

HOME DECOR

Dragon Mama. Step into this charming downtown Hilo spot to find authentic Japanese fabrics, futons, and gifts along with an elegant selection of clothing, sleepwear, slippers, and tea-service accoutrements. Handmade comforters, pillows, and futon pads are sewn of natural fibers on-site. ✉ *266 Kamehameha Ave.* ☎ *808/934–9081* ⊕ *www. dragonmama.com.*

MARKETS

Fodor's Choice

★

Hilo Farmers Market. The 200 vendors here—stretching a couple of blocks—sell a profusion of tropical flowers, locally grown produce, aromatic honey, tangy goat cheese, hot breakfast and lunch items, and fresh baked specialties at extraordinary prices. This colorful, open-air market—the most popular on the island—opens for business Wednesday and Saturday from 6 am to 4 pm. A smaller version on the other

4

days features 20 to 30 vendors. ✉ *Kamehameha Ave. and Mamo St.* ☎ *808/933–1000* ⊕ *www.hilofarmersmarket.com.*

SPAS

Updated by Kristina Anderson

The Big Island's spa directors have produced menus full of "only in Hawaii" treatments well worth a splurge. Local specialties include *lomilomi* massages, hot-lava-stone massages, and scrubs and wraps that incorporate plenty of coconut, ginger, orchids, and macadamia nuts. Also expect to find Swedish and deep-tissue massages and, at some spas, Thai massage. And in romantic Hawaii, couples can be pampered side by side. ■ **TIP→ Lomilomi massage is a quintessential Hawaiian deep-tissue massage, and most practitioners are happy to adjust the pressure to your needs.** Most of the full-service spas on the Big Island are at the resorts. With the exception of the Four Seasons Spa at Hualalai, these spas are open to anyone. In fact, many of the hotels outsource spa management, and there is no price difference for guests and nonguests, although guests can receive in-room services.

KAILUA-KONA

Pau Hana Massage. This classy massage studio, owned and operated by resort-trained massage therapists, is conveniently located in downtown Kona. In addition to traditional massage, you can get a five-star experience—warmed coconut oil scalp massage, lemongrass-ginger hot-stone foot soak, or other tropical specialties—at a fraction of Kohala Coast resort prices. ✉ *75-5741 Kuakini Hwy., Bldg. A, Kailua-Kona* ☎ *808/327–5664* ⊕ *www.pauhanamassage.com* ☞ *$75 60-min massage; $105–$265 packages. Services: Aromatherapy, body scrubs and wraps, massages.*

Fodor'sChoice ★ **The Spa at Hualalai.** For the exclusive use of Four Seasons Resort guests and members, this spa features 19 massage treatment areas. Tropical breezes waft through 10 outdoor massage *hales,* situated in beautiful garden settings. The therapists are top-notch, and a real effort is made to incorporate local traditions. Apothecary services allow you to customize your treatment with ingredients like kukui nuts, Hawaiian salts, and coconut. Massage options range from traditional lomilomi to Thai. ✉ *Four Seasons Resort Hualalai, 72-100 Kaupulehu Dr., Kailua-Kona* ☎ *808/325–8000* ⊕ *www.fourseasons.com* ☞ *$175 50-min massage, $180 body scrub, $175 facials. Hair salon, outdoor hot tub, sauna, steam room. Gym with: Cardiovascular machines, free weights, weight-training equipment. Classes and programs: Personal training, Pilates, Spinning, yoga.*

THE KONA COAST

Mamalahoa Hot Tubs and Massage. Tucked into a residential neighborhood above Kealakekua, this is a welcome alternative to the large Kohala Coast resort spas. It feels like a secret hideaway aglow with tiki torches, and offers Hawaiian lomilomi and hot-stone massages at affordable prices. Soaking tubs, enclosed in their own thatched gazebo with roof portholes for stargazing, are great for a couple's soak. It's open Wednesday to Saturday. ⊠ *81-1016 St. John's Rd., Kealakekua* ☎ *808/323–2288* ⊕ *www.mamalahoa-hottubs.com* ✆ *$30 60-min soak; $95 30-min soak plus 60-min lomilomi, Swedish, or deep-tissue massage; $150 30-min soak plus 90-min hot-stone massage.*

THE KOHALA COAST

Hawaii Island Retreat Maluhia Spa. This peaceful and elegant sanctuary in North Kohala offers three artfully appointed indoor treatment rooms and two outdoor massage platforms that overlook the valley. The spa is first-rate, with handcrafted wooden lockers, rain-style showerheads, and a signature line of lotions and scrubs that's made locally. The owners also create their own scrubs and wraps from ingredients grown on the property. The Papaya Delight lives up to its name, and features roasted ground papaya seeds mixed with goat yogurt and geranium. The slate of massages includes lomilomi, Thai, and deep tissue. The Shirodhara treatment consists of warm oil slowly drizzled over your third eye. ⊠ *250 Maluhia Rd., Kapaau* ☎ *808/889–6336* ⊕ *www. hawaiiislandretreat.com* ✆ *$130 60-minute lomilomi massage, $140 signature facial. Hot tub, infinity pool. Services: Facials, massages. Classes and programs: Aquacise, qigong, yoga.*

Mauna Kea Spa by Mandara. Mandara blends European, Balinese, and indigenous treatments to create the ultimate spa experience. Though this facility is on the smaller side, the excellent treatments are up to the international company's exacting standards. Try the Elemis Tri-Enzyme Resurfacing Facial; the Mandara Four Hand Massage, where two therapists work out the kinks simultaneously; or an outdoor, ocean-cabana massage. Traditional Hawaiian lomilomi is also available. The hotel operates a separate hair salon that offers manicures and pedicures. ⊠ *Mauna Kea Beach Hotel, 69-100 Mauna Kea Beach Dr., Kohala Coast* ☎ *808/882–5630* ⊕ *www.mandaraspa.com* ✆ *$188 50-min lomilomi massage, $288 50-min outdoor massage. Services: Body treatments, facials, massages, waxing.*

Fodor's Choice ★ **Mauna Lani Spa.** This is a one-of-a-kind experience with a mix of traditional standbys (lomilomi massage, moisturizing facials) and innovative treatments influenced by ancient traditions and incorporating local products. Most treatments take place in outdoor thatched *hales* (huts) surrounded by lava rock. An exception is Watsu therapy, in which clients are cradled in the arms of a certified therapist in warm saltwater in a 1,000-square-foot grotto between two lava tubes. (It's great for people with disabilities who can't enjoy traditional massage.) Black volcanic clay applications are offered in a natural lava sauna. Aesthetic treatments incorporate high-end products from Epicuran and Emminence, so facials have lasting therapeutic effects. The spa also offers a full regimen of fitness and yoga classes. ⊠ *Mauna Lani Bay Hotel & Bungalows, 68-1365 Pauoa Rd., Kohala Coast* ☎ *808/881–7922* ⊕ *www. maunalani.com* ✆ *$175 60-min lomilomi massage, $185 50-min Lava Watsu Experience. Hair salon, hot tub, sauna, steam room. Services:*

Aquatic therapy, baths, body wraps, facials, massages, nail treatments, scrubs, tinting, waxing. Gym with: Cardiovascular machines, free weights, weight-training equipment. Classes and programs: Body sculpting, kickboxing, personal training, Pilates, Spinning, weight training, yoga.

Fodor'sChoice **Spa Without Walls at the Fairmont Orchid Hawaii.** This ranks among the
★ best massage facilities on the island, partially due to the superlative setting—private massage areas are situated amid the waterfalls, saltwater pools, and meandering gardens, as well as right on the beach. In fact, the Fairmont Orchid is one of the few resorts to offer beachside massage. Splurge on the 110-minute Alii Experience, offering hot coconut oil treatments, lomilomi, and hot-stone massage. Other great treatments include caviar facials, fragrant herbal wraps, and coffee-and-vanilla scrubs. Where else can you relax to the sounds of cascading waterfalls while watching tropical yellow tang swim beneath you through windows in the floor? ⊠ *Fairmont Orchid Hawaii, 1 N. Kaniku Dr., Kohala Coast* ☎ *808/887–7540, 808/885–2000* ⊕ *www.fairmont.com/ orchid* ☞ *$159–$179 50-min lomilomi massage. Sauna, steam room. Services: Baths, body wraps, facials, massages, scrubs. Classes and programs: Aquaerobics, guided walks, meditation, personal training, yoga.*

HAWAII VOLCANOES NATIONAL PARK AND VICINITY

Hale Hoola Spa in Volcano. Those staying in Volcano or Hilo have easy access to body treatments, massages, and facials at far more reasonable prices than on the other side of the island. Hale Hoola's menu features a bounty of local ingredients and traditional Hawaiian treatments, including *lomi hula*, which is lomilomi massage choreographed to hula music, and *laau hamo*, which blends lomilomi with traditional Hawaiian and Asian healing herbs and plant extracts. *Popokapai* is a divine blend of hot-stone massage and laau hamo, incorporating lomilomi with warm compresses filled with healing herbs. Facials and body scrubs use traditional ginger, coconut, and macadamia nuts, but also some surprises, including taro, vanilla, and volcanic clay. ⊠ *Mauna Loa Estates, 11-3913 7th St., Volcano* ☎ *808/756–2421* ⊕ *www.halehoola. net* ☞ *$75 60-min lomilomi massage, $190 rejuvenation package. Services: Aromatherapy, body scrubs and wraps, facials, hair removal, makeup, massages, waxing.*

ENTERTAINMENT AND NIGHTLIFE

Updated
by Kristina
Anderson

If you're the sort of person who doesn't come alive until after dark, you might be a little lonely on the Big Island. Blame it on the sleepy plantation heritage. People did their cane raising in the morning, thus very limited late-night fun.

Still, there are a few lively bars on the island, a handful of great local playhouses, half a dozen or so movie houses (including those that play foreign and independent films), and plenty of musical entertainment to keep you happy.

Also, many resorts have bars and late-night activities and events, and keep pools and gyms open late so there's something to do after dinner. And let's not forget the luau. These fantastic dance and musical performances are combined with some of the best local food on the island and are plenty of fun for the whole family.

ENTERTAINMENT

DINNER CRUISES AND SHOWS

Luau on the Water Glass Bottom Dinner Cruise. Blue Sea Cruises offers a classier alternative to the booze cruise, with a buffet dinner, tropical cocktails, live entertainment, hula show, and conga dancing in a glass-bottom boat. The focus is on the sunset and the scenery, with the chance to see spinner dolphins and manta rays, as well as whales from November to May. ⊠ *Kailua Pier, Alii Dr., next to Courtyard King Kamehameha's Kona Beach Hotel, Kailua-Kona* ☎ *808/331–8875* ⊕ *www.blueseacruisesinc.com* ✉ *$103* ⊙ *Mon., Wed., Fri., and Sat., departure times vary.*

LUAU AND POLYNESIAN REVUES

KAILUA-KONA

Island Breeze Luau. With traditional dancing showcasing the interconnected Polynesian roots of Hawaii, Samoa, Tahiti, and New Zealand, the "We Are *Ohana* (family)" luau is not a hokey tourist-trap event. These performers take their art seriously. The historic oceanfront location at King Kamehameha's former royal compound near Ahuhena Heiau adds to the authenticity, and the bounty of food includes *kalua* pig cooked in an underground *imu* (oven). ⊠ *75-5660 Palani Rd.* ☎ *866/482–9775* ⊕ *www.islandbreezeluau.com* ✉ *$79.43* ⊙ *Tues., Thurs., and Sun. 5–8.*

Haleo Luau Dinner & Show at Sheraton Kona Resort. On the graceful grounds of the Sheraton Kona Resort, this luau takes you on a journey of song and dance, celebrating the historic Keauhou region, birthplace of King Kamehameha III. Before the show, you can participate in workshops on topics ranging from coconut-frond weaving to poi ball techniques. The excellent buffet is a feast of local favorites, including kalua pig, poi, ahi poke, chicken long rice, fish, and mango chutney. Generous mai tai refills are a plus, and it's all highlighted by a dramatic fire-knife finale. ⊠ *Sheraton Kona Resort & Spa at Keauhou Bay, 78-128 Ehukai St.* ☎ *808/930–4900* ⊕ *www.sheratonkona.com* ✉ *$85.78* ⊙ *Mon. at 5.*

KOHALA COAST

Gathering of the Kings Polynesian Feast at Fairmont Orchid. Offering bang for your buck, this show is slickly produced and well choreographed, incorporating both traditional and modern dance and an array of beautiful costumes. The meal offers the most variety of any island luau, with four buffet tables representing New Zealand, Hawaii, Tahiti, and Samoa, and there's an open bar for mai tai refills. ⊠ *Fairmont Orchid Hawaii, 1 N. Kaniku Dr., Kohala Coast* ☎ *808/885–2000* ⊕ *www.fairmont.com/orchid* ✉ *$109* ⊙ *5pm Sat.*

DID YOU KNOW?

Hilo, on the east side of Big Island, is appropriately nicknamed "The City of Rainbows," as it's surrounded by rain forests and gets about 130 inches of rain per year.

Hapuna Beach Prince Hotel's Let's Go Crabbing. While the Mauna Kea Beach Hotel's clambake gets all the acclaim, this meal is tastier and at a fraction of the price. Held on the hotel's ocean terrace, the all-you-can-eat buffet features everything from prime rib and roasted breast of turkey to Washington mussels, steamed Manila clams, excellent shrimp salads, and corn-and-crab bisque. Expect an array of crab offerings, including wok-fried Dungeness crab and chilled snow-crab claws. Homemade ice cream is the star attraction of the dessert bar, which features hot fudge and other toppings. ⊠ *Hapuna Beach Prince Hotel, 62-100 Kaunaoa Dr., Kohala Coast* ☎ *808/880–1111* ⊕ *www.princeresortshawaii.com* ⌨ *$62* ⊙ *Fri. at 6.*

FAMILY **Legends of the Hawaii Luau at Hilton Waikoloa Village.** Presented outdoors at the Kamehameha Court, this new show is aptly subtitled, "Our Big Island Story." A delicious buffet offers Big Island–grown luau choices as well as more familiar fare and an open tropical bar. Pay a small fee and upgrade to Alii seating for a front-row vantage and your own buffet station. A children's station has kid favorites. Delicious desserts such as haupia cream puffs and Kona-coffee cheesecake top it all off. ⊠ *Hilton Waikoloa Village, 69-425 Waikoloa Beach Dr., Waikoloa* ☎ *808/886–1234* ⊕ *www.hiltonwaikoloavillage.com* ⌨ *$112* ⊙ *Tues., Fri., and Sun. at 6.*

Mauna Kea Beach Hotel Clambake. The weekly clambake here features an extensive menu with oysters on the half shell, Manila clams, Dungeness crab legs, sashimi, and Keahole lobster. There's even prime rib for meat lovers and a dessert station. Live Hawaiian music is often accompanied by a graceful hula dancer. ⊠ *Mauna Kea Beach Hotel, 62-100 Mauna Kea Beach Dr., Kohala Coast* ☎ *808/882–5810, 808/882–7222* ⊕ *www. maunakeabeachhotel.com* ⌨ *$92* ⊙ *Sat. at 6.*

Waikoloa Beach Marriott Sunset Luau. Overlooking beautiful Anaehoomalu Bay, the festivities at this luau include a spectacular Samoan fire dance performance as well as traditional song and dances from various Pacific Island cultures. Traditional dishes are served alongside more familiar Western fare, and there's also an open bar. ⊠ *Waikoloa Beach Marriott, 69-275 Waikoloa Beach Dr., Waikoloa* ☎ *808/886–6789* ⊕ *www. sunsetluau.com* ⌨ *$97* ⊙ *Wed. and Sat. 5–8:15.*

FESTIVALS

There is a festival dedicated to just about everything on the Big Island. Some of them are small community affairs, but a handful of film, food, and music festivals provide quality entertainment for visitors and locals alike. *The following is a list of our favorites:*

King Kamehameha Day Celebration Parade. In this parade, at least 100 Hawaiian horseback riders represent the colorful flora of the Hawaiian Islands. A cultural festival usually follows. ☎ *808/322–9944* ⊕ *www. konaparade.org* ⊙ *June.*

Kona Brewers Festival. At this lively annual celebration, 70 types of ales and lagers are showcased along with cuisine from 35 Hawaii chefs. There's also live music, fashion shows, a fun run, and a golf tournament. The multi-day, sellout event is a community fundraiser and local favorite. ⊠ *Courtyard King Kamehameha's Kona Beach Hotel, 75-5660*

Catch a Big Island sunset while hiking on mountaintops covered with lava fields.

Palani Rd. ☎ *808/331–3033* ⊕ *www.konabrewersfestival.com* ☯ *Early Mar.*

Kona Coffee Cultural Festival. Held over 10 days, the longest-running food festival in Hawaii includes coffee recipe, picking, and label-design contests; cupping competitions; a lecture series; and a colorful community parade featuring the newly crowned Miss Kona Coffee. During the Holualoa Village Coffee and Art Stroll, you can meet artists and sample estate coffees. ☎ *808/323–2006* ⊕ *www.konacoffeefest.com* ☯ *Early Nov.*

Fodor's Choice
★

Merrie Monarch Festival. The mother of all Hawaii festivals, the Merrie Monarch celebrates all things hula and completely overtakes Hilo for one fantastic week a year. The highly popular event honors the legacy of King David Kalakaua, the man responsible for reviving fading Hawaiian cultural traditions such as hula. The festival is staged at the spacious Edith Kanakaole Multi-Purpose Stadium during the first week following Easter Sunday. Hula *halau* (studios) worldwide come to compete in *kahiko* (ancient) and *auana* (modern) dance styles. ■ **TIP→ You must reserve accommodations up to a year in advance. Ticket requests must be mailed after December 26 of the preceding year.** ⊠ *Edith Kanakaole Multi-Purpose Stadium, 350 Kalanikoa St., Hilo* ☎ *808/935–9168* ⊕ *www.merriemonarchfestival.org* ☯ *Apr.*

Taste of the Hawaiian Range. Since 1995, this culinary event has given locals and visitors a taste of what the region's best chefs and ranches have to offer, from grass-fed beef, lamb, and mutton to succulent veal. ☎ *808/981–5199* ⊕ *www.tasteofthehawaiianrange.com* ☯ *Sept. or Oct.*

THEATER

Kahilu Theatre. This intimate theater regularly hosts internationally acclaimed performers. In recent seasons, Mikhail Barishnikov, the Szymanwski Quartet, Terence Blanchard, Ben Vereen, and the Martha Graham Company shared the calendar with regional modern-dance troupes and traditional Hawaiian musicians. Tremendous community support revived the theater after it closed in 2012. ☒ *Parker Ranch Center, 67-1185 Mamalahoa Hwy., Waimea* ☎ *808/885–6868* ⊕ *www. kahilutheatre.org.*

Volcano Art Center. Hawaiian music and dance, as well as theater performances, are hosted by this local art center. Locals drive here from all over the island for concerts. ☒ *19-4744 Old Volcano Rd., Volcano* ☎ *808/967–8222* ⊕ *www.volcanoartcenter.org.*

NIGHTLIFE

KAILUA-KONA

BARS

Humpy's Big Island Alehouse. Beer drinkers appreciate the fine craft brews on tap at this oceanfront restaurant. It's always busy with young, local revelers. Humpy's food can be hit or miss, but it's great for late-hour grill items. Happy-hour specials are available weekdays 3 to 6, and the bar stays open until 2 am. ☒ *75-5815 Alii Dr.* ☎ *808/324–2337* ⊕ *www. humpys.com/kona.*

Fodor's Choice ★ **Kona Brewing Co. Pub & Brewery.** The only genuine brewpub in Kona, this spot is beloved by locals. Good pizzas and salads, great locally brewed beer (go for the sampler and try them all), and an outdoor patio with live music on Sunday night means this place can get crowded, especially on weekends. The main entrance is at the end of Pawai Street, in the Old Industrial area. ☒ *75-5629 Kuakini Hwy.* ☎ *808/334–2739* ⊕ *www.konabrewingco.com.*

CLUBS

Huggo's on the Rocks. Jazz, island, and classic-rock bands perform here, and outside you may see people dancing in the sand. The food can be hit or miss, but the location, on the waterfront by the Royal Kona Resort, is worth it. ☒ *75-5828 Kahakai Rd., at Alii Dr.* ☎ *808/329–1493* ⊕ *www. huggos.com.*

Lulu's. On weekends, a young crowd gyrates to hot dance music under strobes. A DJ spins hip-hop, techno, and electronic beats, and the party lasts well into the wee hours. ☒ *Coconut Grove Marketplace, 75-5819 Alii Dr.* ☎ *808/331–2633* ⊕ *www.lulushawaii.com.*

THE KOHALA COAST

BARS

Luana Lounge. This wood-paneled lounge in the Fairmont Orchid has a large terrace and an impressive view. The bartenders are skilled, service impeccable. The crowd is subdued, so it's a nice place for an early-evening cocktail or after-dinner liqueur. ☒ *Fairmont Orchid, 1 N. Kaniku Dr., Kohala Coast* ☎ *808/885–2000* ⊕ *www.fairmont.com/orchid.*

BEST SUNSET MAI TAIS

Huggo's on the Rocks (Kailua-Kona). Table dining in the sand, plus live music Friday and Saturday.

Kona Inn (Kailua-Kona). Wide, unobstructed view of the Kailua-Kona coastline.

Rays on the Bay at the Sheraton Kona Beach Resort & Spa at

Keauhou Bay (Kailua-Kona). Fantastic sunset views from plush lounge chairs, followed by spotlighted glimpses of manta rays attracted by the lights.

Waioli Lounge in the Hilo Hawaiian Hotel (Hilo). A nice view of Coconut Island; live music Friday and Saturday nights.

4

HILO
BARS
Cronie's Bar & Grill. A sports bar by night and hamburger joint by day, Cronie's is a local favorite. When the lights go down, the bar gets packed. ⊠ *11 Waianuenue Ave.* ☎ *808/935–5158.*

WHERE TO EAT

Updated by Karen Anderson

Between star chefs and myriad local farms, the Big Island restaurant scene has really heated up in the last 10 years. Food writers from national magazines are praising the chefs of the Big Island for their ability to turn the local bounty into inventive blends of the island's cultural heritage. The Big Island has become a destination for vacationing foodies, who are drawn by the innovative offerings and reputations of world-renowned chefs and premier restaurants.

Resorts along the Kohala Coast have long invested in culinary programs that offer memorable dining experiences that include inventive entrées, spot-on wine pairings, and customized chef's table options. But great food on the Big Island doesn't begin and end with the resorts. A handful of cutting-edge chefs have retired from the fast-paced hotel world and opened their own small bistros closer to the farms in Upcountry Waimea, or other places off the beaten track. And, as some historic towns transform into vibrant arts communities, unique and wonderful restaurants have cropped up in Hawi, Kainaliu, and Holualoa, and on the east side of the island in Hilo.

Though the larger, gourmet restaurants (especially those at the resorts) tend to be very pricey, there are still *ono grindz* (Hawaiian slang for tasty local food) to be found at budget prices throughout the island, from greasy plate lunch specials to reasonably priced organic fare at a number of cafés and health food markets. Less populated areas like Kau, the Hamakua Coast, and Puna offer limited choices for dinner, but there are usually at least one or two spots that have a decent plate lunch or surprisingly good food.

BEST BETS FOR BIG ISLAND DINING

Fodor's Choice ★

Beach Tree, $$$, p. 417
Brown's Beach House, $$$$, p. 417
Café Pesto, $$, p. 423
CanoeHouse, $$$$, p. 419
Kona Brewing Co. Pub & Brewery, $, p. 413
Norio's Japanese Steakhouse and Sushi Bar, $$$ p. 420
Sushi Rock, $$, p. 421
Ulu Ocean Grill, $$$, p. 417
Village Burger, $, p. 423

By Price

$

Island Lava Java, p. 412
Kona Brewing Co. Pub & Brewery, p. 413
Lilikoi Café, p. 422

$$

Bamboo Restaurant, p. 417
Jackie Rey's Ohana Grill, p. 413
Keei Café, p. 416
Kenichi Pacific, p. 413
Merriman's Mediterranean Café, p. 420
Sam Choy's Kai Lanai, p. 414

$$$

Beach Tree, p. 417
Kilauea Lodge, p. 427
Ulu Ocean Grill, p. 417

$$$$

Brown's Beach House, p. 417
CanoeHouse, p. 419
KPC (Kamuela Provision Company), p. 419
Manta & Pavilion Wine Bar, p. 420

By Cuisine

PLATE LUNCH

Café 100, $, p. 423
Kaaloa's Super Js Authentic Hawaiian Food, $, p. 416
Verna's Drive-In, $, p. 426

SUSHI

Kenichi Pacific, $$, p. 413
Monstera, $$, p. 420
Norio's Japanese Steakhouse and Sushi Bar, $$$ p. 420
Sansei Seafood Restaurant & Sushi Bar, $$, p. 421

Prices in the reviews are the average cost of a main course at dinner or, if dinner is not served, at lunch.

KAILUA-KONA

$ SEAFOOD 🍴 **Bite Me Fish Market Bar & Grill.** This cool sit-down bar and grill overlooks the boat ramp at Bite Me Fish Market in Honokohau Harbor, where you can pick up some fresh fish on the way out. Sit at the outdoor picnic tables and sip a beer while watching the day's catch get hoisted from the charter boats; chances are it will end up on your plate that day. Sandwiches are named after famous fishing lures in Kona (try the Kaya Bait Fish Reuben). Fish tacos can be ordered à la carte for a couple of bucks. Breakfast includes omelets, French toast, pancakes, and burritos. [$] *Average main: $12* ✉ *Gentrys Kona Marina at Honokohau Harbor, 74-425 Kealakehe Pkwy., No. 17* ☎ *808/327–3474* 🌐 *www.bitemefishmarket.com.*

$$ HAWAIIAN 🍴 **Don the Beachcomber at the Royal Kona Resort.** The "original home of the mai tai," Don the Beachcomber features a retro, tiki-bar setting with the absolute best view of Kailua Bay in town. There is a sizeable lunch and dinner menu at the bar, but dining in the main restaurant

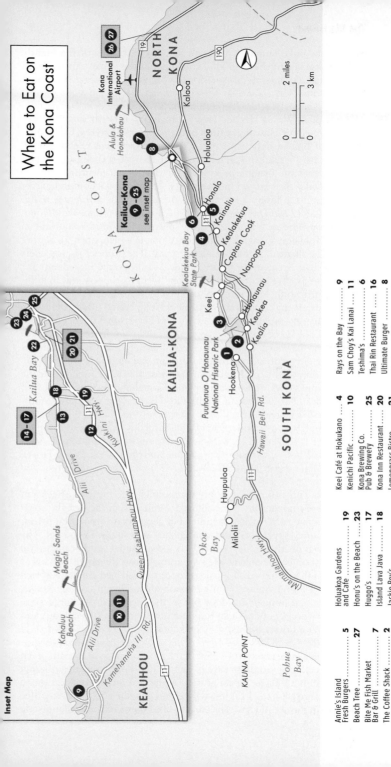

Where to Eat on the Kona Coast

Inset Map

KEAUHOU

KAILUA-KONA

Magic Sands Beach

Kahaluu Beach

Kailua Bay

Alii Drive

Kamehameha III Rd.

Queen Kaahumanu Hwy

Kuakini Hwy.

KONA COAST

NORTH KONA

Kailua-Kona
9 – 25
see inset map

Kona International Airport

Aiula & Honokohau

Kaloa

Kalaoa

Holualoa

Honalo

Kainaliu

Kealakekua

Captain Cook

Napoopoo

Kealakekua Bay State Park

Honaunau

Keokea

Kealia

Keei

Hookena

Puuhonua O Honaunau National Historic Park

SOUTH KONA

Huupuloa

Milolii

Okoe Bay

Hawaii Belt Rd.

Mamalahoa Hwy.

KAUNA POINT

Pohue Bay

0   2 miles
0   3 km

takes place only Thursday through Saturday. Try any of the nightly seafood specials or the Huli Huli chicken, but the Paniolo prime rib is the star attraction, slow roasted for flavor and tenderness. Save room for the Molten Lava Cake. $ *Average main: $20 ⊠ Royal Kona Resort, 75-5852 Alii Dr.* ☎ *808/329–3111* ⊕ *www.royalkona.com/Dining.cfm.*

$$ ✕ **Fish Hopper.** With a bayside view in the heart of Historic Kailua Vil-
SEAFOOD   lage, the open-air Hawaii location of the popular Monterey, California,
FAMILY   restaurant has an expansive menu for breakfast, lunch, and dinner, with inventive fresh-fish specials alongside the fish-and-chips and clam chowder that the original is known for. The lunch menu is tantalizing, especially the seafood pasta entrées. There's also a comprehensive wine list, plus a happy hour menu 2–6 and 8–9:30. $ *Average main: $24 ⊠ 75-5683 Alii Dr.* ☎ *808/326–2002* ⊕ *www.fishhopper.com/kona.*

$$ ✕ **Holuakoa Gardens and Cafe.** This respected slow-food restaurant in
HAWAIIAN   historic Holualoa Village features fine dining in a lush, open-air setting beneath the shade of an old monkeypod tree. The proprietors, top chefs from the Bay Area, strive to use all local and organic ingredients for such dishes as ahi succotash and chicken liver crostini toscani. In addition to serving only local meats plus vegetables harvested each morning, the restaurant makes its own organic pastas, baked goods, and desserts. $ *Average main: $20 ⊠ 76-5900 Old Government Rd., Holualoa* ☎ *808/322–2233* ⊕ *www.holuakoacafe.com* ☾ *No dinner Sun.*

$$$ ✕ **Honu's on the Beach.** Featuring al fresco dining near the sand, this is
HAWAIIAN   one of the only truly beachfront restaurants in Historic Kailua Village. Part of Courtyard King Kamehameha's Kona Beach Hotel, the venue offers prime views of Kailua Pier and Kamakahonu Bay. Steak and seafood dominate the menu, highlighted by Hawaii rancher's "natural" New York steak, fresh catch of the day, and sushi. A prime rib seafood buffet is available Friday and Saturday nights, and a breakfast buffet is served daily, with à la carte options available. $ *Average main: $28 ⊠ Courtyard King Kamehameha's Kona Beach Hotel, 75-5660 Palani Rd.* ☎ *808/329–2911* ⊕ *www.konabeachhotel.com/ dining.htm* ☾ *No lunch.*

$$$$ ✕ **Huggo's.** This is one of the only restaurants in town with prices and
HAWAIIAN   atmosphere comparable to the splurge restaurants at the Kohala Coast resorts. Dinner offerings sometimes fall short, considering the prices, but the *pupus* (appetizers) and small plates are usually a good bet. The dining lanai overlooks the rocks at the ocean's edge, and at night you can almost touch the marine life swimming below. Relax with cocktails for two and feast on fresh local seafood; the certified Angus beef is a cut above USDA Choice. If you're on a budget, **Huggo's on the Rocks,** next door, is a popular outdoor bar in the sand, and the burgers are pretty darn good, too. It's also Kailua-Kona's hot spot for cocktails and live music on Friday nights. $ *Average main: $36 ⊠ 75-5828 Kahakai Rd., off Alii Dr.* ☎ *808/329–1493* ⊕ *www.huggos.com* ☾ *No lunch.*

$ ✕ **Island Lava Java.** Open from 6:30 in the morning to 9:30 at night seven
AMERICAN   days a week, this outdoor café is one of the most popular gathering spots in Kailua Village. Order at the counter and then sit outside at one of the umbrella-shaded tables, where you can sip 100% Kona coffee and take in the ocean view. The variety-filled menu includes island-style

pancakes for breakfast, fresh-fish tacos for lunch, and braised lamb shanks or vegan cioppino for dinner, plus towering, fresh bistro salads. There are also pizzas, sandwiches, and plenty of choices for both vegetarians and meat eaters. Portions are large and most of the menu is fresh, local, and organic. For a quick snack, scones and pastries fill the display case. $ *Average main: $14* ⊠ *75-5799 Alii Dr.* ☎ *808/327–2161* ⊕ *www.islandlavajava.com.*

$$ ✕ **Jackie Rey's Ohana Grill.** This brightly decorated, open-air restaurant
AMERICAN is a favorite lunch and dinner destination of visitors and residents,
FAMILY thanks to generous portions and a nice variety of chef's specials, steaks, and seafood dishes. Meals pair well with selections from Jackie Rey's well-rounded wine list. The lunchtime menu offers great value on items like beer-battered fish-and-chips, a barbecued kalua-pork sandwich, and guava-glazed baby-back ribs. On the lighter side, inventive salads keep it healthy but flavorful. $ *Average main: $23* ⊠ *Pottery Terrace, 75-5995 Kuakini Hwy.* ☎ *808/327–0209* ⊕ *www.jackiereys.com* ☉ *No lunch weekends.*

$ ✕ **Kanaka Kava.** This is a popular local hangout, and not just because
HAWAIIAN the kava makes you mellow. (Used for relaxation, organic kava root is harvested on the Hamakua Coast and transformed into a traditional, slightly bitter brew.) The Hawaiian proprietors also serve traditional Hawaiian food, including fresh poke; bowls of smoky, pulled kalua pork; and healthy organic greens, available in fairly large portions for less than you'll pay elsewhere. In addition, the restaurant offers fresh-fish plates, *opihi* (limpets), vegetarian options, and even traditional Hawaiian *laulau* (pork wrapped in taro leaves and steamed). Seating is at a premium, but don't be afraid to share a table and make friends. $ *Average main: $12* ⊠ *Coconut Grove Marketplace, 75-5803 Alii Dr., Space B6* ☎ *808/327–1660* ⊕ *www.kanakakava.com.*

$$ ✕ **Kenichi Pacific.** With black-lacquer tables and lipstick-red banquettes,
JAPANESE Kenichi offers a more sophisticated dining atmosphere than what's normally found in Kona. Its shopping center location feels like a secret, but it's worth seeking out. This is where residents go when they feel like splurging on top-notch sushi and steak. It's a little on the pricey side, but you'll leave feeling satisfied. The signature rolls are inventive, especially the always-popular Dynamite Shrimp. To save a buck or two, go early for happy hour (5 to 6:30 pm daily), when all sushi rolls are half price, or hang out in the cocktail lounge, where menu items average $6. $ *Average main: $25* ⊠ *Keauhou Shopping Center, 78-6831 Alii Dr., D-125* ☎ *808/322–6400* ⊕ *www.kenichirestaurants.com* ☉ *No lunch. Closed Mon.*

$ ✕ **Kona Brewing Co. Pub & Brewery.** This ultra-popular destination with
AMERICAN outdoor patio features an excellent and varied menu, including pulled-
Fodor's Choice pork quesadillas, gourmet pizzas, and a killer spinach salad with Gor-
★ gonzola cheese, macadamia nuts, and strawberries. The best bet for lunch or dinner is the veggie slice and salad for under $8—the garden salad is generous and the pizza is the best in town. The beer-tasting menu offers a choice of four of the eight available microbrews in miniature glasses that add up to about two regular-size mugs for the price

of one. The Hefeweizen is excellent. If you're staying in town, purchase beer to go in a half-gallon jug ("growler") filled on-site from the brewery's own taps. The Growler Shack also sells beer by the keg. $ *Average main: $12* ⊠ *75-5629 Kuakini Hwy., off Kaiwi St. at end of Pawai Pl.* ☎ *808/329–2739* ⊕ *www.konabrewingco.com.*

$$ ✗ **Kona Inn Restaurant.** This vintage open-air restaurant offers a beautiful, oceanfront setting on Kailua Bay. It's a great place to have a mai tai and some appetizers while watching the sunset, or to enjoy a calamari sandwich, clam chowder, or salad at lunch. Dinner is also available, but the entrées are less than stellar and for the prices there are better options once the sun disappears. $ *Average main: $20* ⊠ *75-5744 Alii Dr.* ☎ *808/329–4455* ⊕ *www.windandsearestaurants.com.*

AMERICAN

$ ✗ **Lemongrass Bistro.** This well-kept secret occupies a small but upscale venue near the Kona Inn Shopping Village. The Asian-fusion menu—everything is made to order—includes Thai, Vietnamese, Japanese, Laotian, and Filipino. Although dishes are presented with resort flair (the proprietor is a former resort chef, and there's a second location at Queens' MarketPlace at Waikoloa Beach Resort), entrées average an afforable $14, with appetizers for $7. Best bets are the ono sashimi and the grilled marinated chicken salad with crispy wonton. This is one of the few restaurants in town open until 11 pm. $ *Average main: $14* ⊠ *75-5742 Kuakini Hwy., Suite 103, across from library* ☎ *808/331–2708* ⊕ *lemongrass-bistro.webs.com.*

ASIAN

$ ✗ **Quinn's Almost by the Sea.** With the bar in the front and the dining patio in the back, Quinn's may seem like a bit of a dive at first glance, but this venerable restaurant serves up the best darn cheeseburger and fries in town. Appropriate for families, the restaurant stays busy for lunch and dinner, while the bar attracts a cast of colorful regulars. The menu has many tasty options, such as fish-and-chips, meat loaf, and beef tenderloin tips. If time gets away from you on a drive to the north beaches, Quinn's, which stays open until 11, awaits your return with a cheap beer and a basket of fried calamari. Drinks are strong—no watered-down cocktails here. Breakfast is sometimes served during football season. ■TIP→ **Park across the street at the Courtyard King Kamehameha's Kona Beach Hotel and get free one-hour parking with validation.** $ *Average main: $15* ⊠ *75-5655 Palani Rd.* ☎ *808/329–3822* ⊕ *quinnsalmostbythesea.com.*

AMERICAN

$$ ✗ **Rays on the Bay.** The Sheraton Kona's signature restaurant overlooks Keauhou Bay, offering nighttime views of the native manta rays that appear nightly beneath the balcony. The dinner menu includes surf and turf, fresh catch, and salads, plus seafood appetizers like sushi rolls and poke. Sit next to one of the many fire pits and soak up the starlit atmosphere. $ *Average main: $25* ⊠ *Sheraton Kona Resort & Spa, 78-128 Ehukai St.* ☎ *808/930–4949* ⊕ *www.raysonthebay.com* ⚐ *Reservations not accepted* ☉ *No lunch.*

SOUTH PACIFIC

$$ ✗ **Sam Choy's Kai Lanai.** Celebrity chef Sam Choy has transformed an old Wendy's perched on a bluff above a shopping center into a beautiful open-air restaurant with a bar that looks like a charter-fishing boat. Granite-topped tables offer ocean views from every seat. Open for lunch and dinner (and breakfast on weekends only), the venue

HAWAIIAN

presents reasonably priced entrées, highlighted by macadamia-nut-crusted chicken, Oriental lamb chops, and Sam's trio of fish served with shiitake-mushroom cream sauce. The ahi salad (served in a deep-fried flour tortilla bowl) is a great deal for $14. *Keiki* (children's) menus accommodate families, and yes, the restaurant can be noisy. Parking is at a premium, so you might have to park in the shopping center below, or opt for valet service. **■TIP→ Arrive at 5 pm to nab the best patio seating.** [$] *Average main: $22* ✉ *Keauhou Shopping Center, 78-6831 Alii Dr., Suite 1000* ☎ *808/333–3434* 🌐 *www.samchoy.com.*

$ THAI 🍴 **Thai Rin Restaurant.** This dependable restaurant adjacent to Island Lava Java on Alii Drive offers an excellent selection of Thai food at decent prices. Everything is cooked to order, and the menu is brimming with choices, including five curries, a green-papaya salad, and a popular platter that combines spring rolls, satay, beef salad, and *tom yum* (lemongrass soup). For a real treat, try the deep-fried fish. Piña colada fans appreciate the excellent cocktails here, and you can't beat the beautiful view of Kailua Bay. Indoor and outdoor seating is available. [$] *Average main: $11* ✉ *75-5799 Alii Dr.* ☎ *808/329–2929* 🌐 *www.aliisunsetplaza.com.*

$ DINER 🍴 **Ultimate Burger.** Located in a Sports Authority shopping complex, this excellent burger joint may look like a chain, but it's an independent, locally owned and operated eatery that serves 100% organic, grass-fed Big Island beef on buns locally made. Be sure to order a side of seasoned Big Daddy fries served with house-made aioli dipping sauce. [$] *Average main: $8* ✉ *Kona Commons Shopping Center, 74-5450 Makala Blvd.* ☎ *808/329–2326.*

$$ JAPANESE 🍴 **Wasabi's.** A tiny place hidden in the back of the Coconut Grove Marketplace on Alii Drive, Wasabi's features indoor and outdoor seating. Prices may seem steep, but the fish is of the highest quality, highlighted by a large selection of rolls and authentic Japanese offerings, along with a few unique inventions. And for those who prefer their seafood cooked, teriyaki, udon, and sukiyaki options abound. The restaurant has recently unveiled a beer garden. [$] *Average main: $18* ✉ *Coconut Grove Marketplace, 75-5803 Alii Dr.* ☎ *808/326–2352* 🌐 *www.wasabishawaii.com.*

4

THE KONA COAST

SOUTH KONA

$ MODERN AMERICAN 🍴 **Annie's Island Fresh Burgers.** At the best Upcountry burger restaurant in Kona, the burgers are made of succulent, 100% island-raised beef. Leather couches, hardwood floors, artwork, and live trees growing through the floor and up through the roof create a casual yet well-appointed feel. The homemade sauces are excellent, as are the onion rings and basil french fries. [$] *Average main: $13* ✉ *Mango Court, 79-7460 Hawaii Belt Rd. #105, Kainaliu* ☎ *808/324–6000.*

$ AMERICAN 🍴 **The Coffee Shack.** Visitors enjoy stopping here for breakfast or lunch after a morning of snorkeling at Kealakekua Bay, and for good reason: the views of the Honaunau coast from this roadside restaurant are stunning. Breads are all homemade, and you get to choose your favorite when ordering a generously sized sandwich brimming with

Black Forest ham and the like. If you're in the mood for a Hawaiian smoothie, iced honey-mocha latte, scone, or homemade luau bread, it's worth the detour, even though the parking lot can be tricky to maneuver. $ *Average main: $11* ⊠ *83-5799 Mamalahoa Hwy., Captain Cook* ☎ *808/328–9555* ⊕ *www.coffeeshack.com* ☉ *No dinner.*

$ ✕ **Kaaloa's Super Js Authentic Hawaiian Food.** It figures that the best *lau-*

HAWAIIAN   *lau* (meat wrapped in taro leaves and ti) in West Hawaii can be found at a roadside hole-in-the-wall rather than at an expensive resort luau. In fact, this humble family-run eatery was featured on the *Food Network*'s "The Best Thing I Ever Ate." Plate lunches "to go" include tender chicken or pork laulau, steamed for up to 10 hours. The kalua pig and cabbage is delicious, and the *lomilomi* salmon features vine-ripened tomatoes. Owners John and Janice Kaaloa grind their own poi sourced from taro in Hilo and Waipio. $ *Average main: $7* ⊠ *83-5409 Mamalahoa Hwy., between mile markers 106 and 107, Honaunau* ☎ *808/328–9566* ▤ *No credit cards* ☉ *Closed Sun.*

$$ ✕ **Keei Café at Hokukano.** This beautiful restaurant, perched above the

ECLECTIC   highway just 15 minutes south of Kailua-Kona, serves delicious dinners with Brazilian, Asian, and European flavors highlighting fresh ingredients from local farmers. Favorites are the Brazilian seafood chowder or peanut-miso salad, followed by pasta primavera smothered with a basil-pesto sauce. There's an extensive wine list. Bob Miyashiro, the owner, is a Kona native, and his wife, Gina, is Brazilian. A husband-and-wife cooking team, also from Brazil, have been with the restaurant since its humble beginnings at its previous location in Honaunau. Toast your friendly hosts with a refreshing mojito before dinner. $ *Average main: $20* ⊠ *79-7511 Mamalahoa Hwy., ½ mile south of Kainaliu, Kealakekua* ☎ *808/322–9992* ⊕ *www.keeicafe.net* ⟁ *Reservations essential* ▤ *No credit cards* ☉ *Closed Sun. and Mon. No lunch.*

$$ ✕ **Mi's Italian Bistro.** This steady presence in the South Kona dining scene

ITALIAN   is a friendly, white-tablecloth establishment in a hole-in-the-wall location next to a liquor store on the mountain (*mauka*) side of Highway 11. The restaurant's husband-and-wife owners prepare homemade pastas and focaccia daily. Specials are always delicious and usually include lasagna, focaccia, and risotto. The homemade herb-cheese ravioli is rich and savory, and even the salad options are a notch above, with ingredients such as candied macadamia nuts, roasted beets, and sautéed haricots verts. Homemade desserts are worth saving room for, particularly the banana-rum flambé. $ *Average main: $18* ⊠ *81-6372 Mamalahoa Hwy., Kealakekua* ☎ *808/323–3880* ⊕ *www.misitalianbistro.com* ☉ *No lunch.*

$ ✕ **Teshima's.** Locals gather at this small, historic restaurant 15 minutes

JAPANESE   south of Kailua-Kona whenever they're in the mood for fresh sashimi, puffy shrimp tempura, or *hekka* (beef and vegetables cooked in an iron pot) at a reasonable price. Teshima's doesn't look like much, inside or out, but it's been a *kamaaina* (local) favorite since 1929 for a reason. You might want to try *teishoku* (tray) No. 3, featuring sashimi, tempura, sukiyaki beef, rice, miso soup, and sunomono, or order the popular bento box lunch. Service is laid-back and friendly. Open for breakfast, lunch, and dinner, the restaurant has been family owned and operated by five generations of Teshimas. $ *Average main: $15* ✉ *79-7251 Mamalahoa Hwy., Honalo* ☎ *808/322–9140.*

NORTH KONA

$$$ ✕ **Beach Tree at the Four Seasons Resort Hualalai.** This beautifully designed
MODERN ITALIAN   venue provides a relaxed and elegant setting for alfresco dining near the
FAMILY   sand, with its boardwalk-style deck, outdoor seating under the trellis,
Fodor's Choice   and enormous vaulted ceiling. Chef Nick Mastrascusa is a transplant
★   from the Four Seasons Hotel New York, bringing Italian and Spanish
influences to his inventive menu. Outstanding entrées include the seafood paella for two and the grilled rib eye with shoestring fries. The
tropical Peletini martini is a favorite, and at dinner, the premium wine
list includes the Beach Tree's own signature reds and whites. There's
also a great children's menu and chalkboard placemats for kids to play
with. Live Hawaiian music is featured nightly. $ *Average main: $35*
✉ *Four Seasons Resort Hualalai, 72-100 Kaupulehu Dr.* ☎ *808/325–8000* ⊕ *www.fourseasons.com/hualalai.*

$$$ ✕ **Ulu Ocean Grill and Sushi Lounge at the Four Seasons Resort Hualalai.**
MODERN   Replacing the flagship Pahuia, this artfully renovated restaurant has the
HAWAIIAN   same spectacular oceanfront setting with a more casual dining experi-
Fodor's Choice   ence that highlights locally grown products. Breakfast can be à la carte
★   or buffet, but nighttime is when the magic happens, starting with an
impressive wine program that includes boutique wines and world-class
imports. Diverse menu choices—from roasted beet salad and corn-and-
coconut soup to Big Island wild boar served with poha berry chutney,
Kona lobster pad thai, and local grass-fed tenderloin—make deciding
what to order a challenge. There's also a full sushi menu. Reserve a table
on the patio and you may spot whales while dining. $ *Average main:
$35* ✉ *Four Seasons Resort Hualalai, 72-100 Kaupulehu Dr., North
Kona* ☎ *808/325–8000* ⊕ *www.fourseasons.com/hualalai* ☻ *No lunch.*

THE KOHALA COAST

$$ ✕ **Bamboo Restaurant.** This popular restaurant in the heart of Hawi pro-
ASIAN   vides a historic setting in which to enjoy a menu brimming with Hawai-
ian country flair. Creative entrées feature fresh island fish prepared
several ways. Try the seafood dish with sesame ginger, chili broth, garlic,
shiitake mushrooms, and Asian noodles; it's best accompanied with a
passion-fruit margarita or passion-fruit iced tea. Bamboo accents, bold
local artwork, and an old unfinished wooden floor make the restau-
rant cozy. Sunday brunch includes omelets, *pupu* (appetizers), salads,
and sandwiches. Local musicians entertain on Friday or Saturday, and
drinks and *pupu* are discounted during Tuesday to Thursday happy
hours, from 4 to 6. $ *Average main: $25* ✉ *55-3415 Akoni Pule Hwy.
(Hwy. 270), Hawi* ☎ *808/889–5555* ⊕ *www.bamboorestaurant.info*
☻ *Closed Mon. No dinner Sun.*

$$$$ ✕ **Brown's Beach House at the Fairmont Orchid Hawaii.** Nestled alongside the
MODERN   resort's sandy bay, Brown's Beach House offers beautiful sunset dining
HAWAIIAN   and innovative cuisine. Attention to detail is evident in the sophisti-
Fodor's Choice   cated menu, like the Alae salt-roasted filet mignon served with kabocha
★   pumpkin mash and truffle foie gras demi-glace. Seafood lovers might

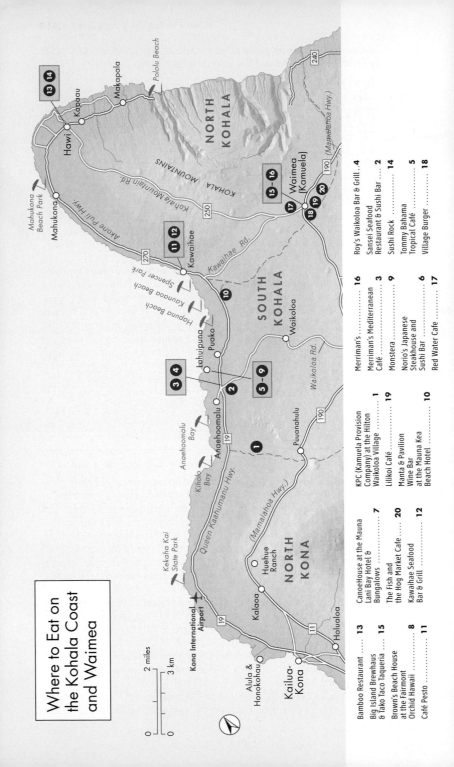

Where to Eat on the Kohala Coast and Waimea

2 miles

3 km

Bamboo Restaurant **13**

Big Island Brewhaus
& Tako Taco Taqueria **15**

Brown's Beach House
at the Fairmont
Orchid Hawaii **8**

Café Pesto **11**

CanoeHouse at the Mauna
Lani Bay Hotel &
Bungalows **7**

The Fish and
the Hog Market Cafe **20**

Kawaihae Seafood
Bar & Grill **12**

KPC (Kamuela Provision
Company) at the Hilton
Waikoloa Village **1**

Lilikoi Café **19**

Manta & Pavilion
Wine Bar
at the Mauna Kea
Beach Hotel **10**

Merriman's **16**

Merriman's Mediterranean
Café **3**

Monstera **9**

Norio's Japanese
Steakhouse and
Sushi Bar **6**

Red Water Cafe **17**

Roy's Waikoloa Bar & Grill ..**4**

Sansei Seafood
Restaurant & Sushi Bar **2**

Sushi Rock **14**

Tommy Bahama
Tropical Café **5**

Village Burger **18**

like the crab-crusted Kona kampachi or the Sustainable Seafood Trio, featuring fresh catch from the Kona Coast. The menu includes choices that accommodate diet-specific preferences such as macrobiotic, raw, vegan, gluten-free, and diabetic—amazingly, these offerings are as flavorful and inventive as everything else on the main menu. $\boxed{\$}$ *Average main: $40 ⊠ Fairmont Orchid Hawaii, 1 N. Kaniku Dr., Kohala Coast* ☎ *808/885–2000* ⊕ *www.fairmont.com/orchid* ☾ *No lunch.*

$$ ✕ **Café Pesto.** In the sleepy harbor town of Kawaihae, the original Café
ITALIAN   Pesto ranks as a hidden find. Gourmet, wood-fired pizzas are topped with eclectic goodies like pork and pineapple, chili-grilled shrimp, shiitake mushrooms, and cilantro crème fraîche. The menu also includes Asian-inspired pastas and risottos, fresh-fish entrées, and an excellent array of salads, including the Volcano Mist, garnished with crisp, local onion rings. Local brews and a full-service bar make this a good place to end the evening, and the lounge-y bar area with sofas and comfy chairs provides a nice place to grab a drink while waiting for a table. $\boxed{\$}$ *Average main: $25 ⊠ Kawaihae Harbor Shopping Center, 61-3665 Akoni Pule Hwy. (Hwy. 270), Kawaihae* ☎ *808/882–1071* ⊕ *www. cafepesto.com.*

$$$$ ✕ **CanoeHouse at the Mauna Lani Bay Hotel & Bungalows.** This landmark
ECLECTIC   restaurant near the ocean showcases the inventive cuisine of Chef Allen
Fodor's Choice   Hess, who previously worked at the famed Merriman's restaurant in
★   Waimea. The progressive menu—divided into the categories of Farmer, Fisherman, and Rancher—draws its influences from locally grown and raised products including grass-fed beef, lamb, fresh catch, shellfish, and homemade sausage and bacon. For appetizers, try the goat tacos served in a crispy bao bun. The Hawaii ranchers tenderloin is a good bet for a main course, as is the furikaki-crusted ono served tataki style. Each table has its own iPad that features a wine list to peruse by touchscreen. Adjacent to the restaurant, The Lounge at the CanoeHouse presents chef's bites, desserts, and signature cocktails from 5:30 to 9. A customized dining program is offered at the Captain's Table. $\boxed{\$}$ *Average main: $42 ⊠ Mauna Lani Bay Hotel & Bungalows, 68-1400 Mauna Lani Dr., Kohala Coast* ☎ *808/885–6622* ⊕ *www.maunalani.com* ☾ *No lunch.*

$$ ✕ **Kawaihae Seafood Bar & Grill.** Upstairs in a structure that dates from
SEAFOOD   the 1850s, this seafood bar has been a hot spot since it opened in 2003, serving up a dynamite and well-priced bar menu with tasty *pupu* (appetizers), and an always expanding dinner menu that includes at least four fresh-fish specials daily. There's fare for landlubbers, too, including boneless braised short ribs, rib-eye steak, specialty pizza, and lots of salad options. Don't miss the escargot, oysters Rockefeller, and ginger steamed clams. At lunch, the menu ranges from sandwiches and burgers to sashimi and poke. Happy hour runs daily from 3 to 6 pm, and again from 10:30 pm until closing (midnight). If you've got the late-night munchies, this is a great spot—food is served until 11. $\boxed{\$}$ *Average main: $19 ⊠ 61-3642 Kawaihae Harbor, Hwy. 270, Kawaihae* ☎ *808/880–9393* ⊕ *www.seafoodbargrill.com.*

$$$$ ✕ **KPC (Kamuela Provision Company) at the Hilton Waikoloa Village.** The
MODERN   breezy lanai has the most spectacular view of the leeward coast of any
HAWAIIAN   restaurant on the Big Island. Get here by 5:30 if you want to score a seat

4

for the sunset. It's the perfect accompaniment to the elegant yet down-to-earth Hawaii regional cuisine. Specialty cocktails, like the mango martini, are great, too. Entrées are on the pricey side, but the ginger-steamed *monchong* (a deep-water Hawaiian fish) is a winner. Among appetizers, the ahi carpaccio does not disappoint. The restaurant's number-one seller is the Kona Coffee Mud Slide, but the Baked Mauna Kea (KPC's take on a baked Alaska) is equally decadent. $ *Average main: $36 ✉ Hilton Waikoloa Village, 69-425 Waikoloa Beach Dr., Waikoloa ☎ 808/886–1234 ⊕ www.hiltonwaikoloavillage.com ⊗ No lunch.*

$$$$
MODERN
HAWAIIAN

✗ **Manta & Pavilion Wine Bar at the Mauna Kea Beach Hotel.** Perched on the edge of a bluff overlooking the sparkling waters of Kaunaoa Beach, the resort's flagship restaurant is a compelling spot for a romantic meal at sunset, especially at one of the outside tables. The Enomatic wine system lets guests sample 48 wines by the glass—from rare dessert wines and ports to premier wines from France, Italy, and Argentina. Executive Chef Peter Pahk's take on Hawaii regional cuisine includes Kona kampachi prepared with black-sesame miso sauce, Japanese apricot oil, and baby arugula salad. Waimea tomatoes, Puna goat cheese, and rainbow chard from a nearby farm are some of the locally grown ingredients. Among Sunday brunch's impressive spread are an omelet station, prime rib, smoked salmon, tempura, lobster bisque, and a build-your-own-sundae bar. $ *Average main: $40 ✉ Mauna Kea Beach Hotel, 62-100 Mauna Kea Beach Dr., Kohala Coast ☎ 808/882–5707 ⊕ www.maunakeabeachhotel.com ⊗ No lunch. No dinner Sun. and Mon.*

$$
MEDITERRANEAN

✗ **Merriman's Mediterranean Café.** From Peter Merriman, one of Hawaii's star chefs, comes a more affordable alternative to his upscale Waimea, Kauai, and Maui restaurants. The Mediterranean-influenced menu includes a variety of pasta dishes, tasty appetizers, and salads teeming with fresh ingredients from nearby Waimea farms. The outdoor patio beckons locals and visitors alike. It's open daily for lunch, followed by happy hour from 3 to 5:30 and dinner until 9. $ *Average main: $25 ✉ Kings' Shops at Waikoloa Beach Resort, 250 Waikoloa Beach Dr., Waikoloa ☎ 808/886–1700 ⊕ www.merrimanshawaii.com/mediterranean-cafe.*

$$
JAPANESE
FAMILY

✗ **Monstera.** It may not be beachfront with a view of the sunset, but this Shops at Mauna Lani eatery is worth a visit for its sophisticated Japanese pub food with a touch of local inspiration. Chef Norio Yamamoto's dinner menu includes his signature Original 69 Roll with Dungeness crab. There are excellent sizzling plate items like short ribs and New York steak, hot and cold noodle dishes, and, of course, outstanding sushi. Most people make a meal out of sharing several small-plate items to sample a bit of everything. For dessert, a tempura banana is drizzled with chocolate and caramel. The *keiki* (children's) menu has chicken nuggets and udon noodles. It's best to make a reservation; you can also get some of the menu to go. $ *Average main: $25 ✉ The Shops at Mauna Lani, 68-1330 Mauna Lani Dr., Waikoloa ☎ 808/887–2711 ⊕ www.monserasushi.com ⊗ No lunch.*

$$$
JAPANESE
Fodor's Choice
★

✗ **Norio's Japanese Steakhouse and Sushi Bar.** On the garden level of the Fairmont Orchid, this restaurant and Chef Darren Ogasawara's cuisine appeal to both steak and seafood lovers, from Australian A6 Wagyu rib eye (seasoned with five different kinds of Hawaiian sea salt) to hamachi-and-avocado sashimi served with ponzu-garlic sauce. Dry-aged meats from Kulana Farms are served on cedar planks, while free-range chicken and sustainably caught Hawaiian seafood round out the offerings. Everything is made from scratch, including the sauces, and the fish is as fresh as it gets. Special dietary considerations are accommodated; the gluten-free vegetable tempura and soy-free udon noodle are as flavorful as the originals. $ *Average main: $35* ✉ *Fairmont Orchid Hawaii, 1 N. Kaniku Dr., Kohala Coast* ☎ *808/885–2000* ⊕ *www.fairmont.com/ orchid* ☾ *Closed Tues. and Wed. No lunch.*

$$$

MODERN HAWAIIAN

✕ **Roy's Waikoloa Bar & Grill.** Overlooking the lake at the Kings' Shops is, granted, not an oceanfront setting, but if you're staying nearby and are looking for decent food, this place fits the bill. In the mood for a light meal? Choose from the enormous selection of great appetizers, paired with something from the extensive wine-by-the-glass list. The three-course meal is a good bet, as is the butterfish or Szechwan ribs, a melt-in-your mouth encounter. The menu changes nightly and has a lot of specials, like ancho-chili-pepper seared sea scallops and grilled Hawaiian ono taco. $ *Average main: $30* ✉ *Kings' Shops at Waikoloa Village, 250 Waikoloa Beach Dr., Kohala Coast* ☎ *808/886–4321* ⊕ *www.roysrestaurant.com* ☾ *No lunch.*

$$

JAPANESE

✕ **Sansei Seafood Restaurant & Sushi Bar.** Heavenly interpretations of sushi and contemporary Asian cuisine are created by famed Hawaii chef D. K. Kodama. More than a few dishes have won awards, including the shrimp dynamite in a creamy garlic masago aioli and unagi glaze, and the panko-crusted ahi sashimi sushi roll. Though it has tried-and-true mainstays, the menu is consistently updated to include new and exciting options, such as the Hawaiian *moi* sashimi rolls and the Japanese yellowtail nori aioli poke. You can certainly make a meal out of appetizers and sushi rolls, but Sansei's entrées, from both land and sea, are great. On Sunday and Monday from 5 to 6 pm, selected menu items are half off (limited seating; first come, first served). Or opt for a late-night meal on Friday and Saturday, when sushi and appetizers are half off from 9:30 until midnight, though you may have to put up with karaoke singers (21 and older). $ *Average main: $20* ✉ *201 Waikoloa Beach Dr., 801 Queens' MarketPlace, Waikoloa* ☎ *808/886–6286* ⊕ *www. sanseihawaii.com* ☾ *No lunch.*

$$

JAPANESE

Fodor's Choice

★

✕ **Sushi Rock.** Located in historic Hawi Town, Sushi Rock isn't big on size—its narrow dining room is brightly painted and casually decorated with Hawaiian and Japanese knickknacks—but discerning locals and *akamai* (in-the-know) visitors come here for some of the island's best sushi. The restaurant prides itself on using local ingredients like grass-fed beef tenderloin, goat cheese, macadamia nuts, and mango in the island-inspired sushi rolls. It also serves up a variety of cooked seafood, chicken, noodle dishes, sandwiches, and salads for lunch and dinner. Everything is plated beautifully and served either at the sushi bar, at one of the handful of indoor tables, or on the covered front patio. Vegetarian, gluten-free, and vegan items are available, and a full bar even has house-infused vodka. $ *Average main: $23* ✉ *55-3435 Akoni Pule Hwy., Hawi* ☎ *808/889–5900* ⊕ *sushirockrestaurant.net.*

4

$$$ MODERN HAWAIIAN 🍴 **Tommy Bahama Tropical Café.** This breezy, open-air restaurant, located upstairs at the Shops at Mauna Lani, offers an excellent roster of appetizers, including seared-scallop sliders and coconut-crusted crab cakes. The chef here has freedom to cook up his own daily specials, and the miso-marinated kampachi is a standout. Other entrées include rustic chicken pasta and crab-stuffed shrimp. Homemade breads and creamy butters set the stage for a nice meal, which most definitely should include one of Tommy's outstanding martinis, the tastiest and strongest anywhere on the island. Desserts are decadent and meant for sharing. There's live music every evening. [$] *Average main: $34* ✉ *The Shops at Mauna Lani, 68-1330 Mauna Lani Dr., No. 102, Kohala Coast* ☎ *808/881–8686* 🌐 *www.tommybahama.com.*

WAIMEA

$ MEXICAN 🍴 **Big Island Brewhaus & Tako Taco Taqueria.** Tako Taco has always been a favorite Waimea eatery, and owner Tom Kerns is a veteran brewer who's now churning out some decent ales, lagers, and specialty beers from his on-site brewery. With a focus on fresh ingredients, Tako Taco whips up excellent tacos, burritos, Mexican salads, enchiladas, rellenos, and quesadillas fresh to order. You'll want refills on the habanero salsa, perhaps accompanied by a top-shelf margarita, either classic or *lilikoi* (passion fruit). And nothing beats a cold local brew to wash down that spicy enchilada. [$] *Average main: $11* ✉ *64-1066A Mamalahoa Hwy.* ☎ *808/887–1717* 🌐 *www.bigislandbrewhaus.com.*

$ ECLECTIC 🍴 **The Fish and the Hog Market Cafe.** Formerly Huli Sue's, this casual little restaurant along the highway serves up generous sandwiches, salads, and melt-in-your-mouth barbecue items, including kiawe-smoked meat like ribs, pork ribs, and brisket. Additional options range from pupu platters, chowders, and crayfish boils to salads made with produce grown in Waimea and a variety of seafood pasta dishes. Because the owners are fisherpeople, the ceviche and poke use fish caught from their boat. The on-site market sells fresh fish, homemade sausage, and freshly made salad dressings and sauces. [$] *Average main: $15* ✉ *64-957 Mamalahoa Hwy. (Hwy. 11)* ☎ *808/885–6268* 🌐 *www.thefishandthehog.com.*

$ EUROPEAN 🍴 **Lilikoi Café.** This gem of a café is tucked away in the back of the Parker Ranch Center. Locals love that it's hard to find because they want to keep its delicious breakfast crepes, freshly made soups, and croissants Waimea's little secret. Owner and chef John Lorda creates an impressive selection of salad choices daily, including chicken curry, beet, fava bean, chicken pesto, and Mediterranean pasta. The Israeli couscous with tomato, red onion, cranberry, and basil is a hit, as is the half avocado stuffed with tuna salad. There's also a nice selection of sandwiches and hot entrées. The food is fresh, many of the ingredients are organic, and everything is homemade. [$] *Average main: $9* ✉ *Parker Ranch Center, 67-1185 Mamalahoa Hwy. (Hwy. 11)* ☎ *808/887–1400* 🕓 *Closed Sun. No dinner.*

$$$$ MODERN HAWAIIAN 🍴 **Merriman's.** Among the best restaurants in Upcountry Waimea, this is the signature restaurant of Peter Merriman, one of the pioneers of Hawaii Regional Cuisine. Merriman's is the home of the original

wok-charred ahi: it's seared on the outside and sashimi on the inside. If you prefer meat, try the Kahua Ranch braised lamb, raised locally to the restaurant's specifications, or the prime bone-in New York steak, grilled to order. The extensive wine list is impressive and includes many selections poured by the glass. Although lunch prices are reasonable, dinner is "resort pricey," so prepare to splurge. $ *Average main: $45* ✉ *Opelo Plaza, 65-1227 Opelo Rd.* ☎ *808/885–6822* ⊕ *www.merrimanshawaii. com* ⌖ *Reservations essential* ⊘ *No lunch weekends.*

$$$
ECLECTIC
FAMILY

✕ **Red Water Cafe.** Chef David Abraham has transformed the former Fujimamas into a place for Hawaiian café food with a twist. The specialty is "multicultural cuisine," like a Thai Caesar salad with crispy calamari croutons that is big enough to share. There's a full sushi bar as well. The Fuji roll has shrimp, ahi, crab, avocado, and cucumber, tempura-battered and deep-fried. Wash it all down with the signature saketini. Lunch is a great bet here, too, with a build-your-own *saimin* (broth with noodles), huge Cobb salad, and juicy 8-ounce burger with lots of fixings. This place is popular among locals and is a nice spot for the whole family—the kids' menu was developed by Abraham's eight-year-old daughter. $ *Average main: $30* ✉ *65-1299 Kawaihae Rd.* ☎ *808/885–9299* ⊕ *www.redwater-cafe.com* ⊘ *Closed Sun.*

$
AMERICAN
Fodor'sChoice
★

✕ **Village Burger.** This little eatery brings a whole new meaning to gourmet hamburgers. It serves up locally raised, grass-fed, hormone-free beef that is ground fresh, hand-shaped daily on-site, and grilled to perfection right before your eyes. Top your burger (be it ahi, veal, Kahua Ranch Wagyu beef, Hamakua mushroom, or Waipio taro) with everything from local avocados, baby greens, and chipotle goat cheese to tomato marmalade. Even the ice cream for the milkshakes is made in Waimea, and the delicious brioche buns that house the juicy burgers are baked fresh in nearby Hawi. $ *Average main: $10* ✉ *Parker Ranch Center, 67-1185 Mamalahoa Hwy.* ☎ *808/885–7319* ⊕ *www. villageburgerwaimea.com.*

HILO

$
HAWAIIAN
FAMILY

✕ **Café 100.** Established in 1948, this family-owned restaurant is famous for its tasty loco moco, prepared in more than three-dozen ways, and its dirt-cheap breakfast and lunch specials. (You can stuff yourself for $3 if you order right.) The word "restaurant," or even "café," is used liberally here—you order at a window and eat on one of the outdoor benches provided—but you come here for the food, prices, and authentic, old Hilo experience. $ *Average main: $6* ✉ *969 Kilauea Ave.* ☎ *808/935– 8683* ⊕ *www.cafe100.com* ⊘ *Closed Sun.*

$$
ITALIAN
Fodor'sChoice
★

✕ **Café Pesto.** Located in a beautiful and historic venue, Café Pesto offers exotic pizzas (with fresh Hamakua mushrooms, artichokes, and rosemary Gorgonzola sauce, for example), Asian-inspired pastas and risottos, fresh seafood, delicious salads, and appetizers you can make a meal of. Products from local farmers feature heavily on the menu— Kulana free-range beef, Kawamata Farms tomatoes, and Kapoho Farms lehua-blossom honey are all made on the island. Local musicians provide entertainment at dinner Wednesday through Sunday. On the island's west side, another Café Pesto is located above Kawaihae

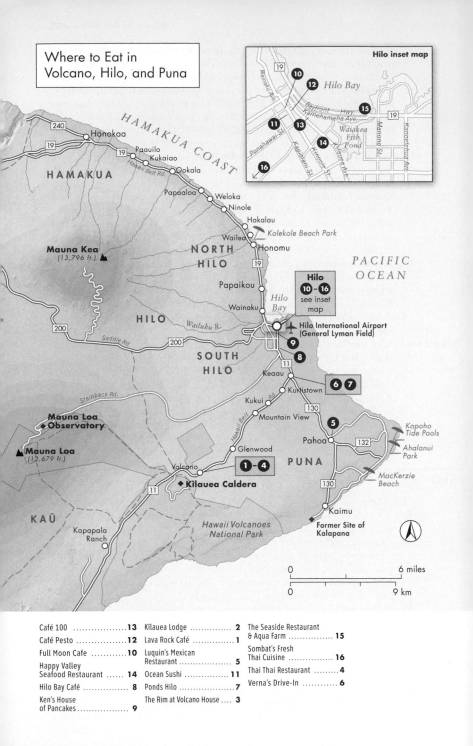

Where to Eat in Volcano, Hilo, and Puna

Hilo inset map

Hilo Bay

Bayfront Kamehameha Ave.

Waiākea Fish Pond

Wainaku Ave.

Ponahawai St.

Kapiolani St.

Kilauea Ave.

Kinoole St.

Manono St.

Kamoleolua Ave.

HAMAKUA COAST

240
Honokaa
19
Paauilo
Kukaiao
Ookala
Hawai'i Belt Rd.

HAMAKUA

Papaaloa
Weloka
Ninole
Hakalau
Wailea
Kolekole Beach Park
Honomu

Mauna Kea
(13,796 ft.)

NORTH HILO
19

PACIFIC OCEAN

Papaikou

Hilo Bay

Wainaku

200

HILO

Wailuku R.

Saddle Rd.

200

SOUTH HILO

Keaau

Hilo
10 – 16
see inset map

Hilo International Airport
(General Lyman Field)

9
8
11

6 7

Stainback Rd.

Kukui
Kurtistown

Mauna Loa
Observatory

Kukui
Mountain View
130

Kapoho Tide Pools

Mauna Loa
(13,679 ft.)

Glenwood

Hawai'i Belt Rd.

5
Pahoa

132

Ahalanui Park

Volcano
1 – 4

PUNA

MacKerzie Beach

Kīlauea Caldera

11

130

KAŪ

Kaimu

Kapapala Ranch

Hawaii Volcanoes National Park

Former Site of Kalapana

0   6 miles
0   9 km

Harbor. $ *Average main: $20* ✉ *308 Kamehameha Ave.* ☎ *808/969–6640* ⊕ *www.cafepesto.com.*

$ ✕ **Full Moon Cafe.** This cozy restaurant in a historic bayfront building
THAI offers a small menu of American choices like burgers, fish, and steak,
but where the eatery stands out is its fresh and tasty traditional Thai
fare. The owners grow their own spices, herbs, and papayas organically
on their Puna farm. The chefs sauté with olive oil to keep things heart-
healthy. Good choices are the hot and sour Tom Yum soup, loaded with
fresh veggies; the pineapple curry; green papaya salad; and steamed
salmon. There's outdoor seating on the lanai, and the adjacent Full
Moon Coffee serves breakfast beginning at 6. $ *Average main: $13*
✉ *51 Kalakaua St.* ☎ *808/961–0599* ⊕ *www.fullmooncafe.net.*

$ ✕ **Happy Valley Seafood Restaurant.** Don't let the name fool you. Though
CHINESE Hilo's best Chinese restaurant does specialize in seafood (the salt-and-
pepper prawns are fantastic), it also offers a wide range of other Cantonese treats, including a sizzling lamb platter, salt-and-pepper pork,
Mongolian beef or chicken, and vegetarian specialties like garlic eggplant and crispy green beans. The food is decent, portions are large, and
the price is right, but don't come here expecting any ambience—this
is a funky and cheap Chinese restaurant, with a few random pieces of
artwork tacked up here and there. $ *Average main: $12* ✉ *1263 Kilauea
Ave., Suite 320* ☎ *808/933–1083* ⊘ *No lunch Sun.*

$$ ✕ **Hilo Bay Café.** This popular restaurant, previously located in a Wal-
AMERICAN Mart strip mall, now overlooks Hilo Bay from its towering perch on
the waterfront. The sophisticated second-floor dining room looks like
it's straight out of Manhattan. While some of the menu items have
changed, old favorites are still available, including the traditional Blue
Bay burger, shoestring fries, and eggplant Parmesan custard. A sushi
bar now complements the excellent selection of fresh fish, gourmet
sake, and premium wines. $ *Average main: $20* ✉ *123 Lihiwai St.*
☎ *808/935–4939* ⊕ *www.hilobaycafe.com* ⊘ *No lunch Sun.*

$ ✕ **Ken's House of Pancakes.** For years, this 24-hour diner on Banyan Drive
DINER between the airport and the hotels has been a gathering place for Hilo
residents and visitors. Breakfast is the main attraction: Ken's serves
11 types of pancakes, plus all kinds of fruit waffles (banana, peach)
and popular omelets, like Da Bradda, teeming with meats. The menu
features 180 other tasty local specialties (loco moco, tripe stew, oxtail
soup) and American-diner-inspired items from which to choose. Sunday
is all-you-can-eat spaghetti night, Tuesday is all-you-can-eat tacos, and
Wednesday is prime rib night. $ *Average main: $10* ✉ *1730 Kame-
hameha Ave.* ☎ *808/935–8711* ⊕ *www.kenshouseofpancakes.com.*

$ ✕ **Ocean Sushi.** What this restaurant lacks in ambience it certainly makes
JAPANESE up for in quality and value. We're talking about light and crispy tem-
pura; tender, moist teriyaki chicken; and about 25 specialty sushi rolls
that, on average, cost a mere $5 per roll. Sushi lovers enjoy the "hospi-
tal roll," with shrimp tempura, cream cheese, cucumber, and spicy ahi,
and the "volcano roll," akin to a California roll topped with flying-fish
eggs, dried fish shavings, green onions, and spicy mayo. Don't let the
low price fool you—the service is quick and the food is fresh and filling.
$ *Average main: $12* ✉ *250 Keawe St.* ☎ *808/961–6625* ⊘ *Closed Sun.*

4

$$ HAWAIIAN FAMILY 🍴 **Ponds Hilo.** Perched on the waterfront overlooking a scenic and serene pond, this restaurant has the look and feel of an old-fashioned, harborside steak house and bar. The menu features a good range—burgers and salads, steak and seafood. Every Thursday is lobster night, with 8-ounce lobster tails served a variety of ways. Live music happens most evenings. [$] *Average main: $20* ✉ *135 Kalanianaole Ave.* ☎ *808/934–7663* 🌐 *www.pondshilohi.com.*

$$ SEAFOOD FAMILY 🍴 **The Seaside Restaurant & Aqua Farm.** The Nakagawa family has been running this eatery since the early 1920s. The latest son to manage it has transformed both the menu and the decor, and that, paired with the setting (on a 30-acre natural, brackish fishpond) makes this one of the most interesting places to eat in Hilo. Islanders travel great distances for the fried *aholehole* (young Hawaiian flagtail), and mullet raised at the aqua farm. Other great dishes from the sea include furikake salmon, miso butterfish, and macadamia nut–crusted mahimahi, but the Pacific Rim menu includes plenty for landlubbers, too, like prime rib, chicken, and salads. Arrive before sunset and request a table by the window for a view of egrets roosting around the fishpond. [$] *Average main: $23* ✉ *1790 Kalanianaole Ave.* ☎ *808/935–8825* 🌐 *www.seasiderestaurant.com* 🕓 *Closed Mon. No lunch.*

$ THAI 🍴 **Sombat's Fresh Thai Cuisine.** There's a reason why locals flock to this hideaway for the best Thai cuisine in Hilo, and the name says it all. Fresh local ingredients highlight proprietor Sombat Saenguthai's menu (many of the herbs come from her own garden) to create authentic and tasty Thai treats like coconut curries, fresh basil rolls, eggplant stir-fry, and green papaya salad. Most dishes can be prepared with your choice of tofu, pork, beef, chicken, squid, or fish. The weekday lunch plate special is a steal ($7–$9). And if you can't leave the island without it, Sombat's famous pad thai sauce is available to take home in jars. [$] *Average main: $13* ✉ *Waiakea Kai Plaza, 88 Kanoelehue Ave.* ☎ *808/969–9336* 🌐 *www.sombats.com* 🕓 *Closed Sun. No lunch Sat.*

$ HAWAIIAN 🍴 **Verna's Drive-In.** Verna's is a favorite among locals, who come for the moist homemade burgers and filling plate lunches. The price is right with a burger combo that includes fries and a drink for just $5.50. If you're hungry for more, try the traditional Hawaiian plate with *laulau*, beef stew, chicken long rice, *lomilomi* salmon; or the smoked meat plate (a local specialty) smothered in onions and served with rice and macaroni salad. Whatever you choose, you won't leave hungry. Late-night revelers take note: Verna's is one of the only joints in Hilo that's open 24 hours every day. [$] *Average main: $8* ✉ *1765 Kamehameha Ave.* ☎ *808/935–2776.*

PUNA

$ MEXICAN 🍴 **Luquin's Mexican Restaurant.** Long an island favorite for tasty, albeit greasy, Mexican grub, this landmark is still going strong in the funky town of Pahoa. Breakfast includes huevos rancheros. Tacos are great (go for crispy), especially when stuffed with grilled, seasoned local fish on occasion. Chips are warm and salty, the salsa's got some kick, and the beans are thick with lard and topped with melted cheese. Not something you'd eat before a long swim, but perfect after a long day of exploring. $ *Average main: $9* ⊠ *15-2942 Pahoa Village Rd., Pahoa* ☎ *808/965–9990* ⊕ *www.luquins.com.*

HAWAII VOLCANOES NATIONAL PARK AND VICINITY

VOLCANO

$$$ ✕ **Kilauea Lodge.** Chef and owner Albert Jeyte combines contemporary
EUROPEAN trends with traditional cooking styles from France and his native Hamburg, Germany. The menu changes daily and features such entrées as venison, duck à l'orange with an apricot-mustard glaze, and lamb provençal garnished with papaya-apple-mint sauce. The coconut-crusted Brie appetizer is melty and delicious, served with papaya salsa and brandied apples. Savory soups and breads are made from scratch. Built in 1937 as a YMCA camp, the restaurant still retains the original Fireplace of Friendship, embedded with coins and plaques from around the world. The roaring fire, koa-wood tables, and intimate lighting are in keeping with this cozy lodge in the heart of Volcano Village. $ *Average main: $30* ⊠ *19-3948 Old Volcano Hwy., Volcano Village* ☎ *808/967–7366* ⊕ *www.kilaualodge.com.*

$ ✕ **Lava Rock Café.** This is an affordable place to grab a sandwich or a
DINER coffee and check your email (Wi-Fi is free with purchase of meal) before
FAMILY heading to Hawaii Volcanoes National Park. The homey, sit-down diner caters to families, serving up heaping plates of pancakes and French toast for breakfast. For lunch, burgers range from bacon-cheese to turkey to Paniolo burgers made with Hawaii grass-fed beef. There are also generous sandwiches, loco moco, and soups; beef or chicken teriyaki; and haupia cake for dessert. A full bar serves draft beer. $ *Average main: $10* ⊠ *19-3972 Old Volcano Hwy., behind Kilauea General Store* ☎ *808/967–8526* ⊘ *No dinner Sun. and Mon.*

$$ ✕ **The Rim at Volcano House.** The reopened Volcano House hotel houses a
HAWAIIAN fine-dining restaurant that overlooks the rim of Kilauea caldera and its fiery glow. Featuring two bars, a lounge, and live entertainment, it highlights island-inspired cuisine and incorporates locally sourced produce and other ingredients. Paired with Hilo coffee-rubbed rack of lamb, the creamy kabocha squash soup warms up a cool Volcano night. The Taste of Hawaii lunch menu comprises a choice of entrée (kalua pork, fresh catch, chicken, or stir-fry) and five local-style side dishes, such as poi, ahi poke wonton, and lilikoi cream puff, plus beverage; at $19, it's a great deal. $ *Average main: $25* ⊠ *Hawaii Volcanoes National Park, Crater Rim Dr.* ☎ *808/756–9625* ⊕ *www.hawaiivolcanohouse.com.*

$$ ✕ **Thai Thai Restaurant.** The food is authentic and the prices are reason-
THAI able at this little Volcano Village find. A steaming hot plate of curry is the perfect antidote to a chilly day at the volcano. The chicken satay is excellent—the peanut dipping sauce a good blend of sweet and spicy. And speaking of spicy, "medium" is more than spicy enough, even for hard-core chili addicts. The service is warm and friendly and the dining room pleasant, with white tablecloths, Thai art, and a couple of silk wall hangings. $ *Average main: $20* ⊠ *19-4084 Old Volcano Rd.* ☎ *808/967–7969* ⊘ *No lunch Wed.*

WHERE TO STAY

Updated
by Karen
Anderson

Even among locals, there is an ongoing debate about which side of the Big Island is "better," so don't worry if you're having a tough time deciding where to stay. Our recommendation? Do both. Each side offers a different range of accommodations, restaurants, and activities.

Consider staying at one of the upscale resorts along the Kohala Coast or in a condo in Kailua-Kona for half of your trip. Then, shift gears and check into a romantic bed-and-breakfast on the Hamakua Coast, South Kona, Hilo, or near the volcano. If you've got children in tow, opt for a vacation home or a stay at one of the island's many family-friendly hotels. On the west side, explore the island's most pristine beaches or try some of the fine-dining restaurants; on the east side, hike through rain forests, witness majestic waterfalls, or go for a plate lunch.

Some locals like to say that the east is "more Hawaiian," but we argue that King Kamehameha himself made Kailua-Kona his final home during his sunset years. Another reason to try a bit of both: your budget. You can justify splurging on a stay at a Kohala Coast resort for a few nights because you'll spend the rest of your time paying one-third that rate at a cozy cottage in Volcano or a vacation rental on Alii Drive. And although food at the resorts is very expensive, you don't have to eat every meal there. Condos and vacation homes can be ideal for a family trip or for a group of friends looking to save money and live like *kamaainas* (local residents) for a week or two. Many of the homes also have private pools and hot tubs, lanai, ocean views, and more—you can go as budget or as high-end as you like.

If you choose a bed-and-breakfast, inn, or an out-of-the-way hotel, explain your expectations fully to the proprietor and ask plenty of questions before booking. Be clear about your travel and location needs. Some places require stays of two or three days. No matter where you stay, you'll want to rent a car. Some rental car companies do have restrictions about taking their vehicles to certain Big Island scenic spots, so make sure to ask about rules before you book.

Prices in the reviews are the lowest price of a standard double room in high season.

For expanded hotel reviews, visit Fodors.com.

KAILUA-KONA

$ RENTAL **Casa de Emdeko.** A large and pretty complex on the *makai* (oceanfront) side of Alii Drive, Casa de Emdeko offers a few more amenities than most condo complexes, including a florist, hair salon, and an on-site convenience store that makes sandwiches. **Pros:** oceanfront fresh- and saltwater pools; hidden from the street; very private. **Cons:** quality and prices depend on owner; not kid-friendly. $ *Rooms from: $110* ⌧ *75-6082 Alii Dr.* ⊕ *www.casadeemdeko.org* ⊃ *106 units* ⧖ *No meals.*

$$ HOTEL **Courtyard King Kamehameha's Kona Beach Hotel.** This landmark hotel by Kailua Pier highlights Kona's rich history, whether on the grounds where King Kamehameha I spent his final years or in the jazzed-up

BEST BETS FOR
BIG ISLAND LODGING

Fodor'sChoice ★

Fairmont Orchid Hawaii,
$$$$, p. 434

**Four Seasons Resort
Hualalai,** $$$$, p. 434

**Mauna Lani Bay Hotel
and Bungalows,** $$$$,
p. 437

Puakea Ranch, $$$, p. 437

Waianuhea, $$, p. 438

By Price

$

**Courtyard King
Kamehameha's Kona
Beach Hotel,** p. 428

Hale Ohia Cottages,
p. 441

Kilauea Lodge, p. 441

Kona Tiki Hotel, p. 432

Manago Hotel, p. 434

Royal Kona Resort,
p. 433

**Sheraton Kona Resort
& Spa at Keauhou Bay,**
p. 433

**Waimea Gardens
Cottage,** p. 438

$$

**Courtyard King
Kamehameha's Kona
Beach Hotel,** p. 428

Hilton Waikoloa Village,
p. 436

Waianuhea, p. 438

$$$

Puakea Ranch, p. 437

$$$$

Fairmont Orchid Hawaii,
p. 434

**Four Seasons Resort
Hualalai,** p. 434

Holualoa Inn, p. 429

Mauna Kea Beach Hotel,
p. 436

**Mauna Lani Bay Hotel
and Bungalows,** p. 437

**Waikoloa Beach Marri-
ott,** p. 437

By Experience

BEST BEACH

**Hapuna Beach Prince
Hotel,** $$$, p. 436

Mauna Kea Beach Hotel,
$$$$, p. 436

**Waikoloa Beach Marri-
ott,** $$$$, p. 437

lobby, which displays an impressive array of historical Hawaiian arti-facts. **Pros:** central location; tastefully appointed rooms; historic ambi-ence; aloha-friendly staff. **Cons:** most rooms have partial ocean views; some rooms face the parking lot. $ *Rooms from: $199 ✉ 75-5660 Palani Rd.* ☎ *808/329–2911* ⊕ *www.konabeachhotel.com* ☞*452 rooms* ⑩ *No meals.*

$$$$
B&B/INN
Fodor'sChoice ★
⊡ **Holualoa Inn.** Six spacious rooms and suites—plus a private, vintage, one-bedroom cottage that's perfect for honeymooners—are available at this beautiful cedar home on a 30-acre coffee-country estate, a few miles above Kailua Bay in the heart of the artists' village of Holualoa. **Pros:** within walking distance of art galleries and cafés; well-appointed, with wood floors, fine art, and lots of windows; panoramic views. **Cons:** not kid-friendly. $ *Rooms from: $380 ✉ 76-5932 Mamalahoa Hwy., Box 222, Holualoa* ☎ *808/324–1121, 800/392–1812* ⊕ *www.holualoainn. com* ☞*6 rooms, 1 cottage* ⑩ *Breakfast.*

$
RESORT
⊡ **Holua Resort at Mauna Loa Village.** Tucked away by Keauhou Bay amid a plethora of coconut trees, this well-maintained enclave of blue-roofed villas offers lots of amenities, including an 11-court tennis center (with a center court, pro shop, and lights), swimming pools, hot tubs, fitness

WHERE TO STAY ON THE BIG ISLAND

	Local Vibe	Pros	Cons
Kailua-Kona	Kailua-Kona is a bustling little village. Alii Drive is brimming with hotels and condo complexes.	Plenty to do, day and night; main drag of shops, historic landmarks, and seaside attractions within easy walking distance of most hotels; many grocery stores in the area.	More traffic than anywhere else on the island; limited number of beaches; traffic noise on Alii Drive.
South Kona and Kau	A great place to stay if you want to be near some of the best water attractions on the island. There are plenty of bed-and-breakfasts and vacation rentals at or near Kealakekua Bay.	Kealakekua Bay is one of the most popular destinations on the island for snorkeling; several good dining options nearby; coffee-farm tours in Captain Cook and Kainaliu towns.	Vog from Kilauea often settles here; fewer sand beaches in the area; farther south, the Kau district is quite remote.
The Kohala Coast	The Kohala Coast is home to most of the Big Island's major resorts. Blue, sunny skies prevail here, along with the island's best beaches.	Beautiful beaches; high-end shopping and dining; lots of activities for adults and children.	Pricey; long driving distances to Volcano, Hilo, and Kailua-Kona.
Waimea	Though it seems a world away, Waimea is only about a 15- to 20-minute drive from the Kohala Coast.	Beautiful scenery, paniolo (cowboy) culture; home to some exceptional local restaurants.	Can be cool and rainy year-round; nearest beaches are a 20-minute drive away.
The Hamakua Coast	The Hamakua Coast is a nice spot for those seeking peace, tranquillity, and an alternative to the tropical-beach-vacation experience.	Close to Waipio Valley; foodie and farm tours in the area; good spot for honeymooners.	Beaches are an hour's drive away; convenience shopping is nonexistent.
Hilo	Hilo is the wetter, more lush eastern side of the Big Island. It is also less touristy than the west side.	Proximity to waterfalls, rain-forest hikes, museums, and botanical gardens; good bed-and-breakfast options.	The best white-sand beaches are on the other side of the island; noise from coqui frogs can be distracting at night.
Puna	Puna doesn't attract nearly as many visitors as other regions on the island, so you'll find good deals on rentals and B&Bs here.	A few black-sand beaches; off the beaten path with lots of outdoor wilderness to explore; lava flows into the sea here.	Few dining and entertainment options; no resorts or resort amenities; noisy coqui frogs at night.
Hawaii Volcanoes National Park and Vicinity	If you are going to visit Hawaii Volcanoes National Park, stay the night at any number of enchanting bed-and-breakfast inns in the fern-shrouded Volcano Village.	Good location for watching lava at night bubbling inside Halemaumau Crater; great for hiking, nature tours, and bike riding; close to Hilo and Puna.	Not many dining options; not much nightlife; can be cold and wet.

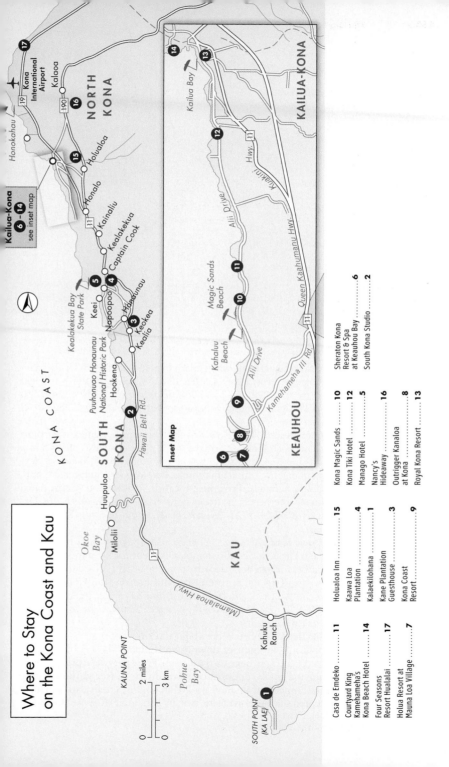

Where to Stay on the Kona Coast and Kau

KONA COAST

SOUTH KONA

NORTH KONA

KAU

KAILUA-KONA

KEAUHOU

Kailua-Kona
6–14
see inset map

Inset Map

Casa de Emdeko 11
Courtyard King
Kamehameha's
Kona Beach Hotel 14
Four Seasons
Resort Hualalai 17
Holua Resort at
Mauna Loa Village 7

Holualoa Inn 15
Kaawa Loa
Plantation 4
Kalaekilohana 1
Kane Plantation
Guesthouse 3
Kona Coast
Resort 9

Kona Magic Sands 10
Kona Tiki Hotel 12
Manago Hotel 5
Nancy's
Hideaway 16
Outrigger Kanaloa
at Kona 8
Royal Kona Resort 13

Sheraton Kona
Resort & Spa
at Keauhou Bay 6
South Kona Studio 2

"We saw lava flowing into the sea. The sun went down, the steam turned shades of red and orange. It was one of the most memorable moments in my life." —disneydan, Fodors.com photo contest participant

center, manicured gardens, waterfalls, covered parking, and a Tuesday-night hula show. **Pros:** tennis center; upscale feeling. **Cons:** no beach. [$] *Rooms from: $129* ✉ *78-7190 Kaleiopapa St.* ☎ *808/324–1550* 🌐 *www.shellhospitality.com/Holua-Resort-at-Mauna-Loa-Village* 🛏 *73 units* 🍴 *No meals.*

$ RENTAL **Kona Coast Resort.** Just below Keauhou Shopping Center, this resort offers furnished condos on 21 acres with pleasant ocean views and a host of on-site amenities including a swimming pool, beach volleyball, cocktail bar, hot tub, tennis courts, hula classes, equipment rental, and children's activites. **Pros:** nice location in Keauhou. **Cons:** dated decor; not on the beach. [$] *Rooms from: $140* ✉ *78-6842 Alii Dr., Keauhou* ☎ *808/324–1721* 🌐 *www.shellhospitality.com* 🛏 *268 units* 🍴 *No meals.*

$ RENTAL **Kona Magic Sands.** Cradled between a lovely grass park and Magic Sands Beach Park, this condo complex is great for swimmers, surfers, and sunbathers. **Pros:** next door to popular beach; affordable; oceanfront view from all units; restaurant and bar on-site. **Cons:** studios only; some units are dated. [$] *Rooms from: $115* ✉ *77-6452 Alii Dr.* ☎ *808/329–9393, 800/622–5348* 🌐 *www.konahawaii.com/ms.htm* 🛏 *37 units* 🍴 *No meals.*

$ HOTEL **Kona Tiki Hotel.** The best thing about this three-story walk-up budget hotel, about a mile south of downtown Kailua Village, is that all the units have lanai right next to the ocean. **Pros:** very low price; oceanfront lanai and pool; room fridges; friendly staff; free parking. **Cons:** older hotel in need of update; no TV in rooms; credit card payment only accepted via hotel website, not in person. [$] *Rooms from: $85*

✉ *75-5968 Alii Dr.* ☎ *808/329–1425* 🌐 *www.konatikihotel.com* 🛏 *16 rooms* 💳 *No credit cards* 🍴 *Breakfast.*

$ RENTAL 🏨 **Nancy's Hideaway.** A few miles up the hill from downtown Kailua-Kona, this charming cottage and studio offer modern comforts; each has its own entrance, a lanai, ocean views, and a wet bar. **Pros:** plenty of privacy; ocean views. **Cons:** Upcountry location in the clouds; not kid-friendly. [$] *Rooms from: $130* ✉ *73-1530 Uanani Pl., off Kaloko Dr.* ☎ *808/325–3132, 866/325–3132* 🌐 *www.nancyshideaway.com* 🛏 *2 rooms.*

$$$ RENTAL 🏨 **Outrigger Kanaloa at Kona.** The 16-acre grounds provide a peaceful and verdant background for this low-rise condominium complex bordering the Keauhou-Kona Country Club and within a five-minute drive of the nearest beaches (Kahaluu and Magic Sands). **Pros:** within walking distance of Keauhou Bay; three pools with hot tubs; shopping center and restaurants nearby. **Cons:** no restaurant on property; mandatory cleaning fee at checkout. [$] *Rooms from: $285* ✉ *78-261 Manukai St.* ☎ *808/322–9625, 808/322–2272, 800/688–7444* 🌐 *www.outrigger.com* 🛏 *63 units* 🍴 *No meals.*

$ RESORT 🏨 **Royal Kona Resort.** This is a great option if you're on a budget—the location is central; the bar, lounge, pool, and restaurant are right on the water; and the rooms feature contemporary Hawaiian decor with Polynesian accents. **Pros:** convenient location; waterfront pool; low prices. **Cons:** can be crowded; parking is tight. [$] *Rooms from: $139* ✉ *75-5852 Alii Dr.* ☎ *808/329–3111, 800/222–5642* 🌐 *www.royalkona.com* 🛏 *436 rooms, 8 suites* 🍴 *No meals.*

$ RESORT FAMILY 🏨 **Sheraton Kona Resort & Spa at Keauhou Bay.** What this big concrete structure lacks in intimacy, it makes up for with its beautifully manicured grounds, historic sense of place, renovated interiors, and stunning location on Keauhou Bay. **Pros:** cool pool; manta rays on view nightly; restaurant; resort style at lower price. **Cons:** no beach; daily resort fee for Wi-Fi and parking. [$] *Rooms from: $169* ✉ *78-128 Ehukai St.* ☎ *808/930–4900* 🌐 *www.sheratonkona.com* 🛏 *485 rooms, 24 suites* 🍴 *No meals.*

KAILUA-KONA CONDO COMFORTS

The **Safeway** at Crossroads Shopping Center (✉ *75-1027 Henry St., Kailua-Kona* ☎ *808/329–2207*) offers an excellent inventory of groceries and produce, although prices can be steep. For pizza, **Kona Brewing Co. Pub & Brewery** (✉ *75-5629 Kuakini Hwy., just past Palani intersection on right, Kailua-Kona* ☎ *808/329–2739*) is the best bet, if you can pick it up. Otherwise, for delivery, try **Domino's** (☎ *808/329–9500*).

THE KONA COAST

SOUTH KONA

$ B&B/INN 🏨 **Kaawa Loa Plantation.** Proprietors Mike Martinage and Greg Nunn operate a grand bed-and-breakfast inn on a 5-acre coffee farm above Kealakekua Bay. **Pros:** nice views; excellent breakfast; Hawaiian steam room. **Cons:** not within walking distance of bay; some rooms share a bath. $ *Rooms from: $129* ⊠ *82-5990 Napoopoo Rd., Captain Cook* ☎ *808/323–2686* ⊕ *www.kaawaloaplantation.com* ⊅ *2 rooms, 1 suite, 1 cottage* ⍝⌷ *Breakfast.*

$ 🏠 **Kane Plantation Guesthouse.** The historic former home of the late leg-
B&B/INN   endary artist Herb Kane, this luxury boutique guesthouse occupies a 16-acre avocado farm overlooking the South Kona coastline. **Pros:** privacy; upscale amenities. **Cons:** not on the beach. $ *Rooms from: $155* ⊠ *84-1120 Telephone Exchange Rd., off Hwy. 11, ¼ mile past mile marker 105, south of Captain Cook, Honaunau* ☎ *808/328–2416* ⊕ *www.kaneplantationhawaii.com* ⊅ *4 suites.*

$ 🏠 **Manago Hotel.** This historic hotel is a good option if you want to
HOTEL   escape the touristy thing but still be close to the water and attractions like Kealakekua Bay and Puuhonua O Honaunau National Histori-cal Park. **Pros:** local color; rock-bottom prices; terrific on-site restau-rant. **Cons:** not the best sound insulation between rooms. $ *Rooms from: $36* ⊠ *81-6155 Mamalahoa Hwy., Box 145, Captain Cook* ☎ *808/323–2642* ⊕ *www.managohotel.com* ⊅ *64 rooms, 42 with bath* ⍝⌷ *No meals.*

$ 🏠 **South Kona Studio.** This little studio is a great find for travelers on a
RENTAL   budget. **Pros:** budget-friendly; snorkel gear included; ocean views; last-minute availability. **Cons:** remote location; two guests max. $ *Rooms from: $79* ⊠ *Kaohe Rd. and Hwy. 11, Captain Cook* ☎ *808/938–1172* ⊅ *1 room.*

NORTH KONA

$$$$ 🏠 **Four Seasons Resort Hualalai.** Beautiful views everywhere, polished
RESORT   wood floors, custom furnishings and linens in warm earth and cool
Fodor'sChoice   white tones, and Hawaiian fine artwork make this resort a peaceful
★   retreat. **Pros:** beautiful location; excellent restaurants. **Cons:** not the best beach among the resorts. $ *Rooms from: $695* ⊠ *72-100 Kaupu-lehu Dr., Box 1269, Kailua-Kona* ☎ *808/325–8000, 800/819–5053, 888/340–5662* ⊕ *www.fourseasons.com/hualalai* ⊅ *243 rooms, 51 suites* ⍝⌷ *No meals.*

THE KOHALA COAST

$$ 🏠 **Aston Shores at Waikoloa.** Villas with terra cotta–tile roofs are set amid
RENTAL   landscaped lagoons and waterfalls at the edge of the championship Waikoloa Village Golf Course. **Pros:** good prices for the area; great loca-tion; fully self-sufficient condos with maid service. **Cons:** no restaurants. $ *Rooms from: $239* ⊠ *69-1035 Keana Pl., Waikoloa* ☎ *808/886–5001, 800/922–7866* ⊕ *www.astonhotels.com* ⊅ *56 units* ⍝⌷ *No meals.*

$$$$ 🏠 **Fairmont Orchid Hawaii.** This first-rate resort overflows with tropical
RESORT   gardens, cascading waterfalls, sandy beach cove, beautiful wings with
Fodor'sChoice   "open sesame" doors, a meandering pool, and renovated rooms with
★   all the amenities. **Pros:** oceanfront location; great restaurants; excellent pool; aloha hospitality. **Cons:** top resort features come at a high price. $ *Rooms from: $569* ⊠ *1 N. Kaniku Dr., Kohala Coast* ☎ *808/885–2000, 800/845–9905* ⊕ *www.fairmont.com/orchid* ⊅ *486 rooms, 54 suites* ⍝⌷ *No meals.*

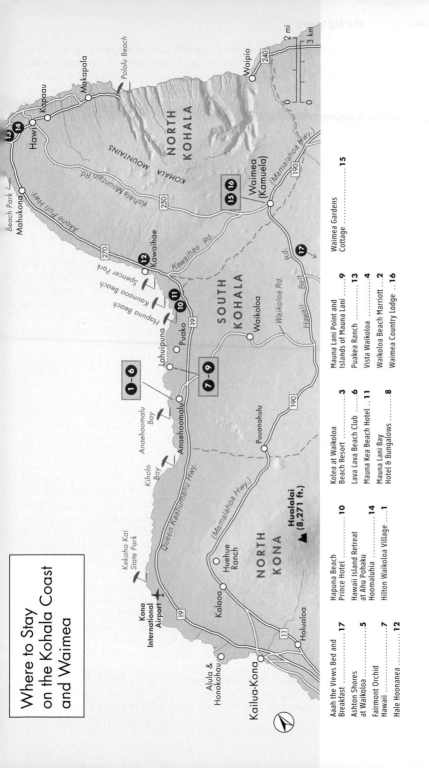

Where to Stay on the Kohala Coast and Waimea

NORTH KOHALA

KOHALA MOUNTAINS

Kohala Mountain Rd.

Akoni Puli Hwy.

Beach Park
Mahukona
Pololu Beach
Makapala
Kapaau
Hawii **14** **13**

Waimea (Kamuela)
15 **16**

240
Waipio

2 mi
3 km

Kawaihae Rd.
(Mamalahoa Hwy.)

190

Spencer Park
Kawaihae **12**

Kaunaoa Beach
Hapuna Beach
10 **11**

SOUTH KOHALA

Kawaihae Rd.

Waikoloa Rd.

Hawaii Belt

17

Puako
Lahuipuna
19

1 – 6

Anaehoomalu Bay
Anaehoomalu
7 – 9

Waikoloa

Kiholo Bay

Kekaha Kai State Park

Queen Kaahumanu Hwy.

Puuanahulu

190

Huehue Ranch

NORTH KONA

Hualalai
▲ (8,271 ft.)

(Mamalahoa Hwy.)

Kona International Airport

Kaloaa

Holualoa

Alula &
Honokohau

11

Kailua-Kona

Aaah the Views Bed and
Breakfast **17**
Ashton Shores
at Waikoloa **5**
Fairmont Orchid
Hawaii **7**
Hale Hoonanea **12**

Hapuna Beach
Prince Hotel **10**
Hawaii Island Retreat
at Ahu Pohaku
Hoomaluhia **14**
Hilton Waikoloa Village **1**

Kolea at Waikoloa
Beach Resort **3**
Lava Lava Beach Club **6**
Mauna Kea Beach Hotel .. **11**
Mauna Lani Bay
Hotel & Bungalows **8**

Mauna Lani Point and
Islands of Mauna Lani **9**
Puakea Ranch **13**
Vista Waikoloa **4**
Waikoloa Beach Marriott .. **2**
Waimea Country Lodge .. **16**

Waimea Gardens
Cottage **15**

$
B&B/INN
FAMILY

▣ **Hale Hoonanea.** A comfortable home with two detached guest suites, this 3-acre property in the Kohala Estates, above Kawaihae Harbor, lives up to the English translation of its name, "House of Relaxation." **Pros:** detached suites for maximum privacy; panoramic ocean views from private lanai; good price for the neighborhood. **Cons:** not within walking distance to restaurants; no pool. $ *Rooms from: $110 ⊠ Kohala Estates, 59-513 Ala Kahua Dr., Kawaihae ☎ 808/882–1653, 877/882–1653 ⊕ www.houseofrelaxation.com ➫ 2 suites �†○⦙ Breakfast.*

$$$
RESORT
FAMILY

▣ **Hapuna Beach Prince Hotel.** More reasonably priced than its neighbor resorts, this hotel occupies the northern corner of the largest sand beach on the Big Island. **Pros:** extra-large rooms, all ocean-facing; direct access to one of island's best beaches. **Cons:** fitness center is a 10-minute walk from the golf course; daily fees for Wi-Fi and parking. $ *Rooms from: $289 ⊠ 62-100 Kaunaoa Dr., Kohala Coast ☎ 808/880–1111, 866/774–6236 ⊕ www.princeresortshawaii.com ➫ 351 rooms, 37 suites �†○⦙ No meals.*

$$$
B&B/INN

▣ **Hawaii Island Retreat at Ahu Pohaku Hoomaluhia.** Here, above the seacliffs in North Kohala's Hawi, sustainability meets luxury without sacrificing comfort. **Pros:** stunning location; ancient Hawaiian spiritual sites; eco-friendly. **Cons:** not within walking distance of restaurants; off the beaten path. $ *Rooms from: $275 ⊠ 250 Maluhia Rd., off Hwy. 270 in Hawi, Kapaau ☎ 808/889–6336 ⊕ www.hawaiiislandretreat.com ➫ 9 rooms, 7 yurts ⊙⦙ Breakfast.*

$$
RESORT
FAMILY

▣ **Hilton Waikoloa Village.** Dolphins swim in the lagoon; pint-size guests zoom down the 175-foot waterslide; a bride poses on the grand staircase; a fire-bearing runner lights the torches along the seaside path at sunset—these are some of the typical scenes at this 62-acre megaresort. **Pros:** family-friendly; lots of restaurant and activity options. **Cons:** gigantic, crowded; lots of kids; restaurants are pricey. $ *Rooms from: $229 ⊠ 69-425 Waikoloa Beach Dr., Waikoloa ☎ 808/886–1234, 800/445–8667 ⊕ www.hiltonwaikoloavillage.com ➫ 1,241 rooms, 58 suites ⊙⦙ No meals.*

$$$
RENTAL
FAMILY

▣ **Kolea at Waikoloa Beach Resort.** These modern, impeccably furnished condos appeal to the high-end visitor typically associated with the Mauna Lani Bay Hotel & Bungalows. **Pros:** high design; close to beach and activities; resort amenities of nearby Hilton. **Cons:** pricey; no on-property restaurants. $ *Rooms from: $300 ⊠ Waikoloa Beach Resort, 69-1000 Kolea Kai Circle, Waikoloa ☎ 808/987-4519 ⊕ www.waikoloavacationrentals.com/kolea-rentals ➫ 40 villas, 4 houses ⊙⦙ No meals.*

$$$$
RENTAL

▣ **Lava Lava Beach Club.** Spend the day swimming steps away from your private lanai and fall asleep to the sound of the ocean at these four artfully decorated one-room cottages, on the beach at Anaehoomalu Bay. **Pros:** on the beach; fully air-conditioned; free Wi-Fi. **Cons:** beach is public, so there will be people on it in front of cottage. $ *Rooms from: $475 ⊠ 69-1081 Kuualii Pl., Waikoloa ☎ 808/769–5282 ⊕ www.lavalavabeachclub.com ➫ 4 cottages.*

$$$$
RESORT

▣ **Mauna Kea Beach Hotel.** The grande dame of the Kohala Coast has long been regarded as one of the state's premier vacation resort hotels, and it borders one of the island's finest white-sand beaches, Kaunaoa. **Pros:**

beautiful beach; premier tennis center; extra-large contemporary rooms; on-site restaurants. **Cons:** small swimming pool; overpriced sundries shop. $ *Rooms from: $445* ⊠ *62-100 Mauna Kea Beach Dr., Kohala Coast* 🕿 *808/882–7222, 866/977–4589* ⊕ *www.maunakeabeachhotel. com* ⬅ *254 rooms, 10 suites* ◯❙ *No meals.*

$$$$
RESORT
Fodor's Choice
★
Mauna Lani Bay Hotel & Bungalows. Popular with honeymooners and anniversary couples for decades, this elegant Kohala Coast classic is still one of the most beautiful resorts on the island, highlighted by a breathtaking, open-air lobby with cathedral-like ceilings, Zen-like koi ponds, and illuminated sheets of cascading water. **Pros:** beautiful design; award-winning spa; no hidden fees; complimentary valet parking. **Cons:** no luau. $ *Rooms from: $400* ⊠ *68-1400 Mauna Lani Dr., Kohala Coast* 🕿 *808/885–6622, 800/367–2323* ⊕ *www.maunalani.com* ⬅ *318 rooms, 18 suites, 5 bungalows* ◯❙ *No meals.*

$$$
RENTAL
Mauna Lani Point and Islands of Mauna Lani. Surrounded by the emerald greens of a world-class ocean-side golf course, spacious two-story suites at Islands of Mauna Lani offer a private, independent home, while Mauna Lani Point villas are closer to the beach. **Pros:** privacy; soaking tubs; extra-large units. **Cons:** pricey. $ *Rooms from: $275* ⊠ *68-1050 Mauna Lani Point Dr., Kohala Coast* 🕿 *808/885–5022, 800/642–6284* ⊕ *www.maunalanipoint.com* ⬅ *72 units* ◯❙ *No meals.*

$$$
RENTAL
Fodor's Choice
★
Puakea Ranch. Four beautifully restored ranch houses and bungalows occupy this historic country estate in Hawi, where guests enjoy their own private swimming pools, horseback riding, round-the-clock concierge availability, and plenty of fresh fruit to pick from the orchards. **Pros:** horseback lessons and trail riding; charmingly decorated; beautiful bathrooms; private swimming pools. **Cons:** not on the beach $ *Rooms from: $289* ⊠ *56-2864 Akoni Pule Hwy., Kohala Coast* 🕿 *808/315–0805* ⊕ *www.puakearanch.com* ⬅ *4 bungalows, 2 cottages* ◯❙ *No meals.*

$
RENTAL
Vista Waikoloa. Older and more reasonably priced than most of the condo complexes along the Kohala Coast, the well-appointed, two-bedroom, two-bath Vista condos offer ocean views and two lanai per unit. **Pros:** centrally located; reasonably priced; very large units; 75-foot lap pool. **Cons:** hit or miss on decor because each unit is individually owned. $ *Rooms from: $180* ⊠ *Waikoloa Beach Resort, 69-1010 Keana Pl., Waikoloa* 🕿 *808/886–3594* ⬅ *122 units* ◯❙ *No meals.*

$$$$
RESORT
FAMILY
Waikoloa Beach Marriott. Covering 15 acres with ancient fishponds, historic trails, and petroglyph fields, the Marriott has rooms with sleek modern beds, bright white linens, Hawaiian art, and private lanai. **Pros:** more low-key than the Hilton Waikoloa; sunset luau Wednesday and Saturday; sand-bottom pool for kids. **Cons:** only one restaurant. $ *Rooms from: $410* ⊠ *69-275 Waikoloa Beach Dr., Waikoloa* 🕿 *808/886–6789, 800/228–9290* ⊕ *www.marriott.com* ⬅ *525 rooms, 22 suites* ◯❙ *No meals.*

WAIMEA

$
B&B/INN
Aaah the Views Bed and Breakfast. The name aptly sums up the experience at this tranquil, stream-side inn built specifically to be a bed-and-breakfast—and it's the only lodging in Waimea that hosts a full, sit-down breakfast. **Pros:** away from it all; friendly hosts; beautiful

countryside views; free beach gear. **Cons:** no pool. [$] *Rooms from: $139* ✉ *66-1773 Alaneo St., off Akulani St., just past mile marker 60 on Hwy. 19* ☎ *808/885-3455* 🌐 *www.aaahtheviews.com* 🛏 *3 suites* 🍴 *Breakfast.*

$ HOTEL 🏨 **Waimea Country Lodge.** In the heart of cowboy country, this modest ranch house–style lodge offers views of the green, rolling slopes of Mauna Kea. **Pros:** affordable; large rooms equipped with kitchenettes. **Cons:** rooms could use some updating; no pool. [$] *Rooms from: $135* ✉ *65-1210 Lindsey Rd.* ☎ *808/885-4100, 800/367-5004* 🌐 *www.castleresorts.com* 🛏 *21 rooms* 🍴 *No meals.*

$ B&B/INN 🏨 **Waimea Gardens Cottage.** Surprisingly luxe, yet cozy and quaint, three charming country cottages at this historic Hawaiian homestead are surrounded by flowering private gardens and a backyard stream. **Pros:** no detail left out; beautiful self-contained cottages; gardens; complete privacy. **Cons:** requires payment in full six weeks prior to arrival. [$] *Rooms from: $155* ☎ *808/885-8550* 🌐 *www.waimeagardens.com* 🛏 *2 cottages, 1 studio* 💳 *No credit cards* 🍴 *Breakfast.*

THE HAMAKUA COAST

$$ B&B/INN 🏨 **The Palms Cliff House Inn.** This handsome Victorian-style mansion, 15 minutes north of downtown Hilo and a few minutes from Akaka Falls, is perched on the sea cliffs 100 feet above the crashing surf of the tropical coast. **Pros:** stunning views; terrific breakfast; comfortable rooms with every amenity; all rooms have private entrances from the exterior. **Cons:** no pool; no lunch or dinner on-site; remote location means you have to drive to Hilo for dinner. [$] *Rooms from: $239* ✉ *28-3514 Mamalahoa Hwy., Honomu* ☎ *866/963-6076, 808/963-6076* 🌐 *www.palmscliffhouse.com* 🛏 *4 rooms, 4 suites* 🍴 *Breakfast.*

$$ B&B/INN Fodor's Choice ★ 🏨 **Waianuhea.** Defining Hawaiian Upcountry elegance, this gorgeous country inn, which is fully self-contained and runs off solar power, sits in a forested area on the Hamakua Coast in Ahualoa. **Pros:** eco-friendly hotel; hot and healthy breakfast; beautiful views of Mauna Kea. **Cons:** very remote location; unreliable phone access. [$] *Rooms from: $225* ✉ *45-3503 Kahana Dr., Box 185, Honokaa* ☎ *888/775-2577, 808/775-1118* 🌐 *www.waianuhea.com* 🛏 *4 rooms, 1 suite* 🍴 *Breakfast.*

HILO

$ B&B/INN 🏨 **The Bay House.** Overlooking Hilo Bay and just steps away from the Singing Bridge near Hilo's historic downtown area, this small, quiet bed-and-breakfast is vibrantly decorated, with Hawaiian-quilted beds and private lanai in each of the three rooms. **Pros:** free Wi-Fi; ample parking; cliffside hot tub; Hilo Bay views. **Cons:** only two people per room. [$] *Rooms from: $175* ✉ *42 Pukihae St.* ☎ *888/235-8195, 808/961-6311* 🌐 *www.bayhousehawaii.com* 🛏 *3 rooms* 🍴 *Breakfast.*

$ HOTEL FAMILY 🏨 **Dolphin Bay Hotel.** Units in this circa-1950s motor lodge are modest, but charming, clean, and inexpensive. **Pros:** great value; full kitchens in all units; extremely helpful and pleasant staff; weekly rates are a good deal. **Cons:** no pool; no phones in the rooms. [$] *Rooms from: $119*

✉ *333 Iliahi St.* ☎ *808/935–1466* ⊕ *www.dolphinbayhotel.com* ⌁ *18 rooms, 12 studios, 4 1-bedroom units, 1 2-bedroom unit* ⦿ *No meals.*

$ **Hale Kai.** On a bluff above
B&B/INN Honolii surf beach, this modern 5,400-square-foot home is 2 miles from downtown Hilo and features four rooms—each with patio, deluxe bedding, and grand ocean views within earshot of the surf. **Pros:** delicious hot breakfast; pool; panoramic views of Hilo Bay; hot tub; free Wi-Fi; smoke-free property. **Cons:** no kids under 13. $ *Rooms from: $165* ✉ *111 Honolii Pl.* ☎ *808/935–6330* ⊕ *www.halekaihawaii.com* ⌁ *3 rooms, 1 suite* ⦿ *Breakfast.*

$$ **Hilo Hawaiian Hotel.** This recently
HOTEL renovated landmark hotel has large bay-front rooms offering spectacular views of Mauna Kea and Coconut Island on Hilo Bay. **Pros:** Hilo Bay views; private lanai in most rooms; large rooms. **Cons:** Daily fee for in-room Internet. $ *Rooms from: $245* ✉ *71 Banyan Dr.* ☎ *808/935–9361, 800/367–5004 from mainland, 800/272–5275 interisland* ⊕ *www.castleresorts.com* ⌁ *264 rooms, 21 suites* ⦿ *No meals.*

$ **Hilo Seaside Hotel.** A bit noisy due to its proximity to the airport, this
HOTEL local-flavor destination is a friendly, laid-back, and otherwise peaceful place, with tropical rooms that have private lanai. **Pros:** private lanai, friendly staff. **Cons:** noise from overhead planes can be disruptive. $ *Rooms from: $155* ✉ *126 Banyan Way* ☎ *808/935–0821, 800/560–5557* ⊕ *www.hiloseasidehotel.com* ⌁ *135 rooms.*

$$ **Shipman House Bed & Breakfast Inn.** This historic bed-and-breakfast on
B&B/INN 5½ verdant acres on Reed's Island is furnished with antique koa and period pieces, some dating from the days when Queen Liliuokalani came to tea. **Pros:** 10-minute walk to downtown Hilo; historic home; friendly and knowledgeable local hosts. **Cons:** not a great spot for kids; two-night minimum. $ *Rooms from: $219* ✉ *131 Kaiulani St.* ☎ *808/934–8002, 800/627–8447* ⊕ *www.hilo-hawaii.com* ⌁ *5 rooms* ⦿ *Breakfast.*

PUNA

$ **Coconut Cottage Bed & Breakfast.** This cottage has quickly become a
B&B/INN favorite for its beautiful grounds, the hosts' attention to detail, and its proximity to different island adventures. **Pros:** great breakfast; convenient to the lava-flow area, black-sand beach, and Kapoho tide pools for snorkeling; free Wi-Fi; laundry facility. **Cons:** some may have a hard

---

KOHALA COAST CONDO COMFORTS

If you require anything not provided by the management, both the **Kings' Shops** (✉ *250 Waikoloa Beach Dr., Waikoloa* ☎ *808/886–8811*) and the **Queens' Marketplace** (✉ *201 Waikoloa Beach Dr., Waikoloa* ☎ *808/886–8822*) in the Waikoloa Beach Resort are good places to go. There are a small grocery store, a liquor store, and several nice restaurants at the Kings' Shops. The newer Queens' Marketplace also has a food court, as well as a gourmet market where you can get pizza baked to order. It's not exactly cheap, but you're paying for the convenience of not having to drive into town.

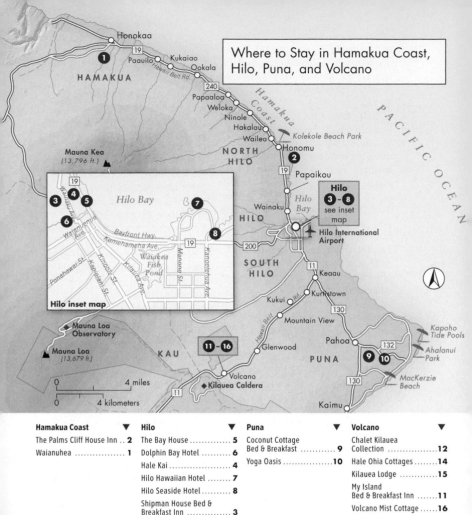

Where to Stay in Hamakua Coast, Hilo, Puna, and Volcano

time sleeping with the coqui frogs chirping. $ *Rooms from: $140 ✉ 13-1139 Leilani Ave., Pahoa* ☎ *808/965–0973, 866/204–7444* ⊕ *www.coconutcottagehawaii.com* ➯ *3 rooms, 1 bungalow* ⦿*Breakfast.*

$
B&B/INN

⚏ **Yoga Oasis.** With its exposed redwood beams, Balinese doorways, and imported art, Yoga Oasis draws those who seek relaxation and rejuvenation, and perhaps a free morning yoga lesson or two. **Pros:** daily yoga; focus on relaxation; breakfast and other meals may be available; very low prices. **Cons:** remote location; rooms in main building share bathrooms. $ *Rooms from: $65 ✉ Box 1935, 13-677 Pohoiki Rd., Pahoa* ☎ *808/936-7710, 800/274–4446* ⊕ *www.yogaoasis.org* ➯ *4 rooms with shared bath, 4 cabins, 2 houses* ⦿*No meals.*

HAWAII VOLCANOES NATIONAL PARK AND VICINITY

4

$
HOTEL

⚏ **Chalet Kilauea Collection.** Comprising three inns and lodges in and around Volcano Village, the collection has rooms and suites ranging from a historic lodge with no-frills, basic bedrooms to a deluxe inn with themed rooms and its own six-person hot tub. **Pros:** free Wi-Fi at all facilities; free afternoon tea at main office; friendly front desk; large variety of lodging types to choose from; hot tub; fireplace. **Cons:** office closes at 5 pm—late arrivals allowed with formal check-in the following morning. $ *Rooms from: $55 ✉ 19-4178 Wright Rd.* ☎ *808/967-7786, 800/937–7786* ⊕ *www.volcano-hawaii.com* ➯ *14 rooms, 3 suites, 5 houses* ⦿*No meals.*

$
RENTAL

⚏ **Hale Ohia Cottages.** A stately and comfortable Queen Anne–style mansion, Hale Ohia was built in the 1930s as a summer home for a wealthy Scotsman (the property is listed on the State Historic Register). **Pros:** unique architecture; central, quiet location; free Wi-Fi and parking; privacy. **Cons:** no TVs. $ *Rooms from: $115 ✉ 11-3968 Hale Ohia Rd., off Hwy. 11* ☎ *808/967–7986, 800/455–3803* ⊕ *www.haleohia.com* ➯ *4 rooms, 3 cottages, 1 suite* ⦿*Breakfast.*

$
HOTEL

⚏ **Kilauea Lodge.** A mile from the entrance of Hawaii Volcanoes National Park, this lodge was initially built as a YMCA camp in the 1930s; now it is a pleasant inn, tastefully furnished with European antiques. **Pros:** great restaurant; close to volcano; fireplaces. **Cons:** no TV or phone in lodge rooms. $ *Rooms from: $180 ✉ 19-3948 Old Volcano Rd., 1 mile northeast of Volcano Store, Box 116* ☎ *808/967-7366* ⊕ *www.kilauealodge.com* ➯ *12 rooms, 4 cottages (off property)* ⦿*Breakfast.*

$
B&B/INN

⚏ **My Island Bed & Breakfast Inn.** This three-story, family-operated inn occupies a historic home built in 1886 by the Lyman missionary family and set on a 7-acre botanical estate. **Pros:** historic home; full breakfast. **Cons:** some shared bathrooms; not every room has a TV. $ *Rooms from: $94 ✉ 19-3896 Old Volcano Hwy., Volcano Village* ☎ *808/967-7216* ⊕ *www.myislandinnhawaii.com* ➯ *6 rooms, 1 guesthouse* ⦿*Breakfast.*

$$$
RENTAL

⚏ **Volcano Mist Cottage.** Both rustic and Zen, this magical cottage in the rain forest features cathedral ceilings, spruce walls, cork flooring, and amenities not usually found at Volcano vacation rentals, like bathrobes, a Bose home theater system, and Trek mountain bikes. $ *Rooms from: $275 ✉ 11-3932 9th St., Volcano Village* ☎ *808/895-8359* ⊕ *www.volcanomistcottage.com* ➯ *1 cottage.*

$ RENTAL 🏨 **Volcano Places.** A collection of lovely vacation rental cottages, these accommodations range from a simple cottage in the rain forest to the stunning cedar-paneled Nohea, with its own hot tub. **Pros:** unique architecture; accommodates families; competitively priced, with discounts for three or more nights. **Cons:** no nightlife nearby. [$] *Rooms from: $135* ✉ *Volcano Village* ☎ *808/967–7990, 877/967–7990* 🌐 *www.volcanoplaces.com* 🛏 *2 2-bedroom cottages, 1 1-bedroom unit, 1 studio* 🍴 *No meals.*

KAU

$$ B&B/INN 🏨 **Kalaekilohana.** You wouldn't really expect to find a top-notch bed-and-breakfast in Kau, but just up the road from South Point, this grand yellow residence offers large, comfortable private suites with beautiful, locally harvested hardwood floors, private lanai with ocean and mountain views, and big, comfy beds decked out with high-thread-count sheets and fluffy down comforters. **Pros:** luxurious beds; beautiful decor reminscent of old Hawaii; delicious breakfast; dinner Friday and Saturday. **Cons:** not for children under 10; no pool. [$] *Rooms from: $249* ✉ *94-2152 South Point Rd., Naalehu* ☎ *808/939–8052* 🌐 *www.kau-hawaii.com* 🛏 *4 rooms* 🍴 *Multiple meal plans.*

5

KAUAI

WELCOME TO KAUAI

TOP REASONS TO GO

★ **Napali Coast:** On foot, by boat, or by air—explore what is unarguably one of the most beautiful stretches of coastline in all Hawaii.

★ **Kalalau Trail:** Hawaii's ultimate adventure hike will test your endurance but reward you with lush tropical vegetation, white-sand beaches, and unforgettable views.

★ **Kayaking:** Kauai is a hub for kayakers, with four rivers plus the spectacular coastline to explore.

★ **Waimea Canyon:** Dramatic, colorful rock formations and frequent rainbows make this natural wonder one of Kauai's most stunning features.

★ **Birds:** Birds thrive on Kauai, especially at the Kilauea Point National Wildlife Refuge.

1 North Shore. Dreamy beaches, green mountains, breathtaking scenery, and abundant rain, waterfalls, and rainbows characterize the North Shore, which includes the communities of Kilauea, Princeville, and Hanalei.

2 East Side. This is Kauai's commercial and residential hub, dominated by the island's largest town, Kapaa. The airport, harbor, and government offices are found in the county seat of Lihue.

3 South Shore. Peaceful landscapes, sunny weather, and beaches that rank among the best in the world make the South Shore the resort capital of Kauai. The Poipu resort area is here, along with the main towns of Koloa, Lawai, and Kalaheo.

Hae
Kalalau Trail

NAPALI COAST

Kalalau Lookout

Kokee State Park

550

WAIMEA CANYON

WEST SIDE
4

552

550

Kaulakahi Channel

50

Kekaha

Waimea

TO NIIHAU

0   8 mi
0   8 km

50

Hanapepe

Ele

Hanapepe Bay

Hanalei
Bay

Princeville

560
Hanalei   **1**
NORTH SHORE

Kilauea

Anahola

56

Waialeale
5,148 ft.

581

Kapaa

580

Wailua
Bay

EAST SIDE
2

583

56

Kilohana Crater
1,138 ft.

Hanamaulu

Lihue   ✈ **Lihue Airport**

50

58

Nawiliwili Bay

Kalaheo

520

530

Koloa

Kauai Channel

SOUTH SHORE
3

Poipu

GETTING ORIENTED

Despite its small size—about 550 square miles—Kauai has four distinct regions, each with its own unique characteristics. The windward coast, which catches the prevailing trade winds, consists of the North Shore and East Side, while the drier, leeward coast encompasses the South Shore and West Side. One main road nearly encircles the island, except for a 15-mile stretch of sheer cliffs called Napali Coast. The center of the island—Mt. Waialeale, completely inaccessible by car and rarely viewable except from above due to nearly year-round cloud cover—is reputedly the wettest spot on Earth, getting about 450 inches of rain per year.

5

4 West Side. Dry, sunny, and sleepy, the West Side includes the historic towns of Hanapepe, Waimea, and Kekaha. This area is ideal for outdoor adventurers because it's the entryway to the Waimea Canyon and Kokee State Park, and the departure point for most Napali Coast boat trips.

GREAT ITINERARIES

As small as Kauai may be, you still can't do it all in one day: hiking Kalalau Trail, kayaking Wailua River, showering in a waterfall, watching whales at Kilauea Lighthouse, waking to the sunrise above Kealia, touring underwater lava tubes at Tunnels, and shopping for gifts at Koloa Town shops. Rather than trying to check everything off your list in one fell swoop, we recommend choosing your absolute favorite and devoting a full day to the experience.

A Bit of History

Hawaiian beliefs are traditionally rooted in nature. If you're interested in archaeological remains where sacred ceremonies were held, focus on the Wailua River area. Your best bet is to take a riverboat tour—it's full of kitsch, but you'll definitely walk away with a deeper understanding of ancient Hawaii. Then, head to Lihue's Kauai Museum, where you can pick up a memento of authentic Hawaiian artistry at the gift shop. End your day at Gaylord's restaurant and meander through the historic Kilohana Plantation sugar estate.

Adventure Galore

For big-time adventure, kayak Napali Coast or skydive over the ocean and island for a once-in-a-lifetime experience. For those whose idea of adventure is a good walk, take the flat, coastal trail along the East Side—you can pick it up just about anywhere starting at the southern end of Lydgate Park, heading north. It'll take you all the way to Anahola, if you desire. After it's all over, recuperate with a massage by the ocean—or in the comfort of your own room, so you can crash immediately afterward.

A Day on the Water

Start your day before sunrise and head west to Port Allen Marina. Check in with one of the tour-boat operators—who will provide you with plenty of coffee to jumpstart your day—and cruise Napali Coast before heading across the Kaulakahi Channel to snorkel the fish-rich waters of Niihau. Slather up with sunscreen and be prepared for a long—and sometimes big—day on the water; you can enjoy a couple of mai tais on the return trip. Something about the sun and the salt air conspires to induce a powerful sense of fatigue—so don't plan anything in the evening. The trip also helps build a huge appetite, so stop at Grinds in Eleele on the way home.

Coastal Drives

If you're staying on the East Side or North Shore, the best drive for ocean vistas is, hands down, Highway 560, which begins at Princeville on the main highway where Highway 56 ends. Stop at the first lookout overseeing Hanalei River valley for a few snapshots; then head down the hill, across the one-lane bridge—taking in the taro fields—and through the town of Hanalei and on to the end of the road at Kee Beach. If you're up for it, enjoy a bit of unparalleled hiking on the Kalalau Trail, go snorkeling at Kee, or simply soak up the sun on the beach, if it's not too crowded. If you're staying on the South Shore or West Side, follow Highway 50 west. You'll start to catch distant ocean vistas from the highway as you head out of the town of Kalaheo and from the coffee fields of Kauai Coffee. Stop here for a sample. You'll come closer to the ocean—and practically reach out and touch it—after you pass through Waimea en route to Kekaha. Although this isn't great swimming water—it's unprotected, with no reef—there is a long stretch of beach here perfect for walking, running, or simply meandering. Once the paved road ends—if you're brave and your car-rental agreement allows—keep going and you'll eventually come to Polihale, a huge, deserted beach. It'll feel like the end of the world here, so it's a great place to spend a quiet afternoon and witness a spectacular sunset. Just be sure to pack plenty of food, water, and sunscreen before you depart Kekaha—and gas up the car.

Shop Till You Drop

You could actually see a good many of the island's sights by browsing in our favorite island shops. Of course, you can't see the entire island, but this itinerary will take you through Kapaa and north to Hanalei. Don't miss Marta's Boat—high-end clothing for mom and child—across from Foodland in Waipouli. A mile north, Kela's Glass has great art pieces. From there, a leisurely drive north will reveal the rural side of Kauai. If you enjoy tea, sake, or sushi, stop at Kilauea's Kong Lung, where you can stock up on complete place settings for each. Then, head down the road to Hanalei. If you're inspired by surf, stop in Hanalei Surf Company. Our favorite for one-of-a-kind keepsakes—actually antiques and authentic memorabilia—is Yellow Fish Trading Company, and we never head into Hanalei without stopping at On the Road to Hanalei.

Relax Kauai-Style

If you're headed to Kauai for some peace and quiet, you'll want to start your day with yoga at Yoga Hanalei (⊕ *www. yogahanalei.com*) or Kapaa's Bikram Yoga Kauai (⊕ *www.bikramyogakapaa. com*). If you're staying on the South Shore, try yoga on the beach (actually a grassy spot just off the beach) with longtime yoga instructor Joy Zepeda (⊕ *www.kauaioceanfrontyoga.com*). If it happens to be the second or last Sunday of the month, you might then head to the Lawai International Center (⊕ *www. lawaicenter.org*) for an afternoon stroll among 88 Buddhist shrines. On the North Shore, Limahuli Gardens is the perfect place to wander among native plants. Then watch the sun slip into the sea on any west-facing beach and call it a day with a glass of wine.

Have a Little Romance

We can't think of a better way to ensure a romantic vacation for two than to pop a bottle of champagne and walk the Mahaulepu shoreline at sunrise, hand in hand with a loved one. Make this a Sunday and follow your walk with brunch at the Grand Hyatt. Then spend the afternoon luxuriating with facials, body scrubs, and massage in the Hyatt ANARA Spa's Garden Treatment Village, in a private, thatched hut just for couples. That'll put you in the mood for a wedding ceremony or renewal of vows on the beach followed by a sunset dinner overlooking the ocean at the Beach House restaurant. Can it get any more romantic than this?

5

Even a nickname like "The Garden Island" fails to do justice to Kauai's beauty. Verdant trees grow canopies over the few roads, and brooding mountains are framed by long, sandy beaches, coral reefs, and sheer sea cliffs. Pristine trade winds moderate warm daily temperatures while offering comfort for deep, refreshing sleep through gentle nights.

For adventure seekers, Kauai offers everything from difficult hikes to helicopter tours. The island has top-notch spas and golf courses, and its beaches are known to be some of the most beautiful in the world. Even after you've spent days lazing around drinking mai tais or kayaking your way down a river, there's still plenty to do, as well as see: plantation villages, a historic lighthouse, wildlife refuges, a fern grotto, a colorful canyon, and deep rivers are all easily explored.

GEOLOGY
Kauai is the oldest and northernmost of the main Hawaiian Islands. Five million years of wind and rain have worked their magic, sculpting fluted sea cliffs and whittling away at the cinder cones and caldera that prove its volcanic origin. Foremost among these is Waialeale, one of the wettest spots on Earth. Its approximate 450-inch annual rainfall feeds the mighty Wailua River, the only navigable waterway in Hawaii. The vast Alakai Swamp soaks up rain like a sponge, releasing it slowly into the watershed that gives Kauai its emerald sheen.

FLORA AND FAUNA
Kauai offers some of the best birding in the state, due in part to the absence of the mongoose. Many nene (the endangered Hawaiian state bird) reared in captivity have been successfully released here, along with an endangered forest bird called the puaiohi. The island is also home to a large colony of migratory nesting seabirds and has two refuges protecting endangered Hawaiian waterbirds. Kauai's most noticeable fowl, however, is the wild chicken. A cross between jungle fowl (*moa*) brought by the Polynesians and domestic chickens and fighting cocks that escaped during the last two hurricanes, they are everywhere, and

the roosters crow when they feel like it, not just at dawn. Consider yourself warned.

HISTORY

Kauai's residents have had a reputation for independence since ancient times. Called "The Separate Kingdom," Kauai alone resisted King Kamehameha's charge to unite the Hawaiian Islands. In fact, it was only by kidnapping Kauai's king, Kaumualii, and forcing him to marry Kamehameha's widow that the Garden Isle was joined to the rest of Hawaii. That spirit lives on today as Kauai residents try to resist the lure of tourism dollars captivating the rest of the Islands. Local building tradition maintains that no structure be taller than a coconut tree, and Kauai's capital, Lihue, is still more small town than city.

KAUAI PLANNER

5

GETTING HERE AND AROUND

AIR TRAVEL

All commercial and cargo flights use the Lihue Airport, 2 miles east of the town of Lihue.

GROUND TRANSPOR- TATION

Unless you plan to stay strictly at a resort or do all your sightseeing as part of guided tours, you'll need a rental car. There is bus service on the island, but the bumpy buses tend to run limited hours.

You most likely won't need a four-wheel-drive vehicle anywhere on the island, so save yourself the money. And although convertibles look like fun, the frequent, intermittent rain showers and intense tropical sun make hardtops a better (and cheaper) choice.

If possible, avoid the "rush" hours when the local workers go to and from their jobs. Kauai has some of the highest gas prices in the Islands.

DRIVING TIMES	
Haena to Hanalei	5 miles/15 mins
Hanalei to Princeville	4 miles/10 mins
Princeville to Kilauea	5 miles/10 mins
Kilauea to Anahola	8 miles/12 mins
Anahola to Kapaa	5 miles/10 mins
Kapaa to Lihue	10 miles/20 mins
Lihue to Poipu	13 miles/25 mins
Poipu to Kalaheo	8 miles/15 mins
Kalaheo to Hanapepe	4 miles/8 mins
Hanapepe to Waimea	7 miles/10 mins

ISLAND DRIVING TIMES

Driving around Kauai will take longer than you'd expect, and Kauai roads are subject to some heavy traffic, especially going through Kapaa and Lihue.

RESTAURANTS

Kauai's cultural diversity is apparent in its restaurants, which offer authentic Vietnamese, Chinese, Korean, Japanese, Thai, Mexican, Italian, and Hawaiian specialties. Less specialized restaurants cater to the tourist crowd, serving standard American fare—burgers, pizza, sandwiches, surf-and-turf combos, and so on. Kapaa offers the best selection of restaurants, with options for a variety of tastes and budgets; most fast-food joints are in Lihue.

Parents will be relieved to encounter a tolerant attitude toward children, even if they're noisy. Men can leave their jackets and ties at home; attire tends toward informal. But if you want to dress up, you can. Reservations are accepted in most places and required at some of the top restaurants.

Prices in the reviews are the average cost of a main course at dinner or, if dinner is not served, at lunch.

HOTELS

If you want to golf, play tennis, or hang at a spa, stay at a resort. You'll also be more likely to find activities for children at resorts, including camps that allow parents a little time off. The island's hotels tend to be smaller and older, with fewer on-site amenities. Some of the swankiest places to stay on the island are the St. Regis Princeville Resort on the North Shore, where rooms run more than $1,000 per night in high season, and the Grand Hyatt Kauai on the South Shore for a bit less; of course, those with views of the ocean book faster than those without.

Condos and vacation rentals on Kauai tend to run the gamut from fabulous luxury estates to scruffy little dives. It's buyer-beware in this totally unregulated sector of the visitor industry, though the County of Kauai is still in the process of developing new regulations for these types of properties, particularly those in agricultural and rural areas. If you're planning to stay at one of these, be sure to contact the operator prior to traveling to ensure it's still open.

Properties managed by individual owners can be found on online vacation-rental directories such as CyberRentals and Vacation Rentals By Owner, as well as on the Kauai Visitors Bureau's website. There are also several Kauai-based management companies with vacation rentals.

The island's bed-and-breakfasts allow you to meet local residents and more directly experience the aloha spirit. Many have oceanfront settings and breakfasts with everything from tropical fruits and juices, Kauai coffee, and macadamia-nut waffles to breads made with local bananas and mangoes. Some have pools, hot tubs, services such as *lomilomi* massage, and breakfasts delivered to your lanai. Some properties have stand-alone units on-site.

Prices in the reviews are the lowest cost of a standard double room in high season. For expanded hotel reviews visit www.Fodors.com.

VISITOR INFORMATION

The Kauai Visitors Bureau has an office at 4334 Rice Street, Lihue's main thoroughfare, near the Kauai Museum.

Information Kauai Visitors Bureau ✉ *4334 Rice St., Suite 101, Lihue*
☎ *808/245–3971, 800/262–1400* ⊕ *www.kauaidiscovery.com.* **Poipu Beach
Resort Association** ☎ *808/742–7444, 888/744–0888* ⊕ *www.poipubeach.org.*

EXPLORING

Updated by
Charles E.
Roessler

The main road tracing Kauai's perimeter takes you past much more
scenery than would seem possible on one small island. Chiseled mountains, thundering waterfalls, misty hillsides, dreamy beaches, lush vegetation, and small towns make up the physical landscape. Perhaps the
most stunning piece of scenery is a place no road will take you—the
breathtakingly beautiful Napali Coast, which runs along the northwest
side of the island.

■TIP➜ While exploring the island, try to take advantage of the many
roadside scenic overlooks and pull over to take in the constantly changing view. Don't try to pack too much into one day. Kauai is small, but
travel is slow. The island's sights are divided into four geographic areas,
in clockwise order: the North Shore, the East Side, the South Shore,
and the West Side.

THE NORTH SHORE

The North Shore of Kauai includes the environs of Kilauea, Princeville,
Hanalei, and Haena. Traveling north on Route 56 from the airport, the
coastal highway crosses the Wailua River and the busy towns of Wailua
and Kapaa before emerging into a decidedly rural and scenic landscape, with expansive views of the island's rugged interior mountains.
As the two-lane highway turns west and narrows, it winds through
spectacular scenery and passes the posh resort community of Princeville
before dropping down into Hanalei Valley. Here it narrows further and
becomes a federally recognized scenic roadway, replete with one-lane
bridges (the local etiquette is for six or seven cars to cross at a time,
before yielding to those on the other side), hairpin turns, and heart-
stopping coastal vistas. The road ends at Kee, where the ethereal rain
forests and fluted sea cliffs of Napali Coast Wilderness State Park begin.

In winter Kauai's North Shore receives more rainfall than other areas
of the island. Don't let this deter you from visiting. The clouds drift
over the mountains of Namolokama creating a mysterious mood and
then, in a blink, disappear, rewarding you with mountains laced with
a dozen waterfalls or more. The views of the mountain—as well as the
sunsets over the ocean—from the St. Regis Bar, adjacent to the lobby
of the St. Regis Princeville Resort, are fantastic.

HANALEI, HAENA, AND WEST
Haena 40 miles northwest of Lihue; Hanalei 5 miles east of Haena.

Crossing the historic one-lane bridge into Hanalei reveals old-world
Hawaii, including working taro farms, poi making, and evenings of
throwing horseshoes at Black Pot Beach Park—found unmarked (as
many places are on Kauai) at the east end of Hanalei Bay Beach Park.
Although the current real-estate boom on Kauai has attracted mainland

millionaires to build estate homes on the few remaining parcels of land in Hanalei, there's still plenty to see and do. It's *the* gathering place on the North Shore. Restaurants, shops, and people-watching here are among the best on the island, and you won't find a single brand name, chain, or big-box store around—unless you count surf brands like Quiksilver and Billabong.

The beach and river at Hanalei offer swimming, snorkeling, bodyboarding, surfing, and kayaking. Those hanging around at sunset often congregate at the Hanalei Pavilion, where a husband-and-wife-slack-key-guitar-playing combo makes impromptu appearances. There's an old rumor, since quashed by the local newspaper, the *Garden Island*, that says Hanalei was the inspiration for the song "Puff the Magic Dragon," performed by the 1960s singing sensation Peter, Paul & Mary. Even with the newspaper's clarification, some tours still point out the shape of the dragon carved into the mountains encircling the town.

Once you pass through Hanalei town, the road shrinks even more as you skirt the coast and pass through Haena. Blind corners, quick turns, and one-lane bridges force slow driving along this scenic stretch across the Lumahai and Wainiha valleys.

GETTING HERE AND AROUND

There is only one road leading beyond Princeville to Kee Beach at the western end of the North Shore: Route 560. Hanalei's commercial stretch fronts this route, and you'll find parking at the shopping compounds on each side of the road. After Hanalei, parking is restricted to two main areas, Haena Beach Park and a new lot at Haena State Park, and there are few pullover areas along Route 560. Traffic and especially parking have become major concerns as the North Shore has gained popularity, so be prepared to be patient.

TOP ATTRACTIONS

Hanalei Valley Overlook. Dramatic mountains and a patchwork of neat taro farms bisected by the wide Hanalei River make this one of Hawaii's loveliest sights. The fertile Hanalei Valley has been planted in taro since perhaps AD 700, save for a century-long foray into rice that ended in 1960. (The historic Haraguchi Rice Mill is all that remains of the era.) Many taro farmers lease land within the 900-acre Hanalei National Wildlife Refuge, helping to provide wetland habitat for four species of endangered Hawaiian waterbirds. ⊠ *Rte. 56, across from Foodland, Princeville.*

Limahuli Garden. Narrow Limahuli Valley, with its fluted mountain peaks and ancient stone taro terraces, creates an unparalleled setting for this botanical garden and nature preserve. Dedicated to protecting native plants and unusual varieties of taro, it represents the principles of conservation and stewardship held by its founder, Charles "Chipper" Wichman. Limahuli's priomordial beauty and strong *mana* (spiritual power) eclipse the extensive botanical collection. It's one of the most gorgeous spots on Kauai and the crown jewel of the National Tropical Botanical Garden, which Wichman now heads. Call ahead to reserve a guided tour, or tour on your own. Be sure to check out the quality gift shop and revolutionary compost toilet, and be prepared to

DID YOU KNOW?

You'll find a welcome respite
at gorgeous and secluded
Kalalau Beach when you
reach the end of the arduous
11-mile Kalalau Trail.

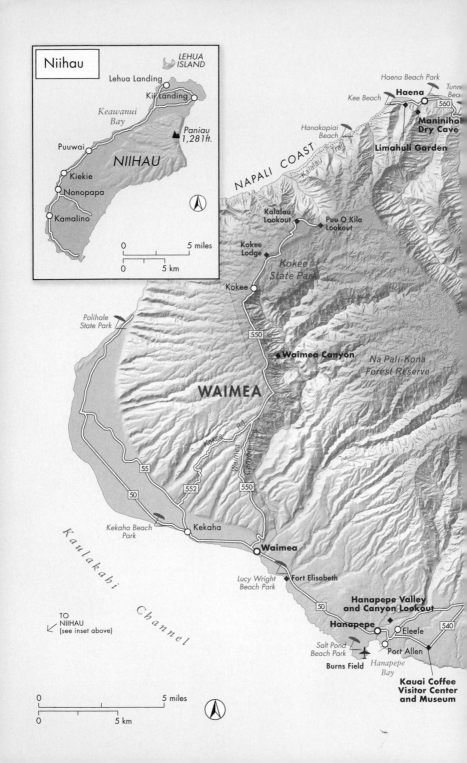

Niihau

LEHUA
ISLAND

Lehua Landing

Kii Landing

*Keawanui
Bay*

Puuwai

▲ Paniau
1,281ft.

NIIHAU

Kiekie

Nonopapa

Kamalino

0 _____ 5 miles

0 _____ 5 km

Haena Beach Park

Kee Beach   **Haena**   Tunn
Bea

560

**Maniniho
Dry Cave**

*Hanakapiai
Beach*

Limahuli Garden

NAPALI COAST

Kalalau Trail

**Kalalau
Lookout**   ◆ Puu O Kila
Lookout

**Kokee
Lodge**

*Kokee
State Park*

Kokee

550

*Na Pali-Kona
Forest Reserve*

◆ **Waimea Canyon**

*Polihale
State Park*

WAIMEA

Kokee Rd.

Waimea Canyon

55

552

50

550

*Kekaha Beach
Park*

Kekaha

Waimea

*Lucy Wright
Beach Park*   ◆ Fort Elisabeth

Kaulakahi   Channel

50

**Hanapepe Valley
and Canyon Lookout**

Hanapepe   ◆

○ Eleele   540

TO
NIIHAU
(see inset above)

*Salt Pond
Beach Park*

Port Allen

Burns Field   *Hanapepe
Bay*

**Kauai Coffee
Visitor Center
and Museum**

0 _____ 5 miles

0 _____ 5 km

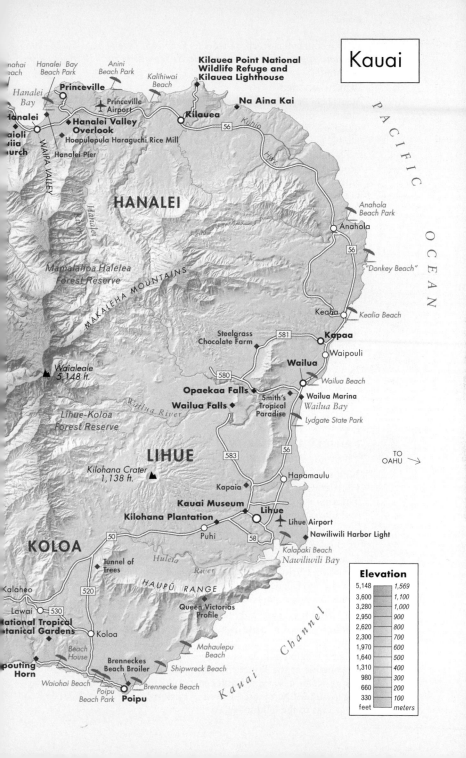

walk a somewhat steep hillside. ⊠ *Rte. 560, Haena* ☎ *808/826–1053* ⊕ *www.ntbg.org* 🎫 *Self-guided tour $15, guided tour $30 (reservations required)* 🕙 *Tues.–Sat. 9:30–4.*

WORTH NOTING

Maniniholo Dry Cave. Kauai's North Shore caves echo an enchanting, almost haunting, alternative to sunny skies and deep blue seas. Steeped in legend, Maniniholo Dry Cave darkens and becomes more claustrophobic as you glide across its sandy floor, hearing the drips down the walls and wondering at its past. Legend has it that Maniniholo was the head fisherman of the Menehune—Kauai's quasi-mythical first inhabitants. After gathering too much food to carry, his men stored the excess in the dry cave overnight. When he returned in the morning, the food had vanished and he blamed the imps living in the cracks of the cave. He and his men dug into the cliff to find and destroy the imps, leaving behind the cave. Across the highway from Maniniholo Dry Cave is Haena State Park. ⊠ *Rte. 560, Haena.*

Waioli Huiia Church. Designated a National Historic Landmark, this little church—affiliated with the United Church of Christ—doesn't go unnoticed right alongside Route 560 in downtown Hanalei, and its doors are often wide open (from 9 to 5, give or take) inviting inquisitive visitors in for a look around. Like the Waioli Mission House next door, it's an exquisite representation of New England architecture crossed with Hawaiian thatched buildings. During Hurricane Iniki's visit in 1992, which brought sustained winds of 160 mph and wind gusts up to 220 mph, this little church was lifted off its foundation but, thankfully, lovingly restored. Services are held at 10 am on Sunday with many hymns sung in Hawaiian and often accompanied by piano and ukulele. ⊠ *5-5393A Kuhio Hwy., Hanalei* ☎ *808/826–6253* ⊕ *www.hanaleichurch.org.*

PRINCEVILLE, KILAUEA, AND AROUND

Princeville 4 miles east of Hanalei; Kilauea 5 miles east of Princeville.

Built on a bluff offering gorgeous sea and mountain vistas, including Hanalei Bay, Princeville is the creation of a 1970s resort development. The area is anchored by a few large hotels, world-class golf courses, and lots of condos and time-shares.

Five miles down Route 56, a former plantation town, Kilauea, maintains its rural flavor in the midst of unrelenting gentrification encroaching all around it. Especially noteworthy are its historic lava-rock buildings, including **Christ Memorial Episcopal Church** on Kolo Road and, on Keneke and Kilauea Road (commonly known as Lighthouse Road), the Kong Lung Company, which is now an expensive shop.

GETTING HERE AND AROUND

There is only one main road through the Princeville resort area, so maneuvering a car here can be a nightmare. If you're trying to find a smaller lodging unit, be sure to get specific driving directions. Parking is available at the Princeville Shopping Center at the entrance to the resort. Kilauea is about 5 miles east on Route 56. There's a public parking lot in the town center as well as parking at the end of Kilauea Road for access to the lighthouse.

Stop by the farmers' market in Kapaa to pick up locally grown mangoes and other fruits.

TOP ATTRACTIONS

Fodor's Choice ★ **Kilauea Point National Wildlife Refuge and Kilauea Lighthouse.** A beacon for sea traffic since it was built in 1913, this National Historic Landmark just celebrated its centennial and has the largest clamshell lens of any lighthouse in the world. It's within a national wildlife refuge, where thousands of seabirds soar on the trade winds and nest on the steep ocean cliffs. Seeing endangered nene geese, white- and red-tailed tropic birds, and more (all identifiable by educational signboards) as well as native plants, dolphins, humpback whales, huge winter surf, and gorgeous views of the North Shore are well worth the modest entry fee. The gift shop has a great selection of books about the island's natural history and an array of unique merchandise, with all proceeds benefiting education and preservation efforts. ✉ *Kīlauea Lighthouse Rd., Kilauea* ☎ *808/828–0168* ⊕ *www.kilaueapoint.org OR www.fws.gov/kilaueapoint* ✐ *$5* ☻ *Daily 10–4.*

Fodor's Choice ★ **Na Aina Kai.** One small sign along the highway is all that promotes this once-private garden gone big time. Joyce and Ed Doty's love for plants and art now spans 240 acres and includes many different gardens, a hardwood plantation, a canyon, lagoons, a Japanese teahouse, a poinciana maze, a waterfall, and a sandy beach. Throughout are more than 160 bronze sculptures, reputedly one of the nation's largest collections. One popular feature is a children's garden with a 16-foot-tall Jack and the Beanstalk bronze sculpture, gecko maze, tree house, kid-size train and, of course, a tropical jungle. Located in a residential neighborhood and hoping to maintain good neighborly relations, the garden, which is now a nonprofit organization, limits tours (guided only). Tour lengths vary widely, from 1½ to 5 hours. Reservations are required. ✉ *4101 Wailapa Rd., Kilauea* ☎ *808/828–0525.*

THE EAST SIDE

The East Side encompasses Lihue, Wailua, and Kapaa. It's also known as the Coconut Coast, as there was once a coconut plantation where today's aptly named Coconut Marketplace is located. A small grove still exists on both sides of the highway. *Mauka* (toward the mountains), a fenced herd of goats keeps the grass tended; on the *makai* (toward the ocean) side, you can walk through the grove, although it's best not to walk directly under the trees—falling coconuts can be dangerous. Lihue is the county seat, and the whole East Side is the island's center of commerce, so early-morning and late-afternoon drive times (or rush hour) can get very congested. (Because there's only one main road, if there's a serious traffic accident, the entire roadway may be closed, with no way around. Not to worry; it's a rarity.)

KAPAA AND WAILUA

Kapaa 16 miles southeast of Kilauea; Wailua 3 miles south of Kapaa.

Old Town Kapaa was once a plantation town, which is no surprise—most of the larger towns on Kauai once were. Old Town Kapaa is made up of a collection of wooden-front shops, some built by plantation workers and still run by their progeny today. Kapaa houses the two biggest grocery stores on the island, side by side: Foodland and Safeway. It also offers plenty of dining options for breakfast, lunch, and dinner, and gift shopping. If the timing is right, plan to cruise the town on the first Saturday evening of each month when the bands are playing and the town's wares are on display. To the south, Wailua comprises a few restaurants and shops, a few midrange resorts along the coastline, and a housing community *mauka.*

GETTING HERE AND AROUND

Turn to the right out of the airport at Lihue for the road to Wailua. Careful, though—the zone between Lihue and Wailua has been the site of many car accidents. Two bridges—under which the very culturally significant Wailua River gently flows—mark the beginning of Wailua. It quickly blends into Kapaa; there's no real demarcation. Pay attention and drive carefully, always knowing where you are going and when to turn off.

TOP ATTRACTIONS

Opaekaa Falls. The mighty Wailua River produces many dramatic waterfalls, and Opaekaa (pronounced oh-pie-kah-ah) is one of the best. It plunges hundreds of feet to the pool below and can be easily viewed from a scenic overlook with ample parking. Opaekaa means "rolling shrimp," which refers to tasty native crustaceans that were once so abundant they could be seen tumbling in the falls. ■**TIP**➔ Just before reaching the parking area for the waterfalls, turn left into a scenic pull-out for great views of the Wailua River valley and its march to the sea. ✉ *Kuamoo Rd. From Rte. 56, turn mauka onto Kuamoo Rd. and drive 1½ miles, Wailua.*

Continued on page 462

HAWAII'S PLANTS 101

Hawaii is a bounty of rainbow-colored flowers and plants. The evening air is scented with their fragrance. Just look at the front yard of almost any home, travel any road, or visit any local park and you'll see a spectacular array of colored blossoms and leaves. What most visitors don't know is that many of the plants they are seeing are not native to Hawaii; rather, they were introduced during the last two centuries as ornamental plants, or for timber, shade, or fruit.

Hawaii boasts nearly every climate on the planet, excluding the two most extreme: arctic tundra and arid desert. The Islands have wine-growing regions, cactus-speckled ranchlands, icy mountaintops, and the rainiest forests on earth.

Plants introduced from around the world thrive here. The lush lowland valleys along the windward coasts are predominantly populated by non-native trees including yellow- and red-fruited **guava**, silvery-leafed **kukui**, and orange-flowered **tulip trees**.

The colorful **plumeria flower**, very fragrant and commonly used in lei making, and the giant multicolored **hibiscus flower** are both used by many women as hair adornments, and are two of the most common plants found around homes and hotels. The umbrella-like **monkeypod tree** from Central America provides shade in many of Hawaii's parks including Kapiolani Park in Honolulu. Hawaii's largest tree, found in Lahaina, Maui, is a giant **banyan tree.** Its canopy and massive support roots cover about two-thirds of an acre. The native **ohia tree**, with its brilliant red brush-like flowers, and the **hapuu**, a giant tree fern, are common in Hawaii's forests and are also used ornamentally in gardens.

Bougainvillea

Guava

Monkeypod

Banyan

Ohia Lehua*

Tulip Tree

Plumeria

Pandanus

Hibiscus

Anthurium

Kukui

Hapuu

*endemic to Hawaii

DID YOU KNOW?

More than 2,200 plant species are found in the Hawaiian Islands, but only about 1,000 are native. Of these, 320 are so rare, they are endangered. Hawaii's endemic plants evolved from ancestral seeds arriving in the Islands over thousands of years as baggage with birds, floating on ocean currents, or drifting on winds from continents thousands of miles away. Once here, these plants evolved in isolation, creating many new species known nowhere else in the world.

Wailua Falls. You may recognize this impressive cascade from the opening sequences of the *Fantasy Island* television series. Kauai has plenty of noteworthy waterfalls, but this one is especially gorgeous, easy to find, and easy to photograph. ⊠ *End of Rte. 583, 4 miles from Rte. 56, Kapaa.*

WORTH NOTING

FAMILY **Smith's Tropical Paradise.** Nestled next to Wailua Marina along the mighty Wailua River, this 30-acre botanical and cultural garden offers a glimpse of exotic foliage, including fruit orchards, a bamboo rain forest, and tropical lagoons. Take the tram and enjoy a narrated tour or stroll along the mile-long pathways. It's a popular spot for wedding receptions and other large events, and its four-times-weekly luau is one of the island's oldest and best. ⊠ *Rte. 56, just south of Wailua River, Kapaa* ☎ *808/821–6895* ⊕ *smithskauai.com.*

Steelgrass Chocolate Farm. Hawaii is the only state in the country where *theobroma cacao* grows. As every chocolate connoisseur knows, the tree that grows the precious seed that becomes chocolate is the cacao tree. The Lydgates are on a mission to grow enough cacao on their family farm with the hope that one day they will produce an identifiable Kauai Homegrown Chocolate. For now, you can tour this organic farm (in addition to cacao, they grow vanilla, timber, bamboo, and many tropical fruits) and learn how chocolate is made, "from branch to bar," as they put it. The three-hour tour includes, of course, plenty of chocolate tastings. Reservations are required for the morning tour, which begins Monday, Wednesday, and Friday at 9 am. Children 12 and under are free. Driving directions are provided when you make a reservation. ⊠ *Off Rte. 581* ☎ *808/821–1857* ⊕ *www.steelgrass.org* 🗨 *$60* ⊙ *Mon., Wed., Fri. for tours only.*

LIHUE
7 miles southwest of Wailua.

The commercial and political center of Kauai County, which includes the islands of Kauai and Niihau, Lihue is home to the island's major airport, harbor, and hospital. This is where you can find the state and county offices that issue camping and hiking permits and the same fast-food eateries and big-box stores that blight the mainland. The county is seeking help in reviving the downtown; for now, once your business is done, there's little reason to linger in lackluster Lihue.

GETTING HERE AND AROUND
Route 56 leads into Lihue from the north and Route 50 comes here from the south and west. The road from the airport (where Kauai's car-rental agencies are) leads to the middle of Lihue. Many of the area's stores and restaurants are on and around Rice Street, which also leads to Kalapaki Bay and Nawiliwili Harbor.

WORTH NOTING
Kauai Museum. Maintaining a stately presence on Rice Street, the historic museum building is easy to find. It features a permanent display, "The Story of Kauai," which provides a competent overview of the Garden Island and Niihau, tracing the islands' geology, mythology, and cultural history. Local artists are represented in changing exhibits in the

KAUAI SIGHTSEEING TOURS

Aloha Kauai Tours. You get *way* off the beaten track on these four-wheel-drive van excursions. Choose from several options, including the half-day Backroads Tour covering mostly haul-cane roads behind the locked gates of Grove Farm Plantation, and the half-day Rainforest Tour, which follows the Wailua River to its source, Mt. Waialeale. The expert guides are some of the best on the island. Rates are $80. ⊠ *Check in at 1702 Haleukana St. in Puhi, 1702 Haleukana, St.* ☎ *808/245–6400, 800/452–1113* ⊕ *www. alohakauaitours.com.*

Roberts Hawaii Tours. The Round-the-Island Tour, sometimes called the Wailua River–Waimea Canyon Tour, gives a good overview of half the island, including Fort Elisabeth and Opaekaa Falls. Guests are transported in air-conditioned, 25-passenger minibuses. The $79.50 trip includes a boat ride up the Wailua River to the Fern Grotto and a visit to the lookouts above Waimea Canyon. ☎ *808/245–9101, 800/831–5541* ⊕ *www.robertshawaii.com.*

Waimea Historic Walking Tour. Led by a *kupuna*, a respected Hawaiian elder, this 2½- to 3-hour tour begins promptly at 9:30 am, every Monday at the West Kauai Visitor Center. While sharing her personal remembrances, Aletha Kaohi leads an easy walk that explains Waimea's distinction as a recipient of the 2006 National Trust for Historic Preservation Award. The tour is free, but a reservation is required. ⊠ *Waimea* ☎ *808/338–1332.*

second-floor mezzanine gallery. The expanded gift shop alone is worth a visit, with a fine collection of authentic Niihau shell lei, feather hatband lei, hand-turned wooden bowls, reference books, and other quality arts, crafts, and gifts, many of them locally made. ⊠ *4428 Rice St., Lihue* ☎ *808/245–6931* ⊕ *www.kauaimuseum.com* ☜ *$10* ☉ *Mon.–Sat. 9–5, closed Sun.*

FAMILY **Kilohana Plantation.** This estate dates back to 1850, shortly after the "Great Mahele"—the division of land by the Hawaiian people. Plantation manager Albert Spencer Wilcox developed it as a working cattle ranch, and his nephew, Gaylord Parke Wilcox, took over in 1936, building Kauai's first mansion. Today the 16,000-square-foot, Tudor-style home houses specialty shops, art galleries, and Gaylord's, a pretty restaurant with courtyard seating and a spiffy new bar. Nearly half the original furnishings remain, and the gardens and orchards were replanted according to the original plans. You can tour the grounds for free; children enjoy visiting the farm animals and feeding the wild pigs in residence. A train runs 2½ miles on the hour through 104 acres of lands representing the agricultural story of Kauai as well as surviving as a working farm. ⊠ *3-2087 Kaumualii Hwy., Lihue* ☎ *808/245–5608* ⊕ *www.kilohanakauai.com* ☉ *Mon.–Sat. 9:30–9:30, Sun. 9:30–3:30.*

THE SOUTH SHORE

As you follow the main road south from Lihue, the landscape becomes lush and densely vegetated before giving way to drier conditions that characterize Poipu, the South Side's major resort area. Poipu owes much of its popularity to a steady supply of sunshine and a string of sandy beaches, although the beaches are smaller and more covelike than those on the West Side. With its extensive selection of accommodations, services, and activities, the South Shore attracts more visitors than any other area of Kauai. It also attracted developers with big plans for the onetime sugarcane fields that are nestled in this region and enveloped by mountains. There are few roads in and out, and local residents are concerned about increased traffic as well as noise and dust pollution as a result of chronic construction. If you're planning to stay on the South Side, be sure to ask if your hotel, condo, or vacation rental will be impacted by the development during your visit.

Both Poipu and nearby Koloa (site of Kauai's first sugar mill) can be reached via Route 520 (Maluhia Road) from the Lihue area. Route 520 is known locally as Tree Tunnel Road, due to the stand of eucalyptus trees lining the road that were planted at the turn of the 20th century by Walter Duncan McBryde, a Scotsman who began cattle ranching on Kauai's South Shore. The canopy of trees was ripped to literal shreds twice—in 1982 during Hurricane Iwa and again in 1992 during Hurricane Iniki. And, true to Kauai, both times the trees grew back into an impressive tunnel. It's a distinctive way to announce, "You are now on vacation," for there's a definite feel of leisure in the air here. There's still plenty to do—snorkel, bike, walk, horseback ride, take an ATV tour, surf, scuba dive, shop, and dine—everything you'd want on a tropical vacation. From the west, Route 530 (Koloa Road) slips into downtown Koloa, a string of fun shops and restaurants, at an intersection with the only gas station on the South Shore.

POIPU

13 miles southwest of Lihue.

Thanks to its generally sunny weather and a string of golden-sand beaches dotted with oceanfront lodgings, Poipu is a top choice for many visitors. Beaches are user-friendly, with protected waters for *keiki* (children) and novice snorkelers, lifeguards, restrooms, covered pavilions, and a sweet coastal promenade ideal for leisurely strolls. Some experts have even ranked Poipu Beach Park number one in the nation. It depends on your preferences, of course, though it certainly does warrant high accolades.

GETTING HERE AND AROUND

Poipu is the one area on Kauai where you could get by without a car, though that could mean an expensive taxi ride from the airport and limited access to other parts of the island. To reach Poipu by car, follow Poipu Road south from Koloa. After the traffic circle, the road curves to follow the coast, leading to some of the popular South Shore beaches.

TOP ATTRACTIONS

National Tropical Botanical Gardens (*NTBG*). Tucked away in Lawai Valley, these gardens include lands and a cottage once used by Hawaii's Queen Emma for a summer retreat. Visitors can take a self-guided tour of the rambling 252-acre **McBryde Gardens** to see and learn about plants collected throughout the tropics. It is known as a garden of "research and conservation." The 100-acre **Allerton Gardens,** which can be visited only on a guided tour, artfully display statues and water features that were originally developed as part of a private estate. Reservations are requested for tours of Allerton Gardens, but not for the self-guided tours of McBryde Gardens. The visitor center has a high-quality gift shop with botany-theme merchandise.

Besides harboring and propagating rare and endangered plants from Hawaii and elsewhere, NTBG functions as a scientific research and education center. The organization also operates gardens in Limahuli, on Kauai's North Shore, and in Hana, on Maui's east shore, as well as one in Florida. ⊠ *3530 Lawai Rd., Poipu* ☎ *808/742–2623* ⊕ *www. ntbg.org* 🕮 *McBryde self-guided tour $15, Allerton guided tour $35, Discover tour $45.* ⊗ *Allerton Gardens tours (by reservation) daily at 9, 10, 1, 2 and 3. Sunset Tour Tues., Thurs., Sat. ($70).*

Spouting Horn. If the conditions are right, you can see a natural blowhole in the reef behaving like Old Faithful, shooting saltwater high into the air and making a cool, echoing sound. It's most dramatic during big summer swells, which jam large quantities of water through an ancient lava tube with great force. Vendors hawk inexpensive souvenirs and collectibles in the parking lot. You may find good deals on shell jewelry, but some vendors also carry exotic Niihau-shell creations with prices up to $12,000. ⊠ *End of Lawai Rd., Poipu.*

QUICK BITES

Brennecke's Beach Broiler. Stop in at Brennecke's Beach Broiler, a longtime fixture on the beach in Poipu. After a day of sun, this is a perfect spot to chill out with a mango margarita or mai tai, paired with a yummy pupu (appetizers) platter. ⊠ *2100 Hoone Rd., Poipu* ☎ *808/742–7588* ⊕ *www.brenneckes.com.*

THE WEST SIDE

Exploring the West Side is akin to visiting an entirely different world. The landscape is dramatic and colorful: a patchwork of green, blue, black, and orange. The weather is hot and dry, the beaches are long, the sand is dark. Niihau, a private island and the last remaining place in Hawaii where Hawaiian is spoken exclusively, can be glimpsed offshore. This is rural Kauai, where sugar is making its last stand and taro is still cultivated in the fertile river valleys. The lifestyle is slow, easy, and traditional, with many folks fishing and hunting to supplement their diets. Here and there modern industry has intruded into this pastoral scene: huge generators turn oil into electricity at Port Allen; seed companies cultivate experimental crops of genetically engineered plants in Kekaha and Waimea; the navy launches rockets at Mana to test the "Star Wars" missile defense system; and NASA mans a tracking

"Jungle fowl were all over some of the scenic stops in Kauai. They had beautiful colors, and it was cool just to see them walking around."—jedivader

station in the wilds of Kokee. It's a region of contrasts that simply shouldn't be missed.

Heading west from Lihue or Poipu, you pass through a string of tiny towns, plantation camps, and historic sites, each with a story to tell of centuries past. There's Hanapepe, whose coastal salt ponds have been harvested since ancient times; Kaumakani, where the sugar industry still clings to life; Fort Elisabeth, from which an enterprising Russian tried to take over the island in the early 1800s; and Waimea, where Captain Cook made his first landing in the Islands, forever changing the face of Hawaii.

From Waimea town you can head up into the mountains, skirting the rim of magnificent Waimea Canyon and climbing higher still until you reach the cool, often-misty forests of Kokee State Park. From the vantage point at the top of this gemlike island, 3,200 to 4,200 feet above sea level, you can gaze into the deep, verdant valleys of the North Shore and Napali Coast. This is where the "real" Kauai can still be found: the native plants, insects, and birds that are found nowhere else on Earth.

HANAPEPE
15 miles west of Poipu.

In the 1980s Hanapepe was fast becoming a ghost town, its farm-based economy mirroring the decline of agriculture. Today it's a burgeoning art colony with galleries, crafts studios, and a lively art-theme street fair on Friday nights. The main street has a new vibrancy enhanced by the restoration of several historic buildings. The emergence of Kauai Coffee as a major West Side crop and expanded activities at Port Allen,

SUNSHINE MARKETS

If you want to rub elbows with the locals and purchase fresh produce and flowers at reasonable prices, head for Sunshine Markets, also known as Kauai's farmers' markets. These busy markets are held weekly, usually in the afternoon, at locations all around the island. They're good fun, and they support neighborhood farmers. Arrive a little early, bring dollar bills to speed up transactions and your own shopping bags to carry your produce, and be prepared for some pushy shoppers. Recently, many smaller markets have popped up around the island—look for them on handmade signs pointing the way. Farmers are usually happy to educate visitors about unfamiliar fruits and veggies. ☎ 808/241-6303 ⊕ www.kauai.gov.

North Shore Sunshine Markets
⊠ Waipa, mauka of Rte. 560 north of Hanalei after mile marker 3,

Hanalei ⊗ Tues. 2 pm ⊠ Kilauea Neighborhood Center, on Keneke St., Kilauea ⊗ Thurs. 4:30 pm ⊠ Hanalei Community Center ⊗ Sat. 9:30 am–noon.

East Side Sunshine Markets
⊠ Vidinha Stadium, Lihue, ½ mile south of airport on Rte. 51 ⊗ Fri. 3 pm ⊠ Kapaa ✛ Turn mauka on Rte. 581/Olohena Rd. for 1 block ⊗ Wed. 3 pm.

South Shore Sunshine Markets
⊠ Ballpark, Koloa, north of intersection of Koloa Rd. and Rte. 520 ⊗ Mon. noon.

West Side Sunshine Markets
⊠ Kalaheo Community Center, on Papalina Rd. just off Kaumualii Hwy., Kalaheo ⊗ Tues. 3 pm ⊠ Hanapepe Park, Hanapepe ⊗ Thurs. 3 pm ⊠ Kekaha Neighborhood Center, Elepaio Rd., Kekaha ⊗ Sat. 9 am.

now the main departure point for tour boats, also gave the town's economy a boost.

GETTING HERE AND AROUND

Hanapepe, locally known as Kauai's "biggest little town," is just past the Eleele Shopping Center on the main highway (Route 50). A sign leads you to the town center, where street parking is easy and there's an enjoyable walking tour.

WORTH NOTING

Hanapepe Valley and Canyon Lookout. This dramatic divide and fertile river valley once housed a thriving Hawaiian community of taro farmers, with some of the ancient fields still in cultivation today. From the lookout, you can take in the farms on the valley floor with the majestic mountains as a backdrop. ⊠ Rte. 50, Hanapepe.

Kauai Coffee Visitor Center and Museum. Two restored camp houses, dating from the days when sugar was the main agricultural crop on the Islands, have been converted into a museum, visitor center, and gift shop. About 3,100 acres of McBryde sugar land have become Hawaii's largest coffee plantation, producing over 50% of the state's beans. You can walk among the trees, view old grinders and roasters, watch a video to learn how coffee is processed, sample various estate roasts, and check out the gift store. The center offers a 15-minute or so self-guided tour with well-marked signs through a small coffee grove as well as free

The sunny South Shore beaches have some good surf breaks. Head to Poipu Beach for board rentals or lessons.

guided tours daily. From Kalaheo, take Highway 50 in the direction of Waimea Canyon (west) and veer left onto Highway 540. It's located 2½ miles from the Highway 50 turnoff. ⊠ *870 Halawili Rd., Kalaheo* ☎ *808/335–0813* ⊕ *www.kauaicoffee.com* ⊠ *Free* ⊙ *Daily 9–5.*

QUICK BITES

Lappert's Ice Cream. It's not ice cream on Kauai if it's not Lappert's Ice Cream. Guava, mac nut, pineapple, mango, coconut, banana—Lappert's is the ice-cream capital of Kauai. Warning: Even at the factory store in Hanapepe, the prices are no bargain. But, hey, you gotta try it. ⊠ *1-3555 Kaumualii Hwy., Hanapepe* ☎ *808/335–6121* ⊕ *www.lappertshawaii.com.*

WAIMEA, WAIMEA CANYON, AND AROUND
Waimea 7 miles northwest of Hanapepe; Waimea Canyon 10 miles northeast of Waimea.

Waimea is a serene, pretty town that has the look of the old West and the feel of old Hawaii, with a lifestyle that's decidedly laid-back. It's an ideal place for a refreshment break while sightseeing on the West Side. The town has played a major role in Hawaiian history since 1778, when Captain James Cook became the first European to set foot on the Hawaiian Islands. Waimea was also the place where Kauai's King Kaumualii acquiesced to King Kamehameha's unification drive in 1810, averting a bloody war. The town hosted the first Christian missionaries, who hauled in massive timbers and limestone blocks to build the sturdy Waimea Christian Hawaiian and Foreign Church in 1846. It's one of many lovely historic buildings preserved by residents who take great pride in their heritage and history.

Waimea Canyon: You don't have to hike to see sweeping Waimea Canyon vistas. Many overlooks, like the one pictured above, are reachable by car, right off the main road.

North of Waimea town, via Route 550, you'll find the vast and gorgeous Waimea Canyon, also known as the Grand Canyon of the Pacific. The spectacular vistas from the lookouts along the road culminate with an overview of Kalalau Valley. There are various hiking trails leading to the inner heart of Kauai. A camera is a necessity in this region.

GETTING HERE AND AROUND

Route 50 continues northwest to Waimea and Kekaha from Hanapepe. You can reach Waimea Canyon and Kokee State Park from either town—the way is clearly marked. Some pull-off areas on Route 550 are fine for a quick view of the canyon, but the designated lookouts have bathrooms and parking.

TOP ATTRACTIONS

Kalalau Lookout. At the end of the road, high above Waimea Canyon, Kalalau Lookout marks the start of a 1-mile (one-way) hike to **Puu o Kila Lookout.** On a clear day at either spot, you can see a dreamy landscape of gaping valleys, sawtooth ridges, waterfalls, and turquoise seas, where whales can be seen spouting and breaching during the winter months. If clouds block the view, don't despair—they tend to blow through fast, giving you time to snap that photo of a lifetime. You may spot wild goats clambering on the sheer, rocky cliffs, and white tropic birds. If it's very clear to the northwest, look for the shining sands of Kalalau Beach, gleaming like golden threads against the deep blue of the Pacific. ⊠ *Waimea Canyon Dr., 4 miles north of Kokee State Park.*

Kokee State Park. This 4,345-acre wilderness park is 4,000 feet above sea level, an elevation that affords you breathtaking views in all directions. You can gain a deeper appreciation of the island's rugged terrain and dramatic beauty from this vantage point. Large tracts of native ohia and koa forest cover much of the land, along with many varieties of exotic plants. Hikers can follow a 45-mile network of trails through diverse landscapes that feel wonderfully remote—until the tour helicopters pass overhead. A few years ago, the state introduced a 20-year master plan for the park that included significant development (think a 40- to 60-room lodge in a sacred meadow), but after community input meetings, the plan was scaled back. ⊠ *Kaumakani-Hanapepe, Hanapepe* ⊕ *www.kokee.org.*

Kokee Natural History Museum. When you arrive at the park, Kokee Natural History Museum is a great place to start your visit. The friendly staff is knowledgeable about trail conditions and weather, while informative displays and a good selection of reference books can teach you more about the unique attributes of the native flora and fauna. You may also find that special memento or gift you've been looking for. ⊠ *Rte. 550, Kauai* ☎ *808/335–9975* 🖼 *Donations accepted* ☉ *Daily 9–4:30.*

Fodor's Choice
★

Waimea Canyon. Carved over countless centuries by the Waimea River and the forces of wind and rain, Waimea Canyon is a dramatic gorge nicknamed the "Grand Canyon of the Pacific"—but not by Mark Twain, as many people mistakenly think. Hiking and hunting trails wind through the canyon, which is 3,600 feet deep, 2 miles wide, and 10 miles long. The cliff sides have been sharply eroded, exposing swatches of colorful soil. The deep red, brown, and green hues are constantly changing in the sun, and frequent rainbows and waterfalls enhance the natural beauty. This is one of Kauai's prettiest spots, and it's worth stopping at both the **Puu ka Pele** and **Puu hinahina** lookouts. Clean public restrooms and parking are at both lookouts. ⊠ *Kokee Rd., Waimea* ☎ *808/587–0300.*

QUICK BITES
Kokee Lodge. There's only one place to buy food and hot drinks in Kokee State Park, and that's the dining room of rustic Kokee Lodge. It's known for its corn bread, of all things. Peruse the gift shop for T-shirts, postcards, or campy Kokee memorabilia. ⊠ *Kokee State Park, 3600 Kokee Rd., mile marker 15, Kokee* ☎ *808/335–6061* ⊕ *www.thelodgeatkokee.net* ☉ *No dinner.*

BEACHES

Updated by Joan Conrow

With more sandy beaches per mile of coastline than any other Hawaiian Island, Kauai could be nicknamed the Sandy Island just as easily as it's called the Garden Island. Totaling more than 50 miles, Kauai's beaches make up 44% of the island's shoreline—almost twice that of Oahu, second on this list.

It is, of course, because of Kauai's age as the eldest sibling of the inhabited Hawaiian Islands, allowing more time for water and wind erosion to break down rock and coral into sand.

But not all Kauai's beaches are the same. Each beach is unique unto itself. Conditions, scenery, and intrigue can change throughout the day

Kauai Beaches

Puu Poa Beach
Palikekua Beach (Hideaways)
Haena Beach Park
Lumahai Beach
Anini Beach Park
Kalihiwai Beach
Kee Beach
Hanalei Bay
Kauapea Beach
Hanakapiai Beach
Kahili Beach
North Shore
Haena
Princeville
Kilauea
Larsen's Beach
NAPALI COAST
Kalalau
Kalalau Trail
Honalei
Kilauea Lighthouse
Handlei Bay Beach Park
Aliomanu Beach
Kalalau Lookout
Kokee State Park
Anahola Beach Park
Anahola
Donkey Beach
olihale ate Park
WAIMEA CANYON
Waialeale 5,148 ft.
East Side
Kealia Beach
581
Kealia
Kapaa
Baby Beach
580
Wailua Beach
Wailua Bay
Lydgate State Park
552 550
Kilohana Crater 1,138 ft.
583
56
Hanamaulu
Lihue
Lihue Airport
Kekaha each Park
Kekaha
Waimea
50
Kalapaki Beach
58
Nawiliwili Bay
Lucy Wright Beach Park
50
Kalaheo
Mahaulepu Beach
ulakahi Channel
Hanapepe
Eleele
South Shore
Koloa
Beach House
Hanapepe Bay
Lawai Kai
Keoniloa (Shipwreck Beach)
Brennecke Beach
Kauai Channel
Kukuiula Small Boat Harbor
Waiohai Beach
Poipu
Poipu Beach Park

0 _____ 10 mi
0 _____ 10 km

and certainly throughout the year, transforming, say, a tranquil lakelike ocean setting in summer into monstrous waves drawing internationally ranked surfers from around the world in winter.

There are sandy beaches, rocky beaches, wide beaches, narrow beaches, skinny beaches, and alcoves. Generally speaking, surf kicks up on the North Shore in winter and the South Shore in summer, although summer's southern swells aren't nearly as frequent or big as the northern winter swells that attract those surfers. Kauai's longest and widest beaches are found on the North Shore and West Side and are popular with beachgoers, although during winter's rains, everyone heads to the dryer South and West sides. The East Side beaches tend to be narrower and have onshore winds less popular with sunbathers, yet fishers abound. Smaller coves are characteristic of the South Shore and attract all kinds of water lovers year-round, including monk seals.

In Hawaii, all beaches are public, but their accessibility varies greatly. Some require an easy ½-mile stroll, some require a four-wheel-drive vehicle, others require boulder-hopping, and one takes an entire day of serious hiking. And then there are those "drive-in" beaches adjacent to parking areas. Kauai is not Disneyland, so don't expect much signage to help you along the way. One of the top-ranked beaches in the whole world—Hanalei—doesn't have a single sign in town directing you to

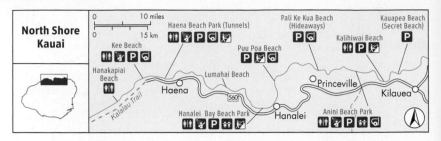

the beach. Furthermore, the majority of Kauai's beaches on Kauai's vast coastline are remote, offering no facilities. It's important to note that drownings are common on Kauai, in part because many beaches have no lifeguards and tricky ocean conditions. When in doubt, stay out. ■TIP→ **If you want the convenience of restrooms, picnic tables, lifeguards and the like, stick to county beach parks.**

THE NORTH SHORE

If you've ever dreamed of Hawaii—and who hasn't—you've dreamed of Kauai's North Shore. Lush, tropical, and abundant are just a few words to describe this rugged and dramatic area. And the views to the sea aren't the only attraction—the inland views of velvety-green valley folds and carved mountain peaks will take your breath away. Rain is the reason for all the greenery on the North Shore, and winter is the rainy season. Not to worry, though; it rarely rains *everywhere* on the island at one time. ■TIP→ **The rule of thumb is to head south or west when it rains in the north.**

The waves on the North Shore can be big—and we mean huge—in winter, drawing crowds to witness nature's spectacle. By contrast, in summer the waters can be completely serene.

FAMILY **Anini Beach Park.** A great family park, Anini features one of the longest and widest fringing reefs in all Hawaii, creating a shallow lagoon that is good for snorkeling and kids splashing about. It is safe in all but the highest of winter surf. The reef follows the shoreline for some 2 miles and extends 1,600 feet offshore at its widest point. There's a narrow ribbon of sandy beach and lots of grass and shade, as well as a campground at the western end and a small boat ramp. **Amenities:** parking; showers; toilets; lifeguard. **Best for:** walking; swimming; sunrise. ⊠ *Anini Rd., off Rte. 56, Princeville.*

Fodor'sChoice **Haena Beach Park** (*Tunnels Beach*). This is a drive-up beach park popu-
★ lar with campers year-round. The wide bay here—named Makua—is bordered by two large reef systems creating favorable waves for skilled surfers during peak winter conditions. In July and August, waters at this same beach usually are as calm as a lake. To the east of the park is a popular snorkeling area nicknamed Tunnels for its underwater lava tubes. Entering the water can be dangerous in winter when the big swells roll in. ■TIP→ **During the summer months only, this is a premier snorkeling site on Kauai.** It's not unusual to find a food vendor parked here selling sandwiches and drinks out of a converted bread van.

Amenities: lifeguards; parking; showers; toilets; food and drink. **Best for:** walking; snorkeling; surfing. ✉ *Near end of Rte. 560, across from Maniniholo Dry Cave, Haena.*

FAMILY

Fodor's Choice

★

Hanalei Bay Beach Park. This 2-mile crescent beach cradles a wide bay in a setting that is quintessential Hawaii. The sea is on one side, and behind you are the mountains, often ribboned with waterfalls and changing color in the shifting light. In winter, Hanalei Bay boasts some of the biggest onshore surf breaks in the state, attracting world-class surfers, and the beach is plenty wide enough for sunbathing and strolling. In summer, the bay is transformed—calm waters lap the beach, sailboats moor in the bay, and outrigger-canoe paddlers ply the sea. Pack the cooler, haul out the beach umbrellas, and don't forget the beach toys, because Hanalei Bay is worth scheduling for an entire day, maybe two. To reach Hanalei Bay Beach Park from Hanalei, turn *makai* (toward the ocean) at Aku Rd. and drive one block to Weli Weli Rd. Parking areas are on the *makai* side of Weli Weli Rd. **Amenities:** lifeguards; parking; showers; toilets. **Best for:** surfing; swimming; walking; sunsets. ✉ *Weli Weli Rd., Hanalei.*

Fodor's Choice

★

Kalalau Beach. Located at the end of the trail with the same name, Kalalau is a remote beach in the spectacular Napali Coast State Wilderness Park. Reaching it requires an arduous 11-mile hike along sea cliff faces, through muddy coastal valleys, and across sometimes-raging streams. Another option is to paddle a kayak to the beach—summer only, though; otherwise the surf is way too big. The beach is anchored by a *heiau* (a stone platform used as a place of worship) on one end and a waterfall on the other. The safest time to come is summer, when the trail is dry and the beach is wide, cupped by low, vegetated sand dunes and a large walk-in cave on the western edge. Day hikes into the valley offer waterfalls, freshwater swimming pools, and wild, tropical fruits. Though camping permits are required, the valley often has a significant illegal crowd, which has strained park facilities and degraded much of its former peaceful solitude. Helicopter overflights are near-constant in good weather. **Amenities:** none. **Best for:** sunset; nudists; walking. ✉ *Trailhead starts at end of Rte. 560, 7 miles west of Hanalei* ⊕ *www.hawaiistateparks.org.*

Kalihiwai Beach. A winding road leads down a cliff face to picture-perfect Kalihiwai Beach, which fronts a bay of the same name. It's another one of those drive-up beaches, so it's very accessible. Most people park under the grove of ironwood trees, near the stream, where young kids like to splash and older kids like to bodyboard. Though do beware the stream carries leptospirosis, a potentially lethal bacteria that can enter through open cuts. In winter months, beware of a treacherous shore break. Summer is the only truly safe time to swim. There's a favorite locals winter surf spot off the eastern edge of the beach, for advanced surfers only. The toilets here are the portable kind, and there are no showers. **Amenities:** parking; toilets. **Best for:** surfing; swimming; walking. ✉ *Kalihiwai Rd., on Kilauea side of Kalihiwai Bridge, Kilauea.*

Kauapea Beach (*Secret Beach*). This beach went relatively unknown—except by local fishermen, of course—for a long time, hence the common

5

Be sure to set aside time to catch a sunset over Napali Coast from Kee Beach on Kauai's North Shore.

reference to it as "Secret Beach." You'll understand why once you stand on the coarse white sands of Kauapea and see the solid wall of rock 100 feet high, maybe more, that runs the length of the beach, making it fairly inaccessible. For the hardy, there is a steep hike down the western end. From there, you can walk for a long way in either direction in summer. During winter, big swells cut off access to sections of the beach. You may witness dolphins just offshore, and it's a great place to see seabirds, as the Kilauea Point National Wildlife Refuge and its historic lighthouse lie at the eastern end. Nudity is not uncommon. A consistent onshore break makes swimming here typically dangerous. **Amenities:** parking. **Best for:** solitude; walking; sunrise. ⊠ *Kalihiwai Rd., just past the turnoff for Kīlauea, Kilauea.*

Kee Beach. Highway 560 on the North Shore literally dead-ends at this beach, pronounced kay-eh. This is also the start of the famous Kalalau Trail, and a culturally significant area to Native Hawaiians, who still use an ancient *heiau* (temple) dedicated to hula. (It's not appropriate to hang out on the grass platform or leave offerings there.) The setting is gorgeous, with Makana (a prominent peak that Hollywood dubbed "Bali Hai" in the blockbuster musical *South Pacific*) dramatically imposing itself on the lovely coastline and lots of lush tropical vegetation. The small beach is protected by a reef—except during high surf—creating a small sandy-bottom lagoon that's a popular snorkeling spot. There can be a strong current in winter. Unfortunately, it's so heavily visited that parking is difficult, if not impossible. Expect to park quite a distance from the beach. It's a great place to watch the sunset lighting up Napali Coast. **Amenities:** lifeguards; parking; showers,

CLOSE UP

Best Beaches

He says "to-mah-toe," and she says "to-may-toe." When it comes to beaches on Kauai, the meaning behind that axiom holds true: People are different. What rocks one person's world wreaks havoc for another's. Here are some additional tips on how to choose a beach that's right for you.

BEST FOR FAMILIES
Lydgate State Park, East Side. The kid-designed playground, the protected swimming pools, and Kamalani Bridge guarantee you will not hear these words from your child: "Mom, I'm bored."

Poipu Beach Park, Poipu, South Shore. The *keiki* (children's) pool and lifeguards make this a safe spot for kids. The near-perpetual sun isn't so bad, either.

BEST STAND-UP PADDLING
Anini Beach Park, North Shore. The reef and long stretch of beach give beginners to stand-up paddling a calm place to give this new sport a try. You won't get pummeled by waves here.

Wailua Beach, East Side. On the East Side, the Wailua River bisects the beach and heads inland 2 miles, providing stand-up paddlers with a long and scenic stretch of water before they have to figure out how to turn around.

BEST SURFING
Hanalei Bay Beach Park, North Shore. In winter, Hanalei Bay offers a range of breaks, from beginner to advanced. Hanalei is where surfing legends such as Laird Hamilton and the Irons Brothers—international surf champions—began their shredding careers as they grew up surfing these waters.

Waiohai Beach, South Shore. Surf instructors flock to this spot with their students for its gentle, near-shore break. Then, as students advance, they can paddle out a little farther to an intermediate break—if they dare.

BEST SUNSETS
Kee Beach, North Shore. Even in winter, when the sun sets in the south and out of view, you won't be disappointed here, because the "magic hour," as photographers call the time around sunset, paints Napali Coast with a warm gold light.

Polihale State Park, West Side. This due-west-facing beach may be tricky to get to, but it does offer the most unobstructed sunset views on the island. The fact that it's so remote means you won't have strangers in your photos, but you will want to depart right after sunset or risk getting lost in the dark.

BEST FOR SEEING AND BEING SEEN
Haena Beach Park, North Shore. Behind those gated driveways and heavily foliaged yards that line this beach live—at least, part-time—some of the world's most celebrated music and movie moguls. Need we say more?

Hanalei Bay Beach Park, North Shore. We know we tout this beach often, but it deserves the praise. It's a magnet for everyone—regular joes, surfers, fishers, young, old, locals, visitors, and, especially, the famous. You may also recognize Hanalei Bay from the movie *The Descendants.*

5

toilets. **Best for:** swimming; snorkeling; sunset; walking. ⊠ *End of Rte. 560, 7 miles west of Hanalei.*

Lumahai Beach. Famous as the beach where Nurse Nellie washed that man right out of her hair in *South Pacific,* Lumahai's setting is picturesque, with a river and ironwood grove on the western end, and stands of *hala* (pandanus) trees and black lava rock on the eastern side. In between is a long stretch of thick olivine-flecked sand. It can be accessed in two places from the highway; one involves a steep hike from the road. The ocean can be very dangerous here, with a snapping shore break year-round and monster swells in the winter. The current can be strong near the river. Parking is very limited along the road or in a rough dirt lot near the river. **Amenities:** none. **Best for:** solitude; walking; sunset. ⊠ *On winding section of Rte. 560, near mile marker 5, Hanalei.*

THE EAST SIDE

The East Side of the island is considered the *windward* side, a term you'll often hear in weather forecasts. It simply means the side of the island receiving onshore winds. The wind helps break down rock into sand, so there are plenty of beaches here. Unfortunately, only a few of those beaches are protected, so many are not ideal for beginning oceangoers, though they are perfect for long sunrise ambles. On super-windy days, kiteboarders sail along the east shore, sometimes jumping waves and performing acrobatic maneuvers in the air.

FAMILY **Baby Beach.** There aren't many swimming beaches on Kauai's East Side; however, this one usually ranks highly with mothers of small children because there's a narrow lagoonlike area between the beach and the near-shore reef perfect for small children. Of course, in winter, watch for east and northeast swells that would not make this such a safe option. There are no beach facilities—no lifeguards, so watch your babies. There is an old-time shower spigot available to rinse the saltwater. **Amenities:** shower; parking. **Best for:** swimming; sunrise. ⊠ *Moamakai Rd., off Keaka Rd., Kapaa.*

FAMILY **Kalapaki Beach.** Five minutes south of the airport in Lihue, you'll find this wide, sandy-bottom beach fronting the Kauai Marriott. This beach is almost always safe from rip currents and undertows because it's around the back side of a peninsula, in its own cove. There are tons of activities here, including all the usual water sports—beginning and intermediate surfing, bodyboarding, bodysurfing, and swimming—plus, there are two outrigger canoe clubs paddling in the bay and the Nawiliwili Yacht Club's boats sailing around the harbor. **Kalapaki** is the only place on Kauai where sailboats—in this case Hobie Cats—are available for rent (at Kauai Beach Boys, which fronts the beach next to Duke's Canoe Club restaurant). Visitors can also rent snorkel gear, surfboards, bodyboards, and kayaks from Kauai Beach Boys. A volleyball court on the beach is often used by a loosely organized group of local players; visitors are always welcome. ■TIP➔ **Beware the stream on the south side of the beach, though, as it often has high bacteria counts.** Duke's Canoe Club restaurant is one of only a couple of restaurants on the island actually on a beach; the restaurant's lower level is casual, even

welcoming beach attire and sandy feet, perfect for lunch or an afternoon cocktail. **Amenities:** parking; showers; toilets; water sports; food and drink; lifeguard. **Best for:** swimming; surfing; partiers; walking. ⊠ *Off Rice St., Lihue* ⊕ *www.kalapakibeach.org.*

Kealia Beach. A half-mile long and adjacent to the highway heading north out of Kapaa, Kealia Beach attracts bodyboarders and surfers year-round. It's a favorite with locals and visitors alike. Kealia is not generally a great beach for swimming, but it's a place to sunbathe and enjoy the beach scene. The waters are usually rough and the waves crumbly due to an onshore break (no protecting reef) and northeasterly trade winds. A scenic lookout on the southern end, accessed off the highway, is a superb location for saluting the morning sunrise or spotting whales during winter. A level, paved trail with small, covered pavilions runs along the coastline here, and is very popular for walking and biking. **Amenities:** lifeguard; parking; showers; toilets. **Best for:** surfing; swimming; walking; sunrise. ⊠ *Rte. 56, at mile marker 10, Kealia.*

FAMILY **Lydgate State Park.** This is by far the best family beach park on Kauai. The waters off the beach are protected by a hand-built breakwater, creating two boulder-enclosed saltwater pools for safe swimming and snorkeling most of the year. The smaller of the two pools is perfect for *keiki* (children). Behind the beach is Kamalani Playground; children of all ages—that includes you—enjoy the swings, lava-tube slides, tree house, and more. Picnic tables abound in the park, and pavilions for day use and overnight camping are available by permit. The Kamalani Kai Bridge is a second playground, south of the original. (The two are united by a bike and pedestrian path that is part of the Nawiliwili-to-Anahola multi-use path project currently under construction.) ■TIP➔ This park system is perennially popular; the quietest times to visit are early mornings and weekdays. **Amenities:** lifeguards; parking; showers; toilets. **Best for:** partiers; walking; swimming; sunrise. ⊠ *Nalu Rd., just south of Wailua River, Wailua.*

THE SOUTH SHORE

The South Shore's primary access road is Highway 520, a tree-lined, two-lane, windy road. As you drive along it, there's a sense of tunneling down a rabbit hole into another world, à la Alice. And the South Shore is certainly a wonderland. On average, it rains only 30 inches per year, so if you're looking for fun in the sun, this is a good place to start. The beaches with their powdery-fine sand are consistently good year-round,

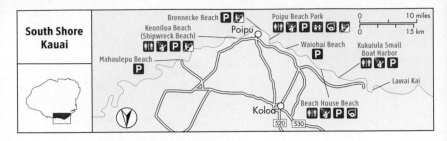

except during high surf, which, if it hits at all, will be in summer. If you want solitude, this isn't it; if you want excitement—well, as much excitement as quiet Kauai offers—this is the place for you.

Brennecke Beach. This beach is synonymous on Kauai with board surfing and bodysurfing, thanks to its shallow sandbar and reliable shore break. Because the beach is small and often congested, surfboards are prohibited near shore. The water on the rocky eastern edge of the beach is a good place to see the endangered green sea turtles noshing on plants growing on the rocks. **Amenities:** parking; food and drink. **Best for:** surfing; sunset. ⊠ *Hoone Rd., off Poipu Rd., Poipu.*

Keoniloa Beach (*Shipwreck Beach*). Few—except the public relations specialists at the Grand Hyatt Kauai Resort and Spa, which backs the beach—refer to this beach by anything other than its common name: Shipwreck Beach. Its Hawaiian name means "long beach." Both make sense. It is a long stretch of crescent-shape beach punctuated by stunning sea cliffs on both ends, and, yes, a ship once wrecked here. With its onshore break, the waters off Shipwreck are best for bodyboarding and bodysurfing; however, the beach itself is plenty big for sunbathing, sandcastle building, Frisbee, and other beach-related fun. The eastern edge of the beach is the start of an interpretive dune walk (complimentary) held by the hotel staff; check with the concierge for dates and times. **Amenities:** parking, showers, toilets; food and drink. **Best for:** surfing; walking; sunrise ⊠ *Ainako Rd. Continue on Poipu Rd. past Hyatt, turn makai on Ainako Rd., Poipu.*

Fodor'sChoice **Lawai Kai.** One of the most spectacular beaches on the South Shore is
★ inaccessible by land unless you tour the National Tropical Botanical Garden's Allerton Garden, which we highly recommend. On the tour, you'll see the beach, but you won't visit it. One way to legally access the beach on your own is by paddling a kayak 1 mile from Kukuiula Harbor. However, you have to rent the kayaks elsewhere and haul them on top of your car to the harbor. Also, the wind and waves usually run westward, making the in-trip a breeze but the return trip a workout against Mother Nature. Another way is to boulder-hop along the coast from Spouting Horn—a long trek over sharp lava rock that we do not recommend. ■TIP➔ Do not attempt this beach in any manner during a south swell. **Amenities:** none. **Best for:** solitude; sunrise. ⊠ *Lawai Rd., off Poipu Rd.*

Fodor'sChoice **Mahaulepu Beach.** This 2-mile stretch of coast, with its sand dunes, lime-
★ stone hills, sinkholes, and caves is unlike any other on Kauai. Remains

of a large, ancient settlement, evidence of great battles, and the discovery of a now-underwater petroglyph field indicate that Hawaiians lived in this area as early as 700 AD. Mahaulepu's coastline is unprotected and rocky, which makes venturing into the ocean hazardous. There are three beach areas with bits of sandy-bottom swimming; however, the best way to experience Mahaulepu is simply to roam, especially at sunrise. ■ TIP→ Access to this beach is via private property. The owner allows access during daylight hours, but be sure to depart before sunset or risk getting locked in for the night. **Amenities:** parking. **Best for:** walking; solitude; sunrise. ⊠ *Poipu Rd., past the Hyatt Hotel, Poipu.*

FAMILY

Fodor's Choice

★

Poipu Beach Park. The most popular beach on the South Shore is Poipu Beach Park. During calm seas, the snorkeling and swimming are good, and when the surf's up, the bodyboarding and surfing are good, too. Frequent sunshine, grassy lawns and easy access add to the appeal, especially with families. The beach is frequently crowded and great for people-watching. Even the endangered Hawaiian monk seal often makes an appearance. **Amenities:** lifeguards; parking; showers; toilets; food and drink. **Best for:** swimming and snorkeling; partiers; walking. ⊠ *Hoone Rd., off Poipu Rd., Poipu* 🕾 808/742–7444.

Waiohai Beach. The first hotel built in Poipu in 1962 overlooked this beach, adjacent to Poipu Beach Park. Actually, there's little to distinguish where one starts and the other begins other than a crescent reef at the eastern end of Waiohai Beach. That crescent, however, is important. It creates a small, protected bay—good for snorkeling and beginning surfers. If you're a beginner, this is the spot. But when a summer swell kicks up, the near-shore conditions become dangerous; offshore, there's a splendid surf break for experienced surfers. The beach itself is narrow and, like its neighbor, gets very crowded in summer. **Amenities:** parking. **Best for:** surfing; sunrise; sunset. ⊠ *Hoone Rd., off Poipu Rd., Poipu.*

THE WEST SIDE

The West Side of the island receives hardly enough rainfall year-round to water a cactus, and because it's also the leeward side, there are few tropical breezes. That translates to sunny and hot with long, languorous, and practically deserted beaches. You'd think the leeward waters—untouched by wind—would be calm, but there's no reef system, so the beach drops off quickly and currents are commons. Rivers often turn the ocean water murky. ■ TIP→ The best place to gear up for the beaches on the West Side is on the South Shore or East Side. Although there's some catering to visitors here, it's not much.

Kekaha Beach Park. This is one of the premier spots on Kauai for sunset walks and the start of the state's longest beach. We don't recommend much water activity here without first talking to a lifeguard: The beach is exposed to open ocean and has an onshore break that can be hazardous any time of year. But there are some excellent surf breaks—for experienced surfers only. Or, if you would like to run on a beach, this is the one—the hard-packed sand goes on for miles, all the way to Napali Coast, but you won't get past the Pacific Missile Range Facility and its post-9/11 restrictions. Another bonus for this beach is its relatively dry

CLOSE UP

Seal-Spotting on the South Shore

When strolling on one of Kauai's lovely beaches, don't be surprised if you find yourself in the rare company of Hawaiian monk seals. These are among the most endangered of all marine mammals, with perhaps fewer than 1,100 remaining. They primarily inhabit the northwestern Hawaiian Islands, although more are showing their faces on the main Hawaiian Islands, especially on Kauai. They're fond of hauling out on the beach for a long snooze in the sun, particularly after a night of gorging on fish. They need this time to rest and digest, safe from predators.

During the past several summers, female seals have birthed young on the beaches around Kauai, where they stay to nurse their pups for upward of six weeks. It seems the seals enjoy particular beaches for the same

reasons we do: the shallow, protected waters.

If you're lucky enough to see a monk seal, keep your distance and let it be. Although they may haul out near people, they still want and need their space. Stay several hundred feet away, and forget photos unless you've got a zoom lens. It's illegal to do anything that causes a monk seal to change its behavior, with penalties that include big fines and even jail time. In the water, seals may appear to want to play. It's their curious nature. Don't try to play with them. They are wild animals—mammals, in fact, with teeth.

If you have concerns about the health or safety of a seal, or just want more information, contact the **Hawaiian Monk Seal Conservation Hui** (☎ *808/651–7668 ⊕ www.kauaiseals. com*).

5

weather year-round. If it's raining where you are, try Kekaha Beach Park. Toilets here are the portable kind. **Amenities:** lifeguards; showers; toilets; parking. **Best for:** sunset; walking; surfing. ⊠ *Rte. 50, near mile marker 27, Kekaha.*

Fodor's Choice
★

Polihale State Park. The longest stretch of beach in Hawaii starts in Kekaha and ends about 15 miles away at the start of Napali Coast. At the Napali end of the beach is the 5-mile-long, 140-acre Polihale State Park. In addition to being long, this beach is 300 feet wide in places and backed by sand dunes 50 to 100 feet tall. It is frequently very hot, with minimal shade and scorching sand in summer. Polihale is a remote beach accessed via a rough, 5-mile haul-cane road (four-wheel drive needed) at the end of Route 50 in Kekaha. ■**TIP**➜ **Be sure to start the day with a full tank of gas and a cooler filled with food and drink.** Though it's a popular camping and day-use beach location, the water here is typically rough and not recommended for recreation. No driving is allowed on the beach. The Pacific Missile Range Facility (PMRF), operated by the U.S. Navy, is adjacent to the beach and access to the coastline in front of the base is restricted. **Amenities:** parking; showers; toilets. **Best for:** walking; solitude; sunset. ⊠ *Dirt road at end of Rte. 50, Kekaha* ☎ *808/587–0300.*

FAMILY **Salt Pond Beach Park.** A great family spot, Salt Pond Beach Park features a naturally made, shallow swimming pond behind a curling finger of

Lydgate State Park is a great place for families. Kids love watching fish in the nearby koi ponds and blowing off steam on the two playgrounds designed by local *keiki* (children).

rock where *keiki* (children) splash and snorkel. This pool is generally safe except during a large south swell, which usually occurs in summer, if at all. The center and western edge of the beach is popular with bodyboarders and bodysurfers. Pavilions with picnic tables offer shade, and there's a campground at the eastern end. On a cultural note, the flat stretch of land to the east of the beach is the last spot in Hawaii where ponds are used to harvest salt in the dry heat of summer. The beach park is popular with locals and it can get crowded on weekends and holidays. **Amenities:** lifeguard; parking; showers, toilets. **Best for:** swimming; sunset; walking. ⊠ *Lolokai Rd., off Rte. 50, Hanapepe.*

WATER SPORTS AND TOURS

Updated by
Joan Conrow

So, you've decided to vacation on an island. That means you're going to run into a little water at some time. Ancient Hawaiians are notorious water sports fanatics—they invented surfing, after all—and that proclivity hasn't strayed far from today's mind-set. Even if you're not into water sports or sports in general, there's only a slim chance that you'll leave this island without getting out on the ocean, as Kauai's top attraction—Napali Coast—is something not to be missed.

BOAT TOURS

Deciding to see Napali Coast by boat is an easy decision. Choosing the outfitter to go with is not. There are numerous boat-tour operators to choose from, and, quite frankly, they all do a good job. Before you even start thinking about whom to go out with, answer these three questions: What kind of boat do I prefer? Where am I staying? Do I want to go in the morning or afternoon? Once you settle on these three, you can easily zero in on the tour outfitter.

First, the boat. The most important thing is to match your personality and that of your group with the personality of the boat. If you like thrills and adventure, the rubber, inflatable rafts—often called Zodiacs, which Jacques Cousteau made famous and which the U.S. Coast Guard uses—will entice you. They're fast, likely to leave you drenched and windswept, and quite bouncy. If you prefer a smoother, more leisurely ride, then the large catamarans are the way to go. The next boat choice is size. Both the rafts and catamarans come in small and large. Again— think smaller, more adventurous; larger, more leisurely. ■TIP➜ Do not choose a smaller boat because you think there will be fewer people. There might be fewer people, but you'll be jammed together sitting atop strangers. If you prefer privacy over socializing, go with a larger boat, so you'll have more room to spread out. The smaller boats will also take you along the coast at a higher rate of speed, making photo opportunities a bit more challenging. One advantage to smaller boats, however, is that—depending on ocean conditions—some may slip into a sea cave or two. If that sounds interesting to you, call the outfitter and ask their policy on entering sea caves. Some won't, no matter the conditions, because they consider the caves sacred or because they don't want to cause any environmental damage.

Boats leave from three points around the island (Hanalei, Port Allen, and Waimea), and all head to the same spot: Napali Coast. Here's the inside skinny on which is the best: If you're staying on the North Shore, choose to depart from the North Shore. If you're staying anywhere else, depart from the West Side. It's that easy. Sure, the North Shore is closer to Napali Coast; however, you'll pay more for less overall time. The West Side boat operators may spend more time getting to Napali Coast; however, they'll spend about the same amount of time along Napali, plus you'll pay less. Finally, you'll also have to decide whether you want to go on a morning tour, which includes a deli lunch and a stop for snorkeling, or an afternoon tour, which does not always stop to snorkel but does include a sunset over the ocean. The morning tours with snorkeling, more popular with families and those who love dolphins, enjoy the "waves" created by the front of the catamarans and might just escort you down the coast. The winter months will also be a good chance to spot some whales breaching, though surf is much rougher along Napali. You don't have to be an expert snorkeler or even have any prior experience, but if it is your first time, note that although there will be some snorkeling instruction, there might not be much. Hawaiian spinner dolphins are so plentiful in the mornings that some tour companies guarantee you'll see them, though you won't get in the water and swim with them. The afternoon tours are more popular with nonsnorkelers—obviously—and photographers interested in capturing the setting sunlight on the coast. ■TIP➜ No matter which tour you select, book it online whenever possible. Most companies offer Web specials, usually around $10 to $20 off per person.

CATAMARAN TOURS

Fodor's Choice **Blue Dolphin Charters.** Blue Dolphin operates 65-foot sailing (rarely raised
★ and always motoring) catamarans designed with three decks of spacious seating with great visibility, as well as motorized rafts. ■TIP→ The
lower deck is best for shade seekers. On Tuesday and Friday a tour of
Napali Coast includes a detour across the channel to Niihau for snorkeling and diving. Morning snorkel tours of Napali include a deli lunch.
Sunset sightseeing tours include a Hawaiian-style buffet. North Shore
and South shore rafting tours are also available, and daily sport fishing
charters of four-to-eight hours for no more than six guests. Blue Dolphin promises dolphin-sightings and the best mai tais "off the island."
Book online for cheaper deals on every tour offered. ⊠ 4353 Waialo
Rd., No. 2-6B7B, Eleele ☎ 808/335–5553, 877/511–1311 ⊕ www.
kauaiboats.com ⊠ From $105–$185. Two-hour whale-watching/sunset tours, winter only, $75.

Capt. Andy's Sailing Adventures. Departing from Port Allen and running
two 55-foot sailing catamarans, Capt. Andy's offers five-hour snorkeling and four-hour sunset tours along Napali Coast. Unlike other charters, they have a 24-foot Zodiac raft that uses hydrophones to hear
whales and other underwater sounds. The longtime Kauai company also
operates a snorkel BBQ sail and dinner sunset sail aboard its *Southern
Star* yacht, originally built for private charters. This boat now operates
as host for two of Capt. Andy's daily sailing trips for an upgraded fee.
For a shorter adventure, they have a two-hour sunset sail, embarking
out of Kukuiula Harbor in Poipu along the South Shore—with live
Hawaiian music—on Monday, Wednesday, and Saturday. ■TIP→ If
the winds and swells are up on the North Shore, this is usually a good
choice—especially if you're prone to seasickness. This is the only tour
boat operator that allows infants on board—but only on the two-hour
trip. Note, if you have reservations for the shorter tour, you'll check
in at their Kukuiula Harbor office. ⊠ 4353 Waiola Rd., Ste. 1A-2A,
Eleele ⊕ www.napali.com ⊠ From $79, discounts for online booking.

Captain Sundown. Sundown has one of the few permits to sail from
Hanalei Bay and operates the only sailing catamaran there. Captain
Bob has been cruising Napali Coast since 1971—six days a week, sometimes twice a day. (And right alongside Captain Bob is his son, Captain
Larry.) To say he knows the area is an understatement. Here's the other
good thing about this tour: they take only 15 to 17 passengers on the
40-foot boat. The breathtaking views of the waterfall-laced mountains
behind Hanalei and Haena start immediately, and then it's around Kee
Beach and the magic of Napali Coast unfolds before you. All the while,
the captains are trolling for fish, and if they catch any, guests get to
reel 'em in. Afternoon sunset sails (summertime only) run three hours
and check in around 3 pm—these are BYOB. ⊠ 5-5134 Kuhio Hwy.,
Hanalei ☎ 808/826–5585 ⊕ www.captainsundown.com ⊠ From $115.

Catamaran Kahanu. Hawaiian-owned-and-operated, Catamaran Kahanu
has been in business since 1985 and runs a 40-foot power catamaran
with 18-passenger seating. It offers seasonal whale-watching, snorkeling, and sunset cruises, ranging from two to five hours, and departs
from Port Allen. The five-hour tour includes snorkeling at Nualolo

Get out on the water and see Napali Coast in style on a luxe cruising yacht.

Kai, plus a deli lunch and soft drinks. The four-hour afternoon tour takes in the sunset and includes a hot dinner. The boat is smaller than most and may feel a tad crowded, but the tour feels more personal, with a laid-back, *ohana* style. Guests can witness the ancient cultural practice of coconut weaving or other Hawaiian craft demonstrations on board. There's no alcohol allowed. ⊠ *4353 Waialo Rd., near Port Allen Marina Center, Eleele* ☎ *808/645–6176, 888/213–7711* ⊕ *www. catamarankahanu.com* ⌑ *From $79.*

HoloHolo Charters. Choose between the 50-foot catamaran called *Leila* for a morning snorkel sail to Napali Coast or the 65-foot *Holo Holo* seven-hour catamaran trip to the "forbidden island" of Niihau. Both boats have large cabins and little outside seating. HoloHolo also offers a seasonal voyage of Napali from Hanalei Bay on its rigid-hull inflatable rafts, specifically for diving and snorkeling. Originators of the Niihau tour, HoloHolo Charters built their 65-foot powered catamaran with a wide beam to reduce side-to-side motion, and twin 425 HP turbo diesel engines specifically for the 17-mile channel crossing to Niihau. ■ TIP→ It's the only outfitter running daily Niihau tours. The *Holo Holo* also embarks on a daily sunset and sightseeing tour of the Napali Coast. Leila can hold 37 passengers, while her big brother can take a maximum of 49. Check-in is at Port Allen Marina Center. ⊠ *4353 Waialo Rd., Ste. 5A, Eleele* ☎ *808/335–0815, 800/848–6130* ⊕ *www.holoholocharters. com* ⌑ *From $100.*

Kauai Sea Tours. This company operates the *Lucky Lady*, a 60-foot sailing catamaran designed almost identically to that of Blue Dolphin Charters—with all the same benefits—including great views and spacious seating. Snorkeling tours anchor near Makole (based on the captain's discretion). If snorkeling isn't your thing, try the four-hour sunset tour, with beer, wine, mai tais, pupu (appetizers), and a hot buffet dinner. Seasonal tours of Napali are offered on inflatable rafts. Check in at Port Allen Marina Center. ⊠ *4353 Waialo Rd., Eleele* ☏ *808/826–7254, 800/733–7997* ⊕ *www.kauaiseatours.com* ✉ *From $135.*

Liko Kauai Cruises. There are many things to like about Liko Kauai Cruises. The 49-foot powered cat will enter sea caves, ocean conditions permitting. Sometimes, even Captain Liko himself—a Native Hawaiian—still takes the captain's helm. We particularly like the layout of his boat—most of the seating is in the bow, so there's good visibility. A maximum of 32 passengers make each trip, which last five hours and include snorkeling, food, and soft drinks. Trips usually depart out of Kikiaola Harbor in Waimea, a bit closer to Napali Coast than those leaving from Port Allen. ⊠ *4516 Alawai Rd., Waimea* ☏ *808/338–0333, 888/732–5456* ⊕ *www.liko-kauai.com* ✉ *$140.*

RAFT TOURS

Kauai Sea Tours. This company holds a special permit from the state to land at Nualolo Kai along Napali Coast, ocean conditions permitting. Here, you'll enjoy a picnic lunch, as well as an archaeological tour of an ancient Hawaiian fishing village, ocean conditions permitting. Kauai Sea Tours operates four 24-foot inflatable rafts—maximum occupancy 14. These are small enough for checking out the insides of sea caves and the undersides of waterfalls. Four different tours are available, including whale-watching, depending on the season. ⊠ *Port Allen Marina Center, 4353 Waialo Rd., Eleele* ☏ *808/826–7254, 800/733–7997* ⊕ *www. kauaiseatours.com* ✉ *From $115.*

Fodor's Choice ★ **Napali Explorer.** These tours operate out of Waimea, a tad closer to Napali Coast than most of the other West Side catamaran tours. The company runs two different sizes of inflatable rubber raft: a 48-foot, 36-passenger craft with an onboard toilet, freshwater shower, shade canopy, and seating in the stern (which is surprisingly smooth and comfortable) and bow (which is where the fun is); and a 26-foot, 14-passenger craft for the all-out fun and thrills of a white-knuckle ride in the bow. The smaller vessel stops at Nualolo Kai and ties up onshore for a tour of the ancient fishing village. Charters are available. ⊠ *9643 Kaumalii Hwy., Waimea* ☏ *808/338–9999* ⊕ *www.napaliexplorer.com* ✉ *From $100.*

Napali Riders. This tour-boat outfitter distinguishes itself in two ways. First, it cruises the entire Napali Coast, clear to Kee Beach and back. Second, it has a reasonable price, because it's a no-frills tour—no lunch provided, just beverages and snacks. The company runs morning and afternoon five-hour snorkeling trips out of Kikiaola Harbor in Waimea on a 30-foot inflatable raft with a 28-passenger maximum—that's fewer than they used to take, but can still be a bit cramped. ⊠ *9600 Kaumualii Hwy., Waimea* ☏ *808/742–6331* ⊕ *www.napaliriders.com* ✉ *$149.*

Z-Tourz. What we like about Z-Tourz is that it's a boat company that makes snorkeling its priority. Its tours include South Shore's abundant offshore reefs, as well as Napali Coast. If you want to snorkel with

Hawaii's tropical reef fish and turtles (pretty much guaranteed), this is your boat. The craft is a 26-foot rigid-hull inflatable (think Zodiac) with a maximum of 16 passengers. These snorkel tours are guided, so someone actually identifies what you're seeing. Rates include lunch and snorkel gear. ⊠ *3417 Poipu Rd., Poipu* ☎ *808/742–7422, 888/998–6879* ⊕ *www.kauaiztours.com* 🖃 *From $100.*

RIVERBOAT TOURS TO FERN GROTTO

Smith's Motor Boat Services. This 2-mile trip up the lush and lovely Wailua River, the only navigable waterway in Hawaii, culminates at a yawning lava tube that is covered with enormous fishtail ferns. During the boat ride, guitar and ukulele players regale you with Hawaiian melodies and tell the history of the river. It's a kitschy bit of Hawaiiana, for a small fee and short duration. Flat-bottom, 150-passenger riverboats (that rarely fill up) depart from Wailua Marina at the mouth of the Wailua River. ■ TIP→ It's extremely rare, but occasionally after heavy rains the tour doesn't disembark at the grotto; if you're traveling in winter, ask beforehand. Round-trip excursions take 1½ hours, including time to walk around the grotto and environs. Tours run at 9:30, 11, 2, and 3:30 daily. ⊠ *5971 Kuhio Hwy, Kapaa* ☎ *808/821–6895* ⊕ *www. smithskauai.com* 🖃 *$20.*

BODYBOARDING AND BODYSURFING

The most natural form of wave riding is bodysurfing, a popular sport on Kauai because there are many shore breaks around the island. Wave riders of this style stand waist-deep in the water, facing shore, and swim madly as a wave picks them up and breaks. It's great fun and requires no special skills and absolutely no equipment other than a swimsuit. The next step up is bodyboarding, also called boogie boarding. In this case, wave riders lie with their upper body on a foam board about half the length of a traditional surfboard and kick as the wave propels them toward shore. Again, this is easy to pick up, and there are many places around Kauai to practice. The locals wear short-finned flippers to help them catch waves, which is a good idea to enhance safety in the water. It's worth spending a few minutes watching these experts as they spin, twirl, and flip—that's right—while they slip down the face of the wave. Of course, all beach safety precautions apply, and just because you see wave riders of any kind in the water doesn't mean the water is safe for everyone. Any snorkeling-gear outfitter also rents bodyboards.

Some of our favorite bodysurfing and bodyboarding beaches are **Brennecke, Wailua, Kealia, Kalihiwai,** and **Hanalei.** *For directions, see Beaches.*

DEEP-SEA FISHING

Simply step aboard and cast your line for mahimahi, ahi, ono, and marlin. That's about how quickly the fishing—mostly trolling with lures—begins on Kauai. The water gets deep quickly here, so there's less cruising time to fishing grounds. Of course, your captain may elect to cruise to a hot location where he's had good luck lately.

There are oodles of charter fishermen around; most depart from Nawili-wili Harbor in Lihue, and most use lures instead of live bait. Inquire about each boat's "fish policy," that is, what happens to the fish if any are caught. Some boats keep all; others will give you enough for a meal or two, even doing the cleaning themselves. On shared charters, ask about the maximum passenger count and about the fishing rotation; you'll want to make sure everyone gets a fair shot at reeling in the big one. Another option is to book a private charter. Shared and private charters run four, six, and eight hours in length.

BOATS AND CHARTERS

Captain Don's Sport Fishing & Ocean Adventure. Captain Don is very flexible and treats everyone like family—he'll stop to snorkel or whale-watch if that's what the group (four to six) wants. Saltwater fly-fishermen (bring your own gear) are welcome. He'll even fish for bait and let you keep part of whatever you catch. The *June Louise* is a 34-foot twin diesel. ⊠ *Nawiliwili Small Boat Harbor, off Nawiliwili Rd., Nawiliwili* ☎ *808/639–3012* ⊕ *www.captaindonsfishing.com* ✉ *From $145 (shared); from $595 (private).*

Kai Bear. The father of this father-and-son duo has it figured out: He lets the son run the business and do all the work. Or so he says. Fish policy: Share the catch. Trips run from a four-hour, shared charter (six fishermen max) up to an eight-hour, keep-all-the-fish-you-want exclusive. What's particularly nice about this company are the boats: the 38-foot Bertram *Kai Bear* and the 42-foot Bertram *Grander*. Very roomy. ⊠ *Nawiliwili Small Boat Harbor, off Nawiliwili Rd., Nawiliwili* ☎ *808/652–4556* ⊕ *www.kaibear.com* ✉ *From $189.*

KAYAKING

Kauai is the only Hawaiian island with navigable rivers. As the oldest inhabited island in the chain, Kauai has had more time for wind and water erosion to deepen and widen cracks into streams and streams into rivers. Because this is a small island, the rivers aren't long, and there are no rapids, which makes them generally safe for kayakers of all levels, even beginners, except when rivers are flowing fast from heavy rains.

For more advanced paddlers, there aren't many places in the world more beautiful for sea kayaking than Napali Coast. If this is your draw to Kauai, plan your vacation for the summer months, when the seas are at their calmest. ■TIP→ Tour and kayak-rental reservations are recommended at least two weeks in advance during peak summer and holiday seasons. In general, tours and rentals are available year-round, Monday through Saturday. Pack a swimsuit, sunscreen, a hat, bug repellent, water shoes (sport sandals, aqua socks, old tennis shoes), and motion sickness medication if you're planning on sea kayaking.

RIVER KAYAKING

Tour outfitters operate on the Huleia, Wailua, and Hanalei rivers with guided tours that combine hiking to waterfalls, as in the case of the first two, and snorkeling, as in the case of the third. Another option is renting kayaks and heading out on your own. Each has its advantages and disadvantages, but it boils down as follows:

If you want to swim at the base of a remote 100-foot waterfall, sign up for a five-hour kayak (4-mile round-trip) and hiking (2-mile round-trip) tour of the **Wailua River.** It includes a dramatic waterfall that is best accessed with the aid of a guide, so you don't get lost. ■**TIP**➜ **Remember—it's dangerous to swim under waterfalls no matter how good a water massage may sound. Rocks and logs are known to plunge down, especially after heavy rains.**

If you want to kayak on your own, choose the **Hanalei River.** It's most scenic from the kayak itself—there are no trails to hike to hidden waterfalls. And better yet, a rental company is right on the river—no hauling kayaks on top of your car.

If you're not sure of your kayaking abilities, head to the **Huleia River;** 3½-hour tours include easy paddling upriver, a nature walk through a rain forest with a cascading waterfall, a rope swing for playing Tarzan and Jane, and a ride back downriver—into the wind—on a motorized, double-hull canoe.

As for the kayaks themselves, most companies use the two-person sit-on-top style that is quite buoyant—no Eskimo rolls required. The only possible danger comes in the form of communication. The kayaks seat two people, which means you'll share the work (good) with a guide, or your spouse, child, parent, or friend (the potential danger part). On the river, the two-person kayaks are known as "divorce boats." Counseling is not included in the tour price.

SEA KAYAKING

In its second year and second issue, *National Geographic Adventure* ranked kayaking Napali Coast second on its list of America's Best 100 Adventures, right behind rafting the Colorado River through the Grand Canyon. That pretty much says it all. It's the adventure of a lifetime in one day, involving eight hours of paddling. Although it's good to have some kayaking experience, feel comfortable on the water, and be reasonably fit, it doesn't require the preparation, stamina, or fortitude of, say, climbing Mt. Everest. Tours run May through September, ocean conditions permitting. In the winter months sea-kayaking tours operate on the South Shore—beautiful, but not as dramatic as Napali.

EQUIPMENT AND TOURS

Kayak Kauai. Based in Hanalei, this company pioneered kayaking on Kauai. It offers guided tours on the Hanalei and Wailua rivers, and along Napali Coast in season. It has a great shop right on the Hanalei River for kayak rentals and camping gear. The guided Hanalei River Kayak and Snorkel Tour starts at the shop and heads downriver, so there's not much to see of the scenic river valley. (For that, rent a kayak on your own.) Instead, this three-hour tour paddles down to the river mouth, where the river meets the sea. Then, it's a short paddle around a point to snorkel at either Princeville Hotel Beach or, ocean conditions permitting, a bit farther at Hideaways Beach. This is a great choice if you want to try your paddle at a bit of ocean kayaking.

In summer you can reach Kalalau Beach by sea kayaking along Napali Coast. "[We had a] great day at the river by Kalalau."—clitopower

A second location on Kuhio Highway in Kapaa offers access to the Kapaa Reef and stand-up paddling on the Kapaa River, while the Wailua River Marina locale gives access to the river and bay. It's not right on the river, however, so shuttling is involved. For rentals, the company provides the hauling gear necessary for your rental car. Snorkel gear, bodyboards, and standup paddleboards also can be rented. ⊠ *5-5070 Kuhio Hwy., 1 mile past Hanalei Bridge, Hanalei* ☎ *808/826–9844, 800/437–3507* ⊕ *www.kayakkauai.com* ✉ *From $45 (river tours) and $145 (sea tours); kayak rentals from $29 per day.* ⊠ *4-1604 Kuhio Hwy, Kapaa.*

Kayak Wailua. We can't quite figure out how this family-run business offers pretty much the same Wailua River kayaking tour as everyone else—except for lunch and beverages, which are BYO—for the lowest price, but it does. They say it's because they don't discount and don't offer commission to activities and concierge desks. Their trips, a 4½-hour kayak, hike, and waterfall swim, are offered four times a day, beginning at 9 am, with the last at 1 pm. With the number of boats going out, large groups can be accommodated. No tours are allowed on Wailua River on Sundays. ⊠ *4565 Haleilio Rd., behind the old Coco Palms hotel, Kapaa* ☎ *808/822–3388* ⊕ *www.kayakwailua.com* ✉ *$50.*

Fodor's Choice
★ **Napali Kayak.** A couple of longtime guides ventured out on their own to create this company, which focuses solely on sea kayaking along the 17-mile Napali Coast from April to October. These guys are highly experienced and still highly enthusiastic about their livelihood—so much so that REI Adventures hires them to run their multiday, multisport tours. You can also rent kayaks. If you're an experienced kayaker

and want to try camping on your own at Kalalau (you'll need permits), Napali Kayak will provide kayaks outfitted with dry bags, extra paddles, and seat backs, while also offering transportation drop-off and pickup. ✉ *5-5075 Kuhio Hwy., next to Postcards Café, Hanalei* ☎ *808/826–6900, 866/977–6900* ⊕ *www.napalikayak.com* ✉ *From $200; kayak rental from $25.*

FAMILY **Outfitters Kauai.** This well-established tour outfitter operates year-round river-kayak tours on the Huleia and Wailua rivers, as well as sea-kayaking tours along Napali Coast in summer and the South Shore in winter. Outfitters Kauai's specialty, however, is the Kipu Safari. This all-day adventure starts with kayaking up the Huleia River and includes a rope swing over a swimming hole, a wagon ride through a working cattle ranch, a picnic lunch by a private waterfall, hiking, and two "zips" across the rain-forest canopy (strap on a harness, clip into a cable, and zip over a quarter of a mile). They then offer a one-of-a-kind Waterzip Zipline at their mountain stream-fed blue pool. The day ends with a ride on a motorized double-hull canoe. It's a great tour for the family, because no one ever gets bored. ✉ *2827-A Poipu Rd., Poipu* ☎ *808/742–9667, 888/742–9887* ⊕ *www.outfitterskauai.com* ✉ *Kipu Safari $184; guided from $104.*

Wailua Kayak & Canoe. This is the only purveyor of kayak rentals right on the Wailua River, which means no hauling your kayak on top of your car (a definite plus). This outfitter promotes itself as "Native Hawaiian owned and operated." No Wailua River tours are offered on Sunday. ✉ *169 Wailua Rd., Kapaa* ☎ *808/821–1188* ⊕ *www. wailuariverkayaking.com* ✉ *$50 for a single, $85 for a double; guided tours from $65.*

KITEBOARDING

Several years ago, the latest wave-riding craze to hit the Islands was kiteboarding, and the sport is still going strong. As the name implies, there's a kite and a board involved. The board you strap on your feet; the kite is attached to a harness around your waist. Steering is accomplished with a rod that's attached to the harness and the kite. Depending on conditions and the desires of the kiteboarder, the kite is played out some 30 to 100 feet in the air. The result is a cross between waterskiing—without the boat—and windsurfing. Speeds are fast and aerobatic maneuvers are involved. Unfortunately, neither lessons nor rental gear is available for the sport on Kauai (Maui is a better bet), so if you aren't a seasoned kiteboarder already, you'll have to be content with watching the pros—who can put on a pretty spectacular show. The most popular year-round spots for kiteboarding are **Kapaa Beach Park, Anini Beach Park,** and **Mahaulepu Beach.** ■ TIP➜ Many visitors come to Kauai dreaming of parasailing. If that's you, make a stop at Maui or the Big Island. There's no parasailing or commercial jet skiing on Kauai.

SCUBA DIVING

The majority of scuba diving on Kauai occurs on the South Shore. Boat and shore dives are available, although boat sites surpass the shore sites for a couple of reasons. First, they're deeper and exhibit the complete symbiotic relationship of a reef system, and second, the visibility is better a little farther offshore.

The dive operators on Kauai offer a full range of services, including certification dives, referral dives, boat dives, shore dives, night dives, and drift dives. ■TIP➔ As for certification, we recommend completing your confined-water training and classroom testing before arriving on the island. That way, you'll spend less time training and more time diving.

BEST SPOTS

The best and safest scuba-diving sites are accessed by boat on the South Shore of the island, right off the shores of Poipu. The captain selects the actual site based on ocean conditions of the day. Beginners may prefer shore dives, which are best at **Koloa Landing** on the South Shore year-round and **Makua (Tunnels) Beach** on the North Shore in the calm summer months. Keep in mind, though, that you'll have to haul your gear a ways down the beach.

For the advanced diver, the island of Niihau—across an open ocean channel in deep and crystal clear waters—beckons and rewards, usually with some big fish. Seasport Divers, Fathom Five, and Bubbles Below venture the 17 miles across the channel in summer when the crossing is smoothest. Divers can expect deep dives, walls, and strong currents at Niihau, where conditions can change rapidly. To make the long journey worthwhile, three dives and Nitrox are included.

EQUIPMENT, LESSONS, AND TOURS

Bubbles Below. Marine ecology is the emphasis here aboard the 36-foot, eight-passenger *Kai Manu*. This longtime Kauai company discovered some pristine dive sites on the West Side of the island where white-tip reef sharks are common—and other divers are not. Thanks to the addition of a 32-foot powered catamaran—the six-passenger *Dive Rocket*—the group also runs Niihau, Napali, and North Shore dives year-round (depending on ocean conditions, of course). They're still known for their South Side trips and lead dives at the East Side walls as well, so they truly do circumnavigate the island. A bonus on these tours is the wide variety of food served between dives. Open-water certification dives, check-out dives, and intro shore dives are available upon request. ⊠ *Port Allen Small Boat Harbor, 4353 Waialo Rd., Eleele* ☎ *808/332–7333* ⊕ *www.bubblesbelowkauai.com* ⊠ *$130 for a two-tank boat dive and up to $30 extra for rental gear; Niihau charter $335.*

Kauai Down Under Dive Team. This company offers boat dives, but specializes in shore diving, typically at Koloa Landing (year-round) and Tunnels (summers). They're not only geared toward beginning divers—for whom they provide a thorough and gentle certification program as well as the Discover Scuba program—but also offer night dives and scooter (think James Bond) dives. Their main emphasis is a detailed review of marine biology, such as pointing out rare dragon eel and

If you get up close with a Hawaiian monk seal, consider yourself lucky—they're endangered. But look, don't touch—it's illegal.

harlequin shrimp tucked away in pockets of coral. ■TIP→ Hands down, we recommend Sacred Seas Scuba for beginners, certification (all levels), and refresher dives. One reason is that their instructor-to-student ratio never exceeds 1:4—that's true of all their dive groups. All dive gear included. ⊠ *Sheraton Kauai Resort, 2440 Hoonani Rd., Koloa* ☎ *877/538–3483, 808/742–9534* ⊕ *www.kauaidownunderscuba.com* ⊠ *From $79 for a one-tank certified dive; $450 for certification.*

Fodor's Choice
★

Ocean Quest Watersports/Fathom Five. This operator offers it all: boat dives, shore dives, night dives, certification dives. They pretty much do what everyone else does with a few twists. First, they offer a three-tank premium charter for those really serious about diving. Second, they operate a Nitrox continuous-flow mixing system, so you can decide the mix rate. Third, they add on a twilight dive to the standard, one-tank night dive, making the outing worth the effort. Fourth, their shore diving isn't an afterthought. Finally, we think their dive masters are pretty darn good, too. They even dive Niihau in the summer aboard their 35-foot *Force.* ■TIP→ In summer, book well in advance. ⊠ *3450 Poipu Rd., Koloa* ☎ *808/742–6991, 800/972–3078* ⊕ *www.fathomfive. com* ⊠ *From $105 for boat dives from $75 for shore dives; $40 for gear rental, if needed.*

Seasport Divers. Rated highly by readers of *Scuba Diving* magazine, Seasport Divers' 48-foot *Anela Kai* tops the chart for dive-boat luxury. But owner Marvin Otsuji didn't stop with that. A second boat—a 32-foot catamaran—is outfitted for diving, but we like it as an all-around charter. The company does brisk business, which means it won't cancel at the last minute because of a lack of reservations, like some other companies, although they may book up to 18 people per boat. ■ TIP→ There are slightly more challenging trips in the morning; mellower dive sites are in the afternoon. The company runs a good-size dive shop for purchases and rentals, as well as a classroom for certification. Night dives are offered, and Niihau trips are available in summer. There's also an outlet in Kapaa. ✉ *2827 Poipu Rd., look for yellow submarine in parking lot, Poipu* ☎ *808/742–9303, 808/823–9222* ⊕ *www. seasportdivers.com* ✉ *From $160; rental gear, $30 extra.*

SNORKELING

Generally speaking, the calmest water and best snorkeling can be found on Kauai's North Shore in summer and South Shore in winter. The East Side, known as the windward side, has year-round, prevalent northeast trade winds that make snorkeling unpredictable, although there are some good pockets. The best snorkeling on the West Side is accessible only by boat.

A word on feeding fish: *Don't.* As Captain Ted with HoloHolo Charters says, fish have survived and populated reefs for much longer than we have been donning goggles and staring at them. They will continue to do so without our intervention. Besides, fish food messes up the reef and—one thing always leads to another—can eliminate a once-pristine reef environment. As for gear, if you're snorkeling with one of the Napali boat-tour outfitters, they'll provide it; however, depending on the company, it might not be the latest or greatest. If you have your own, bring it. On the other hand, if you're going out with SeaFun or Z-Tourz *(see Boat Tours),* the gear is top-notch. If you need to rent, hit one of the snorkel-and-surf shops such as Snorkel Bob's in Koloa and Kapaa, Nukumoi in Poipu, or Seasport in Poipu and Kapaa, or shop Wal-Mart or Kmart if you want to drag it home. Typically, though, rental gear will be better quality than that found at Wal-Mart or Kmart. ■ TIP→ If you wear glasses, you can rent prescription masks at the rental shops—just don't expect them to match your prescription exactly.

BEST SPOTS

Just because we say these are good places to snorkel doesn't mean that the exact moment you arrive, the fish will flock—they are wild, after all.

FAMILY   **Lydgate Beach Park.** Lydgate Beach Park is typically the safest place to snorkel on Kauai, though not the most exciting. With its lava-rock wall creating a protected swimming pool, it's a good spot for beginners, young and old. The fish are so tame here it's almost like swimming in a saltwater aquarium. There is also a lifeguard, a playground for children, plenty of parking, and full-service restrooms with showers. ✉ *4470 Nalu Rd., just south of Wailua River, turn makai off Rte. 56 onto Lehu Dr. and left onto Nalu Rd., Kapaa.*

Fodor's Choice   **Niihau.** With little river runoff and hardly any boat traffic, the waters off
★   the island of Niihau are some of the clearest in all Hawaii, and that's good for snorkeling and excellent for scuba diving. Like Nualolo Kai, the only way to snorkel here is to sign on with one of the tour boats venturing across a sometimes rough open ocean channel: Blue Dolphin Charters and HoloHolo.

Nualolo Kai. Nualolo Kai was once an ancient Hawaiian fishpond and is now home to the best snorkeling along Napali Coast (and perhaps on all of Kauai). The only way to access it is by boat, including kayak. Though many boats stop offshore, only a few Napali snorkeling-tour operators are permitted to come ashore. We recommend Napali Explorer and Kauai Sea Tours.

Tunnels (Makua). The search for Tunnels (Makua) is as tricky as the snorkeling. Park at Haena Beach Park and walk east—away from Napali Coast—until you see a sand channel entrance in the water, almost at the point. Once you get here, the reward is fantastic. The name of this beach comes from the many underwater lava tubes, which always attract marine life. The shore is mostly beach rock interrupted by three sand channels. You'll want to enter and exit at one of these channels (or risk stepping on a sea urchin or scraping your stomach on the reef). Follow the sand channel to a drop-off; the snorkeling along here is always full of nice surprises. Expect a current running east to west. Snorkeling here in winter can be hazardous; summer is the best and safest time for snorkeling. ⊠ *Haena Beach Park, near end of Rte. 560, across from lava-tube sea caves, after stream crossing.*

TOURS

FAMILY

Fodor's Choice

★

SeaFun Kauai. This guided snorkeling tour, for beginners and intermediates alike, is led by a marine expert, so there's instruction plus the guide actually gets into the water with you and identifies marine life. You're guaranteed to spot tons of critters you'd never see on your own. This is a land-based operation and the only one of its kind on Kauai. (Don't think those snorkeling cruises are guided snorkeling tours—they rarely are. A member of the boat's crew serves as lifeguard, not a marine life *guide*.) A half-day tour includes all your snorkeling gear—and a wet suit to keep you warm—and stops at one or two snorkeling locations, chosen based on ocean conditions. They will come pick up customers at some of the resorts, depending on locale and destination. ⊠ *1702 Haleukana St., Lihue* ☎ *808/245–6400, 800/452–1113* ⊕ *www. alohakauaitours.com* ⊟ *$80.*

STAND-UP PADDLING

Unlike kiteboarding, this is a new sport that even a novice can pick up—*and* have fun doing. Technically, it's not really a new sport but a reinvigorated one from the 1950s. Beginners start with a heftier surfboard and a longer-than-normal canoe paddle. And, just as the name implies, stand-up paddlers stand on their surfboards and paddle out from the beach—no timing a wave and doing a push-up to stand. The perfect place to learn is a river (think **Hanalei** or **Wailua**) or a calm lagoon (try **Anini** or **Kalapaki**). But this sport isn't just for beginners. Tried-and-true surfers turn to it when the waves are not quite right for their preferred sport, because it gives them another reason to be on the water. Stand-up paddlers catch waves earlier and ride them longer than longboard surfers. In the past couple of years, professional stand-up paddling competitions have popped up, and surf shops and instructors have adapted to its quick rise in popularity.

EQUIPMENT

Not all surf instructors teach stand-up paddling, but more and more are, like Blue Seas Surf School and Titus Kinimaka Hawaiian School of Surfing *(see Surfing)*.

Back Door Surf Co. Along with its sister store across the street–Hanalei Surf Shop–Back Door Surf Co. provides just about all the rentals necessary for a fun day at Hanalei Bay, along with clothing and new boards. ⊠ *Ching Young Village, 5-5161 Kuhio Hwy., Hanalei* ☎ *808/826–9000* ⊕ *www.hanaleisurf.com.*

Hawaiian Surfing Adventures. This Hanalei location has a wide variety of stand-up boards and paddles for rent, with a few options depending on your schedule. Check in at the storefront and then head down to the beach, where your gear will be waiting. Lessons are also available on the scenic Hanalei River or in Hanalei Bay, and include one hour of instruction and two hours to practice with the board. The company also offers surfboard rentals and surfing lessons. ⊠ *5134 Kuhio Hwy., Hanalei* ☎ *808/482–0749* ⊕ *www.hawaiiansurfingadventures.com* 🏄 *Paddleboard rental, $50; surfboards from $20; lessons from $65.*

Kauai Beach Boys. This outfitter is right on the beach at Kalapaki, so there's no hauling your gear on your car. Classes are also held at Poipu Beach, at the Marriott Waiohai. Stand-up paddle and sailing lessons can be arranged, too. ⊠ *3610 Rice St., Lihue* ☎ *808/742–4442, 808/246–6333* ⊕ *www.kauaibeachboys.com* 🏄 *$75 for 1½-hour surfing lesson.*

SURFING

Good ol' stand-up surfing is alive and well on Kauai, especially in winter's high-surf season on the North Shore. If you're new to the sport, we highly recommend taking a lesson. Not only will this ensure you're up and riding waves in no time, but instructors will provide the right board for your experience and size, help you time a wave, and give you a push to get your momentum going. ■TIP→ **You don't need to be in top physical shape to take a lesson. Because your instructor helps push you into the wave, you won't wear yourself out paddling.** If you're experienced and want to hit the waves on your own, most surf shops rent boards for all levels, from beginners to advanced.

BEST SPOTS

Perennial-favorite beginning surf spots include **Poipu Beach** (the area fronting the Marriott Waiohai Beach Club), **Hanalei Bay,** and the stream end of **Kalapaki Beach.** More advanced surfers move down the beach in Hanalei to an area fronting a grove of pine trees known as **Pine Trees,** or paddle out past the pier. When the trade winds die, the north ends of **Wailua** and **Kealia** beaches are teeming with surfers. Breaks off **Poipu** and **Beach House/Lawai Beach** attract intermediates year-round. During high surf, the break on the cliff side of **Kalihiwai** is for experts only. Advanced riders will head to Polihale to face the heavy West Side waves when conditions are right.

Winter brings big surf to Kauai's North Shore. You can see some of the sport's biggest celebrities catching waves at Haena and Hanalei Bay.

LESSONS

Hanalei Surf Company. You can rent boards here and shop for rash guards, wet suits, and some hip surf-inspired apparel. ⊠ *Hanalei Center, 5-5161 Kuhio Hwy., Hanalei* ☎ *808/826–9000* ⊕ *www.hanaleisurf.com.*

Margo Oberg Surfing School. Seven-time world surfing champion and hall of famer Margo Oberg runs a surf school that meets on the beach in front of the Sheraton Kauaii in Poipu. Margo's staff teaches more than she does these days. ⊠ *2440 Hoonani Rd., Koloa* ☎ *808/332–6100* ⊕ *www.surfonkauai.com* ✉ *$68 for two-hour group lessons; $125 for private sessions.*

Nukumoi Surf Co. Owned by the same folks who own Brennecke's restaurant, this shop offers board (surfing, body, and stand-up paddle) rentals, as well as snorkel and beach gear rental, along with casual clothing. Their primary surf spot is the beach fronting the Sheraton. ⊠ *2100 Hoone Rd., across from Poipu Beach Park, Koloa* ☎ *808/742–8019* ⊕ *www.nukumoi.com* ✉ *$75 for groups for two hours; $175 for private sessions.*

Progressive Expressions. This full-service shop has a choice of rental boards and a whole lotta shopping for clothes, swimsuits, and casual beachwear. ⊠ *5428 Koloa Rd., Koloa* ☎ *808/742–6041.*

Tamba Surf Company. This is Kauai's homegrown surf shop, and your best bet for surfboard and snorkel gear rentals on the East Side. Tamba is a big name in local surf apparel. ⊠ *4-1543 Kuhio Hwy., next to Kojima store, Kapaa* ☎ *808/823–6942* ⊕ *www.tambasurfcompany.com.*

Titus Kinimaka Hawaiian School of Surfing. Famed as a pioneer of big-wave surfing, this Hawaiian believes in giving back to his sport. Beginning, intermediate, and advanced lessons are available. If you want to learn to surf from a living legend, this is the man. ■**TIP➜ He employs other instructors, so if you want Titus, be sure to ask for him. (And good luck, because if the waves are going off, he'll be surfing, not teaching.)** Customers are able to use the board for a while after the lesson is complete. ✉ *Quicksilver, 5-5088 Kuhio Hwy., Hanalei* ☏ *808/652–1116* ⊕ *www. hawaiianschoolofsurfing.com* ✉ *$55, 90-minute group; $65, 90-minute group stand-up paddle.*

EQUIPMENT

Hanalei Surf Company. You can rent boards here and shop for rash guards, wet suits, and some hip surf-inspired apparel. ✉ *Hanalei Center, 5-5161 Kuhio Hwy., Hanalei* ☏ *808/826–9000* ⊕ *www.hanaleisurf.com.*

Progressive Expressions. This full-service shop has a choice of rental boards and a whole lotta shopping for clothes, swimsuits, and casual beachwear. ✉ *5428 Koloa Rd., Koloa* ☏ *808/742–6041.*

Tamba Surf Company. This is Kauai's homegrown surf shop, and your best bet for surfboard and snorkel gear rentals on the East Side. Tamba is a big name in local surf apparel. ✉ *4-1543 Kuhio Hwy., Next to Kojima store, Kapaa* ☏ *808/823–6942* ⊕ *www.tambasurfcompany.com.*

WHALE-WATCHING

Every winter North Pacific humpback whales swim some 3,000 miles over 30 days, give or take a few, from Alaska to Hawaii. Whales arrive as early as November and sometimes stay through April, though they seem to be most populous in February and March. They come to Hawaii to breed, calve, and nurse their young.

Of course, nothing beats seeing a whale up close. During the season, any boat on the water is looking for whales; they're hard to avoid, whether the tour is labeled "whale-watching" or not. Consider the whales a benefit to any boating event that may interest you. If whales are definitely your thing, though, you can narrow down your tour boat decision by asking a few whale-related questions like whether there's a hydrophone on board, how long the captain has been running tours in Hawaii, and if anyone on the crew is a marine biologist or trained naturalist.

Several boat operators will add two-hour, afternoon whale-watching tours during the season that run on the South Shore (not Napali). Operators include **Blue Dolphin, Catamaran Kahanu, HoloHolo,** and **Napali Explorer** *(see Boat Tours).* Trying one of these excursions is a good option for those who have no interest in snorkeling or sightseeing along Napali Coast, although keep in mind, the longer you're on the water, the more likely you'll be to see the humpbacks.

One of the more unique ways to, *possibly,* see some whales is atop a kayak. For such an encounter, try **Outfitters Kauai**'s South Shore kayak trip *(see Kayaking Tours).* There are a few lookout spots around the island with good land-based viewing: Kilauea Lighthouse on the North Shore, the Kapaa Scenic Overlook just north of Kapaa town on the

Humpback whales arrive at Kauai in December and stick around until early April. Head out on a boat tour for a chance to see these majestic creatures breach.

East Side, and the cliffs to the east of Keoniloa (Shipwreck) Beach on the South Shore.

GOLF, HIKING, AND OUTDOOR ACTIVITIES

Updated by
Charles E.
Roessler

For those who love ocean sports but need a little break from all that sun, sand, and salt, there are plenty of options on Kauai to keep you busy on the ground. You can hike the island's many trails, or take your vacation into flight with a treetop zip line. You can have a backcountry adventure in a four-wheel drive, or relax in an inner tube floating down the cane-field irrigation canals.

AERIAL TOURS

If you only drive around Kauai in your rental car, you will not see *all* of Kauai. There is only one way to see it all, and that's by air. Helicopter tours are the favorite way to get a bird's-eye view of Kauai—they fly at lower altitudes, hover above waterfalls, and wiggle their way into areas that a fixed-wing aircraft cannot.

Blue Hawaiian Helicopters. This multi-island operator flies the latest in helicopter technology, the Eco-Star, costing $1.8 million. It has 23% more interior space for its six passengers, has unparalleled viewing, and offers a few extra safety features. As the name implies, the helicopter is also a bit more environmentally friendly, with a 50% noise-reduction rate. Even though flights run a tad shorter than others (50 to 55 minutes instead of the 55 to 65 minutes that other companies

500 <   **Kauai**

tout), they feel complete. A DVD of your tour is available for an additional $25. ⊠ *3651 Ahukini Rd., Heliport 8, Lihue* ☎ *808/245–5800, 800/745–2583* ⊕ *www.bluehawaiian.com* 🖅 *$247, includes taxes and fuel surcharge.*

Inter-Island Helicopters. This company flies Robinson 4 helicopters with 3 passenger seats guaranteeing an unobstructed window seat for each passenger. It can get chilly at higher elevations, so bring a sweater and wear long pants. Tours depart from Hanapepe's Port Allen Airport, so if you're staying on the West Side, this is a good bet. Special group rates available. ⊠ *Port Allen Airport, 3441 Kuiloko Rd., Hanapepe* ☎ *808/335–5009, 800/656–5009* ⊕ *www.interislandhelicopters.com* 🖅 *From $249 per person.*

Fodor's Choice **Jack Harter Helicopters.** Jack Harter was the first company to offer heli-
★ copter tours on Kauai. The company flies the six-passenger ASTAR helicopter with floor-to-ceiling windows, and the four-person Hughes 500, which is flown with no doors. The doorless ride can get windy, but it's the best bet for taking reflection-free photos. Pilots provide information on the Garden Island's history and geography through two-way intercoms. The company flies out of Lihue and has a second office at the Kauai Marriott. Tours are 60 to 65 minutes and 90 to 95 minutes. ⊠ *4231 Ahukini Rd.* ☎ *808/245–3774, 888/245–2001* ⊕ *www.helicopters-kauai.com* 🖅 *From $269.*

Safari Helicopters. This company flies the "Super" ASTAR helicopter, which offers floor-to-ceiling windows on its doors, four roof windows, and Bose X-Generation headphones. Two-way microphones allow passengers to converse with the pilot. A major perk Safari offers is its 90-minute "ecotour," which adds a landing in Olokele Canyon. Passengers are then met by Keith Robinson of *the* Robinson family, who provides a brief tour of the Kauai Wildlife Refuge, with endangered, endemic plants. The once daily tour goes out Monday through Friday at 3:30 p.m. A DVD is available for $40. ⊠ *3225 Akahi St., Lihue* ☎ *808/246–0136, 800/326–3356* ⊕ *www.safarihelicopters.com* 🖅 *From $224.*

Sunshine Helicopter Tours. If the name of this company sounds familiar, it may be because its pilots fly on all the main Hawaiian Islands except Oahu. On Kauai, Sunshine Helicopters departs out of two different locations: Lihue and Princeville. They fly the six-passenger FX STAR from Lihue and super roomy six-passenger WhisperSTAR birds from Princeville. ■ TIP→ Discounts can be substantial by booking online and taking advantage of the "early-bird" seating during off hours. ⊠ *3416 Rice St., Ste 203, Lihue* ☎ *808/240–2577, 888/245–4354* ⊕ *www.sunshinehelicopters.com* 🖅 *From $244 for Lihue flights; from $289 for Princeville flights* ⊠ *Princeville Airport, Princeville.*

ATV TOURS

Although all the beaches on the island are public, much of the interior land—once sugar and pineapple plantations—is privately owned. This is really a shame, because the valleys and mountains that make up the vast interior of the island easily rival the beaches in sheer beauty. The good news is some tour operators have agreements with landowners that make exploration possible, albeit a bit bumpy, and unless you have back troubles, that's half the fun. ■ TIP→ If it looks like rain, book an ATV tour ASAP. That's the thing about these tours: the muddier, the better.

Fodor's Choice ★ **Kauai ATV Tours.** This is *the* thing to do when it rains on Kauai. Consider it an extreme mud bath. Kauai ATV in Koloa is the originator of the island's all-terrain-vehicle tours. The three-hour Koloa tour takes you through a private sugar plantation and historic cane-haul tunnel. The four-hour waterfall tour visits secluded waterfalls and includes a picnic lunch. This popular option includes a hike to secret WWII bunkers and a swim in a freshwater pool at the base of the falls—to rinse off all that mud. You must be 16 or older to operate your own ATV, but Kauai ATV also offers its four-passenger "Ohana Bug" and two-passenger "Mud Bugs" to accommodate families with kids ages five and older. ✉ *3477A Weliweli Rd., Koloa* 🕿 *808/742–2734, 877/707–7088* ⊕ *www.kauaiatv. com* 🖾 *$133 Koala tour; $163 waterfall tour.*

Kipu Ranch Adventures. This 3,000-acre property extends from the Huleia River to the top of Mt. Haupu. *Jurassic Park, Indiana Jones,* and *Mighty Joe Young* were filmed here, and you'll see the locations for all of them on the three-hour Ranch Tour, (depending on the vehicle). The four-hour Waterfall Tour includes a visit to two waterfalls and a picnic lunch. Once a sugar plantation, Kipu Ranch today is a working cattle ranch, so you'll be in the company of bovines as well as pheasants, wild boars, and peacocks. ✉ *235 Kipu Rd., off Hwy. 50, Lihue* 🕿 *808/246–9288* ⊕ *www.kiputours.com* 🖾 *From $120.*

BIKING

Kauai is a labyrinth of cane-haul roads, which are fun for exploring on two wheels. The challenge is finding roads where biking is allowed and then not getting lost in the maze. Maybe that explains why Kauai is not a hub for the sport . . . yet. Still, there are some epic rides for those who are interested—both the adrenaline-rush and the mellower beach-cruiser kind. If you want to grind out some mileage, you could take the main highway that skirts the coastal area, but take caution. There are only a few designated bike lanes. It's hilly, and you'll find that keeping your eyes on the road and not the scenery is the biggest challenge. "Cruisers" should head to Kapaa. A new section of Ke Ala Hele Makalae, a pedestrian and bicycle trail that runs along the East Side of Kauai, was completed in the summer of 2013, extending the multi-use path to about 8 miles. You can rent bikes (with helmets) from the activities desks of certain hotels, but these are not the best quality. You're better off renting from Coconut Coasters or Kauai Cycle in Kapaa,

Outfitters Kauai in Poipu, or Pedal 'n' Paddle in Hanalei. Ask for the "Go Green Kauai" map for a full description of Kauai biking options.

Ke Ala Hele Makalae (*Nawiliwili to Anahola Bike/Pedestrian Path*). For the cruiser, this path follows the coastline on Kauai's East Side. Eventually, it will run some 20 miles and presently offers scenic views, picnic pavilions, and restroom facilities along the way—all in compliance with the Americans with Disabilities Act. For now, there are 2.5 miles of path in Lydgate Beach Park, a connection across the Wailua River to the Coconut Marketplace, a gap of about a half-mile, and the continuous path from the Waipouli Beach Resort to secluded Kuna Bay (aka Donkey Beach). An easy way to access the longest completed section of the path is from Kealia Beach. Park here and head north into rural lands with spectacular coastline vistas or head south into Kapaa for a more interactive experience. ⊠ *Trailhead: 1 mile north of Kapaa; park at north end of Kealia Beach, Kapaa.*

Moalepe Trail. This trail is perfect for intermediate to advanced riders. The first 2 miles of this 5-mile double-track road winds through pastureland. The real challenge begins when you reach the steep and rutted switchbacks, which during a rainy spell can be hazardous. Moalepe dead-ends at the Kuilau Trail. If you choose to continue down the Kuilau Trail, it will end at the Keahua Arboretum stream. ⊠ *Wailua* ✛ *From Kuhio Hwy. in Kapaa drive mauka (toward mountains) on Kuamoo Rd. for 3 miles and turn right on Kamalu Rd. It dead-ends at Olohena Rd. Turn left and follow until the road veers sharply to the right.*

Wailua Forest Management Road. For the novice mountain biker, this is an easy ride, and it's also easy to find. From Route 56 in Wailua, turn *mauka* (toward the mountains) on Kuamoo Road and continue 6 miles to the picnic area, known as Keahua Arboretum; park here. The potholed four-wheel-drive road includes some stream crossings—⚠ **stay away during heavy rains, because the streams flood**—and continues for 2 miles to a T-stop, where you should turn right. Stay on the road for about 3 miles until you reach a gate; this is the spot where the gates in the movie *Jurassic Park* were filmed, though it looks nothing like the movie. Go around the gate and down the road for another mile to a confluence of streams at the base of Mt. Waialeale. Be sure to bring your camera. ⊠ *Kuamoo Rd., Kapaa.*

Waimea Canyon Road. For those wanting a very challenging road workout, climb this road, also known as Route 550. After a 3,000-foot climb, the road tops out at mile 12 adjacent to Waimea Canyon, which will pop in and out of view on your right as you ascend. From here it continues several miles (mostly level) past the Kokee Museum and ends at the Kalalau Lookout. It's paved the entire way, uphill 100%, and curvy. ⚠ **There's not much of a shoulder on either road—sometimes none—so be extra cautious.** The road gets busier as the day wears on, so you may want to consider a sunrise ride. A slightly more moderate uphill climb is Kokee Road, Route 552, from Kekaha, which intersects with Route 550. By the way, bikes aren't allowed on the hiking trails in and around Waimea Canyon and Kokee State Park, but there are

One of the most visited sites on Kauai is Waimea Canyon. Make sure to stop at Puu ka Pele and Puu Hinahina lookouts.

miles of wonderful 4WD roads perfect for mountain biking. Check at Kokee Lodge for a map and conditions. ⊠ *Off Rte. 50, near grocery store, Waimea.*

EQUIPMENT AND TOURS

Kauai Cycle. This reliable, full-service bike shop rents, sells, and repairs bikes. Cruisers, mountain bikes (front- and full-suspension), and road bikes are available for $30 to $60 per day and $110 to $250 per week with directions to trails. The Ke Ala Hele Makalae is right out their back door. ⊠ *4-934 Kuhio Hwy., across from Taco Bell, Kapaa* ☎ *808/821–2115* ⊕ *www.kauaicycle.com.*

Outfitters Kauai. Hybrid "comfort" and mountain bikes (both full-suspension and hardtails), as well as road bikes, are available at this shop in Poipu. You can ride right out the door to tour Poipu, or get information on how to do a self-guided tour of Kokee State Park and Waimea Canyon. The company also leads sunrise and evening coasting tours (under the name **Bicycle Downhill**) from Waimea Canyon past the island's West Side beaches. Stand-up paddle tours are also available. ⊠ *2827-A Poipu Rd., near turnoff to Spouting Horn, Poipu* ☎ *808/742–9667, 888/742–9887* ⊕ *www.outfitterskauai.com* ◫ *Rentals from $15; tours $104 plus tax.*

Pedal 'n' Paddle. This company rents old-fashioned, single-speed beach cruisers and hybrid road bikes. In the heart of Hanalei, this is a great way to cruise the town; the more ambitious cyclist can head to the end of the road. Be careful, though, because there are no bike lanes on the twisting and turning road to Kee. ⊠ *Ching Young Village, 5-5190 Kuhio*

Hwy., Hanalei ☎ *808/826-9069* ⊕ *www.pedalnpaddle.com* ☞ *Rentals from $15 per day and $60 per week.*

GOLF

For golfers, the Garden Isle might as well be known as the Robert Trent Jones Jr. Isle. Four of the island's nine courses, including Poipu Bay—onetime home of the PGA Grand Slam of Golf—are the work of Jones, who maintains a home at Princeville. Combine these four courses with those from Jack Nicklaus, Robin Nelson, and local legend Toyo Shirai, and you'll see that golf sets Kauai apart from the other Islands as much as the Pacific Ocean does. ■ TIP→ Afternoon tee times at most courses can save you big bucks.

Kauai Lagoons Golf Club. After a 2011 renovation the Kiele Moana Nine (ocean) course now features a half-mile of oceanfront golf, the longest stretch of continuous ocean holes in Hawaii. Jack Nicklaus returned to do the initial design work and then saw it to completion. The Kiele Moana Nine is coupled with the Kiele Mauka (toward the mountain) Nine to offer players 18 championship-style holes of golf. For those looking for a more family- and kid-friendly layout, their Waikehe Nine inland course is an economical option. ⊠ *3351 Hoolaulea Way, Lihue* ☎ *808/241–6000, 800/634–6400* ⊕ *www.kauailagoonsgolf.com* ☞ *From $150* ⅄ *18 holes, 7156 yds, par 72.*

Kauai Mini Golf. The only miniature golf course on the island, Kauai Mini Golf is also a full botanical garden. The 18-hole course was designed to be challenging, beautiful, and family-friendly. Replacing the typical clown's nose and spinning wheels are some water features and tropical tunnels. Surrounding each hole is flora and plant life that walks players through different eras of Hawaiian history. A gift shop with local products and a concessions counter make it a fun activity for any time of day. ⊠ *5-273 Kuhio Hwy, Kilauea* ☎ *808/828–2118* ⊕ *www. kauaiminigolf.com* ☞ *$18* ☉ *Tue.–Sun., 11–8.*

Kiahuna Plantation Golf Course. A meandering creek, lava outcrops, and thickets of trees give Kiahuna its character. Robert Trent Jones Jr. was given a smallish piece of land just inland at Poipu, and defends par with smaller targets, awkward stances, and optical illusions. In 2003 a group of homeowners bought the club and brought Jones back to renovate the course (it was originally built in 1983), adding tees and revamping bunkers. The pro here boasts his course has the best putting greens on the island. This is the only course on Kauai with a complete set of junior's tee boxes. ⊠ *2545 Kiahuna Plantation Dr., Koloa* ☎ *808/742–9595* ⊕ *www.kiahunagolf.com* ☞ *$105* ⅄ *18 holes, 6341 yds, par 70.*

Poipu Bay Golf Course. Poipu Bay has been called the Pebble Beach of Hawaii, and the comparison is apt. Like Pebble Beach, Poipu is a links course built on headlands, not true links land. There's wildlife galore. It's not unusual for golfers to see monk seals sunning on the beach below, sea turtles bobbing outside the shore break, and humpback whales leaping offshore. From 1994 to 2006, the course (designed by Robert Trent Jones Jr.) hosted the annual PGA Grand Slam of Golf. Tiger Woods was a frequent winner here. Call ahead to take advantage of varying prices for tee times. ✉ *2250 Ainako St., Koloa* ☎ *808/742–8711* ⊕ *www.poipubaygolf.com* ▣ *$240* ⅄ *18 holes, 6127 yards, par 72.*

Princeville Makai Golf Club. The 27-hole Princeville Makai Golf Club was named for its five ocean-hugging front holes. Designed by golf course architect Robert Trent Jones Jr. in 1971, the 18-hole championship Makai Course underwent extensive renovations from 2008–2010, including new turf throughout, reshaped greens and bunkers, refurbished cart paths and comfort stations, and an extensive practice facility. Since the renovation the Makai Course has consistently been ranked a top golf course in the U.S. The Club offers free rounds for juniors (15 and under) when accompanied by one paying adult. A web check (makaigolf.com) provides varying rates. ✉ *4080 Lei O Papa Rd., Princeville* ⊕ *www.makaigolf.com* ▣ *$239* ⅄ *18-holes, 7223 yards, par 72; Woods Course: 9 holes, 3445 yards, par 36.*

Prince Golf Course. The Prince Course reveals architect Robert Trent Jones Jr. at his finest as it meanders over 390 acres of natural splendor with fairytale vistas and jungly valleys. It's a challenging course that emphasizes touch and precision. Mountain and ocean views frame rolling plateaus and deep ravines with tropical birds and flora serving as natural backdrops. A high-end practice facility morphs into a kid and duffer friendly 6-hole, par 3 course after 4 pm daily. Celebrity chef Roy Yamaguchi's restaurant, The Tavern, complements the upscale ambience of the facility. ✉ *5-3900 Kuhio Hwy., Princeville* ☎ *808/826–5001* ⊕ *www.princeville.com* ▣ *$250* ⅄ *18 holes, 7378 yds, par 72.*

Wailua Municipal Golf Course. Considered by many to be one of Hawaii's best golf courses, this seaside course provides an affordable game with minimal water hazards, but it is challenging enough to have been chosen to host three USGA Amateur Public Links Championships. It was first built as a 9-holer in the 1930s. The second 9 holes were added in 1961. Course designer Toyo Shirai created a course that is fun but not punishing. The trade winds blow steadily on the East Side of the island and provide a game with challenges. An ocean view and affordability make this one of the most popular courses on the island. Tee times are accepted up to seven days in advance and must be paid in cash or traveler's checks. ✉ *3-5350 Kuhio Hwy., Lihue* ☎ *808/241–6666* ▣ *$48 weekdays, $60 weekends; cart rental $20* ⅄ *18 holes, 6585 yds, par 72.*

HIKING

The best way to experience the *aina*—the land—on Kauai is to step off the beach and hike into the remote interior. You'll find waterfalls so tall you'll strain your neck looking, pools of crystal clear water for swimming, tropical forests teeming with plant life, and ocean vistas that will make you wish you could stay forever.

■ **TIP→** For your safety wear sturdy shoes—preferably water-resistant ones. All hiking trails on Kauai are free, so far. There's a development plan in the works that could turn the Waimea Canyon and Kokee state parks into admission-charging destinations. Whatever it may be, it will be worth it.

Hanalei-OkolehaoTrail. *Okolehao* basically translates to "moonshine" in Hawaiian. This trail follows the Hihimanu Ridge, which was established in the days of Prohibition, when this backyard liquor was distilled from the roots of ti plants. The 2-mile hike climbs 1,200 feet and offers a 360-degree view of Hanalei Bay and Waioli Valley. Your ascent begins at the China Ditch off the Hanalei River. Follow the trail through a lightly forested grove and then climb up a steep embankment. From here the trail is well marked. Most of the climb is lined with hala, ti, wild orchid, and eucalyptus. You'll get your first of many ocean views at mile marker 1. ⊠ *Hanalei* ⊹ *Follow Ohiki Rd. (north of the Hanalei Bridge) 5 miles to the U.S. Fish and Wildlife Service parking area. Directly across the street is a small bridge that marks the trailhead.*

Fodor's Choice
★

Kalalau Trail. Of all the hikes on the island, Kalalau Trail is by far the most famous and in many regards the most strenuous. A moderate hiker can handle the 2-mile trek to Hanakapiai Beach, and for the seasoned outdoorsman, the additional 2 miles up to the falls is manageable. But be prepared to rock-hop along a creek and ford waters that can get waist high during the rain. Round-trip to Hanakapiai Falls is 8 miles. This steep and often muddy trail is best approached with a walking stick. If there has been any steady rain, waiting for drier days would provide a more enjoyable trek. The narrow trail will deliver one startling ocean view after another along a path that is alternately shady and sunny. Wear hiking shoes or sandals, and bring drinking water since the creeks on the trail are not potable. Plenty of food is always encouraged on a strenuous hike such as this one. If your plan is to venture the full 11 miles into Kalalau, you need to acquire a camping permit, which can be acquired either online or at the State Building in Lihue for $20 per person per night. It is advisable that you secure a permit well in advance of your trip. ⊹ *Drive north past Hanalei to end of road. Trailhead is directly across from Kee Beach* ⊕ *www.kalalautrail.com.*

Mahaulepu Heritage Trail. This trail offers the novice hiker an accessible way to appreciate the rugged southern coast of Kauai. A cross-country course wends its way along the water, high above the ocean, through a lava field and past a sacred *heiau* (stone structure). Walk all the way to Mahaulepu, 2 miles north for a two-hour round-trip. ⊹ *Drive north on Poipu Rd., turn right at Poipu Bay Golf Course sign. The street name is Ainako, but the sign is hard to see. Drive down to beach and park in lot.* ⊕ *www.hikemahaulepu.org.*

Sleeping Giant Trail. An easily accessible trail practically in the heart of Kapaa, the moderately strenuous Sleeping Giant Trail—or simply Sleeping Giant—gains 1,000 feet over 2 miles. We prefer an early-morning— say, sunrise—hike, with sparkling blue-water vistas, up the East Side trailhead. At the top you can see a grassy grove with a picnic table. Experienced hikers may want to go a step farther, all the way to the giant's nose and chin, which offer 360-degree views of the island. It is a local favorite with many East-Siders meeting here to exercise. ⊠ *Haleilio Rd., off Rte. 56, Wailua.*

Waimea Canyon and Kokee State Parks. This park contains a 50-mile network of hiking trails of varying difficulty that take you through acres of native forests, across the highest-elevation swamp in the world, to the river at the base of the canyon, and onto pinnacles of land sticking their necks out over Napali Coast. All hikers should register at Kokee Natural History Museum, where you can find trail maps, current trail information, and specific directions.

All mileage mentioned below is one-way.

The **Kukui Trail** descends 2½ miles and 2,200 feet into Waimea Canyon to the edge of the Waimea River—it's a steep climb. The **Awaawapuhi Trail**, with 1,600 feet of elevation gains and losses over 3¼ miles, feels more gentle than the Kukui Trail, but it offers its own huffing-and-puffing sections in its descent along a spiny ridge to a perch overlooking the ocean.

The 3½-mile **Alakai Swamp Trail** is accessed via the **Pihea Trail** or a four-wheel-drive road. There's one strenuous valley section, but otherwise it's a pretty level trail—once you access it. This trail is a bird-watcher's delight and includes a painterly view of Wainiha and Hanalei valleys at the trail's end. The trail traverses the purported highest-elevation swamp in the world on a boardwalk so as not to disturb the fragile plant- and wildlife. It is typically the coolest of the hikes due to the tree canopies, elevation, and cloud coverage.

The **Canyon Trail** offers much in its short trek: spectacular vistas of the canyon and the only dependable waterfall in Waimea Canyon. The easy 2-mile hike can be cut in half if you have a four-wheel-drive vehicle. If you were outfitted with a headlamp, this would be a great hike at sunset, as the sun's light sets the canyon walls ablaze in color. ⊠ *Kokee Natural History Museum, 3600 Kokee Rd., Kekaha* ☎ *808/335–9975 for trail conditions.*

EQUIPMENT AND TOURS

Fodor's Choice
★
Kauai Nature Tours. Father and son scientists started this hiking tour business. As such, their emphasis is on education and the environment. If you're interested in flora, fauna, volcanology, geology, oceanography, and the like, this is the company for you. They offer daylong hikes along coastal areas, beaches, and in the mountains. ■TIP→ If you have a desire to see a specific location, just ask. They will do custom hikes to spots they don't normally hit if there is interest. Hikes range from easy to strenuous. Transportation is often provided from your hotel. ⊠ *5162 Lawai Rd., Koloa* ☎ *808/742–8305, 888/233–8365* ⊕ *www.kauainaturetours.com* ⊠ *From $135.*

HORSEBACK RIDING

Most of the horseback-riding tours on Kauai are primarily walking tours with little trotting and no cantering or galloping, so no experience is required. Zip. Zilch. Nada. If you're interested, most of the stables offer private lessons. The most popular tours are the ones including a picnic lunch by the water. Your only dilemma may be deciding what kind of water you want—waterfalls or ocean. You may want to make your decision based on where you're staying. The "waterfall picnic"

Continued on page 516

NAPALI COAST: EMERALD QUEEN OF KAUAI

If you're coming to Kauai, Napali ("cliffs" in Hawaiian) is a major must-see. More than 5 million years old, these sea cliffs rise thousands of feet above the Pacific, and every shade of green is represented in the vegetation that blankets their lush peaks and folds. At their base, there are caves, secluded beaches, and waterfalls to explore.

The big question is how to explore this gorgeous stretch of coastline. You can't drive to it, through it, or around it. You can't see Napali from a scenic lookout. You can't even take a mule ride to it. The only way to experience its magic is from the sky, the ocean, or the trail.

FROM THE SKY

If you've booked a helicopter tour of Napali, you might start wondering what you've gotten yourself into on the way to the airport. Will it feel like being on a small airplane? Will there be turbulence? Will it be worth all the money you just plunked down?

Your concerns will be assuaged on the helipad, once you see the faces of those who have just returned from their journey: Everyone looks totally blissed out. And now it's your turn.

Climb on board, strap on your headphones, and the next thing you know the helicopter gently lifts up, hovers for a moment, and floats away like a spider on the wind—no roaring engines, no rumbling down a runway. If you've chosen a flight with music, you'll feel as if you're inside your very own IMAX movie.

Pinch yourself if you must, because this is the real thing. Your pilot shares history, legend, and lore. If you miss something, speak up: pilots love to show off their island knowledge. You may snap a few pictures (not too many or you'll miss the eyes-on experience!), nudge a friend or spouse, and point at a whale breeching in the ocean, but mostly you stare, mouth agape. There is simply no other way to take in the immensity and greatness of Napali but from the air.

Helicopter flight over Napali Coast

GOOD TO KNOW

Helicopter companies depart from the north, east, and west side of the island. Most are based in Lihue, near the airport.

If you want more adventure—and air—choose one of the helicopter companies that flies with the doors off.

Some companies offer flights without music. Know the experience you want ahead of time. Some even sell a DVD of your flight, so you don't have to worry about taking pictures.

Wintertime rain grounds some flights; plan your trip early in your stay in case the flight gets rescheduled.

IS THIS FOR ME?

Taking a helicopter trip is the most expensive way to see Napali—as much as $300 for an hour-long tour.

Claustrophobic? Choose a boat tour or hike. It's a tight squeeze in the helicopter, especially in one of the middle seats.

Short on time? Taking a helicopter tour is a great way to see the island.

WHAT YOU MIGHT SEE

■ Nualolo Kai (an ancient Hawaiian fishing village) with its fringed reef

■ The 300-foot Hanakapiai Falls

■ A massive sea arch formed in the rock by erosion

■ The 11-mile Kalalau Trail threading its way along the coast

■ The amazing striations of aa and pahoehoe lava flows that helped push Kauai above the sea

FROM THE OCEAN

Napali from the ocean is two treats in one: spend a good part of the day on (or in) the water, and gaze up at majestic green sea cliffs rising thousands of feet above your head.

There are three ways to see it: a mellow pleasure-cruise catamaran allows you to kick back and sip a mai tai; an adventurous raft (Zodiac) tour will take you inside sea caves under waterfalls, and give you the option of snorkeling; and a daylong outing in a kayak is a real workout, but then you can say you paddled 16 miles of coastline.

Any way you travel, you'll breathe ocean air, feel spray on your face, and see pods of spinner dolphins, green sea turtles, flying fish, and, if you're lucky, a rare Hawaiian monk seal.

Napali stretches from Kee Beach in the north to Polihale beach on the West Side. If your departure point is Kee, you are already headed toward the lush Hanakapiai Valley. Within a few minutes, you'll see caves and waterfalls galore. About halfway down the coast just after the Kalalau Trail ends, you'll come to an immense arch—formed where the sea eroded the less dense basaltic rock—and a thundering 50-foot waterfall. And as the island curves near Nualolo State Park, you'll begin to notice less vegetation and more rocky outcroppings.

(left and top right) Kayaking on Napali Coast
(bottom right) Dolphin on Napali Coast

GOOD TO KNOW

If you want to snorkel, choose a morning rather than an afternoon tour—preferably during a summer visit—when seas are calmer.

If you're on a budget, choose a non-snorkeling tour.

If you want to see whales, take any tour, but be sure to plan your vacation for December through March.

If you're staying on the North Shore or East Side, embark from the North Shore. If you're staying on the South Shore, it might not be worth your time to drive to the north, so head to the West Side.

IS THIS FOR ME?

Boat tours are several hours long, so if you have only a short time on Kauai, a helicopter tour is a better alternative.

Even on a small boat, you won't get the individual attention and exclusivity of a helicopter tour.

Prone to seasickness? A large boat can be surprisingly rocky, so be prepared.

WHAT YOU MIGHT SEE

■ Hawaii's state fish—the humuhumunukunukuapuaa—otherwise known as the reef triggerfish

■ Waiahuakua Sea Cave, with a waterfall coming through its roof

■ Tons of marine life, including dolphins, green sea turtles, flying fish, and humpback whales, especially in February and March

■ Waterfalls—especially if your trip is after a heavy rain

FROM THE TRAIL

If you want to be one with Napali—feeling the soft red earth beneath your feet, picnicking on the beaches, and touching the lush vegetation—hiking the Kalalau Trail is the way to do it.

Most people hike only the first 2 miles of the 11-mile trail and turn around at Hanakapiai. This 4-mile round-trip hike takes three to four hours. It starts at sea level and doesn't waste any time gaining elevation. (Take heart—the uphill lasts only a mile and tops out at 400 feet; then it's downhill all the way.) At the half-mile point, the trail curves west and the folds of Napali Coast unfurl.

Along the way you might share the trail with feral goats and wild pigs. Some of the vegetation is native; much is introduced.

After the 1-mile mark the trail begins its drop into Hanakapiai. You'll pass a couple of streams of water trickling across the trail, and maybe some banana, ginger, the native uluhe fern, and the Hawaiian ti plant. Finally the trail swings around the eastern ridge of Hanakapiai for your first glimpse of the valley and then switchbacks down the mountain. You'll have to boulder-hop across the stream to reach the beach. If you like, you can take a 4-mile, round-trip fairly strenuous side trip from this point to the gorgeous Hanakapiai Falls.

(left) Awaawapuhi mountain biker on razor-edge ridge
(top right) Feral goats in Kalalau Valley
(bottom right) Napali Coast

GOOD TO KNOW

Wear comfortable, amphibious shoes. Unless your feet require extra support, wear a self-bailing sort of shoe (for stream crossings) that doesn't mind mud. Don't wear heavy, waterproof hiking boots.

During winter the trail is often muddy, so be extra careful; sometimes it's completely inaccessible.

Don't hike after heavy rain—flash floods are common.

If you plan to hike the entire 11-mile trail (most people do the shorter hike described at left) you'll need a permit to go past Hanakapiai.

IS THIS FOR ME?

Of all the ways to see Napali (with the exception of kayaking the coast), this is the most active. You need to be in decent shape to hit the trail.

If you're vacationing in winter, this hike might not be an option due to flooding—whereas you can take a helicopter year-round.

WHAT YOU MIGHT SEE

■ Big dramatic surf right below your feet

■ Amazing vistas of the cool blue Pacific

■ The spectacular Hanakapiai Falls; if you have a permit don't miss Hanakoa Falls, less than 1/2 mile off the trail

■ Wildlife, including goats and pigs

■ Zany-looking ohia trees, with aerial roots and long, skinny serrated leaves known as hala. Early Hawaiians used them to make mats, baskets, and canoe sails.

tours are on the wetter North Shore, and the "beach picnic" tours take place on the South Side.

Esprit de Corps. If you ride, this is the company for you. Esprit De Corps Riding Academy now offers private two- and three-hour waterfall picnic rides for advanced riders with trotting and cantering. Group rides at a walk, as well as a 90-minute custom ride, are also featured. Lessons with a certified instructor are held in a covered arena for beginner through advanced riders ages six and up, both in English and Western saddles. Weddings on horseback can be arranged (in fact, Dale, the owner, is a wedding officiant and planner). Make sure to call ahead because they are by appointment only. ⊠ *1491 Kualapa Pl., Kapaa* ☎ *808/822–4688* ⊕ *www.kauaihorses.com* ✉ *From $99.*

Fodor's Choice ★ **Princeville Ranch Adventures.** A longtime *kamaaina* (resident) family operates Princeville Ranch. They originated the waterfall picnic tour, which runs three-and-a-half hours and includes a short but steep hike down to Kalihiwai Falls, a dramatic three-tier waterfall, for swimming and picnicking. Princeville also has shorter, straight riding tours and private rides. A popular option is the three-hour combination Ride N' Glide tour with three ziplines. ⊠ *Kuhio Hwy., between mile markers 27 and 28, Princeville* ☎ *808/826–7669* ⊕ *www.princevilleranch.com* ✉ *Ride only from $99; private tours from $245.*

MOUNTAIN TUBING

FAMILY **Kauai Backcountry Adventures.** Popular with all ages, this laid-back adventure can book up two weeks in advance in busy summer months. Here's how it works: you recline in an inner tube and float down fern-lined irrigation ditches that were built more than a century ago—the engineering is impressive—to divert water from Mt. Waialeale to sugar and pineapple fields around the island. They'll even give you a headlamp so you can see as you float through five covered tunnels. The scenery from the island's interior at the base of Mt. Waialeale on Lihue Plantation land is superb. Ages five and up are welcome. The tour takes about three hours and includes a picnic lunch and a swim in a swimming hole. ■TIP→ You'll definitely want to pack water-friendly shoes (or rent some from the outfitter), sunscreen, a hat, bug repellent, and a beach towel. Tours are offered morning and afternoon daily. ⊠ *3-4131 Kuhio Hwy., across from gas station, Hanamaulu* ☎ *808/245–2506, 888/270–0555* ⊕ *www.kauaibackcountry.com* ✉ *$102 per person.*

SKYDIVING

Skydive Kauai. Ten thousand feet over Kauai and falling at a rate of 120 mph is probably as thrilling as it gets while airborne. First, there's the 25-minute plane ride to altitude in a Cessna 182, then the exhilaration of the first step into sky, the sensation of sailing weightless in the air over Kauai, and finally the peaceful buoyancy beneath the canopy of your parachute. A tandem free-fall rates among the most unforgettable experiences of a lifetime. Wed that to the aerial view over Kauai and you've got a winning marriage that you can relive with an HD video memory.

LEPTOSPIROSIS

The sparkling waters of those babbling brooks trickling around the island can be life-threatening, and we're not talking about the dangers of drowning, although they, too, exist. Leptospirosis is a bacterial disease that is transmitted from animals to humans. It can survive for long periods of time in freshwater and mud contaminated by the urine of infected animals, such as mice, rats, and goats. The bacteria enter the body through the eyes, ears, nose, mouth, and broken skin. To avoid infection, do not drink untreated water from the island's streams; do not wade in waters above the chest or submerge skin with cuts and abrasions in island streams or rivers. Symptoms are often mild and resemble the flu—fever, diarrhea, chills, nausea, headache, vomiting, and body pains—and may occur 2 to 20 days after exposure. If you think you have these symptoms, see a doctor right away.

✉ *Port Allen Airport, 3666 Kuiloko Rd., Hanapepe* ☎ *808/335–5859* ⊕ *www.skydivekauai.com* 🖾 *Tandem dive $229.*

TENNIS

If you're interested in booking some court time on Kauai, there are public tennis courts in Waimea, Kekaha, Hanapepe, Koloa, Kalaheo, Puhi, Lihue, Wailua Homesteads, Wailua Houselots, and Kapaa New Park.

Many hotels and resorts have tennis courts on property; even if you're not staying there, you can still rent court time. Rates range from $10 to $20 per person per hour. On the South Shore, try the **Grand Hyatt Kauai** (☎ *808/742–1234*) and Poipu Kai Tennis. On the North Shore try the **Hanalei Bay Resort** (☎ *808/826–6522 Ext. 8225*) or **Princeville Racquet Club** (☎ *808/826–1863*).

For specific directions or more information, call the **County of Kauai Parks and Recreation Office** (☎ *808/241–4463*).

ZIPLINE TOURS

The latest adventure on Kauai is "zipping," or "ziplining." Regardless of what you call it, chances are you'll scream like a rock star while trying it. Strap on a harness, clip onto a cable running from one side of a river or valley to the other, and zip across. The step off is the scariest part. ■TIP➔ Pack knee-length shorts or pants, athletic shoes, and courage for this adventure.

Fodor's Choice ★ **Just Live.** When Nichol Baier and Julie Lester started Just Live in 2003, their market was exclusively school-age children, but soon they added visitor tours. Experiential education through adventure is how they describe it. Whatever you call it, sailing 70 feet above the ground for 3-plus hours will take your vacation to another level. This is the only treetop zipline on Kauai where your feet never touch ground once you're in the air: Seven zips and four canopy bridges make the Tree Top

DID YOU KNOW?

Most of Kauai's land is not accessible by road. You can explore the island's lush interior on a zipline tour.

Tour their most popular one. For the heroic at heart, there's the Zipline Eco Adventure, which includes three ziplines, two canopy bridges, a climbing wall, a 100-foot rappelling tower, and a "Monster Swing." If you're short on time—or courage—you can opt for the Wikiwiki Zipline Tour, which includes three ziplines and two canopy bridges in about two hours. They now have a shop with outdoor gear specifically for the island's activities, although their primary focus remains community programming. Enjoy knowing that money spent here serves Kauai's children. ✉ *Nawiliwili, Anchor Cove, Lihue* ☎ *808/482–1295* ⊕ *www.justlive.org* ✇ *From $79.*

Outfitters Kauai. This company added new zipline offerings in 2009. They still have a half-day, multisport adventure of ziplining, suspension bridge crossings, and aerial walkways with hiking in between. Their most popular tour (Zipline Trek Nui Nui Loa) features an 1,800-foot tandem zip—that's right, you don't have to go it alone. Plus, a unique WaterZip cools things off if you work up a sweat. A shorter version of this adventure—the Zipline Lele Eono—is also offered. Outfitters Kauai also includes ziplining as part of its Kipu Safari tour (*see Kayaking*). ✉ *2827-A Poipu Rd., Poipu* ☎ *808/742–9667, 888/742–9887* ⊕ *www. outfitterskauai.com* ✇ *From $114.*

Princeville Ranch Adventures. The North Shore's answer to ziplining is a nine-zipline course with a bit of hiking, and suspension bridge crossing thrown in for a half-day adventure. The 4½-hour Zip N' Dip tour includes a picnic and swimming at a waterfall pool, while the Zip Express whizzes you through the entire course in three hours. Both excursions conclude with a 1,200-foot tandem zip across a valley. Guides are energetic and fun and can offer good dining and nightlife recommendations. This is as close as it gets to flying; just watch out for the albatross. ✉ *Rte. 56, between mile markers 27 and 28, Princeville* ☎ *808/826–7669, 888/955–7669* ⊕ *www.princevilleranch. com* ✇ *From $125.*

SHOPPING

Updated by
Joan Conrow

There aren't a lot of shops and spas on Kauai, but what you will find here are a handful of places very much worth checking out for the quality of their selection of items sold and services rendered. Many shops now make an effort to sell as many locally made products as possible. When buying an item, ask where it was made or even who made it.

Often you will find that a product handcrafted on the island may not be that much more expensive than a similar product made overseas. You can also look for the purple "Kauai Made" sticker many merchants display.

Along with one major shopping mall, a few shopping centers, and a growing number of big-box retailers, Kauai has some delightful mom-and-pop shops and specialty boutiques with lots of character. The Garden Isle also has a large and talented community of artisans and fine artists, with galleries all around the island showcasing their creations. You can find many island-made arts and crafts in the small shops, and it's worthwhile to stop in at crafts fairs and outdoor markets to look for bargains and mingle with island residents.

If you're looking for a special memento of your trip that is unique to Kauai County, check out the distinctive Niihau shell lei. The tiny shells are collected from beaches on Kauai and Niihau, pierced, and strung into beautiful necklaces, chokers, and earrings. It's a time-consuming and exacting craft, and these items are much in demand, so don't be taken aback by the high price tags. Those made by Niihau residents will have certificates of authenticity and are worth collecting. You often can find cheaper versions made by non-Hawaiians at crafts fairs.

Stores are typically open daily from 9 or 10 am to 5 pm, although some stay open until 9 pm, especially those near resorts. Don't be surprised if the posted hours don't match the actual hours of operation at the smaller shops, where owners may be fairly casual about keeping to a regular schedule.

5

THE NORTH SHORE

The North Shore has three main shopping areas, all in towns off the highway. Hanalei has two shopping centers directly across from each other, which offer more than you would expect in a remote, relaxed town. Princeville Shopping Center is a bustling little mix of businesses, necessities, and some unique, often pricey, shops. Kilauea is a bit more sprawled out and offers a charming, laid-back shopping scene with a neighborhood feel.

SHOPPING CENTERS

Ching Young Village. This popular shopping center looks a bit worn, but that doesn't deter business. Hanalei's only grocery store is here along with a number of other shops useful to locals and visitors, such as a Hawaiian music outlet, jewelry stores, art galleries, a surf shop, and several restaurants. ✉ *5-5190 Kuhio Hwy., near mile marker 2, Hanalei* ⊕ *www.chingyoungvillage.com.*

Hanalei Center. Once an old Hanalei schoolhouse, the Hanalei Center is now a bevy of boutiques and restaurants. You can dig through '40s and '50s vintage memorabilia, find Polynesian artifacts, or search for that unusual gift. Buy beach gear as well as island wear and women's clothing. Find a range of fine jewelry and paper art jewelry. There are a full-service salon and a yoga studio in the two-story modern addition to the center, which also houses a well-stocked health food store. ✉ *5-5161 Kuhio Hwy., near mile marker 2, Hanalei* ☎ *808/826–7677.*

Princeville Shopping Center. The big draws at this small center are a full-service grocery store and a hardware store, but there's also a wine market, bar, a sandal boutique, a small food court, and an ice cream shop. This is also the last stop for gas and banking on the North Shore. ✉ *5-4280 Kuhio Hwy., near mile marker 28, Princeville* ☎ *808/826– 9497* ⊕ *www.princevillecenter.com.*

SHOPS

Kong Lung Co. Sometimes called the Gump's of Kauai, this gift store sells elegant clothing, exotic glassware, ethnic books, gifts, and artwork—all very lovely and expensive. The shop is housed in a beautiful 1892 stone building in the heart of Kilauea. It's the showpiece of the pretty little Kong Lung Center, where everything from handmade soaps to hammocks can be found. A great bakery and pizzeria round out the offerings, along with an exhibit of historical photos. ⊠ *2484 Keneke St., Kilauea* ☎ *808/828–1822* ⊕ *www.konglungkauai.com.*

Village Variety Store. How about a fun beach towel for the folks back home? That's just one of the gifts you can find here, along with shell lei, Kauai shirts, macadamia nuts, and other souvenirs at low prices. The store also has many small, useful items such as envelopes, housewares, and toiletries. ⊠ *Ching Young Village, Kuhio Hwy., Hanalei* ☎ *808/826–6077.*

THE EAST SIDE

KAPAA AND WAILUA

Kapaa is the most heavily populated area on Kauai, so it's not surprising that it has the most diverse shopping opportunities on the island. Unlike the North Shore's retail scene, shops here are not neatly situated in centers; they are spread out along a long stretch of road, with many local retail gems tucked away that you may not find if you're in a rush.

SHOPPING CENTERS

Kauai Village Shopping Center. The buildings of this Kapaa shopping village are in the style of a 19th-century plantation town. **ABC Discount Store** sells sundries; **Safeway** carries groceries and alcoholic beverages; **Longs Drugs** has a pharmacy, health and beauty products, and a good selection of Hawaiian merchandise; **Papaya's** has health foods and an excellent café. There's also a great local clothing boutique, **Kauai Crush,** and a **UPS store.** Other shops sell jewelry, art, and home decor. Check out the **Children of the Land Cultural Center,** which holds workshops, classes, and other events. Restaurants include Chinese, vegetarian, and Vietnamese options, and there's also a **Starbucks** and two bars. ⊠ *4-831 Kuhio Hwy., Kapaa* ☎ *808/822–3777.*

Kinipopo Shopping Village. Kinipopo is a tiny little center on Kuhio Highway. **Korean Barbeque** fronts the highway, as does **Goldsmith's Kauai Gallery,** which sells handcrafted Hawaiian-style gold jewelry. **Monaco's** has authentic Mexican food, and **Cakes by Kristin** is a tasty bakery shop specializing in cakes. There's also a clothing shop, beauty salon, and an art gallery. ⊠ *4-356 Kuhio Hwy., Kapaa* ⊕ *www.kinipopovillage.com.*

SHOPS AND GALLERIES

Deja Vu Surf Outlet. This mom-and-pop operation has a great assortment of surfwear and clothes for outdoor fanatics, including tank tops, visors, swimwear, and Kauai-style T-shirts. They also carry bodyboards and water sport accessories. Good deals can be found at sidewalk sales. ⊠ *4-1419 Kuhio Hwy., Kapaa* ☎ *808/822–4401* ⊕ *www.dejavusurf. com.*

Jim Saylor Jewelers. Jim Saylor has been designing beautiful keepsakes for more than 30 years on Kauai. Gems from around the world, including black pearls, diamonds and more, appear in his unusual settings. ⊠ *1318 Kuhio Hwy., Kapaa* ☎ *808/822–3591.*

Kela's Glass Gallery. The colorful vases, bowls, and other fragile items sold in this distinctive gallery are definitely worth viewing if you appreciate quality handmade glass art. It's expensive, but if something catches your eye, they'll happily pack it for safe transport home. They also ship worldwide. ⊠ *4-1354 Kuhio Hwy., Kapaa* ☎ *808/822–4527* ⊕ *www. glass-art.com.*

Vicky's Fabric Shop. This small store is packed full of tropical and Hawaiian prints, silks, slinky rayons, soft cottons, and other fine fabrics. A variety of sewing patterns and notions are featured as well, making it a must-stop for any seamstress. Check out the one-of-a-kind selection of purses, aloha wear, and other quality hand-sewn items. ⊠ *4-1326 Kuhio Hwy., Kapaa* ☎ *808/822–1746* ⊕ *www.vickysfabrics.com.*

LIHUE

Lihue is the business area on Kauai, as well as home to all the big-box stores (Costco, Home Depot, Wal-Mart, and Big K) and the only real mall. Do not mistake this town as lacking in rare finds, however. Lihue is steeped in history and diversity while simultaneously welcoming new trends and establishments.

SHOPPING CENTERS

Kilohana Plantation. This 16,000-square-foot Tudor mansion contains art galleries, a jewelry store, and the restaurant Gaylord's. Kilohana Plantation is filled with antiques from its original owner, and the restored outbuildings house a craft shop and a Hawaiian-style clothing shop. Train rides on a restored railroad are available, with knowledgeable guides reciting the history of sugar on Kauai. The site is also now the home of Luau Kalamaku and Koloa Rum Company. ⊠ *3-2087 Kaumualii Hwy.* ☎ *808/245–5608* ⊕ *www.kilohanakauai.com.*

Kukui Grove Center. This is Kauai's only true mall. Besides **Kmart,** anchor tenants are **Longs Drugs, Macy's,** and **Times Supermarket.** The mall's stores offer women's clothing, surf wear, art, toys, athletic shoes, jewelry, a hair salon, and locally made crafts. Restaurants range from fast food and sandwiches to Mexican and Korean, with a popular Starbucks and Jamba Juice. The center stage often has entertainment, there is a farmers' market on Mondays, and "Toddler Thursdays" offers entertainment for young children. ⊠ *3-2600 Kaumualii Hwy.* ☎ *808/245–7784* ⊕ *www.kukuigrovecenter.com.*

SHOPS AND GALLERIES

Hilo Hattie, The Store of Hawaii. This is the big name in aloha wear for tourists throughout the Islands, and Hilo Hattie, The Store of Hawaii has only one store on Kauai. Located a mile from Lihue Airport, come here for cool, comfortable aloha shirts and muumuu in bright floral prints, as well as other souvenirs. Also, be sure to check out the line of Hawaii-inspired home furnishings. ⊠ *3252 Kuhio Hwy.* ☎ *808/245–3404* ⊕ *www.hilohattie.com.*

Kauai Community Market. This is no regular farmers' market. Join the locals at the Community College in Lihue on Saturdays, and you'll find fresh produce and flowers, as well as packaged products like breads, goat cheese, pasta, honey, coffee, soaps, lotions and more, all made locally. Seating areas are available to grab a snack or lunch from the food booths and lunch wagons set up there. ⊠ *3-1901 Kaumualii Hwy* ☎ *808/337-9944* ⊙ *Saturdays from 9:30 am to 1:00 pm.*

Fodor's Choice
★
Kapaia Stitchery. Hawaiian quilts made by hand and machine, a beautiful selection of fabrics, quilting kits, and fabric arts fill Kapaia Stitchery, a cute little red plantation-style building. There are also many locally made gifts and quilts for sale. The staff is friendly and helpful, even though a steady stream of customers keeps them busy. ⊠ *3-3551 Kuhio Hwy.* ☎ *808/245–2281* ⊕ *www.kapaia-stichery.com.*

Kauai Fruit and Flower Company. At this shop near Lihue and five minutes away from the airport, you can buy fresh Hawaii Gold pineapple, sugarcane, ginger, tropical flowers, coconuts, local jams, jellies, and honey, plus papayas, bananas, and mangoes from Kauai. All the fruit at Kauai Fruit and Flower Company has been inspected and approved to ship out-of-state. ⊠ *3-4684 Kuhio Hwy.* ☎ *808/245–1814* ⊕ *www. kauaifruit.com.*

Fodor's Choice
★
Kauai Museum. The gift shop at the museum sells some fascinating books, maps, and prints, as well as lovely feather lei hatbands, Niihau shell jewelry, handwoven *lau hala* hats, and koa wood bowls. Also featured at the Kauai Museum are tapa cloth, authentic *tikis* (hand-carved wooden figurines), as well as other good-quality local crafts at reasonable prices. ⊠ *4428 Rice St.* ☎ *808/246–2470* ⊕ *www.kauaimuseum.org.*

Two Frogs Hugging. At Two Frogs Hugging, you'll find lots of interesting housewares, accessories, knickknacks, and hand-carved collectibles, as well as baskets and furniture from Indonesia, the Philippines and China. The shop recently moved to larger quarters in the Lihue Industrial Park. ⊠ *3094 Aukele St.* ☎ *808/246–8777* ⊕ *www.twofrogshugging.com.*

THE SOUTH SHORE

The South Shore, like the North Shore, has convenient shopping clusters, including Poipu Shopping Village and the upscale Kukuiula Shopping Village. There are many high-priced shops but some unique clothing and gift selections.

SHOPPING CENTERS

Poipu Shopping Village. Convenient to nearby hotels and condos on the South Shore, the two-dozen shops at Poipu Shopping Village sell resort wear, gifts, souvenirs, and art. This complex also has great food choices, from hot dog stands to excellent restaurants. There are a few upscale and appealing jewelry stores and fun clothing stores. A Tahitian dance troupe performs in the open-air courtyard Monday and Wednesday at 5 pm. ⊠ *2360 Kiahuna Plantation Dr., Poipu Beach* ☎ *808/742–2831* ⊕ *www.poipushoppingvillage.com.*

The Shops at Kukuiula. This is the South Shore's newest shopping center, with chic, high-end shops, exclusive galleries, several great restaurants, and a gourmet grocery store. Check out the Kauai Culinary Market on Wednesday from 4 to 6, to see cooking demonstrations, listen to live Hawaiian music, visit the beer and wine garden, and browse wares from local vendors. This attractive open-air, plantation-style center is just beyond the roundabout as you enter Poipu. ⊠ *2829 Kalanikaumaka St., Poipu* ☎ *808/742–9545.*

SHOPS AND GALLERIES

Fodor's Choice ★ **Galerie 103.** This gallery sells art, but the owners want you to experience it as well. Sparse and dramatic, the main room at Galerie 103 consists of concrete floors and walls of featured pieces, from internationally acclaimed artists and local Kauai ones. Most of the artwork is contemporary or modern with a focus on environmental issues. ⊠ *2829 Kalanikaumaka Rd., Koloa* ☎ *808/742–0103* ⊕ *www.galerie103.com* ⊗ *Tuesday through Saturday 12–8.*

THE WEST SIDE

5

The West Side is years behind the South Shore in development, offering charming, simple shops with authentic local flavor.

SHOPPING CENTERS

Eleele Shopping Center. Kauai's West Side has a scattering of stores, including those at this no-frills strip-mall, Eleele Shopping Center. It has a bank and health clinic, and is a good place to rub elbows with local folk at **Times Big Save** grocery store. Or grab a quick bite to eat at the casual **Grinds Cafe** or **Tois Thai Kitchen.** ⊠ *4469 Waialo Rd., Eleele.*

Waimea Canyon Plaza. As Kekaha's retail hub and the last stop for supplies before heading up to Waimea Canyon, Waimea Canyon Plaza is a tiny, tidy complex of shops that is surprisingly busy. Look for local foods, souvenirs, and island-made gifts for all ages. ⊠ *Kokee Rd., at Rte. 50, Kekaha.*

SHOPS AND GALLERIES

Kauai Coffee Visitor Center and Museum. Kauai produces more coffee than any other island in the state. The local product can be purchased from grocery stores or here at the Kauai Coffee Visitor Center and Museum, where a sampling of the nearly two-dozen coffees is available. Be sure to try some of the estate-roasted varieties. ⊠ *870 Halawili Rd., off Rte. 50, Kalaheo* ☎ *808/335–0813, 800/545–8605* ⊕ *www.kauaicoffee.com.*

Paradise Sportswear. This is the retail outlet of the folks who invented Kauai's popular "red dirt" shirts, which are dyed and printed with the characteristic local soil. Ask the salesperson at Paradise Sportswear to tell you the charming story behind these shirts. Sizes from infants up to 5X are available. ⊠ *4350 Waialo Rd., Port Allen* ☎ *800/335–5670* ⊕ *www.dirtshirt.com.*

Talk Story Bookstore. Located in a historic building in quiet Hanapepe town, this cozy bookstore becomes the gathering place on busy Friday evenings during the weekly art nights. Local authors sign their books inside while outside there's live music and food trucks for treats. Mostly used books are sold here, one of just two bookstores on Kauai. ⊠ *3785 Hanapepe Rd., Hanapepe* ☎ *808/335* ⊕ *www.talkstorybookstore.com.*

SPAS

Updated by
Joan Conrow

Though most spas on Kauai are associated with resorts, none is restricted to guests only. And there's much by way of healing and wellness to be found on Kauai beyond the traditional spa—or even the day spa. More and more retreat facilities are offering what some would call alternative healing therapies. Others would say there's nothing alternative about them; you can decide for yourself.

Alexander Day Spa & Salon at the Kauai Marriott. This sister spa of Alexander Simson's Beverly Hills spa focuses on body care rather than exercise, so don't expect any fitness equipment or exercise classes, just pampering and beauty treatments. The Alexander Day Spa & Salon at the Kauai Marriott is a sunny, pleasant facility. Massages are available in treatment rooms and on the beach, although the beach locale isn't as private as you might imagine. Wedding-day and custom spa packages can be arranged. ⊠ *Kauai Marriott Resort & Beach Club, 3610 Rice St., Suite 9A, Lihue* ☎ *808/246–4918* ⊕ *www.alexanderspa.com* ⌂ *$70–$200 massage. Facilities: Hair salon and spa. Services: Body treatments—including masks, scrubs, and wraps—facials, hair styling, makeup, manicures, massages, pedicures, waxing.*

Fodor's Choice
★

ANARA Spa. The luxurious ANARA Spa has all the equipment and services you expect from a top resort spa, along with a pleasant, professional staff. Best of all, it has indoor and outdoor areas that capitalize on the tropical locale and balmy weather, further distinguishing it from the Marriott and St. Regis spas. Its 46,500 square feet of space includes the lovely Garden Treatment Village, an open-air courtyard with private thatched-roof huts, each featuring a relaxation area, misters, and open-air shower in a tropical setting. Ancient Hawaiian remedies and local ingredients are featured in many of the treatments, such as a Lokahi Garden facial, and a warm stone and ti leaf lomilomi massage. The open-air lava-rock showers are wonderful, introducing many guests to the delightful island practice of showering outdoors. The spa, which includes a full-service salon, adjoins the Hyatt's legendary swimming pool. ⊠ *Hyatt Regency Kauai Resort and Spa, 1571 Poipu Rd., Poipu* ☎ *808/240–6440* ⊕ *www.anaraspa.com* ⌂ *Massages start at $160 and average $235. Facilities: Hair salon, outdoor hot tubs, sauna, steam room. Gym is 24-hour with: Cardiovascular machines, free weights, weight-training equipment. Services: Body scrubs and wraps, facials, manicures, massage, pedicures. Classes and programs: Aerobics, aquaerobics, body sculpting, fitness analysis, flexibility training, personal training, weight training, yoga.*

Angeline's Muolaulani Wellness Center. It doesn't get more authentic, or rustic, than this. In the mid-1980s Aunty Angeline Locey opened her Anahola home to offer traditional Hawaiian healing practices. Now, her son and granddaughter carry on the tradition. At Angeline's Muolaulani Wellness Center, there's a two-hour treatment ($150) that starts with a steam, followed by a sea-salt-and-clay body scrub and a two-person massage. The real treat, however, is relaxing on Aunty's open-air garden deck. Hot-stone lomi is also available. Aunty's mission is to promote a healthy body image; as such, au naturel is an option here, but if you're nudity-shy, you can stick to the more traditional approach. On second thought, Aunty would say consider it, as *muolaulani* translates to "a place for young buds to bloom." Detailed directions are given when you book a treatment. Cash only and bring your own towel. ⊠ *Kamalomaloo Pl., Anahola* ☎ *808/822–3235* ⊕ *www.angelineslomikauai.com* ☞ *Facilities: steam room. Services: body scrubs, showers, and massage.*

Fodor's Choice **Halelea Spa.** This superb spa at The St. Regis Princeville Resort is ★ indeed a House of Joy, as its Hawaiian name translates. so long as you are prepared to pay handsomely for services. Opened in 2009, the 11,000-square-foot Halelea Spa transports users to a place of tranquillity. The spa's 12 luxurious treatment rooms afford a subdued indoor setting outmatched only by the professional service. Take advantage of the dedicated couples' room and enjoy a taro butter pohaku hot stone massage. Follow that with a few hours sipping tea in the relaxation lounge, sweating in the sauna, and rinsing in an overhead rain shower. There is a qualified wellness consultant, and spa programs are inspired by Native Hawaiian healing rituals. ⊠ *The St. Regis Princeville Resort, 5520 Ka Haku Rd., Princeville* ☎ *877/787–3447, 808/826–9644* ⊕ *www.stregisprinceville.com/* ☞ *Massage $175–$265. Services: Body scrubs and wraps, facials, massage, waxing, full service salon for hair and nails.*

Hanalei Day Spa. As you travel beyond tony Princeville, life slows down. The single-lane bridges may be one reason. Another is the Hanalei Day Spa, an open-air, thatched-roof, Hawaiian-style hut nestled just off the beach on the grounds of Hanalei Colony Resort in Haena. Though this no-frills day spa offers facials, waxing, wraps, scrubs, and the like, its specialty is massage: Ayurveda, Zen Shiatsu, Swedish, four-handed, and even a baby massage (and lesson for Mom, to boot). Owner Darci Frankel teaches yoga, a discipline she started as a young child. That practice led her to start the Ayurveda Center of Hawaii, which operates out of the spa and offers an ancient Indian cleansing and rejuvenation program known as Pancha Karma. Think multiday wellness retreat. ⊠ *Hanalei Colony Resort, Rte. 560, 6 miles past Hanalei, Haena* ☎ *808/826–6621* ⊕ *www.hanaleidayspa.com* ☞ *Massage $105–$205. Services: Body scrubs and wraps, facials, massage, waxing. Classes and programs: Yoga.*

ENTERTAINMENT AND NIGHTLIFE

Updated by
Joan Conrow

Kauai has never been known for its nightlife. It's a rural island, where folks tend to retire early, and the streets are dark and deserted well before midnight. The island does have its nightspots, though, and the after-dark entertainment scene keeps expanding, especially in areas frequented by tourists.

Most of the island's dinner and luau shows are held at hotels and resorts. Hotel lounges are a good source of live music, often with no cover charge, as are a few bars and restaurants around the island.

Check the local newspaper, the *Garden Island,* for listings of weekly happenings, or tune in to community radio station KKCR—found at

90.9, 91.9, or 92.7 on the FM dial, depending on where you are on the island at that moment—for frequent readings of the arts and entertainment calendar. Free publications such as *Kauai Gold, This Week on Kauai,* and *Essential Kauai* also list entertainment events. You can pick them up at Lihue Airport near the baggage claim area, as well as at numerous retail areas on the island.

ENTERTAINMENT

Although luau remain a primary source of evening fun for families on vacation, there are a handful of other possibilities. There are no traditional dinner cruises, but some boat tours do offer an evening buffet with music along Napali Coast. A few times a year, Women in Theater (WIT), a local women's theater group, performs dinner shows at the Hukilau Lanai in Wailua. You can always count on a performance of *South Pacific* at the Kauai Beach Resort, and the Kauai Community College Performing Arts Center draws well-known artists.

Kauai Community College Performing Arts Center. This is a main venue for island entertainment, hosting a concert music series, visiting musicians, dramatic productions, and special events such as educational forums. ⊠ *3-1901 Kaumualii Hwy., Lihue* ☎ *808/245–8352* ⊕ *www.kauai.hawaii.edu/pac.*

DINNER SHOW

South Pacific Dinner Show. It seems a fitting tribute to see the play that put Kauai on the map. Rodgers and Hammerstein's original *South Pacific* has been playing at the Kauai Beach Resort since 2002. The full musical production, accompanied by a buffet dinner, features local talent. ⊠ *Jasmine Ballroom, Kauai Beach Resort, 4331 Kauai Beach Dr., Lihue* ☎ *808/346–6500* ⊕ *www.southpacifickauai.com* ⊠ *$85* ☉ *Wed., doors open at 5:30 pm, show at 6:30.*

LUAU

Although the commercial luau experience is a far cry from the backyard luau thrown by local residents to celebrate a wedding, graduation, or a baby's first birthday, they're nonetheless entertaining and a good introduction to the Hawaiian food that isn't widely sold in restaurants. Besides the feast, there's often an exciting dinner show with Polynesian-style music and dancing. It all makes for a fun evening that's suitable for couples, families, and groups, and the informal setting is conducive to meeting other people. Every luau is different, reflecting the cuisine and tenor of the host facility, so compare prices, menus, and entertainment before making your reservation. Most luau on Kauai are offered only on a limited number of nights each week, so plan ahead to get the luau you want. We tend to prefer those *not* held on resort properties, because they feel a bit more authentic.

Grand Hyatt Kauai Luau. What used to be called Drums of Paradise has a new name and a new dance troupe but still offers a traditional luau buffet and an exceptional performance in a garden setting near majestic Keoneloa Bay. ⊠ *Grand Hyatt Kauai Resort and Spa, 1571 Poipu*

Rd., Poipu ☎ *808/240–6456* ⊕ *www.grandhyattkauailuau.com* ✉ *$99* ⊙ *Thur. and Sun., doors open at 5:45 pm, show begins at 7.*

Luau Kalamaku. Set on historic sugar-plantation land, this luau bills itself as the only "theatrical" luau on Kauai. The luau feast is served buffet-style, there's an open bar, and the performers aim to both entertain and educate about Hawaiian culture. Guests sit at tables around a circular stage; tables farther from the stage are elevated, providing unobstructed views. Additional packages offer visitors the opportunity to tour the 35-acre plantation via train or special romantic perks like a lei greeting and champagne. ✉ *3-2087 Kaumualii St., Lihue* ☎ *877/622–1780* ⊕ *www.luaukalamaku.com* ✉ *$99* ⊙ *Tue. and Fri. Check-in begins at 5:30, dinner at 6:30, show at 7:30.*

Fodor's Choice ★ **Smith's Tropical Paradise Luau.** A 30-acre tropical garden provides the lovely setting for this popular luau, which begins with the traditional blowing of the conch shell and *imu* (pig roast) ceremony, followed by cocktails, an island feast, and an international show in the amphitheater overlooking a torch-lighted lagoon. It's fairly authentic and a better deal than the pricier resort events. ✉ *174 Wailua Rd., Kapaa* ☎ *808/821–6895* ⊕ *www.smithskauai.com* ✉ *$88* ⊙ *Mon., Wed.–Fri.; Nov.–Feb. 4:45, Mar–Oct. 5 pm.*

MUSIC

Check the local papers for outdoor reggae and Hawaiian-music shows, or one of the numbers listed below for more formal performances.

Hanalei Slack Key Concerts. Relax to the instrumental music form created by Hawaiian *paniolo* (cowboys) in the early 1800s. Shows are at Hale Halawai Ohana O Hanalei, which is *mauka* (toward the mountains) down a dirt access road across from St. William's Catholic Church (Malolo Road) and then left down another dirt road. Look for a *hale* (house), several little green plantation-style buildings, and the brown double-yurt community center around the gravel parking lot. ✉ *Hanalei Family Community Center, 5-5299 Kuhio Hwy., Hanalei* ☎ *808/826–1469* ⊕ *www.hawaiianslackkeyguitar.com* ✉ *$20* ⊙ *Fri. at 4, Sun. at 3.*

Kauai Concert Association. This group offers a seasonal program at the Kauai Community College Performing Arts Center that features well-known classical musicians, including soloists and small ensembles. ✉ *3-1901 Kaumualii Hwy., Lihue* ☎ *808/245–7464* ⊕ *www.kauai-concert.org.*

NIGHTLIFE

For every new venue that opens on Kauai, another one closes, mainly because most island residents tend to retire early. It is, after all, a rural island. But still, there are a number of places to shake your booty, hear local music, and simply enjoy a drink. Nightclubs that stay open until the wee hours are rare on Kauai, and the bar scene is limited. The major resorts generally host their own live entertainment and happy hours. All bars and clubs that serve alcohol must close at 2 am, except those with a cabaret license, which allows them to close at 4 am. For information

Continued on page 534

HULA: MORE THAN A FOLK DANCE

Hula has been called "the heartbeat of the Hawaiian people" and also "the world's best-known, most misunderstood dance." Both are true. Hula isn't just dance. It is storytelling.

Chanter Edith McKinzie calls it "an extension of a piece of poetry." In its adornments, implements, and customs, hula integrates every important Hawaiian cultural practice: poetry, history, genealogy, craft, plant cultivation, martial arts, religion, protocol. So when 19th century Christian missionaries sought to eradicate a practice they considered depraved, they threatened more than just a folk dance.

With public performance outlawed and private hula practice discouraged, hula went underground for a generation. The fragile verbal link by which culture was transmitted from teacher to student hung by a thread. Even increasing literacy did not help because hula's practitioners were a secretive and protected circle.

As if that weren't bad enough, vaudeville, Broadway, and Hollywood got hold of the hula, giving it the glitz treatment in an unbroken line from "Oh, How She Could Wicky Wacky Woo" to "Rock-A-Hula Baby." Hula became shorthand for paradise: fragrant flowers, lazy hours. Ironically, this development assured that hundreds of Hawaiians could make a living performing and teaching hula. Many danced *auana* (modern form) in performance; but taught *kahiko* (traditional), quietly, at home or in hula schools.

Today, 30 years after the cultural revival known as the Hawaiian Renaissance, language immersion programs have assured a new generation of proficient—and even eloquent—chanters, songwriters, and translators. Visitors can see more, and more authentic, traditional hula than at any other time in the last 200 years.

Like the culture of which it is the beating heart, hula has survived.

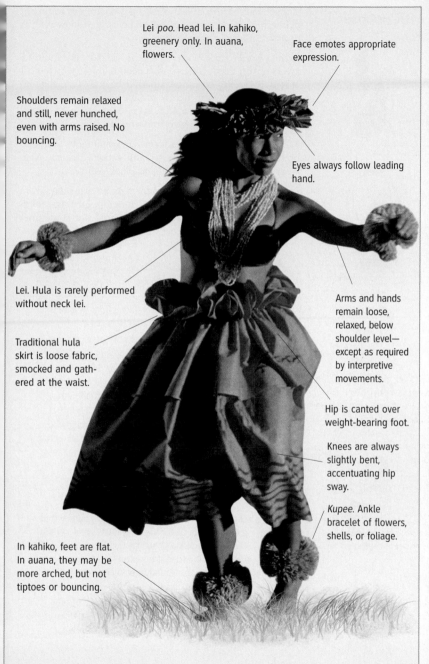

Lei *poo*. Head lei. In kahiko, greenery only. In auana, flowers.

Face emotes appropriate expression.

Shoulders remain relaxed and still, never hunched, even with arms raised. No bouncing.

Eyes always follow leading hand.

Lei. Hula is rarely performed without neck lei.

Arms and hands remain loose, relaxed, below shoulder level—except as required by interpretive movements.

Traditional hula skirt is loose fabric, smocked and gathered at the waist.

Hip is canted over weight-bearing foot.

Knees are always slightly bent, accentuating hip sway.

Kupee. Ankle bracelet of flowers, shells, or foliage.

In kahiko, feet are flat. In auana, they may be more arched, but not tiptoes or bouncing.

BASIC MOTIONS

Speak or Sing

Moon or Sun

Grass Shack or House

Mountains or Heights

Love or Caress

At backyard parties, hula is performed in bare feet and street clothes, but in performance, adornments play a key role, as do rhythm-keeping implements.

In hula *kahiko* (traditional style), the usual dress is multiple layers of stiff fabric (often with a pellom lining, which most closely resembles *kapa*, the paperlike bark cloth of the Hawaiians). These wrap tightly around the bosom but flare below the waist to form a skirt. In pre-contact times, dancers wore only kapa skirts. Men traditionally wear loincloths.

Monarchy-period hula is performed in voluminous muumuu or high-necked muslin blouses and gathered skirts. Men wear white or gingham shirts and black pants.

In hula *auana* (modern), dress for women can range from grass skirts and strapless tops to contemporary tea-length dresses. Men generally wear aloha shirts, but sometimes grass skirts over pants or even everyday gear.

SURPRISING HULA FACTS

■ Grass skirts are not traditional; workers from Kiribati (the Gilbert Islands) brought this custom to Hawaii.

■ In olden-day Hawaii, *mele* (songs) for hula were composed for every occasion—name songs for babies, dirges for funerals, welcome songs for visitors, celebrations of favorite pursuits.

■ Hula *mai* is a traditional hula form in praise of a noble's genitals; the power of the *alii* (royalty) to procreate gave *mana* (spiritual power) to the entire culture.

■ Hula students in old Hawaii adhered to high standards: scrupulous cleanliness, no sex, daily cleansing rituals, certain food prohibitions, and no contact with the dead. They were fined if they broke the rules.

WHERE TO WATCH

If you're interested in "the real thing," there are annual hula festivals on each island. Check the individual island visitors' bureaus websites. The Merrie Monarch Hula Festival—held annually in Hilo (the Big Island) the week after Easter—is the best place to experience hula. Advance planning is required (⊕ www.merriemonarch.com).

If you can't make it to a festival, there are plenty of other hula shows—at most resorts, many lounges, and even at certain shopping centers. Ask your hotel concierge for performance information.

Kauai: Undercover Movie Star

Though Kauai has played itself in the movies, most recently starring in *The Descendants* (2011), most of its screen time has been as a stunt double for a number of tropical paradises. The island's remote valleys portrayed Venezuelan jungle in Kevin Costner's *Dragonfly* (2002) and a Costa Rican dinosaur preserve in Steven Spielberg's *Jurassic Park* (1993). Spielberg was no stranger to Kauai, having filmed Harrison Ford's escape via seaplane from Menehune Fishpond in *Raiders of the Lost Ark* (1981).

The fluted cliffs and gorges of Kauai's rugged Napali Coast play the misunderstood beast's island home in *King Kong* (1976), and a jungle dweller of another sort, in *George of the Jungle* (1997), frolicked on Kauai. Harrison Ford returned to the island for 10 weeks during the filming of *Six Days, Seven Nights* (1998), a romantic adventure set in French Polynesia. Part-time Kauai resident Ben Stiller used the island as a stand-in for the jungles of Vietnam in *Tropic Thunder* (2008) and Johnny Depp came here to film some of *Pirates of the Caribbean: On Stranger Tides* (2011). But these are all relatively contemporary movies. What's truly remarkable is that Hollywood discovered Kauai in 1933 with the making of *White Heat*, which was set on a sugar plantation and—like another more memorable movie filmed on Kauai—dealt with interracial love stories.

Kauai saw no fewer than a dozen movies filmed on the island in the 1950s. Rita Hayworth starred in *Miss Sadie Thompson* (1953) and no one you'd recognize starred in the tantalizing *She Gods of Shark Reef* (1956).

The movie that is still immortalized on the island in the names of restaurants, real estate offices, a hotel, and even a sushi item is *South Pacific* (1957). (You guessed it, right?) That mythical place called Bali Hai is never far away on Kauai.

In the 1960s Elvis Presley filmed *Blue Hawaii* (1961) and *Girls! Girls! Girls!* (1962) on the island. A local movie tour likes to point out the stain on a hotel carpet where Elvis's jelly doughnut fell.

Kauai has welcomed a long list of Hollywood's A-List: John Wayne in *Donovan's Reef* (1963); Jack Lemmon in *The Wackiest Ship in the Army* (1961); Richard Chamberlain in *The Thorn Birds* (1983); Gene Hackman in *Uncommon Valor* (1983); Danny DeVito and Billy Crystal in *Throw Momma from the Train* (1987); and Dustin Hoffman, Morgan Freeman, Renee Russo, and Cuba Gooding Jr. in *Outbreak* (1995).

TV shows, TV pilots, and made-for-TV movies make the list as well, including *Gilligan's Island*, *Fantasy Island*, *Starsky & Hutch*, *Baywatch Hawaii*—even reality TV shows *The Bachelor* and *The Amazing Race 3*.

For the record, just because a movie did some filming here doesn't mean the entire movie was filmed on Kauai. *Honeymoon in Vegas* filmed just one scene here, while the murder mystery *A Perfect Getaway* (2009) was set on the famous Kalalau Trail and featured beautiful Kauaian backdrops but was shot mostly in Puerto Rico.

on events or specials, check out the local newspaper's nightlife section, *Kauai Times* (⊕ *kauaitimes.net*).

THE NORTH SHORE

Hanalei Gourmet. The sleepy North Shore stays awake—until 10:30, that is—each evening in this small, convivial deli and bar inside Hanalei's restored old school building. There's local live Hawaiian, jazz, rock, and folk music on Sunday and Wednesday evening. ⊠ *Hanalei Center, 5-5161 Kuhio Hwy., Hanalei* ☎ *808/826–2524* ⊕ *www. hanaleigourmet.com.*

St. Regis Bar. This spacious and comfortable lounge with a gorgeous view of Hanalei Bay offers drinks daily from 3:30 to 11 and a champagne toast at sunset. Stop by between 5:30 and 10 for *pupu* (hors d'oeuvres), with a popular jazz show from 6:30 to 9 on Sunday nights. ⊠ *Princeville Resort, 5520 Ka Haku Rd., Princeville* ☎ *808/826–9644.*

Tahiti Nui. This venerable and funky institution in sleepy Hanalei still offers its famous luau at 5 on Wednesday evenings, even though the venerable owner and founder Auntie Louise Marston has died. Spirits are always high at this popular hangout for locals and visitors alike, which houses live nightly entertainment, usually Hawaiian music. Open until 1 am. ⊠ *5-5134 Kuhio Hwy., Hanalei* ☎ *808/826–6277.*

THE EAST SIDE

Fodor'sChoice **Caffé Coco.** Nestled in a bamboo forest draped in bougainvillea and
★ flowering vines and hidden from view off the Kuhio Highway is a charming little venue where local musicians perform most evenings. Caffé Coco offers vegan, gluten-free *pupu* (appetizers), entrées, and desserts. It may not have a liquor license, but don't let that stop you from enjoying the entertainment in a pleasant outdoor setting; just bring your own wine or beer. It's open until 9 nightly. ⊠ *4-369 Kuhio Hwy., Wailua* ☎ *808/822–7990* ⊕ *www.caffecocokauai.com.*

Duke's Barefoot Bar. This is one of the liveliest bars in Nawiliwili. Contemporary Hawaiian music is usually performed at this beachside bar and restaurant every day but Tuesday during "Aloha Hours" from 4 to 6 pm. On Thursday, Friday, and Saturday nights, live music is held from 8:30 to 10:30 pm. ⊠ *Kalapaki Beach, 3610 Rice St., Lihue* ☎ *808/246–9599* ⊕ *www.dukeskauai.com.*

Hukilau Lanai. This open-air bar and restaurant is on the property of the Kauai Coast Resort but operates independently. Trade winds trickle through the modest little bar, which looks out into a coconut grove. If the mood takes you, go on a short walk to the sea, or recline in big, comfortable chairs while listening to mellow jazz or Hawaiian slack-key guitar. Live music plays from 6 to 9 every night, though the bar is closed on Monday. Poolside happy hour runs from 3 to 5. Freshly infused tropical martinis—perhaps locally grown lychee and pineapple or a Big Island vanilla bean infusion—are house favorites. ⊠ *520 Aleka Loop, Wailua* ☎ *808/822–0600* ⊕ *www.hukilaukauai.com.*

Rob's Good Times Grill. Let loose at this popular restaurant and sports bar, which features DJs spinning Friday and Saturday from 10 pm to 2 am, preceded by live music on Thursday and Friday. Tuesday offers swing dancing, while Wednesday you can kick up your heels with country line dancing from 8 to 10 pm. Karaoke follows both, while Sunday and Monday are full-on karaoke all night. ⊠ *4303 Rice St., Lihue* ☎ *808/246–0311* ⊕ *www.kauaisportsbarandgrill.com.*

Trees Lounge. This funky bar and restaurant is popular with a middle-aged crowd. It hosts live music nightly, and a late-night DJ on Wednesdays, that gets people out on the tiny dance floor. It's behind the Coconut Marketplace and next to the Kauai Coast Resort in Kapaa. Closed Sunday. ⊠ *440 Aleka Pl., Kapaa* ☎ *808/823–0600* ⊕ *www. treesloungekauai.com.*

THE SOUTH SHORE

Keoki's Paradise. A young, energetic crowd makes this a lively spot on Friday and Saturday nights. There's live music almost every night, usually for two hours between 7 pm and 9 pm. When the dining room clears out, there's a bit of a bar scene for singles. The bar closes at 10:30 pm. ⊠ *Poipu Shopping Village, 2360 Kiahuna Plantation Dr., Poipu* ☎ *808/742–7534* ⊕ *www.keokisparadise.com.*

WHERE TO EAT

Updated by
Joan Conrow

On Kauai, if you're lucky enough to win an invitation to a potluck, baby luau, or beach party, don't think twice—just accept. The best grinds (food) are homemade, and so you'll eat until you're full, then rest, eat some more, and make a plate to take home, too.

But even if you can't score a spot at one of these parties, don't despair. Great local-style food is easy to come by at countless low-key places around the island. As an extra bonus, these eats are often inexpensive, and portions are generous. Expect plenty of meat—usually deep-fried or marinated in a teriyaki sauce and grilled *pulehu*-style (over an open fire)—and starches. Rice is standard, even for breakfast, and often served alongside potato-macaroni salad, another island specialty. Another local favorite is *poke,* made from chunks of raw tuna or octopus seasoned with sesame oil, soy sauce, onions, and pickled seaweed. It's a great *pupu* (appetizer) when paired with a cold beer.

■ TIP→ One cautionary note: Most restaurants stop serving dinner at 8 or 9 pm, so plan to eat early.

Prices in the reviews are the average cost of a main course at dinner or, if dinner is not served, at lunch.

THE NORTH SHORE

Because of the North Shore's isolation, restaurants have enjoyed a captive audience of visitors who don't want to make the long, dark trek into Kapaa town for dinner. As a result, dining in this region has been characterized by expensive fare that isn't especially tasty, either. Fortunately, the situation is slowly improving as new restaurants open and others change hands or menus.

Still, dining on the North Shore can be pricier than other parts of the island, and not especially family-friendly. Most of the restaurants are

BEST BETS FOR KAUAI DINING

Fodor's Choice★	By Price	$$$
Bar Acuda, $$$$, p. 537	**$**	Beach House, p. 546
Beach House, $$$, p. 546	Hamura Saimin, p. 544	Dondero's, p. 546
Dondero's, $$$, p. 546	Joe's on the Green, p. 546	Red Salt, p. 552
Hamura Saimin, $, p. 544	Kilauea Fish Market,	$$$$
Hukilau Lanai, $$, p. 543	p. 540	Bar Acuda, p. 537
Kauai Grill, $$$$, p. 537	**$$**	Kauai Grill, p. 537
Red Salt, $$$, p. 552	Hukilau Lanai, p. 543	Merriman's Fish House, p. 551
Restaurant Kintaro, $$, p. 543	Kauai Pasta, p. 543	Tidepools, p. 552
	Wrangler's Steakhouse, p. 553	

found either in Hanalei town or the Princeville resorts. Consequently, you'll encounter delightful mountain and ocean views, but just one restaurant with oceanfront dining.

$$$$
ECLECTIC
Fodor's Choice
★
✕ **Bar Acuda.** This hip and pricey tapas bar is a top place in Hanalei in terms of tastiness, creativity, and pizzazz. Owner-chef Jim Moffat's brief menu changes regularly: You might find *banderillas* (grilled flank steak skewers with honey and chipotle chili oil), local honeycomb with goat cheese and apple, or seared island fish with macadamia-nut pesto. The food is often organic and consistently remarkable, but it's the subtly intense sauces that elevate the cuisine to outstanding. The dining room is super casual, but chic, with a welcoming bar and a nice porch for outdoor dining. $ *Average main: $40* ⊠ *Hanalei Center, 5-5161 Kuhio Hwy., Hanalei* ☎ *808/826–7081* ⊕ *www.restaurantbaracuda.com.*

$$$$
ECLECTIC
Fodor's Choice
★
✕ **Kauai Grill.** Savor an artful meal created by world-renowned chef Jean-Gorges Vongerichten, surrounded by a dramatic Hanalei Bay scene that's positively stunning at sunset. Located at the luxurious St. Regis Princeville Resort, Kauai Grill has dark-wood decor and an ornate chandelier, the centerpiece of the room. The attention here is on the flavors of robust meat and local, fresh seafood. Meats are simply grilled and paired with exotic sauces. Specials change frequently and use many Hawaiian-grown ingredients. Expect attentive service with the feel of an exclusive nightclub, and an expertly created meal. Vegetarian and gluten-free menus are available. $ *Average main: $45* ⊠ *St. Regis Princeville, 5520 Ka Haku Rd., Princeville* ☎ *808/826–9644* ⊕ *www. kauaigrill.com* ⚶ *Reservations essential* ⊗ *No lunch. Closed Sun.–Mon.*

$$
AMERICAN
FAMILY
✕ **Kilauea Bakery and Pau Hana Pizza.** This bakery is known for its starter of Hawaiian sourdough made with guava as well as its specialty pizzas topped with eclectic ingredients such as smoked *ono* (a Hawaiian fish), Gorgonzola-rosemary sauce, barbecued chicken, goat cheese, and chipotle peppers. Open from 6:30 am, the bakery serves coffee drinks,

Where to Eat
on Kauai

Haena Beach Park
Tunnels Beach
Kee Beach
Haena
560
Princeville
35
Hanalei Bay
33
Hanalei
34
Han
Bea
Pa
WAIPA VALLEY
37

Hanakapiai Beach

NAPALI COAST

Kalalau Trail

Kalalau Lookout
Puu-O-Kila Lookout

Kokee Lodge
Kokee State Park

Kokee

550

WAIMEA CANYON

NaPali-Kona Forest Reserve

Waialeale 5,148 ft.

WAIMEA

Kokee Rd.

Waimea Canyon Dr.

55

552

550

KOLOA

Kekaha Beach Park

Kekaha

Menehune Ditch

1 Waimea

Lucy Wright Beach Park

Kalaheo

3

Lawai

50

540

53

2 Hanapepe
Eleele

Burns Field

Port Allen

Hanapepe Bay

Spouting Horn

Beach House

Kaulakahi Channel

0   5 miles
0   5 km

Mahimahi is a popular fish dish on Kauai. The Beach House adds a macadamia-nut crust for local flavor.

delicious fresh pastries, bagels, and breads in the morning. Late risers beware: breads and pastries sell out quickly on weekends. Pizza (including a gluten-free dough option), soup, and salads can be ordered for lunch or dinner. Service is leisurely. There's free Wi-Fi and a cute courtyard with covered tables. $ *Average main: $20* ⊠ *Kong Lung Center, 2484 Keneke St., Kilauea* ☎ *808/828–2020.*

$ **✗ Kilauea Fish Market.** If you're not in a hurry, this tiny restaurant serves
HAWAIIAN up fresh fish in quality preparations, including tucked into hearty wraps and salads, stir-fried, and grilled with tasty sauces made from scratch. All fish and vegetables are locally purchased. The massive ahi wrap and fish tacos are the most popular selections, while the chicken plate lunch, with a choice of brown or white rice, is the best deal for the budget conscious. After placing your order inside, you can eat outside at covered tables (flies are sometimes a nuisance), or take out. Another location has been added at ⊠ *440 Aleka Place* behind Coconut Marketplace in Kapaa. $ *Average main: $12* ⊠ *Kilauea Lighthouse Rd., Kilauea* ☎ *808/828–6244* ⊘ *Closed Sun.*

$$$$ **✗ Makana Terrace.** Enjoy dining while gazing at a breathtaking pan-
HAWAIIAN oramic view of Hanalei Bay. There's no doubt it's pricey, but you're
FAMILY paying for the view—sit on the terrace if you can—and for an attentive staff. The focus is on local, Hawaiian-grown foods here, including the fish plate of a fresh Pacific catch, which is your best bet for lunch. For breakfast, feast at an extensive buffet or order à la carte. A fantastic and expensive brunch is the only option on Sunday morning and afternoon. The sushi is a good dinner choice—splurge on the petite fillet and lobster tail (around $58) and time your dinner around sunset for an

The Beach House on the South Shore is a prime spot to watch the sun set.

unforgettable Hawaiian vista. Ⓢ *Average main: $40* ✉ *5520 Ka Haku Rd., Princeville* ☎ *808/826–9644.*

$$$
MEDITERRANEAN

✗ **Mediterranean Gourmet.** A trip to this romantic Middle Eastern oasis pays off after a narrow, beach-hugging ride along the exquisite North Shore coastline. Owner-chef Imad Beydoun, a native of Beirut, serves multiple hummus appetizers, stuffed grape leaves, baba ghanoush, crispy spinach and lamb fatayers alongside traditional favorites like chicken and duck kabob, rib eye, and rosemary rack of lamb. Local fish including ahi, ono, and seasonal catches add Pacific Rim touches when combined with fresh local produce. Belly-dancing performances and live music enhance Tuesday's luau (reservations required). The Sunday brunch is a great bet. Ⓢ *Average main: $30* ✉ *Hanalei Colony Resort, 5-7130 Kuhio Hwy., Haena* ☎ *808/826–9875* ⊕ *www.kauaimedgourmet.com.*

$$
AMERICAN

✗ **Postcards Café.** This plantation-cottage restaurant has a menu full of seafood but also offers additive-free vegetarian and vegan options. Top menu picks include taro fritters, wasabi-crusted ahi, tandoori, and baked portabella mushrooms. Desserts are made without refined sugar. Try the chocolate silk pie made with barley malt chocolate, pure vanilla, and creamy tofu with a gingery crust, or even better yet, the warm chocolate volcano. Ⓢ *Average main: $21* ✉ *5-5075A Kuhio Hwy., Hanalei* ☎ *808/826–1191* ⊕ *www.postcardscafe.com* ⊗ *No lunch.*

$$$
AMERICAN
FAMILY

✗ **The Tavern at Princeville.** Roy Yamaguchi's tasteful restaurant overlooks the ocean and the Prince Golf Course, making it ideal for lunch or a sunset meal. The food is distinctive and high-quality, with comfort food specialties like buttermilk fried chicken and braised short ribs with creamy cheese grits. The garlicky escargot is memorable. There are fresh fish and nightly specials, plus steak, burger, and chicken choices. The cocktails are strong and innovative. Kid- and small-group friendly, the Tavern lends itself to a casual come-and-go vibe. $ *Average main: $27* ⊠ *5-3900 Kuhio Hwy, Princeville* ☎ *808/826–8700* ⊕ *www. tavernbyroy.com.*

THE EAST SIDE

Since the East Side is the island's largest population center, it makes sense that it should boast a wide selection of restaurants. It's also a good place to get both cheaper meals and the local-style cuisine that residents favor.

Most of the eateries are found along Kuhio Highway between Kapaa and Wailua; a few are tucked into shopping centers and resorts. In Lihue, it's easier to find lunch than dinner because many restaurants cater to the business crowd.

You'll find all the usual fast-food joints in both Kapaa and Lihue, as well as virtually every ethnic cuisine available on Kauai. Although fancy gourmet restaurants are less abundant in this part of the island, there's plenty of good, solid food, and a few stellar attractions. But unless you're staying on the East Side, or passing through, it's probably not worth the long drive from the North Shore or Poipu resorts to eat here.

KAPAA AND WAILUA

$$$

STEAKHOUSE

✕ **Bull Shed.** The A-frame structure makes this popular restaurant look distinctly rustic from the outside. Inside, light-color walls and a full wall of glass highlight an ocean view that is one of the best on Kauai. Come early for a window seat and watch the surf crashing on the rocks while you study the menu. The food is simple, but they know how to do surf and turf. You can try both in one of several combo dinner platters or order fresh island fish and thick steaks individually. Meals include salad bar. The restaurant is best known for its prime rib and Australian rack of lamb. Longtime visitors and locals love this place, which hasn't changed much in 30 years. Arrive early for the best seats. $ *Average main: $25* ⊠ *796 Kuhio Hwy., Kapaa* ☎ *808/822–3791, 808/822–1655* ⊕ *www.bullshedrestaurant.com* ⊗ *No lunch.*

$$

ECLECTIC

✕ **Caffé Coco.** A restored plantation cottage is the casual setting for this island café. It's set back off the highway near the Bambulei boutique and surrounded by tropical foliage. The menu emphasizes vegetarian, vegan, and gluten-free, and the kitchen uses primarily local ingredients. Outdoor seating in the vine-covered garden is pleasant during nice weather. Acoustic music is offered most evenings, attracting a laid-back local crowd. $ *Average main: $26* ⊠ *4-369 Kuhio Hwy., Wailua* ☎ *808/822–7990* ⊕ *www.caffecocokauai.com* ⊗ *Dinner only.*

$$$

ECLECTIC

✕ **The Eastside.** This restaurant is under new ownership that has continued many of the same menu items, though the quality of the food isn't quite as good as it was. Still, the service is friendly and attentive, and the ambience has brightened up. The kale salad with goat cheese and succulent hulihuli chicken are winners, as are any of the fresh fish choices. For dessert, the *lilikoi* (passion fruit) cheesecake and flourless chocolate cake come in huge portions that are best shared. The small bar is a nice place for a specialty cocktail, and there's live music a few nights a week. [$] *Average main: $28* ✉ *4-1380 Kuhio Hwy., Kapaa* ☎ *808/823–9500* ⏲ *No lunch Sun.-Mon.*

$$ AMERICAN Fodor's Choice ★ 🍴 **Hukilau Lanai.** Relying heavily on super-fresh island fish and locally grown vegetables, this restaurant offers quality food that is competently and creatively prepared. The nightly fish specials—served grilled, steamed, or sautéed with succulent sauces—shine here. Other sound choices are the savory meat loaf and prime rib. Mac nut–crusted chicken and a few pasta dishes round out the menu. The ahi poke nachos appetizer is not to be missed, nor is the warm chocolate cake. The spacious dining room looks out to the ocean, and it's lovely to eat at the outdoor tables when the weather is nice. Overall, it's a great choice for value and consistent quality on the East Side. [$] *Average main: $23* ✉ *Kauai Coast Resort, Coconut Marketplace, 520 Aleka Loop, Kapaa* ☎ *808/822–0600* 🌐 *www.hukilaukauai.com* ⏲ *No lunch. Closed Mon.*

$$ ITALIAN 🍴 **Kauai Pasta.** This simple yet elegant establishment offers some of the best Italian food on the island at moderate prices. Their specials are delicious, and their 10-inch pizzettas make a fine meal for one. The adjacent and chic KP Lounge stays open late, offering a handsome hideout for tasty appetizers such as vine-ripened tomato bruschetta and crispy calamari with togarashi and soy-lemon aioli. Their signature drink menu has a few gems, including a rosemary and ginger margarita, and a basil and coconut mojito. There's a branch in Lihue that also serves lunch and dinner. [$] *Average main: $18* ✉ *4-939B Kuhio Hwy., Kapaa* 🌐 *www.kauaipasta.com.*

$ AMERICAN FAMILY 🍴 **Kountry Kitchen.** If you like a hearty breakfast, try Kountry Kitchen, a family-friendly restaurant that has a cozy, greasy-spoon atmosphere with friendly service. Breakfast and lunch items are served until 1:30 pm daily. Across the street from the library in Kapaa, it's a great spot for omelets, banana pancakes, and eggs Benedict in two sizes. Lunch selections include sandwiches, burgers, and *loco mocos* (a popular local rice, beef, gravy, and eggs concoction). It's very busy at breakfast, so expect a wait on weekends. Take-out orders are also available. [$] *Average main: $12* ✉ *1485 Kuhio Hwy., Kapaa* ☎ *808/822–3511* 🌐 *www.kountrykitchenfamrest.com* ⏲ *No dinner.*

$$ JAPANESE Fodor's Choice ★ 🍴 **Restaurant Kintaro.** If you want to eat at a hip restaurant that's a favorite with locals, visit Kintaro. But be prepared to wait on weekends, because the dining room and sushi bar are always busy. Try the soft-shell crab roll or the unbeatable Bali Hai bomb, a roll of crab and smoked salmon, baked and topped with wasabi mayonnaise. For a traditional Japanese meal, ask for the tempura combination, complete with fish, shrimp, and vegetables. *Teppanyaki* dinners are meat, seafood, and vegetables flash-cooked on tabletop grills in an entertaining display. Tatami-mat seating is available behind shoji screens that provide privacy for groups. The purple haze, a delicious mix of warm sake and framboise liqueur, is a must-have cocktail. [$] *Average main: $22* ✉ *4-370 Kuhio Hwy., Wailua* ☎ *808/822–3341* ⏲ *No lunch. Closed Sun.*

$ INDIAN 🍴 **Shivalik Indian Cuisine.** This eatery provides a refreshing alternative to the typical fish and seafood offerings at most of Kauai's restaurants. Boasting no particular Indian regional style, this small-plaza hideaway with a tandoor oven has delicious curried vegetables, chicken dishes, and naan. Their samosas are especially noteworthy. The atmosphere is pleasant and the service is efficient. An all-you-can eat buffet is offered on Wednesday nights and at lunch on the weekend. [$] *Average main: $17* ✉ *4-771 Kuhio Hwy, Kapaa* ☎ *808/821–2333* 🌐 *www.shivalikindiancuisine.com* 🕒 *No lunch Wed.*

$ MEXICAN 🍴 **Tiki Tacos.** Authentic Mexican food and quality ingredients, many of them organic and locally sourced, place Tiki Tacos a notch above most Kauai taco joints. The corn tortillas are housemade, and so are the tamales and slow-cooked meats. The fish tacos are popular, as are those filled with spicy steak or fire-roasted vegetables. Tacos are about $5 each, and they're very large. Outside tables face a parking lot; inside is a tiny, warm dining room. [$] *Average main: $8* ✉ *4-971 Kuhio Hwy., Kapaa* ☎ *808/823–8226* 🕒 *Closed Sun.*

LIHUE

$$$ ECLECTIC 🍴 **Gaylord's.** Located in what was once Kauai's most expensive plantation estate, Gaylord's pays tribute to the elegant dining rooms of 1930s high society. Although the food is satisfying, Gaylord's is primarily about ambience. Tables with candlelight sit on a cobblestone patio that surrounds a fountain and overlooks a wide lawn. The menu is eclectic, ranging from tender seared scallops served in a fennel cream with potato croquettes to buttermilk fried chicken with a thick country gravy. Try the fish-packed cioppino or the tender hoisin-glazed pork short ribs. The pineapple shortcake is a tasty twist on an old favorite. Lunch mostly consists of pricey burgers, crepes, and salads. The lavish Sunday brunch buffet includes an ahi tuna Benedict, blackened steak and eggs, and a waffle station. Before or after dining you can stroll the estate grounds. [$] *Average main: $30* ✉ *Kilohana Plantation, 3-2087 Kaumualii Hwy.* ☎ *808/245–9593* 🌐 *www.gaylordskauai.com.*

$ ASIAN Fodor's Choice ★ 🍴 **Hamura Saimin.** Folks just love this funky old plantation-style diner. Locals and tourists stream in and out all day long, and neighbor islanders stop in on their way to the airport to pick up take-out orders for friends and family back home. Their famous *saimin* soup is the big draw, and each day the Hiraoka family dishes up about 1,000 bowls of steaming broth and homemade noodles, topped with a variety of garnishes. The barbecued chicken and meat sticks adopt a smoky flavor during grilling. The landmark eatery is also famous for its *lilikoi* (passion fruit) chiffon pie. ■ **TIP→ This is one of the few island restaurants open late—8:30 pm on weeknights and midnight on Friday and Saturday.** [$] *Average main: $7* ✉ *2956 Kress St.* ☎ *808/245–3271* 💳 *No credit cards.*

$$$ AMERICAN 🍴 **JJ's Broiler.** This spacious, low-key restaurant serves hearty fare, with dinner specials such as lobster and Slavonic steak, a broiled sliced tenderloin dipped in buttery wine sauce and local-style kalua pig and cabbage. The grilled cajun-style prime rib is also pretty good. On sunny afternoons, ask for a table on the lanai overlooking Kalapaki Bay and try one of the generous salads or appetizers and a drink. The upstairs section is currently only available for private events, but you can still eat at the restaurant's lower level, which is open-air and casual. JJ's is a relaxed place to enjoy lunch, dinner, or just sit at the bar for a

Some of the best eats on Kauai come from the sea. Ask what the local catch of the day is for the freshest option.

drink, with one of the best ocean views in Lihue. $ *Average main: $30* ✉ *Anchor Cove, 3416 Rice St., Nawiliwili* ☎ *808/246–4422* ⊕ *www. jjsbroiler.com.*

$$ ✕ **Kalapaki Joe's.** The original Kalapaki Joe's at Nawiliwili Harbor in
AMERICAN Lihue is the place for sports fans who like a rip-roaring happy hour. The appetizer menu is extensive, or choose from burgers, salads, sandwiches, fish tacos, steaks, ribs, and fresh fish specials. This place is typically packed with a boisterous crowd from late afternoon on into the night. The second-story location has a postcard-perfect view of Kalapaki Bay. $ *Average main: $20* ✉ *3501 Rice St, No. 208* ☎ *808/245–6266* ⊕ *www.kalapakijoes.com.*

$$ ✕ **Kukui's Restaurant and Bar.** The meals at Kukui's feature Hawaiian,
ECLECTIC Asian, and contemporary American influences, and the open-air setting makes it a pleasant place to dine. It's very spacious, and not as busy and noisy as the other eateries at the Marriott, making it well-suited to families and those who want a relaxed setting. The menu includes slow-roasted prime rib, fresh fish, and pasta dishes. You can also order from the Toro Tei sushi bar, or from the bar menu. A full breakfast buffet is offered every morning, or choose from the à la carte menu. $ *Average main: $25* ✉ *Kauai Marriott Resort & Beach Club, 3610 Rice St., Kalapaki Beach* ☎ *808/245–5050* ⊕ *kukuiskauaimarriott.com.*

$ ✕ **Lihue Barbecue Inn.** Few Kauai restaurants are more beloved than this
ECLECTIC family-owned eatery, a mainstay of island dining since 1940. The menu runs from traditional American to Asian, and you can dine in comfy booths. The Japanese side of the menu is generally satisfying, as are fresh fish specials and the fish salads. Prices are a bit high for the food, but meals include a good miso soup or fresh fruit cup and dessert. The

homemade cream pie is a winner, in any flavor. $ *Average main: $15* ✉ *2982 Kress St.* ☎ *808/245–2921* ⊘ *Closed Sun.*

THE SOUTH SHORE

Most South Shore restaurants are more upscale and located within the Poipu resorts. If you're looking for a gourmet meal in a classy setting, the South Shore is where you'll find it. Poipu has a number of excellent restaurants in dreamy settings and decidedly fewer family-style, lower-price eateries.

$$$
ASIAN
Fodor's Choice
★

✕ **Beach House.** This restaurant partners a dreamy ocean view with impressive cuisine, and is one of the best places on the island for a romantic dinner, open-air lunch, or cocktail and appetizer. Few Kauai experiences are more delightful than sitting at one of the Beach House's outside tables and savoring a delectable meal while the sun sinks into the glassy blue Pacific and surfers slice the waves. Cobble up a meal from tasty sides like crab cakes, sweet-spicy braised pork, arugula–goat cheese salad, and an excellent ceviche. Or pick a wasabi-crusted fresh fish sauté or braised lamb shank with truffle-asparagus risotto. The fire-grilled filet mignon with blue cheese is remarkable. Our dessert favorites include the warm molten chocolate cake, the bananas Foster, and the carrot cake with pineapple, macadamia nuts, and cream cheese frosting. Gluten-free and vegan choices are also available. $ *Average main: $35* ✉ *5022 Lawai Rd., Koloa* ☎ *808/742–1424* ⊕ *www.the-beach-house. com* ⌂ *Reservations essential.*

$$$
ITALIAN
Fodor's Choice
★

✕ **Dondero's.** With a beautiful setting, outstanding food, a remarkable wine list, and impeccable service, Dondero's is one of Kauai's best restaurants. The inlaid marble floors, ornate tile work, and Italianate murals that compose the elegant interior at this restaurant compete with a stunning ocean view. The elegant tasting menu features Italian dishes, including homemade pastas, risotto, and flatbread pizza. Try the ricotta gnocchi primavera; melt-in-your-mouth osso buco; seafood cioppino with scallops, mussels, fresh fish, lobster, and shrimp; or any of the outstanding pasta, meat, fish, and vegetarian choices. Many menu items are gluten-free, and a scoop of passion fruit or pineapple sorbetti is a refreshing ending to the meal. The food is beautifully executed, and the waitstaff earns special praise for thoughtful, personalized service. It's delightful to sit outside beneath twinkling lights. $ *Average main: $33* ✉ *Grand Hyatt Kauai Resort and Spa, 1571 Poipu Rd., Koloa* ☎ *808/240–6456* ⊘ *No lunch.*

$
AMERICAN

✕ **Joe's on the Green.** Eat an open-air breakfast or lunch with an expansive vista of Poipu. Located on the Kiahuna Golf Course, this restaurant boasts such favorites as eggs Benedict, tofu scramble, and banana-macadamia-nut pancakes. For lunch, try the quarter-pound hot dog, the Reuben sandwich, the ribs, or build your own salad. Happy hour, which often features live music, offers local favorites like manapua dumplings and ahi poke, along with sliders, ribs, and homemade chili nachos. With a casual atmosphere and generous portions, Joe's is a refreshing alternative to the pricier hotel brunch venues in this area. $ *Average main: $12* ✉ *2545 Kiahuna Plantation Dr., Poipu* ☎ *808/742–9696* ⊕ *www. joesonthegreen.com* ⊘ *No dinner.* Continued on page 551

LUAU: A TASTE OF HAWAII

The best place to sample Hawaiian food is at a backyard luau. Aunts and uncles are cooking, the pig is from a cousin's farm, and the fish is from a brother's boat.

But even locals have to angle for invitations to those rare occasions. So your choice is most likely between a commercial luau and a Hawaiian restaurant.

Some commercial luau are less authentic; they offer little of the traditional diet and are more about umbrella drinks, spectacle, and fun.

For greater culinary authenticity, folksy experiences, and rock-bottom prices, visit a Hawaiian restaurant (most are in anonymous storefronts in residential neighborhoods). Expect rough edges and some effort negotiating the menu.

In either case, much of what is known today as Hawaiian food would be as foreign to a 16th-century Hawaiian as risotto or chow mein. The pre-contact diet was simple and healthy—mainly raw and steamed seafood and vegetables. Early Hawaiians used earth ovens and heated stones to cook seafood, taro, sweet potatoes, and breadfruit and seasoned their food with sea salt and ground kukui nuts. Seaweed, fern shoots, sweet potato vines, coconut, banana, sugarcane, and select greens and roots rounded out the diet.

Successive waves of immigrants added their favorites to the ti leaf–lined table. So it is that foods as disparate as salt salmon and chicken long rice are now Hawaiian—even though there is no salmon in Hawaiian waters and long rice (cellophane noodles) is Chinese.

AT THE LUAU: KALUA PORK

The heart of any luau is the *imu*, the earth oven in which a whole pig is roasted. The preparation of an imu is an arduous affair for most families, who tackle it only once a year or so, for a baby's first birthday or at Thanksgiving, when many Islanders prefer to imu their turkeys. Commercial luau operations have it down to a science, however.

THE ART OF THE STONE
The key to a proper imu is the *pohaku*, the stones. Imu cook by means of long, slow, moist heat released by special stones that can withstand a hot fire without exploding. Many Hawaiian families treasure their imu stones, keeping them in a pile in the backyard and passing them on through generations.

PIT COOKING
The imu makers first dig a pit about the size of a refrigerator, then lay down *kiawe* (mesquite) wood and stones, and build a white-hot fire that is allowed to burn itself out. The ashes are raked away, and the hot stones covered with banana and ti leaves. Well-wrapped in ti or banana leaves and a net of chicken wire, the pig is lowered onto the leaf-covered stones. *Laulau* (leaf-wrapped bundles of meats, fish, and taro leaves) may also be placed inside. Leaves—ti, banana, even ginger—cover the pig followed by wet burlap sacks (to create steam). The whole is topped with a canvas tarp and left to steam for the better part of a day.

OPENING THE IMU
This is the moment everyone waits for: The imu is unwrapped like a giant present and the imu keepers gingerly wrestle out the steaming pig. When it's unwrapped, the meat falls moist and smoky-flavored from the bone, looking just like Southern-style pulled pork, but without the barbecue sauce.

WHICH LUAU?
Most resort hotels have luau on their grounds that include hula, music, and, of course, lots of food and drink. Each island also has at least one "authentic" luau. For lists of the best luau on each island, visit the Hawaii Visitors and Convention Bureau website: ⊕*www.gohawaii.com*.

MEA AI ONO
GOOD THINGS TO EAT

LAULAU
Steamed meats, fish, and taro leaf in ti-leaf bundles: fork-tender, a medley of flavors; the taro resembles spinach.

LOMI LOMI SALMON
Salt salmon in a piquant salad or relish with onions, tomatoes.

POI
Poi, a paste made of pounded taro root, may be an acquired taste, but it's a must-try during your visit.

Consider: The Hawaiian Adam is descended from *kalo* (taro). Young taro plants are called "keiki"–children. Poi is the first food after mother's milk for many Islanders. Ai, the word for food, is synonymous with poi in many contexts.

Not only that, we love it. "There is no meat that doesn't taste good with poi," the old Hawaiians said.

But you have to know how to eat it: with something rich or powerfully flavored. "It is salt that makes the poi go in," is another adage. When you're served poi, try it with a mouthful of smoky kalua pork or salty lomi lomi salmon. Its slightly sour blandness cleanses the palate. And if you don't like it, smile and say something polite. (And slide that bowl over to a local.)

Laulau

Lomi Lomi Salmon

Poi

E HELE MAI AI! COME AND EAT!

Hawaiian restaurants tend to be inconveniently located in well-worn storefronts with little or no parking, outfitted with battered tables and clattering Melmac dishes, but they personify aloha, invariably run by local families who welcome tourists who take the trouble to find them.

Many are cash-only operations and combination plates are a standard feature: one or two entrées, a side such as chicken long rice, choice of poi or steamed rice and—if the place is really old-style—a tiny portion of coarse Hawaiian salt and some raw onions for relish.

Most serve some foods that aren't, strictly speaking, Hawaiian, but are beloved of kamaaina, such as salt meat with watercress (preserved meat in a tasty broth), or *akubone*

(skipjack tuna fried in a tangy vinegar sauce).

Our favorite: **Dani's Restaurant** (✉ 4201 Rice St., Lihue, ☎ 808/245–4991).

MENU GUIDE

Much of the Hawaiian language encountered during a stay in the Islands will appear on restaurant menus and lists of luau fare. Here's a quick primer.

ahi: *yellowfin tuna.*

aku: *skipjack, bonito tuna.*

amaama: *mullet; it's hard to get but tasty.*

bento: *a box lunch.*

chicken luau: *a stew made from chicken, taro leaves, and coconut milk.*

haupia: *a light, pudding-like sweet made from coconut.*

imu: *the underground oven in which pigs are roasted for luau.*

kalua: *to bake underground.*

kimchee: *Korean dish of fermented cabbage made with garlic, hot peppers, and other spices.*

Kona coffee: *coffee grown in the Kona district of the Big Island.*

laulau: *literally, a bundle. Laulau are morsels of pork, chicken, butterfish, or other ingredients wrapped with young taro leaves and then bundled in ti leaves for steaming.*

lilikoi: *passion fruit, a tart, seedy yellow fruit that makes delicious desserts, juice, and jellies.*

lomi lomi: *to rub or massage; also a massage. Lomi lomi salmon is fish that has been rubbed with onions and herbs; commonly served with minced onions and tomatoes.*

luau: *a Hawaiian feast; also the leaf of the taro plant used in preparing such a feast.*

luau leaves: *cooked taro tops with a taste similar to spinach.*

mahimahi: *mild-flavored dolphinfish, not the marine mammal.*

mai tai: *potent rum drink with orange liqueurs and pineapple juice, from the Tahitian word for "good."*

malasada: *a Portuguese deep-fried doughnut without a hole, dipped in sugar.*

manapua: *steamed chinese buns filled with pork, chicken, or other fillings.*

niu: *coconut.*

onaga: *pink or red snapper.*

ono: *a long, slender mackerel-like fish; also called wahoo.*

ono: *delicious; also hungry.*

opihi: *a tiny limpet, found on rocks.*

papio: *a young ulua or jack fish.*

poha: *Cape gooseberry. Tasting a bit like honey, the poha berry is often used in jams and desserts.*

poi: *a paste made from pounded taro root, a staple of the Hawaiian diet.*

poke: *cubed raw tuna or other fish, tossed with seaweed and seasonings.*

pupu: *appetizers or small plates.*

saimin: *long thin noodles and vegetables in broth, often garnished with small pieces of fish cake, scrambled egg, luncheon meat, and green onion.*

sashimi: *raw fish thinly sliced and usually eaten with soy sauce.*

ti leaves: *a member of the agave family. The leaves are used to wrap food while cooking and removed before eating.*

uku: *deep-sea snapper.*

ulua: *a member of the jack family that also includes pompano and amberjack. Also called crevalle, jack fish, and jack crevalle.*

$$$ CONTEMPORARY 🍴 **Josselin's Tapas Bar & Grill.** Chef Jean-Marie Josselin, one of the pioneers of Hawaiian regional cuisine, has a winner with this fun, sophisticated small-plates restaurant. After the roaming sangria cart rolls up with concoctions containing *lilikoi* (passion fruit) and lychee, the feast is on. The menu changes frequently, but expect a wide range of Hawaiian-influenced, Asian, and Western choices to satisfy all palates. The idea is to share a variety of choices. The tempura ahi roll with beurre blanc is especially tasty. Or try the Kauai shrimp and duck tacos with pineapple salsa, the pumpkin ravioli, or the sesame-crusted mahi and braised pork belly with apple kimchi. The only drawback is the very noisy dining room. [$] *Average main: $30* ✉ *Kukuiula shopping center, upstairs, 2829 Ala Kalani Kaumaka St., Koloa* ☎ *808/742–7117* 🌐 *josselins.com* 🕒 *No lunch.*

$ AMERICAN 🍴 **Kalaheo Café & Coffee Co.** Folks love this roadside café, especially for breakfast, though it's good for lunch and a simple dinner, too. It's a casual atmosphere, and is frequently busy, especially on weekend mornings. Order up front and then find a seat inside or out on the lanai. Favorites include the Kahili Breakfast, scrambled eggs served with Portuguese sausage, ham, and green onions; and the Longboard sandwich, with fried egg, bacon, lettuce, tomato, and melted provolone cheese. The dinner menu has some really good salads, ribs, meatloaf, chicken, fish, burgers, and weekly specials. Lots of local products are used here, including Anahola Granola, local fish, and Kauai coffee, which you can buy by the pound. It's a solid choice in an area with limited restaurants. [$] *Average main: $17* ✉ *2-2560 Kaumualii Hwy. (Rte. 50), Kalaheo* ☎ *808/332–5858* 🌐 *www.kalaheo.com* 🕒 *No Dinner Mon.*

$$ ASIAN FAMILY 🍴 **Keoki's Paradise.** Built to resemble a dockside boathouse, this active, boisterous place fills up quickly at night thanks to a busy bar and frequent live music. Seafood appetizers span the tide from sashimi to Thai shrimp sticks, crab cakes, and potstickers. The day's fresh catch is available in various styles and sauces, along with scallops, seafood risotto, and lobster. The imu-roasted pork ribs are popular, as is the prime rib. The ice cream and Oreo cookie hula pie is a classic, but the chocolate crème brûlée should not be overlooked. There's a gluten-free menu, and lighter fare at the bar. The *keiki* (children's) menu includes tropical drinks. [$] *Average main: $25* ✉ *Poipu Shopping Village, 2360 Kiahuna Plantation Dr., Koloa* ☎ *808/742–7534* 🌐 *www.keokisparadise.com.*

$$$$ MODERN HAWAIIAN 🍴 **Merriman's Fish House.** The regional food served up at chef Peter Merriman's namesake restaurant is enhanced by a sophisticated setting and lovely views from a pretty second-floor dining room. Start at the bar, where fine wines are offered by the glass, and try the crispy crab cakes or raw fish poke. The dinner menu states the origin of the fish, lamb, beef, chicken, and veggies. Wok-charred ahi is the signature dish, though the sesame-crusted opah and Hanalei taro-jalapeño cakes with honey sour cream also shine. Smaller portions of two entrées also can be ordered. The banana lumpia with a vanilla gelato and housemade chocolate sauce is a deliciously decadent ending. [$] *Average main: $38* ✉ *2829 Ala Kalanikaumaka St., G-149, Koloa* ☎ *808/742–8385* 🌐 *www.merrimanshawaii.com* 🕒 *No lunch.*

5

$ ITALIAN FAMILY 🍴 **Pizzetta.** This family-style Italian restaurant serves up hearty portions of pasta, calzones, and pizza, along with kalua pork and cabbage, grilled fish, and barbecue ribs, all of which can find their way into pizza toppings. The berry cobbler with vanilla gelato is a nice finish. The menu is quite extensive, and the food is generally good. Meals are served in a casual, lively setting, with an open-air deck. Neighborhood delivery is available. [$] *Average main: $15* ✉ *5408 Koloa Rd., Koloa* ☎ *808/742–8881* 🌐 *www.pizzettarestaurant.com.*

$$ AMERICAN FAMILY 🍴 **Poipu Tropical Burgers.** Families will appreciate the children's menu, bottomless soft drinks, and wide variety of choices at this no-frills eatery in the Poipu Shopping Village. The food is simple, and the gourmet half-pound burgers use local beef. Veggie and fish burgers, sandwiches, soups, and hearty salads round out the choices. Pasta, steaks, fresh fish, and other specials are added at dinner. The dining room is airy and casual. The service can be slow. [$] *Average main: $18* ✉ *Poipu Shopping Village, 2360 Kiahuna Plantation Dr., Koloa* ☎ *808/742–1808.*

$$$ ECLECTIC Fodor's Choice ★ 🍴 **Red Salt.** A smart, sophisticated decor and exceptional food paired with professional service make Red Salt a great choice for leisurely fine dining. Lobster ravioli sits atop saffron pasta, while the seared rack of lamb is enlivened by mango chutney and the ono is nestled on a king crab potato hash. The root beer float and pineapple cotton candy are fun desserts, but the dark chocolate macadamia nut torte is memorable. The presentation is exquisite, making this a feast for the eyes as well as the tastebuds. [$] *Average main: $32* ✉ *Koa Kea Resort, 2251 Poipu Rd., Koloa* ☎ *808/742–4288.*

$$$$ SEAFOOD 🍴 **Tidepools.** Of the Grand Hyatt's many notable restaurants, Tidepools is definitely the most tropical and campy, sure to appeal to folks seeking a bit of island-style romance and adventure. Private grass-thatch huts seem to float on a koi-filled pond beneath starry skies while torches flicker in the lushly landscaped grounds nearby. The equally distinctive food has an island flavor that comes from the chef's advocacy of Hawaii regional cuisine and extensive use of Kauai-grown products including fresh herbs from the resort's organic garden. You won't go wrong ordering the soy-ginger-glazed catch of the day, macadamia nut–crusted mahimahi, or the wasabi-crusted beef fillet. Start with jumbo lump crab cakes or heirloom tomato salad to wake up your taste buds. The roasted peach tart with macadamia-nut ice cream is a memorable dessert. [$] *Average main: $40* ✉ *Grand Hyatt Kauai Resort and Spa, 1571 Poipu Rd., Koloa* ☎ *808/240–6456* ⏲ *No lunch.*

$$ ASIAN 🍴 **Yum Cha Asian Eatery.** Sightly off the grounds of the Grand Hyatt, at the Poipu Bay Golf Course, Yum Cha offers an appealing mix of Chinese, Japanese, and Thai cuisine, with such distinctive offerings as soy-ginger-glazed "spoon tender" short ribs, noodle and rice dishes, and kung pao chicken. More eclectic choices include green curry with spinach soba and fiddlehead fern soup. It's an easy walk, or take the hotel shuttle, and go early to enjoy a lovely view of the greens. Make a satisfying meal from crab cakes, spring rolls, pot stickers, chicken satay, and roasted duck bao. The warm fried malasada, a favorite local Portuguese donut served with chocolate-coffee pot au creme, and the ginger crème brûlée are dynamite desserts. Also choose from a sake menu and

specialty cocktails. $ *Average main: $25* ✉ *Grand Hyatt Kauai, 2250 Ainako St., Koloa* ⊘ *No lunch. Closed Sun. and Mon.*

THE WEST SIDE

When it comes to dining on the West Side, pickings are mighty slim. Fortunately, the eateries that are here are generally worth patronizing, so you won't go too far wrong if your hunger demands to be satisfied while you're out enjoying the sights.

$ ✕ **Little Fish Coffee.** For a wholesome breakfast or lunch on the West
CAFÉ Side, Little Fish Coffee is the spot. The coffee is good, with each cup individually dripped, and the fresh bagels come with housemade cream cheese. The fruit and granola bowls, sandwiches, and wraps are recommendable, too. Smoothies and juices add to the healthy cuisine. This place is small, friendly, funky, and fun, right down to the marking pens that allow you to leave your own graffiti on the bathroom wall. Seating is very limited inside, but the courtyard in the back is a nice spot to dine. $ *Average main: $8* ✉ *3900 Hanapepe Rd., Hanapepe* ☎ *808/335–5000* ⊘ *No dinner. Closed Sun.*

$$ ✕ **Wrangler's Steakhouse.** Denim-covered seating, decorative saddles, and
STEAKHOUSE a stagecoach in a loft helped to transform the historic Ako General Store in Waimea into a West Side steak house. You can eat under the stars on the deck out back or inside the old-fashioned, wood-panel dining room. The 16-ounce New York steak comes sizzling, and the rib eye is served with capers. A trip to the tiny salad bar is included. Those with smaller appetites might consider the vegetarian tempura or the ahi served on penne pasta. Local folks love the special lunch: rice, beef teriyaki, and shrimp tempura with kimchi served in a three-tier *kaukau* tin, or lunch pail, just like the ones sugar-plantation workers once carried. There's live music on Saturday night. $ *Average main: $25* ✉ *9852 Kaumualii Hwy., Waimea* ☎ *808/338–1218* ⊘ *No lunch Sat. Closed Sun.*

WHERE TO STAY

Updated by
Joan Conrow

The Garden Isle has lodgings for every taste, from swanky resorts to rustic cabins, and from family-friendly condos to romantic bed-and-breakfasts. The savvy traveler can also find inexpensive places that are convenient, safe, and accessible to Kauai's special places and activities.

When you're choosing a place to stay, location is an important consideration. Kauai may seem small on a map, but because it's circular with no through roads, it can take more time than you think to get from place to place. If at all possible, stay close to your desired activities. This way, you'll save time to squeeze in all the things you'll want to do.

Time of year is also a factor. If you're here in winter or spring, consider staying on the South Shore, as the surf on the North Shore and East Side tends to be rough, making many ocean beaches dangerous for swimming or water sports.

Before booking accommodations, think hard about what kind of experience you want to have for your island vacation. There are several

BEST BETS FOR KAUAI LODGING

Fodor's Choice★	By Price	$$
Grand Hyatt Kauai Resort and Spa, $$$$, p. 559	**$**	**Hanalei Bay Resort**, p. 554
Kauai Coast Resort, $, p. 555	**Aston Aloha Beach Hotel**, p. 555	**Waimea Plantation Cottages**, p. 561
Koa Kea Hotel and Resort, $$$$, p. 559	**Garden Island Inn**, p. 557	**$$$**
Sheraton Kauai Resort, $$, p. 561	**Garden Isle Cottages**, p. 559	**Hanalei Colony Resort**, p. 554
St. Regis Princeville Resort, $$$$, p. 555	**Hotel Coral Reef**, p. 555	**$$$$**
Waimea Plantation Cottages, $$, p. 561	**Kauai Coast Resort**, p. 555	**Grand Hyatt Kauai Resort and Spa**, p. 559
	Kauai Palms Hotel, p. 559	**St. Regis Princeville Resort**, p. 555
	Kokee Lodge, p. 561	**Whalers Cove**, p. 561

top-notch resorts to choose from, and Kauai also has a wide variety of condos, vacation rentals, and bed-and-breakfasts. The Kauai Visitors Bureau provides a comprehensive listing of accommodation choices to help you decide.

Prices shown in reviews are the lowest price of a standard double room in high season. Rental prices are the one-bedroom rate per night.

For expanded hotel reviews, visit Fodors.com.

THE NORTH SHORE

$$
RESORT
FAMILY
Hanalei Bay Resort. This lovely condominium resort overlooks Hanalei Bay and Napali Coast. **Pros:** beautiful views; tennis courts on property; children's tennis program; tropical pool. **Cons:** steep walkways; long walk to beach. $ *Rooms from: $199* ✉ *5380 Honoiki Rd., Princeville* ☎ *808/826–6522, 877/507–1428* ⊕ *www.hanaleibayresort.com* ⌑ *134 units* ‖○‖ *No meals.*

$$$
HOTEL
Hanalei Colony Resort. The only true beachfront resort on Kauai's North Shore, Hanalei Colony is a laid-back, go-barefoot kind of resort sandwiched between towering mountains and the sea. **Pros:** oceanfront setting; private, quiet; seventh night free. **Cons:** remote location; poor cell phone reception; damp in winter. $ *Rooms from: $307* ✉ *5-7130 Kuhio Hwy., Haena* ☎ *808/826–6235, 800/628–3004* ⊕ *www.hcr.com* ⌑ *48 units* ‖○‖ *No meals.*

$
RENTAL
Hanalei Inn. If you're looking for lodgings that won't break the bank a block from gorgeous Hanalei Bay, look no further, as this is literally the only choice among the town's pricey vacation rentals. **Pros:** quick walk to beach: bus stop; shops; full kitchen. **Cons:** strict cancellation policy; daytime traffic noise. $ *Rooms from: $180* ✉ *5-5468 Kuhio*

Hwy., Hanalei ☎ *808/826–9333, 888/773-4730* 🌐 *www.hanaleiinn.com* 🛏 *4 studios* 🍴 *No meals.*

$$$$ RESORT FAMILY Fodor's Choice ★ **St. Regis Princeville Resort.** Built into the cliffs above Hanalei Bay, this swanky Starwood resort offers expansive views of the sea and mountains, including Makana, the landmark peak immortalized as mysterious Bali Hai island in the film *South Pacific*. **Pros:** great views; excellent restaurants; attractive lobby. **Cons:** minimal grounds; beach not ideal for swimming; extremely expensive. [$] *Rooms from: $490* ✉ *5520 Ka Haku Rd., Princeville* ☎ *877/787–3447, 808/826–9644* 🌐 *www.stregisprinceville.com* 🛏 *201 rooms, 51 suites* 🍴 *No meals.*

THE EAST SIDE

KAPAA AND WAILUA

$ RESORT **Aston Aloha Beach Hotel.** Nestled alongside Wailua Bay and the Wailua River, this low-key, low-rise hotel is a convenient and very inexpensive place to stay. **Pros:** close to ocean; convenient locale; mini-refrigerators. **Cons:** occasional foul smell from wastewater treatment plant nearby; restaurant meals are average. [$] *Rooms from: $89* ✉ *3-5920 Kuhio Hwy., Kapaa* ☎ *808/823–6000, 888/823–5111* 🌐 *www.astonhotels.com* 🛏 *216 rooms, 10 suites, 24 beach cottages* 🍴 *Multiple meal plans.*

$$ RESORT **Courtyard By Marriott at Coconut Beach.** This popular hotel, one of the few true oceanfront properties on Kauai, sits on a ribbon of sand in Kapaa. **Pros:** convenient location; close to ocean; pleasant grounds. **Cons:** coastline not conducive to swimming; small pool; high daily parking fee. [$] *Rooms from: $229* ✉ *650 Aleka Loop, Kapaa* ☎ *808/822–3455, 800/760–8555* 🌐 *www.marriott.com* 🛏 *311 rooms* 🍴 *No meals.*

$ HOTEL FAMILY **Hotel Coral Reef.** This small hotel has been in business since 1956 and is something of a Kauai beachfront landmark. **Pros:** free parking; oceanfront setting; convenient location. **Cons:** located in a busy section of Kapaa; ocean swimming is marginal. [$] *Rooms from: $125* ✉ *4-1516 Kuhio Hwy., Kapaa* ☎ *808/822–4481, 800/843–4659* 🌐 *www.hotelcoralreefresort.com* 🛏 *19 rooms, 2 suites* 🍴 *Breakfast.*

$ RENTAL **Kapaa Sands.** An old rock etched with Japanese characters known as *kanji* reminds you that the site of this condominium gem was formerly occupied by a Shinto temple. **Pros:** discounts for extended stays; walking distance to shops, restaurants, and beach; turtle and monk seal sightings common. **Cons:** no-frills lodging; small bathrooms; traffic noise in rear units. [$] *Rooms from: $119* ✉ *380 Papaloa Rd., Kapaa* ☎ *808/822–4901, 800/222–4901* 🌐 *www.kapaasands.com* 🛏 *24 units* 🍴 *No meals.*

$ RENTAL FAMILY Fodor's Choice ★ **Kauai Coast Resort.** Fronting an uncrowded stretch of beach, this three-story primarily time-share resort is convenient and a bit more upscale than nearby properties. **Pros:** central location; nice sunrises; free parking. **Cons:** beach is narrow; ocean not ideal for swimming. [$] *Rooms from: $146* ✉ *520 Aleka Loop, Kapaa* ☎ *808/822–3441, 866/678–3289* 🌐 *www.shellhospitality.com* 🛏 *108 units* 🍴 *No meals.*

$ HOTEL **Kauai Sands.** This oceanfront inn has been transformed into an affordable boutique hotel, thanks to a much-needed renovation of its guest rooms and public spaces. **Pros:** convenient location; free Wi-Fi; great

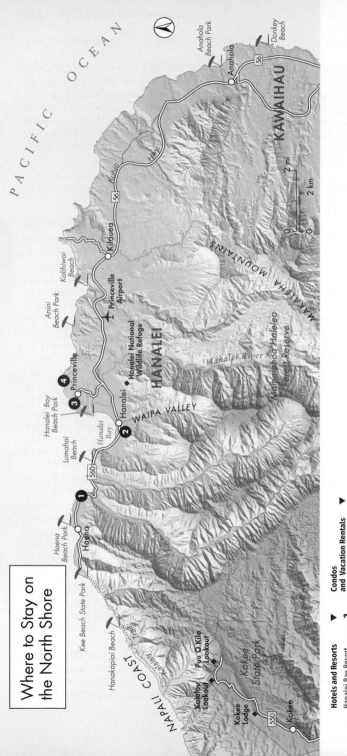

Where to Stay on the North Shore

Hotels and Resorts ▼
Hanalei Bay Resort **3**
Hanalei Colony Resort **1**
St. Regis
Princeville Resort **4**

**Condos
and Vacation Rentals** ▼
Hanalei Inn **2**

WHERE TO STAY IN KAUAI

	Local Vibe	**Pros**	**Cons**
The North Shore	Properties here have the "wow" factor with ocean and mountain beauty; laid-back Hanalei and Princeville set the high-end pace.	When the weather is good (summer) this side has it all. Epic winter surf, gorgeous waterfalls, and verdant vistas create some of the best scenery in Hawaii.	Lots of rain (being green has a cost) means you may have to travel south to find the sun; expensive restaurants and shopping offer few deals.
The East Side	The most reasonably priced area to stay for the practical traveler; lacks the pizzazz of expensive resorts on North and South shores; more traditional Hawaiian hotels.	The best travel deals show up here; more direct access to the local population; plenty of decent restaurants with good variety, along with delis in food stores.	Beaches aren't the greatest (rocky, reefy) at many of the lodging spots; bad traffic at times; some crime issues in parks.
The South Shore	Resort central; plenty of choices where the consistent sunshine is perfect for those who want to do nothing but play golf or tennis and read a book by the pool.	Beautiful in its own right; many enchanted evenings with stellar sunsets; summer surf easier for beginners to handle.	Some areas are deserty with scrub brush; construction can be brutal on piece of mind.
The West Side	There are few options for lodging in this mostly untouristlike setting with contrasts such as the extreme heat of a July day in Waimea to a frozen winter night up in Kokee.	A gateway area for exploration into the wilds of Kokee or for boating trips on Napali Coast; main hub for boat and helicopter trips; outstanding sunsets.	Least convenient side for most visitors; daytime is languid and dry; river runoff can ruin ocean's clarity.

sunrises. **Cons:** coral reef makes ocean swimming marginal; modest property; no resort amenities. [$] *Rooms from: $75* ✉ *420 Papaloa Rd., Kapaa* ☎ *808/822–4951, 800/560–5553* 🌐 *www.kauaisandshotel.com* 🛏 *200 rooms, 2 suites* 🍴 *Breakfast.*

$$ RENTAL 🏨 **Outrigger at Lae Nani.** Ruling Hawaiian chiefs once returned from ocean voyages to this spot, now host to condominiums comfortable enough for minor royalty. **Pros:** nice beach; walking distance to playground; attractively furnished. **Cons:** third floor is walk-up; no Wi-Fi; cleaning fee. [$] *Rooms from: $209* ✉ *410 Papaloa Rd., Kapaa* ☎ *808/822–4938, 866/956-4262* 🌐 *www.outrigger.com* 🛏 *84 units* 🍴 *No meals.*

LIHUE

$ HOTEL 🏨 **Garden Island Inn.** Budget travelers love this three-story inn near Kalapaki Bay and Anchor Cove shopping center. **Pros:** walk to beach, restaurants, and shops; good for extended stays and budget travel. **Cons:** some traffic noise; near a busy harbor; limited grounds; no pool. [$] *Rooms from: $119* ✉ *3445 Wilcox Rd., Kalapaki Beach* ☎ *808/245–7227, 800/648–0154* 🌐 *www.gardenislandinn.com* 🛏 *21 rooms* 🍴 *No meals.*

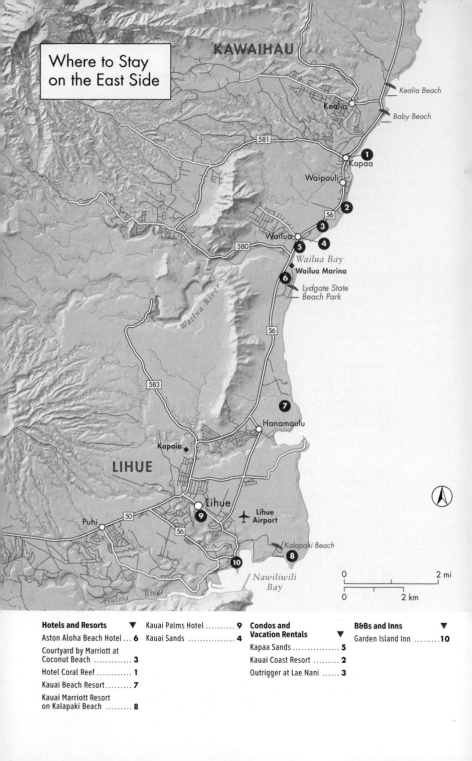

Where to Stay on the East Side

KAWAIHAU

Kealia Beach

Baby Beach

Kealia

581

Kapaa **1**

Waipouli

56

2

3

Wailua

580

4

5

Wailua Bay

Wailua Marina

6

Lydgate State Beach Park

56

583

7

Hanamaulu

Kapaia

LIHUE

Lihue

9

Lihue Airport

Puhi

50

56

Kalapaki Beach

8

10

Nawiliwili Bay

Huleia River

| 0 | | | 2 mi |
| 0 | | | 2 km |

$$ **Kauai Beach Resort.** This plantation-style hotel recently came under
RESORT the management of Aqua Hotels and Resorts and was given a $14
million renovation that upgraded the amenities to provide a relaxing,
upscale experience. **Pros:** unique pool; quiet; resort amenities; shuttle
services. **Cons:** not a good swimming beach; windy at times. $ *Rooms
from: $219* ✉ *4331 Kauai Beach Dr.* ☎ *888/805–3843* ⊕ *www.
kauaibeachresorthawaii.com* ⮌ *350 rooms, 7 suites* ¶○¶ *No meals.*

$$$ **Kauai Marriott Resort on Kalapaki Beach.** An elaborate tropical garden,
RESORT waterfalls right off the lobby, Greek statues and columns, and an enor-
FAMILY mous 26,000-square-foot swimming pool characterize the grand—and
grandiose—scale of this resort on Kalapaki Beach, which looks out at
the dramatic Haupu Ridge. **Pros:** oceanfront setting; numerous restaurants; convenient location; airport shuttle. **Cons:** distant airport noise;
ocean water quality can be poor at times. $ *Rooms from: $319* ✉ *3610
Rice St., Kalapaki Beach* ☎ *808/245–5050, 800/220–2925* ⊕ *www.
kauaimarriott.com* ⮌ *356 rooms, 11 suites.*

$ **Kauai Palms Hotel.** This low-cost alternative is close to the airport and
HOTEL priced right for the frugal traveler. **Pros:** clean; inexpensive; centrally
located. **Cons:** bare-bones amenities; smallish rooms. $ *Rooms from:
$89* ✉ *2931 Kalena St.* ☎ *808/246–0908* ⊕ *www.kauaipalmshotel.com*
⮌ *33 rooms* ¶○¶ *Breakfast.*

THE SOUTH SHORE

$ **Garden Isle Cottages.** Tropical fruit trees and flower gardens sur-
RENTAL round this spacious two-unit condominum, with a unit upstairs and
another downstairs. **Pros:** gorgeous view; oceanfront setting; comfortable accommodations. **Cons:** no sandy beach; cleaning fee. $ *Rooms
from: $159* ✉ *2658 Puuholo Rd., Koloa* ☎ *808/639–9233, 800/742–
6711* ⊕ *www.oceancottages.com* ⮌ *2 cottages* ▭ *No credit cards* ¶○¶ *No
meals.*

$$$$ **Grand Hyatt Kauai Resort and Spa.** Dramatically handsome, this clas-
RESORT sic Hawaiian low-rise is built into the cliffs overlooking an unspoiled
FAMILY coastline. **Pros:** fabulous pool; excellent restaurants; Hawaiian ambi-
Fodor'sChoice ence. **Cons:** poor and somewhat dangerous swimming beach during
★ summer swells; small balconies. $ *Rooms from: $440* ✉ *1571 Poipu
Rd., Koloa* ☎ *808/742–1234, 800/633–7313* ⊕ *www.grandhyattkauai.
com* ⮌ *602 rooms, 37 suites* ¶○¶ *No meals.*

$ **Kauai Cove Cottages.** Three modern studio cottages sit side by side
RENTAL at the mouth of Waikomo Stream, about two blocks from the beach
in a residential neighborhood. **Pros:** clean; great snorkeling nearby.
Cons: not on beach. $ *Rooms from: $145* ✉ *2672 Puuholo Rd., Poipu*
☎ *808/742–2562, 800/624–9945* ⊕ *www.kauaicove.com* ⮌ *3 cottages*
¶○¶ *No meals.*

$$$$ **Koa Kea Hotel and Resort.** This boutique property offers a high-end
RESORT experience without the bustle of many larger resorts, making it a great
Fodor'sChoice place to forget it all, and a perfect romantic getaway. **Pros:** incred-
★ ibly comfortable beds; great food at Red Salt restaurant; romantic spa.
Cons: not much for children. $ *Rooms from: $369* ✉ *2251 Poipu Rd.,
Koloa* ☎ *808/828–8888, 800/230-4134* ⊕ *www.koakea.com* ⮌ *121
rooms* ¶○¶ *No meals.*

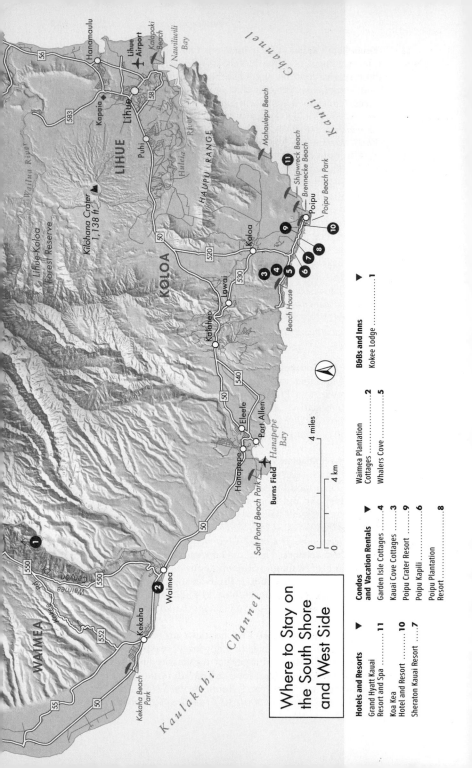

Where to Stay on the South Shore and West Side

Hotels and Resorts ▶
Grand Hyatt Kauai
Resort and Spa **11**

Koa Kea
Hotel and Resort **10**

Sheraton Kauai Resort **7**

**Condos
and Vacation Rentals** ▶
Garden Isle Cottages **4**

Kauai Cove Cottages **3**

Poipu Crater Resort **9**

Poipu Kapili **6**

Poipu Plantation
Resort **8**

Waimea Plantation
Cottages **2**

Whalers Cove **5**

B&Bs and Inns ▶
Kokee Lodge **1**

$$ **RENTAL** [building icon] **Poipu Crater Resort.** These two-bedroom individually owned condominium units are fairly spacious, and the large windows and high ceilings add to the sense of space and light. **Pros:** attractive and generally well kept; pretty setting. **Cons:** beach isn't good for swimming; few resort amenities. [$] *Rooms from: $185* ✉ *2330 Hoohu Rd., Poipu* ☎ *808/742–7400* 🛏 *30 units* 🍴 *No meals.*

$$$$ **RENTAL** [building icon] **Poipu Kapili.** This resort offers spacious one- and two-bedroom condo units that are minutes from Poipu's restaurants and across the street from a nice beach. **Pros:** units are roomy; good guest services; property is small. **Cons:** units are ocean-view but not oceanfront. [$] *Rooms from: $410* ✉ *2221 Kapili Rd., Koloa* ☎ *808/742–6449, 800/443–7714* 🌐 *www.poipukapili.com* 🛏 *60 units* 🍴 *No meals.*

$ **RENTAL** [building icon] **Poipu Plantation Resort.** Plumeria, ti, and other tropical foliage create a lush landscape for this resort, which rents four rooms in a bed-and-breakfast–style plantation home and seven one- and two-bedroom cottage apartments. **Pros:** attractively furnished; full breakfast at B&B. **Cons:** three-night minimum. [$] *Rooms from: $154* ✉ *1792 Pee Rd., Poipu* ☎ *808/742–6757, 800/634–0263* 🌐 *www.poipubeach.com* 🛏 *4 rooms, 7 cottages* 🍴 *Breakfast.*

5

$$ **RESORT** **Fodor's Choice** ★ [building icon] **Sheraton Kauai Resort.** The Sheraton's ocean-wing accommodations are so close to the water you can practically feel the spray of the surf as it hits the rocks below. **Pros:** ocean-view pool; quiet; great restaurant with spectacular views. **Cons:** somewhat businesslike ambience. [$] *Rooms from: $236* ✉ *2440 Hoonani Rd., Poipu Beach, Koloa* ☎ *808/742–1661, 888/488–3535* 🌐 *www.sheraton-kauai.com* 🛏 *394 rooms, 11 suites* 🍴 *No meals.*

$$$$ **RENTAL** [building icon] **Whalers Cove.** Perched about as close to the water's edge as they can get, these condos are the most luxurious on the South Shore, available in one-, two-, or three-bedroom units. **Pros:** on-site staff; outstanding setting; fully equipped spacious units. **Cons:** rocky beach not ideal for swimming; no air-conditioning. [$] *Rooms from: $349* ✉ *2640 Puuholo Rd., Koloa* ☎ *808/742–7571, 800/225–2683* 🌐 *www.whalerscoveresort.com* 🛏 *39 units* 🍴 *No meals.*

THE WEST SIDE

$ **B&B/INN** [building icon] **Kokee Lodge.** If you're an outdoors enthusiast, you can appreciate Kauai's mountain wilderness from the 12 rustic cabins that make up this lodge. **Pros:** outstanding setting; more refined than camping; cooking facilities. **Cons:** very austere; no restaurants for dinner; remote. [$] *Rooms from: $65* ✉ *3600 Kokee Rd., at mile marker 15, Waimea* ☎ *808/335–6061* 🌐 *www.thelodgeatkokee.net* 🛏 *12 cabins* 🍴 *No meals.*

$$ **RENTAL** **Fodor's Choice** ★ [building icon] **Waimea Plantation Cottages.** History buffs will adore these relocated and refurbished sugar-plantation cottages, which were originally built in the early 1900s. **Pros:** homey lodging; quiet and low-key; free Wi-Fi. **Cons:** not a white-sand beach; rooms are not luxurious; no air-conditioning. [$] *Rooms from: $249* ✉ *9400 Kaumualii Hwy., Box 367, Waimea* ☎ *808/338–1625, 877/997–6667* 🌐 *www.waimeaplantation.com* 🛏 *60 cottages* 🍴 *No meals.*

MOLOKAI

WELCOME TO MOLOKAI

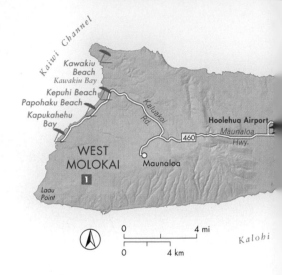

TOP REASONS TO GO

★ **Kalaupapa Peninsula:**
Hike or take a mule ride
down the world's tallest
sea cliffs to a fascinating,
historic community that
still houses a few former
Hansen's disease patients.

★ **A waterfall hike
in Halawa:** A fascinat-
ing guided hike through
private property takes
you past ancient ruins,
restored taro patches, and
a sparkling cascade.

★ **Deep-sea fishing:** Sport
fish are plentiful in these
waters, as are gorgeous
views of several islands.
Fishing is one of the
island's great adventures.

★ **Closeness to nature:**
Deep valleys, sheer cliffs,
and the untamed ocean
are the main attrac-
tions on Molokai.

★ **Papohaku Beach:** This
3-mile stretch of golden
sand is one of the most
sensational beaches in all
of Hawaii. Sunsets and
barbecues are perfect here.

1 West Molokai. The
most arid part of the island,
known as the west end,
has two inhabited areas:
the coastal stretch includes
a few condos and luxury
homes and the largest
beaches on the island.
Nearby is the fading hilltop
hamlet of Maunaloa.

2 Central Molokai. The
island's only true town,
Kaunakakai, with its mile-
long wharf, is here. Nearly
all the island's eateries and
stores are in or close to
Kaunakakai. Highway 470
crosses the center of the
island, rising to the top of
the sea cliffs and the Kalaupapa overlook. At the base
of the cliffs is Kalaupapa
National Historical Park, a
top attraction.

PACIFIC OCEAN

Kalaupapa
Airfield

KALAUPAPA
PENINSULA

Kalaupapa

Kalaupapa National
Historical Park

Halawa
Beach

olehua

Halawa

Moaula Falls ◆

Kualapuu

470

**CENTRAL
MOLOKAI**

2

Kamakou
Preserve

3 **EAST
MOLOKAI**

MOKUHOC
ISLANI

450

Kaunakakai

450

Waialua
Waialua
Beach Park

6

Kamiloloa
Heights

Kawela

Pauwalu

Kamehameha V. Hwy.

Pukoo

el

One Alii
Beach Park

Kaluaaha

Ualapue

Pailolo Channel

---

3 **East Molokai.** The scenic drive on Route 450 around this undeveloped area, also called the east end, passes through the green pastures of Puu O Hoku Ranch and climaxes with a descent into Halawa Valley. As you continue east, the road becomes increasingly narrow and the island ever more lush.

GETTING ORIENTED

Shaped like a long bone, Molokai is about 10 miles wide on average and four times that long. The north shore thrusts up from the sea to form the tallest sea cliffs on Earth, while the south shore slides almost flat into the water, then fans out to form the largest shallow-water reef system in the United States. Kaunakaki, the island's main town, has most of the stores and restaurants. Surprisingly, the highest point on Molokai rises to only 4,970 feet.

Updated by
Heidi Pool

With sandy beaches to the west, sheer sea cliffs to the north, and a rainy, lush eastern coast, Molokai offers a bit of everything, including a peek at what the Islands were like 50 years ago. Large tracts of land from Hawaiian Homeland grants have allowed the people to retain much of their traditional lifestyle. A favorite expression is "Slow down, you're on Molokai." Exploring the great outdoors and visiting the historic Kalaupapa Peninsula, where St. Damien and St. Marianne Cope helped people with leprosy, are attractions for visitors.

Molokai is generally thought of as the last bit of "real" Hawaii. Tourism has been held at bay by the island's unique history and the pride of its predominantly native Hawaiian population. Only 38 miles long and 10 miles wide at its widest point, Molokai is the fifth-largest island in the Hawaiian archipelago. Eight thousand residents call Molokai home, nearly 60% of whom are Hawaiian.

Molokai is a great place to be outdoors. There are no tall buildings, no traffic lights, no streetlights, no stores bearing the names of national chains, and nothing at all like a resort. You will, however, find 15 parks and more than 100 miles of shoreline to play on. At night the whole island grows dark, creating a velvety blackness and a wonderful, rare thing called silence.

GEOLOGY

Roughly 1½ million years ago, two large volcanoes—Kamakou in the east and Mauna Loa in the west—broke the surface of the Pacific Ocean and created the island of Molokai. Shortly thereafter a third and much smaller caldera, Kauhako, popped up to form the Makanalua Peninsula on the north side. After hundreds of thousands of years of rain, surf, and wind, an enormous landslide on the north end sent much of the mountain into the sea, leaving behind the sheer sea cliffs that make Molokai's north shore so spectacularly beautiful.

HISTORY

Molokai is named in chants as the child of the moon goddess Hina. For centuries the island was occupied by native people, who took advantage of the reef fishing and ideal conditions for growing taro.

When leprosy broke out in the Hawaiian Islands in the 1840s, the Makanalua Peninsula, surrounded on three sides by the Pacific and accessible only by a steep trail, was selected as the place to exile people suffering from the disease. The first patients were thrown into the sea to swim ashore as best they could, and left with no facilities, shelter, or supplies. In 1873 a missionary named Father Damien arrived and began to serve the peninsula's suffering inhabitants. He died in 1889 from leprosy and was canonized as a saint by the Catholic Church in 2009. In 1888, a nun named Mother Marianne Cope moved to Kalaupapa to care for the dying Father Damien and continue his vital work. Mother Marianne stayed at Kalaupapa until her death in 1918 (not from leprosy), and was canonized in 2012.

Though leprosy, now known as Hansen's disease, is no longer contagious and can be remitted, the buildings and infrastructure created by those who were exiled here still exist, and some longtime residents have chosen to stay in their homes. Today the area is Kalaupapa National Historical Park. Visitors are welcome but must prebook a tour operated by Damien Tours of Kalaupapa. You can reach the park by plane, by hiking, or by taking a mule ride down the steep Kalaupapa Trail.

THE BIRTHPLACE OF HULA

Tradition has it that, centuries ago, Lailai came to Molokai and lived on Puu Nana at Kaana. She brought the art of hula and taught it to the people, who kept it secret for her descendants, making sure the sacred dances were performed only at Kaana. Five generations later, Laka was born into the family and learned hula from an older sister. She chose to share the art and traveled throughout the Islands teaching the dance, though she did so without her family's consent. The yearly Ka Hula Piko Festival, held on Molokai in May, celebrates the birth of hula at Kaana.

PLANNING

WHEN TO GO

If you're keen to explore Molokai's beaches, coral beds, or fishponds, summer is your best bet for nonstop calm seas and sunny skies. The weather mimics that of the other Islands: low to mid-80s year-round, slightly rainier in winter. As you travel up the mountainside, the weather changes with bursts of downpours. The strongest storms occur in winter, when winds and rain shift to come in from the south.

For a taste of Hawaiian culture, plan your visit around a festival. In January, islanders and visitors compete in ancient Hawaiian games at the Ka Molokai Makahiki Festival. The Molokai Ka Hula Piko, an annual daylong event in May, draws premier hula troupes, musicians, and storytellers. Long-distance canoe races from Molokai to Oahu are in late

September and early October. Although never crowded, the island is busier during these events—book accommodations and transportation six months in advance.

GETTING HERE AND AROUND

AIR TRAVEL

If you're flying in from the mainland United States or one of the Neighbor Islands, you must first make a stop in Honolulu. From there, it's a 25-minute trip to Molokai. Molokai's transportation hub is Hoolehua Airport, a tiny airstrip 8 miles west of Kaunakakai and about 18 miles east of Maunaloa. An even smaller airstrip serves the little community of Kalaupapa on the north shore.

From Hoolehua Airport it takes about 10 minutes to reach Kaunakakai and 25 minutes to reach the west end of the island by car. There's no public bus. A taxi will cost about $27 from the airport to Kaunakakai with Hele Mai Taxi. Shuttle service costs about $28 per person from Hoolehua Airport to Kaunakakai. For shuttle service, call Molokai Outdoors. Keep in mind, however, that it's difficult to visit the island without a rental car.

Contacts Hele Mai Taxi ☎ 808/336–0967, 808/646–9060 ⊕ www.molokaitaxi. com. **Molokai Outdoors** ☎ 808/553–4477, 877/553–4477 ⊕ www.molokai-outdoors.com.

CAR TRAVEL

If you want to explore Molokai from one end to the other, you must rent a car. With just a few main roads to choose from, it's a snap to drive around here. The gas stations are in Kaunakakai. Ask your rental agent for a free *Molokai Drive Guide.*

Alamo maintains a counter at Hoolehua Airport, and will pick you up at Kaunakakai Harbor. Make arrangements in advance, because the number of rental cars on Molokai is limited. Be sure to check the vehicle to make sure the four-wheel drive is working before departing from the agency. There is a $75 surcharge for taking a four-wheel-drive vehicle off-road. *See Travel Smart Maui for more information on renting a car and driving.*

Contact Alamo ☎ 888/826–6893 ⊕ www.alamo.com.

FERRY TRAVEL

The Molokai Ferry crosses the channel every day between Lahaina (Maui) and Kaunakakai. Boats depart from Lahaina daily at 6 pm and Monday to Saturday at 7:15 am, and from Kaunakakai daily at 4 pm and Monday to Saturday at 5:15 am. The 1½-hour trip takes passengers but not cars, so arrange ahead of time for a car rental or tour at the arrival point.

Contact Molokai Ferry ☎ 808/661–3392, 866/307–6524 ⊕ www.molokaiferry. com.

RESTAURANTS

Dining on Molokai is more a matter of eating. There are no fancy restaurants, just pleasant low-key places to eat out. Paddlers' Inn has the best dinner offerings. Other options include burgers, plate lunches, pizza, coffee shop–style sandwiches, and make-it-yourself fixings. *Prices in the reviews are the average cost of a main course at dinner or, if dinner is not served, at lunch.*

HOTELS

Molokai appeals most to travelers who appreciate genuine Hawaiian ambience rather than swanky digs. Most hotel and condominium properties range from adequate to funky. Visitors who want to lollygag on the beach should choose one of the condos or home rentals in West Molokai. Travelers who want to immerse themselves in the spirit of the island should seek out a condo or cottage, the closer to East Molokai the better. *Prices in the reviews are the lowest cost of a standard double room in high season. For expanded reviews, facilities, and current deals, visit Fodors.com.*

Destination Molokai Visitors Bureau. Ask about a brochure with up-to-date listings of vacation rentals operated by this company's members. ☎ *808/553–3876* ⊕ *www.gohawaii.com/molokai.*

Molokai Vacation Properties. This company handles condo rentals and can act as an informal concierge, including arranging for a rental car, during your stay. There is a three-night minimum on all properties. Private rental properties, from beach cottages to large estates, are also available. ☎ *800/367–2984, 808/553–8334* ⊕ *www.molokai-vacation-rental.net.*

COMMUNICATIONS

There are many locations on the island where cell-phone reception is difficult, if not impossible, to obtain. Your best bet for finding service is in Kaunakakai.

VISITOR INFORMATION

Contacts Destination Molokai Visitors Bureau ⊠ *12 Kamoi St., Ste. 200, Kaunakakai* ☎ *808/553–3876, 800/800–6367* ⊕ *www.gohawaii.com/molokai.* **Maui Visitors Bureau** ☎ *808/244–3530, 800/525–6284* ⊕ *www.visitmaui.com.*

EXPLORING MOLOKAI

The first thing to do on Molokai is to drive everywhere. It's a feat you can accomplish comfortably in two days. Depending on where you stay, spend one day exploring the west end and the other day exploring the east end. Basically you have one 40-mile west–east highway (two lanes, no stoplights) with three side trips: the nearly deserted little west-end town of Maunaloa; the Highway 470 drive (just a few miles) to the top of the north shore and the overlook of Kalaupapa Peninsula; and the short stretch of shops in Kaunakakai town. After you learn the general lay of the land, you can return to the places that interest you most. ■TIP→ **Directions on the island are often given as mauka (toward the mountains) and makai (toward the ocean).**

Kapuaiwa Coconut Grove in central Molokai is a survivor of royal plantings from the 19th century.

WEST MOLOKAI

Papohaku Beach is 17 miles west of the airport; Maunaloa is 10 miles west of the airport.

The remote beaches and rolling pastures on Molokai's west end are presided over by Mauna Loa, a dormant volcano, and a sleepy little former plantation town of the same name. Papohaku Beach, the Hawaiian Islands' second-longest white-sand beach, is one of the area's biggest draws. *For information about Papohaku Beach, see Beaches.*

GETTING HERE AND AROUND

The sometimes winding paved road through West Molokai begins at Highway 460 and ends at Kapukahehu Bay. The drive from Kaunakakai to Maunaloa is about 30 minutes.

WORTH NOTING

Kaluakoi. Although the late-1960s Kaluakoi Hotel and Golf Club is closed and forlorn, some nice condos and a gift shop are operating nearby. Kepuhi Beach, the white-sand beach along the coast, is still worth a visit. ⊠ *Kaluakoi Rd.*

Maunaloa. Built in 1923, this quiet community at the western end of the highway once housed workers for the island's pineapple plantation. Many businesses have closed, but it's the last place to buy supplies when you're exploring the nearby beaches. If you're in the neighborhood, stop at Maunaloa's Big Wind Kite Factory. You'll want to talk story with Uncle Jonathan, who has been making and flying kites here for more than three decades. ⊠ *Maunaloa Hwy.*

CENTRAL MOLOKAI

Kaunakakai is 8 miles southeast of the airport.

Most residents live centrally, near the island's one and only true town, Kaunakakai. It's just about the only place on the island to get food and supplies. It *is* Molokai. Go into the shops along and around Ala Malama Street. Buy stuff. Talk with people. Take your time, and you'll really enjoy being a visitor. Also in this area, on the north side, are Coffees of Hawaii, a 500-acre coffee plantation, and the Kalaupapa National Historical Park, one of the island's most notable sights.

MOLOKAI VIBES

Molokai is one of the last places in Hawaii where most of the residents are living an authentic rural lifestyle and wish to retain it. Many oppose developing the island for visitors or outsiders, so you won't find much to cater to your needs, but if you take time and talk to the locals, you will find them hospitable and friendly. Some may even invite you home with them. It's a safe place, but don't interrupt private parties on the beach or trespass on private property. Consider yourself a guest in someone's house, rather than a customer.

GETTING HERE AND AROUND

Central Molokai is the hub of the island's road system, and Kaunakakai is the commercial center. Watch for kids, dogs, and people crossing the street in downtown Kaunakakai.

TOP ATTRACTIONS

Coffees of Hawaii. Visit the headquarters of a 500-acre Molokai coffee plantation, where the espresso bar serves freshly made sandwiches, *lilikoi* (passion fruit) cheesecake, and java in artful ways. The "Mocha Mama" is a special Molokai treat. This is the place to pick up additions to your picnic lunch if you're headed to Kalaupapa. The Blue Monkey gift shop offers a wide range of Molokai handicrafts, memorabilia, and, of course, coffee. Live music is performed on the covered lanai every Sunday from 4 to 6 pm. ⊠ *1630 Farrington Hwy., off Rte. 470, Kualapuu* ☎ *877/322–3276, 808/567–9490* ⊕ *www.coffeesofhawaii. com* ⊙ *Café and gift shop weekdays 6 am–5 pm, Sat. 8–8, Sun. 8–5.*

Fodor's Choice ★ **Kalaupapa.** *See photo feature, Kalaupapa Peninsula: A Tale of Tragedy and Triumph.*

Fodor's Choice ★ **Kalaupapa Guided Mule Tour.** Mount a friendly, well-trained mule and wind along a thrilling 3-mile, 26-switchback trail to reach the town of Kalaupapa, which was once home to patients with leprosy who were exiled to this remote spot. The path was built in 1886 as a supply route for the settlement below. Once in Kalaupapa, you take a guided tour of the town and enjoy a light picnic lunch. The trail traverses some of the highest sea cliffs in the world, and views are spectacular. ■TIP➔ Only those in good shape should attempt the ride, as two hours each way on a mule can take its toll. You must be at least 16 years old and weigh no more than 249 pounds; pregnant women are not allowed. The entire event takes seven hours. Make reservations ahead of time, as space is limited. The same outfit can arrange for you to hike down or fly in. No

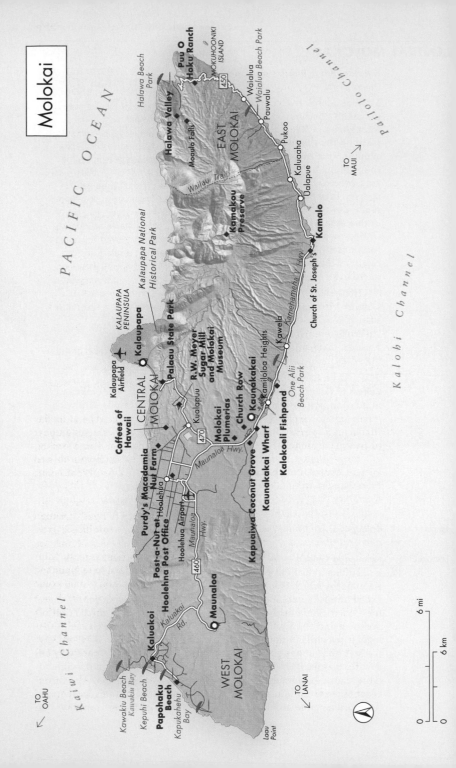

one is allowed in the park or on the trail without booking a tour; hikers must be down in the park by 10 am. *See Kalaupapa Peninsula: A Tale of Tragedy and Triumph photo feature for more information.* ✉ *100 Kalae Hwy., Kualapuu* ☎ *808/567–6088, 800/567–7550* ⊕ *www.muleride. com* 💲 *$199* ⊙ *Mon.–Sat. at 8 am (returns at 3 pm).*

Kaunakakai. Central Molokai's main town looks like a classic 1940s movie set. Along the one-block main drag is a cultural grab bag of restaurants and shops, and many people are friendly and willing to supply directions. The preferred dress is shorts and a tank top, and no one wears anything fancier than a cotton skirt or aloha shirt. ✉ *Rte. 460, 3 blocks north of Kaunakakai Wharf.*

HAWAII'S FIRST SAINT

A long-revered figure on Molokai and in Hawaii, Father Damien, who cared for the desperate patients at Kalaupapa, was elevated to sainthood in 2009. Plans call for a small museum and bookstore in his honor in Kaunakakai, and refurbishment of the three churches in the Catholic parish is currently underway. Visitors who cannot visit Kalaupapa can find information on St. Damien at the Damien Center in Kaunakakai, and may worship at Our Lady of Seven Sorrows (just west of Kaunakakai) or at St. Vincent Ferrer in Maunaloa.

QUICK BITES

Kamoi Snack-n-Go. Stop for some of Dave's Hawaiian Ice Cream at the Kamoi Snack-n-Go. Sit in the refreshing breeze on one of the benches outside for a Molokai rest stop. Snacks, crack seed, cold drinks, and water are also available. ✉ *28 Kamoi St.* ☎ *808/553–3742.*

Molokai Plumerias. The sweet smell of plumeria surrounds you at this ten-acre orchard containing thousands of these fragrant trees. Purchase a lei to go, or for $25 owner Dick Wheeler will give you a basket, set you free to pick your own blossoms, and then teach you how to string your own lei. ✉ *1342 Maunaloa Hwy.* ☎ *808/553–3391* ⊕ *www. molokaiplumerias.com* ⊙ *Weekdays 9:30–noon.*

Palaau State Park. One of the island's few formal recreation areas, this 233-acre retreat sits at a 1,000-foot elevation. A short path through an ironwood forest leads to **Kalaupapa Lookout,** a magnificent overlook with views of the town of Kalaupapa and the 1,664-foot-high sea cliffs protecting it. Informative plaques have facts about leprosy, Saint Damien, and the colony. The park is also the site of **Kaule O Nanahoa** (the phallus of Nanahoa)—where women in old Hawaii would come to the rock to enhance their fertility, and it is said some still do. It is a sacred site, so be respectful and don't deface the boulders. The park is well maintained, with trails, camping facilities, restrooms, and picnic tables. To get here, take Highway 460 west from Kaunakakai and then head *mauka* (toward the mountains) on Highway 470, which ends at the park. ✉ *Hwy. 470* 💲 *Free* ⊙ *Daily dawn–dusk.*

Purdy's Macadamia Nut Farm. Molokai's only working macadamia-nut farm is open for educational tours hosted by the knowledgeable and entertaining owner. A family business in Hoolehua, the farm takes up

DID YOU KNOW?

The Kalaupapa Guided Mule Tour down the 3-mile trail to Kalaupapa includes multiple switchbacks near high sea cliffs. The views are stunning, but this mule ride is not for the faint of heart or out of shape.

1½ acres with a flourishing grove of 50 original trees that are more than 90 years old, as well as several hundred younger trees. The nuts taste delicious right out of the shell, home roasted, or dipped in macadamia-blossom honey. Look for Purdy's sign behind Molokai High School. ⊠ *Lihi Pali Ave., Hoolehua* ☎ *808/ 567–6601* ⊕ *www.molokai-aloha. com/macnuts* ⌨ *Free* ☉ *Weekdays 9:30–3:30, Sat. 10–2.*

WORD OF MOUTH

"My sons and I spent a week on Molokai and we talk about it all the time. We spent days driving around and just enjoying being part of the local lifestyle. After dinner we would get ice cream at the drive-in, then watch the locals play baseball. Within two nights we were part of their families. I think of all the Hawaiian Islands— and I have visited all of them but Lanai—Molokai is my favorite."

—leanna

R. W. Meyer Sugar Mill and Molokai Museum. Built in 1877, the three-room, fully restored sugar mill has been reconstructed as a testament to Molokai's agricultural history. It is located next to the Molokai Museum and is usually included in the museum tour. Several interesting machines from the past are on display, including a mule-driven cane crusher and a steam engine. The museum contains changing exhibits on the island's early history and has a gift shop. ⊠ *Rte. 470, 2 miles southwest of Palaau State Park, Kualapuu* ☎ *808/567–6436* ⌨ *$5* ☉ *Mon.–Sat. 10–2.*

WORTH NOTING

Church Row. Standing together along the highway are several houses of worship with primarily native Hawaiian congregations. Notice the unadorned, boxlike architecture so similar to missionary homes. ⊠ *Rte. 460, 5½ miles south of airport.*

Kapuaiwa Coconut Grove. From far away this spot looks like a sea of coconut trees. Closer up you can see that the tall, stately palms are planted in long rows leading down to the sea. This is a remnant of one of the last surviving royal groves planted for Prince Lot, who ruled Hawaii as King Kamehameha V from 1863 until his death in 1872. Watch for falling coconuts. ⊠ *Rte. 460, 5½ miles south of airport.*

Kaunakakai Wharf. Once bustling with barges exporting pineapples, these docks now host visiting boats, the ferry from Lahaina, and the twice-weekly barge from Oahu. The wharf is also the starting point for fishing, sailing, snorkeling, whale-watching, and scuba diving excursions. It's a nice place at sunset to watch fish rippling on the water. To get here, take Kaunakakai Place, which dead-ends at the wharf. ⊠ *Rte. 450, at Ala Malama St.*

Post-A-Nut at Hoolehua Post Office. At this small, rural post office you can mail a coconut to anywhere in the world. Postmaster Gary Lam provides the coconuts and colored markers. You decorate and address your coconut, and Gary affixes eye-catching stamps on it from his extensive collection. Costs vary according to destination, but for domestic addresses they start around $10. The office is open weekdays 8:30 am to 4 pm; closed 12 to 12:30 for lunch. ⊠ *69-2 Puupeelua Ave., Hoolehua* ☎ *808/567–6144.*

DID YOU KNOW?

Taro, grown in engineered ponds called *loi,* is a Hawaiian food staple; the pounded root is used to make *poi.* The taro plant is revered as an ancestor of the Hawaiian people.

EAST MOLOKAI

Halawa Valley is 36 miles northeast of the airport.

On the beautifully undeveloped east end of Molokai you can find ancient fishponds, a magnificent coastline, splendid ocean views, and a fertile valley that's been inhabited for 14 centuries. The eastern uplands are flanked by Mt. Kamakou, the island's highest point at 4,961 feet and home to the Nature Conservancy's Kamakou Preserve. Mist hangs over waterfall-filled valleys, and ancient lava cliffs jut out into the sea.

GETTING HERE AND AROUND

Driving the east end is a scenic adventure, but the road narrows and becomes curvy after the 20-mile marker. Take your time, especially in the seaside lane, and watch for oncoming traffic. Driving at night is not recommended.

TOP ATTRACTIONS

Fodor's Choice ★ **Halawa Valley.** Hawaiians lived in this valley as far back as AD 650, making it the oldest recorded habitation on Molokai. Inhabitants grew taro and fished until the 1960s, when an enormous flood wiped out the taro patches and forced old-timers to abandon their traditional lifestyle. Now, a new generation of Hawaiians has begun the challenging task of restoring the taro fields. Much of this work involves rerouting streams to flow through carefully engineered level ponds called *loi.* The taro plants, with their big, dancing leaves, grow in the submerged mud of the *loi,* where the water is always cool and flowing. Hawaiians believe that the taro plant is their ancestor and revere it both as sustenance and as a spiritual necessity. The Solatorio Ohana (family) leads hikes through the valley, which is home to two sacrificial temples, many historic sites, and the trail to **Moaula Falls,** a 250-foot cascade. The $60 fee supports the restoration efforts. The 3.4-mile round-trip hike is rated intermediate to advanced and includes two moderate river crossings. ✉ *Eastern end of Rte. 450* ☎ *808/551–5538, 808/551–1055* ⊕ *www.halawavalleymolokai.com* ✉ *$60.*

OFF THE BEATEN PATH **Kamakou Preserve.** Tucked away on the slopes of Mt. Kamakou, Molokai's highest peak, this 2,774-acre rain-forest preserve is a dazzling wonderland full of wet *ohia* (hardwood trees of the myrtle family, with red blossoms called *lehua* flowers) forests, rare bogs, and native trees and wildlife. Guided hikes, limited to eight people, are held one Saturday each month between March and October. Reserve well in advance. You can visit the park without a tour, but you need a good four-wheel-drive vehicle (hard to find on the island), and it's not recommended. If you are determined to go it alone, the Nature Conservancy requests that you sign in at the office and get directions first. The office is at Molokai

6

Industrial Park, about 3 miles west of Kaunakakai. ⊠ *23 Pueo Pl., Kualapuu* ☎ *808/553–5236* ⊕ *www.nature.org* ⌧ *Free.*

WORTH NOTING

Kalokoeli Fishpond. With its narrow rock walls arching out from the shoreline, Kalokoeli is typical of the numerous fishponds that define southern Molokai. Many were built around the 13th century under the direction of powerful chiefs. This early type of aquaculture, particular to Hawaii, exemplifies the ingenuity of native Hawaiians. One or more openings were left in the wall, where gates called *makaha* were installed. These gates allowed seawater and tiny fish to enter the enclosed pond but kept larger predators out. The tiny fish would then grow too big to get out. At one time there were 62 fishponds around Molokai's coast. ⊠ *Rte. 450, 6 miles east of Kaunakakai.*

Kamalo. A natural harbor used by small cargo ships during the 19th century and a favorite fishing spot for locals, Kamalo is also the location of the **Church of St. Joseph's,** a tiny white church built by Saint Damien of the Kalaupapa colony in the 1880s. It's a state historic site and place of pilgrimage. The door is often open; if it is, slip inside and sign the guest book. The congregation keeps the church in beautiful condition. ⊠ *Rte. 450, 11 miles east of Kaunakakai.*

QUICK
BITES

Manae Goods & Grindz. The best place to grab a snack or picnic supplies is this store, 16 miles east of Kaunakakai. It's the only place on the east end where you can find essentials such as ice and bread, and not-so-essentials such as seafood plate lunches, bentos, burgers, and shakes. Try a refreshing smoothie while here. ⊠ *Rte. 450* ☎ *808/558–8498, 808/558–8186.*

Puu O Hoku Ranch. A 14,000-acre private ranch in the highlands of East Molokai, Puu O Hoku was developed in the 1930s by wealthy industrialist Paul Fagan. Route 450 ambles right through this rural treasure with its pastures and grazing horses and cattle. As you drive slowly along, enjoy the splendid views of Maui and Lanai. The small island off the coast is Mokuhooniki, a favorite spot among visiting humpback whales, and a nesting seabird sanctuary. The ranch has limited accommodations, too. ⊠ *Rte. 450, 25 miles east of Kaunakakai* ☎ *808/558–8109* ⊕ *www.puuohoku.com.*

BEACHES

Molokai's unique geography gives the island plenty of drama and spectacle along the shorelines but not so many places for seaside basking and bathing. The long north shore consists mostly of towering cliffs that plunge directly into the sea and is inaccessible except by boat, and even then only in summer. Much of the south shore is enclosed by a huge reef, which stands as far as a mile offshore and blunts the action of the waves. Within this reef you can find a thin strip of sand, but the water here is flat, shallow, and at times clouded with silt. This reef area is best suited to wading, pole fishing, kayaking, or learning how to windsurf.

Continued on page 583

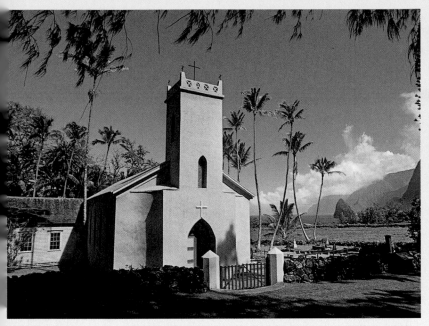

Father Damien's Church, St. Philomena

KALAUPAPA PENINSULA: TRAGEDY & TRIUMPH

For those who crave drama, there is no better destination than Molokai's Kalaupapa Peninsula—but it wasn't always so. For 100 years this remote strip of land was "the loneliest place on earth," a feared place of exile for those suffering from leprosy (now known as Hansen's Disease).

The world's tallest sea cliffs, rain-chiseled valleys, and tiny islets dropped like exclamation points along the coast emphasize the passionate history of the Kalaupapa Peninsula. Today, it's impossible to visit this stunning National Historical Park and view the evidence of human ignorance and heroism without responding. You'll be tugged by emotions—awe and disbelief for starters. But you'll also glimpse humorous facets of everyday life in a small town. Whatever your experience here may be, chances are you'll return home feeling that the journey to present-day Kalaupapa is one you'll never forget.

THE SETTLEMENT'S EARLY DAYS

Father Damien with patients outside St. Philomena church.

IN 1865, PRESSURED BY FOREIGN RESIDENTS, the Hawaiian Kingdom passed "An Act to Prevent the Spread of Leprosy." Anyone showing symptoms of the disease was to be permanently exiled to Kalawao, the north end of Kalaupapa Peninsula—a spot walled in on three sides by nearly impassable cliffs. The peninsula had been home to a fishing community for 900 years, but those inhabitants were evicted and the entire peninsula declared settlement land.

The first 12 patients were arrested and sent to Kalawao in 1866. People of all ages and many nationalities followed, taken from their homes and dumped on the isolated shore. Officials thought the patients could become self-sufficient, fishing and farming sweet potatoes in the stream-fed valleys. That was not the case. Settlement conditions were deplorable.

Belgian missionary Father Damien was one of four priests who volunteered to serve the leprosy settlement at Kalawao on a rotating basis. There were 600 patients at the time. His turn came in 1873; when it was up, he refused to leave. Father Damien is credited with turning the settlement from a merciless exile to a place where hope could be heard in the voices of his recruited choir. He organized the building of the St. Philomena church (and other churches on the island), nearly 300 houses, and a home for boys. A vocal advocate for his adopted community, he pestered the church for supplies, administered medicine, and oversaw the nearly daily funerals. Sixteen years after his arrival, in 1889, he died from the effects of leprosy, having contracted the disease during his service. Known around the world for his sacrifice, Father Damien was beatified by the Catholic Church in 1995, and canonized in 2009.

Mother Marianne Cope heard of the mission while working at a hospital in Syracuse, New York. Along with six other Franciscan Sisters, she volunteered to work with those with leprosy in the Islands. They sailed to the Kalaupapa Peninsula in 1888. Like the Father, the Sisters were considered saints for their work. Mother Marianne stayed at Kalaupapa until her death in 1918; she was beatified by the Catholic Church in 2005, and canonized in 2012.

VISITING KALAUPAPA TODAY

Kalaupapa Peninsula

FROZEN IN TIME, Kalaupapa's one-horse town has bittersweet charm. Signs posted here and there remind residents when the bankers will be there (once monthly), when to place annual barge orders for nonperishable items, and what's happening around town. It has the nostalgic, almost naive ambience expected from a place almost wholly segregated from modern life.

About 8 former patients remain at Kalaupapa (by choice, as the disease is controlled by drugs and the patients are no longer carriers), but many have traveled to other parts of the world and all are over the age of 70. They never lost their chutzpah, however. Having survived a lifetime of prejudice and misunderstanding, Kalaupapa's residents haven't been willing to be pushed around any longer—in past years, several made the journey to Honolulu from time to time to testify before the state legislature about matters concerning them.

To get a feel for what residents' lives were like, visit the National Park Service Web site (⊕ *www.nps.gov/kala/history culture/*) or buy one of several heartbreaking memoirs at the park's library-turned-bookstore.

THE TRUTH ABOUT HANSEN'S DISEASE

■ A cure for leprosy has been available since 1941. Multidrug therapy, a rapid cure, has been available since 1981.

■ With treatment, none of the disabilities traditionally associated with leprosy need occur.

■ Most people have a natural immunity to leprosy. Only 5% of the world's population is even susceptible to the disease.

■ There are still about 228,000 new cases of leprosy each year; the majority are in India.

■ All new cases of leprosy are treated on an outpatient basis.

■ The term "leper" is offensive and should not be used. It is appropriate to say "a person is affected by leprosy" or "by Hansen's Disease."

GETTING HERE

The Kalaupapa Trail and Peninsula are all part of Kalaupapa National Historical Park (☎ 808/567–6802 ⊕ www.nps.gov/kala/), which is open every day but Sunday for tours only. Keep in mind, there are no public facilities (except an occasional restroom) anywhere in the park. Pack your own food and water, as well as light rain gear, sunscreen, and bug repellent.

TO HIKE OR TO RIDE?

There are two ways to get down the Kalaupapa Trail: in your hiking boots, or on a mule.

Hiking: Hiking allows you to travel at your own pace and stop frequently for photos—not an option on the mule ride. The hike takes about 1 hour down and 1½ hours up. You must book a tour in order to access the trail. **Damien Tours** ☎ 808/567–6171.

Kalaupapa Beach & Peninsula

THE KALAUPAPA TRAIL

Unless you fly (flights are available through Makani Kai Air [☎ 808/834–1111 ⊕ www.makanikaiair.com]), the only way into Kalaupapa National Historical Park is on a dizzying switchback trail. The switchbacks are numbered—26 in all—and descend 1,700 feet to sea level in just under 3 miles. The steep trail is more of a staircase, and most of the trail is shaded. Keep in mind, however, that footing is uneven and there is little to keep you from pitching over the side. If you don't mind heights, you can stare straight down to the ocean for most of the way. *Access Kalaupapa Trail off Hwy. 470 near the Kalaupapa Overlook. There is ample parking near end of Hwy. 470.*

Mule-Skinning: You'll be amazed as your mule trots up to the edge of the switchback, swivels on two legs, and completes a sharp-angled turn—26 times. The guides tell you the mules can do this in their sleep, but that doesn't take the fear out of the first few switchbacks. Make reservations well in advance. **Kalaupapa Guided Mule Tour** ☎ 808/567–6088 or 808/567–7550 ⊕ www.muleride.com.

IMPORTANT INFORMATION

Daily tours are offered Monday through Saturday through Damien Tours or the Kalaupapa Guided Mule Tour. Be sure to reserve in advance. Visitors ages 16 and under are not allowed at Kalaupapa, and photographing patients without their written permission is forbidden.

The big, fat, sandy beaches lie along the west end. The largest of these—the second largest in the Islands—is Papohaku Beach, which fronts a grassy park shaded by a grove of *kiawe* (mesquite) trees. These stretches of west-end sand are generally unpopulated. At the east end, where the road hugs the sinuous shoreline, you encounter a number of pocket-size beaches in rocky coves, good for snorkeling. Don't venture too far out, however, or you can find yourself caught in dangerous currents. The island's east-end road ends at Halawa Valley with its unique double bay, which is not recommended for swimming.

If you need beach gear, head to Molokai Fish and Dive at the west end of Kaunakakai's only commercial strip, or rent kayaks from Molokai Outdoors at Kaunakakai Wharf.

> ## BEACH SAFETY
>
> Unlike protected shorelines such as Kaanapali on Maui, the coasts of Molokai are exposed to rough sea channels and dangerous rip currents. The ocean tends to be calmer in the morning and in summer. No matter what the time, however, always study the sea before entering. Unless the water is placid and the wave action minimal, it's best to stay on shore, even though locals may be in the water. Don't underestimate the power of the ocean. Protect yourself with sunblock. Cool breezes make it easy to underestimate the power of the sun as well.

Department of Parks, Land and Natural Resources. All of Hawaii's beaches are free and public. None of the beaches on Molokai have telephones or lifeguards, and they're all under the jurisdiction of the Department of Parks, Land and Natural Resources. ☎ *808/587–0300* ⊕ *www. hawaiistateparks.org.*

WEST MOLOKAI

Molokai's west end looks across a wide channel to the island of Oahu. Crescent-shaped, this cup of coastline holds the island's best sandy beaches as well as the sunniest weather. Remember: all beaches are public property, even those that front developments, and most have public access roads. *Beaches below are listed from north to south.*

Kawakiu Beach. Seclusion is yours at this remote beach, accessible by four-wheel-drive vehicle (through a gate that is sometimes locked) or a 45-minute walk. The white-sand beach is beautiful. To get here, drive to Paniolo Hale off Kaluakoi Road and look for a dirt road off to the right. Park here and hike in or, with a four-wheel-drive vehicle, drive along the dirt road to beach. ⚠ **Rocks and undertow make swimming extremely dangerous at times, so use caution. Amenities:** none. **Best for:** solitude. ⊠ *Off Kaluakoi Rd., Maunaloa.*

Kepuhi Beach. The Kaluakoi Hotel is closed, but its half mile of ivory sand is still accessible. The beach shines against the turquoise sea, black outcroppings of lava, and magenta bougainvillea blossoms. When the sea is perfectly calm lava ridges in the water make good snorkeling spots. With any surf at all, however, the water around these rocky places churns and foams, wiping out visibility and making it difficult to avoid

Lava ridges make Kepuhi Beach beautiful, but swimming is hard unless the water is calm.

being slammed into the jagged rocks. **Amenities:** showers; toilets. **Best for:** snorkeling; walking. ⊠ *Kaluakoi Rd., Maunaloa.*

FodorsChoice ★ **Papohaku Beach.** One of the most sensational beaches in Hawaii, Papohaku is a 3-mile-long strip of light golden sand, the longest of its kind on the island. ■**TIP→ Swimming is not recommended, as there's a dangerous undertow except on exceptionally calm summer days.** There's so much sand here that Honolulu once purchased barge loads of the stuff to replenish Waikiki Beach. A shady beach park just inland is the site of the Ka Hula Piko Festival, held each year in May. The park is also a great sunset-facing spot for a rustic afternoon barbecue. A park ranger patrols the area periodically. **Amenities:** showers; toilets. **Best for:** sunset; walking. ⊠ *Kaluakoi Rd., 2 miles south of the former Kaluakoi Hotel, Maunaloa.*

Kapukahehu Bay. The sandy protected cove is usually completely deserted on weekdays but can fill up when the surf is up. The water in the cove is clear and shallow with plenty of well-worn rocky areas. These conditions make for excellent snorkeling, swimming, and bodyboarding on calm days. Locals like to surf in a break called Dixie's or Dixie Maru. **Amenities:** none. **Best for:** snorkeling; surfing; swimming. ⊠ *End of Kaluakoi Rd., 3½ miles south of Papohaku Beach, Maunaloa.*

CENTRAL MOLOKAI

The south shore is mostly a huge, reef-walled expanse of flat saltwater edged with a thin strip of gritty sand and stones, mangrove swamps, and the amazing system of fishponds constructed by the chiefs of ancient

Molokai. From this shore you can look out across glassy water to see people standing on top of the sea—actually, way out on top of the reef—casting fishing lines into the distant waves. This is not a great area for beaches but is a good place to snorkel or wade in the shallows.

One Alii Beach Park. Clear, close views of Maui and Lanai across the Pailolo Channel dominate One Alii Beach Park (*One* is pronounced *o-nay,* not *won*), the only well-maintained beach park on the island's south-central shore. Molokai folks gather here for family reunions and community celebrations; the park's tightly trimmed expanse of lawn could almost accommodate the entire island's population. Swimming within the reef is perfectly safe, but don't expect to catch any waves. Nearby is the restored One Alii fishpond. **Amenities:** showers; toilets. **Best for:** partiers; swimming. ⊠ *Rte. 450, east of Hotel Molokai, Kaunakakai.*

EAST MOLOKAI

The east end unfolds as a coastal drive with turnouts for tiny cove beaches—good places for snorkeling, shore fishing, or scuba exploring. Rocky little Mokuhooniki Island marks the eastern point of the island and serves as a nursery for humpback whales in winter and nesting seabirds in spring. The road loops around the east end, then descends and ends at Halawa Valley.

Halawa Beach Park. The vigorous water that gouged the steep, spectacular Halawa Valley also carved out two adjacent bays. Accumulations of coarse sand and river rock have created some protected pools that are good for wading or floating around. You might see surfers, but it's not wise to entrust your safety to the turbulent open ocean along this coast. Most people come here to hang out and absorb the beauty of Halawa Valley. The valley itself is private property, so do not wander without a guide *(See East Molokai Exploring).* **Amenities:** toilets. **Best for:** solitude. ⊠ *End of Rte. 450, Kaunakakai.*

Waialua Beach Park. Also known as Twenty Mile Beach, this arched stretch of sand leads to one of the most popular snorkeling spots on the island. The water here, protected by the flanks of the little bay, is often so clear and shallow that even from land you can watch fish swimming among the coral heads. Watch out for traffic when you enter the highway. ■TIP→ **This is a pleasant place to stop on the drive around the east end. Amenities:** none. **Best for:** snorkeling; swimming. ⊠ *Rte. 450, near mile marker 20.*

WATER SPORTS AND TOURS

Molokai's shoreline topography limits opportunities for water sports. Sea cliffs dominate the north shore; the south shore is largely encased by a huge, taming reef. ⚠ **Open-sea access at west-end and east-end beaches should be used only by experienced ocean swimmers, and then with caution, because seas are rough, especially in winter.** Generally speaking, there's no one around—certainly not lifeguards—if you get into trouble. For this reason alone, guided excursions are recommended.

DID YOU KNOW?

Long, sandy, and golden, Papohaku Beach on Molokai's west end is one of Hawaii's most spectacular for sunning and sunsets. The ocean is generally calmer in summer and in the morning.

At least be sure to ask for advice from outfitters or residents. Two kinds of water activities predominate: kayaking within the reef area, and open-sea excursions on charter boats, most of which tie up at Kaunakakai Wharf.

BODY BOARDING AND BODYSURFING

You rarely see people body boarding or bodysurfing on Molokai, and the only surfing is for advanced wave riders. The best spots for body boarding, when conditions are safe (occasional summer mornings), are the west-end beaches. Another option is to seek out waves at the east end around mile marker 20.

DEEP-SEA FISHING

For Molokai people, as in days of yore, the ocean is more of a larder than a playground. It's common to see residents fishing along the shoreline or atop South Shore Reef, using poles or lines. Deep-sea fishing by charter boat is a great Molokai adventure. The sea channels here, though often rough and windy, provide gorgeous views of several islands. Big fish are plentiful in these waters, especially mahimahi, marlin, and various kinds of tuna. Generally speaking, boat captains will customize the outing to your interests, share a lot of information about the island, and let you keep some or all of your catch.

EQUIPMENT

Molokai Fish and Dive. If you'd like to try your hand at fishing, you can rent or buy equipment and ask for advice here. ⊠ *53 Ala Malama St., Kaunakakai* ☎ *808/553–5926* ⊕ *molokaifishanddive.com.*

BOATS AND CHARTERS

Alyce C. This 31-foot cruiser runs excellent sportfishing excursions in the capable hands of Captain Joe. The cost for the six-passenger boat is $550 for a full-day trip, $450 for four to five hours. Gear is provided. It's a rare day when you don't snag at least one memorable fish. ⊠ *Kaunakakai Wharf, Kaunakakai Pl., Kaunakakai* ☎ *808/558–8377* ⊕ *www.alycecsportfishing.com.*

Fun Hogs Sportfishing. Trim and speedy, the 27-foot flybridge boat named *Ahi* offers four-hour ($450), six-hour ($550), and eight-hour ($600) sportfishing excursions. Skipper Mike Holmes also provides one-way or round-trip fishing expeditions to Lanai, as well as sunset cruises and whale-watching trips in winter. ⊠ *Kaunakakai Wharf, Kaunakakai Pl., Kaunakakai* ☎ *808/567–6789, 808/336–0047* ⊕ *www.molokaifishing. com.*

Molokai Action Adventures. Walter Naki has traveled (and fished) all over the globe. He will create customized fishing expeditions and gladly share his wealth of experience. He will also take you to remote beaches for a day of swimming. If you want to explore the north side under the great sea cliffs, this is the way to go. His 21-foot *Boston Whaler* is usually seen in the east end at the mouth of Halawa Valley. ⊠ *Kaunakakai* ☎ *808/558–8184.*

KAYAKING

Molokai's south shore is enclosed by the largest reef system in the United States—an area of shallow, protected sea that stretches over 30 miles. This reef gives inexperienced kayakers an unusually safe, calm environment for shoreline exploring. ⚠ **Outside the reef, Molokai waters are often rough, and strong winds can blow you out to sea. Kayakers out here should be strong, experienced, and cautious.**

BEST SPOTS

South Shore Reef. Inside the South Shore Reef area is superb for flat-water kayaking any day of the year. It's best to rent a kayak from Molokai Outdoors in Kaunakakai and slide into the water from Kaunakakai Wharf. Get out in the morning before the wind picks up and paddle east, exploring the ancient Hawaiian fishponds. When you turn around to return, the wind will usually give you a push home. ⊠ *Kaunakakai.*

EQUIPMENT, LESSONS, AND TOURS

Molokai Fish and Dive. At the west end of Kaunakakai's commercial strip, this all-around outfitter offers guided kayak excursions inside the South Shore Reef. One excursion paddles through a mangrove forest and explores a hidden ancient fishpond. If the wind starts blowing hard, the company will tow you back with its boat. The fee is $69 for the half-day trip, which includes sodas and water. ⊠ *53 Ala Malama St., Kaunakakai* ☎ *808/553–5926* ⊕ *molokaifishanddive.com.*

Molokai Outdoors. This is the place to rent a kayak for exploring on your own. Kayaks rent for $42 per day or $210 per week, and extra paddles are available. ⊠ *9 Hio Pl., Kaunakakai* ☎ *808/553–4477, 877/553–4477* ⊕ *www.molokai-outdoors.com.*

SCUBA DIVING

Molokai Fish and Dive is the only PADI-certified dive company on Molokai. Shoreline access for divers is extremely limited, even nonexistent in winter. Boat diving is the way to go. Without guidance, visiting divers can easily find themselves in risky situations with wicked currents. Proper guidance, though, opens an undersea world rarely seen.

Molokai Fish and Dive. Owners Tim and Susan Forsberg can fill you in on local dive sites, rent you the gear, or hook you up with one of their PADI-certified guides to take you to the island's best underwater spots. Their 32-foot dive boat, the *Ama Lua,* can take eight divers and their gear. Two-tank dives lasting about five hours cost $145. Three-tank dives lasting around six hours cost $295. They know the best blue holes and underwater-cave systems, and can take you swimming with hammerhead sharks. ⊠ *53 Ala Malama St., Kaunakakai* ☎ *808/553–5926* ⊕ *molokaifishanddive.com.*

SNORKELING

During the times when swimming is safe—mainly in summer—just about every beach on Molokai offers good snorkeling along the lava outcroppings in the island's clean and pristine waters. Rough in winter,

Kepuhi Beach is a prime spot in summer. Certain spots inside the South Shore Reef are also worth checking out.

BEST SPOTS

During the summer, **Kepuhi Beach,** on Molokai's west end, offers excellent snorkeling opportunities. The ½-mile-long stretch has plenty of rocky nooks that swirl with sea life. Take Kaluakoi Road all the way to the west end, park at the now-closed Kaluakoi Resort, and walk to the beach. Avoid Kepuhi Beach in winter, as the sea is rough here.

At **Waialua Beach Park,** on Molokai's east end, you'll find a thin curve of sand that rims a sheltered little bay loaded with coral heads and aquatic life. The water here is shallow—sometimes so shallow that you bump into the underwater landscape—and it's crystal clear. Pull off the road near mile marker 20.

EQUIPMENT AND TOURS

Rent snorkel sets from either Molokai Outdoors or Molokai Fish and Dive in Kaunakakai. Rental fees are nominal—$7 to $10 a day. All the charter boats carry snorkel gear and include dive stops.

Fun Hogs Sportfishing. Mike Holmes, captain of the 27-foot *Ahi*, knows the island waters intimately, likes to have fun, and is willing to arrange any type of excursion—for example, one dedicated entirely to snorkeling. His two-hour snorkel trips leave early in the morning and explore rarely seen fish and turtle sites outside the reef. Bring your own food and drinks; the trips cost $70 per person. ⊠ *Kaunakakai Wharf, Kaunakakai Pl., Kaunakakai* ☎ *808/567–6789, 808/336–0047* ⊕ *www.molokaifishing.com.*

Molokai Fish and Dive. Climb aboard a 31-foot twin-hull PowerCat for a snorkeling trip to Molokai's pristine barrier reef. Trips cost $79 per person and include equipment, water, and soft drinks. ⊠ *53 Ala Malama St., Kaunakakai* ☎ *808/553–5926* ⊕ *www.molokaifishanddive.com.*

WHALE-WATCHING

Although Maui gets all the credit for the local wintering humpback-whale population, the big cetaceans also come to Molokai from December to April. Mokuhooniki Island at the east end serves as a whale nursery and courting ground, and the whales pass back and forth along the south shore. This being Molokai, whale-watching here will never involve floating amid a group of boats all ogling the same whale.

BOATS AND CHARTERS

Alyce C. Although this six-passenger sportfishing boat is usually busy hooking mahimahi and marlin, the captain will gladly take you on a three-hour excursion to admire the humpback whales. The price, around $75 per person, is based on the number of people in your group. ⊠ *Kaunakakai Wharf, Kaunakakai Pl., Kaunakakai* ☎ *808/558–8377* ⊕ *www.alycecsportfishing.com.*

Ama Lua. The crew of this 31-foot dive boat, which holds up to 12 passengers, is respectful of the whales and the laws that protect them. A two-hour whale-watching trip is $79 per person; it departs from Kaunakakai Wharf at 7 am from December to April. Call Molokai

Bikers on Molokai can explore the north-shore sea cliffs overlooking the Kalaupapa Peninsula.

Fish and Dive for reservations. ✉ *53 Ala Malama St., Kaunakakai* ☎ *808/553–5926, 808/552–0184* ⊕ *molokaifishanddive.com.*

Fun Hogs Sportfishing. The *Ahi*, a flybridge sportfishing boat, takes you on 2½-hour whale-watching trips in the morning from December to April. The cost is $70 per person. Bring your own snacks and drinks. ✉ *Kaunakakai Wharf, Kaunakakai Pl., Kaunakakai* ☎ *808/567–6789, 808/336–0047* ⊕ *www.molokaifishing.com.*

GOLF, HIKING, AND OUTDOOR ACTIVITIES

Activity vendors in Kaunakakai are a good source of information on outdoor adventures on Molokai. For a mellow round of golf, head to the island's only golf course, Ironwood Hills, where you'll likely share the green with local residents. Molokai's steep and uncultivated terrain offers excellent hikes and some stellar views. Although the island is largely wild, all land is owned, so get permission before hiking.

BIKING

Cyclists who like to eat up the miles love Molokai, since its few roads are long, straight, and extremely rural. You can really go for it—there are no traffic lights and most of the time no traffic.

Molokai Bicycle. You can rent a bike here for $25–$35 per day, depending on the model, with reductions for additional days or weeklong rentals. Bike trailers (for your drinks cooler, perhaps) are also available for $12 a day or $60 for a week. ⊠ *80 Mohala St., Kaunakakai* ☎ *808/553–5740, 800/709–2453* ⊕ *www.mauimolokaibicycle.com.*

GOLF

Molokai is not a prime golf destination, but the single 9-hole course makes for a pleasant afternoon.

Ironwood Hills Golf Course. Like other 9-hole plantation-era courses, Ironwood Hills is in a prime spot, with basic fairways and not-always-manicured greens. It helps if you like to play laid-back golf with locals and can handle occasionally rugged conditions. On the plus side, most holes offer ocean views. Fairways are *kukuya* grass and run through pine, ironwood, and eucalyptus trees. Carts and clubs are rented on the honor system; there's not always someone there to assist you. Bring your own water. Access is via a bumpy, unpaved road. ⊠ *Kalae Hwy., Kualapuu* ☎ *808/567–6000* ⊕ *www.molokaigolfcourse.com* ⌥ *$18 for 9 holes, $24 for 18 holes* 🏌 *9 holes, 3088 yards, par 34.*

HIKING

6

Rural and rugged, Molokai is an excellent place for hiking. Roads and developments are few. The island is steep, so hikes often combine spectacular views with hearty physical exertion. Because the island is small, you can come away with the feeling of really knowing the place. And you won't see many other people around. Much of what may look like deserted land is private property, so be careful not to trespass—seek permission or use an authorized guide.

BEST SPOTS

Kalaupapa Trail. You can hike down to the Kalaupapa Peninsula and back via this 3-mile, 26-switchback route. The trail is often nearly vertical, traversing the face of the high sea cliffs. You can reach Kalaupapa Trail off Highway 470 near Kalaupapa Overlook. Only those in excellent condition should attempt it. You can also arrange a guided hike with Molokai Outdoors. ⊠ *Off Hwy. 470, Kualapuu.*

Kamakou Preserve. The Nature Conservancy of Hawaii manages the 2,774-acre Kamakou Preserve, one of the last stands of Hawaii's native plants and birds. A long, rough dirt road, which begins not far from Kaunakakai, leads to the preserve. This is the landscape of prediscovery Hawaii and can be a mean trek; a four-wheel-drive vehicle is essential. On your way up, be sure to stop at Waikolu Overlook, which gazes into a precipitous canyon. Once inside the preserve, the trail of choice—and you can drive right to it—is the 1½-mile boardwalk trail through Pepeopae Bog, an ecological treasure. Be aware that incoming fog can blot out your trail and obscure markers. The road to the Kamakou Preserve is not marked, so you must check in with the Nature Conservancy prior to embarking upon this somewhat risky journey. ⊠ *23 Pueo Pl., 3 miles west of Kaunakakai* ⊕ *www.nature.org.*

GOING WITH A GUIDE

Fodor's Choice **Halawa Valley Falls Cultural Hike.** This gorgeous, steep-walled valley was
★ carved by two rivers and is rich in history. Site of the earliest Polynesian
settlement on Molokai, Halawa is a sustained island culture with its
ingeniously designed *loi,* or taro fields. Because of a tsunami in 1948
and changing cultural conditions in the 1960s, the valley was largely
abandoned. The Solatorio Ohana (family) is restoring the *loi* and taking visitors on guided hikes through the valley, which includes two
of Molokai's *luakini heiau* (sacred temples), many historic sites, and
the trail to **Moaula Falls**, a 250-foot cascade. Bring water, food, and
insect repellent, and wear sturdy shoes that can get wet. The 3½-mile
round-trip hike is rated intermediate to advanced and includes two
moderate river crossings. ☎ *808/551–5538, 808/551–1055* ⊕ *www.*
halawavalleymolokai.com ⌲ *$60.*

Molokai Outdoors. This company can arrange guided hikes that fit your
schedule and physical condition. The staff will take you down into
Kalaupapa and arrange for a plane to pick you up. ✉ *9 Hio Pl., Kaunak-*
akai ☎ *808/553–4477, 877/553–4477* ⊕ *www.molokai-outdoors.com.*

SHOPPING

6

Molokai has one main commercial area: Ala Malama Street in Kaunakakai. There are no department stores or shopping malls, and the clothing is typical island wear. Local shopping is friendly, and you may find
hidden treasures. A very few family-run businesses define the main drag
of Maunaloa, a rural former plantation town. Most stores in Kaunakakai are open Monday through Saturday between 9 and 6.

WEST MOLOKAI

ARTS AND CRAFTS

Big Wind Kite Factory and Plantation Gallery. The factory has custom-made
kites you can fly or display. Designs range from Hawaiian petroglyphs
to *pueo* (owls). Also in stock are paper kites, minikites, and wind socks.
Ask to go on the factory tour, or take a free kite-flying lesson. The
adjacent gallery carries an eclectic collection of merchandise, including
locally made crafts, Hawaiian books and CDs, jewelry, handmade batik
sarongs, and an elegant line of women's linen clothing. ✉ *120 Maunaloa*
Hwy., Maunaloa ☎ *808/552–2364* ⊕ *www.bigwindkites.com.*

FOOD

Maunaloa General Store. Stocking meat, produce, beverages, and dry
goods, this shop is a convenient stop if you're planning a picnic at one
of the west-end beaches. It's open Monday through Saturday 9 to 6 and
Sunday 9 to noon. ✉ *200 Maunaloa Hwy., Maunaloa* ☎ *808/552–2346.*

No traffic lights here: Molokai's rural, uncrowded roads have wide-open views.

CENTRAL MOLOKAI

ARTS AND CRAFTS

Molokai Art From the Heart. A small downtown shop, this arts and crafts co-op has locally made folk art like dolls, clay flowers, silk sarongs, and children's items. The shop also carries original art by Molokai artists and Giclée prints, jewelry, locally produced music, and Saint Damien keepsakes. Store hours are weekdays 10 to 4:30 and Saturday 9:30 to 2. ⊠ *64 Ala Malama St., Kaunakakai* ☎ *808/553–8018* ⊕ *www. molokaigallery.com.*

CLOTHING AND SHOES

Imports Gift Shop. Across from Kanemitsu Bakery, this one-stop shop offers fancy and casual island-style wear, including Roxy and Quicksilver for men, women, and children. The store is open Monday to Saturday 9 to 6 and Sunday 9 to 1. ⊠ *82 Ala Malama St., Kaunakakai* ☎ *808/553–5734.*

FOOD

Friendly Market Center. The best-stocked supermarket on the island has a slogan—"Your family store on Molokai"—that is truly credible. Sun-and-surf essentials keep company with fresh produce, meat, groceries, and liquor. Locals say the food is fresher here than at the other major supermarket. It's open weekdays 8:30 to 8:30 and Saturday 8:30 to 6:30. ⊠ *90 Ala Malama St., Kaunakakai* ☎ *808/553–5595.*

Home Town Groceries & Drygoods. For those staying at a condo in Molokai, this store will come in handy. It carries bulk items, like a mini-Costco. ⊠ *93 Ala Malama St., Kaunakakai* ☎ *808/553–3858.*

Kumu Farms. This is the most diverse working farm on Molokai, and *the* place to purchase fresh produce, herbs, and gourmet farm products. They're open Tuesday to Friday from 9 to 4. ⊠ *Hua Ai Rd., off Maunaloa Hwy., near Molokai Airport, Kaunakakai* ☎ *808/567–6480* ⊕ *www.kumufarms.com.*

JEWELRY

Imports Gift Shop. You'll find soaps and lotions, a small collection of 14-karat-gold chains, rings, earrings, and bracelets, and a jumble of Hawaiian quilts, pillows, books, and postcards at this local favorite. The shop also special-orders (takes approximately one week) Hawaiian heirloom jewelry, inspired by popular Victorian pieces and crafted here since the late 1800s. ⊠ *82 Ala Malama St., Kaunakakai* ☎ *808/553–5734.*

SPAS

Molokai Acupuncture & Massage. This relaxing retreat offers acupuncture, massage, herbal remedies, wellness treatments, and private yoga sessions by appointment only. The professional staff also services the spa at the Hotel Molokai. ⊠ *40 Ala Malama St., Kaunakakai* ☎ *808/553–3930* ⊕ *www.molokai-wellness.com.*

Molokai Lomi Massage. Allana Noury of Molokai Lomi Massage has studied natural medicine for more than 35 years and is a licensed massage therapist, master herbalist, and master iridologist. She will come to your hotel or condo by appointment. ☎ *808/553–8034* ⊕ *www. molokaimassage.com.*

ENTERTAINMENT AND NIGHTLIFE

Local nightlife consists mainly of gathering with friends and family, sipping a few cold ones, strumming ukuleles and guitars, singing old songs, and talking story. Still, there are a few ways to kick up your heels. Pick up a copy of the weekly Molokai *Dispatch* and see if there's a concert, church supper, or dance.

The bar at the Hotel Molokai is always a good place to drink. The "Aloha Friday" weekly gathering here from 4 to 6 pm is a must-see event, featuring Na Kapuna, a group of accomplished *kupuna* (old-timers) with guitars and ukuleles.

For something truly casual, stop in at Kanemitsu Bakery on Ala Malama Street in Kaunakakai for the nightly hot bread sale (Tuesday through Sunday beginning at 8:30 pm). You'll meet everyone in town, and you can take some hot bread home for a late-night treat.

WHERE TO EAT

During a week's stay, you might easily hit all the dining spots worth a visit and then return to your favorites for a second round. The dining scene is fun because it's a microcosm of Hawaii's diverse cultures. You can find locally grown vegetarian foods, spicy Filipino cuisine, and

Hawaiian fish with a Japanese influence—such as tuna, mullet, and moonfish that's grilled, sautéed, or mixed with seaweed to make *poke* (salted and seasoned raw fish).

Most eating establishments are on Ala Malama Street in Kaunakakai. If you're heading to West Molokai for the day be sure to stock up on provisions, as there is no place to eat there. If you are on the east end, stop by Manae Goods & Grindz (☎ 808/558–8186) near mile marker 16 for good local seafood plates, burgers, and ice cream.

Prices in the reviews are the average cost of a main course at dinner or, if dinner is not served, at lunch.

CENTRAL MOLOKAI

Central Molokai offers most of the island's dining options.

$ ✕**Kanemitsu Bakery and Restaurant.** Stop at this Molokai institution for
CAFÉ morning coffee and some of the round Molokai bread—a sweet, pan-
Fodor'sChoice style white loaf that makes excellent cinnamon toast. Take a few loaves
★ with you for a picnic or a condo breakfast. You can also try a taste of *lavosh,* a pricey flatbread flavored with sesame, taro, Maui onion, Parmesan cheese, or jalapeño. $ *Average main: $6* ⊠ *79 Ala Malama St., Kaunakakai* ☎ *808/553–5855* ▭ *No credit cards* ⊘ *Closed Tues.*

$ ✕**Kualapuu Cookhouse.** The only restaurant in rural Kualapuu, this local
HAWAIIAN favorite is a classic, refurbished, green-and-white plantation house with a shady lanai. Inside, local photography and artwork enhance the simple furnishings. Typical fare is an inexpensive plate of chicken or pork served with rice, but at dinner there's also the more expensive spicy crusted ahi. This laid-back diner sits across the street from the Kualapuu Market. $ *Average main: $10* ⊠ *Farrington Hwy., 1 block west of Rte. 470, Kualapuu* ☎ *808/567–9655* ▭ *No credit cards* ⊘ *No dinner Sun. and Mon.*

$ ✕**Molokai Burger.** Clean and cheery, Molokai Burger offers both drive-
BURGER through and eat-in options. Burgers may be ordered on a whole-wheat bun. Healthier items include breakfast sandwiches without cheese and mayonnaise, and salads featuring Kumu Farms certified-organic veggies. $ *Average main: $6* ⊠ *20 Kamehameha V Hwy., Kaunakakai* ☎ *808/553–3533* ⊕ *www.molokaiburger.com* ⊘ *Closed Sun.*

$ ✕**Molokai Drive Inn.** Fast food Molokai-style is served at this walk-up
HAWAIIAN counter. Burgers, fries, and sundaes are on the menu, but residents usu-
ally choose the foods they grew up on, such as *saimin* (thin noodles and vegetables in broth), plate lunches, shave ice, and the beloved *loco moco* (rice topped with a hamburger and a fried egg and covered in gravy). $ *Average main: $7* ⊠ *15 Kamoi St., Kaunakakai* ☎ *808/553–5655* ▭ *No credit cards.*

$ ✕**Molokai Pizza Cafe.** Cheerful and busy, this is a popular gathering spot
AMERICAN for local families and a good place to pick up food for a picnic. Pizza, sandwiches, salads, pasta, and fresh fish are simply prepared and served without fuss. Kids keep busy at the nearby arcade, and art by local artists decorates the lavender walls. $ *Average main: $12* ⊠ *Kaunakakai Pl., at Wharf Rd., Kaunakakai* ☎ *808/553–3288* ▭ *No credit cards.*

$ 🍴 **Paddlers' Inn.** There aren't many dinner options on Molokai, but this
AMERICAN popular spot is a great place to grab a decent meal while rubbing elbows with locals. Hearty portions of ribs, pork chops, and chicken-fried steak come with two side dishes at a reasonable price. Fish options include salmon and mahimahi. There is live music on Tuesday, Thursday, and Saturday at 6:30 pm. Don't be surprised if the bass player is also a teacher at the local elementary school. [$] *Average main: $14* ✉ *10 N. Mohala St., Kaunakakai* ☎ *808/553–3300* 🌐 *www.molokaipaddlersinn.com.*

$ 🍴 **Sundown Deli.** Small and clean, this deli focuses on freshly made take-
DELI out food. Sandwiches come on a half dozen types of bread, and the Portuguese bean soup and chowders are rich and filling. It's open weekdays from 10:30 am to 2 pm. [$] *Average main: $8* ✉ *145 Ala Malama St., Kaunakakai* ☎ *808/553–3713* 💳 *No credit cards* 🕒 *Closed weekends. No dinner.*

WHERE TO STAY

For expanded hotel reviews, visit Fodors.com.

The coastline along Molokai's west end has ocean-view condominium units and luxury homes available as vacation rentals. Central Molokai offers seaside condominiums. The only lodgings on the east end are some guest cottages in magical settings and the cottages and ranch lodge at Puu O Hoku. Note that room rates do not include 13.42% sales tax.

Note: Maui County has regulations concerning vacation rentals; to avoid disappointment, always contact the property manager or the owner and ask if the accommodations have the proper permits and are in compliance with local ordinances.

Prices in the reviews are the lowest price of a standard double room in high season. Prices for rentals are the lowest per-night cost for a one-bedroom unit in high season.

WEST MOLOKAI

If you want to stay in West Molokai so you'll have access to unspoiled beaches, your only choices are condos or vacation homes. Keep in mind that units fronting the abandoned Kaluakoi golf course present a bit of a dismal view.

$ 🏨 **Ke Nani Kai.** These pleasant, spacious, one- and two-bedroom condos
RENTAL have ocean views and nicely maintained tropical landscaping. **Pros:** on island's secluded west end; uncrowded pool. **Cons:** amenities vary from unit to unit; far from commercial center; some units overlook abandoned golf course. [$] *Rooms from: $105* ✉ *50 Keuphi Beach Rd., Maunaloa* ☎ *808/553–8334, 800/367–2984* 🌐 *www.molokai-vacation-rental.net* 🛏 *120 units* 🍽 *No meals.*

$ 🏨 **Paniolo Hale.** Perched high on a ridge overlooking a favorite local
RENTAL surfing spot, this is Molokai's best condominium property. **Pros:** close
Fodor's Choice ★ to beach; quiet surroundings; perfect if you are an expert surfer. **Cons:** amenities vary; far from shopping; golf course units front abandoned

course. [$] *Rooms from: $125* ✉ *100 Lio Pl., Kaunakakai* ☎ *808/553–8334, 800/367–2984* 🌐 *www.molokai-vacation-rental.net* 🛏 *77 units* 🍴 *No meals.*

CENTRAL MOLOKAI

There are two condo properties in this area, one close to shopping and dining in Kaunakakai, and the other on the way to the east end.

$ RENTAL 🏨 **Molokai Shores.** Many of the units in this three-story condominium complex have a view of the ocean. **Pros:** convenient location; some units upgraded; near water. **Cons:** older accommodations; units close to highway can be noisy. [$] *Rooms from: $105* ✉ *1000 Kamehameha V Hwy., Kaunakakai* ☎ *808/553–5954, 800/535–0085* 🌐 *www.molokai-vacation-rental.net* 🛏 *100 units* 🍴 *No meals.*

$ RENTAL 🏨 **Wavecrest.** This 5-acre oceanfront condominium complex is convenient if you want to explore the east side of the island—it's 13 miles east of Kaunakakai—with access to a beautiful reef, excellent snorkeling, and kayaking. **Pros:** convenient location for divers; good value; nicely maintained grounds. **Cons:** amenities vary; far from shopping; area sometimes gets windy. [$] *Rooms from: $105* ✉ *Rte. 450, near mile marker 13, Kaunakakai* ☎ *800/367–2984, 808/553–8334* 🌐 *www.molokai-vacation-rental.net* 🛏 *126 units* 🍴 *No meals.*

EAST MOLOKAI

Puu O Hoku Ranch, a rental facility on East Molokai, is the main lodging option on this side of the island. The ranch is quite far from the center of the island.

$$ B&B/INN 🏨 **Puu O Hoku Ranch.** At the east end of Molokai, these ocean-view accommodations are on 14,000 isolated acres of pasture and forest—a remote and serene location for people who want to get away from it all or meet in a retreat atmosphere. **Pros:** ideal for large groups; authentic working ranch; great hiking. **Cons:** on remote east end of island; road to property is narrow and winding. [$] *Rooms from: $200* ✉ *Rte. 450, near mile marker 25, Kaunakakai* ☎ *808/558–8109* 🌐 *www.puuohoku.com* 🛏 *3 cottages, 1 lodge* 🍴 *No meals.*

7

LANAI

Visit Fodors.com for advice, updates, and bookings

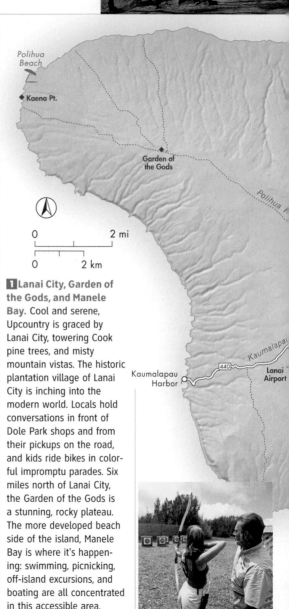

WELCOME TO LANAI

TOP REASONS TO GO

★ **Seclusion and serenity:** Lanai is small; local motion is slow motion. Get into the spirit and go home rested instead of exhausted.

★ **Garden of the Gods:** Walk amid the eerie red-rock spires that Hawaiians still believe to be a sacred spot. The ocean views are magnificent, too; sunset is a good time to visit.

★ **A dive at Cathedrals:** Explore underwater pinnacle formations and mysterious caverns illuminated by shimmering rays of light.

★ **Dole Park:** Hang out in the shade of the Cook pines in Lanai City and talk story with the locals for a taste of old-time Hawaii.

★ **Hit the water at Hulopoe Beach:** This beach may have it all: good swimming, a shady park for perfect picnicking, great reefs for snorkeling, and sometimes schools of spinner dolphins.

1 Lanai City, Garden of the Gods, and Manele Bay. Cool and serene, Upcountry is graced by Lanai City, towering Cook pine trees, and misty mountain vistas. The historic plantation village of Lanai City is inching into the modern world. Locals hold conversations in front of Dole Park shops and from their pickups on the road, and kids ride bikes in colorful impromptu parades. Six miles north of Lanai City, the Garden of the Gods is a stunning, rocky plateau. The more developed beach side of the island, Manele Bay is where it's happening: swimming, picnicking, off-island excursions, and boating are all concentrated in this accessible area.

GETTING ORIENTED

Unlike the other Hawaiian Islands with their tropical splendors, Lanai looks like a desert: *kiawe* trees right out of Africa, red-dirt roads, and a deep blue sea. Lanaihale (house of Lanai), the mountain that bisects the island, is carved into deep canyons by rain and wind on the windward side, and the drier leeward side slopes gently to the sea, where waves pound against surf-carved cliffs. The town of Lanai City is in the center of the island, Upcountry. Manele Bay, on the south side of the island, is popular for swimming and boating.

Shipwreck Beach

Hwy.

2

WINDWARD LANAI

Keomuku

Keomuku Beach

Halepalaoa

Four Seasons Resort Lanai, The Lodge at Koele

Lanai City

Mt. Lanaihale
▲ 3,370 ft.

1

UPCOUNTRY

Manele

Lopa Beach

Palawai Basin

440

Rd.

Naha Beach

Four Seasons Resort Lanai at Manele Bay

Manele Bay

Hulopoe Beach

2 Windward Lanai. This area is the long white-sand beach at the base of Lanaihale. Now uninhabited, it was once occupied by thriving Hawaiian fishing villages and a sugarcane plantation.

Updated by
Heidi Pool

Mostly privately owned, Lanai is the smallest inhabited island in the Hawaiian Islands, and is a true getaway for slowing down and enjoying serenity along with world-class comforts. The two resorts on the island are run by Four Seasons. If you yearn for a beach with amenities, a luxury resort, and golf course, the Four Seasons Resort Lanai at Manele Bay beckons from the shoreline. Upcountry, the grand Four Seasons Resort Lodge at Koele provides cooler pleasures. This leaves the rest of the 100,000-acre island to explore.

With no traffic or traffic lights and miles of open space, Lanai seems suspended in time, and that can be a good thing. Small (141 square miles) and sparsely populated, it has just 3,500 residents, most of them living Upcountry in Lanai City. An afternoon strolling around Dole Park in historic Lanai City offers shopping, dining, and the opportunity to mingle with locals. Though it may seem a world away, Lanai is separated from Maui and Molokai by two narrow channels, and is easily accessed by commercial ferry from Maui.

FLORA AND FAUNA

Lanai bucks the "tropical" trend of the other Hawaiian Islands with African *kiawe* trees, Cook pines, and eucalyptus in place of palm trees, and deep blue sea where you might expect shallow turquoise bays. Abandoned pineapple fields are overgrown with drought-resistant grasses, Christmas berry, and lantana; native plants *aalii* and *ilima* are found in uncultivated areas. Axis deer from India dominate the ridges, and wild turkeys lumber around the resorts. Whales can be seen December through April, and a family of resident spinner dolphins rests and fishes regularly in Hulopoe Bay.

ON LANAI TODAY

Despite its fancy resorts, Lanai still has that languid-Hawaii feel. The island is 97% owned by billionaire Larry Ellison, who is in the process of revitalizing the island. Old-time residents are a mix of just about everything: Hawaiian, Chinese, German, Portuguese, Filipino, Japanese, French, Puerto Rican, English, Norwegian—you name it. When Dole owned the island in the early 20th century and grew pineapples, the plantation was divided into ethnic camps, which helped retain cultural cuisines. Potluck dinners feature sashimi, Portuguese bean soup, *laulau* (morsels of pork, chicken, butterfish, or other ingredients steamed in *ti* leaves), potato salad, teriyaki steak, chicken *hekka* (a gingery Japanese chicken stir-fry), and Jell-O. The local language is pidgin, a mix of words as complicated and rich as the food. Newly arrived residents have added to the cultural mix.

PLANNING

WHEN TO GO

Lanai has an ideal climate year-round, hot and sunny at the sea and a few delicious degrees cooler Upcountry. In Lanai City and Upcountry the nights and mornings can be almost chilly when a fog or harsh trade winds settle in. Winter months are known for *slightly* rougher weather—periodic rain showers, occasional storms, and higher surf.

As higher mountains on Maui capture the trade-wind clouds, Lanai receives little rainfall and has a near-desert ecology. Consider the wind direction when planning your day. If it's blowing a gale on the windward beaches, head for the beach at Hulopoe or check out Garden of the Gods. Overcast days, when the wind stops or comes lightly from the southwest, are common in whale season. At that time, try a whale-watching trip or the windward beaches.

Whales are seen off Lanai's shores from December through April. A Pineapple Festival on the July 4 Saturday in Dole Park features traditional entertainment, a pineapple-eating contest, and fireworks. Buddhists hold their annual outdoor Obon Festival, honoring departed ancestors with joyous dancing, local food, and drumming, in early July. During hunting-season weekends, from mid-February through mid-May, and mid-July through mid-October, watch out for hunters on dirt roads even though there are designated safety zones. Sunday is a day of rest in Lanai City, and shops and most restaurants are closed.

GETTING HERE AND AROUND
AIR TRAVEL

Island Air and Mokulele Airlines are the only commercial airlines serving Lanai City. Direct flights are available from Oahu and Maui; if you're flying to Lanai from any other Hawaiian island, you'll make a stop in Honolulu.

If you're staying at the Hotel Lanai, either Four Seasons hotel, or renting a Jeep or minivan from Lanai City Service, you'll be met at the airport or ferry dock by a bus that shuttles between the resorts and Lanai City. If you're visiting for the day, a shuttle pass is available for $10 per person. At the ferry dock, line up at the concierge podium and you'll be directed to the proper bus. Advance reservations aren't necessary (or even possible), but there's usually plenty of space.

Information Island Air ☎ 800/652–6541 ⊕ www.islandair.com. **Mokulele Airlines** ☎ 866/260–7070 ⊕ www.mokuleleairlines.com.

CAR TRAVEL

Lanai has only 30 miles of paved roads. Keomuku Highway starts just past The Lodge at Koele and runs northeast to the dirt road that goes to Shipwreck Beach and Lopa Beach. Manele Road (Highway 440) runs south down to Manele Bay, the Four Seasons Resort Lanai at Manele Bay, and Hulopoe Beach. Kaumalapau Highway (also Highway 440) heads west to Kaumalapau Harbor. The rest of your driving takes place on bumpy, dusty roads that remain unpaved and unmarked. Driving in thick mud is not recommended, and the rental agency will charge a stiff cleaning fee. Watch out for blind curves on narrow roads.

Renting a four-wheel-drive vehicle is expensive but almost essential if you'd like to explore beyond the resorts and Lanai City. Make reservations far in advance of your trip, because Lanai's fleet of vehicles is limited. Lanai City Service, where you'll find a branch of Dollar Rent A Car, is open daily 7 to 7.

Bring along a good topographical map, and keep in mind your directions. Stop from time to time to find landmarks and gauge your progress. Never drive or walk to the edge of lava cliffs, as rock can give way under you. Directions on the island are often given as *mauka* (toward the mountains) and *makai* (toward the ocean).

Information Lanai City Service ✉ 1036 Lanai Ave., Lanai City ☎ 808/565–7227, 800/533–7808.

FERRY TRAVEL

Ferries operated by Expeditions cross the channel five times daily between Lahaina on Maui to Manele Bay Harbor on Lanai. The crossing takes 45 minutes and costs $30. Be warned: passage can be rough, especially in winter.

Contact Expeditions ☎ 808/661–3756, 800/695–2624 ⊕ www.go-lanai.com.

SHUTTLE TRAVEL

A shuttle transports hotel guests between the Hotel Lanai, the Four Seasons Resort Lanai, The Lodge at Koele, the Four Seasons Resort Lanai at Manele Bay, and the airport. A fee ranging from $35 to $47.50 added to the room rates covers all transportation during the length of your stay.

RESTAURANTS

Lanai has a wide range of choices for dining, from simple plate-lunch local eateries to fancy, upscale, gourmet resort restaurants. *Prices in the reviews are the average cost of a main course at dinner or, if dinner is not served, at lunch.*

Ocean views provide a backdrop to the eroded rocks at Garden of the Gods.

HOTELS

The range of lodgings is limited on Lanai. Essentially there are only three options: the two Four Seasons Resorts Lanai (at Manele Bay and Upcountry at The Lodge at Koele) and the venerable Hotel Lanai. A good alternative is looking into house rentals, which give you a feel for everyday life on the island. Make sure to book far in advance. **Note:** Maui County has regulations concerning vacation rentals; to avoid disappointment, always contact the property manager or owner and ask if the accommodation has the proper permits and is in compliance with local laws. *Prices in the reviews are the lowest cost of a standard double room in high season. For expanded reviews, facilities, and current deals, visit Fodors.com.*

EXPLORING LANAI

You can easily explore Lanai City and the island's two resorts without a car; just hop on the hourly shuttle. A small fee applies. To access the rest of this untamed island, rent a four-wheel-drive vehicle. Take a map, be sure you have a full tank, and bring a snack and plenty of water. Ask the rental agency or your hotel's concierge about road conditions before you set out. Although roads may be dry on the coast they may be impassable upland. It's always good to carry a cell phone. The main road on Lanai, Highway 440, refers to both Kaumalapau Highway and Manele Road.

LANAI CITY, GARDEN OF THE GODS, AND MANELE BAY

Lanai City is 3 miles northeast of the airport; Manele Bay is 9 miles southeast of Lanai City; Garden of the Gods is 6 miles northwest of Lanai City.

With its charming plantation-era shops and restaurants having received new paint jobs and landscaping, Lanai City is worthy of whiling away a lazy Lanai afternoon. This pedestrian-oriented town (the only town on the entire island) is situated around the perimeter of Dole Park, which, with its stately Cook pine trees, serves as the community gathering place.

Pineapples once blanketed the Palawai, the great basin south of Lanai City. Although it looks like a volcanic crater, it isn't. Some say that the name Palawai is descriptive of the mist that sometimes fills the basin at dawn and looks like a huge shining lake.

Manele Bay is an ocean-lover's dream: Hulopoe Beach offers top-notch snorkeling, swimming, picnicking, tide pools, and, sometimes, spinner dolphins. Off-island ocean excursions depart from nearby Manele Small Boat Harbor. Take the short but rugged hike to the Puu Pehe (Sweetheart Rock) overlook, and you'll enjoy a bird's-eye view of this iconic Lanai landmark.

The area northwest of Lanai City is wild; the other-worldly Garden of the Gods is one of its highlights.

GETTING HERE AND AROUND

Lanai City serves as the island's hub, with roads leading to Manele Bay, Kaumalapau Harbor, and windward Lanai. Garden of the Gods is usually possible to visit by car, but beyond that you will need four-wheel drive.

TOP ATTRACTIONS

Fodor's Choice ★ **Garden of the Gods.** This preternatural plateau is scattered with boulders of different sizes, shapes, and colors, the products of a million years of wind erosion. Time your visit for sunset, when the rocks begin to glow—from rich red to purple—and the fiery globe sinks to the horizon. Magnificent views of the Pacific Ocean, Molokai, and, on clear days, Oahu, provide the perfect backdrop for photographs.

The ancient Hawaiians shunned Lanai for hundreds of years, believing the island was the inviolable home of spirits. Standing beside the oxide-red rock spires of this strange, raw landscape, you might be tempted to believe the same. This lunar savanna still has a decidedly eerie edge, but the shadows disappearing on the horizon are those of mouflon sheep and axis deer, not the fearsome spirits of lore. According to tradition, Kawelo, a Hawaiian priest, kept a perpetual fire burning on an altar at the Garden of the Gods, in sight of the island of Molokai. As long as the fire burned, prosperity was assured for the people of Lanai. Kawelo was killed by a rival priest on Molokai and the fire went out. The Hawaiian name for this area is Keahiakawelo, meaning the "fire of Kawelo."

Garden of the Gods is 6 miles north of Lanai City. From the Stables at Koele, follow a dirt road through a pasture, turn right at a crossroad marked by carved boulder, and head through abandoned fields and

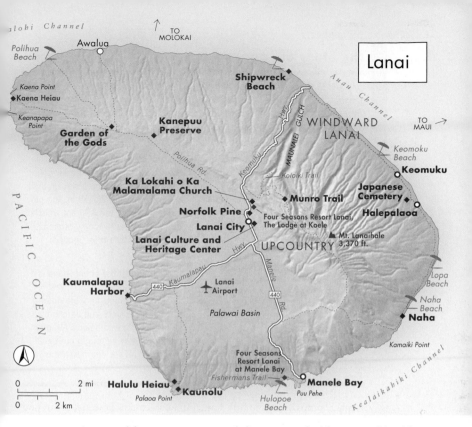

ironwood forests to an open red-dirt area marked by a carved boulder. ⊠ *Off Polihua Rd.*

Ka Lokahi o Ka Malamalama Church. Built in 1938, this picturesque painted wooden church provided services for Lanai's growing population. (For many people, the only other Hawaiian church, in coastal Keomuku, was too far away.) A classic structure of ranching days, the one-room church was moved from its original site when the Lodge at Koele was built. It's open all day and Sunday services are still held in Hawaiian and English; visitors are welcome but are requested to attend quietly. The church is north of the entrance to the Four Seasons Resort Lodge at Koele. ⊠ *1 Keomuku Hwy.*

Kanepuu Preserve. Hawaiian sandalwood, olive, and ebony trees characterize Hawaii's largest example of a rare native dryland forest. Thanks to the combined efforts of volunteers at the Nature Conservancy and Castle & Cooke Resorts, the 590-acre remnant forest is protected from the axis deer and mouflon sheep that graze on the land beyond its fence. More than 45 native plant species, including *nau*, the endangered Hawaiian gardenia, can be seen here. A short, self-guided loop trail, with eight signs illustrated by local artist Wendell Kahoohalahala, reveals this ecosystem's beauty and the challenges it faces. The reserve

The Story of Lanai

Rumored to be haunted by hungry ghosts, Lanai was sparsely inhabited for many centuries. Most of the earliest settlers lived along the shore and made their living from fishing the nearby waters. Others lived in the Uplands near seasonal water sources and traded their produce for seafood. The high chiefs sold off the land bit by bit to foreign settlers, and by 1910 the island was owned by the Gay family.

When the Hawaiian Pineapple Company purchased Lanai for $1.1 million in 1922, it built the town of Lanai City, opened the commercial harbor, and laid out the pineapple fields. Field workers came from overseas to toil in what quickly became the world's largest pineapple plantation. Exotic animals and birds were imported for hunting. Cook pines were planted to catch the rain, and eucalyptus windbreaks anchored the blowing soil.

Everything was stable for 70 years, until the plantation closed in 1992. When the resorts opened their doors, newcomers arrived, homes were built, and other ways of life set in. The old pace, marked by the 6:30 am whistle calling everyone to the plantation, was replaced by a more modern schedule.

Because almost the entire island is now owned by Larry Ellison, vast areas remain untouched and great views abound. Deer and birds provide glimpses of its wild beauty. Although the ghosts may be long gone, Lanai still retains its ancient mysterious presence.

---

is adjacent to the sacred hill, Kane Puu, dedicated to the Hawaiian god of water and vegetation. ⊠ *Polihua Rd., 4.8 miles north of Lanai City.*

Fodor's Choice **Lanai City.** A tidy plantation town, built in 1924 by Jim Dole to accommodate workers for his pineapple business, Lanai City is home to old-time residents, recently arrived resort workers, and second-home owners. A simple grid of roads is lined with stately Cook pines. Despite recent growth, the pace is still calm and the people are friendly. **Dole Park,** in the center of Lanai City, is surrounded by small shops and restaurants and is a favorite spot among locals for sitting, strolling, and talking story. Try a picnic lunch in the park and visit the **Lanai Culture and Heritage Center** in the Old Dole Administration Building to glimpse this island's rich past, purchase historical publications and maps, and get directions to anywhere on the island.

Manele Bay. The site of a Hawaiian village dating from AD 900, Manele Bay is flanked by lava cliffs hundreds of feet high. Ferries from Maui dock five times a day, and visiting yachts pull in here, as it's the island's only small boat harbor. Public restrooms, grassy lawns, and picnic tables make it a busy pit stop—you can watch the boating activity as you rest.

Just offshore to the west is **Puu Pehe.** Often called Sweetheart Rock, the isolated 80-foot-high islet carries a romantic Hawaiian legend that is probably not true. The rock is said to be named after Pehe, a woman so beautiful that her husband kept her hidden in a sea cave. One day, the surf surged into the cave and she drowned. Her grief-stricken husband buried her on this rock and jumped to his death. A more likely story is that the enclosure on the summit is a shrine to birds, built by bird-catchers. Protected shearwaters nest in the nearby sea cliffs from July through November. ⊠ *Hwy. 440, 9 miles south of Lanai City.*

WORTH NOTING

Halulu Heiau. The well-preserved remains of an impressive *heiau* (temple) at Kaunolu village, which was actively used by Lanai's earliest residents, attest to this spot's sacred history. As late as 1810, this hilltop temple was considered a place of refuge, where those who had broken *kapu* (taboos) were forgiven and where women and children could find safety in times of war. If you explore the area, be respectful and leave nothing behind. Be sure to bring along water and wear sturdy shoes.

This place is hard to find, and hard to reach. The four-wheel-drive-only road is alternately rocky, sandy, and soft at the bottom. From Lanai City, follow Highway 440 west toward Kaumalapau Harbor. Past the airport, look for a carved boulder on the hill on your left. Turn left on the dirt road and follow it 3 miles to another carved boulder, where you'll turn right and head downhill. ⊠ *On a dirt road off Hwy. 440.*

Kaunolu. Close to the island's highest cliffs, Kaunolu was once a prosperous fishing village. This important archaeological site includes a major *heiau* (temple), stone floors, and house platforms. The impressive 65-foot drop to the ocean through a gap in the lava rock is called **Kahekili's Leap.** Warriors made the dangerous leap into the shallow water below to prove their courage. King Kamehameha came here for the superb fishing and to collect taxes. The road is rocky, then gets soft and sandy at the bottom. A four-wheel-drive vehicle is essential. From Lanai City, follow Highway 440 west past the airport. At a carved boulder on your left, turn left onto an unmarked dirt road. Continue 3 miles until you reach the second carved boulder, then go downhill 3 miles to village. At the end of the road, walk across the streambed and up the hill. Take water and wear sturdy shoes. Hawaiians request that you do not move or stack rocks. ⊠ *On a dirt road off Hwy. 440.*

Lanai Culture and Heritage Center. Small and carefully arranged, this historical museum features artifacts and photographs from Lanai's varied and rich history. Plantation-era clothing and tools, ranch memorabilia, old maps, precious feather lei, poi pounders, and family portraits combine to give you a good idea of the history of the island and its people. Postcards, maps, books, and pamphlets are for sale. The friendly staff can orient you to the island's historical sites and provide directions. This is the best place to start your explorations of the island. ⊠ *730 Lanai Ave., Lanai City* ☎ *808/565–7177* ⊕ *www.lanaichc.org* 🎫 *Free* ⊙ *Weekdays 8:30–3:30, Sat. 9–1.*

Norfolk Pine. Considered the "mother" of all the pines on the island, this 160-foot-tall tree was planted here, at the former site of the ranch manager's house, in 1875. Almost 30 years later, George Munro, the manager, observed how, in foggy weather, water collected on its foliage, dripping off rain. This led Munro to supervise the planting of Cook pines along the ridge of Lanaihale and throughout the town in order

The calm crescent of Hulopoe Beach is perfect for swimming, snorkeling, or just relaxing.

to add to the island's water supply. This majestic tree is just in front of the south wing of Four Seasons Resort Lodge at Koele. ⊠ *Four Seasons Resort Lodge at Koele, 1 Keomuku Hwy.*

WINDWARD LANAI

9 miles northeast of The Lodge at Koele to end of paved road.

The eastern shore of Lanai is mostly deserted. A few inaccessible *heiau*, or temples, rock walls and boulders marking old shrines, and a restored church at Keomuku reveal traces of human habitation. Four-wheel-drive vehicles are a must to explore this side of the isle. Be prepared for hot, rough conditions. Pack a picnic lunch, a hat and sunscreen, and plenty of drinking water. A cell phone is also a good idea.

GETTING HERE AND AROUND

Once you leave paved Keomuku Highway and turn left toward Shipwreck Beach or right to Naha, the roads are dirt and sand; conditions vary with the seasons. Mileage doesn't matter much here, but figure on 20 minutes from the end of the paved road to Shipwreck Beach, and about 45 minutes to Lopa Beach.

For information about Shipwreck Beach and Lopa Beach, see Beaches, below.

TOP ATTRACTIONS

Munro Trail. This 12.8-mile four-wheel-drive trail along a fern- and pine-clad narrow ridge was named after George Munro, manager of the Lanai Ranch Company, who began a reforestation program in the 1950s to restore the island's much-needed watershed. The trail climbs

Lanaihale (House of Lanai), which, at 3,370 feet, is the island's highest point; on clear days you'll be treated to a panorama of canyons and almost all the Hawaiian Islands. ■ TIP➔ **The road gets very muddy, and trade winds can be strong. Watch for sheer drop-offs, and keep an eye out for hikers.** You can also hike the Munro Trail, although it's steep, the ground is uneven, and there's no water. From the Four Seasons Resort Lodge at Koele, head north on Highway 440 for 1¼ miles, then turn right onto Cemetery Road. Keep going until you're headed downhill on the main dirt road. It's a one-way road, but you may meet jeeps coming from the opposite direction. ⊠ *Cemetery Rd., Lanai City.*

WORTH NOTING

Halepalaoa. Named for the whales that once washed ashore here, Halepalaoa, or the "House of Whale Ivory," was the site of the wharf used by the short-lived Maunalei Sugar Company in 1899. Some say the sugar company failed because the sacred stones of nearby **Kahea Heiau** were used for the construction of the cane railroad. The brackish well water turned too salty, forcing the sugar company to close in 1901, after just two years. The remains of the *heiau* (temple), once an important place of worship for the people of Lanai, are now difficult to find through the *kiawe* (mesquite) overgrowth. There's good public-beach access here and clear shallow water for swimming, but no other facilities. Take Highway 440 (Keomuku Highway) to its eastern terminus; then turn right on the dirt road and continue south for 5½ miles. ⊠ *Dirt road off Hwy. 440, Lanai City.*

Japanese Cemetery. In 1899 sugarcane came to this side of Lanai. The 2,400-acre plantation promised to be a profitable proposition, but that same year disease wiped out the labor force. This Buddhist shrine commemorates the Japanese workers who died, and the local congregation comes down to clean this sacred place each year. Take Highway 440 to its eastern terminus, then turn right on the dirt road and continue south for 6½ miles. The shrine is uphill on your right. ⊠ *Dirt road off Hwy. 440.*

Keomuku. There's a peaceful beauty about the former fishing village of Keomuku. During the late 19th century this small Lanai community served as the headquarters of Maunalei Sugar Company. After the company failed, the land was abandoned. Although there are no other signs of previous inhabitation, its church, **Ka Lanakila O Ka Malamalama,** built in 1903, has been restored by volunteers. Visitors often leave some small token, a shell or lei, as an offering. Take Highway 440 to its eastern terminus, then turn right onto a dirt road and continue south for 5 miles. The church is on your right in the coconut trees. ⊠ *Dirt road off Hwy. 440.*

Naha. An ancient rock-walled fishpond—visible at low tide—lies where the sandy shore ends and the cliffs begin their rise along the island's shores. Accessible by four-wheel-drive vehicle, the beach is a frequent dive spot for local fishermen. ■ TIP➔ **Treacherous currents make this a dangerous place for swimming.** Take Highway 440 to its eastern terminus, then turn right onto a sandy dirt road and continue south

7

for 11 miles. The shoreline dirt road ends here. ⊠ *Dirt road off Hwy. 440, Lanai City.*

BEACHES

Lanai offers miles of secluded white-sand beaches on its windward side, plus the moderately developed Hulopoe Beach, which is adjacent to the Four Seasons Resort Lanai at Manele Bay. Hulopoe is accessible by car or hotel shuttle bus; to reach the windward beaches you need a four-wheel-drive vehicle. Reef, rocks, and coral make swimming on the windward side problematic, but it's fun to splash around in the shallow water. Expect debris on the windward beaches due to the Pacific convergence of ocean currents. Driving on the beach itself is illegal and can be dangerous. *Beaches in this chapter are listed alphabetically.*

> ### THE COASTAL ROAD
>
> Road conditions can change overnight and become impassable due to rain in the Uplands. Car-rental agencies should be able to give you updates before you hit the road. Some of the spur roads leading to the windward beaches from the coastal dirt road cross private property and are closed off by chains. Look for open spur roads with recent tire marks (a fairly good sign that they are safe to drive on). It's best to park on firm ground and walk in to avoid getting your car mired in the sand.

Fodor's Choice
★

Hulopoe Beach. A short stroll from the Four Seasons Resort Lanai at Manele Bay, Hulopoe is one of the best beaches in Hawaii. The sparkling crescent of this Marine Life Conservation District beckons with calm waters safe for swimming almost year-round, great snorkeling reefs, tide pools, and sometimes spinner dolphins. A shady, grassy beach park is perfect for picnics. If the shore break is pounding, or if you see surfers riding big waves, stay out of the water. In the afternoon, watch Lanai High School students heave outrigger canoes down the steep shore break and race one another just offshore. To get here, take Highway 440 south to the bottom of the hill and turn right. The road dead-ends at the beach's parking lot. **Amenities:** parking (no fee); showers; toilets. **Best for:** snorkeling; swimming; surfing. ⊠ *Off Hwy. 440, Lanai City.*

Lopa Beach. A difficult surfing spot that tests the mettle of experienced locals, Lopa is also an ancient fishpond. With majestic views of West Maui and Kahoolawe, this remote white-sand beach is a great place for a picnic. ⚠ **Don't let the sight of surfers fool you: the channel's currents are too strong for swimming.** Take Highway 440 to its eastern terminus, turn right onto a dirt road, and continue south for 7 miles. **Amenities:** none. **Best for:** solitude; sunrise; walking. ⊠ *Dirt road off Hwy. 440.*

Polihua Beach. This often-deserted beach features long, wide stretches of white sand and unobstructed views of Molokai. The northern end of the beach ends at a rocky lava cliff with some interesting tide pools, and sea turtles that lay their eggs in the sand. (Do not drive on the beach and endanger their nests.) However, the dirt road leading here has deep, sandy places that are difficult in dry weather and impassable when it rains. In addition, strong currents and a sudden drop in the ocean floor make swimming dangerous, and strong trade winds can make walking uncomfortable. Thirsty wild bees sometimes gather around your car. To get rid of them, put out water some distance away and wait. The beach is in windward Lanai, 11 miles north of Lanai City.

To get here, turn right onto the marked dirt road past Garden of the Gods. **Amenities:** none. **Best for:** solitude; sunrise; walking. ⊠ *East end of Polihua Rd., Lanai City.*

Shipwreck Beach. The rusting World War II tanker abandoned off this 8-mile stretch of sand adds just the right touch to an already photogenic beach. Strong trade winds have propelled vessels onto the reef since at least 1824, when the first shipwreck was recorded. Beachcombers come to this fairly accessible beach for shells and washed-up treasures, and photographers take great shots of Molokai, just across the Kalohi Channel. A deserted plantation-era fishing settlement adds to the charm. It's still possible to find glass-ball fishing floats as you wander along. Kaiolohia, its Hawaiian name, is a favorite local diving spot. Beyond the beach, about 200 yards up a trail past the Shipwreck Beach sign, are the Kukui Point petroglyphs, marked by reddish-brown boulders. ■TIP→ An offshore reef and rocks in the water mean that it's not for swimmers, though you can play in the shallow water on the shoreline. To get here, take Highway 440 to its eastern terminus, then turn left onto a dirt road and continue to the end. **Amenities:** none. **Best for:** solitude; star gazing; windsurfing. ⊠ *Off Hwy. 440, Lanai City.*

WATER SPORTS AND TOURS

The easiest way to enjoy the water on Lanai is to wade in at Hulopoe Beach and swim or snorkel. If you prefer an organized excursion, a fishing trip is a good bet (you keep some of the fish). Snorkel trips are a great way to see the island, above and below the surface, and scuba divers can marvel at one of the top cave-dive spots in the Pacific.

DEEP-SEA FISHING

Some of the best fishing grounds in Maui County are off the southwest shoreline of Lanai, the traditional fishing grounds of Hawaiian royalty. Pry your eyes open and go deep-sea fishing in the early morning, with departures at 6 or 6:30 am from Manele Harbor. Console yourself with the knowledge that Maui anglers have to leave an hour earlier to get to the same prime locations. Peak seasons are spring and summer, although good catches have been landed year-round. Mahimahi, *ono*

Lanai has miles of good coasts for a variety of water sports.

(a mackerel-like fish; the word means "delicious" in Hawaiian), *ahi* (yellowfin tuna), and marlin are prized catches and preferred eating.

Spinning Dolphin Charters of Lanai. The 36-foot Twin-Vee *Fish-n-Chips* with a tuna tower will get you to the fishing grounds in comfort. Friendly Captain Jason will do everything except reel in the big one for you. Plan on trolling along the south coast for ono and around the point at Kaunolu for mahimahi or marlin. A trip to the offshore buoy often yields skipjack tuna or big ahi. Whales are often spotted during the season. Fishing gear, soft drinks, and water are included. A four-hour charter (six-passenger maximum) is $700; each additional hour costs $110. Guests can keep a third of all fish caught. Shared charters on Sunday are $150 per person. ✉ *Lanai City* ☎ *808/565–7676* ⊕ *www. sportfishinglanai.com.*

SCUBA DIVING

When you have a dive site such as Cathedrals—with eerie pinnacle formations and luminous caverns—it's no wonder that scuba-diving buffs consider exploring the waters off Lanai akin to having a religious experience.

BEST SPOTS

Cathedrals. Just outside Hulopoe Bay, Cathedrals is the best cavern dive site in Lanai. Shimmering light makes the many openings resemble stained-glass windows. A current generally keeps the water crystal clear, even if it's turbid outside. In these unearthly chambers, large *ulua* and small reef sharks add to the adventure. Tiger sharks may appear in certain seasons. ⊠ *Manele*.

Sergeant Major Reef. Off Kamaiki Point, Sergeant Major Reef is named for big schools of yellow- and black-striped *manini* (sergeant major fish) that turn the rocks silvery as they feed. There are three parallel lava ridges separated by rippled sand valleys, a cave, and an archway. Depths range 15 to 50 feet. Depending on conditions, the water may be clear or cloudy. ⊠ *Lanai City*.

EQUIPMENT, LESSONS, AND TOURS

Trilogy Ocean Sports Lanai. Serious certified divers should go for Trilogy's four-hour, two-tank dive. Locations depend on the weather. The $189 fee includes a light breakfast of cinnamon rolls and coffee, wet suits, and all the equipment you need. Noncertified beginners over age 11 can try a one-tank introductory dive lasting 20 to 30 minutes for $102. You can wade into Hulopoe Bay with an instructor at your side. Certified divers can choose a 35- to 40-minute wade-in dive at Hulopoe, also for $102. ⊠ *Manele Small Boat Harbor, Manele Rd., Manele* ☎ *808/874–5649* ⊕ *www.scubalanai.com*.

SNORKELING

Snorkeling is the easiest ocean sport available on the island, requiring nothing but a snorkel, mask, fins, and good sense. Borrow equipment from your hotel or purchase some in Lanai City if you didn't bring your own. Wait to enter the water until you are sure no big sets of waves are coming; and observe the activity of locals on the beach. If little kids are playing in the shore break, it's usually safe to enter. ■ TIP➜ To get into the water safely, always swim in past the breakers, and in the comparative calm put on your fins, then mask and snorkel.

BEST SPOTS

The best snorkeling on Lanai is at **Hulopoe Beach** and **Manele Small Boat Harbor.** Hulopoe, which is an exceptional snorkeling destination, has schools of *manini* (sergeant major fish) that feed on the coral and coat the rocks with flashing silver. You can also easily view *kala* (unicorn fish), *uhu* (parrot fish), and *papio* (small trevally) in all their rainbow colors. Beware of rocks and surging waves. At Manele Harbor, there's a wade-in snorkel spot beyond the break wall. Enter over the rocks, just past the boat ramp. ■ TIP➜ Do not enter if waves are breaking.

EQUIPMENT, LESSONS, AND TOURS

Trilogy Ocean Sports Lanai. A 3½-hour snorkeling trip aboard a spacious catamaran explores Lanai's pristine coastline with this company's experienced captain and crew. The trip includes lessons, equipment, and lunch served on board. Tours are offered Monday, Wednesday, Friday, and Saturday for $181 per person. ⊠ *Manele Small Boat Harbor, Manele Rd., Manele* ☎ *808/874–5649* ⊕ *www.scubalanai.com*.

7

SURFING

Surfing on Lanai can be truly enjoyable. Quality, not quantity, characterizes this isle's few breaks. Be considerate of the locals and they will be considerate of you—surfing takes the place of megaplex theaters and pool halls here, serving as one of the island's few recreational luxuries.

BEST SPOTS

Don't try to hang 10 at **Hulopoe Bay** without watching the conditions for a while. When it "goes off," it's a tricky left-handed shore break that requires some skill. Huge summer south swells are for experts only. The southeast-facing breaks at **Lopa Beach** on the east side are inviting for beginners, but hard to get to. Give them a try in summer, when the swells roll in nice and easy.

EQUIPMENT AND LESSONS

Lanai Surf School. Nick Palumbo offers the only surf instruction on the island. Sign up for his "4x4 Safari"—a four-hour adventure that includes hard- or soft-top boards, snacks, and transportation to windward "secret spots." Palumbo, who was born on Lanai, is a former Hawaii State Surfing Champion. Lessons are $200 (minimum of two people). Experienced riders can rent boards overnight for $58. Palumbo also has the only paddleboard permit for Hulopoe Bay, and gives lessons and rents equipment. He will pick you up at your hotel. ✉ *Lanai City* ☎ *808/649–0739* ⊕ *www.lanaisurfsafari.com.*

GOLF, HIKING, AND OUTDOOR ACTIVITIES

The island's two world-class championship golf courses will certainly test your skill on the green. Experienced hikers can choose from miles of dirt roads and trails, but note that you're on your own—there's no water or support. Remember that Lanai is privately owned, and all land-based activities are at the owner's discretion.

BIKING

Many of the same red-dirt roads that invite hikers are excellent for biking, offering easy, flat terrain and long clear views. There's only one hitch: you may have to bring your own bike, as there are no rentals or tours available except at the resorts.

BEST SPOTS

A favorite biking route is along the fairly flat red-dirt road northward from Lanai City through the old pineapple fields to Garden of the Gods. Start your trip on Keomuku Highway in town. Take a left just before The Lodge at Koele's tennis courts, and then a right where the road ends at the fenced pasture, and continue on to the north end and the start of Polihua and Awalua dirt roads. If you're really hardy you could bike down to Polihua Beach and back, but it would be a serious all-day trip. In wet weather these roads turn to mud and are not advisable. Go in the early morning or late afternoon, because the sun gets hot in the middle of the day. Take plenty of water, spare parts, and snacks.

For the exceptionally fit, it's possible to bike from town down the Keomuku Highway to the windward beaches and back, or to bike the Munro Trail *(see Hiking)*. Experienced bikers also travel up and down the Manele Highway from Manele Bay to town.

GOLF

Lanai has two gorgeous resort courses that offer very different environments and challenges. They are so diverse that it's hard to believe they're on the same island, let alone just 20 minutes apart by resort shuttle.

The Challenge at Manele. Designed by Jack Nicklaus in 1993, this course sits right over the water of Hulopoe Bay. Built on lava outcroppings, it features three holes on cliffs that use the Pacific Ocean as a water hazard. The five-tee concept challenges the best golfers—tee shots over natural gorges and ravines must be precise. This unspoiled natural terrain is a stunning backdrop, and every hole offers ocean views. Early-morning tee times are recommended to avoid the midday heat. ✉ *Four Seasons Resort Lanai at Manele Bay, Challenge Dr., Manele* ☎ *808/565–2222* ⊕ *www.fourseasons.com/manelebay/golf* 🗹 *$210 for guests, $225 for nonguests* 🕵 *18 holes. 7039 yds. Par 72.*

The Experience at Koele. Designed by Greg Norman in 1991, this challenging layout begins at an elevation of 2,000 feet. The front 9 move dramatically through ravines wooded with pine, koa, and eucalyptus trees; seven lakes and streams with cascading waterfalls dot the course. No other course in Hawaii offers a more incredible combination of highland terrain, inspired landscape architecture, and range of play challenges. Beware of the superfast greens and high winds on the back 9. Note that this course will be closed for renovations in 2014, with reopening planned for January 2015. ✉ *Four Seasons Resort Lodge at Koele, 1 Keomuku Hwy., Lanai City* ☎ *808/565–4653* ⊕ *www.fourseasons.com/koele/golf* 🗹 *$210 for guests, $225 for nonguests* 🕵 *18 holes. 7014 yds. Par 72* ☉ *Closed Mon. and Tues.*

HIKING

Only 30 miles of Lanai's roads are paved, but red-dirt roads and trails, ideal for hiking, will take you to sweeping overlooks, isolated beaches, and shady forests. Take a self-guided walk through Kane Puu, Hawaii's largest native dryland forest. You can also explore the Munro Trail over Lanaihale with views of plunging canyons, hike along an old coastal fisherman trail, or head out across Koloiki Ridge. Wear hiking shoes, a hat, and sunscreen, and carry a windbreaker, cell phone, and plenty of water.

BEST SPOTS

Koloiki Ridge. This marked trail starts behind the Lodge at Koele and takes you along the cool and shady Munro Trail to overlook the windward side, with impressive views of Maui, Molokai, Maunalei Valley, and Naio Gulch. The average time for the 5-mile round trip is two hours. Bring snacks, water, and a windbreaker; wear good shoes; and take your time. A map is available from the concierge at the Four

Some holes at The Challenge at Manele use the Pacific Ocean as a water hazard.

Seasons Resort Lodge at Koele, and notify them you are taking the hike. You can also arrange for a guided hike at the Lodge. *Moderate.* ⊠ *Lanai City.*

Lanai Fisherman Trail. Local anglers still use this trail to get to their favorite fishing spots. The trail takes about 1½ hours and follows the rocky shoreline below the Four Seasons Resort at Lanai Manele Bay. The marked trail entrance begins at the west end of Hulopoe Beach. Keep your eyes open for spinner dolphins cavorting offshore and the silvery flash of fish feeding in the pools below you. The condition of the trail varies with weather and frequency of maintenance; it can be slippery and rocky. Take your time, wear a hat and enclosed shoes, and carry water. *Moderate.* ⊠ *Manele.*

Fodor's Choice
★

Munro Trail. This is the real thing: a strenuous 12.8-mile trek that begins behind the Four Seasons Resort Lodge at Koele and follows the ridge of Lanaihale through the rain forest. The island's most demanding hike, it has an elevation gain of 1,400 feet and leads to a lookout at the island's highest point, Lanaihale. It's also a narrow dirt road; watch for careening four-wheel-drive vehicles. The trail is named after George Munro, who supervised the planting of Cook pine trees and eucalyptus windbreaks. Mules used to wend their way up the mountain carrying the pine seedlings. Unless you arrange for someone to pick you up at the trail's end, you have a 3-mile hike back through the Palawai Basin to return to your starting point. The summit is often cloud-shrouded and can be windy and muddy, so check conditions before you start. *Difficult.* ⊠ *Four Seasons Resort Lodge at Koele, 1 Keomuku Hwy., Lanai City.*

Puu Pehe Trail. Beginning to the left of Hulopoe Beach, this trail travels a short distance around the coastline, and then climbs up a sharp, rocky rise. At the top, you're level with the offshore stack of Puu Pehe and can overlook miles of coastline in both directions. The trail is not difficult, but it's hot and steep. Be aware of nesting seabirds and don't approach their nests. ⚠ Stay away from the edge, as the cliff can easily give way. The hiking is best in the early morning or late afternoon, and it's a perfect place to look for whales in season (December–April). Wear a hat and enclosed shoes, and take water so you can spend some time at the top admiring the view. *Moderate.* ⊠ *Manele, Lanai City.*

GOING WITH A GUIDE

Hike Lanai. Many of Lanai's best hiking trails can be difficult to find and negotiate on your own. This outfit has guides who will drive you to and from the trailhead; educate you on island culture, history, flora, and fauna; and share little-known facts and insights. Its Kaunolu Ancient Shoreline Hike ($125 per person) takes you to the largest surviving example of a prehistoric Hawaiian village. The Kaiholena Ridge/Munro Trail Hike ($110 per person) traverses through a forest of native Hawaiian plants to a scenic ridge with views of neighboring Maui and Molokai. ⊠ *Lanai City* ☎ *808/258–2471* ⊕ *www.hikelanai.com.*

HORSEBACK RIDING

GOING WITH A GUIDE

Stables at Koele. The subtle beauty of the high country slowly reveals itself to horseback riders. Two-hour adventures traverse leafy trails with scenic overlooks. Well-trained horses take riders (must be over 8 years old and under 225 pounds) of all skill levels. Prices range from $130 for a 90-minute group ride to $300 for a two-hour private ride. A four-person carriage ride is $150 an hour. Lessons are also available. Book rides at the Four Seasons Resort Lanai, The Lodge at Koele, or with Lanai Grand Adventures. ⊠ *1 Keomuku Hwy., Lanai City* ☎ *808/563–9385* ⊕ *www.lanaigrandadventures.com.*

SPORTING CLAYS AND ARCHERY

For something different, you can try your hand at clay shooting or archery.

Lanai Pine Sporting Clays and Archery Range. Outstanding rustic terrain, challenging targets, and a well-stocked pro shop make this sporting-clays course top-flight in experts' eyes. Sharpshooters can complete the meandering 14-station course in 1½ hours, with the help of a golf cart. There are group tournaments, and even kids can enjoy skilled instruction at the archery range and compressed-air rifle gallery. The $60 archery introduction includes an amusing "pineapple challenge"—contestants are given five arrows with which to hit a paper pineapple target. The winner takes home a crystal pineapple as a nostalgic souvenir of the old Dole Plantation days. Prices depend on amount of ammunition and activity. The range is on the Keomoku Road just past Cemetery

Road on the windward side of island. ⊠ *1 Keomoku Hwy., Lanai City* ☎ *808/565–9385* ⊕ *www.lanaigrandadventures.com.*

SHOPPING

A cluster of Cook pines in the center of Lanai City surrounded by small shops and restaurants, Dole Park is the closest thing to a mall on Lanai. Except for the high-end resort boutiques and pro shops, it's the island's only shopping. A morning or afternoon stroll around the park offers an eclectic selection of gifts and clothing, plus a chance to chat with friendly shopkeepers. Well-stocked general stores are reminiscent of the 1920s, and galleries and a boutique have original art and fashions for everyone.

ARTS AND CRAFTS

Dis 'n Dat. This tiny, jungle-green shop packs in thousands of gift and jewelry items in a minuscule space enlivened by a glittering crystal ceiling. Fanciful garden ornaments and Asian antiques add to the inventory. ⊠ *418 8th St., Lanai City* ☎ *808/565–9170* ⊕ *www.disndatshop.com.*

Island Treasures. This well-stocked boutique is chock-full of appealing souvenirs, including an array of vintage Lanai travel posters that owner Gail Allen will ship right to your door. Gail is always up for a bit of local conversation and advice as well. ⊠ *733 7th St., Lanai City* ☎ *808/565–6255.*

CLOTHING

Cory Labang Studio. This tiny studio shop near Dole Park reflects its owner's lifelong love of vintage clothing. Cory Labang's old piano and her Hawaiian family photos are a nice backdrop for handmade bags and clutches in antique fabrics. Crystal glassware, glittering costume jewelry, and one-of-a-kind accessories complete this unique collection. ⊠ *431A 7th St., Lanai City* ☎ *808/315–6715* ⊕ *www.corylabangstudio. com.*

Fodor'sChoice
★
The Local Gentry. Spacious and classy, this store has clothing for every need, from casual men's and women's beachwear to evening resort wear, shoes, jewelry, and hats. There are fancy fashions for tots as well. A selection of original Lanai-themed clothing is also available, including the signature "What happens on Lanai everybody knows" T-shirts. Proprietor Jenna Gentry Majkus will mail your purchases. ⊠ *363 7th St., Lanai City* ☎ *808/565–9130.*

FOOD

Pine Isle Market. One of Lanai City's two all-purpose markets, Pine Isle stocks everything from beach toys and electronics to meats and vegetables. The staff is friendly, and it's the best place around to buy fresh fish. The market is closed Sunday. ⊠ *356 8th St., Lanai City* ☎ *808/565–6488.*

Richard's. Along with fresh meats, fine wines, and imported gourmet items, Richard's stocks everything from camping gear to household items. ⊠ *434 8th St., Lanai City* ☎ *808/565–3780.*

GALLERIES

Lanai Art Center. Local artists display their work at this dynamic center staffed by volunteers. Workshops in pottery, photography, woodworking, and painting welcome visitors. The gift shop sells Lanai handicrafts and special offerings like handmade Swarovski crystal bracelets, whose sale underwrites children's art classes. There are occasional concerts and special events. It's closed on Sunday. ⊠ *339 7th St., Lanai City* ☎ *808/565-7503* ⊕ *www.lanaiart.org.*

Fodor'sChoice **Mike Carroll Gallery.** The dreamy, soft-focus oil paintings of award-win-
★ ning painter Mike Carroll are inspired by island scenes. His work is showcased along with those of other local artists and visiting Plein Air painters. You can also find handcrafted jewelry and antiques. ⊠ *443 7th St., Lanai City* ☎ *808/565-7122* ⊕ *www.mikecarrollgallery.com.*

GENERAL STORES

International Food and Clothing Center. This old-fashioned emporium stocks everything from fishing and camping gear to fine wine to imported beer. It's a good place to pick up last-minute items when other stores are closed on Sunday. ⊠ *833 Ilima Ave., Lanai City* ☎ *808/565-6433.*

Lanai City Service. In addition to being Lanai's only gas station and auto-parts store, this outfit sells resort wear, *manapua* (steamed buns with pork filling), hot dogs, beer, soda, and bottled water. It's open 6:30 am to 10 pm daily. ⊠ *1036 Lanai Ave., Lanai City* ☎ *808/565-7227.*

SPAS

If you're looking for rejuvenation, the whole island could be considered a spa, though currently the only full spa is at the Four Seasons Resort Lanai at Manele Bay.

The Spa at Manele. Granite floors, eucalyptus steam rooms, and private cabanas set the scene for indulgence. State-of-the-art pampering enlists a panoply of oils and lotions that would have pleased Cleopatra. The Makai Ritual includes a *hehi lani* foot treatment, signature Makala massage, and scalp-conditioning massage. The banana-coconut scrub and pineapple-citrus polish treatments are delicious. Afterward, relax in the sauna or steam room. Massages in private oceanfront *hale* (houses) are available for singles or couples. ⊠ *Four Seasons Resort Lanai at Manele Bay, 1 Manele Bay Rd., Manele* ☎ *808/565-2088* ⊕ *www.fourseasons. com/manelebay/spa* ☞ *$165–$190 50-min massage; $345 per person Makai Ritual. Gym with: Cardiovascular equipment, free weights. Services: Aromatherapy, body wraps, facials, hair salon, hair care, reflexology, waxing. Classes and programs: Core strengthening, guided hikes, hydrotone, meditation, personal training, Spinning, yoga, Zumba.*

NIGHTLIFE

When it comes to nightlife, Lanai is beginning to come alive. A handful of places now feature live music and stay open past 9 pm. At the resorts, pianists add to the romantic settings. An alternative is stargazing from the beaches or watching the full moon rise from secluded vantage points.

The Bar. This intimate lounge at the Four Seasons Resort Lodge at Koele has a lively atmosphere. It's open until 11 pm, so you can enjoy a late-night cocktail and plan your next day's activities. The resort also features quiet music every evening in its Great Hall, as well as performances by well-known Hawaiian entertainers and local hula dancers. ⊠ *Four Seasons Resort Lodge at Koele, 1 Keomuku Hwy., Lanai City* ☎ *808/565–4000* ⊕ *www.fourseasons.com.*

Hotel Lanai. A visit to this small, lively bar lets you chat with locals and find out more about the island. Enjoy performances by local and visiting musicians in the big green tent on Friday nights. Get here early, as last call is at 9:30. ⊠ *Hotel Lanai, 828 Lanai Ave., Lanai City* ☎ *808/565–7211* ⊕ *www.hotellanai.com.*

Sports Bar. At the Four Seasons Resort Lanai at Manele Bay, the oceanfront Sports Bar is an open-air lounge serving such casual fare as chicken wings and burgers. Pool tables, shuffleboard courts, and a 46-inch TV make for an amusing time out. An added bonus: dolphins play in the bay below. ⊠ *Four Seasons Resort Lanai at Manele Bay, 1 Manele Bay Rd., Manele* ☎ *808/565–2000* ⊕ *www.fourseasons.com.*

WHERE TO EAT

Lanai's own version of Hawaii regional cuisine draws on the fresh bounty provided by local farmers and fishermen, combined with the skills of well-regarded chefs. The upscale menus at the Four Seasons Resort Lanai, The Lodge at Koele and the Four Seasons Resort Lanai at Manele Bay encompass European- and Asian-inspired cuisine as well as innovative preparations of international favorites and vegetarian delights. All Four Seasons Resort restaurants offer children's menus. Lanai City's eclectic ethnic fare runs from construction-worker-size local plate lunches to *poke* (raw fish), pizza, and pasta. ■TIP➔ Lanai "City" is really a small town; restaurants sometimes close their kitchens early, and only a few are open on Sunday.

Prices in the reviews are the average cost of a main course at dinner or, if dinner is not served, at lunch.

MANELE BAY

Dining at Manele Bay offers the range of options provided by Four Seasons Lanai resorts, from informal poolside meals to relaxed, eclectic dining.

$$ ✕ **The Challenge at Manele Clubhouse.** A stunning view of the legend-
AMERICAN   ary Puu Pehe rock only enhances the imaginative fare of this open-air

restaurant. Spot frolicking dolphins from the terrace. Tuck into a Hulopoe Bay prawn BLT, or the crispy battered fish-and-chips with Meyer lemon tartar sauce. The blackened-fish tacos are splendid, and specialty drinks add to the informal fun. $ *Average main: $25* ⊠ *Four Seasons Resort Lanai at Manele Bay, 1 Manele Bay Rd., Manele* ☎ *808/565–2230* ⊕ *www.fourseasons.com/manelebay* ☾ *No dinner.*

$$$
ITALIAN
✕ **Kailani.** Poolside at the Four Seasons Resort Lanai at Manele Bay, Kailani offers contemporary Italian cuisine in a setting with a stunning view of Hulopoe Bay. The big umbrellas are cool and cheerful, and upholstered chairs comfortable. If you're a coffee drinker, a Kona cappuccino freeze by the pool is a must. For a satisfying lunch try the crunchy fish-and-chips or an old-fashioned burger. House-made spaghetti carbonara with applewood slab bacon and Parmigiano-Reggiano, or lava-salt-crusted ahi are good choices for dinner. The service is the brand of cool aloha always offered by the Four Seasons. $ *Average main: $35* ⊠ *Four Seasons Resort Lanai at Manele Bay, 1 Manele Bay Rd., Manele* ☎ *808/565–2092* ⊕ *www.fourseasons.com/manelebay* ⟋ *Reservations essential.*

$$$
JAPANESE
✕ **Nobu.** Chef Nobuyuki "Nobu" Matsuhisa offers his signature new-style Japanese cuisine in this open-air, relaxed luxury venue. This is fine dining without the stress, as black-clad waiters present dish after dish of beautifully seasoned, raw and lightly cooked seafood flown in directly from Alaska and Japan. Pale-gray wicker couches on the veranda provide comfortable sink-in seating, while inside diners relax around natural wood tables. An *omakase* (chef's choice) multicourse menu makes it easy for first-timers. This simple yet elegant establishment is as much about the experience as it is about the food itself, but brace yourself for a significant bill at meal's end. $ *Average main: $30* ⊠ *1 Manele Bay Rd., Manele* ☎ *808/565–2832* ⊕ *www.noburestaurants.com/lanai* ⟋ *Reservations essential* ☾ *No lunch.*

$$$$
AMERICAN
✕ **One Forty.** Named after the island's 140 square miles, this ocean-view restaurant offers an extensive steak and seafood menu that emphasizes local ingredients. Prime cuts of beef and the freshest local fish are served in airy comfort on the hotel terrace, which overlooks the wide sweep of Hulopoe Bay. Retractable awnings provide shade on sunny days. Comfy rattan chairs, potted palms, and tropical decor create an inviting backdrop. At breakfast, fresh-baked pastries and made-to-order omelets ensure that your day starts well. $ *Average main: $45* ⊠ *Four Seasons Resort Lanai at Manele Bay, 1 Manele Bay Rd., Manele* ☎ *808/565–2290* ⊕ *www.fourseasons.com/manelebay* ⟋ *Reservations essential* ☾ *No lunch.*

LANAI CITY AND UPCOUNTRY

In Lanai City you can enjoy everything from local-style plate lunches to upscale gourmet meals. For a small area, there are a number of good places to eat and drink, but remember that Lanai City mostly closes down on Sunday.

$
AMERICAN
✕ **Anuenue Juice Bar & Cafe.** Congenial owner Tammy Ringbauer whips up healthy juice concoctions in her whirring blender, like the Liquid

Sunshine (orange, carrot, pineapple, and lemon juices with ginger), and Can You Feel the Beet (beet, apple, grapefruit, orange, and carrot juices). Add-ons include bee pollen, spirulina, and chia seeds. She also creates tasty smoothies, salads, and açai bowls, all with Lanai-grown ingredients. Pull up a stool at the small high-top bar, or enjoy your fresh blend outside under one of the shady umbrellas. $ *Average main: $10* ⊠ *338 8th St., Lanai City* ☎ *808/250–0633* ⊕ *www.anuenuejuicebar. com* ⚠ *Reservations not accepted* ⊘ *Closed Wed. No dinner.*

$ × **Blue Ginger Café.** Owners Joe and Georgia Abilay made this cheery
HAWAIIAN place into a Lanai City institution with simply prepared, consistent, tasty food. Local paintings and photos line the walls inside, while townspeople parade by the outdoor tables. For breakfast, try the Lanai omelet with Portuguese sausage. Lunch selections range from burgers to such local favorites as saimin noodles. For dinner you can sample generous portions of shrimp tempura or roasted pork. Phone ahead for takeout. $ *Average main: $12* ⊠ *409 7th St., Lanai City* ☎ *808/565–6363* ⊕ *www.bluegingercafelanai.com* ⚠ *Reservations not accepted* ▭ *No credit cards.*

$$$$ × **The Dining Room.** Reflecting the resort's country-manor ambience, this
HAWAIIAN peaceful and romantic octagonal restaurant is fine dining at its infor-
Fodor'sChoice mal best. Terra-cotta walls and soft peach lighting flatter everyone,
★ and intimate tables are spaced to allow for private conversations. The four-course tasting menu, with optional wine pairings, changes weekly, and features such delicacies as Hawaii Island Kahua Ranch beef or lamb, Molokai venison, Kona fish or shellfish, and Hamakua mushrooms. Service is quietly attentive. $ *Average main: $95* ⊠ *Four Seasons Resort Lodge at Koele, 1 Keomuku Hwy., Lanai City* ☎ *808/565–4580* ⊕ *www.fourseasons.com/koele* ⚠ *Reservations essential* ⊘ *Closed Wed. and Thurs. No lunch.*

$ × **565 Café.** Named after the oldest telephone prefix on Lanai, 565 Café
HAWAIIAN is a convenient stop for plate lunches, sandwiches like Palawai chicken breast on freshly baked focaccia, or platters of chicken *katsu* (Japanese-style breaded and fried) to take along for an impromptu picnic. Phone ahead to order pizza. Bring your own beer or wine for lunch or dinner. The patio and outdoor tables are kid-friendly. $ *Average main: $10* ⊠ *408 8th St., Lanai City* ☎ *808/565–6622* ⚠ *Reservations not accepted* ⊘ *Closed Sun.*

$$$$ × **Lanai City Grille.** Simple white walls hung with local art, lazily turn-
AMERICAN ing ceiling fans, and unobtrusive service provide the backdrop for a
Fodor'sChoice menu designed and supervised by celebrity-chef Beverly Gannon. Crab
★ cakes, pulled-pork wontons, or steamed manila clams are a great way to start the evening. Baby field greens are artfully presented. The entrées are on the meaty side for Hawaii, and should satisfy serious appetites. The dining room is a friendly and comfortable alternative to the Four Seasons, and a convenient, if sometimes noisy, gathering place for large parties. $ *Average main: $36* ⊠ *Hotel Lanai, 828 Lanai Ave., Lanai City* ☎ *808/565–4700* ⊕ *www.hotellanai.com* ⚠ *Reservations essential* ⊘ *Closed Mon. and Tues. No lunch.*

$ × **Coffee Works.** A block from Dole Park, this Northern California–style
AMERICAN café offers an umbrella-covered deck where you can sip cappuccinos

and get in tune with the slow pace of life. Bagels with lox, deli sandwiches, and pastries add to the caloric content, while blended espresso shakes and gourmet ice cream complete the coffee-house vibe. [$] *Average main: $8* ✉ *604 Ilima St., Lanai City* ☎ *808/565–6962* ✍ *Reservations not accepted* 🕑 *Closed Sun. No dinner.*

$ HAWAIIAN 🍴 **Lanai Ohana Poke Market.** This is the closest you can come to dining on traditional cuisine on Lanai. Enjoy fresh food prepared by a Hawaiian family and served in a cool, shady garden. The emphasis is on *poke,* which is raw ahi tuna flavored with Hawaiian salt and seaweed. Hawaiian plate lunches, take-out kimchi shrimp, and ahi and aku tuna steaks complete the menu. The place also caters picnics and parties. [$] *Average main: $9* ✉ *834A Gay St., Lanai City* ☎ *808/559–6265* ✍ *Reservations not accepted* 💳 *No credit cards* 🕑 *Closed weekends. No dinner.*

$ HAWAIIAN FAMILY 🍴 **No Ka Oi Grindz Lanai.** A local favorite, this lunchroom-style café has a shaded picnic table in the landscaped front yard and five more tables in the no-frills interior. The innovative menu, which changes frequently, includes such delicacies as kimchi fried rice, pork fritter sandwiches, and massive plate lunches. Sit outside and watch the town drive by. [$] *Average main: $10* ✉ *335 9th St., Lanai City* ☎ *808/565–9413* ✍ *Reservations not accepted* 💳 *No credit cards* 🕑 *Closed Sun.*

$$ ITALIAN 🍴 **Pele's Other Garden.** Small and colorful, Pele's is a deli and bistro all in one. For lunch, sandwiches or daily hot specials satisfy hearty appetites. At night it's transformed into a busy bistro, complete with tablecloths and soft jazz. Designer beers and fine wines enhance an Italian-inspired menu. Start with bruschetta, then choose from a selection of pizzas or pasta dishes. An intimate back-room bar add to the liveliness, and entertainers often drop in for impromptu jam sessions. [$] *Average main: $19* ✉ *811 Houston St., at 8th St., Lanai City* ☎ *808/565–9628, 888/764–3354* 🌐 *www.pelesothergarden.com* ✍ *Reservations essential* 🕑 *Closed Sun.*

$$$$ AMERICAN 🍴 **The Terrace.** Floor-to-ceiling glass doors at this spacious lounge open onto formal gardens and lovely vistas of the mist-clad mountains. A comfort-food menu features a hearty breakfast to start the day, and braised beef with pearl onions to finish it. The Sunday brunch is a special treat. In the evening the soothing sounds of Hawaiian music or the grand piano in the Great Hall complete the ambience. [$] *Average main: $38* ✉ *Four Seasons Resort Lodge at Koele, 1 Keomuku Hwy., Lanai City* ☎ *808/565–4500* 🌐 *www.fourseasons.com/koele* ✍ *Reservations essential.*

WHERE TO STAY

Though Lanai has few properties, it does have a range of price options. Four Seasons manages both The Lodge at Koele and Four Seasons Resort Lanai at Manele Bay. Although the room rates are different, guests can partake of all the resort amenities at both properties. If you're on a budget, consider the Hotel Lanai. Note that room rates do not include 13.42% sales tax.

Prices in the reviews are the lowest cost of a standard double room in high season.

$$$$
RESORT
FAMILY
Fodor's Choice
★

⛻ **Four Seasons Resort Lanai at Manele Bay.** Overlooking Hulopoe Bay, this sublime retreat offers beachside urban chic with stunning views of the deep blue sea and astonishing rocky coastline. **Pros:** fitness center with ocean views; nearby beach; outstanding restaurants. **Cons:** 20 minutes from town; need a car to explore the area. $ *Rooms from: $459* ✉ *l Manele Rd., Manele* ☎ *808/565–2000, 800/321–4666* ⊕ *www.fourseasons.com/manelebay* ↩ *215 rooms, 21 suites* ⎟◎⎟ *No meals.*

$$$$
RESORT
Fodor's Choice
★

⛻ **Four Seasons Resort Lanai, The Lodge at Koele.** In the highlands above Lanai City, this grand country estate exudes luxury and romance with paths meandering through formal gardens, a huge reflecting pond, and an orchid greenhouse. **Pros:** beautiful surroundings; impeccable service; walking distance to Lanai City. **Cons:** doesn't seem much like Hawaii; can get chilly, especially in winter; not much to do in rainy weather. $ *Rooms from: $389* ✉ *1 Keomoku Rd., Lanai City* ☎ *808/565–4000, 800/321–4666* ⊕ *www.fourseasons.com/koele* ↩ *94 rooms, 8 suites* ⎟◎⎟ *No meals.*

$
HOTEL

⛻ **Hotel Lanai.** Built in 1923 to house visiting pineapple executives, this historic inn has South Pacific–style rooms with country quilts, ceiling fans, and bamboo shades. **Pros:** historic atmosphere; walking distance to town. **Cons:** rooms are a bit plain; noisy at dinnertimes; no room phones or TVs. $ *Rooms from: $149* ✉ *828 Lanai Ave., Lanai City* ☎ *808/565–7211, 800/795–7211* ⊕ *www.hotellanai.com* ↩ *10 rooms, 1 cottage* ⎟◎⎟ *Breakfast.*

TRAVEL SMART
HAWAII

GETTING HERE AND AROUND

▌ AIR TRAVEL

Flying time to Hawaii is about 10 hours from New York, 8 hours from Chicago, and 5 hours from Los Angeles.

Hawaii is a major destination link for flights traveling between the U.S. mainland and Asia, Australia, New Zealand, and the South Pacific. Although the Neighbor Islands' airports are smaller and more casual than Honolulu International, during peak times they can also be quite busy. Allot extra travel time to all airports during morning and afternoon rush-hour traffic periods.

Plan to arrive at the airport at least 60 minutes before departure for interisland flights.

Plants and plant products are subject to regulation by the Department of Agriculture, both on entering and leaving Hawaii. Upon leaving the Islands, you'll have to have your bags X-rayed and tagged at one of the airport's agricultural inspection stations before you proceed to check-in. Pineapples and coconuts with the packer's agricultural inspection stamp pass freely; papayas must be treated, inspected, and stamped. All other fruits are banned for export to the U.S. mainland. Flowers pass except for gardenia, rose leaves, jade vine, and mauna loa. Also banned are insects, snails, soil, cotton, cacti, sugarcane, and all berry plants.

You'll have to leave dogs and other pets at home. A 120-day quarantine is imposed to keep out rabies, which is nonexistent in Hawaii. If specific pre- and postarrival requirements are met, animals may qualify for a 30-day or five-day-or-less quarantine.

Airline Security Issues Transportation Security Administration ⊕ www.tsa.gov.

Air Travel Resources in Hawaii State of Hawaii Department of Transportation— Airports Division ☎ 808/836–6413 ⊕ hidot. hawaii.gov/airports.

AIRPORTS

All of Hawaii's major islands have their own airports, but Honolulu's International Airport is the main stopover for most domestic and international flights. From Honolulu, there are flights to the Neighbor Islands almost every half-hour from early morning until evening. In addition, some carriers now offer non-stop service directly from the mainland to Maui, Kauai, and the Big Island on a limited basis. No matter the island, all of Hawaii's airports are "open-air," meaning you can enjoy those trade-wind breezes up until the moment you step on the plane.

HONOLULU/OAHU AIRPORT

Hawaii's major airport is Honolulu International, on Oahu, 20 minutes (9 miles) west of Waikiki. When traveling interisland from Honolulu, you will depart from either the interisland terminal or the commuter-airline terminal, located in two separate structures adjacent to the main overseas terminal building. The airport operates a free shuttle system between the terminals from 6 am to 10 pm every day.

Airport Information Honolulu International Airport (HNL) ⊠ Honolulu ☎ 808/836–6411 ⊕ www.hawaii.gov/hnl.

MAUI AIRPORTS

Maui has two main airports. Kahului Airport handles major airlines and interisland flights; it's the only airport on Maui that has direct service from the mainland. If you're arriving from another island and you're staying in West Maui, you can avoid the hour drive from the Kahului Airport by flying into the much smaller Kapalua–West Maui Airport, which is served by Mokulele Airlines. The tiny town of Hana in East Maui also has an airstrip, served by Pacific Wings, Mokulele Airlines, and charter flights from Kahului and Kapalua. Flying here from one of the other airports is a great option if you want to avoid the long and winding drive to Hana.

Airport Information Hana Airport (HNM)
☏ 808/248–4861 ⊕ hawaii.gov/hnm. **Kahului Airport (OGG)** ☏ 808/872–3830 ⊕ hawaii. gov/ogg. **Kapalua–West Maui Airport (JHM)** ☏ 808/665–6108 ⊕ hawaii.gov/jhm.

BIG ISLAND AIRPORTS
Those flying to the Big Island of Hawaii regularly land at one of two fields. Kona International Airport at Keahole, on the west side, best serves Kailua-Kona, Keauhou, and the Kohala Coast. Hilo International Airport is more appropriate for those going to the east side. Waimea-Kohala Airport, called Kamuela Airport by residents, is used primarily for commuting among the Islands.

Airport Information Hilo International Airport (ITO) ☏ 808/961–9300 ⊕ hawaii.gov/ ito. **Kona International Airport at Keahole (KOA)** ☏ 808/327–9520 ⊕ hawaii.gov/koa. **Waimea-Kohala Airport (MUE)** ☏ 808/887–8126 ⊕ hawaii.gov/mue.

KAUAI AIRPORT
On Kauai, visitors fly into Lihue Airport, on the East Side of the island.

Airport Information Lihue Airport (LIH) ☏ 808/274–3800 ⊕ hawaii.gov/lih.

MOLOKAI AND LANAI AIRPORTS
Molokai Airport is small and centrally located, as is Lanai Airport. Both rural airports handle a limited number of flights per day. Visitors coming from the mainland to these Islands must first stop in Maui or Oahu and change to an interisland flight.

Information Molokai Airport (MKK) ☏ 808/567–9660 ⊕ hawaii.gov/mkk. **Lanai Airport (LNY)** ☏ 808/565–7942 ⊕ hawaii. gov/lny.

FLIGHTS
US Airways, American, and United fly into Oahu, Maui, Kauai, and the Big Island. Alaska flies into Oahu, Maui, Kauai, and the Big Island. Delta serves Oahu (Honolulu), Maui, and the Big Island. Hawaiian Airlines flies direct into Oahu from many cities in the western United States. In 2012 it added direct service from New York's JFK Airport.

Hawaiian Airlines, go! Airlines, Mokulele Airlines, Island Air, and Pacific Wings offer regular service between the Islands. All have frequent-flier programs, which will entitle you to rewards and upgrades the more you fly. Be sure to compare prices offered by all the interisland carriers. Interisland fares have increased in recent years, but if you are somewhat flexible with your dates and times you may find a lower fare.

If you prefer, you can take a charter flight between the Islands. Pacific Wings serves Oahu, Lanai, Maui, Molokai, and the Big Island. Services include premiere (same-day departures on short notice), premium (24-hour notice), group, and cargo/courier.

Airline Contacts Alaska Airlines ☏ 800/252–7522 ⊕ www.alaskaair.com. **American Airlines** ☏ 800/433–7300 ⊕ www.aa.com. **Delta Airlines** ☏ 800/221–1212 ⊕ www.delta.com. **United Airlines** ☏ 800/864–8331 ⊕ www.united.com. **US Airways** ☏ 800/428–4322 ⊕ www.usairways. com.

Interisland Flights go! Airlines ☏ 888/435–9462 ⊕ www.iflygo.com. **Hawaiian Airlines** ☏ 800/367–5320 ⊕ www. hawaiianairlines.com. **Mokulele Airlines** ☏ 866/260–7070 ⊕ www.mokuleleairlines. com. **Pacific Wings** ☏ 888/575–4546 ⊕ www. pacificwings.com.

▌ BOAT TRAVEL

There is daily ferry service between Lahaina, Maui, and Manele Bay, Lanai, with Expeditions Lanai Ferry. The 9-mile crossing costs $60 round-trip, per person, and takes 45 minutes or so, depending on ocean conditions (which can make this trip a rough one). Molokai Ferry offers twice-daily ferry service between Lahaina, Maui, and Kaunakakai, Molokai. Travel time is about 90 minutes each way and the one-way fare is $69.55 per person; a book of six one-way tickets costs $321.69.

Reservations are recommended for both ferries.

Information **Expeditions Lanai Ferry** ☎ *808/214–1467, 800/695–2624* ⊕ *www. go-lanai.com.* **Molokai Ferry** ☎ *877/307–6524* ⊕ *www.molokaiferry.com.*

▌BUS TRAVEL

OAHU

While bus service is not as practical on some of the Neighbor Islands, getting around by bus is a convenient and affordable option on Oahu.

You can go all around the island or just down Kalakaua Avenue for $2.50 on Honolulu's municipal transportation system, affectionately known as TheBus. It's one of the island's best bargains. Taking TheBus in the Waikiki and downtown Honolulu areas is especially easy, with buses making stops in Waikiki every 15 minutes to take passengers to nearby shopping areas, such as Ala Moana Shopping Center.

You're entitled to one free transfer per fare if you ask for it when boarding. Exact change is required, and dollar bills are accepted. A four-day pass for visitors costs $35 and is available at ABC convenience stores in Waikiki and in the Ala Moana Shopping Center. Monthly passes cost $60.

You can find privately published route booklets at most drugstores and other convenience outlets. The important route numbers for Waikiki are 2, 8, 19, 20, 23, and City Express Route A. If you venture farther afield, you can always get back on one of these.

The Waikiki Trolley has four lines and dozens of stops that allow you to design your own itinerary while riding on brass-trimmed, open-air trolleys. The Red Line Historic Honolulu Sightseeing Tour travels between Waikiki and the Bishop Museum and includes stops at Aloha Tower, Ala Moana, and downtown Honolulu, among others. The Blue Line Panoramic Coastline Tour provides a tour of Oahu's southeastern coastline, including Diamond Head Crater, Hanauma Bay, and Sea Life Park. The Blue Line also has an express trolley to Diamond Head that runs twice daily. The Pink Line Waikiki/Ala Moana Shopping Shuttle stops at the Ala Moana Shopping Center, DFS Galleria, and the Royal Hawaiian Shopping Center among others.

A one-day pass for the Red, Green, and Pink lines is $32 if purchased online, or $35 in person. A four-day pass for the same three lines is $54 online, or $57 in person. And a seven-day pass good for the same three lines is $59 when purchased online, or $73 in person. A one-day Blue Line pass is $18 online, or you can combine it with the other three lines passes range for $42 to $69 (online prices). In Waikiki, there also are a number of brightly painted private buses, many of which are free, that will take you to such commercial attractions as dinner cruises, garment factories, and the like.

Bus Information **TheBus** ☎ *808/848–5555, 808/848–4500* ⊕ *www.thebus.org.* **Waikiki Trolley** ☎ *808/591–2561, 800/824–8804* ⊕ *www.waikikitrolley.com.*

MAUI

Maui Bus, operated by Roberts Hawaii, offers 11 routes in and between various Central, South, and West, and Upcountry Maui communities, seven days a week, including all holidays. Passengers can travel in and around Wailuku, Kahului, Lahaina, Kaanapali, Kapalua, Kihei, Wailea, Maalaea, the North Shore (Paia), and Upcountry (including Pukalani, Makawao, Haliimaile, and Haiku). The Upcountry and Haiku Islander routes include a stop at Kahului Airport. All one-way tickets are $2.

For travelers who prefer not to rent a car, Maui Bus is a great way to go. It runs from early morning to late evening daily, and stops at most of the major towns and sightseeing destinations. And, you can't beat the price. Maps and schedules are available online.

Bus Contact Maui Bus ☎ 808/871–4838 ⊕ www.mauicounty.gov/bus.

BIG ISLAND

In Hawaii County, the Hele-On Bus provides public transportation around the island, including a four-hour trip from Kona to Hilo (each way) three times each day. The fare is $2, or $15 for 10 tickets. The county Transit Agency offers a shared-ride taxi program that provides door-to-door service. Participating companies charge as little as $2 per person for trips between one and four miles and as little as $4 per person for trips between 4 and 9 miles (the longest trip covered by the program). Fares are paid with prepurchased vouchers. Maps, schedules, and taxi details are available online.

Bus Contact Hele-On Bus ☎ 808/961–8744 ⊕ www.heleonbus.org.

KAUAI

The Kauai Bus operates a route from Hanalei (on the North Shore) to Kekaha (on the West Side) daily except Sunday. It runs once each hour from early morning until the evening, and provides a lunch-time shuttle around Lihue. The fare is $2. Children six and under travel free.

Bus Contact The Kauai Bus ☎ 808/246–8110 ⊕ www.kauai.gov/transportation.

▌ CAR TRAVEL

Technically, the Big Island of Hawaii is the only island you can completely circle by car, but each island offers plenty of sightseeing from its miles of roadways.

Oahu can be circled except for the roadless northwest-shore area around Kaena Point. Elsewhere, major highways follow the shoreline and traverse the island at two points. Rush-hour traffic (6:30 to 8:30 am and 3:30 to 6 pm) can be frustrating around Honolulu and the outlying areas, as many thoroughfares allow no left turns.

Traffic on Maui can be very bad branching out from Kahului to and from Paia, Kihei, and Lahaina. Drive here during peak hours and you'll know why local residents are calling for restrictions on development. Parking along many streets is curtailed during these times, and towing is strictly practiced. Read curbside parking signs before leaving your vehicle, even at a meter.

On Kauai, the 15-mile stretch of the Napali Coast is the only part of the island's coastline that's not accessible by car. Otherwise, one main road can get you from Barking Sands Beach on the West Side to Haena on the North Shore.

Although Molokai and Lanai have fewer roadways, car rental is still worthwhile and will allow plenty of interesting sightseeing. A four-wheel-drive vehicle is best on these Islands.

Asking for directions will almost always produce a helpful explanation from the locals, but you should be prepared for an Islands term or two. Instead of using compass directions, remember that Hawaii residents refer to places as being either *mauka* (toward the mountains) or *makai* (toward the ocean) from one another.

Other directions depend on your location: in Honolulu, for example, people say to "go Diamond Head," which means toward that famous landmark to your east, or to "go *ewa*," meaning in the opposite direction, toward a town in leeward (West) Oahu. A shop on the *mauka*–Diamond Head corner of a street is on the mountain side of the street on the corner closest to Diamond Head. It all makes perfect sense once you get the lay of the land.

GASOLINE

Gasoline is widely available everywhere but the farthest corners of the main Islands. National chains like 76, Chevron, 7-Eleven, and Shell are ubiquitous, and accept all major credit cards right at the pump or inside the station. Prices can range from $4 to $5 for one gallon of "regular" fuel, which is sufficient for all models of rental cars. Gasoline is generally more expensive closer to the airports, where you'll need to refuel before returning your car. Neighbor Islands have higher gasoline prices than Oahu.

Information Hawaii Gas Prices ⊕ *www. hawaiigasprices.com.*

ROAD CONDITIONS

It's difficult to get lost in most of Hawaii. Although their names may challenge a visitor's tongue, roads and streets are well marked; just watch out for the many one-way streets in Waikiki. Keep an eye open for the Hawaii Visitors and Convention Bureau's red-caped King Kamehameha signs, which mark attractions and scenic spots. Ask for a map at the car-rental counter. Free publications containing high-quality road maps can be found on all Islands. And, of course, a GPS or your passenger's smartphone are great ways to find your way around, too.

Many of Hawaii's roads are two-lane highways with limited shoulders—and yes, even in paradise, there is traffic, especially during the morning and afternoon rush hour. In rural areas, it's not unusual for gas stations to close early. If you see that your tank is getting low, don't take any chances; fill up when you see a station. In Hawaii, turning right on a red light is legal, except where noted. Use caution during heavy downpours, especially if you see signs warning of falling rocks. If you're enjoying views from the road or need to study a map, pull over to the side. Remember the aloha spirit when you are driving; allow other cars to merge, don't honk (it's considered extremely rude in the Islands), leave a comfortable distance between your car and the car ahead of you; use your headlights, especially during sunrise and sunset, and use your turn signals.

ROADSIDE EMERGENCIES

If you find yourself in an emergency or accident while driving on any of the Islands, pull over if you can. If you have a cell phone with you, call the roadside assistance number on your rental car contract or AAA Help. If you find that your car has been broken into or stolen, report it immediately to your rental car company and they can assist you. If it's an emergency and someone is hurt, call 911 immediately and stay there until medical personnel arrive.

Emergency Services AAA Help ☎ *800/222–4357.*

RULES OF THE ROAD

Be sure to buckle up. Hawaii has a strictly enforced seat-belt law for all passengers—front and backseat. Always strap children under age four into approved child-safety seats. Hawaii's Child Restraint Law requires that all children three years and younger be in an approved child-safety seat in the backseat of a vehicle. Children ages four to seven must be seated in a rear booster seat or child restraint such as a lap and shoulder belt. Children 18 and under are also required by state law to use seat belts.

The highway speed limit is usually 55 mph. In-town traffic moves from 25 to 40 mph. Jaywalking is common, so be particularly watchful for pedestrians, especially in congested areas such as Waikiki. Unauthorized use of a parking space reserved for persons with disabilities can net you a $150 fine. All four Hawaii counties have implemented bans on handheld cell phone use by drivers. If you must use the phone, pull to the side of the road to avoid a costly ticket.

CAR RENTAL

If you plan to do lots of sightseeing, it's best to rent a car. Even if all you want to do is relax at your resort, you may want to hop in the car to check out a popular restaurant. All the big national rental car agencies have locations throughout Hawaii, but Dollar is the only company that has offices on all the major Hawaiian Islands. There also are several local rental car companies so be sure to compare prices before you book. While in the

Islands, you can rent anything from an econobox to a Ferrari. On the Big Island, Lanai, and Molokai, four-wheel-drive vehicles are recommended for exploring off the beaten path. Rates are usually better if you reserve through a rental agency's website. It's wise to make reservations far in advance and make sure that a confirmed reservation guarantees you a car, especially if visiting during peak seasons or for major conventions or sporting events. It's not uncommon to find several car categories sold out during major events on some of the smaller Islands.

Rates begin at about $25 to $35 a day for an economy car with air-conditioning, automatic transmission, and unlimited mileage, depending on your pickup location. This does not include the airport concession fee, general excise tax, rental vehicle surcharge, or vehicle license fee.

When you reserve a car, ask about cancellation penalties and drop-off charges should you plan to pick up the car in one location and return it to another.

In Hawaii you must be 21 years of age to rent a car and you must have a valid driver's license and a major credit card. Those under 25 will pay a daily surcharge of $15 to $27. Your unexpired mainland driver's license is valid for rental for up to 90 days. Request car seats and extras such as GPS when you make your reservation. Car seats and boosters range from $5 to $8 per day.

Since many island roads are two lanes, be sure to allow plenty of time to return your vehicle so that you can make your flight. Traffic can be bad during morning and afternoon rush hour. Give yourself about 2½ hours before departure time to return your vehicle.

CAR RENTAL RESOURCES

Automobile Associations

U.S.: American Automobile Association	☎ 800/736–2886 Most contact with the organization is through state and regional members.	⊕ www.aaa.com
National Automobile Club	☎ 800/622–2136 Membership is open to California residents only.	⊕ www.thenac.com

Local Agencies

Advantage Rent-A-Car (Oahu, Maui, Kauai, Big Island)	☎ 800/777–5500	⊕ www.advantage.com
Adventure Lanai EcoCentre	☎ 808/565–7373	⊕ www.adventurelanai.com
Aloha Campers (Maui)	☎ 808/281–8020	⊕ www.alohacampers.com
Discount Hawaii Car Rental	☎ 800/292–1930	⊕ www.discounthawaiicarrental.com
Happy Campers Hawaii (Big Island)	☎ 888/550–3918	⊕ www.happycampershawaii.com
Harper Car and Truck Rental (Big Island)	☎ 800/852–9993	⊕ www.harpershawaii.com
Hawaii Car Rental	☎ 800/655–7989	⊕ www.hawaiicarrental.com
Hawaiian Discount Car Rentals	☎ 800/955–3142	⊕ www.hawaiidrive-o.com
JN Car and Truck Rentals (Oahu)	☎ 800/363–4036	⊕ www.jnrentalshawaii.com
Molokai Rental Car (Molokai)	☎ 866/666–3304	⊕ www.molokairentalcar.com

Major Agencies

Alamo	☎ 877/222–9075	⊕ www.alamo.com
Avis	☎ 800/331–1212	⊕ www.avis.com
Budget	☎ 800/527–0700	⊕ www.budget.com
Dollar	☎ 800/800–3665	⊕ www.dollar.com
Enterprise	☎ 800/261–7331	⊕ www.enterprise.com
Hertz	☎ 800/654–3131	⊕ www.hertz.com
National Car Rental	☎ 877/222–9058	⊕ www.nationalcar.com
Thrifty	☎ 800/847–4389	⊕ www.thrifty.com

ESSENTIALS

■ ACCOMMODATIONS

Hawaii truly offers something for everyone. Are you looking for a luxurious oceanfront resort loaded with amenities, an intimate two-room bed-and-breakfast tucked away in a lush rain forest, a house with a pool and incredible views for your extended family, a condominium just steps from the 18th hole, or even a campsite at a national park? You can find all these and more throughout the Islands.

Most hotels and other lodgings require you to give your credit-card details before they will confirm your reservation. Get confirmation in writing and have a copy of it handy when you check in. Be sure you understand the hotel's cancellation policy. Some places allow you to cancel without any kind of penalty—even if you prepaid to secure a discounted rate—if you cancel at least 24 hours in advance. Others require you to cancel a week in advance or penalize you the cost of one night. Small inns and bed-and-breakfasts are most likely to require you to cancel far in advance. Most hotels allow children under a certain age to stay in their parents' room at no extra charge, but others charge for them as adults; find out the cutoff age for discounts.

Prices in the reviews are the lowest cost of a standard double room in high season. For expanded hotel reviews, visit www. Fodors.com.

BED-AND-BREAKFASTS

For many travelers, nothing compares to the personal service and guest interaction offered at bed-and-breakfasts. There are hundreds of bed-and-breakfasts throughout the Islands; many even invite their guests to enjoy complimentary wine tastings and activities such as lei making and basket weaving. Each island's website also features a listing of member B&Bs that are individually owned.

Contacts Bed and Breakfast.com
☎ 512/462–2632 ⊕ *www.bedandbreakfast. com.* **Bed & Breakfast Inns Online**
☎ 800/215–7365 ⊕ *www.bbonline.com.*
Better Bed and Breakfasts ⊕ *www. betterbedandbreakfasts.com.* **BnB Finder.com**
☎ 888/547–8226, 888/469–6663 ⊕ *www. bnbfinder.com.* **Hawaii's Best Bed & Breakfasts** ☎ 808/263–3100 ⊕ *www.bestbnb.com.*

CONDOMINIUM AND HOUSE RENTALS

Vacation rentals are perfect for couples, families, and friends traveling together who like the convenience of staying at a home away from home. Properties managed by individual owners can be found on online vacation-rental listing directories such as CyberRentals and Vacation Rentals By Owners, as well as on the visitors bureau website for each island. There also are several Islands-based management companies with vacation rentals.

Compare companies, as some offer Internet specials and free night stays when booking. Policies vary, but most require a minimum stay, usually greater during peak travel seasons.

Contacts CyberRentals ☎ 512/684–1098
⊕ *www.cyberrentals.com.* **Vacation Rentals By Owner** ⊕ *www.vrbo.com.*

HOME EXCHANGES

With a direct home exchange you stay in someone else's home while they stay in yours. *The exchange clubs listed below feature dozens of Hawaii homes available for exchange.* Many are on the beach or have ocean views.

Exchange Clubs HomeExchange.com. A three-month membership is $47.85; a twelve-month membership is $119.40. ☎ 800/877–8723, 310/798–3864 ⊕ *www.homeexchange. com.* **HomeLink International.** This company charges an $89 annual membership fee, or $39 for USA exchanges only. ☎ 800/638–3841, 954/566–2687 ⊕ *www.homelink.org.* **Intervac.** This company charges $99 for a one-year membership. ☎ 800/756–4663 ⊕ www. intervac-homeexchange.com.

HOTELS

All hotels listed have private bath unless otherwise noted.

▮ COMMUNICATIONS

INTERNET

If you've brought your laptop with you to the Islands, you should have no problem connecting to the Internet. Major hotels and resorts offer high-speed access in rooms and/or lobbies. In some cases there will be an hourly or daily charge billed to your room. If you're staying at a small inn or vacation home without Internet access (a rarity these days), ask for the nearest café or coffee shop with wireless access.

Contacts Cybercafes. This site lists more than 4,000 Internet cafés worldwide. ⊕ www. cybercafes.com.

▮ EATING OUT

Whether you're looking for a dinner for two in a romantic oceanfront dining room or a family get-together in a hole-in-the-wall serving traditional Hawaiian fare like *kalua* (cooked in an underground oven) pig, you'll find it throughout the Islands. When it comes to eating, Hawaii has something for every taste bud and every budget. With chefs using locally grown fruits and vegetables, vegetarians often have many exciting choices for their meals. And because Hawaii is a popular destination for families, restaurants almost always have a children's menu. When making a reservation at your hotel's dining room, ask about free or reduced-price meals for children.

MEALS AND MEALTIMES

Breakfast is usually served from 6 or 7 am to 9:30 or 10 am.

Lunch typically runs from 11:30 am to around 1:30 or 2 pm, and will include salads, sandwiches, and lighter fare. The "plate lunch," a favorite of many locals, usually consists of an Asian protein, like shoyu chicken, seared ahi, or teriyaki beef—served with two scoops of white rice and a scoop of macaroni or potato salad. The phrase "broke da mouth," often used to describe these plates, refers not only to their size, but also their tastiness.

Dinner is usually served from 5 to 9 pm and, depending on the restaurant, can be a simple or lavish affair. Stick to the chefs' specials if you can because they usually represent the best of the season. *Poke* (marinated raw tuna) is a local specialty and can often be found on *pupu* (appetizer) menus.

Meals in resort areas are pricey and only sometimes excellent. The restaurants we include are the cream of the crop in each price category. Unless otherwise noted, the restaurants listed are open daily for lunch and dinner.

Prices in the reviews are the average cost of a main course at dinner or, if dinner is not served, at lunch.

For guidelines on tipping, see Tipping.

RESERVATIONS AND DRESS

Hawaii is decidedly casual. Aloha shirts and shorts or long pants for men and island-style dresses or casual resort wear for women are standard attire for evenings in most hotel restaurants and local eateries. T-shirts and shorts will do the trick for breakfast and lunch. We mention dress only when men are required to wear a jacket or a jacket and tie.

Regardless of where you are, it's a good idea to make a reservation if you can. In some places, it's expected. We only mention reservations specifically when they are essential or when they are not accepted. For popular restaurants, book as far ahead as you can (often a month or more), and reconfirm as soon as you arrive. Large parties should always call ahead to check the reservations policy.

WINE, BEER, AND SPIRITS

Hawaii has a new generation of micro-breweries, including on-site microbreweries at many restaurants. The drinking age in Hawaii is 21 years of age, and a photo ID must be presented to purchase alcoholic beverages. Bars are open until 2 am; venues with a cabaret license can stay open until 4 am. No matter what you might see in the local parks, drinking alcohol in public parks or on the beaches is illegal. It's also illegal to have open containers of alcohol in motor vehicles.

▮ HEALTH

Hawaii is known as the Health State. The life expectancy here is 82.7 years, the longest in the nation. Balmy weather makes it easy to remain active year-round, and the low-stress aloha attitude certainly contributes to general well-being. When visiting the Islands, however, there are a few health issues to keep in mind.

The Hawaii State Department of Health recommends that you drink 16 ounces of water per hour to avoid dehydration when hiking or spending time in the sun. Use sunblock, wear UV-reflective sunglasses, and protect your head with a visor or hat for shade. If you're not acclimated to warm, humid weather, you should allow plenty of time for rest stops and refreshments.

When visiting freshwater streams, be aware of the tropical bacterial infection leptospirosis, which is spread by animal urine and carried into streams and mud. It's rare but the symptoms include fever, headache, body aches, nausea, sweating and chills, weakness and loss of appetite, and red eyes. If you or someone you're with exhibits any of these symptoms, you should seek medical attention. However, the best thing to do is to avoid such contact. Don't swim or wade in freshwater streams or ponds if you have open sores and don't drink from any freshwater streams or ponds, especially after it has rained.

On the Islands, fog is a rare occurrence, but there can often be "vog," an airborne haze of gases released from volcanic vents on the Big Island. During certain weather conditions such as "Kona Winds," the vog can settle over the Islands and cause discomfort for those with respiratory and other health conditions, especially asthma or emphysema. If susceptible, stay indoors and get medical assistance if needed.

The Islands have their share of bugs and insects that enjoy the tropical climate as much as visitors do. Most are harmless but annoying. When planning to spend time outdoors in hiking areas, wear long-sleeve clothing and pants and use mosquito repellent containing DEET. In very damp places, you may encounter the dreaded local centipede. On the Islands they usually come in two colors, brown and blue, and they range from the size of a worm to an 8-inch cigar. Their sting is very painful, and the reaction is similar to bee- and wasp-sting reactions. When camping, shake out your sleeping bag before climbing in, and check your shoes in the morning, as the centipedes like cozy places. If planning on hiking or traveling in remote areas, always carry a first-aid kit and appropriate medications for sting reactions.

▮ HOURS OF OPERATION

Even people in paradise have to work. Local business hours are generally weekdays 8 to 5. Banks are usually open Monday through Thursday 8:30 to 4 and until 6 on Friday. Some banks have Saturday-morning hours. Grocery and department stores, as well as shopping malls and boutiques, are open seven days a week.

Many self-serve gas stations stay open around the clock, with full-service stations usually open from around 7 am until 9 pm. U.S. post offices are open weekdays 8:30 am to 4:30 pm and Saturday 9 to 11 am. On Oahu, the Ala Moana post office branch is the only branch, other than the main Honolulu International

Airport facility, that stays open until 4 pm on Saturday.

Most museums generally open their doors between 9 am and 10 am and stay open until 5 pm Tuesday through Saturday. Many museums operate with afternoon hours only on Sunday and close on Monday. Visitor-attraction hours vary throughout the state, but most sights are open daily with the exception of major holidays such as Christmas. Check local newspapers upon arrival for attraction hours and schedules if visiting over holiday periods. The local dailies carry a listing of "What's Open/What's Not" for those time periods.

Stores in resort areas sometimes open as early as 8, while shopping centers open at 9:30 or 10 on weekdays and Saturday, a bit later on Sunday. Bigger malls stay open until 9 pm weekdays and Saturday and close between 5 and 6 pm on Sunday. Boutiques in resort areas may stay open as late as 11.

▌ MONEY

Prices are given for adults. Substantially reduced fees are almost always available for children, students, and senior citizens.

ATMS AND BANKS

Automatic teller machines for easy access to cash are everywhere on the Islands. ATMs can be found in shopping centers, small convenience and grocery stores, and inside hotels and resorts, as well as outside most bank branches.

CREDIT CARDS

It's a good idea to inform your credit-card company before you travel, especially if you're going abroad and don't travel internationally very often. Otherwise, the credit-card company might put a hold on your card owing to unusual activity—not a good thing halfway through your trip. Record all your credit-card numbers—as well as the phone numbers to call if your cards are lost or stolen—in a safe place, so you're prepared should something go wrong. Both MasterCard and Visa have general numbers you can call if your card is lost, but you're better off calling the number of your issuing bank, since MasterCard and Visa usually just transfer you to your bank; your bank's number is usually printed on your card.

▌ PACKING

Hawaii is casual: sandals, bathing suits, and comfortable, informal clothing are the norm. In summer, synthetic slacks and shirts, although easy to care for, can be uncomfortably warm. Only a few upscale restaurants require a jacket for dinner. The aloha shirt is accepted dress in Hawaii for business and most social occasions. Shorts are standard daytime attire, along with a T-shirt or polo shirt. There's no need to buy expensive sandals on the mainland—here you can get flip-flops for a couple of dollars and off-brand sandals for $20. Golfers should remember that many courses have dress codes requiring a collared shirt. If you're not prepared, you can pick up appropriate clothing at resort pro shops. If you're visiting in winter or planning to visit a high-altitude area, bring a sweater or light- to medium-weight jacket. A polar fleece pullover is ideal.

One of the most important things to tuck into your suitcase is sunscreen. Hats and sunglasses offer important sun protection, too. All major hotels in Hawaii provide beach towels.

You might also want to pack a light raincoat or folding umbrella, as morning rain showers are not uncommon. And on each of the Islands' windward coasts, it can be rainy, especially during the winter months. If you're planning on doing any exploration in rain forests or national parks, bring along a sturdy pair of hiking boots.

SAFETY

Hawaii is generally a safe tourist destination, but it's still wise to follow commonsense safety precautions. Hotel and visitor-center staff can provide information should you decide to head out on your own to more remote areas. Don't leave any valuables in your rental car, not even in a locked trunk. Avoid poorly lighted areas, beach parks, and isolated areas after dark as a precaution.

When hiking, stay on marked trails, no matter how alluring the temptation might be to stray. Weather conditions can cause landscapes to become muddy, slippery, and tenuous, so staying on marked trails will lessen the possibility of a fall or getting lost. Be sure to heed flash flood watches or warnings. Never try to cross a stream, either on food or in a vehicle, during these weather conditions.

Ocean safety is of the utmost importance when visiting an island destination. Don't swim alone, and follow the international signage posted at beaches that alerts swimmers to strong currents, man-of-war jellyfish, sharp coral, high surf, sharks, and dangerous shore breaks. At coastal lookouts along cliff tops, heed the signs indicating that waves can climb over the ledges. Check with lifeguards at each beach for current conditions, and if the red flags are up, indicating swimming and surfing are not allowed, don't go in. Waters that look calm on the surface can harbor strong currents and undertows.

Be wary of those hawking "too good to be true" prices on everything from car rentals to attractions. Many of these offers are just a lure to get you in the door for time-share presentations. When handed a flier, read the fine print before you make your decision to participate.

Women traveling alone are generally safe on the Islands, but always follow the same precautions you would use in any major destination. When booking hotels, request a room closest to the elevator, and always keep your hotel-room door and balcony doors locked. Stay away from isolated areas after dark; camping and hiking solo are not advised. If you stay out late visiting nightclubs and bars, use caution when exiting nightspots and returning to your lodging.

TAXES

There's a 4.16% statewide sales tax on all purchases, including food (it's actually half a percent higher on Oahu to pay for a proposed rail project). An additional hotel room tax, combined with the sales tax, equals a 13.42% rate added onto your hotel bill on most Islands, and a 13.96% rate on Oahu. A $3-per-day road tax is also assessed on each rental vehicle.

TIME

Hawaii is on Hawaiian Standard Time, five hours behind New York, two hours behind Los Angeles, and 10 hours behind London.

When the U.S. mainland is on daylight saving time, Hawaii is not, so add an extra hour of time difference between the Islands and U.S. mainland destinations. You may also find that things generally move more slowly here. That has nothing to do with your watch—it's just the Islands' laid-back way.

TIPPING

As this is a major vacation destination and many of the people who work in the service industry rely on tips to supplement their wages, tipping is not only common, but expected. Consider a tip of 18 to 20% for excellent restaurant service, even at casual eateries. It's customary to tip all service folk at hotels and resorts, from bellmen to valets to housekeepers. Keeping a stash of "singles" in your wallet or handbag makes this easy.

TIPPING GUIDELINES FOR HAWAII

Bartender	$1 to $5 per round of drinks, depending on the number of drinks
Bellhop	$2 to $5 per bag, depending on the level of the hotel and whether you have bulky items like golf clubs, surfboards, etc.
Hotel Concierge	$10 or more, depending on the service
Hotel Doorman	$1 to $5 if he helps you get a cab or helps with bags, golf clubs, etc.
Hotel Maid	$2 to $5 a day, depending on the level of the hotel (either daily or at the end of your stay, in cash)
Hotel Room-Service Waiter	$2 to $5 per delivery, even if a service charge has been added
Porter/Skycap at Airport	$2 to $3 per bag
Spa Personnel	15% to 20% of the cost of your service
Taxi Driver	15% to 20%, but round up the fare to the next dollar amount
Tour Guide	10% of the cost of the tour
Valet Parking Attendant	$2 to $5, each time your car is brought to you
Waiter	15% to 20%, with 20% being the norm at high-end restaurants; nothing additional if a service charge is added to the bill

▮ TOURS

Atlas Cruises & Tours. For customized travel experiences, this established and experienced agency works with many tour companies—like Globus, Tauck, Trafalgar—to create personalized vacations. They offer more than a dozen Hawaii trips, ranging from 7 to 12 nights. ☎ 800/942–3301 ⊕ www.atlastravelweb. com ✉ From $2,100.

Globus. This agency has seven Hawaii itineraries ranging from 10 to 13 days, including an escorted cruise on Norwegian Cruise Lines' *Pride of America*. ☎ 866/755–8581 ⊕ www.globusjourneys. com ✉ From $2,259.

Perillo Tours. This agency has been offering tours to Hawaii for decades and boasts knowledgeable planners and guides. Choose from fully escorted seven- and ten-day tours to two or three Islands (Oahu, Maui, Kauai) with the option of adding the Big Island for additional nights. ☎ 800/431–1515 ⊕ www.perillotours. com ✉ From $999.

Tauck Travel. "The Best of Hawaii" is the name of this experienced company's 12-day tour of the four major islands. Highlights include a gourmet cooking class on Maui, private catamaran sale on the Big Island, and cocktails and dinner at Iolani Palace in Honolulu. ☎ 800/788–7885 ⊕ www.tauck.com ✉ From $5,090.

Trafalgar. The four different itineraries offered by this company range from the 8-day Hawaiian Explorer to the 13-day Hawaii Four Island Adventure; they all offer an insider's view of local culture. In addition to first-class accommodations and transportation, the tours come complete with a professional travel director and, in some cases, local guides. ☎ 866/544–4434 ⊕ www.trafalgar.com ✉ From $2,595.

YMT Vacations. Billing itself the best choice in affordable travel, YMT offers three all-inclusive vacation packages: a 12-day, four-island tour; a 13-day, four-island agricultural tour; and a Hawaiian Islands cruise and tour. ☎ 888/922–9000, 800/736–7300, 800/888–8204 ⊕ www. ymtvacations.com ✉ From $1,549.

SPECIAL-INTEREST TOURS
BIRD-WATCHING
There are more than 150 species of birds that live in the Hawaiian Islands.

Field Guides. Experienced guides take small groups of bird-watching enthusiasts on ten-day, three islands expeditions (Oahu, Kauai, and the Big Island). The focus is on locating birds endemic to Hawaii as well as specialty seabirds. ☎ *800/728–4953, 512/263–7295* ⊕ *www.fieldguides.com* ✉ *From $4,575.*

Victor Emanuel Nature Tours. Small-group birding tours are offered every fall and spring by this well-established company. Tours cover three islands (Oahu, Kauai, and the Big Island) in nine days, focusing on native habitats that are off the beaten path. ☎ *800/328–8368, 512/328–5221* ⊕ *www.ventbird.com* ✉ *From $3,895.*

CULTURE

Road Scholar. With 18 different tours of the Hawaiian Islands, Road Scholar (educational adventures created by Elderhostel) offers more than a dozen different guided tours of the Hawaiian Islands for older adults (and some intergenerational programs). Each provides in-depth looks into the culture, history, and beauty of the Islands. The eight-night "Best of Oahu and Maui" tour highlights historic sites and museums; the six-night "Molokai the Friendly Isle Is a Classroom" tour includes fishing, crafts, and a trip to Kalaupapa Peninsula; the nine-night "Snorkeling Hawaii's Spectacular Marine Environments" tour lets you immerse yourself in Hawaii's fascinating marine life; and the "Tropical Splendor" tour offers a cruise through the Islands. For those with time to spare, there's also a 31-night tour that includes the islands of French Polynesia. ☎ *800/454–5768* ⊕ *www.roadscholar.org* ✉ *From $1,475.*

HIKING

The World Outdoors. Designed for nature lovers, this company offers a six-day hiking tour of Maui and Kauai. In addition to moderately easy hikes, there's time built in for snorkeling and enjoying the beach, too. ☎ *800/488–8483* ⊕ *www.theworldoutdoors.com* ✉ *From $3,398.*

▌ TRIP INSURANCE

Comprehensive trip insurance is valuable if you're booking a very expensive or complicated trip (particularly to an isolated region like Hawaii) or if you're booking far in advance. Comprehensive policies typically cover trip cancellation and interruption, letting you cancel or cut your trip short because of illness, or, in some cases, acts of terrorism in your destination. Such policies might also cover evacuation and medical care. Some also cover you for trip delays because of bad weather or mechanical problems as well as for lost or delayed luggage.

Another type of coverage to consider is financial default—that is, when your trip is disrupted because a tour operator, airline, or cruise line goes out of business. Generally you must buy this when you book your trip or shortly thereafter, and it's available to you only if your operator isn't on a list of excluded companies.

Always read the fine print of your policy to make sure that you're covered for the risks that most concern you. Compare several policies to be sure you're getting the best price and range of coverage available.

Insurance Comparison Info Insure My Trip ☎ *800/487–4722* ⊕ *www.insuremytrip.com.* **Square Mouth** ☎ *800/240–0369* ⊕ *www.squaremouth.com.*

Comprehensive Insurers Allianz Travel Insurance ☎ *866/884–3556* ⊕ *www.allianztravelinsurance.com.* **CSA Travel Protection** ☎ *800/873–9855* ⊕ *www.csatravelprotection.com.* **Travel Guard** ☎ *800/826–4919* ⊕ *www.travelguard.com.* **Travelex Insurance** ☎ *800/228–9792* ⊕ *www.travelexinsurance.com.* **Travel Insured International** ☎ *800/243–3174* ⊕ *www.travelinsured.com.*

▌ VISITOR INFORMATION

Before you go, contact the Hawaii Visitors & Convention Bureau for general information on each island. You can request via phone or online, "Islands of Aloha," a free visitor guide with information on accommodations, transportation, sports and activities, dining, arts and entertainment, and culture. The website has a calendar section that allows you to see what local events are in place during the time of your stay.

You might also want to check out ⊕ *www.ehawaii.gov*, the state's official website, for information on camping, fishing licenses, and other visitor services. Each island has its own website as well: ⊕ *www.gohawaii.com/big-island* (Big Island Visitors Bureau); ⊕ *www.gohawaii.com/maui* (Maui Visitors & Conventions Bureau); ⊕ *www.gohawaii.com/oahu* (Oahu Visitors Bureau); ⊕ *www.gohawaii.com/kauai* (Kauai Visitors Bureau); ⊕ *www.gohawaii.com/lanai* (Lanai Visitors Bureau); and ⊕ *www.gohawaii.com/molokai* (Molokai Visitors Association).

Visit ⊕ *www.insideouthawaii.com* to check out the local Honolulu arts, entertainment and dining scenes; ⊕ *www.honolulu.gov*, from the City and County of Honolulu with calendar of events for Blaisdell Arena and Concert Hall and the Royal Hawaiian Band; ⊕ *www.hawaiimuseums.org*, the website of the Hawaii Museums Association. Be sure to check out ⊕ *www.nps.gov* for

FODORS.COM CONNECTION

Before your trip, be sure to check out what other travelers are saying in Fodor's Travel Talk Forums on ⊕ *www.fodors.com*.

information on the eight parks managed by the National Park Service.

The Hawaii Ecotourism website (⊕ *www.alternative-hawaii.com*) provides listings of everything from ecoculture events on the Islands to Hawaii Heritage tour guides, and the Hawaii Ecotourism Association (⊕ *www.hawaiiecotourism.org*) has an online directory of more than 100 member companies offering tours and activities. The Hawaii Department of Land and Natural Resources (⊕ *www.hawaii.gov/dlnr*) has information on hiking, fishing, and camping permits and licenses; online brochures on hiking safety and mountain and ocean preservation; as well as details on volunteer programs.

Contact Hawaii Visitors & Convention Bureau ☎ *808/923–1811, 800/464–2924* ⊕ *www.gohawaii.com*.

Although an understanding of Hawaiian is by no means required on a trip to the Aloha State, a *malihini,* or newcomer, will find plenty of opportunities to pick up a few of the local words and phrases. Traditional names and expressions are widely used in the Islands. You're likely to read or hear at least a few words each day of your stay.

With a basic understanding and some uninhibited practice, anyone can have enough command of the local tongue to ask for directions and to order from a restaurant menu. One visitor announced she would not leave until she could pronounce the name of the state fish, the *humuhumunukunukuāpua'a.*

Simplifying the learning process is the fact that the Hawaiian language contains only eight consonants—*H, K, L, M, N, P, W,* and the silent *'okina,* or glottal stop, written '—plus one or more of the five vowels. All syllables, and therefore all words, end in a vowel. Each vowel, with the exception of a few diphthongized double vowels such as *au* (pronounced "ow") or *ai* (pronounced "eye"), is pronounced separately. Thus *'Iolani* is four syllables (ee-oh-la-nee), not three (yo-la-nee). Although some Hawaiian words have only vowels, most also contain some consonants, but consonants are never doubled.

Pronunciation is simple. Pronounce *A* "ah" as in *father; E* "ay" as in *weigh; I* "ee" as in *marine; O* "oh" as in *no; U* "oo" as in *true.*

Consonants mirror their English equivalents, with the exception of *W.* When the letter begins any syllable other than the first one in a word, it is usually pronounced as a *V. 'Awa,* the Polynesian drink, is pronounced "ava," *'ewa* is pronounced "eva."

Almost all long Hawaiian words are combinations of shorter words; they are not difficult to pronounce if you segment them. *Kalaniana'ole,* the highway running east from Honolulu, is easily understood as *Kalani ana 'ole.* Apply the standard pronunciation rules—the stress falls on the next-to-last syllable of most two- or three-syllable Hawaiian words—and Kalaniana'ole Highway is as easy to say as Main Street.

Now about that fish. Try *humu-humu nuku-nuku āpu a'a.*

The other unusual element in Hawaiian language is the *kahakō,* or macron, written as a short line (¯) placed over a vowel. Like the accent (´) in Spanish, the kahakō puts emphasis on a syllable that would normally not be stressed. The most familiar example is probably *Waikīkī.* With no macrons, the stress would fall on the middle syllable; with only one macron, on the last syllable, the stress would fall on the first and last syllables. Some words become plural with the addition of a macron, often on a syllable that would have been stressed anyway. No Hawaiian word becomes plural with the addition of an *S,* since that letter does not exist in the language.

The Hawaiian diacritical marks are not printed in this guide.

'a'ā: rough, crumbling lava, contrasting with *pāhoehoe,* which is smooth.

'ae: yes.

aikane: friend.

āina: land.

akamai: smart, clever, possessing savoir faire.

akua: god.

ala: a road, path, or trail.

ali'i: a Hawaiian chief, a member of the chiefly class.

aloha: love, affection, kindness; also a salutation meaning both greetings and farewell.

'ānuenue: rainbow.

'a'ole: no.

'apōpō: tomorrow.

'auwai: a ditch.

auwē: alas, woe is me!

'ehu: a red-haired Hawaiian.

'ewa: in the direction of 'Ewa plantation, west of Honolulu.

hala: the pandanus tree, whose leaves (*lau hala*) are used to make baskets and plaited mats.

hālau: school.

hale: a house.

hale pule: church, house of worship.

ha mea iki or **ha mea 'ole:** you're welcome.

hana: to work.

haole: ghost. Since the first foreigners were Caucasian, *haole* now means a Caucasian person.

hapa: a part, sometimes a half; often used as a short form of *hapa haole,* to mean a person who is part-Caucasian.

hau'oli: to rejoice. *Hau'oli Makahiki Hou* means Happy New Year. *Hau'oli lā hānau* means Happy Birthday.

heiau: an outdoor stone platform; an ancient Hawaiian place of worship.

holo: to run.

holoholo: to go for a walk, ride, or sail.

holokū: a long Hawaiian dress, somewhat fitted, with a yoke and a train. Influenced by European fashion, it was worn at court, and at least one local translates the word as "expensive mu'umu'u."

holomū: a post–World War II cross between a *holokū* and a mu'umu'u, less fitted than the former but less voluminous than the latter, and having no train.

honi: to kiss; a kiss. A phrase that some tourists may find useful, quoted from a popular hula, is *Honi Ka'ua Wikiwiki:* Kiss me quick!

honu: turtle.

ho'omalimali: flattery, a deceptive "line," bunk, baloney, hooey.

huhū: angry.

hui: a group, club, or assembly. A church may refer to its congregation as a *hui* and a social club may be called a *hui.*

hukilau: a seine; a communal fishing party in which everyone helps to drive the fish into a huge net, pull it in, and divide the catch.

hula: the dance of Hawai'i.

iki: little.

ipo: sweetheart.

ka: the. This is the definite article for most singular words; for plural nouns, the definite article is usually *nā.* Since there is no S in Hawaiian, the article may be your only clue that a noun is plural.

kahuna: a priest, doctor, or other trained person of old Hawai'i, endowed with special professional skills that often included prophecy or other supernatural powers; the plural form is kāhuna.

kai: the sea, saltwater.

kalo: the taro plant from whose root *poi* (paste) is made.

kamā'aina: literally, a child of the soil; it refers to people who were born in the Islands or have lived there for a long time.

kanaka: originally a man or humanity, it is now used to denote a male Hawaiian or part-Hawaiian, but is occasionally taken as a slur when used by non-Hawaiians. *Kanaka maoli,* originally a full-blooded Hawaiian person, is used by some native Hawaiian rights activists to embrace part-Hawaiians as well.

kāne: a man, a husband. If you see this word on a door, it's the men's room. If you see *kane* on a door, it's probably a misspelling; that is the Hawaiian name for the skin fungus tinea.

kapa: also called by its Tahitian name, *tapa,* a cloth made of beaten bark and usually dyed and stamped with a repeat design.

kapakahi: crooked, cockeyed, uneven. You've got your hat on *kapakahi.*

kapu: keep out, prohibited. This is the Hawaiian version of the more widely known Tongan word *tabu* (taboo).

kapuna: grandparent; elder.

kēia lā: today.

keiki: a child; *keikikāne* is a boy, *keiki-wahine* a girl.

kona: the leeward side of the Islands, the direction (south) from which the *kona* wind and *kona* rain come.

kula: upland.

kuleana: a homestead or small plot of ground on which a family has been installed for some generations without necessarily owning it. By extension, *kuleana* is used to denote any area or department in which one has a special interest or prerogative. You'll hear it used this way: If you want to hire a surfboard, see Moki; that's his *kuleana*.

lā: sun.

lamalama: to fish with a torch.

lānai: a porch, a balcony, an outdoor living room. Almost every house in Hawaii has one. Don't confuse this two-syllable word with the three-syllable name of the island, Lāna'i.

lani: heaven, the sky.

lau hala: the leaf of the *hala,* or pandanus tree, widely used in handicrafts.

lei: a garland of flowers.

limu: sun.

lolo: stupid.

luna: a plantation overseer or foreman.

mahalo: thank you.

makai: toward the ocean.

malihini: a newcomer to the Islands.

mana: the spiritual power that the Hawaiian believed inhabited all things and creatures.

manō: shark.

manuwahi: free, gratis.

mauka: toward the mountains.

mauna: mountain.

mele: a Hawaiian song or chant, often of epic proportions.

Mele Kalikimaka: Merry Christmas (a transliteration from the English phrase).

Menehune: a Hawaiian pixie. The *Menehune* were a legendary race of little people who accomplished prodigious work, such as building fishponds and temples in the course of a single night.

moana: the ocean.

mu'umu'u: the voluminous dress in which the missionaries enveloped Hawaiian women. Now made in bright printed cottons and silks, it is an indispensable garment. Culturally sensitive locals have embraced the Hawaiian spelling but often shorten the spoken word to "mu'u." Most English dictionaries include the spelling "muumuu."

nani: beautiful.

nui: big.

ohana: family.

'ono: delicious.

pāhoehoe: smooth, unbroken, satiny lava.

Pākē: Chinese. This *Pākē* carver makes beautiful things.

palapala: document, printed matter.

pali: a cliff, precipice.

pānini: prickly pear cactus.

paniolo: a Hawaiian cowboy, a rough transliteration of *español,* the language of the Islands' earliest cowboys.

pau: finished, done.

pilikia: trouble. The Hawaiian word is much more widely used here than its English equivalent.

puka: a hole.

pupule: crazy, like the celebrated Princess Pupule. This word has replaced its English equivalent in local usage.

pu'u: volcanic cinder cone.

waha: mouth.

wahine: a female, a woman, a wife, and a sign on the ladies' room door; the plural form is *wāhine.*

wai: freshwater, as opposed to saltwater, which is *kai.*

wailele: waterfall.

wikiwiki: to hurry, hurry up (since this is a reduplication of *wiki,* quick, neither W is pronounced as a V).

Note: Pidgin is the unofficial language of Hawaii. It is a Creole language, with its own grammar, evolved from the mixture of English, Hawaiian, Japanese, Portuguese, and other languages spoken in 19th-century Hawaii, and it is heard everywhere.

INDEX

PHOTO CREDITS

ABOUT OUR WRITERS

Karen Anderson is a Kona resident who enjoys horseback riding in the hills of the Big Island. She is the managing editor of *At Home, Living with Style in West Hawaii* and has written for a variety of publications including *West Hawaii Today, Big Island Weekly, HAWAII* magazine and the Kona-Kohala Chamber of Commerce. She's also the best-selling author of *The Hawaii Home Book, Practical Tips for Tropical Living*, which received an excellence award from the Hawaii Book Publishers Association. Her monthly editor's column and chef/restaurant profiles are known throughout West Hawaii. For this edition, Karen updated the Shops and Spas, Entertainment and Nightlife, Where to Eat, and Where to Stay sections of the Big Island chapter.

Kristina Anderson has been writing professionally for more than 25 years. After working as an advertising copywriter and creative director in Southern California for more than a decade, she moved to Hawaii in 1992, freelancing copy and broadcast for Hawaii agencies. Since 2006, she's written for national and regional publications, most notably for *At Home in West Hawaii* magazine, which profiles a variety of homes—from coffee shacks to resort mansions—and for USAToday.com Travel Tips. She also fills in here and there as a substitute teacher, which keeps her busy, as does being a single mom to two teenage boys. When there's time, she paddles outrigger canoes competitively and plays tennis very noncompetitively. For this book, Kristina updated the Experience; Golf, Hiking, and Outdoor Activities; and Travel Smart sections of the Big Island chapter.

Michele Bigley splits her time between California and Hawaii. She has contributed to more than two-dozen guidebooks and travel apps. Her work has appeared in the *Los Angeles Times, San Francisco Chronicle, Boston Globe,* CNN, and more. Michele updated the Exploring and Where to Stay sections of the Maui chapter. Her Maui favorites include snorkeling in Napili Bay, lunch at Oo Farms, and sampling banana bread along the Hana Highway.

James Cave is a writer, editor, and founder of the *Offsetter,* an arts and culture website in Honolulu. He has covered the arts, entertainment, and culture of Honolulu for publications such as the *Honolulu Weekly, HI Luxury, Waikiki Magazine,* and *Honolulu Magazine.* James updated the Entertainment and Nightlife section of the Oahu chapter.

Joan Conrow is a Kauai-based independent journalist and blogger who has written about Hawaii politics, culture, environment, and lifestyles for many regional and national publications. She helped write the original Fodor's guide to Kauai and updated the Shops and Spas, Where to Eat, Where to Stay, Water Sports and Tours, Beaches, and Entertainment and Nightlife sections of the Kauai chapter.

Eliza Escaño-Vasquez was raised in Manila, Philippines, and lived in California before falling deeply in aloha with Maui in 2005. She is a contributing writer for *Modern Luxury Hawaii,* and finds inspiration from the Islands' thriving culinary and creative arts collectives. She updated the Water Sports and Tours, Shops and Spas, and Entertainment and Nightlife sections of the Maui chapter. An ocean ninja in training, Eliza currently resides in Maui with her family, who makes living in paradise even more blissful than it sounds.

Bonnie Friedman, a native New Yorker, has made her home on Maui for more than 30 years. A well-published freelance writer, she also owns and operates Grapevine Productions, a public relations company. She updated the Experience and Where to Eat sections of the Maui chapter, adding some of her favorite places. She also updated the Experience Hawaii and Travel Smart chapters of this guide.

Lesa Griffith was born and raised on Oahu and also spent childhood years in Ghana, the Congo, Jordan, and Indonesia—which she believes developed her no-flavors-barred palate. A freelance food writer, she lives in Honolulu and equally enjoys a good *laulau* (sprinkled with chili pepper water) and Iranian caviar. She updated the Where to Eat section of the Oahu chapter.

Trina Kudlacek fell in love with Hawaii while on vacation 20 years ago. She now has the best of all possible worlds as she splits her time between her home in Hawaii, where she is a lecturer at the University of Hawaii, and Italy, where she is a tour guide. She updated the Beaches, Water Sports and Tours, and Golf, Hiking, and Outdoor Activities sections of the Oahu chapter.

Chris Oliver, though U.K.-born, has been a resident of Oahu for 30 years. As a reporter and travel editor for *The Honolulu Advertiser,* she wrote about the Hawaiian Islands, as well as national and international destinations, with an eye for what visitors would most enjoy on a visit to Hawaii. Coming from a different country, climate, and culture has given her an enthusiasm for the exotic. She currently edits a newsletter, writes for *HAWAII* magazine, and divides her time between Hawaii and the United Kingdom. She updated the Shopping section of the Oahu chapter.

Heidi Pool is a freelance writer and personal fitness trainer who moved to Maui in 2003 after having been a frequent visitor for the previous two decades. An avid outdoor enthusiast, Heidi enjoys playing tour guide when friends or family members come to visit. She updated the Beaches and Golf, Hiking, and Outdoor Activities sections for the Maui chapter. She also updated the Molokai and Lanai chapters.

Charles E. Roessler is a long-time Kauai resident who was an editor for the *Japan Times* and the *Buffalo News*

after teaching English and journalism for 10 years. He contributes to the *New York Times* as a stringer/freelancer and loves Kauai, especially playing tennis and swimming at Anini Beach. Charles updated the Experience, Exploring, and Golf, Hiking, and Outdoor Activities sections of the Kauai chapter.

Catherine E. Toth was born and raised in Oahu and has worked as a newspaper reporter in Hawaii since 2004. She continues to freelance as a writer and multimedia journalist—in between surfing, hiking, and eating everything in sight—for such print and online publications as *Forbes Travel Guide, Alaska Airlines Magazine, HAWAII,* and *Modern Luxury Hawaii.* She updated the Where to Stay and Spas sections of the Oahu chapter.

Anna Weaver is a sixth-generation *kama-aina,* born and raised in Kailua, Oahu, when it was a bit sleepier than it is now that the president takes his winter break there. She can never get enough Spam *musubi, malassadas,* or hiking time in her home state. Anna has written for *Slate,* as well as such Hawaii publications as *The Honolulu Advertiser* (now *Star-Advertiser*), *Honolulu Magazine,* and *Pacific Business News.* She updated the Exploring and Travel Smart sections of the Oahu chapter.